Fifth Canadian Edition

PUBLIC FINANCE
in Canada

Harvey S. Rosen

Jean-François Wen

Tracy Snoddon

Mc
Graw
Hill
Education

PUBLIC FINANCE IN CANADA
Fifth Canadian Edition

ISBN 13: 978-1-25903077-2
ISBN 10: 1-25-903077-6

6 7 8 9 10 11 WEB 22 21 20 19

Printed and bound in Canada.

Product Managers: James Booty/Kevin O'Hearn

Product Developer: Lori McLellan

Product Team Associate: Stephanie Giles

Product Developer, Digital: Adam Wagner

Supervising Editor: Cathy Biribauer/Janie Deneau

Plant Production Coordinator: Michelle Saddler

Manufacturing Production Coordinator: Emily Hickey

Inside Design: Michelle Losier

Composition: Aptara®, Inc.

Cover Design: Michelle Losier

Cover Photo: JP Andersen Images/Getty Images

Printer: Webcom

ABOUT THE AUTHORS

Harvey S. Rosen

Harvey S. Rosen is the John L. Weinberg Professor of Economics and Business Policy at Princeton University. Professor Rosen, a Fellow of the Econometric Society and a Research Associate of the National Bureau of Economic Research, is well known for his contributions to the fields of Public Finance, Labor Economics, and Applied Microeconomics. From 1989 to 1991, he served as Deputy Assistant Secretary (Tax Analysis) at the U.S. Treasury. His articles have appeared in such journals as *Econometrica, American Economic Review,* and *Journal of Political Economy*. He is currently on the editorial boards of the *National Tax Journal, International Tax and Public Finance,* and *Regional Science and Urban Economics.*

Jean-François Wen

Jean-François Wen is a Professor of Economics and a Research Fellow of the School of Public Policy at the University of Calgary. His research focuses on taxation, social insurance, and growth. His articles have appeared in the *Canadian Journal of Economics, The Economic Journal, The Review of Economics and Statistics, and the Journal of Public Economic Theory,* among others. Dr. Wen has served as a technical advisor on World Bank tax policy missions in various countries. He was an economist at the Bank of Canada before obtaining his Ph.D. at Queen's University and he holds the Chartered Financial Analyst (CFA) designation. Dr. Wen moved to Canada at the age of eight and grew up in New Brunswick.

Tracy Snoddon

Tracy Snoddon is an Associate Professor of Economics at Wilfrid Laurier University in Waterloo, Ontario. Her research is concentrated in the areas of public economics and public policy, emphasizing issues relating to fiscal federalism, intergovernmental grants, and equalization. Recent work examines the effects of implementing overlapping climate change policies in a decentralized federation. Dr. Snoddon's research has been published in *Canadian Public Policy, Economics of Governance, Policy Options,* and the *Canadian Journal of Regional Science*. She has been invited to participate in numerous policy roundtables and workshops on fiscal federalism issues, including events hosted by the University of Calgary's School of Public Policy, Finance Canada, the C. D. Howe Institute, the Institute for Research on Public Policy, and the Expert Panel on Equalization. Dr. Snoddon currently serves as the Associate Director of Laurier's Viessmann European Research Centre. She is married to Peter Shawn Taylor and has two sons, Daniel and Patrick.

BRIEF TABLE OF CONTENTS

TABLE OF CONTENTS

PART FIVE: A FRAMEWORK FOR TAX ANALYSIS 279

CHAPTER 14:
TAXATION AND INCOME DISTRIBUTION

CHAPTER 15:
TAXATION AND EFFICIENCY

CHAPTER 16:
EFFICIENT AND EQUITABLE TAXATION

PART SIX: THE CANADIAN REVENUE SYSTEM

CHAPTER 17:
THE PERSONAL INCOME TAX

PREFACE

The field of public finance has been changing rapidly in recent years. On the theoretical side, one of the main achievements has been to integrate the analysis of government spending and taxing more closely with basic economic theory. A prime example is the literature on optimal taxation, which has attempted to derive prescriptions for government fiscal behaviour using standard economic tools, rather than to annunciate a set of ad hoc "principles" for tax design. On the empirical side, the most exciting development has been the widespread application of the tools of econometrics to understand how expenditure and tax policies affect individual behaviour and how the government sets its policies.

The results of modern research have been slow entering traditional texts. This book takes its readers to many of the frontiers of current research. The approach to the material, while accessible to undergraduates, is the same as the approach shared by most economists active in the field.

The development of public finance has not proceeded free of controversy. In this book, disputes concerning both methodological and substantive issues are discussed at length. One reviewer of an early draft of the manuscript warned against displaying too much of the profession's dirty laundry in public. My feeling, however, is that "full disclosure" should apply not only in the market for securities, but also in the market for ideas.

There is some tendency for economic analysis to lose touch with the reality it is supposed to describe. I have tried to avoid this tendency. The relevant institutional and legal settings are described in ample detail. Moreover, the links between economic analysis and current political issues are constantly emphasized.

This book is designed for use in undergraduate curricula as well as in graduate programs in public administration. It is assumed that readers are familiar with microeconomic theory at the level of the standard introductory course. Because some use is made of indifference curve analysis, a topic that is not covered in all introductory courses, indifference curves are carefully explained in the chapter "Microeconomics Background for the Study of Public Finance," which is available on the McGraw-Hill Ryerson website, www.mcgrawhill.ca/olc/rosen. This chapter also provides a brief review of other topics in basic microeconomics, including the supply and demand model and marginal analysis. This review should be adequate to refresh the memories of readers who have been away from microeconomics for a while. Finally, a glossary of key terms appears at the end of the book.

The British statesman Edmund Burke noted that, "To read without reflecting is like eating without digesting." To facilitate this digestive process, each chapter ends with a set of discussion questions and problems. Their purpose is to encourage students to apply and extend the principles that they have learned.

Harvey S. Rosen

WHAT'S NEW IN THE FIFTH CANADIAN EDITION?

In the fifth edition of *Public Finance in Canada*, we have undertaken substantial revisions to enhance the currency of the textbook, including coverage of recent theoretical and empirical developments in the literature and major updating of the data. A new feature of this edition is the inclusion of learning objectives at the start of each chapter to help focus the student's attention on the chapter's key concepts, lessons, and applications. Also new to this edition is the inclusion of an encapsulated "In the News" piece in each chapter, which is intended as both an interesting diversion for readers and a demonstration of the application of the chapters' materials in the media. Another major change is the reintegration of cost–benefit analysis into the book, as Chapter 3 (in the previous edition this was an Internet chapter). Some commentators on previous editions indicated their wish to have a simple treatment of efficiency based on the concepts of marginal benefit and marginal cost, while others preferred the more advanced exposition contained in "Fundamentals of Welfare Economics" in Chapter 2. By placing the topic of cost–benefit analysis early in the textbook, we are able to present an alternative discussion of efficiency and distribution in a way that feels natural; after all, cost–benefit analysis is the application of welfare economics to policy issues. In this way, instructors who wish to bypass Chapter 2 can still discuss the basic ideas of welfare economics using Chapter 3.

In Part Two, Chapter 4 contains a new discussion of privatization, based on waste collection in Ontario municipalities. Chapter 5 on externalities now includes a more thorough treatment of how cost-effective emissions reductions can be achieved using either an emissions fee or a permit-trading scheme, illustrated with a simple, two-firm numerical example. The chapter also contains an expanded discussion of public responses to positive externalities. In Chapter 6, income inequality and poverty indicators are now presented in distinct sections to help students more clearly differentiate between the two concepts and how they are measured. The Gini coefficient and the income share of the richest 1 percent of the population have been added to the discussion of common measures of income inequality, while the poverty section focuses on measures of the incidence, and depth, of poverty.

In Part Three, Chapter 7 contains new material on rent-seeking, with an application to the Canadian dairy industry. The coverage of federal grants to provinces in Chapter 8 has been substantially revised to reflect major policy changes since the previous edition.

In Part Four, Chapter 9 on health care now contains a discussion of the Affordable Care Act in the United States in the context of the theory of insurance markets and adverse selection. The systematic exposition on insurance markets in this chapter reflects our view that social insurance is an essential topic for understanding government expenditures in Canada. Chapter 10 now contains a simple model of the labour market search to frame the discussion of how Employment Insurance can affect the unemployment rate. Chapter 11 updates the discussion of intergenerational redistribution from public pensions, and contains a completely rewritten section on empirical estimates of the effect of public pensions on savings. Additions to Chapter 12 should help students to understand the effects of earnings exemptions and benefit clawbacks in welfare-related programs. Chapter 13 on education has been reorganized to better guide the student through the material.

The tax chapters in Parts Five and Six offer some improvements as well. Chapter 17 now describes Tax-Free Savings Accounts and the Working Income Tax Benefit and provides an end-of-chapter exercise on calculating the benefit. Chapter 19 has been reorganized to emphasize Canada's GST rather than the proposals for a flat tax, which are more topical in the United States where there is no national sales tax. Chapter 19 also provides an updated discussion of the insights from optimal tax theory as they pertain to the GST. Revisions to Chapter 21 bring the assessment of the integration between personal and corporate taxation in Canada up to date in light of the new tax rates and the enhanced investment tax credit. Internet Chapter 3 on deficit finance has also been brought up to date.

SUPPLEMENTARY MATERIAL

MARKET LEADING TECHNOLOGY
connect

Learn without Limits

McGraw-Hill Connect® is an award-winning digital teaching and learning platform that gives students the means to better connect with their coursework, with their instructors, and with the important concepts that they will need to know for success now and in the future. With Connect, instructors can take advantage of McGraw-Hill Education's trusted content to seamlessly deliver assignments, quizzes, and tests online. McGraw-Hill Connect is a learning platform that continually adapts to each student, delivering precisely what they need, when they need it, so class time is more engaging and effective. Connect makes teaching and learning personal, easy, and proven.

Connect Key Features:

▉ ║SMARTBOOK®

As the first and only adaptive reading experience, SmartBook is changing the way students read and learn. SmartBook creates a personalized reading experience by highlighting the most important concepts a student needs to learn at that moment in time. As a student engages with SmartBook, the reading experience continuously adapts by highlighting content based on what each student knows and doesn't know. This ensures that he or she is focused on the content needed to close specific knowledge gaps, while it simultaneously promotes long-term learning.

▉ connect INSIGHT

Connect Insight is Connect's new, one-of-a-kind visual analytics dashboard—now available for instructors—that provides at-a-glance information regarding student performance, which is immediately actionable. By presenting assignment, assessment, and topical performance results together with a time metric that is easily visible for aggregate or individual results, Connect Insight gives instructors the ability to take a just-in-time approach to teaching and learning, which was never before available. Connect Insight presents data that helps instructors improve class performance in a way that is efficient and effective.

Simple Assignment Management With Connect, creating assignments is easier than ever, so instructors can spend more time teaching and less time managing.

· Assign SmartBook learning modules.
· Instructors can edit existing questions and create their own questions.
· Draw from a variety of text-specific questions, resources, and test bank material to assign online.
· Streamline lesson planning, student progress reporting, and assignment grading to make classroom management more efficient than ever.

Smart Grading When it comes to studying, time is precious. Connect helps students learn more efficiently by providing feedback and practice material when they need it, where they need it.

· Automatically score assignments, giving students immediate feedback on their work and comparisons with correct answers.
· Access and review each response; manually change grades or leave comments for students to review.
· Track individual student performance—by question, assignment, or in relation to the class overall—with detailed grade reports.
· Reinforce classroom concepts with practice tests and instant quizzes.
· Integrate grade reports easily with Learning Management Systems including Blackboard, D2L, and Moodle.

Instructor Library The Connect Instructor Library is a repository for additional resources to improve student engagement in and out of the class. It provides all the critical resources instructors need to build their course.

· Access Instructor resources.
· View assignments and resources created for past sections.
· Post your own resources for students to use.

INSTRUCTOR RESOURCES

Instructor Resources

- Instructor's Manual
- Instructor's Solutions Manual
- Computerized Test Bank
- Microsoft® PowerPoint® Lecture Slides

SUPERIOR LEARNING SOLUTIONS AND SUPPORT

The McGraw-Hill Education team is ready to help instructors assess and integrate any of our products, technology, and services into your course for optimal teaching and learning performance. Whether it's helping your students improve their grades, or putting your entire course online, the McGraw-Hill Education team is here to help you do it. Contact your Learning Solutions Consultant today to learn how to maximize all of McGraw-Hill Education's resources.

For more information, please visit us online: http://www.mheducation.ca/he/solutions.

ACKNOWLEDGEMENTS

We gratefully acknowledge the contributions of Professors Boothe, Dahlby, and Smith, whose work on the first and second Canadian editions laid the foundations for the current Canadian edition.

We would like to thank the undergraduate students in the public finance courses at the University of Calgary and Wilfrid Laurier University. Special thanks to Christine Neill from Wilfrid Laurier University and Wade Locke from Memorial University for their helpful suggestions on selected chapters.

Finally, we are grateful to the following reviewers who offered helpful suggestions on various drafts of the manuscript:

Kul Bhatia, University of Western Ontario

Gervan Fearon, York University

Irwin Lipnowski, University of Manitoba

Trien Nguyen, University of Waterloo

Balbir Sahni, Concordia University

Mary Anne Sillamaa, University of Toronto

Frances Woolley, Carleton University

Jean-François Wen

Tracy Snoddon

PART ONE
Introduction

People's views on how the government should conduct its financial operations are heavily influenced by their political philosophies. Some people care most about individual freedom, whereas others care more about promoting the well-being of the community as a whole. Philosophical differences can and do lead to disagreements as to the appropriate scope for government economic activity.

However, forming intelligent opinions about governmental activity requires not only a political philosophy, but also an understanding of what the government actually does. Where does the legal power to conduct economic policy reside? What does government spend money on, and how does it raise revenue?

Chapter 1 discusses how political views affect attitudes toward public finance and outlines the operation of the Canadian system of public finance. This chapter provides a broad perspective that is useful to remember as we discuss various details in the rest of the book. Chapter 2 examines normative analysis in terms of welfare economics and discusses the economic roles of government. Chapter 3 discusses how the more conceptual framework of welfare economics provides a basis for cost-benefit analysis, a set of procedures for guiding public expenditure decisions in practice.

CHAPTER 1

Introduction to Public Finance in Canada

It shall be lawful for the Queen, by and with the Advice and Consent of the Senate and House of Commons, to make Laws for the Peace, Order, and good Government of Canada, in relation to all Matters not coming within the Classes of Subjects by this Act assigned exclusively to the Legislatures of the Provinces.

—1867 Constitution Act as amended (to 1991)

AFTER READING THIS CHAPTER, THE STUDENT SHOULD BE ABLE TO:

LO1 Summarize the legal framework within which governments in Canada conduct their economic activities.

LO2 Describe the process of how the size of government is measured using annual expenditures.

LO3 Discuss the importance of taking into account population growth, inflation, and growth in the economy when examining how the size of government has changed over time.

LO4 Explain why conventional government budget expenditures may not fully capture the extent to which society's resources are under government control.

LO5 Identify the spending categories that account for the largest share of government spending for the different levels of government—federal and provincial plus local.

LO6 Identify the largest revenue sources for the different levels of government—federal and provincial plus local.

The dawn of civilization, and thus of public finance history, in the third millennium BC is recorded on clay tablets excavated at Lagash, in Sumer, a region that is now known as modern Iraq:

> The people of Lagash instituted heavy taxation during a terrible war, but when the war ended, the tax men refused to give up their taxing powers. From one end of the land to the other, these clay cones say, "there were the tax collectors." Everything was taxed. Even the dead could not be buried unless a tax was paid. The story ends when a good king, named Urukagina, "established the freedom" of the people, and once again, "There were no tax collectors." This may not have been a wise policy, because shortly thereafter the city was destroyed by foreign invaders. (Adams, 1993: 2)

As the above passage from Charles Adams' *For Good and Evil* illustrates, an ambivalence about government is apparent in even the most ancient of civilizations. In this example, the king burdens the people with taxes, but without taxes an army cannot be provided and the city is vulnerable.

Many centuries have passed but mixed feelings about government and its taxing and spending activities remain. This book is about these government activities, a subject usually called public finance but sometimes referred to as public sector economics or public economics. Our focus is on the microeconomic functions of government, the way government affects the allocation of resources and the distribution of income. The macro-economic functions of government—the use of taxing, spending, and monetary policies to affect the overall level of unemployment and the price level—are usually taught in separate courses.

The topics considered in public finance include some of the major questions of our time:

- What are the roles of the public and private sectors in the delivery of health care?
- How can social assistance be provided for the poor without curbing incentives for self-reliance?
- How much should government subsidize post-secondary education?
- How can governments help in the wake of disasters such as the earthquake in Japan in 2011?
- How is the tax burden distributed and what are the implications of globalization for tax policies?
- Are locally raised taxes a good way to pay for services provided by provincial and local governments?

These are among the issues examined in this book.

VIEWPOINT OF THIS BOOK

Public finance economists analyze not only the effects of actual government taxing and spending activities, but also what these activities ought to be. Views of how government should function in the economic sphere are influenced by general attitudes toward the relationship between the individual and the state. The notion that the individual rather than the group is paramount is relatively new, and as a political philosophy is stronger in some countries, such as the United States, than in others, such as Canada or Sweden. Historian Lawrence Stone (1977: 4–5) notes that a different political philosophy was dominant before the modern period:

> It was generally agreed that the interests of the group, whether that of kin, the village, or later the state, took priority over the wishes of the individual and the achievement of his particular ends. "Life, liberty and the pursuit of happiness" were personal ideals which the average, educated 16th-century man would certainly have rejected as the prime goals of a good society.

Since then, however, the view that government is a contrivance created by individuals to better achieve their individual goals has come to dominate Anglo-American political thought. However, its dominance is not total—as reflected in the Canadian commitment to "peace, order, and good government." Anyone who claims that something must be done in the "national interest," without reference to the welfare of some individual or group of individuals, is implicitly taking the view that the individual has significance only as part of the community, and that the good of individuals is defined with respect to the good of the whole. More generally, even in highly individualistic societies, people sometimes feel it necessary to act on behalf of, or even sacrifice their lives for, the nation. As Kenneth Arrow (1974: 15) observes, "The tension between society and the individual is inevitable. Their claims compete within the individual conscience as well as in the arena of social conflict."

Not surprisingly, Anglo-American economic thought has also developed along individualistic lines, although less so in Canada than in the United States. Individuals and their wants are the main focus in mainstream economics, a view reflected in this text. However, as stressed earlier, within the individualistic tradition there is much controversy with respect to how active a role government should take. As an example, Canada, in contrast to the United States, has long embraced a major role for government in the provision of health care, and federal equalization payments, embedded in the Canadian Constitution, ensure "sufficient revenues to provide reasonably comparable levels of public services at reasonably comparable levels of taxation" regardless of the province of residence.

The desirability of a given course of action inevitably depends in part on ethical and political judgments. However, ideology by itself is insufficient to determine whether any particular economic intervention should be undertaken. An analysis of the economic consequences of a policy and of the general evolution of economic institutions are also essential parts of policy assessment.[1]

---

[1] See North (1990) for example.

CANADA'S GOVERNMENT AT A GLANCE

It is useful to have a broad overview of the Canadian system of public finance–the basic "facts" about the fiscal system and how it operates. However, before doing so, it is necessary to briefly discuss the legal framework within which government conducts its economic activities. We also consider some problems that arise in attempts to quantify the role of government in the economy.

The Legal Framework

According to Perry (1990: 17), "the first recorded taxes under the French regime were export taxes on furs–half of the beaver and one-tenth of the moose, first levied about 1650." As trade increased, taxes on imports (referred to as customs duties or tariffs) and excise taxes on items such as tobacco supplanted export taxes as the main source of government revenues. By 1847, taxes set by the colonies on imported goods had replaced the Imperial tariffs, and the colonies were in control of their taxes. Revenues from the taxes were being used to finance roads, canals, ports, bridges, and other public infrastructure.

Canada's initial Constitution, the 1867 British North America Act (now the Constitution Act, 1982), specifies the taxing and spending powers of the federal and provincial governments. We first look at the provisions relating to the taxing and spending powers of the federal government and then turn to the provinces.

Federal Government

Section 91 of the 1867 Constitution Act gives the federal government the power "to make laws for the peace, order, and good government of Canada." This includes the power to raise money by any system or mode of taxation, although Section 125 prevents the federal government from levying taxes on provincial lands and property.

The main sources of tax revenues in Canada at the time of Confederation were taxes on imports and excise taxes. Although the provinces raised 99 percent of their tax revenues (77 percent of total revenues) from these two sources in 1866, the Constitution excluded provinces from future use of these and other "indirect" taxes; customs duties, excise duties and taxes, and other indirect taxes were reserved for the federal government. The Fathers of Confederation planned for a strong federal government and for most of the taxing power to reside at the federal level. Direct taxes–income taxes, taxes on estates and inheritances at time of death, and property taxes–which could also be used by provincial governments were unpopular and little used in the 1860s.

With the federal taxing power went major responsibilities that had previously resided with the provinces. What were these?

The first half of the nineteenth century in North America saw growing appreciation for government's role. According to Donald Creighton (1939: 67), "the philosophy of 'public improvements' made very rapid progress among colonial populations which were otherwise still addicted to negative views of the state." Infrastructure was needed to move people and goods. Adequate private capital was unavailable. Nova Scotia, New Brunswick, Ontario, and Quebec had, prior to 1867, incurred debt to build ports, railways, roads, canals, wharfs, lighthouses, and bridges; in 1866, 29 percent of provincial expenditures were for debt servicing. With Confederation, the federal government assumed the existing debts of the provinces and the responsibility for servicing and repaying these debts. The federal government was also given responsibility for national defence, navigation and shipping, regulation of trade and commerce, the criminal justice system, and money and banking, among other areas.

The intent was to balance responsibilities with revenues. To achieve this, the federal government provided statutory subsidies to provinces for general government, justice, education, welfare, and internal transport services. These subsidies were specified at the time of Confederation, and any future growth in subsidies was to be strictly limited. The Fathers of Confederation did not foresee the extent to which federal grants to provinces would grow and change.

Revenues from customs and excise duties effectively met federal government needs for the first 50 years following Confederation. Today's major taxes remained unused. World War I introduced an excess profits tax and taxes on corporate (1916) and personal incomes (1917) and it was not until 1920 that the federal government introduced a general sales tax. As late as 1919, excise and customs duties accounted for 78 percent of federal tax revenues. Given the prominence of the GST (Goods and Services Tax) and the personal income tax in today's tax discussions, it may seem surprising that income taxes and a broad-based sales tax had no role in federal government finance for more than half a century after Confederation.

Although there was no change to the Constitution Act, the federal government managed to extend its spending powers into areas of provincial responsibility through the use of conditional grants, first in 1912 in the area of agricultural education, education being an area of exclusive provincial jurisdiction. By 1928, conditional grants were being made for employment services, highway construction, technical education, and disease prevention, all areas for which the provinces had major responsibility. And in 1927, the federal government provided conditional grants for old age pensions. The Great Depression of the 1930s created the need to greatly expand federal conditional grants to provinces for social assistance. The terms of the social assistance grants varied according to the needs of individual provinces. By 1936–37, conditional grants accounted for $69 million of the $90 million transferred by the federal government to the provinces. By providing support for provincial action in specified areas, the federal government encouraged provincial governments to use their own limited resources, although only in certain ways. As long as provinces are free to choose whether to participate through their own legislation, and the federal government does not become involved in providing services that are a provincial responsibility, the conditional grants do not appear to violate the Constitution.

A 1940 amendment (Section 91(2A)) to the 1867 Constitution Act gave the federal government responsibility for unemployment insurance, and another amendment in 1951 (Section 94A) provided for shared jurisdiction with provinces for old age pensions. One result flowing from these two measures has been rapid growth in payroll tax rates and revenues over the past several decades.[2]

The expansion of federal powers into areas reserved to the provinces has been protested by many of the provinces, and most strongly by Quebec, over the years. This has led to "opting out" arrangements whereby provinces that choose not to participate in a conditional grant program obtain increased tax room, or taxing power, in order to finance a similar program of their own.[3]

Income taxes, payroll taxes, and the federal sales tax, all unknown at the time of Confederation, grew from 37 percent of federal revenues in 1934 to 87 percent by 2012. Customs and excise tax revenues now pale in comparison. The federal government has used the flexibility provided by the Fathers of Confederation to meet the demand for growing revenues.

Government bills to tax and to spend must originate in the House of Commons (Section 53 of the 1867 Constitution Act), and must be introduced to the House by a minister of the government. They cannot originate in the Senate, a clear distinction between the powers held by the elected House and by the appointed Senate.

Expenditure estimates for the broad range of federal programs must be prepared and approved annually for new and old programs. Tax measures, in contrast, continue to generate revenues without yearly action. The government introduces budgets that include changes in tax legislation more or less as often as economic and political conditions dictate.

As Canada's substantial federal debt so emphatically demonstrates, the federal government is not required to finance all its expenditures by taxation. If expenditures exceed revenues, the government is empowered to "the borrowing of Money on the Public Credit" (Section 91(4)). In 1873, the gross public debt that had been assumed by the Dominion at Confederation stood at $93.7 million ($27 per capita). Although this had risen to $612 billion ($17,482 per capita) by 2013–14, federal government spending required to service the debt was about 10 percent of total spending in 2014, as compared with about 27 percent 130 years earlier.

Provincial and Local Governments

The 1867 Constitution Act limited provinces to the use of direct taxation within the province in order to raise revenue for provincial purposes.[4] Provinces were not given the power to inhibit interprovincial trade through the use of indirect taxes; statutory subsidies to the provinces compensated for the prohibition on indirect taxes. Per capita subsidies, federal grants to operate government and legislatures, licences and fees, the sale of goods and

---

[2] Di Matteo and Shannon (1995) provide a useful overview of payroll tax evolution in Canada over the past several decades; Lin (2001) offers a more recent update.

[3] The transfer of tax room is accomplished in theory by the federal government reducing its tax rate while the provincial and territorial government that is "opting out" increases its tax rate by an equivalent amount.

[4] A "direct" tax is one that is imposed on the individual who is expected to bear the tax. Thus, the personal income tax is a direct tax. Sales taxes and excise are generally classified by economists as "indirect" taxes; although the person selling or producing the good or service has the statutory obligation to pay the tax, the tax is expected to be borne by the final consumer of the good or service.

services, and revenues from provincial lands and natural resources were to fund the necessary provincial services. Property taxes, income taxes, and succession duties, little used at the time, were also available to provinces.

Federal subsidies, which accounted for about 60 percent of provincial revenues in 1867, fell to 10 percent by 1930. Increased demand for welfare, health, and education services and for intraprovincial transport accompanied economic development and urbanization and led provinces to seek new sources of revenue. British Columbia (1876) and Prince Edward Island (1894) were the first provinces to enact taxes on personal incomes. Ontario, following the example of New York and Pennsylvania, introduced a succession duty in 1892 in order to increase revenues, and by 1896 all provinces had succession duties. Taxes on gasoline and motor vehicle licences were introduced by the 1920s as a way to finance the road systems that were needed with the increasing use of automobiles and trucks.

Provinces held primary responsibility for social welfare, and the Great Depression placed enormous strain on provincial finances. Federal transfers rose from 10 percent in 1930 to 25 percent of provincial revenues by 1937 (Eggleston and Kraft, 1939) due to increasing welfare needs. By 1940, financial pressures had forced all provinces to introduce taxes on personal and corporate incomes, with Saskatchewan and Quebec also using retail sales taxes.[5] Thus, by the time of World War II, both the federal and provincial governments were using corporate and personal income taxes as well as a general sales tax.

Growing disparity between provincial financial needs and resources and an overlap in major revenue sources led the Royal Commission on Dominion-Provincial Relations (Canada, 1940) to recommend that the federal government be the sole user of taxes on personal and corporate income and of successions duties, that it assume responsibility for provincial debts, and that it provide adequate transfers to provincial governments. But it was World War II, rather than the royal commission's recommendations, that led the provinces to relinquish their use of the personal and corporate income taxes. Following the war, a series of federal-provincial agreements provided for federal transfers to provinces based on a combination of per capita grants and a share of the revenues from the income taxes. Per capita grants and statutory subsidies provided an element of equalization among provinces prior to 1957. The 1957-62 agreement included unconditional (equalization) grants based on the per capita yield of the personal and corporate income taxes and succession duties in the two wealthiest provinces–Ontario and British Columbia. The grants were based on these provinces in order to guarantee that per capita provincial revenue would reach a certain standard for all Canadians. Subsequent agreements expanded the basis for equalization payments. By 2006 equalization included 33 provincial revenue sources. A number of changes were made to equalization in the federal government's budget for 2007, including reducing the number of provincial tax bases used to calculate equalization from 33 to 5. Section 36(2) of the 1982 Constitution Act, which entrenches the concept of equalization payments in the Canadian Constitution, states:

> Parliament and the government of Canada are committed to the principle of making equalization payments to ensure that provincial governments have sufficient revenues to provide reasonably comparable levels of public services at reasonably comparable levels of taxation.

The 1982 Constitution Act also amended the Constitution to give provinces greater control over their natural resources, explicitly allowing them to levy indirect taxes on natural resources. Provinces may now raise money by "any mode or system of taxation in respect of . . . nonrenewable resources and forestry resources in the province and the primary production there from . . ." (Section 92A).

As we shall see, the provincial role in public finance in Canada has grown significantly relative to that of the federal government. There has been a dramatic fall in the ratio of federal to provincial government expenditures, from 4.9 to 1 in 1946 to 0.72 to 1 by 2009. The ratio of federal government revenue to provincial revenue (net of federal grants) also fell sharply during this time, from 4.86 to 1 in 1946 to 1.32 to 1 in 2009. Rapid growth in key areas of provincial responsibility–health, education, welfare–during the past half century, and the fact that both federal and provincial governments have access to all major taxes, have also contributed to

---

[5] In contrast to the generally accepted classification of retail sales taxes and excise taxes on gasoline or tobacco products as indirect taxes, courts in Canada have classified these taxes as direct taxes in interpreting the 1867 Constitution Act. The seller of the good is deemed as the agent designated to collect the tax from the consumer who pays and bears the tax in proportion to the amount of the good consumed.

this shift. Although the Fathers of Confederation may have intended the federal government to dominate the provinces, the distribution of taxing and spending among levels of government is very different than at the time of Confederation.

The Constitution Act (formerly the 1867 Constitution Act) does not refer to local governments. Local authorities have only those taxing and spending powers that provincial governments choose to delegate to them. One result is that there is substantial variation across provinces in local taxing and spending decisions. The dominant revenue source for local authorities was, and is, the property tax. Local government own-source revenues, which were more than double provincial own-source revenues in 1926, were less than 25 percent of provincial own-source revenues in 2009. As provincial reliance on sales and income tax revenues grew rapidly, local governments increasingly relied on transfers from provincial governments. Grants from federal and provincial governments, which accounted for 6.7 percent of local revenues in 1926, accounted for about 40 percent in 2008. In sum, since the time of Confederation the role of provincial governments has increased sharply relative not only to the federal government but to local governments as well.

The Size of Government

What has been the result of these legal prescriptions and trends for government taxing and spending activities? The first item that belongs in any such description is a measure of the magnitude of these activities. Just how big is government? The whole public debate concerning the government's size presupposes that there is some way of measuring it. For now, we will examine some of the measures and measurement issues relating to government size; we return to the issue of how to *explain* the growth in government size in Chapter 7.

One measure often used by politicians and journalists to determine the size of government is the number of workers in the public sector. However, inferences about the size of government drawn from the number of workers it employs can be misleading. Imagine a country where a few public servants operate a powerful computer that guides all economic decisions. In this country, the number of individuals on the government payroll certainly underestimates the importance of government. Similarly, it would be easy to construct a scenario in which a large number of workers is associated with a relatively weak public sector. Although there are many reasons why it is useful to know the number of public sector employees, it does not cast light on the central issue—the extent to which society's resources are subject to the control of government.

A more sensible (and common) approach is to measure the size of government by the volume of its annual expenditures. There are basically three types:

1. *Purchases of goods and services.* The government buys a wide variety of items, everything from fighter planes to services provided by forest rangers.
2. *Transfers of income to people, businesses, or other governments.* The government takes income from some individuals or organizations and gives it to others. Examples are welfare programs such as the Guaranteed Income Supplements under the Old Age Security Act and farm programs that guarantee prices for certain commodities.
3. *Interest payments.* The government often borrows to finance its activities and, like any borrower, must pay interest for the privilege of doing so.

The budget is presented by the federal minister of finance each year, traditionally in February, outlining anticipated changes in tax and spending programs and setting forth the anticipated revenues and expenditures for the coming fiscal year. The April 21, 2015, federal budget predicted that spending would exceed revenues by $2.1 billion in fiscal year 2014–15. The federal deficit has fallen in recent years, especially in comparison to the deficits recorded in the years immediately following the 2008 recession. Each provincial finance minister goes through a similar budgetary process. Local authorities also approve their tax and spending programs set forth in an annual budget. Consolidated financial data for government spending and revenues are available, but often with a lag. The latest available consolidated data for federal, provincial, and local governments, for 2008–09, show $633.7 billion in revenue and $631.3 billion in spending, or $18,947 in per capita spending with a per capita surplus of $73.

Typically, if government spending (in total or in per capita terms) increases, people conclude that government has grown. Unfortunately, conventional budget expenditures can convey a misleading impression of the

CANADA'S MILITARY SPENDING GETS A BOOST FROM FEDERAL BUDGET

The federal government has substantially increased its military spending over the past 15 years. The current build-up began in 1999, but it accelerated as a result of Canada's participation in the war in Afghanistan following the terrorist attack in the United States on September 11, 2001, until the Canadian combat mission ended in 2011. In 2014–15, Canada spent $20.1 billion funding its military. Canada now spends more (in inflation-adjusted terms) than at any time since the end of World War II. The cost of the war in Afghanistan is estimated to have been at least $18 billion—and that does not include the cost of caring for veterans and their families or the loss of Canadian soldiers and personnel who died as a result of the conflict.

Pundits will continue to debate whether the mission in Afghanistan was worth it. But the ongoing turmoil and armed conflict in the world suggests that Canada's spending on its military forces will remain at relatively elevated levels for the foreseeable future. Indeed, the 2015 federal budget announced a boost of $11.8 billion to its baseline military funding over the next decade, which does not include incremental funding for special missions.

Based on Robinson (2011), Starr (2015), and "What Canada did – and did not – achieve in Afghanistan." Editorial. *The Globe and Mail.* Mar. 14, 2014.

Complete references for this feature can be found in the References section on page 473.

extent to which society's resources are under government control. There are at least two reasons for this: the methods of accounting for off-budget items, and hidden costs of government.

Accounting Issues

Several complications arise in the computation of government expenditures. Some of these are due to the government's role in lending programs. The government provides **loan guarantees** for individuals, Crown corporations and other businesses, and nonprofit institutions. Because of the government guarantee, the loans are at lower rates than otherwise. In the case of default, the government is on the hook. The total amount outstanding for guarantees by the federal government was $407 billion as of March 31, 2014.[6] In order to attract investments, provincial governments also provide loan guarantees, and make direct loans in some cases. These too lead to future draws on the public purse if loans default.

How should these credit programs be treated for budgetary purposes? One possibility would be to recognize payments and receipts associated with these programs only in the year they are made or arrive. To see the problems with this approach, suppose that the government guarantees some student loans this year and the loans do not come due for four years. The loan guarantees would not show up on this year's budget. However, there will be defaults on at least some of these loans in the future, so by making the loan guarantees now, the government is committing itself to some expenditures in the future. A sensible approach, then, would be so-called accrual accounting, which takes into account the future liabilities created by present decisions. Public accounts normally provide for such liabilities, but high levels of uncertainty may accompany the size of any such provision.[7]

---

[6] See Table 11.5, Canada (2014), page 335.

[7] Similar issues arise in the context of government insurance activities, which are also sizable. The Canada Deposit Insurance Corporation (CDIC) protects hundreds of billions of dollars ($665 billion in 2013–14) in individual deposits in banks and trust and loan companies. Bank failures in the early 1980s resulted in a CDIC loss of $650 million in 1983 on insured deposits of about $150 billion (all in current dollars). Losses could have been larger in this tumultuous period, although in the sixteen years from 1967 to 1982 there had been virtually no losses and during the economic expansion of the 1990s losses were nominal or non-existent. Any CDIC losses incurred are partially offset by the premiums paid by member institutions. In 2013–14, member institutions paid $192 million in premiums. (Working Committee on Canada Deposit Insurance Corporation, *Final Report,* Ottawa, 1985; Canada Deposit Insurance Corporation, *Annual Report 2014* (Ottawa, 2014); http://www.cdic.ca/CDIC/FinRpts/Pages/AR2014.aspx

Government pension plans, including the Canada and Quebec Pension Plans (CPP and QPP), also result in contingent liabilities. Governments have an obligation to pay pensions to individuals who have been paying into the pension plans, and the government's net liability changes from year to year depending on the number and age of the contributors. Through accrual accounting, an increase in liability would be reflected as an expenditure commitment, which may increase a deficit or decrease a surplus. If, instead, increased pension payments show up on the government accounts only at the time they are paid, the public accounts may show a lower level of expenditure, and a lower level of accumulated debt.

The government should also fully account for contingent environmental liabilities associated with contaminated sites and the contingent liabilities of aboriginal claims. High levels of uncertainty may well exist. A further problem identified by the Auditor General (http://www.oag-bvg.gc.ca) is that the disbursements under the Child Tax Benefit program should be considered as program *spending* rather than as an offset to personal income tax revenues, as the government is now doing.

We conclude, then, that the size of the official government budget depends on some rather arbitrary accounting decisions concerning whether and how certain items are to be included. Hence, considerable caution is required in interpreting budgetary figures.

Hidden Costs of Government

Some government activities have substantial effects on resource allocation but may involve minimal explicit outlays. For example, issuing regulations per se is not very expensive, but compliance with the rules can be costly. Airbags and other safety requirements raise the cost of cars. Regulations ensuring sanitary conditions in slaughterhouses, dairies, and bakeries were among Canada's early health regulations that raised costs for businesses. Permit and inspection fees increase the price of housing. Banks, insurance companies, brokerage firms, stock markets, and other financial institutions are subject to extensive regulation. Health and safety regulations for workers increase the cost of labour. Expensive testing required of the drug industry slows the pace and increases the price at which new drugs become accessible to consumers, while patent laws encourage (possibly excessive) research for new drugs.

Unfortunately, it is exceedingly difficult to compute the total costs of regulation. We can easily imagine even pharmaceutical experts disagreeing on what new cures would have been developed in the absence of drug regulation. Similarly, it is hard to estimate how much government-mandated safety procedures in the workplace increase production costs. As with other government activity, the benefits may far outweigh the costs. Nonetheless, through regulatory activity the government sector has a major impact on society and the economy; private costs of compliance may, in some cases, add as much to total costs as do tax liabilities.[8]

Two other "hidden" aspects that deserve mention are (a) **tax expenditures**, and (b) the flow of current services from capital investments. Tax expenditures refer to the value of incentives and preferences given through the tax system for purposes that could be achieved through direct expenditures. For example, a government may choose to provide a direct payment to individuals who are 65 or older, or it may allow a deduction of $1,000 from pension income that would otherwise be taxable. Similarly, the government could make a grant of $250 to a business for every $1,000 invested on Cape Breton, or it could give a tax credit of 25 percent. Although tax expenditures and direct expenditures may reflect comparable levels of government activity and involvement, in the case of direct expenditures this is reflected in the annual budget; in the case of tax expenditures it is not.[9]

The government does not distinguish between capital and current expenditures in the way the private sector does. Capital investments are usually consumed, or depleted, over several years as the capital is used to produce

---

[8] One estimate for Canada suggests that if price and output regulation are taken into account when calculating government spending as a percentage of GDP, its share would increase by at least an additional 10 percentage points [See Cross (2014)].

[9] The Department of Finance first published estimates of tax expenditures in December 1979. Their most recent publication is *Tax Expenditures and Evaluations, 2014* (Ottawa: Department of Finance) http://www.fin.gc.ca/taxexp-depfisc/2014/taxexp14-eng.asp. The estimates include federal tax expenditures made through the corporate income tax and the Goods and Services Tax (GST) as well as the personal income tax. Several provinces have provided estimates of provincial tax expenditures at the time of their annual budgets. According to Sheikh (2014), including federal-provincial tax expenditures increases the size of government in 2009 from 44 to 54 percent of GDP.

goods and services. A high level of capital spending by a company in a given year does not mean it is more active or productive in that year than in any other year, because it may be replacing worn-out equipment. Private accounting practices recognize this by depreciating the equipment over a period of years. In contrast, with no government capital accounts, large capital expenditures appear to reflect a high level of government activity when in fact the involvement is more accurately reflected in the services from schools, roads, canals, dams, hospitals, and water systems that occur over many years. A related problem is that of valuing the services as they are consumed. The value is assumed to be the amount spent by the government, which may or may not be a good approximation.

Some Numbers

We reluctantly conclude that there is no feasible way to summarize in a single number the magnitude of government's impact on the economy. Having made this admission, we are still left with the practical problem of finding some reasonable indicator of government's size that can be used to estimate trends in the growth of government. Most economists are willing to accept conventionally defined government expenditure as a rough but useful measure. Like many other imperfect measures, it yields useful insights as long as its limitations are understood.

With all the appropriate caveats in mind, we present in Table 1.1 data on expenditures made by all levels of Canadian government since 1991. The first column indicates that annual expenditures have grown by 119 percent since 1991. This figure is however a misleading indicator of the growth of government over the past 25 years for several reasons:

1. Because of inflation, the dollar has decreased in value over time. The nominal data in column 1 partly reflects inflation—a general rise in the price level over a period of time. In column 2, the expenditure figures are expressed in 2007 dollars. In real terms, however, government expenditure has grown by about 39 percent between 1991 and 2014.

2. The population has also grown over time. By itself, an increasing population creates demands for a larger public sector. (For example, more roads and sewers are required to accommodate more people.) Column 3 shows real government expenditure per capita. Over the past 25 years, real, per capita government spending has grown by about 9.6%.

3. For some purposes, it is useful to examine government expenditure compared to the size of the economy. If government doubles in size but at the same time the economy triples, then, in a relative sense, government has shrunk. Column 4 shows government expenditure as a percentage of gross domestic product (GDP), the market value of goods and services produced by the economy during the year. In 1991, the figure was 51 percent, and in 2014 it was 39.6 percent. Relative to the economy, the size of government has fallen since 1991.

TABLE 1.1

Local, Provincial, and Federal Government Expenditures, Selected Years

	Total Expenditure ($ millions)	2007 Dollars ($ millions)	In 2007 $ Per Capita	Percentage of GDP
1991	352,796	493,421	17,599	50.9%
1995	390,496	511,790	17,466	47.5%
1999	418,762	524,764	17,261	41.8%
2003	493,117	557,194	17,610	39.6%
2007	589,927	589,927	17,937	37.7%
2011	720,678	667,913	19,448	40.9%
2014	774,877	685,732	19,294	39.6%

Sources: Statistics Canada. CANSIM data from the following series v52531007, v62471023, v466668, v62471340 series.

Ferris and Winer (2007) show that the decline in the size of government relative to GDP is a relatively new phenomenon. Using historical data for the period 1929 to 2004, they show that the ratio of government spending to GDP reached a peak of 51.7 percent in 1992, increasing considerably from 15 percent in 1929.

Although these data convey a false sense of precision, it is evident that historically the economic role of government has grown tremendously and, with roughly 40 percent of GDP going through the public sector today, government is an enormous economic force.

To put the Canadian data in perspective, it helps to make some international comparisons. Figure 1.1 shows government expenditure relative to gross domestic product for several developed countries for 1989, 2000, and 2014. The data indicate that Canada is not alone in having an important public sector. Compared with France and Italy, Canada's public sector share in 2014 is relatively small. And, while the public sector share was quite a bit larger in Canada than in the United States in 1989 (45 percent as compared to 36 percent), the size of this gap has shrunk considerably by 2014.

FIGURE 1.1

GOVERNMENT EXPENDITURES AS A PERCENTAGE OF GDP, SELECTED COUNTRIES

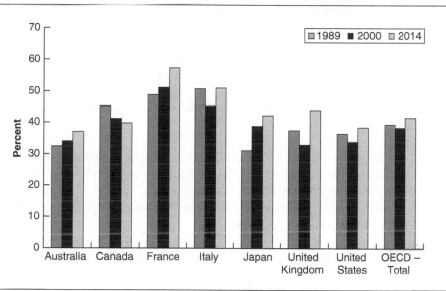

Sources: OECD (2014), "OECD Economic Outlook, annual data", OECD Economic Outlook: Statistics and Projections (database). DOI: http://dx.doi.org/10.1787/data-00729-en (Accessed on 02 June 2015).

EXPENDITURES

We now turn from the overall magnitude of government expenditures to their composition.[10] The major categories of total government expenditure for 1965 and 2009 are shown in Figure 1.2. The following aspects of the figure are noteworthy:

1. Health and social welfare have become important areas of government activity. The combined share of total spending devoted to these two areas has increased by 20 percentage points, from 29 percent in 1965 to close to 50 percent in 2009. Rising costs of health care, a publicly provided health care system, and an

---

[10] This section uses the most recent data available that is suitable for a comparison of the composition of government spending and revenues across time and by level of government. The federal government discontinued these Financial Management System (FMS) data after 2009. Although Statistics Canada is moving to a new system, the Canadian Government Finance Statistics (CGFS), data that allows for comparisons across province and across levels of government after 2009 is not yet available. And to date there has been no indication of whether Statistics Canada intends to revise the historical data in line with the new accounting system.

FIGURE 1.2

COMPOSITION OF TOTAL GOVERNMENT EXPENDITURES, 1965 AND 2009 (PERCENT OF TOTAL)

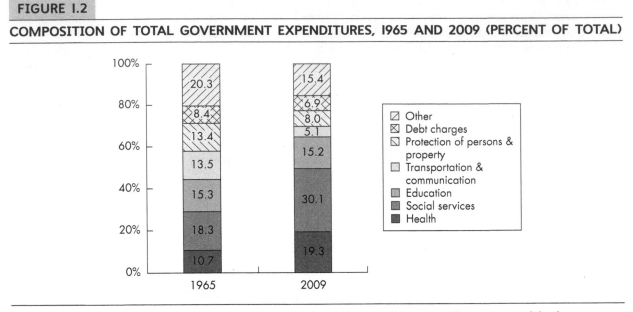

Notes: Total government spending refers here to government spending at all levels of government (known as consolidated government spending). Expenditures include CPP/QPP and nets out intergovernmental transfers.

Sources: Data for 1965 are from M. C. Urquhart and K. A. H. Buckley, *Historical Statistics of Canada,* 2nd ed. (Ottawa, 1983), pp. H148–160; data for 2009 are from Statistics Canada's CANSIM II database http://cansim2.statcan.ca Table 385-0001.

aging population all contribute to health care costs. Federal unemployment compensation and income security programs for the aged and provincial welfare systems for others who are unable to earn sufficient income are the major welfare (social services) programs.

2. The 15 percent share of government spending allocated to education, primarily a provincial spending responsibility, has not changed between 1965 and 2009.

3. While transportation, communication, and the protection of persons and property have historically been important areas of government spending in Canada, the combined share for these areas in 2009 is less than half of what it was in 1965.

4. About 7 percent of spending is absorbed by debt charges.

Some fast-growing or large areas, such as social welfare, are relatively fixed in the sense that they are determined by previous decisions. Indeed, much of the government budget consists of so-called *entitlement* programs—programs whose cost is determined not by fixed dollar amounts, but by the number of people who qualify. Laws governing the Canada Pension Plan and many public programs, such as unemployment insurance, include rules that determine who is entitled to benefits as well as the size of those benefits. Expenditures on entitlement programs are therefore out of the hands of the current government, unless it changes the rules. Similarly, debt payments are determined by interest rates and previous deficits, again mostly out of the control of current decision makers. Much of the federal budget is relatively uncontrollable. In Chapter 7, we discuss whether government spending is out of control and, if so, what can be done about it.

Figure 1.2 shows government spending by all levels of government but, as we have seen, the Constitution confers specific spending powers on the federal and provincial governments. Provinces in turn determine which taxing and spending powers to delegate to local governments. How do the different levels of government allocate their spending? Figure 1.3 shows the composition of total expenditures by level of government. In 2009, health and education accounted for 50 percent of the combined expenditures of provincial and local governments. In contrast, the federal share devoted to these two areas is about 13 percent. Adding social

FIGURE 1.3

COMPOSITION OF GOVERNMENT EXPENDITURES BY LEVEL OF GOVERNMENT, 2009 (PERCENT OF TOTAL)

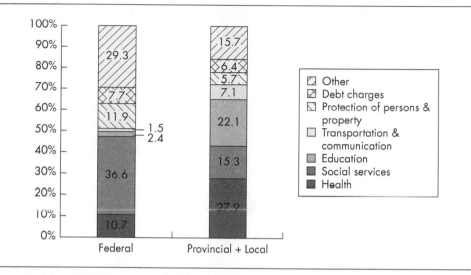

Notes: In the disaggregated data, CPP/QPP are not included and federal spending on transfers to lower levels of government are included. These transfers show up in the "other" category for the federal government.

Sources: Data are from Statistics Canada's CANSIM II database http://cansim2.statcan.ca Table 385-0001.

services spending to health and education, the share of provincial/local spending allocated to these activities increases to 65 percent. Social services actually accounts for a sizeable share of spending at both levels of government. Finally, we observe that the 12 percent share of federal spending on the protection of persons and property (which includes spending on national defence) is about double the share allocated at the provincial/local level.

REVENUES

How are government expenditures financed? We focus on tax revenues since roughly 80 percent of total government revenue comes from taxes. Figure 1.4 shows the percentage of tax revenues attributable to each of the major taxes for 1965 and 2009. The personal income tax is the single most important source of revenue, accounting for more than 36 percent of taxes raised by all levels of government. Payroll taxes include contributions to public pension plans, unemployment insurance, and provincial workers' compensation programs, accounting for about 18 percent of total government tax revenues. Social welfare expenditures have been increasing and so have the taxes that need to be raised to pay for them. The fall in the relative importance of the corporate income tax since the 1960s is also of some interest. In 1965, it accounted for 16.2 percent of all revenue collected, but by 2009 this figure was down to 9.7 percent.[11] Finally, consumption tax revenue (including revenues from sales taxes and excise taxes on gasoline, tobacco, and alcohol) is an important revenue source, currently accounting for one-fifth of total tax revenues.

Do different levels of government rely on different mixes of taxes? Figure 1.5 shows the shares of the major taxes by level of government for 2009. Two key observations can be made. First, the federal government relies

---

[11] As discussed in Chapter 21, a major force driving this change is the globalization of capital markets. The ability of capital to migrate to countries with the lowest taxes has created tax competition and downward pressure on corporate income taxes.

FIGURE 1.4

COMPOSITION OF TOTAL GOVERNMENT TAX REVENUE, 1965 AND 2009 (PERCENT OF TOTAL)

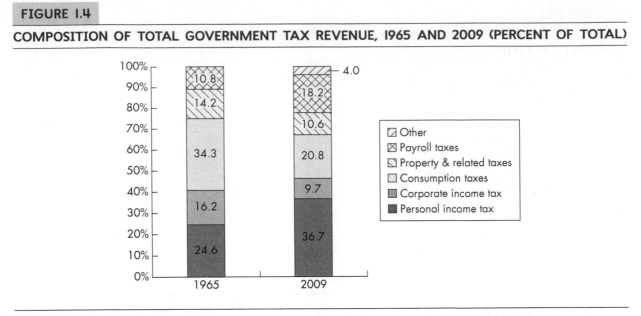

Notes: Total government tax revenue refers here to tax revenue at all levels of government (known as consolidated government revenue). Payroll taxes include CPP/QPP contributions.

Sources: Data for 1965 are from M. C. Urquhart and K. A. H. Buckley, *Historical Statistics of Canada,* 2nd ed. (Ottawa, 1983), pp. H148–160; data for 2009 are from Statistics Canada's CANSIM II database http://cansim2.statcan.ca Table 385-0001.

heavily on the personal income tax, collecting more than half of its tax revenues from this source. Second, in contrast to the subnational (i.e., provincial and local) level, the federal government does not receive any revenue from property taxes. This tax is exclusively in the domain of provincial (and local) governments and accounts for about 22 percent of their tax revenues.

FIGURE 1.5

COMPOSITION OF GOVERNMENT TAX REVENUE BY LEVEL OF GOVERNMENT, 2009 (PERCENT OF TOTAL)

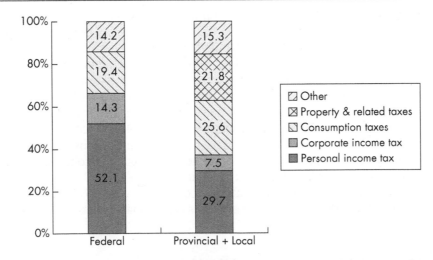

Notes: In the disaggregated data, CPP/QPP are not included.

Sources: Data are from Statistics Canada's CANSIM II database http://cansim2.statcan.ca Table 385-0001.

TRANSFERS

We have looked at measures of the overall size of government in Canada and of the composition of government spending (and tax revenue) by category and by level of government. However, these data overlook an important and persistent feature of government activity in Canada. As shown in Table 1.2, the federal government collected more than 50 percent of all revenues but only accounted for about one-third of government spending at all levels in 2009. In comparison, subnational governments accounted for two-thirds of all government spending whereas their share of total revenue, in 2009, was about 47 percent. Although these shares have changed somewhat over time, the imbalances have persisted.

Federal transfers to provinces (and provincial transfers to local governments) address the persistent gaps in revenue and expenditure shares. A significant amount of federal spending, about 25 percent, takes the form of transfers to provincial, territorial, and local governments. This spending shows up in Figure 1.3 in the "other" category. Federal transfers have been important since Canada was founded and are often the subject of tension between Ottawa and the provinces. We discuss these tensions as well as the purpose and effects of intergovernmental transfers in more detail in Chapter 8.

Provincial and local governments are clearly important players. The provincial role, in particular, has grown significantly over time. Subnational governments account for the bulk of spending on items such as police and fire protection, health, education, transportation, and environmental policy. Substantial public welfare expenditures are also made through the provinces. There can be complications associated with the different fiscal activities of different levels of government, which are also discussed in Chapter 8.

TABLE 1.2

Government Revenues and Expenditures by Level of Government* (percent of total)					
	1926		1960		2009	
	Rev.	Exp.	Rev.	Exp.	Rev.	Exp.
Federal	44.9	37.8	60.8	50.5	53.3	33.2
Provincial	18.0	20.2	21.8	24.8	40.3	46.2
Local	37.1	42.0	17.3	24.7	6.4	20.6
TOTAL	100.0	100.0	100.0	100.0	100.0	100.0

* Includes hospitals with provincial revenues and expenditures and CPP/QPP with federal revenues and expenditures, and excludes grants by governments to other levels of government.

Source: Karin Treff and Deborah Ort, *Finances of the Nation, 2010* (Toronto: Canadian Tax Foundation, 2011), tables B.3 and B.5.

Changes in the Real Value of Debt

In popular discussions, taxes are usually viewed as the only source of government revenue. However, when the government is a debtor and the price level changes, changes in the real value of the debt may be an important source of revenue. To understand why, suppose that at the beginning of the year you owe a creditor $1,000, which does not have to be repaid until the end of the year. Suppose further that during the year prices rise by 10 percent. The dollars you use to repay your creditor are then worth 10 percent less than those you borrowed from him. In effect, inflation has reduced the real value of your debt by $100 (10 percent of $1,000). Alternatively, your real income has increased by $100 as a consequence of inflation. Of course, at the same time, your creditor's real income has fallen by $100.[12]

---

[12] If the inflation is anticipated by borrowers and lenders, one expects that the interest rate charged will be increased to take inflation into account. This phenomenon is discussed in Chapter 17 under "Taxes and Inflation."

At the end of fiscal year 2014, the federal government's net public debt was around $682 billion, with inflation running around 2 percent. Applying the same logic as before, 2 percent inflation will reduce the real value of the federal debt by $13.6 billion ($682 billion × 0.02) in one year. In effect, this is as much a receipt for the government as any of the taxes shown in Figure 1.5. However, the government's accounting procedures exclude gains due to inflationary erosion of the debt on the revenue side of the account.

AGENDA FOR STUDY

This chapter has set forth a collection of basic "facts"—facts on governmental fiscal institutions, on the size and scope of government spending, and on the methods used by government to finance itself. Parts of the rest of this book are devoted to presenting more facts—filling in the rather sketchy picture of how our fiscal system operates. Just as important, we explore the significance of these facts, asking whether the status quo has led to desirable outcomes, and if not, how it can be improved.

SUMMARY

- Public finance, also known as public sector economics or public economics, focuses on the taxing and spending activities of government and their influence on the allocation of resources and the distribution of income.

- Public finance economists both analyze actual policies and develop guidelines for government activities. In the latter role, economists are influenced by their attitudes toward the role of government in society.

- Individual decision making is the focus of much economics and is consistent with the view that the government is a contrivance created by individuals to better achieve their individual goals. Although this is the view adopted in this book, it does not eliminate controversy over the appropriate role of the government in our economy.

- Legal constraints on federal and provincial government economic activity are embodied in the 1867 Constitution Act and the 1982 Constitution Act.

- The federal government may use any form of taxation and may incur debt to finance its expenditures. Although some major expenditure areas (e.g., education and health) are reserved for provincial governments, the federal government is, and has been, involved in these areas through conditional grants.

- The 1867 Constitution Act forbids provincial governments to use indirect taxes. They may levy "direct taxes within the province in order to raise revenue for provincial purposes." Courts have opened the field of sales and excise taxes to provincial governments by interpreting them as "direct" taxes. Provinces may not, however, use customs duties or other taxes that directly inhibit the flow of interprovincial trade.

- All common measures of the size of government—employees, expenditures, revenues, etc.—involve some deficiency. In particular, these items miss the impact of off-budget activities such as tax expenditures and regulatory costs. Nonetheless, there is strong evidence that the impact of the government on the allocation of national resources has increased over time.

- The level of government expenditures has increased in both nominal and real absolute terms, and in per capita terms. Government spending as a percentage of gross domestic product has fallen since the early 1990s.

- The share of spending on public welfare and health has increased in importance. The nature of the entitlement programs in these spending areas reduces governments' control over the annual level of expenditures.

- Personal income taxes, payroll taxes, and consumption taxes are currently the largest sources of government revenue.

EXERCISES

1. In *The End of Liberalism,* Theodore Lowi (1979: xii) offers the following article as part of a present-day constitution: "The public interest shall be defined by the satisfaction of voters in their constituencies. The test of the public interest is reelection." What does this imply about the role of government in society? Do you agree or disagree? Why?

2. Areas of public debate that have highlighted the tension between individual rights and social control include gun control and the required registration of guns, local antismoking bylaws, and laws to fight terrorism. Can you think of other areas of debate that reflect this tension? Discuss in terms of individual rights and social benefits.

3. In each of the following circumstances, decide whether the impact of government on the economy increases or decreases and why. In each case, how does your answer compare to that given by standard measures of the size of government?

   a. Provincial governments mandate that employers provide daycare centres for the use of their employees.

   b. Provincial governments subsidize daycare centres with parents paying $5 in user fees per day.

   c. Provincial governments open government-run daycare centres.

   d. The federal budget is brought into balance by reducing grants to provincial governments.

4. High and rising health care expenditures are one important element that has contributed to provincial government deficits. New, or additional, payroll taxes may be one way to finance the higher health care costs. If adopted, how would the higher payroll taxes affect the size of the provincial budgets? How would this affect the role of government in the economy?

5. Proponents argue that the government guarantees on loans to students do not result in an increase in government spending since only "loans" are involved. The same claim is heard from corporations that receive government guarantees on billions of dollars of loans by (private) banks for private sector projects. Evaluate these claims.

6. Use the data in Table 1.1 to calculate the following: the rate of growth in total government expenditures, in real government spending, and in real, per capita spending over the period from 2000 to 2009.

   (i) What do the data tell you about the growth in government spending relative to population growth in Canada over this nine-year period?

   (ii) Based on the data for the period 2000 to 2009, would you argue that the size of government has increased or decreased over this period? Explain.

7. Consider the data presented in the table below. Suppose that the federal government increases grants to provincial governments by $6 billion in 2010. Does the increase in grants necessarily lead to an increase in total government spending? Why or why not?

	Federal Government		Provincial Governments		Local Governments		Total
Government Expenditures before and after Intergovernmental Grants (millions of dollars)							
	Including Grants	Excluding Grants	Including Grants	Excluding Grants	Including Grants	Excluding Grants	Excluding Grants
2009	258,209	193,130	377,313	324,778	144,736	144,589	662,497

Source: Data taken from Karin Treff and Deborah Ort, *Finances of the Nation, 2010* (Toronto: Canadian Tax Foundation, 2011), B5. Note that for this example CPP and QPP have not been included in the total. "Excluding grants" refers to grants made to other levels of government.

APPENDIX

Doing Research in Public Finance

Throughout the text, we cite many books, articles, and websites. These references are useful for those who want to delve into the various subjects in more detail. Students interested in writing term papers or theses on subjects in public finance should also consult the following journals that specialize in the field:

- *Journal of Public Economics*
- *Canadian Tax Journal*
- *National Tax Journal*
- *Public Finance*
- *Public Finance Quarterly*
- *International Tax and Public Finance*
- *Journal of Public Economic Theory*
- *Economics of Governance*

In addition, all the major general-interest economics journals frequently publish articles that deal with public finance issues. These include, but are not limited to, the following:

- *Canadian Journal of Economics*
- *American Economic Review*
- *Canadian Public Policy*
- *Journal of Economic Perspectives*
- *Journal of Political Economy*
- *Review of Economics and Statistics*
- *Canadian Business Economics*
- *Journal of Economic Literature*

Vast amounts of data are available on government spending and taxing activities. Publications of the Canadian Tax Foundation are a particularly useful source. These include the following:

- *The National Finances* (annually until 1994)
- *Provincial and Municipal Finances* (biannually to 1993)
- *Finances of the Nation* (beginning in 1995)

In addition, the research monographs published by the Canadian Tax Foundation are valuable references. The website for the Canadian Tax Foundation is http://www.ctf.ca. A number of other Canadian research institutes interested in public finance issues have websites. These include the Canadian Centre for Policy Alternatives at http://www.policyalternatives.ca, the C.D. Howe Institute at http://www.cdhowe.org, the Fraser Institute at http://www.fraserinstitute.ca, and the Institute for Research on Public Policy at http://www.irpp.org. These institutes provide alternative views and analysis by public finance scholars.

Budget papers prepared annually by the federal minister of finance and counterparts at the provincial level provide additional data, and the Department of Finance publishes occasional papers on various topics. The website for the Department of Finance is http://www.fin.gc.ca. Statistics Canada, http://www.statcan.ca, regularly publishes detailed federal and provincial public finance data in *Public Sector Statistics*, and in 1992 published *Public Finance Historical Data, 1965–66 to 1991–92. Historical Statistics of Canada*, 2nd ed., by M. C. Urquhart and K. A. H. Buckley (Ottawa: Supply and Services, 1983) provides early Canadian public finance data. Recent taxation statistics can be found at http://www.canadacustoms.ca.

Reports by three royal commissions—the Royal Commission on Dominion–Provincial Relations, 1940 (Rowell–Sirois), the Royal Commission on Taxation, 1966 (Carter), and the Royal Commission on the Economic Union and Development Prospects for Canada, 1985 (Macdonald)—and research papers prepared for these commissions are an additional valuable source.

Canadian tax and expenditure policies are much influenced by U.S. policies. The student of public finance in Canada is well advised to be acquainted with the U.S. situation. In particular, students should consult the volumes published by the Brookings Institution, http://www.brookings.edu. These books include careful and up-to-date discussions of important public finance issues using relatively nontechnical language. The working paper series of the National Bureau of Economic Research, http://www.nber.org, available in many Canadian libraries is another good source of recent research on public finance. The technical difficulty of these papers is sometimes considerable, however.

CHAPTER 2

Fundamentals of Welfare Economics

*[The goals of government] should be to realize maximum human dignity,
maximum human welfare, maximum environmental quality and minimum
violence in human relationships.*

—Pierre Elliott Trudeau

AFTER READING THIS CHAPTER, THE STUDENT SHOULD BE ABLE TO:

LO1 Draw the contract curve in an Edgeworth Box diagram.

LO2 Define a Pareto improvement in the allocation of resources.

LO3 Explain the efficiency conditions for an economy with variable production.

LO4 State the First Fundamental Theorem of Welfare Economics.

LO5 State the Second Fundamental Theorem of Welfare Economics.

LO6 Identify which condition for efficiency is violated when producers have monopoly power.

LO7 Provide examples of the nonexistence of markets.

LO8 Identify the allocation that maximizes social welfare.

LO9 Describe two controversial assumptions of welfare economics.

As citizens we are called on to evaluate a constant flow of proposals concerning government's role in the economy. Should income taxes be raised? Is it sensible to change the age at which Canada Pension Plan payments begin? Should there be stricter controls on auto emissions? The list is virtually endless. Given the enormous diversity of the government's economic activities, some kind of systematic framework is needed to organize thoughts about the desirability of various government actions. Without such a framework, each government program ends up being evaluated on an ad hoc basis, and a coherent economic policy becomes impossible to achieve.[1]

WELFARE ECONOMICS

The framework used by most public finance specialists is **welfare economics**, the branch of economic theory concerned with the social desirability of alternative economic states.[2] This approach uses the concepts of efficiency and equity to evaluate the alternatives. In this chapter we sketch the fundamentals of welfare economics. The theory is used to distinguish the circumstances under which markets can be expected to perform well from those under which markets fail to produce desirable results.

Pure Exchange Economy

We begin by considering a very simple economy: two people who consume two commodities with fixed supplies. The only economic problem here is to allocate amounts of the two goods between the two people.

---

[1] The method of evaluating policies according to certain ethical criteria is called **normative analysis**. In contrast, **positive analysis** refers to the method of predicting the consequences of policies.

[2] Welfare economics relies heavily on certain basic economic tools, particularly indifference curves.

FIGURE 2.1

EDGEWORTH BOX

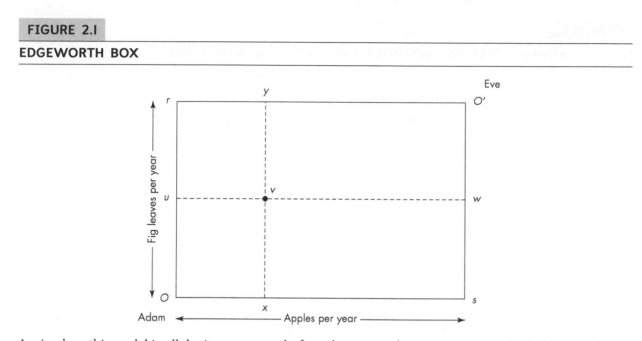

As simple as this model is, all the important results from the two goods–two person case also hold in economies with many people and commodities. We analyze the two-by-two case because of its simplicity.

The two people are Adam and Eve, and the two commodities are apples (food) and fig leaves (clothing). An analytical device known as the **Edgeworth Box** depicts the distribution of apples and fig leaves between Adam and Eve.[3] In Figure 2.1, the length of the Edgeworth Box, Os, represents the total number of apples available in the economy; the height, Or, is the total number of fig leaves. The amounts of the goods consumed by Adam are measured by distances from point O; the quantities consumed by Eve are measured by distances from O'. For example, at point v, Adam consumes Ou fig leaves and Ox apples, while Eve consumes $O'y$ apples and $O'w$ fig leaves. Thus, any point within the Edgeworth Box represents some allocation of apples and fig leaves between Adam and Eve.

Now assume Adam and Eve each have a set of conventionally shaped indifference curves that represent their preferences for apples and fig leaves. In Figure 2.2, both sets of indifference curves are superimposed

FIGURE 2.2

INDIFFERENCE CURVES IN AN EDGEWORTH BOX

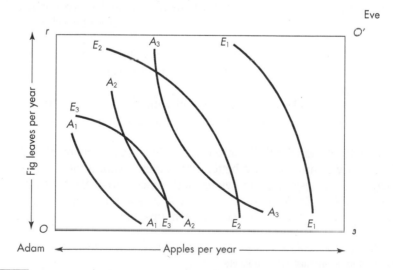

---

[3] Named after the great nineteenth-century economist F. Y. Edgeworth.

FIGURE 2.3

MAKING ADAM BETTER OFF WITHOUT EVE BECOMING WORSE OFF

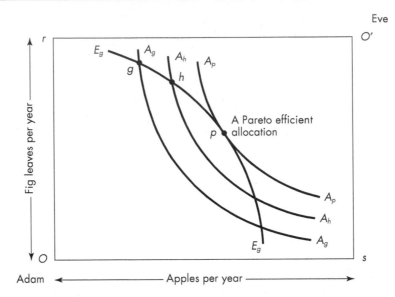

onto the Edgeworth Box. Adam's are labelled with A's; Eve's are labelled with E's. Indifference curves with greater numbers represent higher levels of happiness (utility). Adam is happier on indifference curve A_3 than on A_2 or A_1, and Eve is happier on indifference curve E_3 than on E_2 or E_1. In general, Eve's utility increases as her position moves toward the southwest, while Adam's utility increases as he moves toward the northeast.

Suppose some arbitrary distribution of apples and fig leaves is selected–say point g in Figure 2.3. A_gA_g is Adam's indifference curve that runs through point g, and E_gE_g is Eve's. Now pose the following question. Is it possible to reallocate apples and fig leaves between Adam and Eve in such a way that Adam is made better off, while Eve is made no worse off? A moment's thought suggests such an allocation, at point h. Adam is better off at this point because indifference curve A_hA_h represents a higher utility level for him than A_gA_g. On the other hand, Eve is no worse off at h because she is on her original indifference curve, E_gE_g.

Can Adam's welfare be further increased without doing any harm to Eve? That is possible, as long as Adam can be moved to indifference curves farther to the northeast while still remaining on E_gE_g. This process can be continued until Adam's indifference curve is just touching E_gE_g, which occurs at point p in Figure 2.3. The only way to put Adam on a higher indifference curve than A_pA_p would be to put Eve on a lower one. An allocation such as point p, at which the only way to make one person better off is to make another person worse off, is called **Pareto efficient**.[4] Pareto efficiency is often used as the standard for evaluating the desirability of an allocation of resources. If the allocation is not Pareto efficient, it is "wasteful" in the sense that it is possible to make someone better off without hurting anybody else. When economists use the word *efficient*, they usually have the notion of Pareto efficiency in mind.

A related notion is that of a **Pareto improvement**–a reallocation of resources that makes one person better off without making anyone else worse off. In Figure 2.3, the move from g to h is a Pareto improvement, as is the move from h to p.

Point p is not the only Pareto efficient allocation that could have been reached by starting at point g. Figure 2.4 examines whether we can make Eve better off without lowering the utility of Adam. Logic similar to that surrounding Figure 2.3 suggests moving Eve to indifference curves farther to the southwest, provided that the allocation remains on A_gA_g. In doing so, a point like p_1 is isolated. At p_1, the only way to improve Eve's welfare is to move Adam to a lower indifference curve. Then, by definition, p_1 is a Pareto efficient allocation.

---

[4] Named after the nineteenth-century economist Vilfredo Pareto.

FIGURE 2.4

MAKING EVE BETTER OFF WITHOUT ADAM BECOMING WORSE OFF

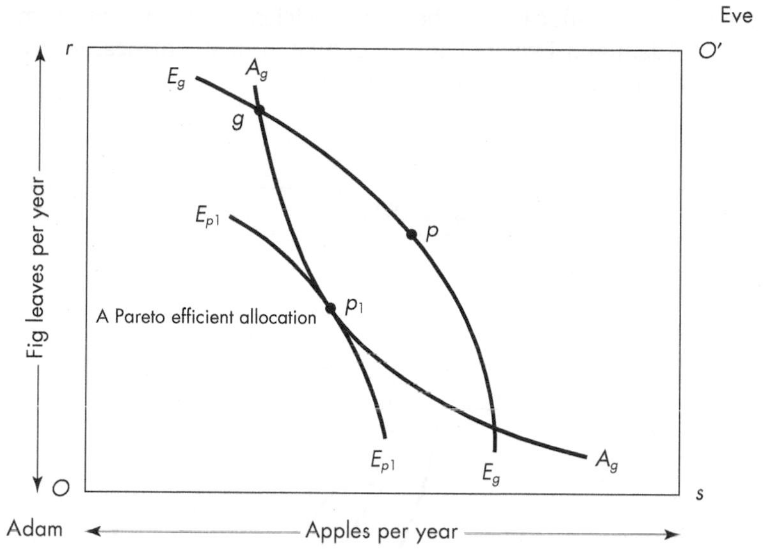

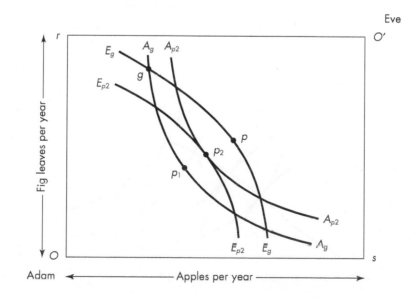

So far, we have been looking at moves that make one person better off and leave the other at the same level of utility. In Figure 2.5 we consider reallocations from point g that make *both* Adam and Eve better off. At p_2, for example, Adam is better off than at point g ($A_{p2}A_{p2}$ is farther to the northeast than A_gA_g) and so is Eve ($E_{p2}E_{p2}$ is farther to the southwest than E_gE_g). Point p_2 is Pareto efficient, because at that point it is impossible to make either individual better off without making the other worse off. It should now be clear that, starting at point g, a whole set of Pareto efficient points can be found. They only differ with respect to how much each of the parties gains from the reallocation of resources.

FIGURE 2.5

MAKING BOTH ADAM AND EVE BETTER OFF

Recall that the initial point *g* was selected arbitrarily. We can repeat the procedure for finding Pareto efficient allocations with any starting point. Had point *k* in Figure 2.6 been the original allocation, Pareto efficient allocations like p_3 and p_4 could have been isolated. This exercise reveals a whole set of Pareto efficient points in the Edgeworth Box. The locus of all the Pareto efficient points is called the **contract curve**, and is denoted *mm* in Figure 2.7. Note that for an allocation to be Pareto efficient (to be on *mm*), it must be a point at which the indifference curves of Adam and Eve are barely touching. In mathematical terms, the indifference curves are tangent—the slopes of the indifference curves are equal.

FIGURE 2.6

STARTING FROM A DIFFERENT INITIAL POINT

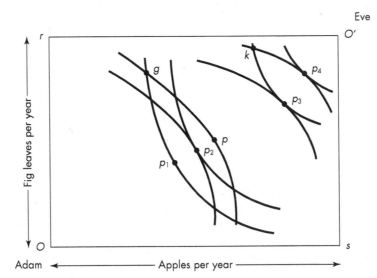

FIGURE 2.7

THE CONTRACT CURVE

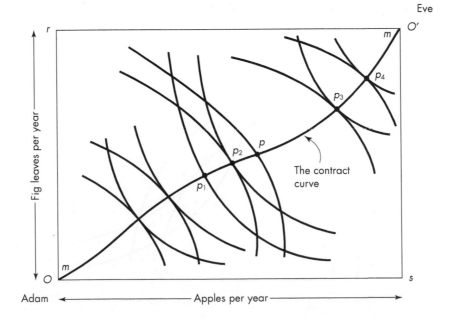

In economic terms, the absolute value of the slope of the indifference curve indicates the rate at which the individual is willing to trade one good for an additional amount of another, called the *marginal rate of substitution* (MRS). Hence, Pareto efficiency requires that marginal rates of substitution be equal for all consumers:

$$MRS_{af}^{Adam} = MRS_{af}^{Eve} \qquad (2.1)$$

where MRS_{af}^{Adam} is Adam's marginal rate of substitution of apples for fig leaves, and MRS_{af}^{Eve} is Eve's.

An Economy with Production

The production possibilities curve. So far, we have assumed that supplies of all the commodities are fixed. Consider what happens when productive inputs can shift between the production of apples and fig leaves, so the quantities of the two goods are alterable. Provided the inputs are efficiently used, if more apples are produced, then fig leaf production must necessarily fall, and vice versa. The **production possibilities curve** shows the maximum quantity of fig leaves that can be produced along with any given quantity of apples.[5] A typical production possibilities curve is depicted as CC in Figure 2.8. As shown in Figure 2.8, one option available to the economy is to produce Ow fig leaves and Ox apples. The economy can increase apple production from Ox to Oz, distance xz. To do this, inputs have to be removed from the production of fig leaves and devoted to apples. Fig leaf production must fall by distance wy if apple production is to increase by xz. The ratio of distance wy to distance xz is called the **marginal rate of transformation** of apples for fig leaves (MRT_{af}) because it shows the rate at which the economy can transform apples into fig leaves. Just as MRS_{af} measures the absolute value of the slope of an indifference curve, MRT_{af} measures the absolute value of the slope of the production possibilities curve.

It is useful to express the marginal rate of transformation in terms of **marginal cost** (*MC*)—the incremental production cost of one more unit of output. To do so, recall that society can increase apple production by xz only by giving up wy fig leaves. In effect, then, the distance wy represents the incremental cost of producing apples, which we denote MC_a. Similarly, the distance xz is the incremental cost of producing fig leaves, MC_f. By definition, the absolute value of the slope of the production possibilities curve is distance wy divided by

FIGURE 2.8

PRODUCTION POSSIBILITIES CURVE

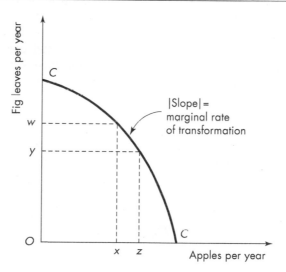

---

[5] The production possibilities curve can be derived from an Edgeworth Box whose dimensions represent the quantities of inputs available for production.

xz, or MC_a/MC_f. But also by definition, the slope of the production possibilities curve is the marginal rate of transformation. Hence, we have shown that

$$MRT_{af} = \frac{MC_a}{MC_f} \qquad (2.2)$$

Efficiency conditions with variable production. When the supplies of apples and fig leaves are variable, the condition for Pareto efficiency in Equation (2.1) must be extended. The condition becomes

$$MRT_{af} = MRS_{af}^{Adam} = MRS_{af}^{Eve} \qquad (2.3)$$

A simple arithmetic example demonstrates why the first equality in Equation (2.3) must hold. Suppose that at a given allocation Adam's MRS_{af} is 1/3, and the MRT_{af} is 2/3. By the definition of MRT_{af}, at this allocation, two additional fig leaves could be produced by giving up three apples. By the definition of MRS_{af}, if Adam lost three extra apples, he would require only one fig leaf to maintain his original utility level. Therefore, Adam could be made better off by giving up three apples and transforming them into two fig leaves, and no one else would be made worse off in the process. Such a trade is *always* possible as long as the marginal rate of substitution does not equal the marginal rate of transformation. Only when the slopes of the curves for each are equal is it impossible to make a Pareto improvement. Hence, $MRT_{af} = MRS_{af}$ is a necessary condition for Pareto efficiency. The rate at which apples can be transformed into fig leaves (MRT_{af}) must equal the rate at which consumers are willing to trade apples for fig leaves (MRS_{af}).

Using Equation (2.2), the conditions for Pareto efficiency can be reinterpreted in terms of marginal cost. Just substitute (2.2) into (2.3), which gives us

$$\frac{MC_a}{MC_f} = MRS_{af}^{Adam} = MRS_{af}^{Eve} \qquad (2.4)$$

as a necessary condition for Pareto efficiency.

THE FIRST FUNDAMENTAL THEOREM OF WELFARE ECONOMICS

Now that we have described the necessary conditions for Pareto efficiency, we may ask whether a real-world economy will achieve this apparently desirable state. It depends on what assumptions we make about the operations of the economy. Suppose that 1) all producers and consumers act as perfect competitors—that is, no one has any market power—and 2) a market exists for each and every commodity. Under these circumstances, the so-called *First Fundamental Theorem of Welfare Economics* states that a Pareto efficient allocation of resources emerges. In effect, this stunning result tells us that a competitive economy "automatically" allocates resources efficiently, without any need for centralized direction. (Think of Adam Smith's "invisible hand.") In a way, the first welfare theorem merely formalizes an insight that has long been recognized: when it comes to providing goods and services, free enterprise systems are amazingly productive.[6]

A rigorous proof of the fundamental theorem requires fairly sophisticated mathematics, but we can provide an intuitive justification. The essence of competition is that all people face the same prices—each consumer and producer is so small relative to the market that his or her actions alone cannot affect prices. In our example, this means Adam and Eve both pay the same prices for fig leaves (P_f) and apples (P_a). A basic result from the theory of rational choice is that a necessary condition for Adam to maximize utility is

$$MRS_{af}^{Adam} = \frac{P_a}{P_f} \qquad (2.5)$$

---

[6] "The bourgeoisie, during its rule of scarce 100 years, has created more massive and more colossal productive forces than have all preceding generations together," according to Karl Marx and Friedrich Engels in *The Communist Manifesto*, Part I (Tucker, 1978: 477).

Similarly, Eve's utility-maximizing bundle is characterized by

$$MRS_{af}^{Eve} = \frac{P_a}{P_f} \tag{2.6}$$

Equations (2.5) and (2.6) together imply that

$$MRS_{af}^{Adam} = MRS_{af}^{Eve}$$

This condition, though, is identical to Equation (2.1), one of the necessary conditions for Pareto efficiency.

However, as emphasized in the preceding section, we must consider the production side as well. A basic result from economic theory is that a profit-maximizing competitive firm produces output up to the point at which marginal cost and price are equal. In our example, this means $P_a = MC_a$ and $P_f = MC_f$, or

$$\frac{MC_a}{MC_f} = \frac{P_a}{P_f} \tag{2.7}$$

But recall from Equation (2.2) that MC_a/MC_f is just the marginal rate of transformation. Thus, we can rewrite (2.7) as

$$MRT_{af} = \frac{P_a}{P_f} \tag{2.8}$$

Now, consider Equations (2.5), (2.6), and (2.8), and notice that P_a/P_f appears on the right-hand side of each. Hence, these three equations together imply that $MRS_{af}^{Adam} = MRS_{af}^{Eve} = MRT_{af}$, which is the necessary condition for Pareto efficiency. Competition, along with maximizing behaviour on the part of all individuals, leads to an efficient outcome. The necessary condition for Pareto efficiency holds in a competitive economy because all consumers and producers face the same prices.

Finally, we can take advantage of Equation (2.4) to write the conditions for Pareto efficiency in terms of marginal cost. Simply substitute (2.5) or (2.6) into (2.4) to find

$$\frac{P_a}{P_f} = \frac{MC_a}{MC_f} \tag{2.9}$$

Pareto efficiency requires that prices be in the same ratios as marginal costs, and competition guarantees this condition is met. The marginal cost of a commodity is the additional cost to society of providing it. According to Equation (2.9), efficiency requires that the additional cost of each commodity be reflected in its price.

FAIRNESS AND THE SECOND FUNDAMENTAL THEOREM OF WELFARE ECONOMICS

If properly functioning competitive markets allocate resources efficiently, what role does the government have to play in the economy? Only a very small government would appear to be appropriate. Its main function would be to establish a setting in which property rights are protected so that competition can work. Government provides law and order, a court system, and national defence. Anything more is superfluous. However, such reasoning is based on a superficial understanding of the fundamental theorem. Things are really much more complicated. For one thing, it has been assumed that efficiency is the only criterion for deciding if a given allocation of resources is good. It is not obvious, however, that Pareto efficiency by itself is desirable.

To see why, let us return to the simple model in which the total quantity of each good is fixed. Consider Figure 2.9, which reproduces the contract curve mm derived in Figure 2.7. Compare the two allocations p_5 (at the lower left-hand corner of the box) and q (located near the centre). Because p_5 lies on the contract curve, by definition it is Pareto efficient. On the other hand, q is inefficient. Is allocation p_5 therefore better? That depends on what is meant by better. To the extent that society prefers a relatively equal distribution of real income, q might be preferred to p_5, even though q is not Pareto efficient. On the other hand, society might not care about distribution at all, or it might care more about Eve than Adam. In this case, p_5 would be preferred to q.

FIGURE 2.9

EFFICIENCY VERSUS EQUITY

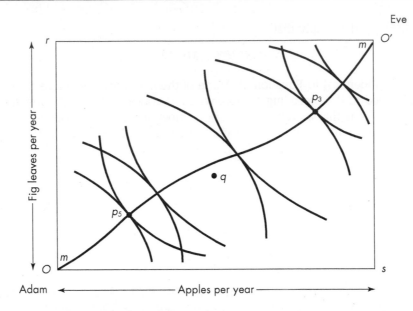

The key point is that the criterion of Pareto efficiency by itself is not enough to rank alternative allocations of resources. Rather, explicit value judgments are required on the fairness of the distribution of utility. To formalize this concept, note that the contract curve implicitly defines a relationship between the maximum amount of utility that Adam can attain for each level of Eve's utility. In Figure 2.10, Eve's utility is plotted on the horizontal axis, and Adam's utility is recorded on the vertical axis. Curve *UU* is the **utility possibilities curve** derived from the contract curve.[7] It shows the maximum amount of one person's utility given the other individual's utility level.

FIGURE 2.10

UTILITY POSSIBILITIES CURVE

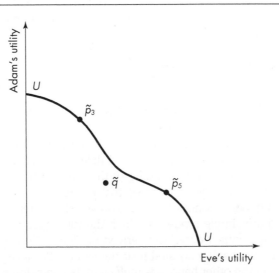

---

[7] The production possibilities curve in Figure 2.8 is drawn on the reasonable assumption that the absolute value of its slope continually increases as we move downward along it. The more apples produced, the more fig leaves given up to produce an apple. However, there is no reason to assume this holds for the trade-off between individuals' utilities. This is why *UU* in Figure 2.10 is wavy rather than smooth.

Point $\widetilde{p}_5$ corresponds to point p_5 on the contract curve in Figure 2.9. Here, Eve's utility is relatively high compared to Adam's. Point $\widetilde{p}_3$ in Figure 2.10, which corresponds to p_3 in Figure 2.9, is just the opposite. Point $\widetilde{q}$ corresponds to point q in Figure 2.9. Because q is off the contract curve, $\widetilde{q}$ must be inside the utility possibilities curve, reflecting the fact that it is possible to increase one person's utility without decreasing the other's.

All points on or below the utility possibilities curve are attainable by society; all points above it are not attainable. By definition, all points on UU are Pareto efficient, but they represent very different distributions of real income between Adam and Eve. Which point is best? The conventional way to answer this question is to postulate a **social welfare function**, which embodies society's views on the relative deservedness of Adam and Eve. Imagine that just as an *individual's* welfare depends on the quantities of commodities he or she consumes, society's welfare depends on the utilities of each of its members. Algebraically, social welfare (W) is some function (F) of each individual's utility:

$$W = F(U^{Adam}, U^{Eve}) \tag{2.10}$$

We assume the value of social welfare increases as either U^{Adam} or U^{Eve} increases—society is better off when any of its members becomes better off. Note that we have said nothing about how society manifests these preferences. Under some conditions, members of society may not be able to agree on how to rank each other's utilities, and the social welfare function does not even exist. For the moment, we simply assume it does exist.

Just as an individual's utility function for commodities leads to a set of indifference curves for those commodities, so does a social welfare function lead to a set of indifference curves between people's utilities. Figure 2.11 depicts a typical set of social indifference curves. Their downward slope indicates that if Eve's utility decreases, the only way to maintain a given level of social welfare is to increase Adam's utility, and vice versa. The level of social welfare increases as we move toward the northeast reflecting the fact that an increase in any individual's utility increases social welfare, other things being the same.

In Figure 2.12, the social indifference curves are superimposed on the utility possibilities curve from Figure 2.10. Point i is not as desirable as point ii (point ii is on a higher social indifference curve than point i) even though point i is Pareto efficient and point ii is not. Here, society's value judgments, embodied in the social welfare function, favour a more equal distribution of real income, inefficient though it may be. Of course, point iii is preferred to either of these. It is both efficient and "fair."

Now, the First Fundamental Theorem of Welfare Economics indicates that a properly working competitive system leads to some allocation on the utility possibilities curve. There is no reason, however, for it to be the

---

FIGURE 2.11

SOCIAL INDIFFERENCE CURVES

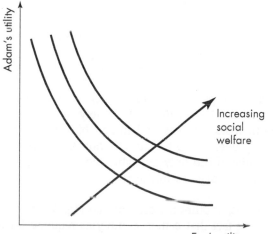

MAXIMIZING SOCIAL WELFARE

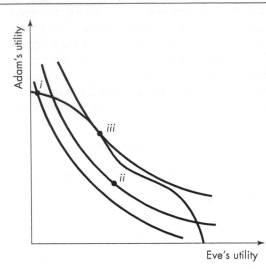

particular point that maximizes social welfare. We conclude that, even if the economy generates a Pareto efficient allocation of resources, government intervention may be necessary to achieve a "fair" distribution of utility.

Does the government have to intervene directly in markets in order to move the economy to the welfare maximizing point? For example, does it have to impose ceilings on the prices of commodities consumed by the poor? The answer is no. According to the *Second Fundamental Theorem of Welfare Economics*, society can attain any Pareto efficient allocation of resources by making a suitable assignment of initial endowments and then letting people freely trade with each other, as in our Edgeworth Box model. Roughly speaking, by redistributing income suitably and then getting out of the way and letting markets work, the government can attain any point on the utility possibility frontier.

Author Tim Harford (2006: 73–74) explains the Second Fundamental Theorem of Welfare Economics by using the analogy of a 100-metre race. He writes,

> If your goal is to have all the sprinters cross the line together, you could just change the rules of the race, ordering the fast runners to slow down and everyone to hold hands as they crossed the finish line. A waste of talent. Or you could move some starting blocks forward and some back, so that although each sprinter was running as fast as he could . . . the fastest had to cover enough extra ground that he would end up breaking the tape neck-and-neck with the slowest.

Achieving equity through such policies as a tax on income is similar to requiring the fast runners to slow down, because it punishes income-enhancing behaviour. But a reassignment of initial endowments (for example, by simply taking away some apples from Adam and giving them to Eve) is similar to moving the starting blocks of the runners. The Second Fundamental Theorem of Welfare Economics shows that this can achieve equity without inhibiting efficiency.

The Second Welfare Theorem is important because it shows that, at least in theory, the issues of efficiency and distributional fairness can be separated. If society determines that the current distribution is unfair, it need not interfere with market prices and impair efficiency. Rather, society need only transfer resources among people in a way deemed to be fair. Of course, the government needs some way to reallocate resources, and problems arise if the only available mechanism for doing so (such as income taxes) themselves induce inefficiencies. We discuss further the relationship between efficiency and fairness in Chapter 16.

In addition to distributional issues, another reason why the First Welfare Theorem need not imply a minimal government has to do with the fact that certain conditions required for its validity may not be satisfied by real-world markets. An absence of these conditions may lead free markets to allocate resources inefficiently.

AIRBNB, UBER, AND THE SHARING ECONOMY

The internet and mobile apps have facilitated the creation of new markets for people to achieve gains from trade. The so-called sharing economy, exemplified by companies like Airbnb and Uber, allows individuals to rent out their underused personal assets, such as cars and homes, to earn additional income. Ratings and reviews are solicited to develop trust among users. Unlike traditional markets, where consumers purchase goods and services at established businesses locations, online platforms cut the cost of peer-to-peer transacting between strangers. These "virtual markets" are growing rapidly. One study estimates that global revenues from sharing economy companies will rise from roughly $15 billion today to $335 billion by 2025. However, the rise of the sharing economy is controversial, because of safety concerns, highlighted by disagreements over insurance and licensing. The City of Toronto filed a legal action against Uber in late 2014, arguing that the company is operating illegally and should be shut down. Airbnb was in the news in 2014 when a Calgary home was trashed by its guests. The potential efficiency gains from the sharing economy are evident, but regulatory issues still need to be sorted out.

Based on CBC News (2014), Kerr (2015), and "Court case between Toronto, Uber pushed back until June." *The Globe and Mail,* May 11, 2015.

Complete references for this feature can be found in the References section on page 473.

MARKET FAILURE

In the famous film *Casablanca,* whenever something seems amiss, the police chief gives an order to "round up the usual suspects." Similarly, whenever markets appear to be failing to allocate resources efficiently, economists round up the same group of possible causes for the supposed failure. A market economy may fail to generate an efficient allocation of resources for two general reasons: market power and nonexistence of markets.

Market Power

The First Welfare Theorem holds only if all consumers and firms are price takers. If some individuals or firms are price makers (they have the power to affect prices), then the allocation of resources will generally be inefficient. Why? A firm with market power may be able to raise price above marginal cost by supplying less output than a competitive firm would. Thus, one of the necessary conditions for Pareto efficiency—that relative prices equal relative marginal costs of production—is violated. An insufficient quantity of resources is devoted to the commodity.

Price-making behaviour can arise in several contexts. An extreme case is a **monopoly**, where there is only one firm in the market and entry of new firms is blocked. Even in the less extreme case of oligopoly (a few sellers), the firms in an industry may be able to increase price above marginal cost. Finally, some industries have many firms, but each firm has some market power because the firms produce differentiated products. For example, a lot of firms produce running shoes, yet many consumers view Reebok, Nike, and Adidas shoes as distinct commodities.

A *natural monopoly* occurs when the production of some good or service is subject to continually decreasing average costs—the greater the level of output, the lower the cost per unit. Consequently, any given output can be produced at the minimum total cost if it is produced by one firm. Some examples are the provision of water, electricity, and high-speed Internet access. A natural monopoly creates a role for government either in the form of regulation or public ownership of the firm.

Nonexistence of Markets

The proof behind the First Welfare Theorem assumes a market exists for every commodity. After all, if a market for a commodity does not exist, then we can hardly expect the market to allocate it efficiently. In reality, markets for certain commodities may fail to emerge. Consider, for instance, insurance, a very important commodity in a world of uncertainty. Despite the existence of firms such as The Co-operators and Allstate, there are certain events for which insurance simply cannot be purchased on the private market. For example, suppose you wanted to purchase insurance against the possibility of becoming poor. Would a firm in a competitive market ever find it profitable to supply "poverty insurance"? The answer is no, because if you purchased such insurance, you might decide not to work very hard. To discourage such behaviour, the insurance firm would have to monitor your behaviour to determine whether your low income was due to bad luck or to goofing off. However, to perform such monitoring would be very difficult or impossible. Hence, there is no market for poverty insurance—it simply cannot be purchased.

Basically, the problem here is **asymmetric information**—one party in a transaction has information that is not available to another. One rationalization for governmental income support programs is that they provide poverty insurance that is unavailable privately. The premium on this "insurance policy" is the taxes you pay when you are able to earn income. In the event of poverty, your benefit comes in the form of welfare payments.

Another type of inefficiency that may arise due to the nonexistence of a market is an **externality**, a situation in which one person's behaviour affects the welfare of another in a way that is outside existing markets. For example, suppose your roommate begins smoking large cigars, polluting the air and making you worse off. Why is this an efficiency problem? Your roommate uses up a scarce resource, clean air, when he smokes cigars. However, there is no market for clean air that forces him to pay for it. In effect, he pays a price of zero for the clean air and therefore "overuses" it. The price system is failing to provide correct signals about the opportunity cost of a commodity.

Externalities have a simple interpretation in the analytics of welfare economics. In the derivation of Equation (2.9), it was implicitly assumed that marginal cost meant social marginal cost—it embodied the incremental value of all of society's resources used in production. In the example above, however, your roommate's private marginal cost of smoking is less than the social marginal cost because he does not have to pay for the clean air he uses. The price of a cigar, which reflects its private marginal cost, is not correctly reflecting its social marginal cost. Hence, Equation (2.9) is not satisfied, and the allocation of resources is inefficient. Incidentally, an externality can be positive—confer a benefit—as well as negative. Think of a molecular biologist who publishes a paper about a novel gene-splicing technique that can be used by a pharmaceutical firm. When a positive externality exists, the market generates an inefficiently low amount of the beneficial activity.

Closely related to an externality is the case of a **public good**, a commodity that is *nonrival* and *nonexcludable* in consumption. Nonrival means that the fact that one person consumes it does not prevent anyone else from doing so as well. Nonexcludable means that it is either impossible or very expensive to prevent anyone from consuming it. The classic example of a public good is a lighthouse. When the lighthouse turns on its beacon, all the ships in the vicinity benefit. The fact that one person takes advantage of the lighthouse's services does not keep anyone else from doing so simultaneously, and it is very difficult to prevent any ship that is passing the lighthouse from using the signal for navigation.

People may have an incentive to hide how much they value a public good. Suppose that the lighthouse benefits you. You know, however, that once the beacon is lit, you can enjoy its services whether you pay for them or not. Therefore, you may claim that the lighthouse means nothing to you, hoping to get a "free ride" after other people pay for it. Unfortunately, everyone has the same incentive, so the lighthouse may not get built, even though its construction could be very beneficial. The market mechanism may fail to force people to reveal their preferences for public goods, and possibly result in insufficient resources being devoted to them.

Governments can provide public goods that will not be provided by the private sector because governments can coerce payments from individuals. Through taxation and other means, governments can force individuals to contribute to the provision of public goods. Furthermore, governments can regulate, promote, or discourage private sector activities that generate externalities. A detailed discussion of the provision of public goods and the regulation of externalities is contained in Chapters 4 and 5.

Overview

The First Fundamental Theorem of Welfare Economics states that a properly working competitive economy generates a Pareto efficient allocation of resources without any government intervention. However, we have just shown that in real-world economies competition may not hold, and markets for some goods and services may not exist (or may function inadequately) because of asymmetric information or the presence of externalities and public goods. Hence, the market-determined allocation of resources is unlikely to be efficient. There are, then, opportunities for government to intervene and enhance economic efficiency.[8]

It must be emphasized that while efficiency problems provide opportunities for government intervention in the economy, they do not require it. The fact that the market-generated allocation of resources is imperfect does not mean that the government is capable of doing better. For example, in certain cases, the costs of setting up a government agency to deal with an externality could exceed the cost of the externality itself. Moreover, governments, like people, can make mistakes. Some argue that government is inherently incapable of acting efficiently, so while in theory it can improve on the status quo, in practice it never will. While this argument is extreme, it highlights the fact that the First Welfare Theorem is helpful only in identifying situations in which intervention *may* lead to greater efficiency.

BUYING INTO WELFARE ECONOMICS

In recent years, vigorous debates have occurred about how to organize an economy in countries as diverse as India, China, and Iraq. Nevertheless, the same issues arise in developed nations as well; how much of the national economy should be devoted to the public sector, and which taxes should finance expenditures? The theory of welfare economics introduced in this chapter provides the standard framework for thinking about public policies. There are, however, some controversies surrounding the theory.

First, the underlying outlook is highly individualistic, with a focus on people's utilities and how to maximize them. This is brought out starkly in the formulation of the social welfare function, Equation (2.10). The basic view expressed in that equation is that a good society is one whose members are happy. As suggested in Chapter 1, however, other societal goals are possible—to maximize the power of the state, to glorify God, and so on. Welfare economics does not have much to say to people with such goals. It is no surprise that Iran's Ayatollah Khomeini used to say that economics is for donkeys.

Because welfare economics puts people's preferences at centre stage, it requires that these preferences be taken seriously. It assumes that people know best what gives them satisfaction. If one believes that individuals' preferences are ill-formed or corrupt, a theory that shows how to maximize their utility is essentially irrelevant.

Musgrave (1959) developed the concept of **merit goods** to describe commodities that ought to be provided even if the members of society do not demand them. Government support of the fine arts is often justified on this basis. Operas and concerts should be provided publicly if individuals are unwilling to pay enough to meet their costs. But as Baumol and Baumol (1981: 426–27) have noted,

> The term *merit good* merely becomes a formal designation for the unadorned value judgment that the arts are good for society and therefore deserve financial support . . . [the] merit good approach is not really a justification for support—it merely invents a bit of terminology to designate the desire to do so.

Another possible problem with the welfare economics framework is its concern with *results*. Situations are evaluated in terms of the allocation of resources, and not of *how* the allocation was determined. Perhaps a society should be judged by the *processes* used to arrive at the allocation, not the actual results. Are people free to enter contracts? Are public processes democratic? If this view is taken, welfare economics loses its normative significance.

On the other hand, the great advantage of welfare economics is that it provides a coherent framework for thinking about the appropriateness of various government interventions. Every government intervention, after

---

[8] The macroeconomic stabilization role of government in the face of persistent unemployment is now normally covered in undergraduate macroeconomic courses and is not discussed at any length in this book. However, the effects of macroeconomic fluctuations on employment and employment insurance are discussed in Chapter 10.

all, involves a reallocation of resources, and the whole purpose of welfare economics is to evaluate alternative allocations. The framework of welfare economics impels us to ask three key questions whenever a government activity is proposed:

· Will it have desirable distributional consequences?
· Will it enhance efficiency?
· Can it be done at a reasonable cost?

If the answer to these questions is no, the market should probably be left alone. Of course, to answer these questions may require substantial research and, in the case of the first question, value judgments as well. But just asking the right questions provides an invaluable structure for the decision-making process. It forces people to make their ethical values explicit, and it facilitates the detection of frivolous or self-serving programs.

SUMMARY

• Welfare economics is the study of the desirability of alternative economic states.

• A Pareto efficient allocation occurs when no person can be made better off without making another person worse off. A necessary condition for Pareto efficiency is that each person's marginal rate of substitution between two commodities equals the marginal rate of transformation. Pareto efficiency is the economist's benchmark of efficient performance for an economy.

• The First Fundamental Theorem of Welfare Economics states that, under certain conditions, competitive market mechanisms lead to Pareto efficient outcomes.

• Despite its appeal, Pareto efficiency has no obvious claim as an ethical norm. Society may prefer an inefficient allocation on the basis of equity, justice, or some other criterion. This provides one possible reason for government intervention in the economy.

• A social welfare function summarizes society's preferences concerning the utility of each of its members. It may be used to find the allocation of resources that maximizes social welfare.

• The Second Fundamental Theorem of Welfare Economics states that society can attain any Pareto efficient allocation of resources by making a suitable assignment of initial endowments and then letting people freely trade with each other.

• In addition to distributional concerns, another possible justification for government intervention is market failure, which may occur in the presence of market power or when some markets do not exist.

• The fact that the market does not allocate resources perfectly does not necessarily mean that the government can do better. Each case must be evaluated on its own merits.

• Welfare economics is based on an individualistic social philosophy. It does not pay much attention to the processes used to achieve results. Thus, although it provides a coherent and useful framework for analyzing policy, welfare economics is controversial.

EXERCISES

1. In which of the following markets do you expect efficient outcomes? Why?
   a. Hurricane insurance for beach houses
   b. Medical care
   c. Stock market
   d. MP3 players
   e. Loans for students who wish to attend college
   f. Housing

2. Hamlet will trade two pizzas for one six-pack of beer and be equally happy. At the same time, Ophelia will gladly exchange two of her six-packs for six pizzas. Is the allocation of beer and pizza Pareto efficient? Illustrate using an Edgeworth Box.

3. Imagine a simple economy comprising only two people, Augustus and Livia.

   a. Let the social welfare function be

   $$W = U_L + U_A$$

   where U_L and U_A are the utilities of Livia and Augustus, respectively. Graph the social indifference curves.

   b. Repeat (a) when

   $$W = U_L + 2U_A$$

   c. Assume that the utility possibility frontier is as depicted in the accompanying figure.

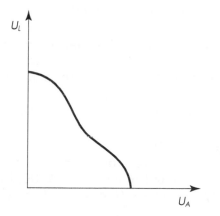

   Graphically show how the optimal solution differs between the welfare functions given in parts (a) and (b). Contrast these solutions with the position taken by an egalitarian—one who holds that the optimum is the point on the frontier where the utilities of Augustus and Livia are the same.

4. Consider an economy with two people, Henry and Catherine, who consume two commodities, bread and water. Suppose that, due to a drought, the authorities decided to allocate exactly half the available water to each person. In order to prevent one person from "exploiting" the other, neither person may trade away any water to the other in exchange for more bread. Set up an Edgeworth Box to depict this situation and explain why it is unlikely to be Pareto efficient. Can this framework be used to analyze the Canadian policy of banning exports of water to the United States?

5. The government of France taxes movies that are produced outside of the country and subsidizes domestically produced movies. Is this policy consistent with a Pareto efficient allocation of resources? (*Hint:* Consider a model in which consumers choose between two goods, "foreign movies" and "domestic movies." How does the marginal rate of substitution between the goods compare to the marginal rate of transformation?)

6. Consider a simple economy with two individuals, John and Marsha. The economy is endowed with 30 kilograms of cheese and 30 loaves of bread each month. John and Marsha's preferences for bread and cheese are given by their marginal rates of substitution of bread for cheese:

$$MRS_{bc}^J = \frac{10}{x_b^J}$$

$$MRS_{bc}^M = \frac{5}{x_b^M}$$

where x_b^J is the quantity of bread consumed by John and x_b^M is the quantity of bread consumed by Marsha.

    a. If each individual only had one loaf of bread, how much cheese would each individual be willing to give up in order to have another loaf of bread?

    b. In the initial allocation, each individual has 15 kilograms of cheese and 15 loaves of bread. Draw the Edgeworth Box diagram for this economy and explain whether the initial allocation of cheese and bread is Pareto efficient.

    c. Draw the contract curve for this economy.

7. Your airplane crashes in the Pacific Ocean. You land on a desert island with one other passenger. A box containing 100 little bags of peanuts also washes up on the island. The peanuts are the only thing to eat.

    In this economy with two people, one commodity, and no production, represent the possible allocations in a diagram, and explain why every allocation is Pareto efficient. Is every allocation fair?

8. Suppose the government imposes a quota restricting the production of apples to an amount less than the competitive market equilibrium quantity. Illustrate this situation on a production possibilities curve for fig leaves and apples and explain which condition for efficiency is violated.

9. A new health minister proposes to distribute an apple a day (at no cost) to every citizen. To be effective, the legislation states that the free apples may not be traded or sold. Explain why this "no-trade" policy would violate the efficiency condition (2.1).

10. [This problem is for readers who know some calculus.] Suppose that there are only two people in society, Mark and Judy, who must split a fixed amount of income of $300. Mark's utility function is U_M and his income is I_M. Judy's utility function is U_J and her income is I_J. Suppose that

$$U_M = 100 \times I_M^{1/2} \quad \text{and} \quad U_J = 200 \times I_J^{1/2}.$$

    Let the social welfare function be $W = U_M + U_J$.

    What distribution of the total income between Mark and Judy maximizes social welfare?

11. Suppose that Tang and Wilson must split a fixed 400 kilograms of food between them. Tang's utility function is $U_T = \sqrt{F_1}$ and Wilson's utility function is $U_W = 1/2\sqrt{F_2}$, where F_1 and F_2 are kilograms of food to Tang and Wilson, respectively.

    a. How much utility will Tang and Wilson receive if the food is distributed evenly between them?

    b. If the social welfare function is $U_T + U_W$, then what distribution of food between Tang and Wilson maximizes social welfare?

    c. If social welfare is maximized when they each obtain the same level of utility, then what is the distribution of food between Tang and Wilson that maximizes social welfare?

12. Suppose that Hannah's utility function is $U_H = 3T + 4C$ and that Jose's utility function is $U_J = 4T + 3C$, where T is kilograms of tea and C is kilograms of coffee per year. Suppose there are fixed amounts of 28 kilograms of coffee per year and 21 kilograms of tea per year. Suppose also that the initial allocation is 15 kilograms of coffee to Hannah (leaving 13 kilograms to Jose) and 10 kilograms of tea to Hannah (leaving 11 kilograms to Jose).

    a. What do the utility functions say about the marginal rate of substitution of coffee for tea?

    b. Draw the Edgeworth Box showing the indifference curves and the initial allocation.

    c. Draw the contract curve on the Edgeworth Box. Explain why it looks different from the contract curve depicted in the text.

    d. Is the initial allocation of coffee and tea Pareto efficient?

13. Indicate whether each of the following statements is true, false, or uncertain, and justify your answer.

   a. If everyone has the same marginal rate of substitution, then the allocation of resources is Pareto efficient.

   b. If the allocation of resources is Pareto efficient, then everyone has the same marginal rate of substitution.

   c. A policy change increases social welfare if, and only if, it represents a Pareto improvement.

   d. A reallocation from a point within the utility possibilities curve to a point on the utilitiy possibilities curve results in a Pareto improvement.

CHAPTER 3

Cost–Benefit Analysis

Paris is well worth a Mass.

—attributed to Henri IV of France

AFTER READING THIS CHAPTER, THE STUDENT SHOULD BE ABLE TO:

LO1 Distinguish between a Pareto improving allocation of resources and a potential Pareto improvement.

LO2 Calculate the present value of future cash flows.

LO3 State the present value criteria for project evaluation.

LO4 Distinguish between the social discount rate and rates based on private sector returns.

LO5 Explain how to estimate the shadow prices of commodities.

LO6 Explain how to use changes in consumer surplus to estimate a project's benefits.

LO7 Infer the value of non-traded goods by observing economic behaviour.

LO8 Define the certainty equivalent of a risky benefit or cost.

LO9 State three common pitfalls in conducting cost–benefit analysis.

Governments provide many policies and projects to try to improve on market outcomes. An example of a major project of the federal government is the new airport planned in Pickering to serve the Greater Toronto Area starting in 2027. The decision to construct the airport is controversial. Critics point to the financial and environmental costs, and to rivalry with the Hamilton airport. The federal government argues that the airport is necessary to meet future travel demands. Is the airport worth its $2 billion price tag? How many runways should it have? Such questions require a systematic approach for making these decisions.

Suppose that the government is presented with a project—building a road, starting a job-training program, or subsidizing mass transit—and must determine whether to pursue it. The theory of welfare economics provides a framework for dealing with such problems; evaluate the social welfare function before and after the project, and see whether social welfare increases. If it does, then do the project.

This methodology is correct, but not very useful. The amount of information required to specify and evaluate a social welfare function is enormous. While social welfare functions are valuable for thinking through certain conceptual problems, they are generally not much help for the day-to-day problems of project evaluation. However, welfare economics does provide the basis for **cost–benefit analysis**—a set of practical procedures for guiding public expenditure decisions.[1]

Most government projects and policies result in the private sector having more of some scarce commodities and less of others. At the core of cost–benefit analysis is a set of systematic procedures for valuing these commodities, which allows policy analysts to determine whether a project is, on balance, beneficial. Cost–benefit analysis allows policy-makers to attempt to do what well-functioning markets do automatically—allocate

---

[1] Boardman, Greenberg, Vining, and Weimer (2011) discuss the links between welfare economics and cost–benefit analysis.

resources to a project as long as the social marginal benefit exceeds the social marginal cost. However, cost-benefit analysis is not a panacea that provides a definitive "scientific" answer to every question. For example, when it comes to assigning dollar values to such intangibles as national security or environmental purity, the tools of cost-benefit analysis provide no easy solutions. Nevertheless, using a cost-benefit analysis helps to ensure consistent decision making that focuses on the right issues.

ECONOMIC EFFICIENCY

Recall from Chapter 2 that when resources are allocated inefficiently, then there is a Pareto improvement available: someone can gain and no one need lose. Now suppose the benefits of a project exceed its costs, thereby increasing the "size of the economic pie." In that case, the beneficiaries of the project can fully compensate the losers and still have some benefits left over. The initial project, together with the compensation payments to those incurring the costs (and not receiving the benefits), generate a Pareto improvement. Thus the difference between benefits B and costs C can be regarded as the contribution of a project to economic efficiency:

$$\text{Net Return} = B - C \tag{3.1}$$

The same form of reasoning underpins the First Welfare Theorem about the efficiency of competitive markets (see Chapter 2). Figure 3.1 depicts a competitive market equilibrium for apples at the intersection of the demand curve (D_a) and the supply curve (S_a). The demand curve shows the maximum amount that individuals would be willing to pay for each apple they consume. The supply curve is the marginal cost of output in perfect competition. It shows the value of resources used to produce additional apples. The equilibrium quantity Q_a^* is efficient because at any other amount a Pareto improvement is possible.[2]

To see this, consider an output Q_1 that is less than Q_a^* in Figure 3.1. At Q_1 consumers are willing to pay a price, P_1, for an additional apple, which exceeds the marginal cost MC_1 of producing it. This implies that consumers (those benefiting from apples) can compensate producers (those bearing the costs of apples) by paying them for more apple production while still having some gain left over. Increasing the output of apples from Q_1 generates a Pareto improvement. The possibility of gainers compensating the losers is exhausted at Q_a^*, where the marginal gain to consumers (the price P_a^*) equals the marginal cost. A similar argument can be constructed to demonstrate why any quantity of apples exceeding Q_a^* gives rise to Pareto improving reductions in production. Consider the quantity Q_2 which lies to the right of Q_a^* in Figure 3.1. The marginal apple is worth P_2 to consumers and costs MC_2 to produce. The cost savings of producers from reducing their production

FIGURE 3.1

EFFICIENCY OF THE COMPETITIVE EQUILIBRIUM

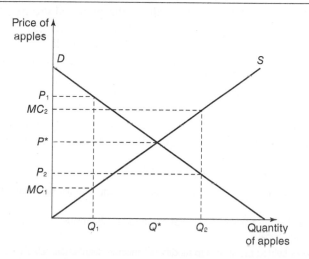

---

[2] The discussion of Figure 3.1 is based on partial equilibrium analysis, which focuses on a single market by ignoring the feedback in prices and quantities across the various markets in the economy. See Chapter 2 for the more general case in which all markets are in equilibrium.

is more than enough to compensate consumers for their loss of apples. The same logic apples for any quantity greater than Q_a^*. Therefore, Q_a^* is the Pareto efficient quantity of apples.

The efficiency of the competitive equilibrium assumes that the demand and supply curves reflect *social* marginal benefits and *social* marginal costs, respectively. As noted in Chapter 2, social marginal values can deviate from private ones in certain circumstances, such as the presence of externalities. Indeed, it is precisely the deviation between social and private marginal values that often warrants a public sector project.

DISTRIBUTIONAL CONSIDERATIONS

So far, we have not considered the distributional effects of public projects. Instead, we assumed that those incurring the losses (and not sharing in the benefits) would be compensated. However, in the absence of such compensation, a public project is not Pareto improving if it imposes net losses on some individuals.

In the private sector, normally no consideration is given to the question of who receives the benefits and bears the costs of a project. A dollar is a dollar, regardless of who is involved. Some economists have argued that the same view be taken in public project analysis. If the net return of a project is positive, it should be undertaken regardless of who gains and loses. This is because as long as the net return is positive the gainers *could* compensate the losers and still enjoy a net increase in utility. This notion, sometimes called a **potential Pareto improvement** or the **Hicks–Kaldor criterion**,[3] thus bases project selection on *potential* gains in social welfare.[4] The actual compensation does not have to take place. That is, it is permissible to impose costs on some members of society if that provides greater net benefits to someone else.

Others believe that because the goal of government is to maximize social welfare (not profit), the distributional implications of a project should be taken into account. Moreover, because it is the actual pattern of benefits and costs that really matters, the Hicks–Kaldor criterion does not provide a satisfactory escape from grappling with distributional issues.

One way to avoid the distributional problem is to assume the government can and will costlessly correct any undesirable distributional aspects of a project by making the appropriate transfers between gainers and losers.[5] The government works continually in the background to ensure that income stays optimally distributed, so the cost–benefit analyst need be concerned only with computing net returns. Again, reality gets in the way. The government may have neither the power nor the ability to distribute income optimally (see Chapter 6).[6]

Suppose the policy-maker believes that some group in the population is especially deserving. This distributional preference can be taken into account by assuming that a dollar benefit to a member of this group is worth more than a dollar going to others in the population.[7] This, of course, tends to bias the selection of projects in favour of those that especially benefit the preferred group. Although much of the discussion of distributional issues has focused on income as the basis for classifying people, presumably characteristics such as race, ethnicity, and gender can be used as well.

After the analyst is given the criteria for membership in the preferred group, he or she must face the question of precisely how to weight benefits to members of that group relative to the rest of society. Is a dollar to a poor person counted twice as much as a dollar to a rich person, or fifty times as much? The resolution of such issues depends on value judgments. All the analyst can do is induce the policy-maker to state explicitly his or her value judgments and understand their implications.

A potential hazard of introducing distributional considerations is that political concerns come to dominate the cost–benefit exercise. Depending on how weights are chosen, any project can generate a positive present value, regardless of how inefficient it is. In addition, incorporating distributional considerations substantially increases the information requirements of cost–benefit analysis. The analyst needs to estimate not only benefits

---

[3] Named after the economists John Hicks and Nicholas Kaldor.

[4] For example, lump-sum taxes could be imposed on those who gain and lump-sum transfers could be paid to those who lose to achieve a Pareto improvement.

[5] "Costlessly" in this context means that the transfer system costs nothing to administer and the transfers are done in such a way that they do not distort people's economic behaviour.

[6] Moreover, as the government works behind the scenes to modify the income distribution, relative prices probably change. But as relative prices change, so do the benefit and cost calculations. Hence, efficiency and equity issues cannot be separated as neatly as suggested here.

[7] The method reflects the equity concerns embodied in social welfare functions (see Chapter 2).

and costs, but also how they are distributed across the population. However, it is often very difficult to assess the distributional implications of government fiscal activities.

PRESENT VALUE

Project evaluation usually requires comparing costs and benefits from different time periods. For example, a program of preschool education for poor children requires substantial expenditures in the present and then yields returns in the future. In this section, we discuss problems that arise when comparing dollar amounts from different time periods. Initially, we assume that no price inflation occurs. We show later how to take inflation into account.

Projecting Present Dollars into the Future

Suppose that you take $100 to the bank and deposit it in an account that yields 5 percent interest after taxes. At the end of one year, you will have $(1 + .05) \times \$100 = \$105$–the $100 initially deposited, plus $5 in interest. Suppose further that you let the money sit in the account for another year. At the end of the second year, you will have $(1 + .05) \times \$105 = \$110.25$. This can also be written as $(1 + .05) \times (1 + .05) \times 100 = (1 + .05)^2 \times 100$. Similarly, if the money is deposited for three years, it will be worth $(1 + .05)^3 \times \$100$ by the end of the third year. More generally, if R is invested for T years at an interest rate of r, at the end of T years it will be worth $\$R \times (1 + r)^T$. This formula shows the future value of money invested in the present.

Discounting Future Dollars into the Present

Now suppose that someone offers a contract that promises to pay you $100 *one year from now*. The person is trustworthy, so you do not have to worry about default. (Also, remember there is no inflation.) What is the maximum amount that you should be willing to pay *today* for this promise? It is tempting to say that a promise to pay $100 is worth $100. But this ignores the fact that the promised $100 is not payable for a year, and in the meantime you are forgoing the interest that could be earned on the money. Why should you pay $100 today to receive $100 a year from now if you can receive $105 a year from now simply by putting the $100 in the bank today? Thus, the value today of $100 payable one year from now is *less* than $100. The **present value** of a future amount of money is the maximum amount you would be willing to pay today for the right to receive the money in the future.

To find the very most you would be willing to give up now in exchange for $100 payable one year in the future, you must find the number that, when multiplied by $(1 + .05)$, just equals $100. By calculation, this is $\$100/(1 + .05)$, or approximately $95.24. Thus, when the interest rate is 5 percent, the present value of $100 payable one year from now is $\$100/(1 + .05)$. Note the symmetry with the familiar problem of projecting money into the future that we discussed already. To find the value of money today one year in the future, you *multiply* by one plus the interest rate; to find the value of money one year in the future today, you *divide* by one plus the interest rate.

Next, consider a promise to pay $100 *two* years from now. In this case, the calculation has to take into account the fact that if you invested $100 yourself for two years, at the end it would be worth $\$100 \times (1 + .05)$. The most you would be willing to pay today for $100 in two years is the amount that when multiplied by $(1 + .05)^2$ yields exactly $100: $\$100/(1 + .05)^2$, or about $90.70.

In general, when the interest rate is r, the present value of a promise to pay R in T years is simply $\$R/(1 + r)^T$.[8] Thus, even in the absence of inflation, a dollar in the future is worth less than a dollar today and must be "discounted" by an amount that depends on the interest rate and when the money is receivable. For this reason, r is often referred to as the **discount rate**. Similarly, $(1 + r)^T$ is called the **discount factor** for money T periods into the future. Note that the further into the future the promise is payable (the larger is T), the smaller the present value. Intuitively, the longer you have to wait for a sum to be paid, the less you are willing to pay for it today, other things being the same.

Finally, consider a promise to pay R_0 today, *and* R_1 one year from now, *and* R_2 two years from now, and so on for T years. How much is this deal worth? By now, it is clear that the naive answer $(\$R_0 + \$R_1 + \cdots + \$R_T)$ is wrong because it assumes that a dollar in the future is exactly equivalent to a dollar in the present. Without dividing by the discount factor, adding up dollars from different points in time is like adding apples and oranges. The correct approach is to convert each year's amount to its present value and *then* add them.

---

[8] This assumes the interest rate is constant at r. Suppose that the interest rate changes over time, so in year 1 it is r_1, in year 2, r_2, and so on. Then the present value of a sum R_T payable T years from now is $\$R_T/[(1 + r_1) \times (1 + r_2) \times \cdots \times (1 + r_T)]$.

TABLE 3.1

Calculating Present Value			
Dollars Payable	**Years in Future**	**Discount Factor**	**Present Value**
R_0	0	1	R_0
R_1	1	$(1 + r)$	$R_1/(1 + r)$
R_2	2	$(1 + r)^2$	$R_2/(1 + r)^2$
.	.	.	.
.	.	.	.
.	.	.	.
R_T	T	$(1 + r)^T$	$R_T/(1 + r)^T$

Table 3.1 shows the present value of each year's payment. To find the present value (*PV*) of the income stream $\$R_0$, $\$R_1$, $\$R_2$, . . . , $\$R_T$, we simply add the figures in the last column:

$$PV = R_0 + \frac{R_1}{(1 + r)} + \frac{R_2}{(1 + r)^2} + \cdots + \frac{R_T}{(1 + r)^T} \qquad (3.2)$$

The importance of computing present values is hard to overestimate. Serious errors can be made if it is ignored. In particular, failure to discount makes ventures that yield returns in the future appear more valuable than they really are. For example, consider a project that yields a return of $1 million twenty years from now. If the interest rate is 5 percent, the present value is $376,889 [= $1,000,000/(1.05)^{20}]. If $r = 10$ percent, the present value is only $148,644 [= $1,000,000/(1.10)^{20}].

Inflation

We now consider how to modify the procedure when the price level is expected to increase in the future. To begin, consider a project that, in present prices, yields the same return each year. Call this return $\$R_0$. Now, assume that inflation occurs at a rate of 7 percent per year, and the dollar value of the return increases along with all prices. Therefore, the dollar value of the return one year from now, $\$\widetilde{R}_1$, is $(1.07) \times \$R_0$. Similarly, two years into the future, the dollar value is $\$\widetilde{R}_2 = (1.07)^2 R_0$. In general, this same return has a dollar value in year T of $\$\widetilde{R}_T = (1 + .07)^T R_0$.

The dollar values $\$\widetilde{R}_0$, $\$\widetilde{R}_1$, $\$\widetilde{R}_2$, . . . , $\$\widetilde{R}_T$ are referred to as **nominal amounts**. Nominal amounts are valued according to the level of prices in the year the return occurs. It is possible to measure these returns in terms of the prices that exist in a single year. These are called **real amounts** because they do not reflect changes that are due merely to alterations in the price level. In our example, the real amount was assumed to be a constant $\$R_0$ measured in present prices. More generally, if the real returns in present year prices are $\$R_0$, $\$R_1$, $\$R_2$, . . . , $\$R_T$, and inflation occurs at a rate of π per year, then the nominal returns are $\$R_0$, $\$R_1 \times (1 + \pi)$, $\$R_2 \times (1 + \pi)^2$, . . . , $\$R_T \times (1 + \pi)^T$.

But this is not the end of the story. When prices are expected to rise, lenders are no longer willing to make loans at the interest rate r that prevailed when prices were stable. Lenders realize they are going to be paid back in discounted dollars, and to keep even in real terms their first year's payment must also be inflated by $(1 + \pi)$. Similarly, the second year's payment must be inflated by $(1 + \pi)^2$. In other words, the market interest rate may be expected to increase by an amount approximately equal to the expected rate of inflation, from r percent to $r + \pi$ percent.[9]

We see, then, that when inflation is anticipated, *both* the stream of returns and the discount rate are increased. When expressed in *nominal* terms, the present value of the income stream is thus

$$PV = R_0 + \frac{(1 + \pi)R_1}{(1 + \pi)(1 + r)} + \frac{(1 + \pi)^2 R_2}{(1 + \pi)^2(1 + r)^2} + \cdots + \frac{(1 + \pi)^T R_T}{(1 + \pi)^T(1 + r)^T} \qquad (3.3)$$

---

[9] The product of $(1 + r)$ and $(1 + \pi)$ is $1 + r + \pi + r\pi$. Thus, the nominal rate actually exceeds the real rate by $\pi + r\pi$. However, for numbers of reasonable magnitude, $r\pi$ is negligible in size, so $r + \pi$ is a good approximation of the nominal rate. There are circumstances under which nominal interest rates may fail to rise by exactly the rate of inflation. See Chapter 17 under "Taxes and Inflation."

A glance at Equation (3.3) indicates that it is equivalent to Equation (3.2) because all the terms involving $(1 + \pi)$ cancel out. The moral of the story is that the *same answer* is obtained whether real or nominal magnitudes are used. It is crucial, however, that dollar magnitudes and discount rates be measured consistently. If real values are used for the Rs, the discount rate must also be measured in real terms–the market rate of interest *minus* the expected inflation rate. Alternatively, if the market rate of interest is used for discounting, returns should be measured in nominal terms.

Private Sector Project Evaluation

As we noted at the beginning of the chapter, the central problem in cost–benefit analysis is valuing the inputs and outputs of government projects. A useful starting point is to consider the same problem from a private firm's point of view.

Suppose a firm is considering two mutually exclusive projects, X and Y. The real benefits and costs of project X are B^X and C^X, respectively; and those for project Y are B^Y and C^Y. For both projects, the benefits and costs are realized immediately. The firm must answer two questions. First, should either project be done at all; are the projects *admissible*? (The firm has the option of doing neither project.) Second, if both projects are admissible, which is *preferable*? Because both benefits and costs occur immediately, answering these questions is simple. Compute the net return to project X, $B^X - C^X$, and compare it to the net return to Y, $B^Y - C^Y$. A project is admissible only if its net return is positive; that is, the benefits exceed the costs. If both projects are admissible, the firm should choose the project with the higher net return.

In reality, most projects involve a stream of real benefits and returns that occur over time rather than instantaneously. Suppose that the initial benefits and costs of project X are B_0^X and C_0^X, those at the end of the first year are B_1^X and C_1^X, and those at the end of the last year are B_T^X and C_T^X. We can characterize project X as a stream of net returns (some of which may be negative):

$$\left(B_0^X - C_0^X\right), \left(B_1^X - C_1^X\right), \left(B_2^X - C_2^X\right), \ldots, \left(B_T^X - C_T^X\right).$$

The present value of this income stream (PV^X) is

$$PV^X = B_0^X - C_0^X + \frac{B_1^X - C_1^X}{(1 + r)} + \frac{B_2^X - C_2^X}{(1 + r)^2} + \cdots + \frac{B_T^X - C_T^X}{(1 + r)^T}$$

where r represents the real rate of return that is generally available to the firm, the opportunity cost of its funds.

Similarly, suppose that project Y generates streams of costs and benefits B^Y and C^Y over a period of T' years. (There is no reason for T and T' to be the same.) Project Y's present value is

$$PV^Y = B_0^Y - C_0^Y + \frac{B_1^Y - C_1^Y}{(1 + r)} + \frac{B_2^Y - C_2^Y}{(1 + r)^2} + \cdots + \frac{B_{T'}^Y - C_{T'}^Y}{(1 + r)^{T'}}$$

Since both projects are now evaluated in present value terms, we can use the same rules that were applied to the instantaneous project described earlier. There are two **present value criteria** for project evaluation:

- A project is admissible only if its present value is positive.
- When two projects are mutually exclusive, the preferred project is the one with the higher present value.

The discount rate plays a key role in the analysis. Different values of r can lead to very different conclusions concerning the admissibility and comparability of projects.

Consider the two projects shown in Table 3.2, a research and development program (R&D) and drilling a new oil well. Both require an initial outlay of $1,000. The R&D program produces a return of $600 at the end of the first year and $550 at the end of the third year. The well, on the other hand, has a single large payoff of $1,200 in three years.

The calculations show the discount rate chosen is important. For low values of r, the oil well is preferred to R&D. However, higher discount rates weigh against the oil well (where the returns are concentrated further into the future) and may even make the project inadmissible.

Thus, one must take considerable care that the value of r represents as closely as possible the firm's actual opportunity cost of funds. If the discount rate chosen is too high, it tends to discriminate against projects with returns that come in the relatively distant future, and vice versa. The firm's tax situation is relevant in

TABLE 3.2

			Comparing the Present Values of Two Projects			
		Annual Net Return			**Present Value**	
Year	R&D	Oil Well	$r =$	R&D	Oil Well	
0	−$1,000	−$1,000	0.00	$150	$200
1	600	0	0.01	128	165
2	0	0	0.03	86	98
3	550	1,200	0.05	46	37
			0.07	10	−21

this context. If the going market rate of return is 10 percent, but the firm's tax rate is 25 percent, its after-tax return is only 7.5 percent. Because the after-tax return represents the firm's opportunity cost, it should be used for r.

Several criteria other than present value are often used for project evaluation. As we will see, they can sometimes give misleading answers, and therefore the present value criteria are preferable. However, these other methods are popular, so it is necessary to understand them and to be aware of their problems.

Internal Rate of Return

A firm is considering the following project. It spends $1 million today on an advertising campaign and reaps a benefit of $1.04 million in increased profits a year from now. If you were asked to compute the advertising campaign's "rate of return," you would probably respond, "4 percent." Implicitly, you calculated that figure by finding the value of ρ that solves the following equation:

$$-\$1,000,000 + \frac{1,040,000}{(1 + \rho)} = 0$$

We can generalize this procedure as follows. If a project yields a stream of benefits (B) and costs (C) over T periods, the **internal rate of return** (ρ) is defined as the ρ that solves the equation

$$B_0^X - C_0^X + \frac{B_1^X - C_1^X}{(1 + \rho)} + \frac{B_2^X - C_2^X}{(1 + \rho)^2} + \cdots + \frac{B_T^X - C_T^X}{(1 + \rho)^T} = 0 \qquad (3.4)$$

The internal rate of return is the discount rate that would make the present value of the project just equal to zero.

An obvious admissibility criterion is to accept a project if ρ exceeds the firm's opportunity cost of funds, r. For example, if the project earns 4 percent while the firm can obtain 3 percent on other investments, the project should be done. The corresponding comparability criterion is that if two mutually exclusive projects are both admissible, choose the one with the higher value of ρ.

Project selection using the internal rate of return can, however, lead to bad decisions. Consider project X that requires the expenditure of $100 today and yields $110 a year from now, so that its internal rate of return is 10 percent. Project Y requires $1,000 today and yields $1,080 in a year, generating an internal rate of return of 8 percent. (Neither project can be duplicated.) Assume that the firm can borrow and lend freely at a 6 percent rate of interest.

On the basis of its internal rate of return, X is clearly preferred to Y. However, the firm makes only a $4 profit on X ($10 minus $6 in interest costs), while it makes a $20 profit on Y ($80 minus $60 in interest costs). Contrary to the conclusion implied by the internal rate of return, the firm should prefer Y, the project with the higher profit. In short, when projects differ in size, the internal rate of return can give poor guidance. In contrast, the present value rule gives correct answers even when the projects differ in scale. The present value of X is −100 + 110/1.06 = 3.77, while that of Y is −1,000 + 1080/1.06 = 18.87. The present value criterion says that Y is preferable, as it should.

Benefit–Cost Ratio

Suppose that a project yields a stream of benefits $B_0, B_1, B_2, \ldots, B_T$, and a stream of costs $C_0, C_1, C_2, \ldots, C_T$. Then the present value of the benefits, B, is

$$B = B_0 + \frac{B_1}{(1 + r)} + \frac{B_2}{(1 + r)^2} + \cdots + \frac{B_T}{(1 + r)^T}$$

and the present value of the costs, C, is

$$C = C_0 + \frac{C_1}{(1 + r)} + \frac{C_2}{(1 + r)^2} + \cdots + \frac{C_T}{(1 + r)^T} \tag{3.5}$$

The **benefit–cost ratio** is defined as B/C.

Admissibility requires that a project's benefit–cost ratio exceed one. Application of this rule always gives correct guidance. To see why, note simply that $B/C > 1$ implies that $B - C > 0$, which is equivalent to the present value criterion for admissibility.

As a basis for comparing admissible projects, however, the benefit–cost ratio is virtually useless. Consider a community that is studying two methods for disposing of toxic wastes. Method I is a toxic waste dump with $B = \$250$ million, $C = \$100$ million, and therefore a benefit–cost ratio of 2.5. Method II involves sending the wastes in a rocket to Saturn, which has $B = \$200$ million, $C = \$100$ million, and therefore a benefit–cost ratio of 2. The town's leaders choose the dump because it has the higher value of B/C. Now suppose that in their analysis of the dump the analysts inadvertently neglected to take into account an induced crop damage of $40 million. If the $40 million is viewed as a reduction in the dump's benefits, its B/C becomes $\$210/\$100 = 2.1$, and the dump is still preferred to the rocket. However, the $40 million can just as well be viewed as an increase in costs, in which case $B/C = \$250/\$140 = 1.79$. Now the rocket looks better than the dump!

We have illustrated that there is an inherent ambiguity in computing benefit–cost ratios because benefits can always be counted as "negative costs" and vice versa. Thus, by judicious classification of benefits and costs, any admissible project's benefit–cost ratio can be made arbitrarily high. In contrast, a glance at Equation (3.2) indicates that such shenanigans have no effect whatsoever on the present value criterion because it is based on the *difference* between benefits and costs rather than their ratio.

We conclude that the internal rate of return and the benefit–cost ratio can lead to incorrect inferences. The present value criterion is the most reliable guide.

PUBLIC SECTOR DISCOUNT RATE

Sensible decision making by the government also requires present value calculations. However, the public sector should compute costs, benefits, and discount rates differently than the private sector. This section discusses problems in the selection of a public sector discount rate. In the next section, we turn to problems in evaluating costs and benefits.

As suggested previously, the discount rate chosen by private individuals should reflect the rate of return available on alternative investments. Although in practice it may be difficult to pinpoint this rate, from a conceptual point of view there is agreement that the opportunity cost of funds to the firm gives the correct value of r. There is less consensus on the conceptually appropriate discount rate for government projects. We now discuss several possibilities.[10]

Rates Based on Returns in the Private Sector

Suppose the last $1,000 of private investment in the economy yields an annual rate of return of 16 percent. If the government extracts $1,000 from the private sector for a project, and the $1,000 is entirely at the expense of private sector investment, society loses the $160 that would have been generated by the private sector project. Thus, the opportunity cost of the government project is the 16 percent rate of return in the private sector. Because it measures the opportunity cost, the 16 percent should be used as the discount rate. It is irrelevant whether or not this return is taxed. Whether it all stays with the investor or part goes

---

[10] See Tresch (2002, Ch. 24) for further discussion of the alternative views.

to the government, the before-tax rate of return measures the value of output that the funds would have generated for society.

Contrary to the assumption made earlier, it is likely that some of the funds for the government project would come at the expense of consumption as well as investment. As just argued, for those funds coming out of investment, the before-tax rate of return is the opportunity cost and therefore the appropriate discount rate. But this is not so for funds that come at the expense of consumption. Consider Nelson, who is deciding how much to consume and how much to save this year. For each dollar Nelson consumes this year, he gives up one dollar of consumption next year plus the rate of return he would have earned on the dollar saved. Hence, the opportunity cost to Nelson of a dollar of consumption now is measured by the rate of return he would have received if he had saved the dollar. Suppose the before-tax yield on an investment opportunity available to Nelson is 16 percent, but he must pay 50 percent of the return to the government in the form of taxes. All that Nelson gives up when he consumes an additional dollar today is the *after*-tax rate of return of 8 percent. Because the after-tax rate of return measures what an *individual* loses when consumption is reduced, dollars that come at the expense of consumption should be discounted by the after-tax rate of return.

Because funds for the public sector reduce both private sector consumption and investment, a natural solution is to use a weighted average of the before- and after-tax rates of return, with the weight on the before-tax rate equal to the proportion of funds that comes from investment, and that on the after-tax rate the proportion that comes from consumption (see Harberger, 1974). In the preceding example, if one-quarter of the funds came at the expense of investment and three-quarters at the expense of consumption, then the public sector discount rate would be 10 percent (1/4 × 16 percent + 3/4 × 8 percent). Unfortunately, in practice it is hard to determine what the proportions of sacrificed consumption and investment actually are for a given government project. The funds are collected from a variety of taxes, each of which has a different effect on consumption and investment. And even with information on the impact of each tax on consumption and investment, it is difficult in practice to determine which tax is used to finance which project. The inability to determine reliably a set of weights lessens the usefulness of this approach as a practical guide to determining discount rates.

Social Discount Rate

An alternative view is that public expenditure evaluation should involve a **social rate of discount**, which measures the valuation *society* places on consumption that is sacrificed in the present. But why should society's view of the opportunity cost of forgoing consumption differ from the opportunity cost revealed in market rates of return? Several reasons have been suggested for believing that the social discount rate is lower.

Concern for future generations. It is the duty of public sector decision makers to care about the welfare not only of the current generation of citizens, but of future generations as well. The private sector, on the other hand, is concerned only with its own welfare. Hence, from a social point of view, the private sector devotes too few resources to saving—it applies too high a discount rate to future returns. However, the idea of government as the unselfish guardian of the interests of future generations assumes a degree of omniscience and benevolence that is unrealistic. Moreover, even totally selfish individuals often find it in their personal interest to engage in projects that benefit future generations. If future generations are expected to benefit from some project, the anticipated profitability is high, which encourages investment today. Private firms plant trees today in return for profits on wood sales that may not be realized for many years.[11]

Paternalism. Even from the point of view of their own narrow self-interest, people may not be farsighted enough to weigh adequately benefits in the future; they therefore discount such benefits at too high a rate. Pigou (1932, Ch. 2) described this problem as a "defective telescopic faculty." The government should use the discount rate that individuals *would* use if they knew their own good. This is a paternalistic argument—government forces citizens to consume less in the present, and in return they have more in the future, at which time they presumably thank the government for its foresight. Like all paternalistic arguments, it raises the fundamental philosophical question of when public preferences should be imposed on individuals.

Market inefficiency. When a firm undertakes an investment, it generates knowledge and technological know-how that can benefit other firms, a process called **learning by doing** (Arrow, 1962). In a sense, then, investment

---

[11] Why should people invest in a project whose returns may not be realized until after they are dead? Investors can always sell the rights to future profits to members of the younger generation and hence consume their share of the anticipated profits during their lifetimes.

creates positive externalities, and by the usual kinds of arguments, investment is underprovided by private markets (see Chapter 5 under "Positive Externalities"). By applying a discount rate lower than the market's the government can correct this inefficiency. The enormous practical problem here is measuring the actual size of the externality. Moreover, the theory of externalities suggests that a more appropriate remedy would be to determine the size of the external marginal benefit at the optimum and grant a subsidy of that amount (see, again, Chapter 5).

It appears, then, that none of the arguments against using market rates provides much specific guidance with respect to the choice of a public sector discount rate. Where does this leave us? It would be difficult to argue very strongly against any public rate of discount in a range between the before- and after-tax rates of return in the private sector. The Treasury Board Secretariat (2007) recommends the use of a social discount real rate of 8 percent, and of 3 and 10 percent for sensitivity analysis.[12] If the present value of a project is computed over this range of discount rates and it remains positive, then the analyst can feel some confidence that the results are not sensitive to the discount rate.

VALUING PUBLIC BENEFITS AND COSTS

The next step in project evaluation is computing benefits and costs. From a private firm's point of view, their computation is relatively straightforward. The benefits from a project are the revenues received, the costs are the firm's payments for inputs, and both are measured by market prices. The evaluation problem is more complicated for the government because *social* benefits and costs may not be reflected in market prices. There are several possibilities for measuring the benefits and costs of public sector projects.

Market Prices

As noted at the start of the chapter, in a properly functioning competitive economy, the price of a good simultaneously reflects social marginal costs of its production and its marginal value to consumers. It would appear that if the government uses inputs and/or produces outputs that are traded in private markets, then market prices should be used for valuation.

The problem is that real-world markets have many imperfections, such as monopoly, externalities, and so on. In such a world, prices do not necessarily reflect social marginal costs and benefits. The relevant question, however, is not whether market prices are perfect, but whether they are likely to be superior to alternative measures of value. Such measures would either have to be made up or derived from highly complicated—and questionable—models of the economy. And, whatever their problems, market prices provide plenty of information at a low cost. Most economists believe that in the absence of any glaring imperfections, market prices should be used to compute public benefits and costs.

Adjusted Market Prices

The prices of goods traded in imperfect markets generally do not reflect their social marginal cost.[13] The **shadow price** of such a commodity is its underlying social marginal cost. Although market prices of goods in imperfect markets diverge from shadow prices, in some cases the market prices can be used to *estimate* the shadow prices. We discuss the relevant circumstances next. In each case, the key insight is that the shadow price depends on how the economy responds to the government intervention.

Monopoly. Suppose a public project uses a monopolistically produced input. In contrast to perfect competition, under which price is equal to marginal cost, a monopolist's price is above marginal cost (see Chapter 2). Should the government value the input at its market price (which measures its value to consumers) or at its marginal production cost (which measures the incremental value of the resources used in its production)?

The answer depends on the impact of the government purchase on the market. If production of the input is expected to increase by the exact amount used by the project, the social opportunity cost is the value of the resources used in the extra production—the marginal production cost. On the other hand, if no more of the input will be produced, the government's use comes at the expense of private consumers, whose value of the input is measured by the demand price. If some combination of the two responses is expected, a weighted average of price and marginal cost is appropriate. (Note the similarity to the previous discount rate problem.)

---

[12] Boardman, Moore, and Vining (2010) argue that a social discount rate for Canadian projects of 3.5 percent is more appropriate.

[13] For further details, see Boardman, Greenberg, Vining, and Weimer (2011).

Taxes. If an input is subject to a sales tax, the price received by the producer of the input is less than the price paid by the purchaser. This is because some portion of the purchase price goes to the tax collector. When the government purchases an input subject to sales tax, should the producer's or purchaser's price be used in the cost calculations? The basic principle is the same as that for the monopoly case. If production is expected to expand, then the producer's supply price is appropriate. If production is expected to stay constant, the purchaser's price should be used. For a combination of responses, a weighted average is required.

Unemployment. If a worker for a public sector project is hired away from a private job, then the opportunity cost of this worker is the wage rate that she was earning in the private sector. Things are trickier when the project employs someone who is currently involuntarily unemployed. Because hiring an unemployed worker does not lower output elsewhere in the economy, the wage the worker is paid does not represent an opportunity cost. All that is forgone when the worker is hired is the leisure he or she was consuming, the value of which is presumably low if the unemployment is involuntary. There are two complications, however. (1) If the government is running its stabilization policy to maintain a constant rate of employment, hiring an unemployed worker may mean reducing employment and output elsewhere in the economy. In this case, the social cost of the worker is his or her wage. (2) Even if the worker is involuntarily unemployed when the project begins, he or she will not necessarily continue to be so during its entire duration. But forecasting an individual's future employment prospects is difficult. In light of the current lack of consensus on the causes and nature of unemployment, the pricing of unemployed resources remains a problem with no agreed-on solution. In the absence of a major depression, valuation of unemployed labour at the going wage is probably a good approximation for practical purposes.

Consumer Surplus

In many cases, private firms are small relative to the economy. Therefore, they do not have to be concerned that changes in the amount they produce will affect the market price of their product. In contrast, public sector projects can be so large that they induce changes in market prices. For example, a government irrigation project could lower the marginal cost of agricultural production so much that the market price of food falls. But if the market price changes, how should the additional amount of food be valued—at its original price, at its price after the project, or at some price in between?

This situation is depicted in Figure 3.2. Kilograms of food are measured on the horizontal axis, the price per kilogram is measured on the vertical, and D_f is the demand schedule for food. Before the irrigation project, the supply curve is labelled S_f, and market price and quantity are P_0 and F_0, respectively. (The supply curve is drawn horizontally for convenience. The main points would still hold even if it sloped upward.)

Suppose that after more land is brought into production by the irrigation project, the supply curve for food shifts to S_f'. At the new equilibrium, the price falls to P_1, and food consumption increases to F_1. How much better off are consumers? Another way of stating this question is, how much would consumers be willing to pay for the privilege of consuming F_1 kilograms of food at price P_1 rather than F_0 Kilograms at price P_0?

FIGURE 3.2

MEASURING THE CHANGE IN CONSUMER SURPLUS

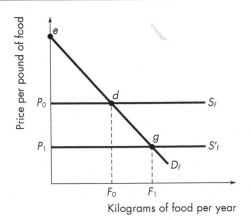

The economic tool for answering this question is **consumer surplus**–the amount by which the sum that individuals would have been willing to pay exceeds the sum they actually have to pay. As shown in the appendix to this chapter, consumer surplus is measured by the area under the demand curve and above a horizontal line at the market price. Thus, when price is P_0, consumer surplus is P_0ed.

When the price of food falls to P_1 because of the irrigation project, consumer surplus is still the area under the demand curve and above a horizontal line at the going price, but because the price is now P_1, the relevant area is P_1eg. Consumer surplus has increased by the difference between areas P_1eg and P_0ed–area P_1P_0dg. Thus, the area behind the demand curve between the two prices measures the value to consumers of being able to purchase food at the lower price. Provided the planner can estimate the shape of the demand curve, the benefit of the project can be measured.

If the supply curve of the commodity under consideration is upward sloping, then changes in producer surplus (also explained in the appendix) can be brought into play. For example, in the cost–benefit analysis of rent controls, the change in landlords' surplus could be estimated given information on the shape of the supply curve of rental housing.

Inferences from Economic Behaviour

So far, we have been dealing with cases in which market data can serve as a starting point for valuing social costs and benefits. Sometimes the good in question is not explicitly traded, so no market price exists. We discuss two examples of how people's willingness to pay for such commodities can be estimated.

The value of time. One benefit of building the Coquihalla Highway in British Columbia is that it saves travellers about two hours per trip in driving from Hope to Kamloops. While it is true that "time is money," to do a cost–benefit analysis we need to know *how much* money the time is worth.[14] A common way to estimate the value of time is to take advantage of the theory of leisure–income choice. People who have control over the amount they work do so up to the point where the subjective value of leisure is equal to the income they gain from one more hour of work–the after-tax wage rate. Thus, the after-tax wage can be used to value the time that is saved.[15]

Although this approach is useful, it has two major problems. (1) Some people cannot choose their hours of work. Involuntary unemployment represents an extreme but common case. (2) Not all uses of time away from the job are equivalent. For example, to avoid spending time on the road, a person who hated driving might be willing to pay at a rate exceeding his or her wage. On the other hand, a person who used the road for pleasure-drives on weekends might not care very much about the opportunity cost of time, particularly if he or she could not work on weekends anyway.

Several investigators have estimated the value of time by looking at people's choices between modes of transportation that involve different travelling times. Suppose that in a given community people can commute to work either by bus or by train. The train takes less time, but is more expensive. By seeing how much extra money people are willing to pay for the train, we can infer how much they are willing to pay to reduce their commuting time, and hence how they value that time. Of course, other characteristics of people, such as their incomes, affect their choice of travel mode. Statistical techniques can be used to take these other variables into account. On the basis of several such studies, a reasonable estimate of the effective cost of travelling time is about 50 percent of the before-tax wage rate (see von Wartburg and Waters, 2004).

The value of life. A physician once saved the life of a passenger on an international flight. The physician submitted a bill to the airline, which the airline refused to pay. In supporting the physician's claim, the fully recovered passenger said, "I feel that he saved my life, and what's the price for a life?" (Goldsmith, 1998). It's a hard question, and even posing it offends most people. Our religious and cultural values suggest that life is priceless. Consider the events that transpired several years ago when a scientist working at the South Pole, Dr. Jerri Nielsen, discovered a lump in her breast and needed treatment. An air force jet was immediately dispatched to airdrop medical supplies for Dr. Nielsen (weather conditions made it impossible for the jet to land). Several months later, when it was determined that Dr. Nielsen required hospitalization, another jet was sent in, this time to land and fly her home. In all of the news accounts of this story, no one questioned the cost of the rescue effort or whether saving Dr. Nielsen's life was worth the cost. Arguing that any price was

---

[14] See Boardman, Mallery, and Vining (1994) for a discussion of the cost-benefit studies on the Coquihalla Highway project.

[15] For further details, see Chapter 18 under "Labour Supply."

too high for saving her life would have been unthinkable. Similarly, if you were asked to value your own life, it would not be surprising if the response indicated that the sky was the limit.

Such a position presents obvious difficulties for cost–benefit analysis. If the value of life is infinite, any project that leads even to a single life being saved has an infinitely high present value. *This leaves no sensible way to determine the admissibility of projects.* If *every* road in Canada were a divided four-lane highway, traffic fatalities would doubtless decrease. Would this be a good project?

Economists have considered two methods for assigning finite values to human life. The first requires measuring the individual's lost earnings; the second requires estimating the value the individual puts on changes in the probability of death.

Lost earnings. The value of life is the present value of the individual's net earnings over a lifetime. If an individual dies as a consequence of a given project, the cost to society is just the expected present value of the output that person would have produced. This approach is often used in law courts to determine how much compensation the relatives of accident fatalities should receive. However, taken literally, this approach means that society would suffer no loss if the aged, infirm, or severely handicapped were summarily executed. This implication is sufficiently bizarre that the method is rejected by most economists.

Probability of death. A second approach has as its starting point the notion that most projects do not actually affect with *certainty* a given individual's prospects for living. Rather, it is more typical for a change in the *probability* of a person's death to be involved. For example, you do not know that cancer research will save *your* life. All that can be determined is that it may reduce the probability of your death. The reason this distinction is so important is that even if people view their lives as having infinite value, they very often accept increases in the probability of death for finite amounts of money. An individual driving a light car is subject to a greater probability of death in an auto accident than someone in a heavy car, other things being the same. People are willing to accept the increased risk of death because of the money they save by purchasing lighter cars.

Another way that people reveal their risk preferences is by their occupational choices. Some jobs involve a higher probability of death than others. Suppose we compare two workers who have identical job qualifications (education, experience, etc.), but one has a riskier job than the other. The individual in the riskier job is expected to have a higher wage to compensate for the higher probability of death. The difference between the two wages provides an estimate of the value that people place on a decreased probability of death. Garen (1988) estimated that increasing by one the number of fatalities per 100,000 workers in an occupation increases the yearly earnings in the occupation by about 0.55 percent.[16]

In the same spirit, there have been many studies of the amounts that people are willing to pay for safety devices, such as smoke alarms, that reduce the probability of death by a given amount. Different studies come up with quite different results, but a rough guess on the basis of such research is that the value of a life is between $4 million and $9 million (Bellavance, Dionne, and Lebeau, 2009). Now, you might think that this range is so great as to be useless. However, these estimates can be very useful in weeding out senseless projects. For example, the regulations relating to the emergency floor lights on commercial planes cost about $900,000 per life saved. These regulations clearly pass the admissibility criterion. On the other hand, asbestos removal rules cost more than $100 million per life saved.

An appealing aspect of this approach is that it puts the analysis on the same willingness-to-pay basis that is so fruitful in other contexts. It remains highly controversial, however. Broome (1978) has argued that the probabilistic approach is irrelevant once it is conceded that *some* people's lives are *certainly* going to be at stake. The fact that we happen to be ignorant of just who will die is beside the point. This position leads us back to where we started, with no way to value projects that involve human life.

This academic controversy has become a matter of public concern because of various proposals to subject government safety and environmental regulations to cost–benefit analysis. Some object to valuing lives in cost–benefit analyses, stating, "There is no price for life because its value is immeasurable" (Ackerman and

---

[16] See Viscusi and Aldy (2003) for further discussion of such estimates. The cost-benefit analyst should also consider the psychological cost of bereavement to families and friends and the changes in financial status of relatives.

NORTHERN GATEWAY PIPELINE

In June 2014 the federal government gave the go-ahead for Enbridge's $7.9 billion Northern Gateway Pipeline Project, subject to 209 conditions. The project would carry diluted heavy oil from Alberta to a tanker port in British Columbia, allowing Canadian oil to be shipped to markets in Asia. The news media reported on the strong reactions of various stakeholders to the announcement of the regulatory decision to approve the project.

"Our position remains unchanged: it is no," said B.C.'s Environment Minister, Mary Polak. She demanded greater environmental safeguards, noting that, "We understand the economic benefits the Northern Gateway pipeline will bring, but it will not be at the cost of our environment." First Nations groups in B.C. objected to the pipeline's intrusion on aboriginal lands, saying in a joint statement of 31 aboriginal organizations, "We will defend our territories whatever the costs may be."

The Northern Gateway Pipeline has been subjected to cost-benefit analyses. One study calculated that the project would generate a net present value of $23.5 billion, assuming a social discount rate of 8 percent. Another study concluded that the benefits of the project would be erased by the inflationary impacts resulting from a domestic oil boom. It is not surprising that the evaluation of the Northern Gateway Pipeline project is controversial. The results are sensitive to the social discount rate used in the calculations, the cleanup and damage costs of oil spills assumed in the analysis, and the prospective demand for Canadian oil. However, the debate over the Northern Gateway Pipeline, as with other high-profile pipeline proposals, such as the Keystone XL and Kinder Morgan projects, is improved by the explicit nature of the assumptions required in a formal cost-benefit analysis of social net benefits.

Based on Hunter and Stueck (2014), Allan (2012), Wright Mansell Research Ltd. (2012), and "Northern Gateway Pipeline approved: B.C. reacts: B.C. reaction is rolling in to the federal government's decision to approve the Enbridge pipeline." *CBC News*, June 11, 2014.

Complete references for this feature can be found in the References section on page 474.

Heinzerling, 2004). Unfortunately, in a world of scarce resources, we have no choice in the matter. The only question is whether or not sensible ways for setting the price are used.

Valuing Intangibles

No matter how ingenious the investigator, some benefits and costs seem impossible to value. One of the benefits of sending Canadian astronauts into space is increased national prestige. Creating national parks gives people the thrill of enjoying beautiful scenery. The mind boggles at putting a dollar value on these "commodities." Three points must be kept in mind when intangible items might be important.

First, intangibles can subvert the entire cost–benefit exercise. By claiming that they are large enough, any project can be made admissible. A journalist commenting on Britain's deliberations about whether to construct a tunnel below the English channel gave this advice: "Build it, not because dreary cost–benefit analysis says it will pay but because Britain needs a big project to arouse it" (Will, 1985). However, presumably anyone who favours a particular project can make a case on the basis of its ability to "arouse." How then does one choose among projects? (Of course, the channel tunnel was ultimately built. When completed in 1994, it cost $15 billion, more than twice the original estimate.)

Second, the tools of cost–benefit analysis can sometimes be used to force planners to reveal limits on how they value intangibles. Suppose a space program's measurable costs and benefits are C and B, respectively, and its intangible benefits, such as national prestige, are an unknown amount X. Then, if the measured costs are greater than measured benefits, X must exceed $(C - B)$ for the program to be admissible. Such information may reveal that the intangible is not valuable enough to merit doing the project. If $(C - B)$ for the space program were $10 million per year, people might agree that its contribution to national prestige was worth it. But if the figure were $10 billion, a different conclusion might emerge.

Finally, even if it is impossible to measure certain benefits, there may be alternative methods of attaining them. If so, systematic study of the costs of the various alternatives should be done to find the cheapest way possible. This is sometimes called **cost-effectiveness analysis**. Thus, while one cannot put a dollar value on national security, it still may be feasible to subject the costs of alternative weapons systems to scrutiny.

Uncertainty

In 2013, the Bow River broke through the levees surrounding the flood plains of Calgary and other cities in Alberta, leading to disastrous flooding. This catastrophe serves as a grim reminder of the fact that the outcomes of public projects are uncertain. Many important debates over project proposals centre around the fact that no one knows how they will turn out. How much will a job-training program increase earnings of welfare recipients? Will new helicopters for the military function properly under Canadian winter conditions?

Suppose that two projects are being considered. They have identical costs, and both affect only one citizen, Smith. Project X guarantees a benefit of $1,000 with certainty. Project Y creates a benefit of zero dollars with a probability of one-half, and a benefit of $2,000 with a probability of one-half. Which project does Smith prefer?

Note that on average, the benefit from Y is equal to that from X. This is because the expected benefit from Y is $1/2 \times \$0 + 1/2 \times \$2,000 = \$1,000$. If Smith is risk averse, she prefers X to Y. This is because project Y subjects Smith to risk, while X is a sure thing. In other words, if Smith is risk averse, she would be willing to trade project Y for a *certain* amount of money less than $1,000–she would give up some income in return for gaining some security. The most obvious evidence that people are in fact willing to pay to avoid risk is the widespread holding of insurance policies of various kinds (see Chapter 9).

Therefore, when the benefits or costs of a project are risky, they must be converted into **certainty equivalents**–the amount of *certain* income the individual would be willing to trade for the set of uncertain outcomes generated by the project. The computation of certainty equivalents requires information on both the distribution of returns from the project and how risk averse the people involved are. The method of calculation is described in Chapter 9.

The calculation of certainty equivalents presupposes that the random distribution of costs and benefits is known in advance. In some cases, this is a reasonable assumption. For example, engineering and weather data could be used to estimate how a proposed dam would reduce the probability of flood destruction. In many important cases, however, it is hard to assign probabilities to various outcomes. There is not enough experience with nuclear reactors to gauge the likelihood of various malfunctions. Similarly, how do you estimate the probability that a new AIDS vaccine will be effective? As usual, the best the analyst can do is to make explicit his or her assumptions and determine the extent to which substantive findings change when these assumptions are modified.

GAMES COST–BENEFIT ANALYSTS PLAY

In addition to the problems we have already discussed, Tresch (2002) has noted a number of common errors in cost–benefit analysis.

The Chain-Reaction Game

An advocate for a proposal can make it look especially attractive by counting secondary profits arising from it as part of the benefits. If the government builds a road, the primary benefits are the reductions in transportation costs for individuals and firms. At the same time, though, profits of local restaurants, motels, and gas stations probably increase. This leads to increased profits in the local food, bed-linen, and gasoline-production industries. If enough secondary effects are added to the benefit side, eventually a positive present value can be obtained for practically any project.

This procedure ignores the fact that the project may induce losses as well as profits. After the road is built, the profits of train operators decrease as some of their customers turn to cars for transportation. Increased auto use may bid up the price of gasoline, decreasing the welfare of many gasoline consumers.

In short, the problem with the chain-reaction game is that it counts as benefits changes that are merely transfers across individuals. The increase in the price of gasoline, for example, transfers income from gasoline consumers to gasoline producers, but it does not represent a net benefit of the project. As noted earlier, distributional considerations may indeed be relevant to the decision maker. But, if so, consistency requires that if secondary benefits are counted, so must be secondary losses.

The Labour Game

Some projects are supported by governments because they "create" employment. Essentially, the wages of the workers employed are viewed as *benefits* of the project. This is absurd, because wages belong on the cost, not the benefit, side of the calculation. Of course, as already suggested, it is true that if workers are involuntarily unemployed, their social cost is less than their wage. Even in an area with high unemployment, it is unlikely that all the labour used in the project would have been unemployed, or that all those who were unemployed would have remained so for a long time.

The Double-Counting Game

Suppose that the government is considering irrigating some land that currently cannot be cultivated. It counts as benefits of the project the sum of (1) the increase in value of the land, *and* (2) the present value of the stream of net income obtained from farming it. The problem here is that a farmer can *either* farm the land and take as gains the net income stream *or* sell the land to someone else. Under competition, the sale price of the land just equals the present value of the net income from farming it. Because the farmer cannot do both simultaneously, counting both (1) and (2) represents a double counting of the true benefits.

This error may seem so silly that no one would ever commit it. However, Tresch (2002: 825) points out that at one time double counting was the official policy of the Bureau of Reclamation within the U.S. Department of the Interior. The bureau's instructions for cost–benefit analysts stipulated that the benefits of land irrigation be computed as the sum of the increase in land value and the present value of the net income from farming it.

AN APPLICATION

In Chapter 9, we note the concerns of Canadians over the high costs of health care. One trend that adversely affects these costs is the increasing demand for single-occupancy acute care hospital rooms compared with double-occupancy rooms. The new Patient Care Centre of the Royal Jubilee Hospital in Victoria, British Columbia, for example, has 83 percent of its 500 beds in single-occupancy rooms, compared with a national average for large multi-purpose hospitals of about 50 percent of beds in single-occupancy rooms. Single-occupancy rooms require relatively more space per bed, and therefore they entail higher hospital costs per patient than do double-occupancy rooms. The question to ask is whether the benefits of single-occupancy, such as increased patient privacy and lower infection rates, are worth the additional costs. Boardman and Forbes (2011) employed the tools of cost–benefit analysis to address this question. Their study illustrates a number of important aspects of cost–benefit analysis, such as discounting and the valuation of non-traded goods.

The Impacts of Private Hospital Rooms

The Boardman and Forbes study is based on a proposed new hospital facility in Vancouver with an estimated capacity of 537 beds and a lifespan of 50 years. The objective of the study is to evaluate the *incremental* net benefits (in 2008 dollars) of building the facility with all the beds in single-occupancy (private) rooms, instead of placing the beds in double-occupancy (semi-private) rooms. There are a number of impacts of single-occupancy that need to be evaluated. Some of these impacts are ongoing annual amounts, which need to be converted into present values by discounting. The authors assume a real discount rate of 3.5 percent in their base case.

Land, construction, operating costs. Private rooms require more space per bed than do semi-private rooms. This section explains how Boardman and Forbes estimated the additional tangible and intangible costs associated with building a relatively larger facility required for placing all the beds in private rooms. These up-front and ongoing incremental costs sum up to $245,806 in present value terms.

Land cost. Based on architectural plans for hospital wards, each private room would require a floor space 436 sq. ft. per bed versus 287 sq. ft. per bed in a semi-private room. These amounts include the corridor space and nursing areas required for each type of ward. Using the amounts developers pay for land in Vancouver ($86.23 per buildable sq. ft. at the proposed location) the authors estimate that the land cost would be $37,596 per private bed, compared to $24,748 per semi-private bed. At the end of the hospital's operation in 50 years the building would be demolished and the land sold, yielding revenues in present value terms of $6,731 per private room and $4,431 per semi-private room. Thus the incremental net present value of the land cost for a private bed is $10,714.

Construction cost. Estimates of the construction costs exist for numerous hospital designs. Excluding the components of construction costs that do not vary with room type, such as landscaping and utilities, the authors assess the construction costs at $442 per sq. ft. Multiplying this amount by the additional floor space required for a bed in a private room yields incremental up-front cost of $65,858 per bed.

Maintenance. The authors report that patient rooms are typically refurbished every 10 years with new fixtures, flooring, wall coverings, and furniture, at a cost of approximately 10 percent of the initial construction costs. On an annualized basis this amounts to an additional cost for a private bed of $659 per year. Discounting the costs over 50 years gives a present value of $15,447.

Housekeeping and operating costs. Figures for the housekeeping and operating costs are taken from the observed costs per square foot at St. Paul's Hospital in Vancouver, but adjusted downward for the new energy efficient design proposed for the new facility. The result is an estimate of $16.52 per sq. ft. for the combined housekeeping and maintenance costs. Multiplying this amount by the space required for each bed implies annual per bed costs of $7,203 for a private room and $4,741 for a semi-private room. The present value of the difference is $57,736.

Patient care costs. Nurses and doctors must spend more time walking between patients located in private rooms than between patients located in semi-private rooms. Given estimates of the average daily nursing time per patient and the distance typically walked by nurses during their shifts, the relatively larger space requirement of private rooms implies that nurses will need to walk 20 minutes more per patient per day if the patients are in private rooms, compared to when they are in semi-private rooms. Based on the salaries of nurses in Vancouver, the extra time nurses would spend walking between patients in private rooms costs $3,726 per bed per year. Factoring in the cost of (the relatively small) additional doctors' time, and adjusting the nursing costs by the expected increase in their real wages in Vancouver, the present value of incremental patient care costs is $96,051.

Patient impacts. Patients value being in single-occupancy rooms not only for the sake of privacy, but also because of fewer disruptions from noise and lower chances of acquiring infections, compared with accommodation in double-occupancy rooms. One way to gauge a patient's incremental willingness to pay for single-occupancy is to examine the price differential between private versus semi-private hospital rooms in British Columbia and the U.S. Surveying price differentials in eight hospitals, the authors arrive at an estimate of $45 per day per patient.[17] Assuming an 80 percent hospital occupancy rate (and hence each bed is occupied only 80 percent of the time), the incremental benefit to patients from being accommodated in private rooms equals $13,140 per year, for a present value of $308,207.

An alternative approach to evaluating patient benefits from private rooms is to try to quantify each impact (noise reduction, privacy, reduced infection) separately. In this section, we explain the authors' techniques for quantifying the patient impacts of non-traded goods one by one.[18]

Noise. Patients in private rooms benefit from relatively less noise arising from the movement of equipment and talking between staff, patients, and visitors. A study in Sweden reports that people are willing to pay about 6.5 percent of their monthly rent per household to decrease noise to a "quiet" level. Based on the average monthly rental charge for a two-bedroom apartment in Vancouver, as well as other corroborating information on people's willingness to pay for reduced noise, the authors estimate that the noise reduction benefit for patients in private rooms compared with semi-private rooms would be $749 per year ($2.57 per day), or $17,570 in present value.

---

[17] A difficulty with using this method to calculate a patient's willingness to pay for a private room is that the "room services" of different hospitals vary and the price of hospital accommodation is at least partially covered by medical insurance rather than out of the patient's pocket.

[18] Boardman and Forbes regard these separate estimates as sensitivity analysis for their base case result of $45/patient-days.

Privacy. Patients may feel embarrassed or irritated by the presence of another patient in a double-occupancy room. A measure of the value of privacy from single occupancy is provided by the average price differential for a private cabin on a cruise ship for singles. This gives an incremental value for privacy of $131 per day per patient, or a present value for the stream of benefits equal to $897,225.[19] While accommodation on a cruise ship is certainly not an identical service to accommodation in a hospital, it may suggest that the $45/patient-day assessment provided above for the *overall* patient benefit of single occupancy is, if anything, too low.

Risk of an adverse event. Studies on inpatient infection rates suggest that private rooms may avoid 0.0002 deaths and 0.008 serious illnesses per bed each year. Estimates of the value of a statistical life (VSL) in the U.S. put the value at $5 million (USD). Converting this amount into Canadian dollars at the prevailing exchange rate and adjusting the amount for historical differences between incomes in the U.S. and Canada yields a VSL in Canada of $4.54 million (CAD). The value of a serious illness avoided is estimated at $300,000. The implication is that private beds might have incremental health benefits of $11,475 per bed per year, which has a present value of $269,146.

Hospital impacts. Private hospital rooms also generate certain cost savings for hospitals relative to semi-private rooms. There are fewer patient transfers and faster patient turnover. The estimated present value of these savings is $7,325 per bed.

Fewer transfers. Boardman and Forbes report that on average 16.7 percent of patients are transferred each week from rooms with multiple occupants to private rooms as a result of complaints or health concerns. Private rooms would reduce the number of transfers to zero. The cost per transfer at a comparable facility is $31. Hence, the cost saving from fewer transfers compared to semi-private rooms is estimated to be $269 per bed each year, which has a present value of $6,314.

Reduced waiting time. Private rooms tend to reduce patients' risk of infection or injury compared with semi-private rooms. An estimate of the reduced probability of an adverse event from staying in a private room is one percentage point per year. Assuming that each adverse event increases the length of stay in a hospital by 16 days, private rooms reduce the usage of each bed by 0.16 days per year. Multiplying this proportion by the incremental cost of a day in an acute care room yields a cost saving of $43 per bed per year, with a present value of $1,011 per bed.

Impacts on the general population. Individuals who are currently healthy may derive a benefit just from knowing that they have the "option" of staying in a private room in the event they have to be hospitalized due to illness or injury. Boardman and Forbes point out that this is an additional benefit from designing the facility with private rooms. However, they do not attempt to quantify the option value.

Summing up the components. Table 3.3 summarizes the present values of the costs and benefits of designing the proposed 537-bed hospital facility in Vancouver with the beds in private rooms instead of in semi-private rooms. The incremental net social benefit is $69,726 per bed, or about $34 million for the facility. Under the alternate estimation of patient impacts, the net social benefit of private rooms is substantially higher. The results support the placement of the beds in private rooms in the proposed new facility, despite the higher up-front costs of doing so.

Comments

The Boardman and Forbes[20] study illustrates some important aspects of practical cost–benefit studies:

1. The analysis is often interdisciplinary because economists alone do not have the technical expertise to evaluate all costs and benefits. Thus, architectural expertise was required to estimate the land and construction costs of alternative hospital designs, and medical research studies were used to predict the risk of inpatient adverse events.

---

[19] The *PV* of privacy benefits based on this alternative method of evaluation is not reported by Boardman and Forbes. Our estimate is obtained by grossing up the amount they report for the case of $45/patient-day by a factor of 2.94 (=$131/$45). However, given that cruise ship passengers may on average have higher incomes than average hospital patients, a more conservative figure for privacy benefits may be more appropriate.

[20] For other applications of cost–benefit analysis in a Canadian context, see Townley (1998). See McHugh (2006) for a cost–benefit analysis of the 2010 Olympic Games in Vancouver.

TABLE 3.3

Net Social Benefits of a Bed in a Private Hospital Room Relative to a Semi-Private Room

	PV of Difference between Private Room and Semi-Private Room (per bed)	PV of Difference using Alternate Estimates of Patient Impacts (per bed)
Costs		
Land	$10,714	
Construction	65,858	
Maintenance	15,447	
Housekeeping and operating	57,736	
Patient care	96,051	
Total Costs	**245,806**	**245,806**
Benefits		
Noise reduction		17,570
Privacy		897,225
Fewer preventable adverse events		269,146
Subtotal benefits	308,207	1,183,941
Patient transfers	6,314	6,314
Patient turnover	1,011	1,011
Option value	Not estimated	Not estimated
Total Benefits	**315,532**	**1,191,266**
Net Social Benefit	**69,726**	**945,460**

Source: Boardman and Forbes (2011) and calculations by the authors based on the article.

2. Evaluation of costs and benefits, especially those arising in the future, is likely to require ad hoc assumptions. The Boardman and Forbes study required a 50-year forecast of wages and salaries (in constant 2008 dollars) to quantify the costs of the longer distances walked by nurses and doctors if rooms were private, and such long-range forecasts are often subject to substantial errors. In general, there is a great deal of uncertainty about the future values of impacts.

3. The evaluation of non-traded goods often requires the use of shadow prices derived from observing consumer behaviour is related markets. In their "alternative" patient benefit estimation, Boardman and Forbes used, for example, the observed price differential between noisy and quiet apartment units to quantify the benefit of noise reduction from accommodation in a private hospital room.

4. For all its limitations, cost–benefit analysis is a remarkably useful way of summarizing information. It also forces analysts to make explicit their assumptions so that the reasons for their ultimate recommendation are clear.

SUMMARY

• Cost–benefit analysis is the practical use of welfare economics to evaluate potential projects.

• A project generates a potential Pareto improvement if the gainers could compensate the losers and still enjoy a net increase in utility.

• Whether distributional considerations belong in cost–benefit analysis is controversial. Some analysts count dollars equally for all persons, while others apply weights that favour projects for selected population groups. Because of the potential for political manipulation, distributional weights must be introduced explicitly.

• Cost–benefit analyses consider net benefits received over time. To make these comparable, the present value of all future net benefits must be computed.

- Other methods—internal rate of return, benefit-cost ratio—can lead to incorrect decisions.
- Choosing the discount rate is critical in cost-benefit analyses. In public sector analyses, three possible measures are the before-tax private rate of return, a weighted average of before- and after-tax private rates of return, and the social discount rate. Choosing among them depends on the type of private activity displaced—investment or consumption—and the degree to which private markets are believed to reflect society's preferences.
- The benefits and costs of public projects may be measured in several ways:
  - Market prices serve well if there is no strong reason to believe that they depart from social marginal costs.
  - Shadow prices adjust market prices for deviations from social marginal costs due to market imperfections.
  - If labour is currently unemployed and will remain so for the duration of the project, the opportunity cost is small. However, forecasting unemployment is difficult. If large government projects change equilibrium prices, consumer surplus can be used to measure the effect on individuals. For non-marketed commodities, no prices are available. In some instances, the values of these commodities can be inferred by observing people's behaviour. Two examples are computing the benefits of saving time and the benefits of a reduced probability of death.
- Certain intangible benefits and costs simply cannot be measured. The safest approach is to exclude these in a cost-benefit analysis and then calculate how large intangibles must be to reverse the decision.
- Cost-benefit analyses sometimes fall prey to several pitfalls:
  - Chain-reaction game—secondary benefits are included to make a proposal appear more favourable, without including the corresponding secondary costs.
  - Labour game—wages are viewed as benefits rather than costs of the project.
  - Double-counting game—benefits are mistakenly counted twice.
- In uncertain situations, individuals favour less risky projects, other things being the same. In general, the costs and benefits of uncertain projects must be adjusted to reflect this.

EXERCISES

1. A cost-benefit study indicated that the Oldman Dam project in southern Alberta had a benefit-cost ratio of 4.9 (Marv Anderson and Associates, 1978: Table 5.2, p. 103). On the basis of this benefit-cost ratio, can you say whether investment in the Oldman Dam was worthwhile? (*Hint:* What other information do you require to render a decision?)

2. The city of Sundown is considering a plan to build a convention centre to revitalize the downtown area. The project requires hiring workers in the construction union. Because of unionization, the workers' wage rate is above the value that would be determined by supply and demand. However, city analysts have econometrically estimated the wage that would prevail if the labour market were competitive.

   a. If the convention centre increases the total number of construction workers employed, what is the appropriate cost of labour?

   b. Suppose instead that total employment is unaffected; workers leave private projects to work on the convention centre. Does your answer to (a) change? Why?

3. A province is considering an emissions testing program for all cars in the province. The waiting time per vehicle for the emissions test is estimated to be between 15 minutes to 2 hours. How should this information be factored into a cost-benefit analysis of the emissions testing program?

4. A project yields an annual benefit of $25 a year, starting next year and continuing forever. What is the present value of the benefits if the interest rate is 10 percent? (*Hint:* The infinite sum $x + x^2 + x^3 + \ldots$ is equal to $x/(1 - x)$, where x is a number less than 1.) Generalize your answer to show that if the perpetual annual benefit is B and the interest rate is r, then the present value is B/r.

5. An outlay of $1,000 today yields an annual benefit of $80 beginning next year and continuing forever. There is no inflation and the market interest rate is 10 percent before taxes and 5 percent after taxes.

   a. What is the internal rate of return?

   b. Taxes levied to fund the project come entirely from consumer spending. Is the project admissible? Why? Suppose instead that taxes are collected by reducing private firms' investments. Is the project admissible in this case? Finally, suppose consumers spend 60 cents of their last dollar and save 40 cents. Is the project admissible now? Explain your calculations.

   c. Suppose the social discount rate is 4 percent. What is the present value of the project?

   d. Now suppose 10 percent annual inflation is anticipated over the next ten years. How are your answers to (a), (b), and (c) affected?

6. Bill rides the subway at a cost of 75 cents per trip, but would switch if the price were any higher. His only alternative is a bus that takes five minutes longer, but costs only 50 cents. He makes ten trips per year. The city is considering renovations of the subway system that would reduce the trip by ten minutes, but fares would rise by 40 cents per trip to cover the costs. The fare increase and reduced travel time both take effect in one year and last forever. The interest rate is 25 percent.

   a. As far as Bill is concerned, what are the present values of the project's benefits and costs?

   b. The city's population consists of 55,000 middle-class people, all of whom are identical to Bill, and 5,000 poor people. Poor people are either unemployed or have jobs close to their homes, so they do not use any form of public transportation. What are the total benefits and costs of the project for the city as a whole? What is the net present value of the project?

   c. Some members of the city council propose an alternative project that consists of an immediate tax of $1.25 per middle-class person to provide "free" legal services for the poor in both of the following two years. The legal services are valued by the poor at a total of $62,500 per year. (Assume this amount is received at the end of each of the two years.) What is the present value of the project?

   d. If the city must choose between the subway project and the legal services project, which should it select?

   e.* What is the "distributional weight" of each dollar received by a poor person that would make the present values of the two projects just equal? That is, how much must each dollar of income to a poor person be weighted relative to that of a middle-class person? Interpret your answer.

7. An article in the *The Economist* (2007, p. 42) tells the story of an economist who once visited China during the rule of Mao Zedong. He saw hundreds of workers building a dam with shovels and asked, "Why don't they use a mechanical digger?" The foreman replied, "That would put people out of work." How does this comment relate to the "labour game" discussed in the chapter?

8. Suppose that the government is debating whether to spend $100 billion today to address climate change. It is estimated that $700 billion of damages will be averted, but these benefits will accrue 100 years from now. A critic of the proposal says that it would be far better to invest the $100 billion, earning an average real return of 5 percent per year, and then use the proceeds in 100 years to repair the damage from climate change. Is this critic correct?

9. A satirical essay recently advocated forcing taxi companies to switch to rickshaws, which are small two-wheeled taxis pulled by a runner or bicyclist. The authors note that this would create new jobs in the form of drivers and producers of rickshaws, and these would be green jobs since rickshaws (unlike taxis) do not produce pollution (Brookes and Foster, 2009). How does this proposal relate to the "labour game" discussed in the chapter?

10. A proposed irrigation project would lower the constant marginal cost of producing rice from \$1,000 to \$600 per unit. The local market for rice is competitive and has a demand curve given by $Q^D = 7,500 - 0.5P$ where P is the price. Draw a graph of the supply and demand for rice to show the change in consumer surplus due to the irrigation project. Calculate the increase in the net benefits to consumers. If the irrigation project will cost taxpayers \$28.1 million, is it worth undertaking?

APPENDIX

Consumer and Producer Surplus

This chapter emphasized that reallocations of resources affect the welfare of individuals. We often want to know not only whether a certain change makes people better or worse off, but also by how much. Suppose, for example, that initially the price of apples is 40 cents per apple, but then it falls to 25 cents. Clearly, apple consumers are better off because of the change. But can we put a dollar figure on the improvement in their welfare? *Consumer surplus* is a tool for obtaining such a dollar measure.

Consumer surplus. To begin our discussion of consumer surplus, consider the demand curve for apples, D_a, depicted in Figure 3A.1. Assume consumers can obtain all the apples they demand at the going market price, 40 cents each. Then the supply curve for apples, S_a, is a horizontal line at this price. According to the diagram, the associated quantity demanded is 65 tonnes.

Suppose now that more land is brought into apple production, and the supply curve shifts to S'_a. At the new equilibrium, the price falls to 25 cents, and apple consumption increases to 100 tonnes. How much better off are consumers? Another way of stating this question is, "How much would consumers be willing to pay for the privilege of consuming 100 tonnes of apples for 25 cents rather than 65 tonnes of apples at 40 cents?"

FIGURE 3A.1

MEASURING CONSUMER SURPLUS

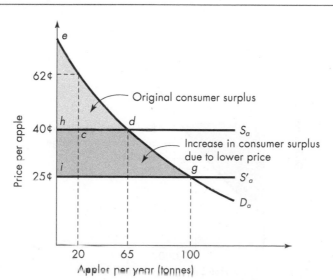

To provide an answer, begin by recalling that the demand curve shows the *maximum* amount that individuals *would* be willing to pay for each apple they consume. Consider some arbitrary quantity of apples, say, 20 tonnes. The most people would be willing to pay for the 20th tonne is the vertical distance up to the demand curve, 62 cents. Initially, consumers in fact had to pay only 40 cents per apple. In a sense then, on their purchase of the 20th tonne, consumers enjoyed a surplus of 22 cents. The amount by which the sum that individuals would have been *willing* to pay exceeds the sum they *actually* have to pay is called the **consumer surplus**.

Of course, the same exercise could be repeated at any quantity, not just at 20 tonnes. When the price is 40 cents per apple, the consumer surplus at each output level equals the distance between the demand curve and the horizontal line at 40 cents. Summing the surpluses for each apple purchased, we find that the total consumer surplus when the price is 40 cents is the area *ehd*. More generally, *consumer surplus is measured by the area under the demand curve and above a horizontal line at the market price.*

When the price falls to 25 cents, consumer surplus is still the area under the demand curve and above a horizontal line at the going price; because the price is now 25 cents, the relevant area is *eig*. Consumer surplus has therefore increased by the difference between areas *eig* and *ehd*, area *higd*. Thus, the area below the demand curve between the two prices measures the value to consumers of being able to purchase apples at the lower price.

To implement this procedure for a real-world problem, an investigator needs to know the shape of the demand curve. Generally, this can be obtained by using one or more of the tools of positive analysis discussed in Web-based Chapter 2 "Tools of Empirical Analysis." Hence, consumer surplus is a very practical tool for measuring the changes in welfare induced by changes in the economic environment.

There is a caveat that may be important under some circumstances. The area under an ordinary demand curve provides only an approximation to the true value of the change in consumer welfare. This is because as price changes, so do people's real incomes, and this may change the value that they place on additions to their income (the marginal utility of income). However, Willig (1976) has shown that measuring consumer surplus by the area under the ordinary demand curve is likely to be a pretty good approximation in most cases, and this approach is used widely in applied work.

Producer surplus. In analogy to consumer surplus, we can define *producer surplus* as the amount of income individuals receive in excess of what they would require to supply a given number of units of a factor. To measure producer surplus, consider Jacob's labour supply curve (*S*), which is represented in Figure 3A.2. Each point on the labour supply curve shows the wage rate required to coax Jacob into supplying the associated number of hours of work. Hence, the distance between any point on the labour supply curve and the wage

FIGURE 3A.2

MEASURING PRODUCER SURPLUS

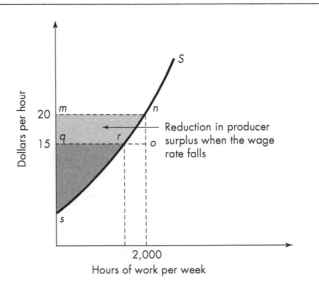

rate is the difference between the minimum payment that Jacob needs to receive for that hour of work and the amount he actually receives (the wage rate). Thus, *the area above the supply curve and below the wage rate is the producer surplus.*

To strengthen your understanding of producer surplus, imagine that initially Jacob works 2,000 hours per year at a wage of $20 per hour, but then his wage falls to $15 per hour. How much worse off is he as a consequence of this fall in wages? One possible answer is that he was working 2,000 hours and is now earning $5 less per hour, so he is worse off by $10,000. This corresponds to area *mqon* in Figure 3A.2. However, producer surplus analysis tells us that this answer is incorrect. Before the wage cut, Jacob's surplus is area *msn*. When the wage rate falls to $15, his surplus falls to *qsr*. Hence, Jacob's loss from the wage cut is area *mqrn*. This is less than the naive answer of *mqon*. Intuitively, the naive answer overstates the loss in welfare because it ignores the fact that when a person's wage falls, he can substitute leisure for consumption. While the increased consumption of leisure certainly does not fully compensate for the wage decrease, it does have some value.

PART TWO

A Framework for the Analysis of Public Expenditure

Market outcomes need be neither efficient nor fair. This part examines how various "market failures" can be remedied by government intervention. We discuss both the normative question of how the government ought to solve a particular problem and the positive question of how government actually changes the status quo.

Chapters 2 and 3 focused our attention on market failure and economic justice as reasons for considering government intervention. The chapters in this part examine these issues in greater detail and provide the conceptual framework for analyzing the expenditure areas examined in Part 4. Chapter 4 examines public goods. Chapter 5 deals with externalities, with a special emphasis on environmental issues. Chapter 6 is devoted to income redistribution and poverty.

CHAPTER 4

Public Goods

Associated or joint activity is a condition of the creation of a community.

—John Dewey

AFTER READING THIS CHAPTER, THE STUDENT SHOULD BE ABLE TO:

LO1 Describe the characteristics of public goods.

LO2 Explain why the private provision of public goods is unlikely to be efficient.

LO3 Derive the condition for an efficient provision of public goods.

LO4 Summarize the procedure of perfect price discrimination for financing a public good.

LO5 Distinguish between public versus private provision and public versus private production.

LO6 Describe the factors that determine the right mix of public and private provision of excludable goods.

LO7 Identify circumstances where private contractors are likely to produce inferior public services.

Which goods and services should the public sector provide, and in what amounts? As the annual debate over the federal budget demonstrates, this question lies at the heart of some of the most important controversies in public policy. How can the Canadian government's decision in 2010 to spend $9 billion for new F-35 fighter jets be evaluated? Is there an economic justification for the $37 million Own the Podium program for Olympic hopefuls in Canada? In this chapter, we discuss the conditions under which public provision of commodities is appropriate. Special attention is devoted to understanding why markets may fail to provide particular goods at Pareto efficient levels.

PUBLIC GOODS DEFINED

What is the difference between national defence and pizza? The question seems silly, but thinking about it leads to a useful framework for determining whether public or private provision of various commodities makes sense. To begin, one big difference between the two commodities is that two people cannot consume a piece of pizza simultaneously—if I eat the piece, you can't. In contrast, your consumption of the protective services provided by the army does nothing to diminish my consumption of the same services. A second major difference arises because I can easily exclude you from consuming my pizza, but excluding you from the benefits of national defence is all but impossible. (It's hard to imagine a situation in which a foreign army is allowed to overrun your home but not mine.)

National defence is an example of a **pure public good**, defined as follows:

- Consumption of the good is *nonrival*—once it is provided, the additional resource cost of another person consuming the good is zero.
- Consumption of the good is *nonexcludable*—to prevent anyone from consuming the good is either very expensive or impossible.

In contrast, a **private good** like pizza is rival and excludable.
Several aspects of our definition of public good are worth noting.

Even though everyone consumes the same quantity of the good, there is no requirement that this consumption be valued equally by all. Consider cleaning up an apartment with many college roommates. This activity is a public good. Everyone benefits from a clean bathroom, and it is hard to exclude anyone from these benefits. Yet some students care about cleanliness much more than others. Indeed, people might differ over whether the value of certain public goods is positive or negative. When a new missile system is constructed, each person has no choice but to consume its services. For those who view the system as an enhancement to their safety, the value is positive. Others believe additional missiles only escalate the arms race and decrease national security. Such individuals value an additional missile negatively. They would be willing to pay to not have it around.

Classification as a public good is not an absolute; it depends on market conditions and the state of technology. Think about the services provided by a lighthouse. Once the beacon is lit, one ship can take advantage of it without impinging on another ship's ability to do the same. Moreover, no particular vessel can be excluded from taking advantage of the signal. Under these conditions, the lighthouse is a pure public good. But suppose that a jamming device were invented that made it possible to prevent ships from obtaining the lighthouse signal unless they purchased a special receiver. In this case, the nonexcludability criterion is no longer satisfied, and the lighthouse is no longer a pure public good. A scenic view can be considered a pure public good when there is a small number of people involved. But as the number of sightseers increases, the area may become congested. The same "quantity" of the scenic view is being "consumed" by each person, but its quality can decrease with the number of people. Hence, the nonrivalness criterion is no longer satisfied.

In many cases, then, it is useful to think of "publicness" as a matter of degree. A pure public good satisfies the definition exactly. Consumption of an **impure public good** is to some extent rival or to some extent excludable. There are not many examples of pure public goods. However, just as analysis of pure competition yields important insights into the operation of actual markets, so the analysis of pure public goods helps us to understand the problems confronting public decision makers.

A commodity can satisfy one part of the definition of a public good and not the other. That is, nonexcludability and nonrivalness do not have to go together. Consider the streets of a downtown urban area during rush hour. In most cases, nonexcludability holds, because it is not feasible to set up enough toll booths to monitor traffic. But consumption is certainly rival, as anyone who has ever been caught in a traffic jam can testify. On the other hand, many people can enjoy a huge seashore area without diminishing the pleasure of others. Despite the fact that individuals do not rival each other in consumption, exclusion is quite possible if there are only a few access roads. Again, however, the characterization of a commodity depends on the state of technology and on legal arrangements. The road congestion example is relevant here. Highway 407 near Toronto is called an "express toll route" because radio waves are used to identify passing cars and automatically charge tolls to drivers' charge accounts. One can imagine using such technology to charge cars as they enter congested city streets—the streets would be excludable. Similarly, plate recognition cameras are now used to implement a London congestion charge in England's heavy traffic areas.

Some things that are not conventionally thought of as commodities have public good characteristics. An important example is honesty. If each citizen is honest in commercial transactions, all of society benefits due to the reduction of the costs of doing business. Such cost reductions are characterized both by nonexcludability and by nonrivalness. Similarly, Thurow (1971) argues that income distribution is a public good. If income is distributed "fairly" each person gains satisfaction from living in a good society, and no one can be excluded from having that satisfaction. Of course, because of disagreements over notions of fairness, people may differ over how a given income distribution should be valued. Nevertheless, consumption of the income distribution is nonrival, and therefore it is a public good.

Private goods are not necessarily provided exclusively by the private sector. There are many *publicly provided private goods*—rival and excludable commodities that are provided by governments. Medical services and housing are two examples of private goods sometimes provided publicly. Similarly, as we see later, public goods can be provided privately. (Think of an individual sponsoring a fireworks display, such as the Kayak Festival Fireworks held annually in Timmins, Ontario.) In short, the label *private* or *public* does not by itself tell us anything about which sector provides the item.

Public provision of a good does not necessarily mean that it is also *produced* by the public sector. Consider garbage collection. Some communities produce this service themselves–public sector managers purchase garbage trucks, hire workers, and arrange schedules. In other communities, the local government hires a private firm for the job and does not organize production itself. For example, in the City of Ottawa, all of the garbage collection is contracted out to private firms.

EFFICIENT PROVISION OF PUBLIC GOODS

What is the efficient amount of defence or of any other public good? To derive the conditions for efficient provision of a public good, it is useful to begin by reexamining private goods from a slightly different point of view from that in Chapter 2. Assume again a society populated by two people, Adam and Eve. There are two private goods, apples and fig leaves. In Figure 4.1A, the quantity of fig leaves (f) is measured on the horizontal axis, and the price per fig leaf (P_f) is on the vertical. Adam's demand curve for fig leaves is denoted by D_f^A. The demand curve shows the quantity of fig leaves that Adam would be willing to consume at each price, other things being the same. Similarly, D_f^E in Figure 4.1B is Eve's demand curve for fig leaves.

Suppose we want to derive the market demand curve for fig leaves. To do so, we simply add together the number of fig leaves each person demands at every price. In Figure 4.1A, at a price of $5, Adam demands one fig leaf, the horizontal distance between D_f^A and the vertical axis. Figure 4.1B indicates that at the same price, Eve demands two fig leaves. The total quantity demanded at a price of $5 is therefore three leaves. The market demand curve for fig leaves is labelled D_f^{A+E} in Figure 4.1C. As we have just shown, the point at which price is $5 and quantity is three lies on the market demand curve. Similarly, finding the market demand at any given price involves summing the horizontal distance between each of the private demand curves and the vertical axis at that price. This process is called **horizontal summation**.

FIGURE 4.1

HORIZONTAL SUMMATION OF DEMAND CURVES

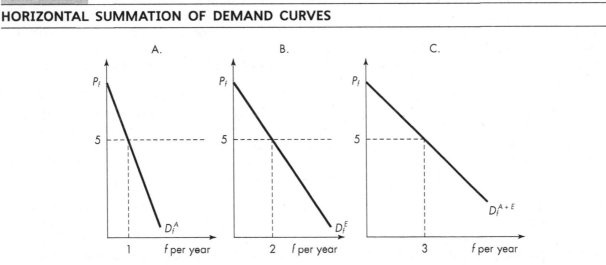

Figure 4.2 reproduces the information from Figure 4.1. Figure 4.2C then superimposes the market supply curve, labelled S_f, on the market demand curve D_f^{A+E}. Equilibrium in the market is at the price where supply and demand are equal. This occurs at a price of $4 in Figure 4.2C. At this price, Adam consumes one-and-one-half fig leaves and Eve consumes three. Note that there is no reason to expect Adam's and Eve's consumption levels to be equal. Due to different tastes, incomes, and other characteristics, Adam and Eve demand different quantities of fig leaves. This is possible because fig leaves are private goods.

The equilibrium in Figure 4.2C has a significant property: the allocation of fig leaves is Pareto efficient. In consumer theory, a utility-maximizing individual sets the marginal rate of substitution of fig leaves for apples (MRS_{fa}) equal to the price of fig leaves (P_f) divided by the price of apples (P_a): $MRS_{fa} = P_f/P_a$. Because only relative prices matter for rational choice, the price of apples can be arbitrarily set at any value. For convenience,

FIGURE 4.2

EFFICIENT PROVISION OF A PRIVATE GOOD

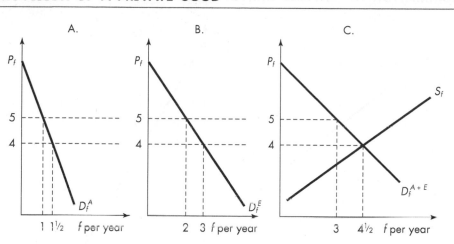

set at $P_a = \$1$. Thus, the condition for utility maximization reduces to $MRS_{fa} = P_f$. The price of fig leaves thus measures the rate at which an individual is willing to substitute fig leaves for apples. Now, Adam's demand curve for fig leaves (D_f^A) shows the maximum price per fig leaf that he would pay at each level of fig leaf consumption. Therefore, the demand curve also shows the MRS_{fa} at each level of fig leaf consumption. Similarly, D_f^E can be interpreted as Eve's MRS_{fa} schedule.

In the same way, the supply curve S_f in Figure 4.2C shows how the marginal rate of transformation of fig leaves for apples (MRT_{fa}) varies with fig leaf production.[1] At the equilibrium in Figure 4.2C, Adam and Eve both set MRS_{fa} equal to four, and the producer also sets MRT_{fa} equal to four. Hence, at equilibrium

$$MRS_{fa}^{Adam} = MRS_{fa}^{Eve} = MRT_{fa} \qquad (4.1)$$

Equation (4.1) is the necessary condition for Pareto efficiency derived in Chapter 2. As long as the market is competitive and functions properly, the First Welfare Theorem guarantees that this condition holds.

Deriving the Efficiency Condition

Having now reinterpreted the condition for efficient provision of a private good, we turn to the case of a public good. Let's develop the efficiency condition intuitively before turning to a formal derivation. Suppose Adam and Eve both enjoy displays of fireworks. Eve's enjoyment of fireworks does not diminish Adam's, and vice versa, and it is impossible for one person to exclude the other from watching the display. Hence, a fireworks display is a public good. The size of the fireworks display can be varied, and both Adam and Eve prefer bigger to smaller displays, other things being the same. Suppose that the display currently consists of 19 rockets and can be expanded at a cost of $5 per rocket, that Adam would be willing to pay $6 to expand the display by another rocket, and that Eve would be willing to pay $4. Is it efficient to increase the size of the display by one rocket? As usual, we must compare the additional value associated with that rocket (the "marginal benefit") with the cost of providing that rocket (the "marginal cost"). To compute the marginal benefit, note that because consumption of the display is nonrival, the 20th rocket can be consumed by *both* Adam and Eve. Hence, the marginal benefit of the 20th rocket is the *sum* of what they are willing to pay, which is $10. Because the marginal cost is only $5, it pays to acquire the 20th rocket. More generally, if the sum of individuals' willingness to pay for an additional unit of a public good exceeds its marginal cost, efficiency requires that the unit be purchased; otherwise, it should not. Hence, efficiency requires that provision of a public good be expanded until the point at which the sum of each person's marginal benefit for the last unit just equals the marginal cost.

---

[1] To see why, note that under competition firms produce up to the point where price equals marginal cost. Hence, the supply curve S_f shows the marginal cost of each level of fig leaf production. As noted in Chapter 2, $MRT_{fa} = MC_f/MC_a$. Because $P_a = \$1$ and price equals marginal cost, then $MC_a = \$1$, and $MRT_{fa} = MC_f$. We can therefore identify the marginal rate of transformation with marginal cost, and hence with the supply curve.

FIGURE 4.3

VERTICAL SUMMATION OF DEMAND CURVES

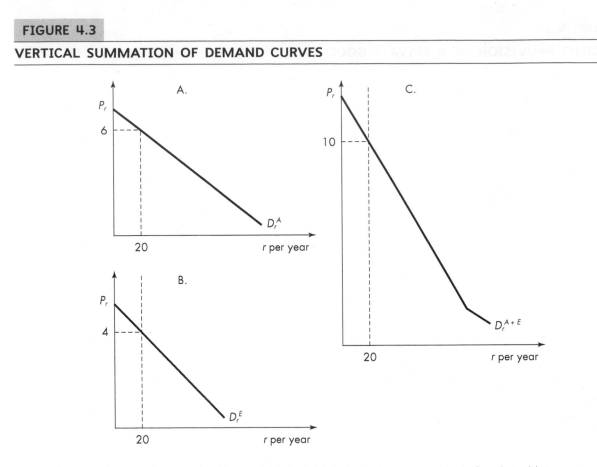

To illustrate this result, consider Figure 4.3A in which Adam's consumption of rockets (r) is measured on the horizontal axis, and the price per rocket (P_r) is on the vertical. Adam's demand curve for rockets is D_r^A. Similarly, Eve's demand curve for rockets is D_r^E in Figure 4.3B. How do we derive the group willingness to pay for rockets? To find the group demand curve for fig leaves—a private good—we horizontally summed the individual demand curves. That procedure allowed Adam and Eve to consume different quantities of fig leaves at the same price. For a private good, this is fine. However, the services produced by the rockets—a public good— *must* be consumed in *equal* amounts. If Adam consumes a 20-rocket fireworks display, Eve must also consume a 20-rocket fireworks display. It makes no sense to try to sum the quantities of a public good that the individuals would consume at a given price.

Instead, to find the group willingness to pay for rockets, we add the prices that each would be willing to pay for a given quantity. The demand curve in Figure 4.3A tells us that Adam is willing to pay $6 per rocket when he consumes 20 rockets. Eve is willing to pay $4 when she consumes 20 rockets. Their group willingness to pay for 20 rockets is therefore $10 per rocket. Thus, if we define D_r^{A+E} in Figure 4.3C to be the group willingness to pay schedule, the vertical distance between D_r^{A+E} and the point $r = 20$ must be 10.[2] Other points on D_r^{A+E} are determined by repeating this procedure for each output level. For a public good, then, the group willingness to pay is found by **vertical summation** of the individual demand curves.

Note the symmetry between private and public goods. With a private good, everyone has the same *MRS*, but people can consume different quantities. Therefore, demands are summed horizontally over the differing quantities. For public goods, everyone consumes the same quantity, but people can have different *MRSs*. Vertical summation is required to find the group willingness to pay. Put another way, for standard private goods, everyone sees the same price and then people decide what quantity they want. For public goods, everyone sees the same quantity and people decide what price they are willing to pay.

---

[2] D_r^{A+E} is not a conventional demand schedule because it does not show the quantity that would be demanded at each price. However, this notation highlights the similarities to the private good case.

FIGURE 4.4

EFFICIENT PROVISION OF A PUBLIC GOOD

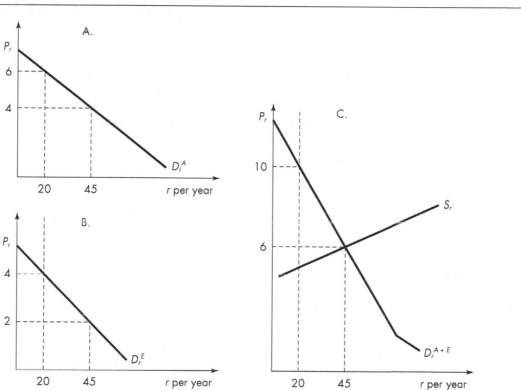

The efficient quantity of rockets is found at the point where Adam's and Eve's willingness to pay for an additional unit just equals the marginal cost of producing a unit. In Figure 4.4C, the marginal cost schedule, S_r, is superimposed on the group willingness to pay curve D_r^{A+E}.[3] The intersection occurs at output 45, where the marginal cost is equal to $6.

Once again, prices can be interpreted in terms of marginal rates of substitution. Reasoning as before, Adam's marginal willingness to pay for rockets is his marginal rate of substitution (MRS_{ra}^{Adam}), and Eve's marginal willingness to pay for rockets is her marginal rate of substitution (MRS_{ra}^{Eve}). Therefore, the sum of the prices they are willing to pay equals $MRS_{ra}^{Adam} + MRS_{ra}^{Eve}$. From the production point of view, price still represents the marginal rate of transformation, MRT_{ra}. Hence, the equilibrium in Figure 4.4C is characterized by the condition

$$MRS_{ra}^{Adam} + MRS_{ra}^{Eve} = MRT_{ra} \tag{4.2}$$

Contrast this with the conditions for efficient provision of a private good described in Equation (4.1). For a private good, efficiency requires that each individual have the same marginal rate of substitution and that this equal the marginal rate of transformation. For a pure public good, the sum of the marginal rates of substitution must equal the marginal rate of transformation. Because everybody must consume the same amount of the public good, its efficient provision requires that the total valuation they place on the last unit provided—the sum of the MRSs—equal the incremental cost to society of providing it—the MRT.

The condition (4.2) for the optimal provision of a public good can also be expressed in terms of the marginal benefit to consumers and the marginal cost of production, expressed in dollar values. Suppose the price of an apple is one dollar. Then the MRS_{ra}^{Adam} can be interpreted as the marginal benefit of a unit of the public good to Adam, MB^{Adam}. Similarly, MRS_{ra}^{Eve} measures the marginal benefit of a unit of the public good to Eve, MB^{Eve}, and MRT_{ra} is the marginal cost of producing a unit of the public good, MC. Therefore the optimality condition is

$$MB^{Adam} + MB^{Eve} = MC \tag{4.3}$$

---

[3] This analysis does not consider explicitly the production possibilities frontier that lies behind this supply curve. See Samuelson (1955).

That is, the public good should be provided up to the point where the **social marginal benefit**—the sum of the marginal benefits to all of the individuals in the society—equals the marginal cost of producing another unit of the public good.

The efficiency condition for a private good described by Equation (4.1) can also be stated in terms of marginal benefit and marginal cost:

$$MB^{Adam} = MB^{Eve} = MC \qquad (4.4)$$

Since the marginal benefit of fig leaves is the same for Adam and Eve at the market equilibrium, we can refer in this case to their common value as the social marginal benefit of a fig leaf.

Provision of Public Goods Financed by Distortionary Taxation

The condition for the optimal provision of public goods, given by Equation (4.2) or (4.3), is based on the assumption that lump-sum taxes are used to pay for the public good. When a public good is financed by distortionary taxation, the cost of providing an additional unit of the public good is affected in two ways. First, increasing distortionary taxes to finance an additional unit of the public good further distorts the allocation of resources in the economy and reduces economic efficiency. The cost of raising an additional dollar of revenue through a distortionary tax is called the marginal cost of public funds (*MCF*), and the *MCF* will generally be greater than one. Thus, the gross cost of providing an additional unit of the public good with distortionary taxation is *MCF* × *MC*. Second, providing an additional unit of the public good may affect the government's tax revenues, thereby affecting the net cost of the public good. For example, the provision of a lighthouse may reduce the cost of shipping goods that might stimulate trade and increase the government's income and sales tax revenues. On the other hand, providing a lighthouse might make it easier to smuggle goods into a country, allowing smugglers to evade tariffs and excise taxes. In this case, the provision of the public good would reduce the government's tax revenues. Let *MR* denote the additional revenue that the government obtains when it provides an additional unit of the public good. *MR* is a positive number if the public good generates more revenues for the government. *MR* is negative if provision of the public good reduces tax revenues. Thus, the net amount of revenue that the government has to raise when it provides an additional unit of the public good is (*MC* − *MR*). This additional net revenue has to be financed through increases in a distortionary tax, and therefore the total cost to the society of providing the additional unit of the public good is *MCF* × (*MC* − *MR*).

The direct marginal benefit of the public good is still given by $MB^{Adam} + MB^{Eve}$, and therefore the optimal provision of the public good is determined by the following condition:[4]

$$MB^{Adam} + MB^{Eve} = MCF \times (MC - MR) \qquad (4.5)$$

In other words, when public good provision is financed by distortionary taxation, the public good should be provided up to the point where the sum of the direct marginal benefits equals the net additional tax revenue that has to be raised times the *MCF*.

This optimality condition could be rewritten in the following form:

$$MB^{Adam} + MB^{Eve} = MCF \times MR = MCF \cdot MC \qquad (4.6)$$

When the *MR* is positive, it can be viewed as an indirect benefit of providing the public good, and this additional benefit should be added to the direct marginal benefit, $MB^{Adam} + MB^{Eve}$, to obtain the total benefit from additional public good provision. Each additional dollar of tax revenue allows us to reduce our reliance on distortionary taxes, and therefore the social value of the additional revenue is *MCF* × *MR*. If the *MR* is negative, then it is an extra cost of providing the public good and should be added to the cost term on the right-hand side of Equation (4.6).

Does the use of distortionary taxation imply that public good provision will be lower than under lump-sum tax financing? Not necessarily. Note that when *MCF* is greater than one and *MR* is positive, *MCF* × (*MC* − *MR*) may be either greater or smaller than *MC*. Thus, with distortionary taxation, the cost to the society of providing public goods may be either greater or less than it would be with lump-sum tax financing. To see this,

---

[4] See Atkinson and Stern (1974) for a formal derivation of this condition. If a government used only lump-sum taxes, then the *MCF* would be one and the *MR* would be zero (because by definition lump-sum tax revenue would not vary with changes in the provision of the public good), and therefore Equation (4.3) can be viewed as a special case of Equation (4.5).

consider the example in Figure 4.4, where the optimal provision of the public good is 45 units with lump-sum tax financing. At this level of provision, the sum of the marginal benefits, $6, is equal to the marginal cost of producing the public good.

Suppose instead that the government financed the public good with distortionary taxation, that *MCF* is 1.33, and that each additional unit of the public good generates $2 in additional tax revenues. When 45 units of the public good are provided, the cost of providing an additional unit of the public good is 1.33 (6 − 2), or $5.33. Since the total direct marginal benefit is $6, more than 45 units should be provided when distortionary taxation is used.[5] On the other hand, if *MR* is less than $1.50, the cost of providing an additional unit of the public good is more than $6, and the optimal provision of the public good with distortionary taxation would be less than 45. Consequently, the use of distortionary taxation may either increase or reduce the optimal provision of the public good, relative to the optimal level with lump-sum taxation.

Problems in Achieving Efficiency

As stressed in Chapter 2, under a certain set of conditions, a decentralized market system provides goods efficiently. Thus, in the absence of imperfections, the market will provide the efficient quantity of fig leaves in Figure 4.2C. Will similar market forces lead to the efficient output level of public goods in Figure 4.4C? The answer depends in part on the extent to which Adam and Eve reveal their true preferences for fireworks. When a private good is exchanged in a competitive market, an individual has no incentive to lie about how much he or she values it. If Eve is willing to pay the going price for a fig leaf, then she has nothing to gain by failing to make the purchase.

However, people may have incentives to hide their true preferences for a public good. Suppose Adam falsely claims that fireworks mean nothing to him. If he can get Eve to foot the entire bill, he can still enjoy the show and yet have more money to spend on apples and fig leaves. This incentive to let other people pay while you enjoy the benefits is known as the **free-rider** problem. Of course, Eve would also like to be a free rider. Where there are public goods, "any one person can hope to snatch some selfish benefit in a way not possible under the self-policing competitive pricing of private goods" (Samuelson, 1955: 389). Hence, the market may fall short of providing the efficient amount of the public good. No automatic tendency exists for markets to reach the efficient allocation in Figure 4.4.

Even if consumption is excludable, market provision of a public good is likely to be inefficient. Suppose now that the fireworks display is excludable; people cannot see the show without purchasing an admission ticket to a stadium. A profit-maximizing entrepreneur sells tickets. Recall from Chapter 2 that Pareto efficiency requires that price equal marginal cost. Because a public good is nonrival in consumption, by definition the marginal cost of providing it to another person is zero. Hence, efficiency requires a price of zero. But if the entrepreneur charges everyone a price of zero, then the entrepreneur cannot stay in business.

Is there a way out? Suppose the following two conditions hold: (1) the entrepreneur knows each person's demand curve for the public good, and (2) it is difficult or impossible to transfer the good from one person to another. Under these two conditions, the entrepreneur could charge each person an individual price based on willingness to pay, a procedure known as **perfect price discrimination**. People who valued the rocket display at only a penny would pay exactly that amount; even they would not be excluded. Thus, everyone who put any positive value on the show would attend, which is an efficient outcome.[6] However, because those who valued the display a lot would pay a very high price, the entrepreneur would still be able to stay in business.

Perfect price discrimination may seem to be the solution until we recall that the first condition requires knowledge of everybody's preferences. But if individuals' demand curves were known, there would be no problem in determining the optimum provision in the first place.[7] We conclude that even if the public good is excludable, private provision is likely to lead to efficiency problems.

[5] The use of distortionary taxation may also affect the individuals' direct *MB*s from the public good. For example, a hotel room tax might reduce the marginal benefit of hiking on National Park trails, since accommodation and recreation are complementary goods.

[6] The outcome is efficient because the price paid by the marginal consumer equals marginal cost.

[7] A number of mechanisms have been designed to induce people to reveal their true preferences to a government agency; see, e.g., Groves and Loeb (1975). The possibility of using of democratic politics to implement the efficient quantity of a public good is discussed in Chapter 7.

UNMANNED AERIAL VEHICLES

Public safety, measured by the reduction in the expected damage from hazards in a community, is an example of a good that is non-rival and non-excludable. An important innovation for producing public safety and policing activities is the use of unmanned aerial vehicles—drones—by the RCMP. Drones are deployed for aerial traffic surveillance, search and rescue, emergency and disaster response, and anti-terrorism. The RCMP currently has 60-plus rotor-propelled drones, costing tens of thousands of dollars each, and are looking to acquire some fixed-wing drones for long endurance flights, which carry a hefty price tag of at least $350,000. The federal government announced in 2015 that it is investing $75 million in research and development of new high-tech cameras and sensors to equip RCMP and military drones. However, civil liberties organizations have expressed concerns that drone usage by law enforcement could breach the right to privacy or be used to spy on demonstrators. According to the policy director of the B.C. Civil Liberties Association, drones exist in a "policy vacuum" without any public consultation about the privacy, safety and cost implications. Clearly, as the application of drone technology shifts from the battlefield to domestic airspace, there are new opportunities for enhancing the public interest, but also new challenges for policymakers to address.

Based on CTVNews.ca (2015), Mackin and Tyee (2013), and "RCMP drone expansion comes with hefty price tag, prompts concerns of 'mission creep'." *National Post*, December 31, 2014.

Complete references for this feature can be found in the References section on page 474.

The Free-Rider Problem

Some suggest that the free-rider problem necessarily leads to inefficient levels of nonexcludable public goods; therefore, efficiency requires government provision of such goods. The argument is that the government can somehow find out everyone's true preferences, and then, using its coercive power, force everybody to pay for public goods. If all this is possible, the government can avoid the free-rider problem and ensure that public goods are optimally provided.

It must be emphasized that free ridership is not a *fact;* it is an implication of the *hypothesis* that people maximize a utility function that depends only on their own consumption of goods. To be sure, one can find examples in which public goods are not provided because people fail to reveal their preferences. On the other hand, much evidence suggests that individuals can and do act collectively without government coercion. Fund drives spearheaded by volunteers have led to the establishment and maintenance of churches, music halls, libraries, scientific laboratories, art museums, hospitals, and other such facilities.[8] One prominent economist has even argued, "I do not know of many historical records or other empirical evidence which show convincingly that the problem of correct revelation of preferences has been of any practical significance" (Johansen, 1977: 147).

These observations do not prove that free ridership is irrelevant. Although some goods that appear to have public characteristics are privately provided, others that "ought" to be provided (on grounds of efficiency) may not be. Moreover, the quantity of those public goods that are privately provided may be insufficient. The key point is that the importance of the free-rider problem is an empirical question whose answer should not be taken for granted.

Several laboratory experiments have been conducted to investigate the importance of free-rider behaviour. In a typical experiment, each of several subjects is given a number of tokens that they can either keep or donate to a "group exchange." For each token he keeps, a subject receives some payoff, say $4. Further, every time someone in the group donates to the group exchange, *everyone* in the group collects some amount of

---

[8] There is even some evidence of successful private provision of that classic public good, the lighthouse. See Coase (1974).

money, say $3, including the person who makes the donation. Clearly, all the subjects would be better off if everyone donated all their tokens to the group exchange. Note, however, that donations to the group exchange provide a nonrival and nonexcludable payoff. The free-rider theory suggests that the subjects might therefore very well decide to make no contributions to the group exchange so that they could benefit from everyone else's donations while putting nothing in themselves.

What do the results show? The findings vary from experiment to experiment, but there are some consistent findings. On average, people do contribute roughly 50 percent of their resources to the provision of the public good. Some free riding therefore is present in the sense that the subjects fail to contribute all their tokens to the group exchange. On the other hand, the results contradict the notion that free riding will lead to zero or trivial amounts of a public good. Some other important results are that (1) the more people repeat the game, the less likely they are to contribute; (2) when players have the opportunity to communicate before the game, cooperation is fostered; and (3) the contribution rates decline when the opportunity cost of giving goes up (i.e., when the reward for keeping a token increases). Cinyabuguma, Page, and Putterman (2005) provide a review of experimental findings.

Although caution must be exercised in interpreting the results of laboratory experiments, the results suggest that people derive a "warm glow" feeling of satisfaction from giving that works counter to the pursuit of the narrow self-interest of free riding.

THE PRIVATIZATION DEBATE

Countries throughout the world are debating the virtues of privatizing governmental functions. **Privatization** means taking services that are supplied by the government and turning them over to the private sector for provision and/or production.[9] Privatizing a publicly provided good is usually possible only when the good in question is excludable. In this section, we first discuss issues relating to *provision* and then turn to *production*.

Public versus Private Provision

Sometimes the services of publicly provided goods can be obtained privately. The commodity "protection" can be obtained from a publicly provided police force. Alternatively, to some extent, protection can also be gained by purchasing strong locks, burglar alarms, and bodyguards, which are obtained privately. A large backyard can serve many of the functions of a public park. Even substitutes for services provided by public courts of law can be obtained privately. For example, because of the enormous costs of using the government's judicial system, companies sometimes bypass the courts and instead settle their disputes before mutually agreed upon neutral advisers or arbitrators.

Over time, the mix between public and private modes of provision has changed substantially. During the nineteenth century, there was much greater private responsibility for education, police protection, libraries, and other functions than there is now. However, there appears to be a trend back to the private sector to provide what we have come to consider publicly provided goods and services. For example, in some U.S. cities homeowners and businesses purchase fire protection and security services from private firms. In Denmark about two-thirds of the country's fire service is provided by a private firm.

What is the right mix of public and private provision? To approach this question, think of publicly and privately provided goods as inputs into the production of some output that people desire. Teachers, classrooms, textbooks, and private tutors are inputs into the production of an output we might call educational quality. Assume that what ultimately matters to people is the level of output, or educational quality, not the particular inputs used to produce it. What criteria should be used to select the amount of each input? There are several considerations:

Relative wage and materials costs. If the public and private sectors pay different amounts for labour and materials, then the less-expensive sector is to be preferred on efficiency grounds, *ceteris paribus*. Input costs faced by public and private sectors may differ if public sector employees are unionized while their private sector counterparts are not. We discuss other differences between public and private production in the next section.

---

[9] See Vickers and Yarrow (1991) for an overview of the issues concerning privatization.

Administrative costs. Under public provision, any fixed administrative costs can be spread over a large group of people. Instead of everyone spending time negotiating an arrangement for garbage collection, the negotiation is done by one office for everybody. The larger the community is, the greater the advantage is to being able to spread these costs.

Diversity of tastes. Households with and without children have very different views about the desirability of financing high-quality education. People who store jewels in their homes may value property protection more than people who do not. To the extent such diversity is present, private provision is more efficient because people can tailor their consumption to their own tastes. However, the benefits of allowing for diversity must be weighed against any possible increases in administrative costs.

Quality of information. If households are poorly informed about the quality of certain goods or their prices, then they cannot make informed choices in the market. Medical care is an example of a type of purchase that can be technically complex and which a household makes infrequently. Grocery shopping, on the other hand, is routine. Thus it is likely that consumers are quite aware of grocery product qualities and prices, but unaware of the available medical interventions and their costs. In general, the more imperfect consumer information is, the stronger the case for public provision.

Distributional issues. The community's notions of fairness may require that some commodities be made available to everybody, an idea sometimes referred to as **commodity egalitarianism**. Commodity egalitarianism may help explain the wide appeal of publicly provided education—people believe everyone should have access to at least some minimum level of schooling. This notion also arises in the ongoing debate over medical care.

Public versus Private Production

People can agree that certain items should be provided by the public sector, but still disagree over whether they should be produced publicly or privately. Part of the controversy stems from fundamental differences regarding the extent to which government should intervene in the economy (see Chapter 1). Part is due to differences of opinion about the relative costs of public and private production. Some argue that public sector managers, unlike their private sector counterparts, do not have to worry about making profits or becoming the victims of takeovers or bankruptcy. Hence, public sector managers have little incentive to monitor the activities of their enterprises carefully.

This notion has an ancient pedigree. In 1776 Adam Smith argued,

> In every great monarchy in Europe the sale of the crown lands would produce a very large sum of money which, if applied to the payments of the public debts, would deliver from mortgage a much greater revenue than any which those lands have ever afforded to the crown . . . When the crown lands had become private property, they would, in the course of a few years, become well improved and well cultivated.[10]

Recent evidence tends to support the view that privately owned firms exhibit greater productivity than government-owned firms. A study by Ehrlich, Gallais-Hamonno, Lui, and Lutter (1994) compares international airlines of different ownership categories from 1973 to 1983 and finds that private ownership leads to lower costs in the long run. See Megginson and Netter (2001) for a survey of empirical studies on privatization.

Opponents of privatization respond that these examples overstate the cost savings of private production. In fact, there is surprisingly little systematic evidence on the cost differences between private and public production. An important reason for this is that the *quality* of the services provided in the two modes may be different, which makes comparisons difficult. Perhaps, for example, private hospitals have lower costs than their public counterparts because the former refuse to admit patients with illnesses that are expensive to treat. This brings us to the central argument of opponents of private production—private contractors produce inferior products.

Incomplete contracts. A possible response to this criticism is that the government can simply write a contract with the private provider, completely specifying the quality of the service that the government wants. However, as Hart, Shleifer, and Vishy (1997) note, it is sometimes impossible to write a contract that is anywhere near

---

[10] Quoted in Sheshinski and Lopez-Calva (1999).

being complete because one cannot specify in advance every possible contingency. For example, a "government would not contract out the conduct of its foreign policy because unforeseen contingencies are a key part of foreign policy, and a private contractor would have enormous power to maximize its own wealth (by, for instance, refusing to send troops somewhere) without violating the letter of the contract" (p. 3). On the other hand, for certain relatively routine activities (garbage collection, snow removal), incomplete contracts are not a serious impediment to private production. In short, in cases where the private sector cost is lower than that in the public sector and relatively complete contracts can be written, a strong case can be made for private production.

Advocates of privatization believe that, even if it is impossible to write a complete contract, there are other mechanisms for getting private firms to refrain from engaging in inefficient cost reductions. If consumers buy the good themselves and there are a number of suppliers, then they can switch if their current supplier is providing shoddy service. Nursing homes are one example. In addition, reputation-building may be important—a private supplier who wants more contracts in the future has an incentive to avoid inefficient cost reductions in the present. Shleifer (1998) argues that the desire to build a good reputation has been of some importance among private producers of prisons.

Market environment. A final important issue in the privatization debate is the market environment in which the public or private enterprise operates. A privately owned monopoly may produce very inefficient results from society's standpoint, while a publicly owned operation that has a lot of competition may produce quite efficiently. Caves and Christensen (1980: 974) came to this conclusion on the basis of an econometric study of CN and CP railway operations in Canada: "The oft-noted inefficiency of government enterprises stems from isolation from effective *competition* rather than public ownership *per se*." Hence, when a government is deciding whether to privatize some service, one important consideration is what kind of market structure will emerge if provision is left to private enterprise.

The contracting out of municipal waste services in Ontario provides an interesting example of the effects of privatization on the cost of service. Waste services include garbage collection and disposal at landfills. The services may be provided by private contractors, by public employees, or by contracting out to other municipal governments. Dachis (2010) examined financial data on waste services for most of Ontario's municipalities covering the period 2001 to 2008. His findings include the following:

* Municipalities with fully contracted waste services (either to private firms or to other municipalities) have substantially lower average costs per household than municipalities with few of their services provided through contracts.
* The market for waste collection services in Ontario is moderately concentrated. Heavy concentration would be problematical because of possible collusion among bidders for service contracts.
* The cost savings from contracting out waste disposal services are independent of whether the contracts are awarded to private firms or to other municipalities. The cost savings emerge just from the contracting process.
* However, in the case of waste collection, municipalities that contract out to private providers achieve significant cost savings, but they derive little savings from contracting out to other municipalities.

The international evidence on cost savings from waste contracting suggests that private ownership alone does not reduce costs. Cost savings can be achieved by either public employees or private contractors as long as there exists competition for contracts. Similarly, mixed public-private service delivery systems, such as in Hamilton, Ontario, where half of the city's garbage is picked up by public workers and half by private companies, can be cost effective, since it may "prevent a monopoly from being developed yet instill a competitive attitude among service providers."[11]

Garbage collection and disposal is a relatively straightforward business. Evaluating the effects of privatization in other areas, such as education, is confounded by the problem of measuring the outputs produced by the public sector. How does one quantify the amount of education produced by a school? Test scores alone will not be sufficient, because schools are also supposed to encourage creativity and to teach self-discipline and good citizenship. Similar problems in measuring outputs arise in comparing public and private costs of producing medical services, police protection, and transportation. It is not an accident that the public sector tends to produce the services that are difficult to measure. But if outputs of many public sector activities cannot be measured

---

[11] From City of Hamilton Committee of the Whole Report TOE01118, Harmonization of Waste Collection Services, p. 12, August 2001.

properly, how can we compare costs of production in the public and private sectors? Obtaining better measures of public sector outputs is one of the most important steps needed to improve the performance of the public sector.

PUBLIC GOODS AND PUBLIC CHOICE

The use of the word *public* to describe commodities that are nonrival and nonexcludable almost seems to prejudge the question of whether they ought to be provided by the public sector. Indeed, we have shown that private markets are unlikely to generate pure public goods in Pareto efficient quantities. Some collective decision must be made regarding the quantity to be supplied. However, in contrast to a pure public good like national defence, sometimes there may be private substitutes for a publicly provided good. But community decision making is also needed in these cases, this time to choose the extent to which public provision will be used. Thus, the subjects of public goods and public choice are closely linked. In Chapter 7 we discuss and evaluate a number of mechanisms for making collective decisions.

SUMMARY

- Public goods are characterized by nonrivalness and nonexcludability in consumption. Thus, each person consumes the same amount, but not necessarily the preferred amount, of the public good.

- With lump-sum taxation, efficient provision of public goods requires that the sum of individuals' *MRSs* equal the *MRT*, unlike private goods where each *MRS* equals the *MRT*. Equivalently, the sum of the individuals' marginal benefits equals the marginal cost of production with the efficient provision of a public good.

- With distortionary taxation, efficient provision of public goods requires that the sum of the individuals' marginal benefits equal the marginal cost of financing the provision of an additional unit of the public good. This is equal to the marginal cost of public funds times the difference between the marginal cost of producing the public good and the additional revenue that is generated when an additional unit of the public good is provided.

- Market mechanisms are unlikely to provide public goods efficiently, even if they are excludable in consumption.

- Casual observation and laboratory studies indicate that people do not fully exploit free-riding possibilities. Nonetheless, in certain cases, free riding is likely to be a significant problem.

- Public goods can be provided privately, and private goods can be provided publicly. The choice between public and private provision should depend on relative wage and materials costs, administrative costs, diversity of tastes for the good, quality of information, and distributional issues.

- Even in cases where public provision of a good is selected, a choice between public and private production must be made. A key factor in determining whether public or private production will be more efficient is the market environment.

EXERCISES

I. Which of the following do you consider public goods? Private goods? Why?
   a. Wilderness areas
   b. Prisons
   c. Peace keeping in Sudan
   d. Public television programs
   e. An Internet site providing information on airline schedules

2. Tarzan and Jane live alone in the jungle and have trained Cheetah both to patrol the perimeter of their clearing and to harvest tropical fruits. Cheetah can collect three kilograms of fruit an hour and currently spends six hours patrolling, eight hours picking, and 10 hours sleeping.

   a. What are the public and private goods in this example?

   b. If Tarzan and Jane are each currently willing to give up one hour of patrol for two kilograms of fruit, is the current allocation of Cheetah's time Pareto efficient? Should he patrol more or less?

3. The global positioning system (GPS) uses satellites to send radio signals that can be picked up by receivers, allowing users to determine their precise locations. The U.S. military, which operates the satellites, originally excluded users by introducing errors in the information sent to receivers held by private individuals. The accurate signals were encrypted and thus available only to the military. In 2000, accurate GPS signals were made available to citizens. From an efficiency standpoint, should accurate GPS signals be available to citizens? Should citizens pay for the GPS signals? Should they pay for the cost of the receivers?

4. The owners of some commercial ships may place a higher value on avoiding dangerous shoals than do other commercial ship owners. Provide a reason why this is likely to be the case and explain how it would affect the value of lighthouses for the different ship owners.

5. Moe, Larry, and Curly are struggling in their drama class and plan to hire an acting coach to help them prepare a stage show. The tutor's wages are $20 per hour. The marginal benefit of each hour of coaching is given in the following table.

Number of Hours	Moe's Marginal Benefit	Larry's Marginal Benefit	Curly's Marginal Benefit
1st hour	12	17	6
2nd hour	10	15	5
3rd hour	8	13	4
4th hour	6	11	3
5th hour	4	9	2
6th hour	2	7	1
7th hour	0	5	0

   a. Sketch the marginal benefit curve of each drama student and construct the marginal social benefit curve.

   b. Determine how many hours Moe, Larry, and Curly should hire the coach.

6. Thelma and Louise are neighbours. During the winter, it is impossible for a snowplow to clear the street in front of Thelma's house without clearing the front of Louise's. Thelma's marginal benefit from snowplowing services is $12 - Z$, where Z is the number of times the street is plowed. Louise's marginal benefit is $8 - 2Z$. The marginal cost of getting the street plowed is $16. Sketch the two marginal benefit schedules and the aggregate marginal benefit schedule. Draw in the marginal cost schedule, and find the efficient level of provision for snowplowing services.

7. Suppose the snowplowing service described in Exercise 6 is financed by distortionary taxation. The *MCF* varies with the amount of tax revenue, R, that is raised:

$$MCF = 1 + 0.0002441R^2$$

If tax revenue is raised only to finance the snowplowing of Thelma and Louise's street, what is the optimal provision of the snowplowing service? (Assume that snowplowing does not affect the amount of revenue generated by the tax system and that the average cost of snowplowing is equal to the marginal cost, $16.)

8. Suppose that there are only two fishermen, Zach and Jacob, who fish along a certain coast. They would each benefit if lighthouses were built along the coast where they fish. The marginal cost of building each additional lighthouse is $100. The marginal benefit to Zach of each additional lighthouse is $90 - Q$, and the marginal benefit to Jacob is $40 - Q$, where Q equals the number of lighthouses.

   a. Explain why we might not expect to find the efficient number of lighthouses along this coast.

   b. What is the efficient number of lighthouses? What would be the net benefits to Zach and Jacob if the efficient number were provided?

9. Should airport security be produced publicly or privately? Use the contracting framework to discuss this question.

CHAPTER 5

Externalities

We have always known that heedless self-interest was bad morals; we know now that it is bad economics.

—Franklin D. Elliott Roosevelt

AFTER READING THIS CHAPTER, THE STUDENT SHOULD BE ABLE TO:

LO1 Describe how positive externalities differ from negative externalities.

LO2 Demonstrate how the presence of an externality may lead to an inefficient allocation of resources.

LO3 Explain how private responses could remedy the externality problem.

LO4 Evaluate the advantages and limitations of various private responses that seek to remedy the externality problem.

LO5 Explain how public responses (government policies) could remedy the externality problem.

LO6 Evaluate the advantages and limitations of various public responses to the externality problem.

LO7 Identify potential distributional implications of private and public responses to the externality problem.

As a by-product of their activities, pulp mills produce dioxin, a chemical that forms when chlorine used for bleaching wood pulp combines with a substance in the pulp. When dioxin is released into the environment, it ends up in everyone's fat tissue and in the milk of nursing mothers. According to some scientists, dioxin is responsible for birth defects and cancer, among other health problems. The burning of fossil fuels to operate machinery, heat homes, and power cars creates as a by-product the greenhouse gas, carbon dioxide. Scientists argue that the accumulation of greenhouse gases (GHG) in the atmosphere leads to warmer surface temperatures and may have serious negative consequences for the environment.

The *First Fundamental Theorem of Welfare Economics* from Chapter 2 suggests that markets allocate resources efficiently. Dioxin and carbon dioxide result from the operation of markets. Does this mean that emitting these substances is efficient? To answer this question, it is helpful to distinguish the different ways in which people can affect each other's welfare.

Suppose large numbers of suburbanites decide they want to live in an urban setting. As they move to the city, the price of urban land increases. Urban property owners are better off, but the welfare of tenants already there decreases. Merchants in the city benefit from increased demand for their products, while their suburban counterparts are worse off. By the time the economy settles into a new equilibrium, the distribution of real income has changed substantially.

In this example, all the effects are transmitted *via changes in market prices*. Suppose that the allocation was Pareto efficient before the change in tastes. The shifts in supply and demand curves change relevant prices, but competition guarantees that the relevant marginal rates of substitution will all be equal to the marginal rates of transformation. Thus, while the behaviour of some people affects the utility of others, there is no market failure. As long as the effects are transmitted by prices, markets are efficient.[1]

---

[1] The new pattern of prices may be more or less desirable from a distributional point of view, depending on one's ethical judgments as embodied in the social welfare function. Effects on welfare that are transmitted via prices are sometimes referred to as **pecuniary externalities**. Mishan (1971) argues convincingly that because such effects are part of the normal functioning of a market, this is a confusing appellation. It is mentioned here only for the sake of completeness and is ignored henceforth.

Dioxin and carbon dioxide emissions embody a different type of interaction than the migration example does. The decrease in the utility of individuals from these emissions is not the result of price changes. Rather, the output decisions of pulp producing firms, and decisions of firms and of individuals regarding how to heat buildings or power machinery, directly affect the welfare of other people. When the activity of one entity (a person or a firm) directly affects the welfare of another in a way that is not transmitted by market prices, that effect is called an **externality**. Unlike effects that are transmitted through market prices, externalities reduce economic efficiency.

In this chapter, we analyze these inefficiencies and examine possible remedies to the externality problem.

THE NATURE OF EXTERNALITIES

Real world applications of externality theory abound; many current and ongoing debates over environmental quality, climate change, crowded roads and congestion, vaccination programs, education, alcohol, and tobacco, among others, have potential externality problems at their core. Externalities have several important characteristics:

Externalities can be produced by consumers as well as by firms. Aluminum-producing firms create GHG emissions as a result of their production processes. A person who smokes or "consumes" a cigar in a crowded room lowers the utility of others by using up fresh air, the common resource.

Externalities are reciprocal in nature. Suppose Bart operates a factory that dumps garbage into a river nobody owns. Lisa makes her living by fishing from this river. Bart's activities make Lisa worse off in a direct way that is not the result of price changes. It seems natural to refer to Bart as the "polluter." However, we could just as well think of Lisa as "polluting" the river with fishers, increasing the social cost of the factory's waste disposal. As an alternative to fishing, using the river for waste disposal is not obviously worse from a social point of view. It depends on the costs of alternatives for both activities.

Externalities can be positive or negative. A **negative externality** is created when the action of a person or firm generates an external cost to others, as is the case with the aluminum firms and the cigar smokers above. If the action generates a benefit to others, then a **positive externality** is created. For example, an individual gets a vaccination for hepatitis A or the flu to lower their risk of contracting the illness. As a by-product of this action, the risk of infection for others is lowered and their utility is, as a result, higher.

The distinction between public goods and externalities is a bit fuzzy. According to Mishan (1971: 2), "the essential feature of the concept of an external effect is that the effect produced is not a deliberate creation but an *unintended* or *incidental* by-product of some otherwise legitimate activity" (emphasis in original). Public goods are activities that are *intentionally produced* to provide benefit to a community, whereas externalities are activities where the effect on the community is the *unintended consequence* of an activity that an individual or firm undertakes for its own benefit. For example, private security services purchased by a homeowner generate a positive externality for the next door neighbour if that neighbour suffers less vandalism and theft as a result; if the entire neighborhood enjoys these benefits then a public good has been provided. Externalities and public goods often occur together. Air pollution, an externality produced as a by-product of various production processes, negatively affects the public good—clean air, or air quality. Although externalities and public goods are quite similar from a formal point of view, in practice it is useful to distinguish between them.

NEGATIVE EXTERNALITIES AND ECONOMIC INEFFICIENCY

To see how the presence of a negative externality can lead to economic inefficiency, consider the factory example above. By dumping garbage into the river that nobody owns, Bart's activities make Lisa worse off in a direct way that is not the result of price changes. In this example, clean water is an input to Bart's production process. Clean water gets used up just like all other inputs, such as land, labour, and capital. Clean water is also a scarce resource with alternative uses, such as fishing by Lisa and swimming. Efficiency thus requires that Bart should pay a price for the water he uses that reflects its value as a scarce resource that can be used for other activities. Instead, Bart pays a zero price and, as a consequence, uses the water in inefficiently large quantities.

Posing the externality problem this way allows us to expose its source. Bart uses his other inputs efficiently because he must pay their owners prices that reflect their value for alternative uses. Otherwise, the owners of the inputs simply sell them elsewhere. However, if no one owns the river, everyone can use it for free. An externality, then, is a consequence of the failure or inability to establish property rights. If someone owned the river, a price would have to be paid for its use, and the externality would not materialize.

If Lisa owned the stream, she could charge Bart a fee for polluting that reflected the damage done to her catch. Bart would take these charges into account when making his production decisions and would no longer use the water inefficiently. On the other hand, if Bart owned the stream, he could make money by charging Lisa for the privilege of fishing in it. The amount of money that Lisa would be willing to pay Bart for the right to fish in the stream would depend on the amount of pollution present. Hence, Bart would have an incentive not to pollute too much. Otherwise, he could not make much money from Lisa.

As long as someone owns a resource, its price reflects the value for alternative uses, and the resource is used efficiently (at least in the absence of any other "market failures"). In contrast, resources that are owned in common may be abused because no one has an incentive to economize in their use.

Figure 5.1 analyzes the Bart–Lisa example. The horizontal axis measures the amount of output, Q, produced by Bart's factory, and the vertical axis measures dollars. The curve labelled *PMB* indicates the *private* marginal benefit to Bart of each level of output; it is assumed to decline as output increases.[2] Also associated with each level of output is some *private* marginal cost, *PMC*. Private marginal cost reflects payments made by Bart for productive inputs and is assumed here to increase with output. As a by-product of its activities, the factory produces pollution that makes Lisa worse off. Assume that as the factory's output increases, so does the amount of pollution it creates. The marginal damage inflicted on Lisa by the pollution at each level of output is denoted by *MD*. *MD* is drawn sloping upward, reflecting the assumption that as Lisa is subjected to additional pollution, she becomes worse off at an increasing rate.

If Bart is a profit maximizer, how much output does he produce? He has an incentive to produce an additional unit of output as long as the private marginal benefit to him exceeds the private marginal cost. Thus, Bart chooses the output Q_1. There is no incentive to increase output beyond Q_1 because the marginal benefit from doing so is less than the additional costs that would be incurred.

From society's point of view, production should occur as long as the marginal benefit *to society* (*SMB*) exceeds the marginal cost *to society* (*SMC*). In this example, the marginal benefit to society is equal to Bart's private marginal benefit. The marginal cost to society has two components, however. First are the inputs purchased by Bart. Their

FIGURE 5.1

A NEGATIVE EXTERNALITY PROBLEM

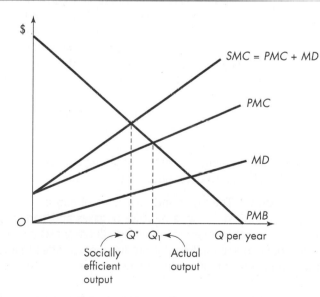

---

[2] If Bart consumes all the output of his factory, then the declining *PMB* reflects the diminishing marginal utility of the output. If Bart sells his output in a competitive market, *PMB* is constant at the market price.

value is reflected in *PMC*. Second is the marginal damage done to Lisa, as reflected in *MD*. Hence, social marginal cost is *PMC plus MD*. Graphically, the social marginal cost schedule is found by adding together the heights of *PMC* and *MD* at each level of output. It is depicted in Figure 5.1 as *SMC*. Note that, by construction, the vertical distance between *SMC* and *PMC* is *MD*. (Because *SMC* = *PMC* + *MD*, it follows that *SMC* − *PMC* = *MD*.)

From a social point of view, efficiency requires production of only those units of output for which *SMB* exceeds *SMC*. Thus, output should be produced just up to the point at which the schedules intersect, at Q^*.

Implications

First, from this model we observe that there is no reason to expect private markets to produce the socially efficient output level when negative externalities are present. In particular, when a good generates a negative externality, too much of it is produced relative to the efficient output.

Second, the analysis implies that, in general, the efficient level of output is positive, not zero. Since production generates pollution, this implies that zero pollution is not socially desirable. Finding the right amount of pollution requires trading off its benefits and costs, and this generally occurs at some positive level of pollution.[3]

Third, the model provides a way to measure the benefits of moving from Q_1 to the efficient level of output Q^*. Figure 5.2 provides a numerical example. To simplify, we assume that Bart consumes all the output he produces. The private marginal benefit, the private marginal cost, and the marginal damage functions are given as $PMB = 200 − 2Q$, $PMC = 20 + Q$, and $MD = Q$, respectively. *SMC* is given by *PMC* + *MD*. Setting *PMB* = *PMC*, we find that Bart's net benefits from consuming Q are highest when $Q = 60$. To see this, note that the total benefit to Bart from 60 units of output is measured as the area under Bart's private marginal benefit curve between 0 and 60 while the total private cost of producing 60 units of output is measured by the area under Bart's private marginal cost schedule between 0 and 60. By producing and consuming 60 units of output, Bart maximizes his net benefits. The socially optimal output level of 45 units is found by setting *SMC* = *SMB* (recall that in this example the marginal benefit to society equals *PMB*).

What is the efficiency gain if Bart is somehow forced to produce at the efficient level? When output is cut from 60 to 45 units, the net benefit to Bart from consuming the output falls. To calculate the size of this loss, note that the net benefit to Bart associated with any unit of output is the difference between his private marginal benefit and private marginal cost. Geometrically, the net benefit on a given unit of output is the vertical distance between *PMB* and *PMC*. If Bart is forced to cut back output, he loses the difference between the *PMB* and *PMC* for each unit of production between 45 and 60 units. This is area *dcg* in Figure 5.2. The dollar value of this loss equals $337.5 (calculated as 0.5 × (60 − 45) × (110 − 65)).

At the same time, Lisa becomes better off because the less Bart produces, the less the damage done to her fishery. For each unit that Bart's output is reduced, Lisa gains an amount equal to the marginal damage associated with that unit of output. In Figure 5.2, Lisa's gain for each unit of output reduction is the vertical distance between *MD* and the horizontal axis. Therefore, Lisa's gain when output is reduced is the area under the marginal damage curve between 45 and 60 units, area *abfe*. Note that *abfe* equals area *cdhg*. This is by construction—the vertical distance between *SMC* and *PMC* is *MD*, which is the same as the vertical distance between *MD* and the horizontal axis. In this example, area *cdhg* is $787.5 (calculated as 0.5 × (60 − 45) × (110 − 65) + 0.5 × (60 − 45) × (140 − 80)). In sum, if output was reduced from 60 to 45 units, Bart would lose area *dcg* and Lisa would gain area *cdhg*. Provided that society views a dollar to Bart as equivalent to a dollar to Lisa, the reduction in output (and the pollution associated with that output) yields a net gain to society equal to the difference between *cdhg* and *dcg*. In dollar terms, this efficiency gain is $450.

To illustrate the negative externality problem, we used simple equations to represent the *MD*, *PMC*, and *PMB* functions. In practice, it can be difficult to determine which pollutants cause harm and by how much.

What activities produce pollutants? The types and quantities of harmful pollution associated with various production processes must be identified. Smog, a mixture of gases and particulates that causes the air to look hazy, is linked to a number of health concerns, including allergies, asthma, and cardiovascular disease, Smog depends on a combination of factors, including the production activities that create the particulates and gases, temperature, and wind. Since the smog-producing pollutants can travel large distances, they can

---

[3] This example assumes that the only way to reduce pollution is to reduce output. In practice, the firm may have other lower-cost ways of reducing pollution, including switching to cleaner inputs or cleaner production technologies. Figure 5.6 considers a more flexible option that does not restrict the firm's choice of how to reduce pollution.

FIGURE 5.2

GAINS AND LOSSES FROM MOVING TO AN EFFICIENT LEVEL OF OUTPUT

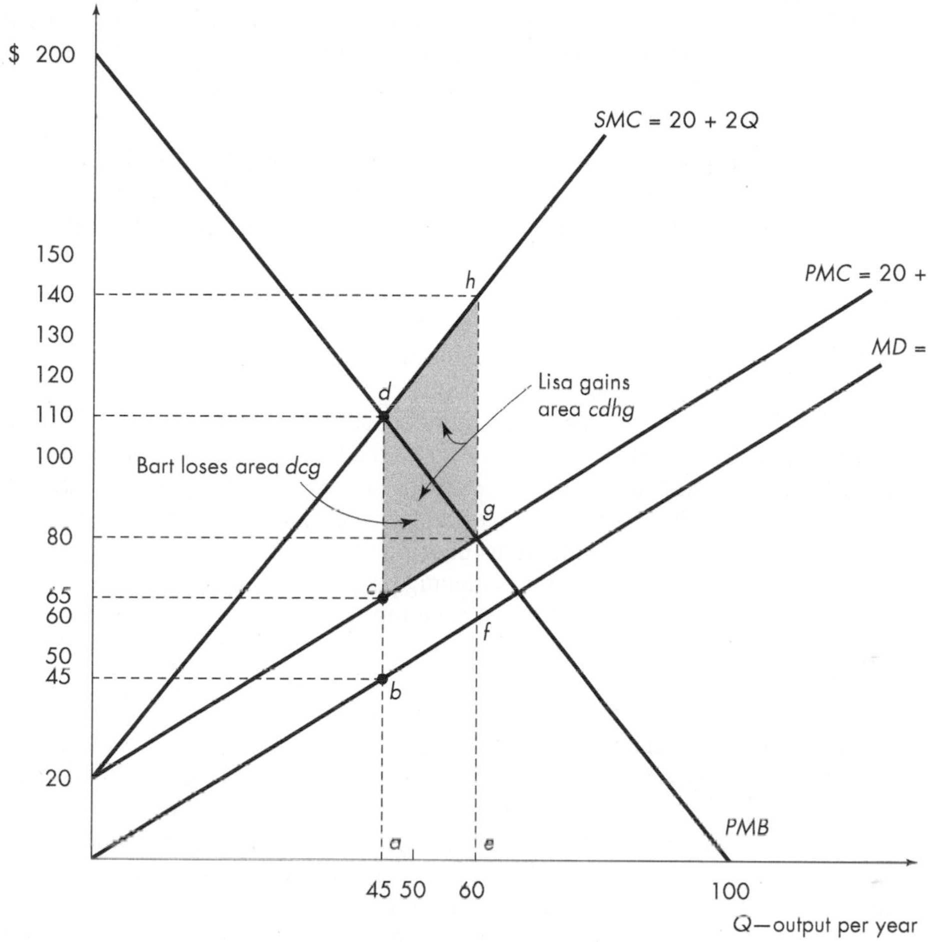

contribute to poor air quality far from where they are emitted. This makes it difficult to determine what activities in fact contribute to a particular smog episode.

The transboundary problem is even greater in the case of acid rain or GHG emissions. GHG emissions contribute to global warming regardless of where in the world the emissions actually occur. Measuring emissions in only one country will lead to a serious underestimation of the impact of emissions on that country as well as globally. For this reason, international cooperation is often required to tackle air and water pollution problems.[4]

Which pollutants do harm? Total suspended particles (TSPs) are widely considered to be the air pollutant most damaging to health. Although several studies have found a correlation between TSPs and mortality rates, it is difficult to establish the causal impact. The difficulty arises because scientists cannot perform randomized studies on the effects of pollution. Instead, investigators undertake studies using cross-sectional or time-series data. These studies could have biased results if other factors that differ across time or location affect both mortality and air pollution. It is also difficult to control for lifetime exposure as individuals move in and out of different cities.

Chay and Greenstone (2003) study the impact of air pollution on infant mortality. They focus on infants because, unlike adults, an infant's lifetime exposure to pollution is easier to measure. They conduct a quasi-experimental analysis, taking advantage of the 1980s recession which led to a reduction in production of TSPs in some areas

---

[4] For example, in an effort to deal with the transboundary pollutants contributing to acid rain, Canada and the United States signed the Canada–United States Air Quality Agreement in 1991. Under the agreement, the two countries agreed to reduce emissions of the two main air pollutants causing acid rain: sulfur dioxide and nitrogen oxides.

of the United States but not in others. They found that a 1 percent reduction in TSPs led to a 0.35 percent reduction in infant mortality rates. This implies that the TSP reductions caused by the 1980–81 recession led to 2,500 fewer infant deaths than would have otherwise been the case.

Using data from California in the 1990s, Currie and Neidell (2005) show that even at relatively low levels air pollution has a significant effect on infant mortality. These researchers focus on three different pollutants—ozone, carbon monoxide, and particulate matter. Their results suggest that carbon monoxide reductions (overlooked by previous studies) contributed significantly to the reduction in the infant mortality rate, illustrating the importance of identifying which pollutants are doing harm.

What is the value of the damage done? The marginal damage schedule shows the dollar value of the external costs imposed by each additional unit of output. Therefore, once the physical damage a pollutant creates is determined, the value of eliminating it must be calculated. When economists think about measuring the value of something, typically they think of people's willingness to pay for it. If you are willing to pay $162 for a bicycle, that is its value to you.

Unlike bicycles, there are generally no explicit markets in which pollution is bought and sold.[5] How then can people's marginal willingness to pay for pollution removal be measured? Some attempts have been made to infer it indirectly by studying housing prices. When people shop for houses, they consider both the quality of the house itself and the characteristics of the neighbourhood, such as the cleanliness of the streets and the quality of schools. Suppose, in addition, that families care about the level of air pollution in the neighbourhood. Consider two identical houses situated in two neighbourhoods, identical in every respect except the first is in an unpolluted area and the second is in a polluted area. We would expect the house in the unpolluted area to have a higher price. This price differential measures people's willingness to pay for clean air.

These observations suggest a natural strategy for estimating people's willingness to pay for cleaner air. Using multiple regression analysis, researchers attempt to estimate the relationship between housing prices and air quality using a sample of houses in a given area or areas.[6] Note that if important determinants of housing prices are omitted from the analysis, the estimated effect of pollution may be unreliable. People may also be unaware of the effects of air pollution on their health, and hence may underestimate the value of it.

The measurement problem is especially acute if we consider GHGs and global warming. While scientists can and do measure GHG emissions associated with various activities in the economy, the damage attributable to these gases is very difficult to measure. There is debate about how the increased stock of greenhouse gases contributes to global warming and about the effects of reductions in such gases on long-run climate trends. Not only are the benefits of reducing emissions hard to measure and uncertain, but they are unlikely to be realized until sometime in the very distant future. In this situation, willingness to pay is not a particularly useful approach to determine the value of damage being done.

Conclusion

To implement the efficient outcome illustrated in Figure 5.1 thus requires the skills of biologists, engineers, ecologists, and health practitioners, among others, in order to derive a reasonable approximation of the marginal damage function. Uncertainty about the long-term effects and the transboundary nature of some types of pollution create serious challenges to the formulation of environmental policy. However, even with superb engineering and biological data, efficient decisions simply cannot be reached without applying the economist's tool of marginal analysis.

POSITIVE EXTERNALITIES AND ECONOMIC INEFFICIENCY

Externalities can also be positive. Vaccination programs, research and development, and gardening are all activities that generate external benefits and increase the utility of others. The analysis of economic inefficiency in the presence of a positive externality is symmetrical to the negative externality example. In general, there is no reason to expect private markets to produce the efficient output level when positive externalities are present. As we will see, when a good or activity generates a positive externality, too little of it is produced relative to the efficient level.

---

[5] There are some exceptions. See the discussion in the section on tradable permit schemes in this chapter.

[6] See the Web-based chapter, "Tools of Empirical Analysis," at www.mcgrawhill.ca/olc/rosen for a description of this statistical technique.

FIGURE 5.3

A POSITIVE EXTERNALITY EXAMPLE

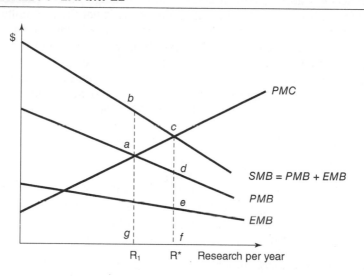

Consider a firm that does research and development (R&D). The private marginal benefit (*PMB*) and the private marginal cost (*PMC*) schedules are as depicted in Figure 5.3. The firm chooses R&D level R_1, where $PMC = PMB$. Assume further that the firm's R&D enables other firms to produce their outputs more cheaply, but that these firms do not have to pay for using the scientific results because they become part of general knowledge.[7] In Figure 5.3, the marginal benefit to other firms of each quantity of research is denoted *EMB* (for external marginal benefit). The social marginal benefit of research is the sum of *PMB* and *EMB*, which is depicted as *SMB*.

Efficiency requires the equality of private marginal cost (which in this case equals the social marginal cost) and social marginal benefit, which occurs at R^*. Hence, not enough R&D is done. If the firm could somehow be forced to increase research and development activity to the efficient level R*, the inefficiency would be eliminated. The dollar value of this gain in efficiency is equal to area *abc* in Figure 5.3, the difference between the additional social benefits generated (area *bcfg*) and the additional costs incurred (*acfg*).

PRIVATE RESPONSES TO EXTERNALITIES

Our analysis has indicated that in the presence of externalities, an inefficient allocation of resources can emerge if nothing is done about it. This section discusses the circumstances under which private individuals, acting on their own, can avoid the inefficiencies of externalities.

Bargaining and the Coase Theorem

Recall our earlier argument that a root cause of the inefficiencies associated with externalities is the absence of property rights. When property rights are assigned, individuals may respond to the externality by bargaining with each other. To see how this works, let's return to our negative externality example. Suppose property rights to the river are assigned to Bart and that it is costless for Lisa and Bart to bargain with each other. Is it possible for the two parties to strike a bargain that will result in output being reduced to the efficient level?

Consider Bart and Lisa's problem as illustrated in Figure 5.2. Bart would be willing not to produce a given unit of output as long as he received a payment that exceeded his net incremental gain from producing that unit (*PMB* − *PMC*). On the other hand, Lisa would be willing to pay Bart not to produce a given unit as long as the payment was less than the marginal damage done to her, *MD*. As long as the amount that Lisa is willing to pay Bart exceeds the cost to Bart of not producing, the opportunity for a bargain exists. Algebraically,

---

[7] Sometimes this type of situation can partially be avoided by patent laws. But in many cases, the results of pure research are not patentable, even though they may be used for commercial purposes.

the requirement is that $MD > (PMB - PMC)$. Figure 5.2 indicates that at 60 units of output $PMB - PMC$ is zero, while MD is positive and equal to $60. Hence, MD exceeds $PMB - PMC$, and there is scope for a bargain.

Similar reasoning indicates that the payment Lisa would be willing to make exceeds $PMB - PMC$ at every output level above the efficient level of 45 units. At output levels lower than 45 units, the amount of money Bart would demand to reduce his output would exceed what Lisa would be willing to pay. Hence, Lisa pays Bart to reduce output just to 45 units, the efficient level. Without more information, we cannot tell exactly how much Lisa will end up paying Bart. This depends on the relative bargaining strengths of the two parties. Given our numerical example in Figure 5.2, the total payment to Bart will be at least equal to cdg, or $337.50 (the amount Bart loses by reducing output from 60 to 45 units) and no greater than $cdhg$, or $787.50 (the amount Lisa gains by having Bart reduce output to 45 units). Regardless of how the gains from the bargain are shared, output ends up at the efficient level.

Suppose instead that Lisa is assigned the property rights to the stream. The bargaining process now consists of Bart paying for Lisa's permission to pollute. Lisa is willing to accept some pollution as long as the payment is greater than the marginal damage (MD) to her fishing enterprise. Bart finds it worthwhile to pay for the privilege of producing as long as the amount is less than the value of $PMB - PMC$ for that unit of output. Reasoning similar to the foregoing suggests that they have every incentive to reach an agreement whereby Lisa sells Bart the right to produce at the efficient output level of 45 units.

Two important assumptions played a key role in the preceding analysis:

1. The costs to the parties of bargaining are low.
2. The owners of resources can identify the source of damages to their property and legally prevent damages.

One way to summarize the implications of this discussion is that, under these assumptions, the efficient solution will be achieved *independently* of who is assigned the property rights, as long as *someone* is assigned those rights. This result, known as the **Coase Theorem** (after Nobel laureate Ronald Coase), implies that once property rights are established, no government intervention is required to deal with externalities (Coase, 1960).

However, externalities such as air pollution involve millions of people (both polluters and pollutees) and it is difficult to imagine them getting together for negotiations at a sufficiently low cost.[8] Even if property rights to air were established, it is not clear how owners would be able to identify which of thousands of potential polluters was responsible for dirtying their airspace and for what proportion of the damage each was liable.[9] Similar obstacles are confronted in the case of climate change. While scientific studies indicate that the accumulation of GHGs in the atmosphere causes warmer surface temperatures, there is considerable uncertainty and debate about the extent of damages from climate change and about the policies that should be adopted to address it. The global nature of the problem is reflected in the ongoing attempts to establish an international agreement on GHG emissions reductions. For instance, in 1998 Canada signed the Kyoto Protocol, an international agreement establishing binding GHG emission reduction targets for the more than 160 countries that ratified it.[10] Over 100 countries, including Canada, have made emission reduction pledges as part of the 2009 Copenhagen Accord.[11]

The Coase Theorem is most relevant for cases in which only a few parties are involved and the sources of the externality are well defined. Even when these conditions hold, the assignment of property rights *is* relevant from the point of view of income distribution. Property rights are valuable; if Lisa owns the stream it will increase her income relative to Bart's, and vice versa.

Assigning property rights along Coasian lines could help solve some significant environmental problems. One commentator, for example, urged that property rights be assigned to rivers in the United States, pointing

[8] There is, however, no guarantee that the transaction costs of implementing a government solution will be less.

[9] Moreover, if the valuation of the external damages (or external benefits) is subjective, an asymmetric information problem may arise, contributing to bargaining costs. As well, some externalities contribute (positively or negatively) to a public good. Pollution reduces air quality. Research and development spending contributes to general knowledge. Both air quality and general knowledge have the joint consumption and nonexcludable characteristics of a pure public good. Individuals may have an incentive to misrepresent their preference and a free riding problem might arise. Such problems will interfere with the emergence of a Coase-like solution.

[10] See Environment Canada (2005) for an overview of the science of climate change. Additional information about the Kyoto Protocol is available from the United Nations Framework Convention on Climate Change website at http://unfccc.int.

[11] In 2010, Canada pledged to reduce its GHG emissions 17 percent below 2005 levels by 2020 as part of the 2009 Copenhagen Accord. See Environment Canada (2010).

out that "in England and Scotland, private ownership of the rivers and waterways has successfully prevented overfishing and controlled water pollution for 800 years. The owners simply charge others for the right to fish in their section of the river. Consequently, the owners have an economic incentive to maintain the fish population and keep the waterway clean" (Conda, 1995: A18).

Another neat application of the Coase Theorem relates to wildlife preservation. In order to conserve elephant populations in Africa, one approach is simply to ban hunting. However, the local villagers have no incentive to obey the ban; they hunt anyway (the law is hard to enforce), and the marginal cost to them of each animal killed is effectively zero. A zero price leads to substantial overhunting. Another approach is to assign individuals the property rights to the animals. In this case, the villagers have an incentive to conserve the herds, because they can make money by selling permission to hunt them. According to Sugg (1996), Kenya banned all hunting in 1977, and its elephant population fell from 167,000 to 16,000 by 1989. In contrast, in 1982, Zimbabwe granted landowners property rights over wildlife; between that time and 1995 its elephant population grew from 40,000 to 68,000. The idea of giving individuals property rights to wild animals on their land has apparently caught on. In southern Africa, many farmers have found it profitable to stop growing food, let their land revert to its natural state, and then charge tourists to view the animals. About 18 percent of the land in the southern third of Africa is now devoted to such ecotourism (Heal, 2003).

Mergers

One way to solve the problems posed by an externality is to "internalize" it by combining the involved parties. Imagine that there is only one polluter and one pollutee, as in our Bart and Lisa example. If Bart took into account the damages he imposed on Lisa's fishery, then a net gain would be possible. In other words, if Bart and Lisa coordinated their activities, then the profit of the joint enterprise would be higher than the sum of their individual profits when they don't coordinate. In effect, by failing to act together, Bart and Lisa are just throwing away money! The market, then, provides a strong incentive for the two firms to merge—Lisa can buy the factory, Bart can buy the fishery, or some third party can buy both of them. Once the two firms merge, the externality is internalized—it is taken into account by the party that generates the externality. For instance, if Bart purchased the fishery, he would willingly produce less output than before, because at the margin doing so would increase the profits of his fishery subsidiary more than it decreased the profits from his factory subsidiary. Consequently, the existence of external effects would not lead to inefficiency. Indeed, an outside observer would not even characterize the situation as an "externality" because all decisions would be made within a single firm.

Private markets or contractual arrangements may develop (as an alternative to merging or joint ownership) to resolve the externality problem. For instance, bees pollinate a variety of different plants, conferring a positive externality to farmers of these crops. Various crops provide nectar for the bees, conferring positive external benefits to beekeepers in the form of more honey production. In the United States, an extensive private market for honey bee pollination services has developed that resolves this reciprocal externality problem.[12]

Social Conventions

Unlike firms, individuals cannot merge to internalize externalities. However, a number of social conventions can be viewed as attempts to force people to take into account the externalities they generate. Schoolchildren are taught that littering is irresponsible and not "nice." If this teaching is effective, children learn that even though they bear a small cost by holding on to a candy wrapper or a banana peel until they find a garbage can, they should incur this cost because it is less than the cost imposed on other people by having to view their unsightly garbage. Think about the golden rule, "Do unto others as you would have others do unto you." A (much) less elegant way of expressing this sentiment is, "Before you undertake some activity, take into account its external marginal benefits and costs." Some moral precepts, then, induce people to empathize with others, and hence internalize the externalities their behaviour may create. In effect, these precepts correct for the absence of missing markets.[13]

---

[12] See Rucker, Thurman, and Burgett (2012) for an examination of this market.

[13] Readers are also referred to the work of Elinor Ostrom who received the Nobel Prize in Economics in 2009 for her research on economic governance.

PUBLIC RESPONSES TO EXTERNALITIES

In cases where individuals acting on their own cannot attain an efficient solution, there are several ways in which government can intervene.[14] Below, we examine a variety of interventions used to remedy negative externalities: taxes, subsidies, emissions fees, tradable permit schemes, and regulation. For positive externalities, we focus on two options: subsidies and regulation.

Taxes and Negative Externalities

In our example, Bart produces inefficiently because the prices he faces for inputs incorrectly signal social costs. Specifically, because his input prices are too low, his private marginal cost of producing output is too low. A natural solution, suggested by the British economist A. C. Pigou, is to levy a tax on the polluter that makes up for the fact that some of his inputs are priced too low. A **Pigouvian tax** is a tax levied on each unit of a polluter's output in an amount just equal to the marginal damage it inflicts *at the efficient level of output*. Figure 5.4 reproduces the example of Figure 5.1. The marginal damage done at the efficient output Q^* is distance cd. This is the Pigouvian tax. (Remember that the vertical distance between SMC and PMC is MD.)

How does Bart react if a tax of cd dollars per unit of output is imposed? The tax raises Bart's effective marginal cost. For each unit he produces, Bart has to make payments both to the suppliers of his inputs (measured by PMC) *and* to the tax collector (measured by cd). Geometrically, Bart's new marginal cost schedule is found by adding cd to PMC at each level of output. This involves shifting up PMC by the vertical distance cd.

To maximize his net benefits from producing and consuming output, Bart produces up to the output at which marginal benefit equals marginal cost. This now occurs at the intersection of PMB and $PMC + cd$, which is at the efficient output Q^*. In effect, the tax forces Bart to take into account the costs of the externality that he generates and induces him to produce efficiently. Note that the tax generates revenue of cd dollars for each of the id units produced ($id = OQ^*$). Hence, tax revenue is $cd \times id$, equal to the area of rectangle $ijcd$ in Figure 5.4. It would be tempting to use these revenues to compensate Lisa, who is still being hurt by Bart's activities, although to a lesser extent than before the tax. However, caution must be exercised. If it becomes known that anyone who fishes along the river receives some money, then some people may choose to fish there who otherwise would not have done so. The result is an inefficiently large amount of fishing done in the river. The key point is that compensation to the victim of the pollution is not necessary to achieve efficiency.

There are practical problems in implementing a Pigouvian tax system. Given the previously mentioned difficulties in estimating the marginal damage function, finding the correct tax rate is bound to be hard. Still,

---

FIGURE 5.4

ANALYSIS OF A PIGOUVIAN TAX

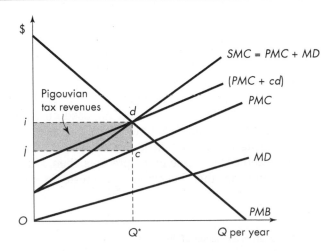

---

[14] The list of possibilities considered here is by no means exhaustive. See Stavins (2003) for a careful discussion of several alternatives.

sensible compromises can be made. Consider the externality of harmful emissions from automobiles. In theory, a tax based on the number of kilometres driven enhances efficiency. Even more efficient would be a tax based on kilometres driven that varies by location and time of day, since pollution is more harmful when emitted in populated areas and during times of high traffic congestion. But such a tax is likely to be prohibitively expensive to administer. The government might instead levy a gasoline tax, even though it is not gasoline use per se that determines the size of the externality. Such a tax would not lead to the most efficient outcome, but it still might be a substantial improvement over the status quo.

Although we have been discussing Pigouvian taxation in the context of environmental damage, it is equally relevant for dealing with other externalities. On crowded roads and highways, every motorist imposes costs on other motorists by increasing congestion. Driving also contributes to accidents and GHG emissions. Motorists are seldom forced to take these external costs into account. A tax on driving equal to the marginal external cost would enhance efficiency. Parry (2009) estimates that a corrective tax on gasoline of $1.23 per gallon (in 2007 dollars) could generate an efficiency gain—the equivalent of area dhg in Figure 5.2—of US$5.9 billion per year if it were applied in the United States. About 75 percent of the corrective tax (roughly 92 cents) is attributable to the marginal damage costs associated with accident and congestion externalities.

Subsidies and Negative Externalities

Under the assumption that the number of polluting firms is fixed, the efficient level of production can be obtained by paying the polluter a subsidy not to pollute. Although this notion may seem peculiar at first, it works much like the tax scheme. This is because a subsidy for not polluting is simply another method of raising the polluter's effective production cost.

Suppose the government announces that it will pay Bart a subsidy of cd for each unit of output that he does not produce. What will Bart do? In Figure 5.5, Bart's private marginal benefit at output level Q_1 is measured by the distance between PMB and the horizontal axis, ge. The marginal cost of producing at Q_1 is the sum of the amount Bart pays for his inputs (which we read off the PMC curve), and the subsidy of cd that he forgoes by producing. Once again, then, the perceived marginal cost schedule is $PMC + cd$. At output Q_1, this is distance ek ($= eg + gk$). But ek exceeds the private marginal benefit, ge. As long Bart's marginal cost exceeds his private marginal benefit, it does not make sense for him to produce the Q_1st unit of output. Instead, he should forgo its production and accept the subsidy. The same line of reasoning indicates that Bart will choose not to produce any output in excess of Q^*. At all output levels to the right of Q^*, the sum of the private marginal cost and the subsidy exceeds the private marginal benefit. On the other hand, at all points to the left of Q^* it is worthwhile for Bart to produce even though he has to give up the subsidy. For these output levels, the total opportunity cost, $PMC + cd$, is less than the private marginal benefit. Hence, the subsidy induces Bart to produce just to Q^*, the efficient output.

FIGURE 5.5

ANALYSIS OF A PIGOUVIAN SUBSIDY

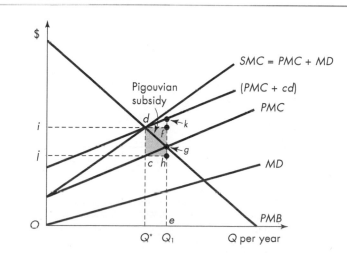

The distributional consequences of the tax and subsidy schemes differ dramatically. Instead of having to pay the tax of *ijcd* (from Figure 5.4), Bart receives a payment equal to the number of units of forgone production, *ch*, times the subsidy per unit, *cd*, which equals rectangle *dfhc* in Figure 5.5.[15] That an efficient solution can be associated with different income distributions is no surprise. It is analogous to the result from Chapter 2–there are an infinite number of efficient allocations in the Edgeworth Box, each of which is associated with its own distribution of real income.

In addition to the problems associated with the Pigouvian tax scheme, the subsidy program has a few of its own. First, recall that the analysis of Figure 5.5 assumes a fixed number of firms. The subsidy leads to higher profits, so in the long run more firms may be induced to locate along the river. The subsidy may cause so many new firms to relocate on the river that total pollution actually increases. Second, the subsidy payments have to be raised by taxes levied somewhere in the economy. In general, taxation distorts people's incentives. And it is not obvious that these distortion effects would be less costly than the externality itself. (The efficiency costs of taxation are discussed in detail in Chapter 15.)

Finally, subsidies may be ethically undesirable. As Mishan (1971: 25) notes:

> It may be argued [that] the freedom to operate noisy vehicles, or pollutive plant, does incidentally damage the welfare of others, while the freedom desired by members of the public to live in clean and quiet surroundings does not, of itself, reduce the welfare of others. If such arguments can be sustained, there is a case . . . for making polluters legally liable.

Emissions Fees and Negative Externalities

Above, we demonstrated how a tax on each unit of Bart's output can lead to the socially efficient outcome. One problem with this approach is that it might not give Bart the proper incentives to search for ways to reduce pollution other than reducing output. Why should Bart install pollution control technology that reduces his emissions per unit of output if doing so won't change his tax bill?

One way to address this problem is to levy a tax on each unit of pollutant instead of each unit of output.[16] This tax is called an **emissions fee**. Figure 5.6 illustrates this approach for our Bart and Lisa example. The horizontal axis measures emissions of the pollutant and the vertical axis is measured in dollars. *MD* denotes

FIGURE 5.6

USING AN EMISSIONS FEE TO REDUCE POLLUTION

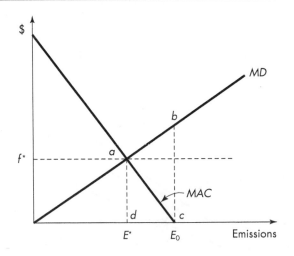

---

[15] In Figure 5.5, Q_1 is the baseline from which Bart's reduction in output is measured. In principle, any baseline to the right of Q^* would do. One potential problem is that firms may attempt to game the system by undertaking inefficient actions so as to increase the baseline output.

[16] In principle, the pollutant could be sulfur dioxide and nitrogen oxides, in the case of acid rain, or CO_2e, in the case of GHG emissions.

the marginal damage schedule and here reflects the marginal damage inflicted on Lisa by the pollutant at each level of *emissions*. Reducing emissions (moving from *right to left* along the *MD* schedule) generates benefits for Lisa since less damage is inflicted on her fishery.

In the absence of the emissions fee, the level of emissions is E_0 (the level of emissions associated with the level of output Q_1 that maximizes Bart's net benefits in Figure 5.1). Bart could reduce emissions by undertaking **abatement activities**, emission-reducing activities that include changing production technology, switching to cleaner inputs, or reducing output. Abatement activities are costly. Bart's **marginal abatement cost**, the additional cost associated with a one unit reduction in emissions, is illustrated as *MAC* in Figure 5.6.

What is the efficient level of emissions? At E_0, the benefit to Lisa from a one-unit reduction in emissions is given by the marginal damage schedule at E_0 whereas the cost to Bart of a one unit reduction in emissions is zero. Clearly, there are net gains to reducing emissions. From an efficiency standpoint, emissions should be reduced as long as the marginal benefit from emissions reductions (avoided damage) exceeds the marginal abatement cost of doing so. For every level of emissions to the right of E^*, *MD* exceeds the *MAC*. To reduce emissions below E^*, however, would impose additional costs on Bart in excess of the additional benefits generated for Lisa. Thus, E* is the efficient level of emissions.

What emissions fee achieves E^*? Suppose the government imposes an emissions fee equal to f^*. Bart has an incentive to reduce emissions below E_0 as long as the amount he saves in fee payments (taxes avoided) exceeds the abatement costs incurred from lowering emissions. At E^*, Bart's *MAC* is equal to f* and Bart has no further incentive to reduce emissions. In moving from E_0 to E*, Bart incurs abatement costs equal to area *acd* while the benefit to Lisa from the reduction in emissions is equal to area *abcd*. The net efficiency gain is equal to area *abc*.[17]

What happens if there is more than one polluter? Suppose that, in addition to Bart, Homer also operates a factory that pollutes the river. Initially, both Bart and Homer emit 90 units of pollution, for a total of 180 per year, and incur no abatement costs. Suppose efficiency requires emissions to fall by 45 units and can be achieved with an emissions fee of $50. How will the emissions reductions be shared between Bart and Homer? Figure 5.7 shows the marginal abatement cost schedules for the two polluters (the marginal abatement cost schedule for Bart is $MAC_B = 180 - 2E_B$; for Homer, the marginal abatement cost is $MAC_H = 225 - 2.5E_H$). Now, each polluter reduces emissions as long as the fees avoided (i.e., the tax savings) exceed the additional abatement costs incurred from reducing emissions. Thus, each polluter reduces emissions until his marginal cost of abatement is just equal to the $50 emissions fee.[18] Since the fee is the same for each polluter, the marginal cost of abatement will be equal across the two polluters. The amount of emissions reduction undertaken by each polluter need not be identical; this will depend on the marginal abatement cost schedule of each polluter. As illustrated in Figure 5.7, Bart reduces emissions by 25 units and pays fees equal to $3250 ($50 × 65 units of emissions). Homer reduces emissions by 20 and pays $3500 in fees.

Reducing emissions is costly—Bart incurs abatement costs of $625 (area *abc* in Figure 5.7), and Homer incurs a cost of $500 (area *def*). To achieve emissions reduction equal to 45 units, the total abatement cost equals $1125. An appealing feature of the emissions fee is that it ensures that this cost is minimized. Consider a different allocation of emissions reductions between Bart and Homer; Bart reduces his emissions to 75 units and Homer to 60 units. The total reduction in emissions is still 45 units. The abatement cost has increased to $1,350.[19] Why? With emissions equal to 75, the cost of an additional one unit reduction in emissions for Bart is $30 (i.e., $MAC_B = 30$). Homer is emitting 60 units; the cost of an additional one-unit reduction in emissions for him is $75. If Bart was to reduce emissions by *one more unit* and Homer by *one unit less*, total abatement cost would fall by about $45 leaving total emissions unchanged. As long as marginal abatement costs differ, total cost can be lowered by reallocating the burden of emissions reduction between polluters. The total cost of emissions reduction is minimized only when the marginal cost of abatement is equal across all polluters. This outcome is **cost-effective**.

---

[17] Note that Bart also makes a tax payment equal to $E^* \times f^*$ to the government. This represents a transfer of surplus from Bart to the government.

[18] Solving for $MAC_B = 50$, we find $E_B = 65$. Solving $MAC_H = 50$, we find that $E_H = 70$.

[19] Total abatement cost is the sum of Bart's cost and Homer's cost. Bart's abatement cost is calculated as the area under MAC_B between 75 and 90 units of emissions. This equals $225 (calculated as $0.5 \times (90 - 75) \times 30$). Homer's cost is calculated as the area under MAC_H between 60 and 90 units of emissions and equals $1,125.

AN EMISSIONS FEE WITH MULTIPLE POLLUTERS

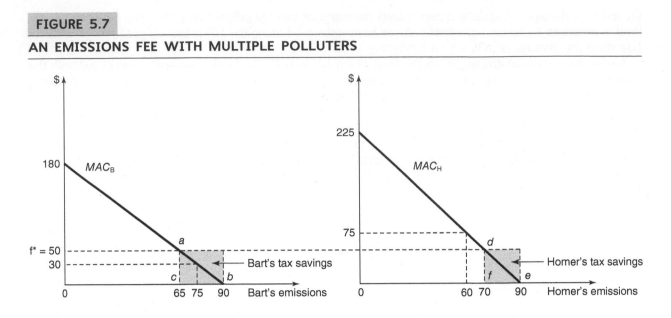

To tackle climate change, some governments have introduced fees, known as carbon taxes, on carbon dioxide equivalent (CO_2e) emissions. Provincial governments in British Columbia and Quebec have introduced modest carbon taxes. At the federal level, former Liberal party leader Stéphane Dion unsuccessfully campaigned in the 2008 federal election on his "Green Shift" plan to introduce a federal carbon tax. In 2012, the Australian carbon tax was introduced by the Labour government. Based on claims of damage to jobs and the economy, the tax was repealed in 2014 by Prime Minister Tony Abbott and his Conservative government, an action endorsed by the Canadian prime minister, Stephen Harper.[20]

A Tradable Permit Scheme and Negative Externalities

As an alternative to an emissions fee, the government could implement a system of tradable pollution permits, known as a **cap and trade** system. Under cap and trade, Bart and Homer must submit one government-issued permit for each unit of pollution they emit. Further, they are allowed to trade these permits with each other. To achieve the 45 unit reduction in emissions in our example illustrated in Figure 5.7, the government would issue 135 permits for the year, setting a cap on total emissions.

How should permits be allocated to Bart and Homer? The government could sell or auction the permits or give them away for free. As long as the permits are tradable, from an efficiency standpoint, how the permits are initially allocated among polluters doesn't matter. To see this, suppose the government decides to give the permits away for free—Bart gets 90 and Homer receives 45. In the absence of permit trading, Bart will not undertake any abatement activities since he has just enough permits to cover his emissions. Homer however will need to reduce emissions from his initial 90 to 45 units, since he only has 45 permits. The situation is illustrated in Figure 5.8. Bart's abatement costs are zero. Homer, on the other hand, reduces emissions by 45 units and incurs a cost equal to $2531.25 or area *abc* in Figure 5.8. The cap ensures that emissions fall by 45 units but the outcome is not cost-effective.

How does permit trading change this outcome? If Bart sold one of his permits to Homer, he would have to lower emissions by one unit and incur additional abatement costs. As long as the price Homer paid Bart for the permit was greater than the added abatement cost Bart would incur, it will be worthwhile for Bart to sell the permit to Homer. By buying the permit, Homer would be able to pollute one more unit (and avoid having to incur the abatement costs associated with eliminating that unit). As long as the permit price was less than Homer's marginal abatement cost, Homer would buy the permit. Note that Bart's marginal abatement cost is zero, given emissions equal to 90. Homer's marginal cost of abatement, given emissions of 45, is $112.5. So, there is scope for a bargain here. Bart will sell one of his permits. By this logic, Bart will continue to sell permits to Homer until the marginal abatement costs of the two polluters are identical. Recall that $MAC_B = MAC_H$

---

[20] See Kennedy (2014).

BRITISH COLUMBIA'S CARBON TAX

Are carbon taxes a good idea? This question has sparked a lively debate in the media. Some commentators argue that a comprehensive carbon tax for Canada is the "least bad option"—easy to administer; fair, if revenue neutral; and effective, if modelled after the carbon tax in British Columbia. BC introduced its carbon tax in 2008, the first jurisdiction in North America to do so. Initially, the tax rate was set at $10 per tonne of carbon dioxide equivalent (CO_2e) emissions; it is now equal to $30 per tonne. It is a broad-based tax, meaning it applies to most fuels, and it is revenue neutral. Revenue neutrality means that the carbon tax revenues collected (about $1.2 billion for 2016/17) will be fully offset with reductions in other taxes.

Those in favour of a carbon tax herald the success of the BC carbon tax, drawing on results from a study by Elgie and McClay (2013). This study finds that over the period 2008 to 2012, per capita fuel consumption in BC declined by 17.4 percent compared to a 1.5 percent increase in the rest of Canada. And between 2008 and 2011, per capita GHG emissions fell by 10 percent in BC but only by 1.1 percent in the rest of Canada. However, some view this evidence with considerable scepticism, arguing that the cause of the dramatic decline in gasoline demand and emissions in B.C. is unclear. Even the study's authors acknowledge that factors other than the carbon tax may be driving the comparatively larger reductions in fuel use and emissions in BC. An economic downturn with different provincial impacts could, for example, be a causal factor. The effectiveness of BC's carbon tax in reducing emissions also depends in part on the extent of the carbon leakage problem, a phenomenon whereby BC emissions fall but emissions in other jurisdictions without a carbon tax increase.

New research can help provide more definitive answers to questions about the effectiveness (and the economic, trade and distributional consequences) of BC's carbon tax. Until then, the lively debate will continue.

Based on Elgie and McClay (2013), Corcoran (2015), Beaty et al. (2014), British Columbia Ministry of Finance (2014), and "A revenue neutral, comprehensive carbon tax is the least bad option." *The Globe and Mail*. November 29, 2013.

Complete references for this feature can be found in the References section on page 475.

FIGURE 5.8

A CAP AND TRADE SCHEME IS COST-EFFECTIVE

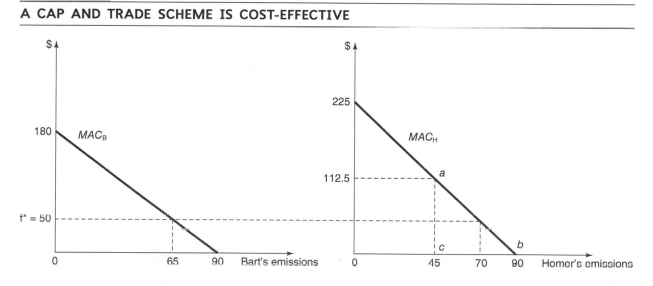

defines a cost-effective outcome. After all gains from trade have been exhausted, Bart will hold 65 permits and Homer will hold 70 permits and the total reduction in emissions is 45 units.

Notice that the same emissions reduction would occur no matter how the government initially allocated the permits to Bart and Homer. Of course, how permits are allocated does affect the distribution of income. From our example, we can see that from the polluter's perspective it is preferable to be a seller of permits rather than a buyer. From the government's perspective, selling or auctioning the permits generates revenue that can be used for other purposes whereas free distribution does not. Finally, we note that the cap and trade system achieves the same cost-effective reduction in emissions (and the same distribution of emissions reductions between Bart and Homer) as the $50 emissions fee discussed above.

The efficient level of pollution can be achieved in principle with either an emissions fee or a cap and trade scheme. How is one to choose between them? Cap and trade has some practical advantages over an emissions fee. One of the most important is that the cap reduces uncertainty about the ultimate level of pollution. If the government is certain about the shapes of the marginal abatement cost and marginal damage schedules in Figure 5.6, then it can safely predict how an emissions fee will affect behaviour. But if there is poor information about these schedules, it is hard to know how much a particular fee will reduce pollution. If lack of information forces policy makers to choose the pollution cap arbitrarily with a system of pollution permits, this level is more likely to be obtained. In addition, under the assumption that firms are profit maximizers, they will find the cost-minimizing technology to attain the standard. When the economy is experiencing inflation, the market price of pollution rights would be expected to keep pace automatically, while changing the emissions fee could require a lengthy administrative procedure.

Auctioning permits has its own problems. Incumbent firms might buy permits in excess of cost-minimizing requirements to deter other firms from entering the market. Whether such strategic behaviour is likely to occur is hard to predict, however. Since the permit price is endogenously determined by market forces, there can also be a great deal of uncertainty about the permit price and the ultimate costs of emissions reductions to firms. A ceiling for permit prices (or safety value) is sometimes proposed to counter this concern.

Cap and trade schemes have been implemented in different contexts. The U.S. Acid Rain Trading Program, introduced in 1990, sets an annual cap for emissions of sulphur dioxide (which combines with nitrogen oxides to form acid rain). Electric utilities, the main producers of sulphur dioxide, must have a permit for each tonne of sulphur dioxide they emit. Total permits are equal to the emissions cap. Initially, the permits are freely distributed among existing electricity producers, after which they can be bought and sold. The interaction between the supply of permits (which is fixed in total) and the market demand for permits determines the market price of a permit. Other examples include the European Union's Greenhouse Gas Emissions Trading System (EUETS) and the Regional Greenhouse Gas Initiative (RGGI) in the U.S.

Regulation and Negative Externalities

Emissions fees and cap and trade schemes are incentive-based approaches to remedying the negative externality problem. Incentive-based approaches provide polluters with market incentives to reduce pollution. Basically, each approach increases the opportunity cost of polluting, forcing polluters to take into account the marginal external damages associated with their behaviour. These approaches give polluters a lot of flexibility in choosing how to reduce emissions—reduce output, switch fuels, and change production technology—because the idea is to find the cheapest way of reducing emissions. They also provide flexibility about *who* reduces emissions. In our permit trading example, Bart can sell his permits to Homer because the cost of reducing a unit of pollution is cheaper for Bart than for Homer. So, Homer essentially pays Bart to reduce pollution for him. Similarly, under an emissions fee, Bart reduces pollution more than Homer, who instead opts to pay more in taxes.

Command and control regulation, as an alternative to the incentive-based approaches, can take a variety of forms, such as a technology or performance standard, but they are all less flexible than incentive-based approaches. A **technology standard** requires polluters to install a certain technology; for example, "scrubbers" in power plants to clean up or reduce emissions. However, the requirement provides no incentive for firms to look for cheaper ways to reduce emissions. A **performance standard** is a type of command and control regulation that sets an emissions goal for each polluter. This approach is more cost-effective than a technology standard as the polluter typically has flexibility in how to meet the standard. However, because the standard sets a fixed emissions reduction goal for each firm, the burden of reducing emissions cannot be shifted to firms that can achieve reductions more cheaply. As a result, performance standards are unlikely to be cost-effective.

A number of empirical studies have sought to compare the costs of using cost-effective versus command and control approaches to obtaining a given reduction in pollution. The particular results depend on the type of pollution being considered and the site of the pollution. One summary of these findings shows that command and control regulations are 1.07 to 22 times more expensive than the cost-effective approach.[21]

A good example of an inefficient command and control approach is the U.S. federal government's corporate average fuel economy standards (CAFE) for all new passenger vehicles. These standards dictate the average gasoline mileage that vehicle fleets must attain (30.2 miles per gallon for cars and 24.1 miles per gallon for light trucks in 2011).[22] CAFE standards have limited flexibility because manufacturers cannot shift the burden among themselves to lower the overall cost. An alternative approach to reducing gasoline consumption would be to levy a tax on gasoline as a form of emissions fee. The Congressional Budget Office compared an increase in CAFE standards with an increase in the gasoline tax that would achieve the same reduction in gasoline consumption and found that CAFE costs about $700 million more per year (CBO, 2004).

The presence of externalities often requires some kind of intervention to achieve efficiency. Implementing any policy entails a host of difficult technical issues. No policy is likely to do a perfect job. However, of the options available, most economists prefer Pigouvian taxes, emissions fees, or pollution permits. These are more likely to achieve efficient outcomes than either subsidies or direct regulation.

Subsidies and Positive Externalities

So far, we have considered public responses to remedy negative externalities. What remedies are available to deal with positive externalities?

Just as a negative externality can be corrected by a Pigouvian tax, a positive externality can be corrected by a Pigouvian subsidy. Let's return to our research and development spending example shown in Figure 5.3. Figure 5.3 shows that left to the private market the level of R&D spending will be too low; if we could somehow induce the market to undertake R* in R&D spending, there would an efficiency gain. Suppose R&D-conducting firms are given a subsidy equal to the external marginal benefit at the efficient level of output—distance cd in Figure 5.3—then it will be induced to produce efficiently.[23] The lesson is clear: when an individual or firm produces positive externalities, the market underprovides the activity or good, but an appropriate subsidy can remedy the situation. Of course, all the problems in measuring the quantity and value of the externality are still relevant. Although estimates vary, research for Canada suggests that the social rate of return to R&D exceeds the private rate of return to R&D by a sizeable margin.[24] If these figures are correct, then the positive externalities associated with R&D are substantial.

Many people who have never heard the term *positive externality* nevertheless have a good intuitive grasp of the concept and its policy implications. They understand that if they can convince the government that their activities create beneficial spillovers, they may be able to dip into the treasury for a subsidy. Requests for such subsidies must be viewed cautiously for two reasons. First, the subsidy has to come from resources extracted from taxpayers. Hence, every subsidy embodies a redistribution of income from taxpayers as a whole to the recipients. Even if the subsidy has good efficiency consequences, the distributional implications may not be desirable. This depends on the value judgments embodied in the social welfare function. Second, when the presence of a beneficial externality is claimed, its precise nature must be determined. The fact that an activity is beneficial per se does not mean that a subsidy is required for efficiency. A subsidy is appropriate only if the market does not allow those performing the activity to capture the full marginal return. For example, a brilliant surgeon who does much good for humanity creates no positive externality as long as the surgeon's salary reflects the incremental value of his or her services.

Regulation and Positive Externalities

In some circumstances, a government may regulate the activity generating the positive externalities. Vaccination programs are one example. A vaccination against a contagious disease, like measles, protects the

[21] Executive Office of the President Council of Economic Advisers (2003), page 153.

[22] Details are available at the U.S. Ministry of Transportation's website: http://www.nhtsa.gov/fuel-economy.

[23] Note that by construction, cd = ef.

[24] See Parsons and Phillips (2007) for a review of Canadian estimates of the social and private rates of return to R&D.

individual who gets vaccinated. If enough people in the community are vaccinated, then the risk of infection to those in the community who have not been vaccinated can also be significantly reduced or eliminated. Some vaccinations are offered free of charge (i.e., a variant of the subsidy option). The government may also make certain vaccinations mandatory. For example, Ontario, New Brunswick, and Manitoba require children to be vaccinated against measles before entering the school system, unless an exemption for religious, medical, and ideological reasons is provided. In the United States, all 50 states have mandatory vaccinations for school-aged children, again with exemptions available under certain circumstances. According to Walkinshaw (2011), one of the most aggressive vaccinations programs can be found in Slovenia, which requires infants to be vaccinated for a number of diseases, including measles and hepatitis B. Exemptions are permitted for medical reasons only and failure to comply results in a fine. Vaccination rates are, as a consequence, high—around 95 percent.

Underlying the debate on the question of mandatory versus voluntary vaccinations is the question of how to balance the freedom of individuals with the protection of the health and safety of others. To illustrate, in 2014, the Alberta Minister of Health stated that he was considering various measures, including mandatory flu vaccinations for health care workers, to improve upon the low vaccination rate for this target group (in 2013, 54 percent of Alberta health care workers got a free flu vaccine).[25] Gardam and Lemieux (2013) argue however that such a policy may be unwarranted. Evidence suggests that the flu vaccine is only moderately effective in preventing the flu. Moreover, the vaccination of health care workers for influenza has not been shown to have a significant effect on influenza-specific patient outcomes.

The regulation of positive externalities comes with challenges similar to those encountered when trying to find the correct Piguovian tax. A substantial amount of information is required to determine the magnitude of external benefits, and uncertainty is a serious issue. Regulation is unlikely to achieve an efficient outcome in any event. For example, **herd immunity** (a situation where enough individuals in the community have been vaccinated so that the risk of infection to anyone else is negligible) may require a minimum vaccination rate of, say, 75 percent. A government subsidy for vaccinations for all school-aged children does not in and of itself ensure that this vaccination rate is achieved. Making such vaccinations compulsory may not help much, depending on compliance rates, conditions for exemptions, and enforcement efforts.

IMPLICATIONS FOR INCOME DISTRIBUTION

Our main focus so far has been on the efficiency aspects of externalities. Welfare economics indicates that we must take distributional as well as efficiency considerations into account. For example, how does the introduction of an emissions fee to improve air quality affect low- and high-income individuals? What are the distributional effects of using distortionary taxes to finance a free vaccination program? Attempts to assess the distributional implications give rise to a number of difficult questions. Below, we outline a few considerations.

Who Benefits?

In our Bart and Lisa example, the distribution of benefits is a trivial issue because there is only one type of pollution and one pollution victim. In reality, there are many different types of individuals who suffer differently from a pollution externality. Some evidence suggests that poor neighbourhoods tend to have more exposure to air pollution than high-income neighbourhoods (Gayer 2000). If this is true, lowering the level of air pollution might make the distribution of real income more equal, other things being the same. On the other hand, the benefits of environmental programs that enhance the quality of recreational areas, such as national parks, probably benefit mainly high-income families, who tend to be their main users.

Knowledge of who is suffering from air pollution is not enough; we need to know how much it is worth to them to have it removed. Suppose a high-income family would be willing to pay more for a given improvement in air quality than a low-income family. Then, even if a cleanup program reduces more of the *physical* amount of pollution for low- than for high-income families, in *dollar* terms the program can end up favouring those with high incomes.

---

[25] Komarnicki (2014).

Positive externalities pose similar challenges. Individuals living in low-income neighbourhoods or countries may be more at risk of a particular disease because of crowding, poor sanitation, and so on. A vaccination program financed by a progressive tax may confer comparatively more benefits to low-income individuals and improve the distribution of real income. But this need not be the case. In Saskatchewan, for example, where the measles vaccine is free (but not mandatory), coverage rates vary by income level. Cushon et al. (2012) found that in Saskatoon the coverage rate in low-income neighbourhoods was significantly lower than in affluent neighbourhoods (43.7 versus 90.6 percent). This result suggest that the policy may unintentionally confer higher benefits to those with higher incomes, especially if the overall vaccination rate is not sufficiently high to achieve herd immunity.

Who Bears the Costs?

Suppose that large numbers of polluting firms are induced to reduce output by government policy. As these firms contract, the demand for the inputs they employ falls, making the owners of these inputs worse off.[26] Some of the polluters' former workers may suffer unemployment in the short run and be forced to work at lower wages in the long run. If these workers have low incomes, environmental cleanup increases income inequality.

Another consideration is that if polluting firms are forced to take into account social marginal costs, their products tend to become more expensive. From an efficiency perspective this is desirable, because otherwise prices give incorrect signals concerning full resource costs. Nevertheless, buyers of these commodities will be made worse off. If the commodities so affected are consumed primarily by high-income groups, the distribution of real income becomes more equal, other things being the same, and vice versa. Thus, to assess the distributional implications of reducing pollution, we also need to know the demand patterns of the goods produced by polluting companies.

A full assessment of the distributional consequences of policies to address externalities would also take into account how revenues generated are disbursed and how subsidies are financed. Subsidies, financed from distortionary taxes, are a redistribution of income from taxpayers as a whole to the recipients. The distribution of income can improve or worsen depending on whether the tax used to finance the subsidy is progressive or not.

Carbon taxes have been shown to impose a disproportionately higher burden on lower income households (Grainger and Kolstad, 2009). These distributional consequences depend on how the revenues from a carbon tax are used. Revenues could be used to reduce taxes that fall more heavily on low-income individuals, which improves the distributional effects. The potentially uneven burden of reducing greenhouse gases across countries adds to the difficulty of achieving an internationally binding agreement. Even within Canada, uneven burden sharing is a serious obstacle. Snoddon and Wigle (2007) and M. K. Jaccard and Associates (2009) find that the provincial welfare effects of reducing Canada's GHG emissions can be quite uneven, depending on how revenues from auctioned permits or from a carbon tax are disbursed.

In summary, correcting externalities can generate efficiency gains but may also give rise to unfavourable distributional consequences. These distributional impacts are often at the forefront of the policy debate on how best to tackle externality problems, creating a dilemma for those who favour both greater efficiency and a more equal income distribution.

SUMMARY

- An externality occurs when the activity of one person affects another person outside of the market mechanism. Externalities may generally be traced to the absence of property rights.

- Externalities cause market price to diverge from social cost, bringing about an inefficient allocation of resources. Negative externalities generally lead to too much of an activity while positive externalities typically result in too little.

---

[26] More specifically, under certain conditions, those inputs used relatively intensively in the production of the polluting good suffer income losses. See Chapter 15 under "General Equilibrium Models."

- The Coase Theorem indicates that private parties may bargain toward the efficient output if property rights are established. However, bargaining costs must be low and the source of the externality easily identified.
- A Pigouvian tax is a tax levied on pollution in an amount equal to the marginal damage at the efficient level. Such a tax gives the producer a private incentive to pollute the efficient amount.
- A subsidy for pollution not produced can induce polluters to produce at the efficient level. However, such subsidies can lead to too much production, are administratively difficult, and are regarded by some as ethically unappealing.
- An emissions fee (a tax levied on each unit of pollution) achieves a given amount of pollution reduction at the lowest feasible cost (i.e., is cost-effective). The cost of emissions reductions is capped by the emissions fee but the level of pollution reduction can be uncertain.
- Pollution rights may be traded in markets. A cap and trade system grants permits to pollute, but allows the permits to be traded. Like the emissions fee, this approach is cost-effective. A cap and trade scheme ensures a particular amount of pollution reduction, an advantage when administrators are uncertain how polluters will respond to Pigouvian taxes or emissions fees. However, the price of permits is uncertain.
- Command and control regulations are less flexible than incentive-based approaches, like emissions fees and permit schemes, and therefore tend to be more costly.
- Positive externalities may be addressed using a subsidy; care must be taken to avoid wasteful subsidies.
- Policies to deal with externalities can have important consequences for the distribution of real income. These distributional consequences are typically difficult to measure and are sometimes unanticipated.

EXERCISES

1. Every year in December, the Smith family decorates their home with a lavish display of Christmas decorations. People come from all over Edmonton to look at the decorations. Consequently, the roads in their part of the city become congested. The Smiths' neighbours complain that at times their streets become impassable and they are virtual prisoners in their homes. Identify the externalities in this situation. Is the allocation of resources efficient?

2. In the accompanying figure, the number of parties that Cassanova gives per month is measured on the horizontal axis, and dollars spent are measured on the vertical. MC_P is the marginal cost of providing parties and MB_P is Cassanova's marginal benefit schedule from having parties.

   a. Graphically, show how many parties Cassanova will host.

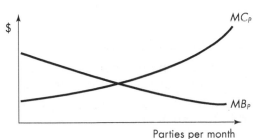

   b. Suppose there is a fixed marginal benefit, $b, per party to Cassanova's friends. Illustrate this on your graph.

c. What is the socially (no pun intended) optimal level of parties? How could the social committee induce Cassanova to host this number of parties?

d. On your graph, show the optimal subsidy per party and the total amount paid to Cassanova. Who gains and loses under this plan?

3*. Consider a hypothetical market for the hepatitis A vaccine. The market demand (or private marginal benefit schedule) is given as: $P = 80 - 0.25Q^d$ where Q^d denotes the number of vaccinations demanded per month and P is the price per vaccination. The market supply for the vaccine (the private marginal cost schedule) is: $P = 15 + 0.4Q^s$ where Q^s denotes the number of vaccinations supplied per month.

a. Sketch a graph of the market and solve for the number of vaccinations purchased per month.

b. The hepatitis A vaccination generates external benefits. Suppose the external marginal benefit schedule is given as: $MEB = 35 - 0.15Q$. Find the efficient number of vaccinations per month.

c. Suppose the government decides to subsidize the price of the hepatitis vaccination. Find the optimal subsidy. Who gains and loses under this plan?

4. For each of the following situations, is the Coase Theorem applicable? Why or why not?

a. A group of university students in a residence shares a communal kitchen. Some of the users of the kitchen never clean up the messes they make when cooking.

b. The pollution from a copper smelter drifts out over a surrounding residential area.

c. Loud gasoline-powered leaf blowers are used by some homeowners for driving leaves and other debris into piles, but also they drive leaves and dust into the yards of neighbours.

5. The government of British Columbia has suggested a "cash-for-clunkers" program. Under this program, the government would buy up "clunkers" (older cars that emit a lot of pollutants and do not meet current pollution standards). Is this a sensible policy? Explain.

6. For each of the following, discuss the nature of the externalities involved and possible government responses:

a. The outbreak of SARS (sudden acute respiratory syndrome) in Toronto in 2003

b. The HINI flu pandemic, as declared by the World Health Organization in June 2009

c. The use of firewood, dung, charcoal, and other unimproved fuels for indoor cooking and heating in rural households in sub-Saharan Africa and China

d. Driving on a (i) congested highway and (ii) uncongested highway

7. The private marginal benefit for commodity X is given by $10 - X$, where X is the number of units consumed. The private marginal cost of producing X is constant at $5. For each unit of X produced, an external cost of $2 is imposed on members of society. In the absence of any government intervention, how much X is produced? What is the efficient level of production of X? What is the gain to society involved in moving from the inefficient to the efficient level of production? Suggest a Pigouvian tax that would lead to the efficient level. How much revenue would the tax raise?

8*. Suppose that in the absence of any corrective measures, the economy generates 750 megatonnes (Mt) of GHG emissions (E) per year. The damage created by an additional Mt of emissions is called the marginal damage. Assume the marginal damage function is $MD = 0.04\,E$. Thus, if $E = 750$ Mt, the additional damage to society associated with one more Mt of emissions is $30. The marginal abatement cost, the additional cost associated with a one Mt reduction in emissions, is given as $MAC = 45 - 0.06\,E$. When there is no abatement, $E = 750$ Mt and the marginal cost of abatement is zero.

---

* Difficult

MD and MAC are illustrated below. Emissions are measured on the horizontal axis in megatonnes per year and the vertical axis is measured in dollars.

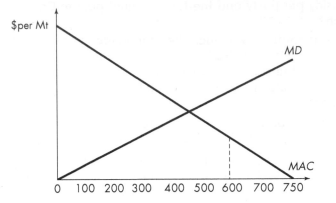

a. If E = 600 Mt, how much abatement (emissions reduction) has occurred? What is the marginal cost associated with lowering emissions by an additional Mt when E = 600? What is the marginal benefit of an additional Mt reduction in emissions when E = 600 (i.e., what is the marginal damage prevented)?

b. If E = 600, calculate total abatement costs as the area below the MAC curve between 600 Mt and 750 Mt. Calculate total benefits from lower emissions as the area under the MD curve between 600 Mt and 750 Mt.

c. For this economy, what is the socially optimal level of emissions, E*? (Hint: From an efficiency standpoint, emissions should continue to be reduced as long as the marginal benefit from emissions reductions exceeds the marginal abatement costs.)

d. Suppose the government imposed a tax on emissions equal to $12 per Mt of greenhouse gas emissions. How does the tax affect total emissions in the economy? Is the tax sufficient to reduce emissions to E*? Why or why not?

9*. Bart and Homer each operate a factory that pollutes the river and and harms Lisa's fishery. Reducing their emissions is costly for both producers. Bart's marginal cost of abatement is $MAC_B = 500 - 10e_B$. Homer's marginal abatement cost is $MAC_H = 1000 - 20e_H$. The government has decided that harmful emissions into the river need to be reduced by 18 units. To achieve this goal, three proposals are under consideration.

Proposal 1: Use a command and control approach. Bart and Homer must share the required emission reductions equally.

Proposal 2: Impose an emissions fee of $120 per unit of pollutant.

Proposal 3: Introduce a cap and trade program. The government issues 82 permits. Bart and Homer each get an equal share of the permits, which are distributed for free.

a. Briefly describe how each of the three proposals works to ensure emissions fall by 18 units.

b. Evaluate the total abatement costs under each proposal. If the government's goal is efficiency, which proposal should it choose? Explain your reasoning.

c. Consider the distributional consequences of each of the three proposals. Rank the three options (least preferred to most preferred) from Bart's perspective? From Homer's perspective? Briefly discuss.

10. Several homeowners in a neighbourhood like to plant gardens in the spring. These gardens generate external benefits for those who reside in or visiting the neighbourhood. No government intervention is needed to remedy the externality; the outcome is efficient. Provide an explanation for why no government response is needed?

CHAPTER 6

Income Redistribution

Income inequality is where the capitalist system is most vulnerable . . . You can't have the capitalist system if an increasing number of people think it is unjust.

—Alan Greenspan[1]

AFTER READING THIS CHAPTER, THE STUDENT SHOULD BE ABLE TO:

LO1 Define market income, total income, and income after taxes and transfers.

LO2 Explain how the Lorenz curve and the Gini coefficient can be used to measure income inequality.

LO3 Summarize how the low income ratio and the low income gap ratio can be used to measure poverty in Canada.

LO4 Describe the alternative views on redistribution that are embedded in the additive social welfare function and the maximin criteria.

LO5 Explain how distortionary taxation affects the policy prescriptions for redistribution given an additive social welfare function and the maximin criteria.

LO6 Describe what Pareto efficient redistribution is and how it differs from the additive and maximin social welfare functions.

LO7 Summarize the arguments made in favour of pursuing redistribution using in-kind transfers rather than cash transfers.

". . . In a state which is desirous of being saved from the greatest of all plagues—not faction, but rather distraction—there should exist among the citizens neither extreme poverty nor, again, excessive wealth, for both are productive of great evil . . . the legislator should determine what is to be the limit of poverty or of wealth."

—From Plato's Laws, Book V (360 B.C.E)

With dramatic and somewhat colourful language, Plato warns of the dangers of extreme income inequality and outlines a role for government in income redistribution. Today, individuals and decision-makers continue to be concerned about income inequality and the government's role in income redistribution. In Canada, the rising income share of the wealthiest 1 percent and growing income inequality have attracted quite a bit of media attention in recent years. Even when they are not explicit, questions of who will gain and who will lose lurk in the background of public policy debates.

This chapter begins with a brief introduction to common measures of income inequality and poverty. Using these measures, we present some data on income inequality and poverty in Canada, highlighting recent trends. Following this, we develop a conceptual framework for thinking about income inequality, poverty, and the normative and positive aspects of government income redistribution policy. This framework is used in Chapter 12 to analyze major government programs for maintaining the incomes of the poor.

---

[1] As quoted in Crutsinger (2007).

DISTRIBUTION OF INCOME

There are several different measures of income inequality. Here, we examine three such indicators: the **Lorenz curve**, the **Gini coefficient**, and the income share of the richest 1 percent of the population.

First, we calculate the **total income** share of the poorest x percent of the population, where x ranges from 0 to 100 percent and total income includes receipts from non-government sources as well as cash transfers from the government. Then, in Figure 6.1, we trace out the cumulative income shares for 2011, yielding the curve *0ab*. This curve is commonly referred to as a Lorenz curve. From Figure 6.1, we see that in 2011 the poorest 20 percent of the population in Canada received 4 percent of total income, the poorest 60 percent 29 percent, and so on. The richest 20 percent received a 47.2 percent income share. Note that if income is distributed equally, the Lorenz curve coincides with the 45° line. The more unequal the distribution of income, the further away the Lorenz curve will lie from the diagonal.

The Lorenz curve is often used to compare the distribution of income over time or across countries. Figure 6.1, for example, shows a Lorenz curve for 2011 and 1980. A comparison of the two curves indicates that the distribution of income in Canada was more unequal in 2011 than in 1980, because the entire 2011 Lorenz curve lies further away from the 45° line than does the curve for 1980.[2, 3] While the richest 20 percent increased its share between 1980 and 2011, the income shares for the other four quintiles declined.

Another common measure of inequality is the Gini coefficient. If income is equally distributed across the population, the Gini coefficient equals 0, corresponding to a Lorenz curve that coincides with the 45° line. The Gini coefficient equals 1 if all income goes to one person.[4] The overall effect of government taxes and transfers in reducing inequality can be seen by comparing the Gini coefficient calculated using **market income** (receipts from employment, investment, retirement pensions, and other non-government sources) with the Gini coefficient based on **income after taxes and transfers**. This is done in Figure 6.2. In 2011, the Gini coefficient based on market income was 0.514 as compared to a Gini coefficient of 0.395 using income after taxes and transfers. Note that the extent to which inequality is reduced through the tax/transfer system does vary over time, as reflected in the variation in the gap between the two Gini coefficients shown in Figure 6.2.

FIGURE 6.1

THE LORENZ CURVE: INCOME INEQUALITY IN CANADA, 1980 AND 2011

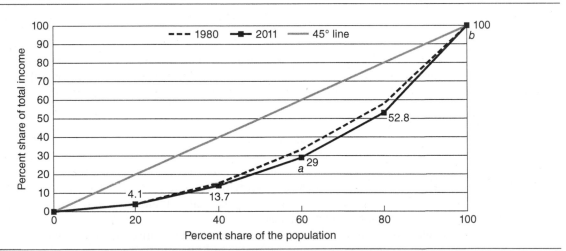

Source: Adapted from the Statistics Canada CANSIM II database http://cansim2.statcan.ca Table 202-0701.

---

[2] When comparing the distribution of income across time or across countries, ambiguities can arise if the Lorenz curves cross.

[3] See, for example, Saez and Veall (2005), Frenette et al. (2006), Veall (2012), and Osberg (2014) for a discussion on income inequality in Canada.

[4] The Gini coefficient is related to the Lorenz curve. In Figure 6.1, define the area above the 2011 Lorenz curve and below the 45° line as A and the area below this Lorenz curve as area B. The Gini coefficient for 2011 can be calculated as the ratio of area A to area (A + B).

FIGURE 6.2

THE GINI COEFFICIENT FOR CANADA (BASED ON MARKET INCOME AND INCOME AFTER TAXES AND TRANSFERS), 1980 TO 2011

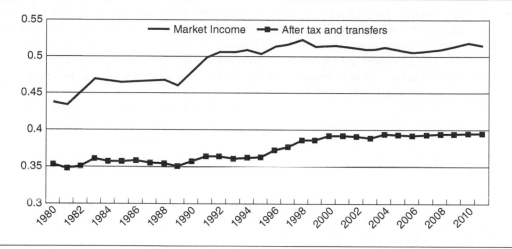

Source: Adapted from the Statistics Canada CANSIM II database http://cansim2.statcan.ca Table 202-0705.

FIGURE 6.3

INCOME SHARE OF TOP ONE PERCENT IN CANADA (1920–2010) AND THE UNITED STATES (1920–2012)*

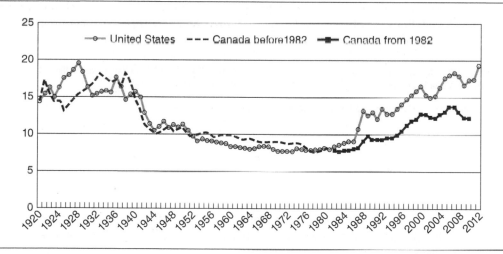

* There is a split in the Canadian data at 1982 reflecting differences in original data sources and methodology.

Source: World Top Incomes Database, retrieved November 19, 2014.

Finally, let's consider the income share of Canada's wealthiest individuals. Figure 6.3 shows the income share of the richest 1 percent for Canada and for the United States for the period from 1920 to 2011. Before 1980, the income share of the top 1 percent was similar in both countries and had been falling for many years. Since 1980, however, the income share of the top 1 percent in Canada has grown significantly. While not as dramatic as in the U.S., this growing gap between Canada's richest 1 percent and its bottom 99 percent is a subject that has received a great deal of attention (see the "In the News" box below).

IN THE NEWS

GROWING INCOME INEQUALITY IN CANADA

The growing gap between the richest 1 percent and everyone else was one of several concerns that spawned the Occupy movement and its protest demonstrations in Canada and in the United States in 2011. Since then, growing income inequality in Canada continues to attract a lot of attention. The release of a 2014 OECD report on top incomes prompted a flurry of newspaper articles discussing Canada's dubious honour as the worst country in the developed world in terms of its widening income gap between top earners and others in society.

Have government policies contributed to the growing income gap in Canada? Some commentators argue that significant cuts to government transfers in the 1990s and 2000s, particularly with respect to employment insurance and social assistance benefits, weakened the redistributive influence of government. Tax reforms, including cuts to top marginal tax rates, are also being scrutinized as a contributing factor. However, some economists are skeptical of the notion that increasing the top tax rates would do much to reduce inequality. Economist Michael Veall cautions that increasing tax rates on those with very high incomes may have adverse incentive effects and may not generate much extra tax revenue. Others, however, argue that refundable tax credits have played a role in improving incomes at the bottom end of the distribution.

What accounts for the increasing disparities in market income? Several possible explanations including globalization, skill-based technical change, and changes in executive compensation packages have all been proposed. Veall argues that the causal evidence for any of these explanations is not yet compelling. Instead, he argues that policies, such as public access to health care and education, that contribute to greater social mobility and help combat some of the negative consequences of income inequality should be prioritized. Economist Lars Osberg counters this view by arguing that Canada's education investment, while valuable for many reasons, has not yet restored the balance in income growth rates necessary for reducing income inequality in the longer term.

Despite the evidence of the widening gap between Canada's richest and poorest and the attention devoted to it, the questions of why income disparities exist and why they are increasing are far from settled.

Based on Davies (2013), Milligan and Osberg (2014), Veall (2012), Jackson (2014), and "Canadian income disparity growing: Income disparity in Canada among fastest growing in the OECD." *Maclean's*, April 30, 2014.

Complete references for this feature can be found in the References section on page 476.

POVERTY

People often focus on the economic position of the poor or those living in poverty in assessing whether income inequality is high or low, increasing or decreasing. **Poverty** can be defined as lacking sufficient resources to meet current needs. From a practical perspective, the difficulty lies in defining "sufficient" and "needs" since these are subjective terms.

Here, we present data on two measures of poverty. We consider the **low income rate**, defined as the percentage of a given population with low income and the **low income gap ratio**, a measure that attempts to capture the depth of poverty.

The low income rate is calculated by determining the percentage of a given population that falls below the **poverty line**, a fixed level of income considered enough to provide a minimally adequate standard of living. In Canada, the most widely used poverty lines are Statistics Canada's low income cut-off lines, commonly referred to as LICO.[5] (Statistics Canada does not refer to them as poverty lines, and they have no official status.)

---

[5] See Statistics Canada (2012) for the 2011 after-tax LICOs.

The low income cut-off lines are threshold levels of income. The thresholds are calculated by finding the income level such that an individual (or family) with that income is spending 20 percentage points more of after-tax income on food, shelter, and clothing than the average individual (or family). An individual with income below this level is deemed to have low income. Statistics Canada calculates threshold income levels for seven family sizes (ranging from 1 to 7+ members) and for different community sizes. For example, the low income cut-off for an unattached individual in 2011 living in an urban area with a population exceeding 500,000 was $19,307, and $12,629 if living in a rural area. For a family of four, it was $36,504 in a large urban area, and $23,879 in a rural area. While there is clearly some arbitrariness in determining what an adequate standard of living is, the notion of a poverty line still provides a useful benchmark.[6]

Figure 6.4 shows the percentage of the population that was below Statistics Canada's low income cut-off lines each year between 1980 and 2011. Overall, the low income rate has fallen from 11.6 percent in 1980 to 8.8 percent in 2011, although it tends to rise during recessions and fall when the economy is recovering. The incidence of poverty among two groups—the young and the old—is a special concern for most people. Figure 6.4 shows that the incidence of low incomes among children was higher than for the population as a whole up until 2008.[7] It rapidly increased over the first half of the 1990s, peaking at 18 percent in 1996. By 2011, the percentage of children living in low income had fallen to 8.5 percent, close to the low income rate for all persons. There has been a long-term decline in the proportion of elderly who are poor, from 21.4 percent in 1980 to 5.2 percent in 2011. Public and private pension benefits have contributed significantly to this decline.

Despite the progress that has been made in reducing the incidence of poverty, especially among the elderly and children, poverty rates for some groups remain high. For instance, the poverty rate among elderly individuals who live alone was 14.9 percent in 2011 as compared to the low income rate of 5.2 percent for all elderly. And for children in a female lone-parent family in 2011, the incidence of low income was 23 percent, more than 2.5 times the poverty rate for children overall.

Measuring the proportion of the population that is poor may obscure the severity of the poverty problem because a household is classified as poor whether it is $1 or $10,000 below the poverty line. One measure of the depth of poverty is the average low income gap ratio. The gap ratio is calculated as the difference in the LICO income and a person's actual income, expressed as a percentage of the LICO. The gap ratio is then averaged over

FIGURE 6.4

LOW INCOME RATES IN CANADA (IN PERCENT)

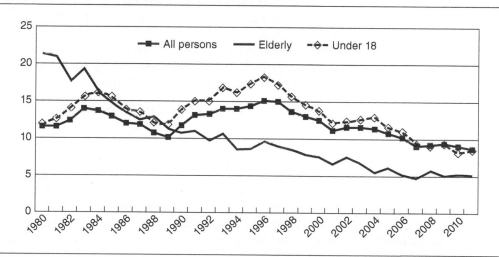

Source: Adapted from the Statistics Canada, CANSIM II database http://cansim2.statcan.ca/, Table 202-0802.

---

[6] Other poverty lines have been devised. Since 1991, for example, Statistics Canada has published before- and after-tax low income measures, based on 50 percent of the average economic family income with adjustments for the size of the family. See, for example, Statistics Canada (2009).

[7] Note that children with low incomes refers to children living in families with low income.

TABLE 6.1

Average Low Income Gap Ratio, 1980 and 2011 (in percent)

	1980	2011
All persons	34	33.3
Persons under age 18	34	24.9
Persons 65 years and over	22.8	18.1

Source: Adapted from the Statistics Canada, CANSIM II database http://cansim2.statcan.ca/ Table 202-0804.

all persons with low income. Table 6.1 shows the average low income gap ratio for all persons, for children, and for the elderly. For children in low income families, and to a lesser extent for elderly persons, the depth of poverty has fallen from 1980 to 2011.

INTREPRETING THE DATA

Data on the distribution of income, income inequality, and poverty receive an enormous amount of attention. It is important therefore to understand some of the conventions used to construct these figures, and their limitations.

The choice of income measure is important. The discussion above makes use of three different income measures: market income, total income, and income after taxes and transfers. Which measure you use depends on what you want to know. Market income is useful as it conveys information about how the market rewards factors of production. Total income provides an indication of income, regardless of source (labour income, investment income, or transfers from government). Finally, income after taxes and transfers is a useful measure of disposable income and the individual's potential to consume.

Some important sources of income are excluded from these data. In-kind transfers, payments made in commodities or services rather than in cash, are excluded from measured income but obviously affect an individual's standard of living. An important source of in-kind income that is excluded is the value of the time that adults devote to their households. Official data miss important differences in the levels of economic resources available to single-parent versus two-parent families, and between two-parent families with both parents working versus those with one parent at home. Gifts, inheritances, and the implicit rental income from owner-occupied housing are other forms of in-kind income that are not included in the Statistics Canada data.[8] The exclusion of these forms of income may understate the incomes received by some groups. (Chapter 17 provides a more detailed discussion of the definition and measurement of income).

The household unit. The data illustrated in Figure 6.1 are not adjusted for family size; both economic families and unattached individuals are included. Economic families are defined by Statistics Canada as a group of individuals sharing a common dwelling and related by blood, marriage (including common-law relationships), or adoption. Unattached individuals are either living alone or living in a household with other unrelated individuals. Comparing the standard of living of families and unattached individuals is challenging because, while families have to spread their income among several individuals, there can also be economies from living together, especially in the consumption of housing. To account for this, Statistics Canada also produces an adjusted after-tax income measure, calculated as total family after-tax income divided by the square root of the number of persons in the family. Obviously, adjusting family income for size is highly judgmental, but some adjustments should be made when we compare households of different sizes.

Time frame. The data in the figures refer to annual income, but it is not obvious what time frame should be used. A daily or weekly measure of income would be absurd, because even a rich individual could have zero

---

[8] A house provides its owner with a flow of housing services. The implicit rental income of these services is equal to the cost to the homeowner of renting a comparable dwelling.

income during some short time periods. It makes much more sense to measure the flow of income over a year, as is customarily done. However, even annual measures may not reflect an individual's true economic position. After all, there can be unexpected fluctuations in income from year to year. From a theoretical point of view, lifetime income would have advantages, but the practical problems in estimating it are enormous.

Although distinguishing between different time periods may seem a mere academic quibble, it is really quite important. People tend to have low incomes when they are young, higher incomes when they are middle-aged, and lower incomes again when they are old and in retirement. Therefore, people who have identical lifetime incomes but are in different stages of the life cycle can show up in the annual data as having unequal incomes. Measures of inequality based on annual income will indicate much more inequality than those constructed on the more appropriate lifetime basis.

Conclusions. The question of why there are large disparities in income has long occupied a central place in economics and is far from definitively settled. The most important reason for inequality in family incomes appears to be differences in the wages and salaries of the family heads; differences in property income (interest, dividends, etc.) account for only a relatively small proportion of overall income inequality. While very important, these observations do not explain income inequality. Why are there large differences in earnings? Earned income depends on items as diverse as physical strength, intelligence, effort, education, marriage decisions, the existence of race and sex discrimination, the presence of public welfare programs, and luck. Many economists believe that a key factor driving the increase in inequality in recent years is an increase in the financial returns from education—because of changes in technology, such as the widespread introduction of computers into the workplace, workers with university educations are now earning relatively more than their low-education counterparts.[9] But no single item can account for every case of poverty. As we see later, this fact has bedevilled attempts to formulate sensible policies for redistributing income.

RATIONALES FOR INCOME REDISTRIBUTION

There is a lot of controversy concerning whether, and to what extent, the government should undertake policies to change the distribution of income (and utilities). In this section, we present a conceptual framework that can be used to discuss some of the different views on the matter.

Before proceeding, we might ask whether government ought to be involved in changing the income distribution. Not everyone would agree with Plato's view, as expressed in the quotation at the beginning of the chapter. In Chapter 1, we discussed some important traditions of political philosophy which argue that government should play no redistributive role. But even the most minimal government action can influence income distribution. For example, when the government purchases materials for public goods, some firms receive contracts and others do not. Presumably the owners of the firms receiving the contracts enjoy increases in their relative incomes. Distributional issues are part and parcel of the government's functioning.

We might also ask whether economists should contribute to this discussion. Notions concerning the "right" income distribution are value judgments, and there is no "scientific" way to resolve differences in matters of ethics. Some argue that discussion of distributional issues is detrimental to objectivity in economics and that economists should restrict themselves to analyzing only the efficiency aspects of social issues. But, as emphasized in Chapter 2, the theory of welfare economics indicates that efficiency alone is not insufficient to rank all alternative allocations of resources; other criteria are needed. Moreover, decision makers care about the distributional implications of policy. If economists ignore distribution, then policy-makers will ignore economists. The economist who systematically takes distribution into account can keep policy-makers aware of both efficiency and distributional issues.

Utilitarianism

We introduced the concept of a social welfare function in Chapter 2. Here, we develop this concept more formally.

---

[9] There is debate about whether this explanation (derived mainly from U.S.-based studies) applies to Canada. See, for example, Burbidge, Magee, and Robb (2002) and Osberg (2008), (2014).

Conventional welfare economics posits that the welfare of society is defined by the well-being of its individual members. Algebraically, if there are n individuals in society and the ith individual's utility is U_i, then social welfare, W, is some function $F(\cdot)$ of individuals' utilities:[10]

$$W = F(U_1, U_2, \ldots, U_n) \tag{6.1}$$

It is assumed that an increase in any of the U_is, other things being the same, increases W. A change that makes someone better off without making anyone worse off increases social welfare.

Equation (6.1) is sometimes referred to as a **utilitarian social welfare function** because of its association with the utilitarian social philosophers of the nineteenth century.[11] Philosophers such as Jeremy Bentham and John Stuart Mill argued that public policies should be guided by the principle of the greatest good for the greatest number. This utilitarian maxim is usually interpreted by economists as implying a social welfare function that is simply the sum of individuals' utilities. It is referred to as an **additive social welfare function**:

$$W = U_1 + U_2 + \cdots + U_n \tag{6.2}$$

What does utilitarianism say about whether the government should redistribute income? The answer is straightforward but not terribly informative–redistribute income as long as it increases W. Alone, this social welfare function tells us little about the appropriate redistribution policy. However, strong results can be obtained if the following assumptions are made:

1. Individuals have identical utility functions that depend only on their incomes.
2. These utility functions exhibit diminishing marginal utility of income–as individuals' incomes increase, they become better off, but at a decreasing rate.
3. The total amount of income available to society is fixed.

Under these assumptions and given the additive social welfare function of Equation (6.2), the government should redistribute income so that *complete equality* is obtained.

To prove this, assume that the society consists of only two people, Peter and Paul. (It is easy to generalize the argument to cases where there are more people.)

In Figure 6.5, the horizontal distance ' measures the total amount of income available in society. Paul's income is measured by the distance to the right of point O; Peter's income is measured by the distance to the left of point O'. Thus, any point along OO' represents some distribution of income between Paul and Peter. The problem is to find the "best" point.

Paul's marginal utility of income is measured vertically, beginning at point O. Following assumption 2, the schedule relating Paul's marginal utility of income to his level of income is downward sloping. It is labelled MU_{Paul}. Peter's marginal utility of income is measured vertically, beginning at point O'. His marginal utility of income schedule is denoted MU_{Peter}. (Remember that movements to the left on the horizontal axis represent *increases* in Peter's income.) Because Peter and Paul have identical utility functions, MU_{Peter} is a mirror image of MU_{Paul}.

Assume that initially Paul's income is Oa and Peter's is $O'a$. Is social welfare as high as possible, or could the sum of utilities be increased if income were somehow redistributed between Paul and Peter? Suppose that ab dollars are taken from Peter and given to Paul. Obviously, this makes Peter worse off and Paul better off. However, the crucial question is what happens to the *sum* of their utilities. Because Peter is richer than Paul, Peter's loss in utility is smaller than Paul's gain, so the sum of their utilities goes up. Geometrically, the area under each person's marginal utility of income schedule measures the change in his utility induced by the income change. Distributing ab dollars to Paul increases his utility by area $abfe$. Taking the ab dollars from Peter decreases his utility by area $abdc$. The sum of their utility therefore increases by shaded area $cefd$.

Similar reasoning suggests that as long as incomes are unequal, marginal utilities will be unequal, and the *sum* of utilities can be increased by distributing income to the poorer individual. Only at point I^*, where incomes and marginal utilities are equal, is social welfare maximized. Full income equality should be pursued.

---

[10] This discussion ignores the problems that arise if the members of a society cannot agree on a social welfare function. See Chapter 7 under "Direct Democracy."

[11] Actually, the utilitarians postulated that social welfare was the sum of utilities, as in Equation (6.2), but the label is now often used to describe the more general formulation expressed in Equation (6.1).

FIGURE 6.5

MODEL OF THE OPTIMAL DISTRIBUTION OF INCOME: THE ADDITIVE SOCIAL
WELFARE FUNCTION

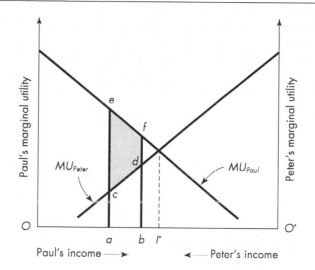

The policy implications of this result are breathtaking, so the assumptions behind it require scrutiny.

Assumption 1. It is fundamentally impossible to determine whether individuals have identical utility functions. It simply cannot be known whether individuals derive the same amount of satisfaction from the consumption of goods, because satisfaction cannot be objectively measured. There are, however, two possible defences for the assumption.

First, although it cannot be *proved* that people derive the same utility from equal amounts of income, it is a reasonable guess. After all, if people generally do not vary wildly in their observable characteristics—weight, height, and so on—why should their utility functions differ? Second, one can interpret the assumption not as a psychological statement, but as an *ethical* one. Specifically, in designing a redistributional policy, government ought to act *as if* all people have the same utility functions, whether they do or not.

Clearly, neither of these defences would convince a skeptic, and the assumption remains troublesome.

Assumption 2. A more technical, but equally important, objection concerns the assumption of decreasing marginal utility of income. While it may be that the marginal utility of any given *good* decreases with its consumption, it is not clear that this is true for *income* as a whole. In Figure 6.5, the results change drastically if the marginal utility of income schedules do not slope down. Suppose the marginal utility of income is instead constant at all levels of income. Then MU_{Peter} and MU_{Paul} are represented by an identical horizontal line. Whenever a dollar is taken from Peter, the loss in his utility is exactly equal to Paul's gain. Thus, the value of the sum of their utilities is independent of the income distribution. Government redistributive policy cannot change social welfare.

Assumption 3. By this assumption, the total amount of income in the society, distance OO', is fixed. The size of the pie does not change as the government redistributes its pieces. Suppose, however, that individuals' utilities depend not only on income, but also on leisure. Each individual chooses how much leisure to surrender (how much to work) to maximize his or her utility. Taxes and subsidies enacted to redistribute income generally change people's work decisions and diminish total real income. Thus, a society whose goal is to maximize the sum of utilities faces an inescapable dilemma. On one hand, it prefers to equalize the distribution of income. On the other hand, in doing so, it reduces the total amount of income available. The optimal income distribution must take into account the costs (in lost real income) of achieving more equality. Some studies suggest these costs may be substantial. Cushing and McGarvey (2003) analyzed a hypothetical program of cash transfers from high income to low income types. They estimate that the welfare losses for those who lose from the policy are 1.11 to 10.97 times greater than the gains to the beneficiaries.[12]

To consider how distortionary taxation affects the optimal income distribution, suppose that all income is earned by Peter and that a transfer to Paul is financed by a proportional income tax on Peter's income. In order to transfer more income to Paul, a higher tax rate has to be imposed on Peter, and it is assumed that the disincentive effects of the higher tax rate cause him to generate less income. As defined in Chapter 4, the marginal cost of public funds, MCF, measures the cost to a society in raising an additional dollar of tax revenue. With a distortionary tax system, the MCF will be greater than one. The optimal income distribution from a utilitarian perspective occurs where the gain to Paul from an additional dollar of transfers, MU_{Paul}, equals the cost imposed on Peter in raising that additional dollar, $MCF \times MU_{Peter}$, or in other words, where:[13]

$$\frac{MU_{Paul}}{MU_{Peter}} = MCF \tag{6.3}$$

Since the MCF is greater than one, MU_{Paul} is greater than MU_{Peter}, which means that Paul's income is less than Peter's income. The more the tax distorts Peter's decision to earn income, the greater the MCF, and the more inequality there will be with the optimal income distribution. Thus, even if we are willing to accept the assumption of identical utility functions and a utilitarian social welfare function, we cannot conclude that the goal of government distributional policy should be to obtain complete equality. The answer depends on the methods used to redistribute income and their effects on people's behaviour.

The Maximin Criterion

The form of the social welfare function plays a crucial role in determining the appropriate governmental redistribution policy. So far, we have examined the utilitarian social welfare function, according to which society is indifferent to the distribution of utilities.[14] If a unit of utility (or "util") is taken away from one individual and given to another, the sum of utilities is unchanged, and by definition, so is social welfare.

Other kinds of social welfare functions do not carry this implication, and hence yield different policy prescriptions. Consider the following social welfare function:

$$W = Minimum(U_1, U_2, \ldots, U_n) \tag{6.4}$$

Because the objective in Equation (6.4) is to maximize the utility of the person with the minimum or lowest level of utility, this social objective is often called the **maximin criterion** because the objective is to maximize the utility of the person with the minimum utility. The maximin criterion implies that the income distribution should be perfectly equal, *except* to the extent that departures from equality increase the welfare of the worst-off person. Consider a society with a rich person, Peter, who employs a poor person, Paul. The government levies a tax on Peter, and distributes the proceeds to Paul. However, when Peter is taxed, he cuts production and fires Paul. Moreover, the income that Paul receives from the government is less than his job-related income loss. In this hypothetical economy, satisfaction of the maximin criterion would still allow for income disparities.

Figure 6.6 illustrates the policy prescriptions for the distribution of income given the additive social welfare function described by Equation (6.2) and the maximin criterion given by Equation (6.4). Peter and Paul are assumed to have identical utility functions and the total income available in the economy is fixed. The utility possibilities curve, KL, is shown in both panel *a* and *b*. Along the 45° line, Peter and Paul would have equal utility (and equal incomes). We assume that the initial distribution of utilities absent government intervention is given by point *i*.

Panel *a* considers the optimal redistribution given the additive social welfare function. Society cares only about the sum of utilities and is indifferent to how a given sum of utilities is distributed between Peter and Paul. These preferences are illustrated using social indifference curves W_0 and W_1 in panel *a*. Since society views the two individuals' utilities as perfect substitutes, the social indifference curves are straight lines with a slope of -1. As discussed above, social welfare is highest at point *c* when incomes (and the resulting utility

---

[12] Research on this topic is still at a formative stage and there is debate on both methodology and interpretation. See Dahlby and Ruggeri (1996) and Browning (2002).

[13] See Dahlby (2008) for a comprehensive treatment of the theory and some applications of the MCF concept.

[14] Equation (6.2) does not imply that society is indifferent to the distribution of incomes, as was proved in the preceding section.

FIGURE 6.6

ALTERNATIVE SOCIAL WELFARE FUNCTIONS AND REDISTRIBUTION

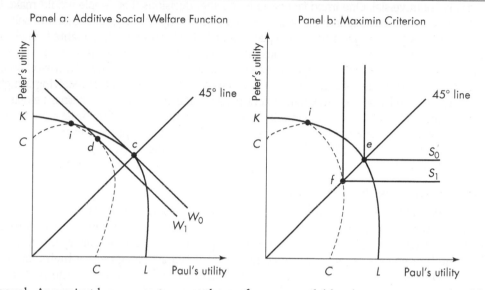

levels) are equal. Assuming lump-sum taxes and transfers are available, the government should redistribute income from Peter to Paul, moving the economy from point *i* to *c*.

In contrast, the utilities of Peter and Paul are not substitutable if society's preferences are captured by the maximin criterion. Any redistribution that reduces a rich person's utility and improves the utility of the least well-off individual, increases social welfare. These preferences are illustrated in panel *b* of Figure 6.6. When society cares only about the utility level of the least well-off individual, social indifference curves, as illustrated by S_0 and S_1, are at right angles to the 45° line. In this case, social welfare is maximized when Peter and Paul have identical utilities (and incomes). Again, assuming that lump-sum taxes and transfers are available, the government should redistribute income so as to achieve complete income (and utility) equality, moving the economy from point *i* to *e*.

So far, the conclusions for redistributive policy are identical; social welfare is highest when Peter and Paul have equal utilities (and income). But this is a special case. Consider what happens if redistribution distorts behaviour (relaxing our earlier assumption of fixed total income). Starting from the initial equilibrium, *CC* shows the combinations of utilities possible when taxes and transfers involve efficiency costs. Note that the curve CC lies inside the utility possibilities frontier. The tax-transfer mechanism used to redistribute income distorts individuals' behaviour, inducing them to work less. Thus, any allocation involving redistributive taxes will be inefficient and lie inside the frontier. Absent these costs, panel *a* shows society's welfare is highest when incomes and utilities are equal, but this allocation is no longer possible. Taking into account the efficiency costs associated with its redistributive policy, society's welfare is now maximized at point *d* where incomes and utility are no longer equal. Redistributive policy moves the economy from point *i* to *d*.[15]

CC is also shown in panel *b*. Here the results for the optimal distribution of income differ. Given the maximin criterion, society's welfare is maximized at point *f* where incomes and utility are equal. Although redistributive taxes and transfer involve efficiency costs, society is willing to incur these costs in order to improve the utility of the worst-off individual, moving the economy from point *i* to *f*.

The maximin criterion has received considerable attention, principally because of philosopher John Rawls' (1971) assertion that it has a special claim to ethical validity. Rawls argument relies on his notion of the **original position**, an imaginary situation in which people have no knowledge of what their place in society is to be. Because of this ignorance as to whether ultimately they will be rich or poor, Rawls believes that in the original position people's opinions concerning distributional goals are impartial and fair. Rawls then argues

---

[15] The CC curve is drawn assuming that when tax rates are relatively low, a higher tax rate generates more tax revenue, which leads to larger transfers. However, after some critical tax rate, tax revenues decline with further tax rate increases. Tax rates above this level make both individuals worse off, so the CC curve has a positive slope at tax rates above this critical level.

that, in the original position, people adopt the maximin social welfare function because of the insurance it provides against disastrous outcomes. People are frightened that they may end up at the bottom of the income distribution and therefore want the level at the bottom as high as possible.

Rawls' analysis is controversial. One important issue is whether decisions that people would make in the hypothetical original position have any superior claim to ethical validity. Why should the amoral and selfish views that individuals have in the original position be given special moral significance? Further, granted Rawls' view on the ethical validity of the original position, it is not obvious that rational self-interest would lead to the maximin criterion. Rawls' decision makers are so averse to risk that they are unwilling to take any chances. However, people might be willing to accept a small probability of being very poor in return for a good chance of receiving a high income.

Finally, critics have noted that the maximin criterion has some peculiar implications. Feldstein (1976: 84) considers the following scenario: "A new opportunity arises to raise the welfare of the least advantaged by a slight amount, but almost everyone else must be made substantially worse off, except for a few individuals who would become extremely wealthy." Because *all* that is relevant is the welfare of the worst-off person, the maximin criterion indicates that society should pursue this opportunity. Intuitively, however, such a course seems unappealing.

Pareto Efficient Income Redistribution

Our discussion of both additive and maximin social welfare functions assumes that redistribution makes some people better off and others worse off. Redistribution was never a Pareto improvement—a change that allowed all individuals to be at least as well off as under the status quo. This is a consequence of the assumption that each individual's utility depends on his or her income only. In contrast, imagine that high-income individuals are **altruistic**, so their utilities depend not only on their own incomes, but those of the poor as well. Under such circumstances, redistribution can actually be a Pareto improvement.

Assume that if (rich) Peter were to give a dollar of income to (poor) Paul, then Peter's increase in satisfaction from doing a good deed would outweigh the loss of his own consumption. At the same time, assume that Paul's utility would increase if he received the dollar. Both individuals would be made better off by the transfer. Indeed, efficiency requires that income be redistributed until Peter's gain in utility from giving a dollar to Paul just equals the loss in Peter's utility caused by lower consumption. Suppose that it is difficult for Peter to bring about the income transfer on his own, perhaps because he lacks enough information to know just who is really poor. Then, if the government costlessly does the transfer for Peter, efficiency is enhanced. In a formal sense, this is just an externality problem. Paul's behaviour (his consumption) affects Peter's welfare in a way that is external to the market. As is usual in such cases, government may be able to increase efficiency.

Pushing this line of reasoning to its logical extreme, the income distribution can be regarded as a public good, because everyone's utility is affected by the degree of inequality.[16] Suppose that each person would feel better off if the income distribution were more equal. No individual acting alone, however, is willing to transfer income to the poor because of the free-rider problem. If the government uses its coercive power to force *everyone* who is wealthy to redistribute income to the poor, economic efficiency increases.

Although altruism doubtless plays an important part in human behaviour, it does not follow that altruistic motives explain the majority of government income redistribution programs. This argument *assumes* that in the absence of coercion, people will contribute less than an efficient amount to the poor. Some argue, however, that if people really want to give to the poor, they do so—witness the millions of dollars in charitable contributions made each year.

There are other reasons self-interest might favour income redistribution. For one, there is always some chance that, through circumstances beyond your control, you will become poor. An income distribution policy is a bit like insurance. When you are well off, you pay "premiums" in the form of tax payments to those who are currently poor. If bad times hit, the "policy" pays off, and you receive relief. The idea that government should provide a safety net is an old one. The seventeenth-century political philosopher Thomas Hobbes (1963/1651: 303–4) noted, "And whereas many men, by *accident* become unable to maintain themselves by their labour; they ought not to be left to the charity of private persons; but to be provided for, as far forth as the necessities of nature require, by the laws of the Commonwealth" (emphasis added).

Finally, some believe that income distribution programs help purchase social stability. If poor people become *too* poor, they may engage in antisocial activities such as crime and rioting. The link between social

---

[16] See Thurow (1971).

stability and changes in income distribution is not totally clear, however. Improvement in the well-being of the poor may increase their aspirations and lead to demands for more radical change.

Nonindividualistic Views

The views of income distribution discussed so far have quite different implications, but they share a common characteristic. In each, social welfare is some function of individuals' utilities, and the properties of the optimal redistribution policy are *derived* from the social welfare function. Some thinkers have approached the problem by specifying what the income distribution should look like independent of individuals' tastes. As Fair (1971: 552) notes, Plato argued that in a good society the ratio of the richest to the poorest person's income should be at the most four to one. Others have suggested that as a first principle, incomes should be distributed equally.[17]

Other Considerations

The positions discussed earlier take for granted that individuals' incomes are common property that can be redistributed as "society" sees fit. No attention is given to the fairness of either the processes by which the initial income distribution is determined or of the procedures used to redistribute it. Some argue that a just distribution of income is defined by the *process* that generated it. For example, many believe that if "equal opportunity" (somehow defined) were available to all, then the ensuing outcome would be fair, *regardless* of the particular income distribution it happened to entail. Hence, if the process generating income is fair, there is no scope for government-sponsored income redistribution.

The philosopher Robert Nozick (1974) has attacked the use of social welfare functions to justify changes in the distribution of income. He argues that how "society" should redistribute its income is a meaningless question because "society" per se has no income to distribute. Only *people* receive income, and the sole possible justification for government redistributive activity is when the pattern of property holdings is somehow improper. Nozick's approach shifts emphasis from the search for a "good" social welfare function to a "good" set of rules to govern society's operation. The problem is how to evaluate social processes. It is hard to judge a process independent of the results generated. If a "good" set of rules consistently generates outcomes that are undesirable, how can the rules be considered good?

An alternative argument against the government undertaking redistribution policies is that, with sufficient social mobility, the distribution of income is of no particular ethical interest. Suppose that those at the bottom of the income distribution (or their children) occupy higher rungs on the economic ladder in future years. At the same time, some other people will move down, at least in relative terms. Then, even distributional statistics that remain relatively constant over time will conceal quite a bit of churning within the income distribution. Even if people at the bottom are quite poor, it may not be a major social problem if the people who are there change over time. For instance, Chen (2009) finds that 30 to 40 percent of the population in Canada moved *up* at least one income decile over a five-year period.

CASH VERSUS IN-KIND TRANSFERS

To this point, it has been assumed that cash transfers are made to the poor. However, many transfer programs involve either the provision or the subsidization of a specific commodity. In addition, many people support public education and health care programs because they think that these programs result in a more equitable distribution of well-being in our society. We will begin by considering the relative merits of cash and in-kind transfers when there is no uncertainty about who deserves a transfer.

Suppose Jones has income equal to Y. Let H be the quantity of housing consumed, measured in square metres, and p_H be the rental price for housing in dollars per square metre. The maximum amount of housing that Jones can consume is Y/p_H. Let C denote Jones's expenditure on the consumption of all other goods. In Figure 6.7, her budget line is AB, and she obtains the maximum utility by consuming H_1 units of housing and spending C_1 on all other goods. Jones is considered to be poor and deserving of a transfer.

Consider two policy options: an in-kind benefit in the form of a housing voucher, and a cash transfer. The housing voucher can be redeemed by the individual to obtain $\hat{H}$ square metres of housing. Jones could choose to spend all her income on other goods; her resulting consumption bundle is K. Alternatively, she could

---

[17] This view is considerably stronger than that of Rawls, who allows inequality as long as it raises the welfare of the worst-off individual.

FIGURE 6.7

CASH VERSUS IN-KIND TRANSFERS

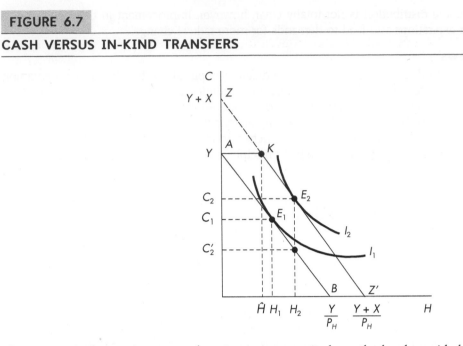

choose to spend some income on housing to increase it above the level provided by the voucher. Given this, Jones' new budget line can be presented as AKZ'. Suppose Jones maximizes her utility given the housing voucher by consuming at point E_2, increasing her consumption of housing from H_1 to H_2 and her expenditures on all other goods from C_1 to C_2. Note that Jones has decided to consume more housing than would be provided by the voucher alone.

In the absence of the voucher, if Jones had consumed H_2, she would only have been able to spend C'_2 on other goods. The fact that she can purchase C_2 instead of C'_2 means that the government is providing her with the additional purchasing power $C_2 - C'_2$. Therefore, the total cost of the housing voucher to the government is equal to $C_2 - C'_2$ or, equivalently, the vertical distance X.

Now suppose that, instead of the housing voucher, the government gave her the equivalent lump-sum cash subsidy X. This would increase her total income to $Y + X$, and her new budget line would be ZZ'. Note that this budget line will also go through the point E_2. Jones' preferred combination on ZZ' is point E_2, where the indifference curve I_2 is tangent to ZZ'.

In this instance the recipient is indifferent to whether the transfer takes the form of a housing voucher or a cash transfer. But this result depends on the individual's preferences and whether the amount of housing transferred with the voucher is greater than the amount of housing the individual prefers to consume. Figure 6.8 illustrates this possibility. The initial budget is AB and, given Jones' preferences, the initial consumption bundle is at E_1. The budget constraint with the housing voucher is AKZ'. The highest indifference curve that Jones can reach is I_2 (which touches the corner of the new budget constraint). She consumes at point K. As before, ZZ' represents the budget constraint for a cash transfer of a dollar amount equal to the housing voucher. With the cash transfer, Jones prefers to consume at E_3 where the budget line is tangent to the indifference curve I_3. In this case, the recipient prefers the cash transfer to the housing voucher; the housing voucher gives more housing than Jones would like to consume. Jones would prefer to trade some of the housing voucher for more spending on other goods but this is not possible. As a result, Jones values the housing voucher less than an equivalent dollar transfer.

Ultimately, whether an in-kind transfer is valued less than a direct cash transfer is an empirical question. One study estimates that a dollar received in food stamps (food vouchers) is worth about 80 cents received in cash (Whitmore, 2002). In-kind benefit programs may also involve higher administrative costs than an equivalent cash transfer. Blanchard et al. (1982: ii) estimated that the administrative costs of the U.S. food stamp program could be reduced by about 36 percent if beneficiaries simply received cheques instead of coupons redeemable for food.

If in-kind transfers are less satisfactory than lump-sum cash from the recipient's point of view and are administratively more costly, why are in-kind transfers so widely used? We consider four possible explanations: asymmetric information, commodity equalitarianism, paternalism, and political motivations.

FIGURE 6.8

AN IN-KIND TRANSFER THAT RESULTS IN A LOWER UTILITY LEVEL THAN A CASH TRANSFER

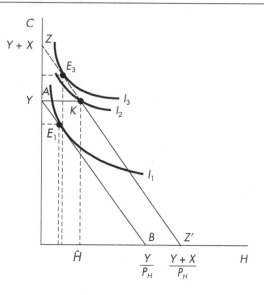

Asymmetric Information

First, consider the effect of imperfect information on the instruments that governments can use to improve the well-being of the poor. A government may have difficulty in distinguishing the "truly needy" who deserve a cash transfer from others who might try to take advantage of a cash transfer program by pretending to be needy. In these cases, an in-kind transfer may help to screen the truly needy from the pretenders. The following model, which is based on Blackorby and Donaldson (1988), illustrates how in-kind transfers can serve this purpose.

Suppose that a society consists of two individuals—Able, who is physically fit, and Bacchus, who has a back problem. For simplicity's sake, it is assumed that the marginal utility of consumption is constant and equal to one for both individuals. If both individuals have the same income, Able has a higher level of utility than Bacchus because Able can enjoy more physical activities than Bacchus. If Bacchus receives physiotherapy treatments, he can enjoy a wider range of physical activities and attain a higher level of utility. The individuals' utility functions are given below:

$$U_A = C_A + H \tag{6.5}$$

$$U_B = C_B + h \cdot T \tag{6.6}$$

C_A is Able's consumption of goods. H is the dollar value that Able attaches to being healthy, and the amount of money that Able would be prepared to spend to stay physically active. C_B is Bacchus's consumption of goods. T is the expenditure on Bacchus's therapy, and h is the marginal utility of a dollar spent on therapy. It is assumed that h is constant, but less than one. In other words, therapy improves Bacchus's well-being, but he would rather spend an additional dollar on consumption because the marginal utility of consumption is one. Let the total value of resources available to this society be R. It is assumed that R is fixed and that transferring income between the two individuals does not affect the amount of resources that are available; that is, there are no disincentive effects from taxes and transfers. The available resources can either be used to provide consumption for Able, consumption for Bacchus, or therapy for Bacchus. (Since Able does not have a bad back, he would never want to have therapy.) Therefore, $R = C_A + C_B + T$.

If society can identify those who have a bad back, it can give different lump-sum transfers to Able and Bacchus. The society's utility possibilities curve is the line *ad* shown in Figure 6.9. Along the utility possibilities curve *ad*, no resources are devoted to therapy because, given our assumption that h is less than one, providing Bacchus with a dollar of therapy is an inefficient way of raising Bacchus's utility. He would

FIGURE 6.9

CASH AND IN-KIND TRANSFERS UNDER ASYMMETRIC INFORMATION

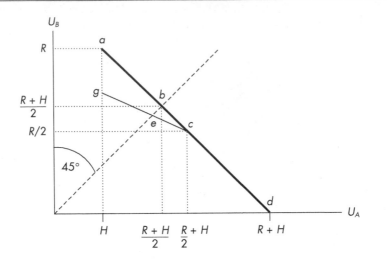

be better off with another dollar of income, which he would spend on the consumption of goods. Some particular points on the utility possibilities curve can be discerned. At a, all of the society's resources are used for Bacchus's consumption, and therefore, $U_B = R$ and $U_A = H$. At b, where the two individuals have the same utility level, Bacchus's income, $(R + H)/2$, exceeds Able's income, $(R - H)/2$, by the amount H. In other words, we equalize their utility levels by giving them unequal incomes. At c, both individuals receive the same income, $R/2$, but Able has a higher level of utility than Bacchus because he has good health. At d, all of the society's resources are devoted to Able's consumption. The preferred distribution of income will depend on the ethical preferences that are used to evaluate distributional issues. For example, given that there are no disincentive effects from income transfers and that the marginal utility of consumption is constant and the same for both individuals, a Rawlsian would choose the equal utility level at b, whereas a utilitarian would be indifferent as to how income was distributed. For a utilitarian, all points on ad are equally desirable because it has been assumed that the marginal utility of consumption is a constant and the same for both individuals. The key point, however, is that regardless of the ethical preferences, cash transfers would be used for redistribution and an in-kind transfer—therapy—would not be used.

Now suppose that we cannot distinguish between someone who has a bad back and someone who pretends to have a bad back. If income transfers were based on whether an individual had a bad back, Able would pretend to have a bad back if it meant that he would receive a higher income. Consequently, the maximum income that Bacchus can receive is $R/2$, the equal income point. We can't raise Bacchus's cash income above $R/2$ because then Able would pretend to have back pain so that he would qualify for a higher income, and this society does not have enough resources to provide both individuals with incomes in excess of $R/2$. On the other hand, Bacchus cannot pretend to be Able, and therefore society could provide Able with more income than Bacchus. This means that, given the asymmetric information problem, society's utility possibilities curve is cd if only lump-sum income transfers are used for redistribution.

Is it possible to raise Bacchus's utility level above $R/2$ by providing him with an in-kind transfer, in this case therapy? The answer is yes as long as a dollar spent on therapy raises Bacchus's utility by more than 0.5. To see this, suppose that, starting at point c, we reduce each individual's income by $0.50 and use the dollar to provide Bacchus with therapy free of charge. While Bacchus's consumption is reduced by 0.5, which reduces his utility by 0.5, he will be better off as long as the marginal utility from therapy, h, exceeds 0.5.[18] In Figure 6.9, it is

---

[18] More generally, the expenditure on therapy will raise the utility of individuals with back pain as long as h is greater than the fraction of the population with back pain.

assumed that $0.5 < h < 1$, and the line gc, which has a slope of $1 - 2h$, shows the utility combinations that can be achieved by providing an in-kind transfer—therapy—to anyone with back pain. The utility combinations along gc cannot be achieved without the in-kind transfer, and the points along gc are Pareto optimal. The preferred point on the utilities possibilities curve gcd will depend on one's ethical preferences. A utilitarian would continue to prefer any allocation along cd, whereas a Rawlsian would prefer the equal utility combination at e where H/h is spent on therapy.[19] The key point is that, with asymmetric information, in-kind transfers may be an efficient policy tool.

Commodity Egalitarianism

Tobin (1970) has suggested that only certain commodities should be distributed equally, a position sometimes called **commodity egalitarianism**. In some cases, this view has considerable appeal. Most people believe that the right to vote should be distributed equally to all, as should the consumption of certain essential foodstuffs during times of war. With cash subsidies, the government cannot ensure that commodities are distributed equally since recipients are free to spend their cash however they please. In-kind transfers can overcome this problem.

Some types of commodity egalitarianism are more controversial than, for example, the right to vote. Should all Canadian children consume the same quality of primary school education? Should everyone receive the same type of health care, or should the rich be able to purchase better quality care? Clearly, limiting the range of the "special" commodities is a difficult problem.

Paternalism

A paternalistic attitude toward the poor, a position that in some cases resembles commodity egalitarianism, can provide a rationale for in-kind transfers within the framework of conventional welfare economics. Assume that Henry cares about Catherine's welfare. Specifically, Henry's utility depends on his own income as well as Catherine's level of *food consumption*, as opposed to her *income*. (This might be due to the fact that Henry does not approve of the other commodities Catherine might consume.) In effect, then, Catherine's food consumption generates a positive externality. Following the logic developed in Chapter 5 on externalities, efficiency may be enhanced if Catherine's food consumption is subsidized, or perhaps if food is provided to her directly. In short, when donors care about recipients' consumption of certain commodities, a policy of redistributing income via these commodities can be viewed as an attempt to correct an externality.

Political Motivations

In-kind transfers may also be attractive politically because they help not only the beneficiary but also the producers of the favoured commodity. A transfer program that increases the demand for housing benefits the building industry, which therefore becomes willing to lend its support to a political coalition in favour of the program. In the same way, the public employees who administer the various in-kind transfer programs can be expected to put their political support behind them. These explanations for in-kind transfers are not mutually exclusive, and they have probably all influenced policy design.

CONCLUSION

This chapter surveys a wide range of opinions concerning whether the government should adopt explicit policies to redistribute income. These views run the gamut from engineering complete equality to doing nothing. The scope of disagreement is not surprising. Setting a distributional objective is no less than formalizing one's views of what a good society should look like, and this is bound to be controversial. Theories on optimal income distribution are normative rather than positive. Actual government policies may be guided by a number of these considerations, but it is not obvious that this is the case. On the whole, we did see that government taxes and transfers reduced income inequality.

---

[19] If utility is equalized, $C_A + H = C_B + hT$, along gc, the individuals have equal incomes so that $C_A = C_B$. Therefore, hT will equal H at e. In other words, at e the individuals will have the same consumption of goods and the same health status.

The chapter also introduced some common indicators of income inequality and poverty. Recent trends show that income inequality has risen in Canada since 1980. We stressed some of the difficulties involved in measuring income accurately and in defining the appropriate time period over which it should be measured. Many important types of income are ignored because of measurement difficulties. Transfers often take the form of in-kind payments on which it is difficult to put a dollar value. There is a widely held view among economists that in-kind transfers are less efficient than cash transfers, but in-kind transfers may be efficient policy instruments if it is difficult to identify the needy or if one does not accept the individuals' preferences as the basis for making transfers.

SUMMARY

- The Lorenz curve, the Gini coefficient, and the income share of the top 1 percent are indicators of income inequality and are sometimes used to compare income inequality over time, across countries, or before and after government taxes and transfers.

- Recent trends indicate that the distribution of income in Canada has become more unequal since 1980.

- The low income rate, a measure of poverty, is calculated as the percentage of a given population with income below a certain threshold income level. A measure of the depth of poverty is the average low income gap ratio for a given population.

- Measuring income inequality and poverty is difficult because income is hard to measure correctly. Some forms of income, such as the implicit rental income from owner-occupied housing, are not included in the official statistics. It is not clear what time period—month, year, lifetime—or what unit of observation—individual, household, family—is appropriate.

- Economists analyze distributional issues to determine the consequences of alternative distributional policies and to draw out the implications of various ethical goals.

- If (1) social welfare is the sum of identical utility functions that depend only on income, (2) there is decreasing marginal utility of income, and (3) the total amount of income is fixed, then income should be equally distributed. These are quite strong assumptions, and weakening them gives radically different results.

- The maximin criterion states that the best income distribution maximizes the utility of the person who has the lowest utility. The ethical validity of this proposition is controversial.

- The income distribution may be like a public good—everyone derives utility from the fact that income is equitably distributed, but government coercion is needed to accomplish redistribution. Pareto efficient redistribution occurs when no one is made worse off as a result of a transfer.

- There are other views of income distribution. Some believe it is a first principle that income, or at least certain goods, be distributed equally. Others argue that the distribution of income is irrelevant as long as the distribution arises from a "fair" process.

- Many government programs provide goods and services directly (in-kind transfers) instead of cash. The value of the in-kind transfer to the recipient will often be less than the market price.

- The prevalence of in-kind transfer programs may be due to asymmetric information, paternalism, commodity egalitarianism, or political attractiveness.

EXERCISES

1. Are the concepts of fairness and equality in the distribution of income synonymous? To what extent is income inequality consistent with fairness? What are the implications of your answer for government expenditure policy?

2. The table below shows the income shares by quintile for Canada in 2011 for different income measures.

Income Quintile	Market Income (Before taxes and transfers)	Total Income (Before taxes and after transfers)	After-tax Income (After transfers)
Lowest quintile	1.0	4.1	4.8
Second quintile	7.2	9.6	10.6
Third quintile	14.6	15.3	16.3
Fourth quintile	24.9	23.8	24.1
Highest quintile	52.3	47.2	44.3

Source: Statistics Canada CANSIM II database http://cansim2.statcan.ca/ Table 202-0701.

a. Calculate the cumulative income shares for all three income measures.

b. Draw the Lorenz curve for each income concept using an Excel spreadsheet or by sketching a graph. According to the data, what contributes more to reducing income inequality in Canada—transfers or taxes? Discuss.

c. Suppose instead of calculating income shares and drawing the Lorenz curves, as above, you use the Gini coefficient to determine the effect of government taxes and transfers on income inequality (for 2011, the Gini coefficient was 0.514 based on market income and 0.395 based on income after taxes and transfers). Briefly discuss the advantages (or disadvantages) of using this approach rather than the Lorenz curve approach to measuring the effect of government policies on income inequality.

3. "I don't care how rich the very rich are. I care if they became rich in an unethical way, or if they use their riches in a particularly vulgar or revolting way. . . . I wouldn't mind if they lost [their wealth] or had it taxed away. But I do find poverty of the very poor unlovely. . . . That condition deserves, in my opinion, our most intensive care. I believe that the present focus on inequality of income diverts national attention from it." (Stein, 1996: A14). Do you agree with this statement? Is it consistent with utilitarianism?

4. "Mobility should play a bigger role in our thinking about poverty. The current standard, preoccupied with income snapshots, only echoes the current welfare formula, with its emphasis on supporting people in poverty rather than helping them to get out" (Jenkins, 1992: A10). Do you agree with this statement? In your answer, discuss how the quote relates to utilitarian criteria for evaluating government distributional problems and to the difficulties present in official statistics on the poverty rate.

5. Suppose there are only two people, Simon and Charity, who must split a fixed income of $100. For Simon, the marginal utility of income is

$$MU_S = 400 - 2I_S$$

whereas for Charity, marginal utility is

$$MU_c = 400 - 6I_c$$

Ic and *Is* are the amounts of income to Charity and Simon, respectively.

a. What is the optimal distribution of income if the social welfare function is additive?

b. What is the optimal distribution if society values only the utility of Charity? What if the reverse is true? Comment on your answers.

c. Finally, comment on how your answers change if the marginal utility of income for both Simon and Charity is constant:

$$MUc = 400$$

$$MUs = 400$$

6.* The economy consists of Will and Grace. They have identical utility functions $U = 100(y_i)^{0.5}$ where the marginal utility of income function is $MU = 50(y_i)^{-0.5}$. The total income available in the economy is fixed and equal to $20,000.

  a. Use an Excel spreadsheet to graph the utilities possibility curve for the economy.

  b. What is the welfare maximizing distribution of income if the social welfare function is $W = U^W + U^G$? What do the social indifference curves look like in this case?

  c. What is the welfare maximizing distribution of income if the social welfare function is $W = min[U^W, U^G]$? What do the social indifference curves look like in this case?

  d. Suppose that Will and Grace do not have identical utility functions. Instead, assume that Will's utility function is $U^W = 200(y_W)^{0.5}$ where marginal utility is given by $MU^W = 100(y_W)^{-0.5}$. Grace's utility is as above. Draw the new utility possibilities curve. What distribution of income maximizes social welfare when the social welfare function is $W = U^W + U^G$? Does the answer change if the social welfare function is given as $W = min[U^W, U^G]$?

7.* Will and Grace are the only two people in the economy. Will's utility is given by $U^W = 100(y_W)^{0.5}$ while Grace's utility depends not only on her own income but also on Will's utility. Her utility function is $U^G = 100(y_G)^{0.5} + 0.8U^W$. The total income available in the economy is fixed and equal to $20,000. If Will and Grace have incomes of $4,000 and $16,000, respectively, what happens to each person's utility if $1,000 is taken from Grace and given to Will? Would Grace undertake the redistribution voluntarily? Explain. If the initial incomes were reversed, would Grace be willing to give up $1,000 to Will? Explain how the concept of Pareto redistribution is relevant here?

8. Philip's demand curve for housing is shown in the figure. (Assume that quantity of housing is measured simply by the number of square metres. Other aspects of quality are ignored.) The market price of housing is P_i; Philip can purchase as much housing as he desires at that price. Alternatively, Philip can live in public housing for a price of P_2 per square metre, but the only apartment available to him has H_2 square metres. Will Philip choose public housing or rent on the private market? Explain carefully. (*Hint:* Compare consumer surplus—see the appendix to Chapter 2—under both possibilities.)

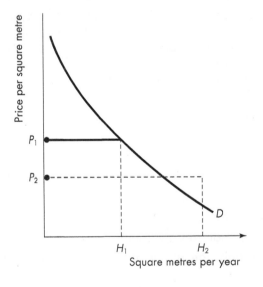

9. An economy consists of two individuals, Lynne and Jonathan, with identical utility functions given by U_L and U_J, respectively. Each individual's utility is assumed to depend only on income.

   a. Suppose that the social welfare function is $W = U_L + U_J$. True or False (explain): Society is indifferent between giving a dollar to Lynne and a dollar to Jonathan.

   b. Now suppose that, instead, the social welfare function is $W = U_L + 8U_J$. True or False (explain): Society values Jonathan's happiness more than Lynne's.

   c. Finally, suppose that the social welfare function is $W = min\ [U_L, U_J]$. True or False (explain): In this society, the optimal distribution of income is complete equality.

PART THREE
Political Economy

This section examines some of the political and constitutional issues that affect public finance in Canada. Decisions made within national or regional jurisdictions may appear complex and, at times, inconsistent. In Chapter 7, on "public choice," we apply economic principles to the understanding of political decision-making. Our discussion examines how "direct democracy" may translate the preferences of voters into collective action, and how governments may behave where "representative democracy" exists. We also offer some possible explanations for the rapid growth of government during the twentieth century and briefly discuss steps that may affect public sector growth.

Canada has one of the most decentralized systems of government in the world. Fiscal federalism, discussed in Chapter 8, is a key aspect of Canadian public finance. Other important federal systems include those of the United States, India, Australia, Brazil, Switzerland, and Germany. The allocation of responsibilities among levels of government in federal systems—with significant responsibilities at the provincial or state level—permits differences in tax and expenditure policies from region to region.

In Canada, with its heterogeneous regions in terms of geography and population characteristics, the case for, and benefits from, a federal system of government may be particularly important. We discuss the advantages and disadvantages of decentralizing revenue raising and program expenditure responsibilities in a country such as Canada. In Chapter 8, we also examine the differing effects of matching (conditional) and non-matching (unconditional) grants made by one level of government to another. Grants from the federal to the provincial governments, and from provincial to local governments, are very important in Canada.

CHAPTER 7

Public Choice

Politics is the skilled use of blunt objects.

—Lester B. Pearson

Textbook discussions of market failures and their remedies tend to convey a rather rosy view of government. With a tax here and an expenditure there, the state readily corrects all market imperfections, meanwhile seeing to it that incomes are distributed in an ethically desirable way. Such a view is at variance with apparent widespread public dissatisfaction with government performance. In a 2015 opinion poll, only 42 percent of Canadians place some trust in political parties, and 62 percent feel politicians only want their vote.[1] Humourist P. J. O'Rourke probably summarized the sentiments of many when he quipped, "Feeling good about government is like looking on the bright side of a catastrophe. When you quit looking on the bright side, the catastrophe is still there."

Perhaps this is merely gratuitous whining. As a matter of definition, in a democracy we get the government we want. Another possibility, however, is that it is inherently difficult for even democratically elected governments to respond to the public interest. This chapter applies economic principles to the understanding of political decision-making, a field known as **public choice**. Public choice models assume that individuals view government as a mechanism for maximizing their well-being. Two points are important regarding this assumption:

- Selfishness does not necessarily lead to inefficient outcomes. As we saw in Chapter 2, under certain conditions the marketplace harnesses self-interest to serve a social end. The question is, "What, if anything, performs that role in the 'political market'?"

- While the maximization assumption may not be totally accurate, just as in more conventional economic settings, it provides a good starting point for analysis.

At the outset, we examine direct democracies and how well they translate the preferences of their members into collective action. We then turn to the complications that arise when decisions are made not by the citizens themselves, but by their elected representatives.

---

[1] "CBC asks: Many Canadians distrustful of federal politics," CBC.ca, March 25, 2015.

DIRECT DEMOCRACY

In democratic societies, various voting procedures are used to decide what quantities of public goods to provide. This section looks at some of these procedures.

Unanimity Rules

Recall from Chapter 4 how the free-rider problem can lead to a disturbing situation—because people are selfish, public goods are under-provided, even though everyone could be made better off if they were provided in efficient amounts. This suggests that, in principle, if a vote were taken on whether to provide the good in an efficient quantity, consent would be unanimous as long as there was a suitable tax system to finance it. A procedure designed to elicit such unanimous agreement was proposed in the early twentieth century by Lindahl (1919, 1958).

To understand Lindahl's procedure, assume again there are two individuals, Adam and Eve, and one public good, rockets for fireworks (r). Suppose Adam is told that his share of the cost of rocket provision will be 30 percent. Then, if the market price per rocket is P_r, Adam's price per rocket is $0.30 \times P_r$. Given this price, the prices of other goods, his tastes, and his income, there is some quantity of rockets that Adam will want to consume. More generally, let S_A denote Adam's share of the cost of rocket provision. For any particular value of S_A, Adam demands some quantity of rockets. As his tax share increases and rockets become more expensive for him, he demands a smaller quantity.

In Figure 7.1, the horizontal axis measures the quantity of rockets. Adam's tax share is measured by the vertical distance from point O. The curve D_r^A shows how the quantity of rockets demanded by Adam decreases as his tax share increases.

In the same way, define S^E as Eve's share of the cost of rockets. (By definition, $S^A + S^E = 1$.) When S^E goes up, the quantity demanded by Eve decreases. In Figure 7.1, Eve's tax share increases as we move down along the vertical axis from O'. (Thus, the distance OO' is 1.) Her demand schedule is denoted D_r^E. It slopes upward because upward movements along the vertical axis represent a lower price to her.

An obvious similarity exists between the role of tax shares in the Lindahl model and market prices in the usual theory of demand. But there is an important difference. Instead of each individual facing the same price, each faces a personalized price per unit of public good, which depends on his or her tax share. The tax shares are referred to as **Lindahl prices**.

An equilibrium is a set of Lindahl prices such that at those prices each person votes for the same quantity of the public good. In Figure 7.1, this occurs when Adam's tax share is OS^* and Eve's tax share is $O'S^*$. At these Lindahl prices, both parties agree that r^* rockets should be provided.

FIGURE 7.1

LINDAHL'S MODEL

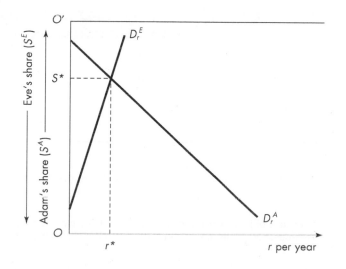

Feasibility of unanimity rules. The Lindahl model shows the tax shares and level of public good provision that are agreeable to all members of society. The big question is how the economy reaches the equilibrium. Imagine that an auctioneer announces some initial set of tax shares. On the basis of their respective demand schedules, Adam and Eve vote for the number of rockets they want. If agreement is not unanimous, the auctioneer announces another set of tax shares. The process continues until Adam and Eve unanimously agree on the quantity of rockets ($r*$, in Figure 7.1). The determination of the quantity of public goods, then, is quite similar to the market process. Like the market outcome, it can be shown that the allocation is Pareto efficient.[2]

As a practical method for providing public goods, Lindahl's procedure has two main problems. First, it assumes people vote sincerely. If Adam can guess the maximum amount that Eve would spend for rockets rather than do without them, he can try to force her to that allocation. Eve has the same incentives. Strategic behaviour may prevent Adam and Eve from reaching the Lindahl equilibrium.

Second, finding the mutually agreeable tax shares may take a lot of time. In this example, there are only two parties. In most important cases, many people are likely to be involved. Getting everyone to agree involves enormous decision-making costs. Indeed, although unanimity rules guarantee that no one will be "exploited," they often lead to situations in which *no* decisions are made. Historically, when organizations adopted a unanimity rule, it was often expressly because the participants wanted to make sure that no actions were taken![3]

Majority Voting Rules

Because unanimity is difficult to attain, voting systems not requiring unanimity may be desirable. With a **majority voting rule**, one more than half of the voters must favour a measure for it to be approved.

Although the mechanics of majority voting are familiar, it is useful to review them carefully. Consider a community with three voters, Denise, Rudy, and Theo, who have to choose among three levels of missile provision, A, B, and C. Level A is small, level B is moderate, and level C is large. The voters' preferences are depicted in Table 7.1. Each column shows how the voter ranks the choices. For example, Rudy most prefers level C, but given a choice between B and A, would prefer B.

Suppose an election were held on whether to adopt A or B. Denise would vote for A, while Rudy and Theo would vote for B. Hence, B would win by a vote of 2 to 1. Similarly, if an election were held between B and C, B would win by a vote of 2 to 1. Level B wins any election against its opposition, and thus is the option selected by majority rule. Note that the selection of B is independent of the order in which the votes are taken.

Majority decision rules do not always yield such clear-cut results. Suppose the preferences for various levels of missile provision are as depicted in Table 7.2. Again, imagine a series of paired elections to determine the most preferred level. In an election between A and B, A would win by a vote of 2 to 1. If an election were held between B and C, B would win by a vote of 2 to 1. Finally, in an election between A and C, C would

TABLE 7.1			
Voter Preferences That Lead to an Equilibrium			
		Voter	
Choice	Denise	Rudy	Theo
First	A	C	B
Second	B	B	C
Third	C	A	A

---

[2] Intuitively, assume $P_a = 1$. Then Eve sets $S^E P_r = MRS_{ra}^{Eve}$, and Adam sets $S^A P_r = MRS_{ra}^{Adam}$. Therefore, $MRS_{ra}^{Eve} + MRS_{ra}^{Adam} = S^E P_r + S^A P_r = P_r(S^E + S^A) = P_r$. But P_r represents MRT_{ra}, so $MRS_{ra}^{Eve} + MRS_{ra}^{Adam} = MRT_{ra}$, which is the necessary condition for Pareto efficiency with a public good in Equation (4.2).

[3] In seventeenth-century Poland, the structure of government was essentially feudal. None of the nobles wanted to lose any power to the monarch. Hence, the monarch had to promise to take no action unless he received the unanimous consent of the Polish parliament (see Massie, 1980: 228).

TABLE 7.2

Voter Preferences That Lead to Cycling			
	Voter		
Choice	**Denise**	**Rudy**	**Theo**
First	A	C	B
Second	B	A	C
Third	C	B	A

win by the same margin. This is a disconcerting result. The first election suggests that *A* is preferred to *B*; the second that *B* is preferred to *C*. Conventional notions of consistency suggest that *A* should therefore be preferred to *C*. But in the third election, just the opposite occurs. Although each individual voter's preferences are consistent, the community's are not. This phenomenon is referred to as the **voting paradox**.

Moreover, with the preferences in Table 7.2, the ultimate outcome depends crucially on the order in which the votes are taken. If the first election is between propositions *A* and *B* and the winner (*A*) runs against *C*, then *C* is the ultimate choice. On the other hand, if the first election is *B* versus *C*, and the winner (*B*) runs against *A*, then *A* is chosen. Under such circumstances, the ability to control the order of voting–the agenda–confers great power. **Agenda manipulation** is the process of organizing the order of votes to assure a favourable outcome.

A related problem is that paired voting can go on forever without reaching a decision. After the election between *A* and *B*, *A* wins. If *C* challenges *A*, then *C* wins. If *B* then challenges *C*, *B* wins. The process can continue indefinitely, a phenomenon called **cycling**. Many important historical cases of cycling have been identified. A good example concerns legislation on abortion in Canada. Bill C-43, proposed by the Conservative government of Brian Mulroney in 1989, made abortion illegal except when pregnancy threatened the life or health of the woman. Since "health" was defined broadly to mean "physical, mental, and psychological health," the bill was viewed as a compromise between pro-life and pro-choice positions. As political scientist Thomas Flanagan explains, "Unwillingness of the extreme blocks, particularly the pro-lifers, to support a compromise turned the situation into a cycle in which any option could be defeated by a coalition of two out of the three blocks" (Flanagan, 1998: 138). Consequently, no new abortion legislation was passed, "even though majorities in both chambers disliked the status quo and wished to legislate."

Clearly, the majority rule does not have to suffer from these problems. After all, the elections associated with Table 7.1 went smoothly. Why the difference? It turns on the structure of individual preferences for various levels of missile procurement. Consider again the people in Table 7.2. Because Denise prefers *A* to *B* to *C*, it follows that *A* gives Denise more utility than *B*, and *B* more than *C*. The schedule denoted Denise in Figure 7.2 depicts this relationship. The schedules labelled Rudy and Theo do the same for the other voters.

We define a **peak** in an individual's preferences as a point at which all the neighbouring points are lower.[4] A voter has **single-peaked preferences** if, as she moves away from her most preferred outcome in any and all directions, her utility consistently falls. She has **double-peaked preferences** if, as she moves away from the most preferred outcome, utility goes down, but then goes up again. Thus, Denise has a single peak at point *A*, Theo has a single peak at point *B*, and Rudy has two peaks: one at *A* and one at *C*. It turns out that Rudy's preferences are the ones that lead to the voting paradox. If Rudy had *any* set of single-peaked preferences, majority voting would lead to a consistent decision. This is why no voting paradox emerges from Table 7.1. There, each voter has single-peaked preferences. More generally, if all voters' preferences are single peaked, no voting paradox occurs.

Because multipeaked preferences can throw a wrench into majority voting, it is important to know whether they are likely to be important as a practical matter. Consider again Rudy's two-peaked preferences in Table 7.2. He prefers either very large or very small missile expenditures to a quantity in the middle. Although such preferences are not necessarily irrational, they do seem a bit peculiar. Perhaps Rudy believes that moderate numbers of missiles will provide little if any real protection so that unless expenditures are large they might as well be close to nothing.

---

[4] The absolute amount of utility associated with each alternative is irrelevant. The vertical distances could change, but as long as the pattern of peaks stays unchanged, so does the election's outcome.

FIGURE 7.2

GRAPHING THE PREFERENCES FROM TABLE 7.2

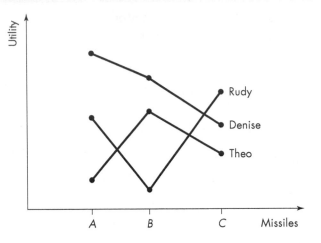

Suppose, however, that instead of missiles, voters are choosing among expenditure levels for a public park–a good for which there are private substitutes. Assume that in the presence of small or medium public park expenditures, voter Vince will join a private country club, but given large expenditures, he will use the public park. If Vince's tax burden increases with park expenditure, he prefers a small to a medium park. Since he will not use these parks, neither of these options benefits Vince, and he prefers the one with the smaller tax burden. But his most preferred outcome might be the large-expenditure public park, depending in part on the associated tax burden compared to the country club membership fee. In short, Vince may prefer either the small or large public park to the medium-sized one. Thus, when there are private substitutes for a publicly provided good, a multipeaked pattern like Rudy's in Figure 7.2 can easily emerge.

Moreover, when issues are not based on a single dimension, multipeaked preferences are also a serious possibility. Suppose that a community is trying to decide how to use a vacant building. Choice *A* is an abortion clinic, choice *B* is an adult book store, and choice *C* is an armed forces recruitment office. Unlike the choice between different levels of missile expenditure, here the alternatives do not represent more or less of a single characteristic. It is easy to imagine multipeaked preferences emerging.

The median voter theorem. Let us now return to the simple case in which all alternatives being considered represent smaller or greater amounts of a single characteristic. People rank each alternative on the basis of this single characteristic. An example is how much of some public good to acquire. Define the **median voter** as the voter whose preferences lie in the middle of the set of all voters' preferences; half the voters want more of the good than the median voter, and half want less. The **median voter theorem** states that as long as all preferences are single peaked, the outcome of majority voting reflects the preferences of the median voter. (With an even number of voters, there may be a tie between two median voters, which must be broken arbitrarily.)

To demonstrate the median voter theorem, assume there are five voters: Donald, Daisy, Huey, Dewey, and Louie. They are deciding how large a party to give together, and each of them has single-peaked preferences for party sizes. The most preferred level for each voter is noted in Table 7.3. *Because preferences are single peaked, the closer an expenditure level is to a given voter's peak, the more he or she prefers it.* A movement from zero party expenditure to $5 would be preferred to no money for parties by all voters. A movement from $5 to $100 would be approved by Daisy, Huey, Dewey, and Louie, and from $100 to $150 by Huey, Dewey, and Louie. Any increase beyond $150 would, however, be blocked by at least three voters: Donald, Daisy, and Huey. Hence, the majority votes for $150. But this is just the amount preferred by Huey, the median voter. The election results mirror the median voter's preferences.

To summarize; when all preferences are single peaked, majority voting yields a stable result, and the choice selected reflects the preferences of the median voter. However, when some voters' preferences are multipeaked,

TABLE 7.3

Preferred Level of Party Expenditure	
Voter	**Expenditure**
Donald	$ 5
Daisy	100
Huey	150
Dewey	160
Louie	700

a voting paradox may emerge.[5] Because multipeaked preferences may be important in many realistic situations, majority voting cannot be depended on to yield consistent public choices. Moreover, as we shall see below, even when majority voting leads to consistent decisions, it may not be efficient in the sense that the net benefits of government action are maximized.

Majority Voting on the Quantity of a Public Good

If the requirements for the median voter rule are satisfied in a direct vote over the quantity of a public good, will the expenditure level that is most preferred by the median voter actually satisfy the efficiency condition described by Equation (4.3) in Chapter 4?

Figure 7.3 depicts the demand curves of Adam, Eve, and Theo for fireworks rockets. As in Chapter 4, the efficient quantity of rockets is determined by the intersection of the group demand curve D_r^{A+E+T} and the marginal cost. In Figure 7.3, the marginal cost is assumed to be constant at $6 and thus the efficient quantity is 60 rockets.

Imagine for now that Adam, Eve, and Theo will split the cost of each rocket equally—that is, each person pays $2 per rocket. In that case, Eve's preferred quantity is 60 rockets. At any quantity less than 60, Eve's

FIGURE 7.3

VOTING ON THE QUANTITY OF A PUBLIC GOOD

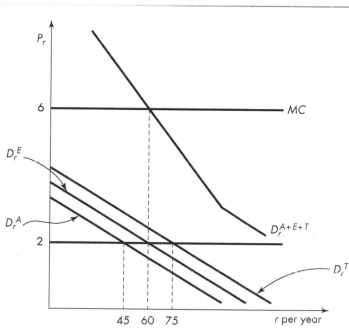

marginal benefit from an extra rocket exceeds her personal marginal cost of $2 per rocket and she prefers more rockets. At any quantity greater than 60 rockets, Eve's marginal benefit is less than $2 and she prefers fewer rockets. Using the same reasoning, we can infer that Adam's best choice is 45 rockets and Theo's is 75 rockets.

If an election is used to choose 60 or 75 rockets, both Adam and Eve would vote for 60 rockets and only Theo would vote for 75. Similarly, if the choice is between 45 and 60 rockets, both Eve and Theo would vote for 60 rockets and only Adam would vote for 45. In each case, the quantity of 60 rockets garners the most votes. This is not a surprise; the outcome of direct voting coincides with the preferred choice of the median voter (Eve).[6]

In Figure 7.3, the outcome of majority voting coincides with the efficient quantity of the public good. But this nice result hinges on some heroic assumptions. In Figure 7.3 the demand curves of Adam and Theo are placed symmetrically around Eve's demand curve and all individuals are assumed to bear the same cost of the public good. There is no reason to believe these assumptions hold in reality. In particular, the taxes used to finance expenditures in Canada are related to personal income and wealth. If the median voter pays less than an equal share of the cost of public goods, then the quantity of the public good selected by majority rule will tend to exceed the efficient quantity.

Logrolling

Another possible problem with simple majority voting is that it does not allow people to register how strongly they feel about the issues. Whether a particular voter just barely prefers *A* to *B* or has an enormous preference for *A* has no influence on the outcome. **Logrolling** systems allow people to trade votes and hence register how strongly they feel about various issues. Suppose that voters Smith and Jones prefer not to have more missiles, but this preference is not strongly felt. Brown, on the other hand, definitely wants more missiles. With a logrolling system, Brown may be able to convince Jones to vote for more missiles if Brown promises to vote for a new road to go by Jones's factory.

Vote trading is controversial. Its proponents argue that trading votes leads to efficient provision of public goods, just as trading commodities leads to efficient provision of private goods. Proponents also emphasize its potential for revealing the intensity of preferences and establishing a stable equilibrium. Moreover, the compromises implicit in vote trading are necessary for a democratic system to function. As the English statesman Edmund Burke noted, "All government—indeed, every human benefit and enjoyment, every virtue and every prudent act—is founded on compromise and barter."

A numerical example helps illustrate these advantages of logrolling. Suppose a community is considering three projects: a hospital, a library, and a swimming pool. The community has three voters: Melanie, Rhett, and Scarlet. Table 7.4 shows their benefits for each project. (A minus sign indicates a net loss; that is, the costs exceed the benefits.)

The first thing to notice about the table is that the total net benefit for each project is positive. Thus, by definition, the community as a whole would be better off if each project were adopted.[7] But what would happen if the projects were voted on *one at a time*? Melanie would vote for the hospital because her net benefit

TABLE 7.4

Logrolling Can Improve Welfare				
	Voter			
Project	**Melanie**	**Rhett**	**Scarlet**	**Total Net Benefits**
Hospital	200	−50	−55	95
Library	−40	150	−30	80
Pool	−120	−60	400	220

---

[6] It is common in Switzerland to use referendums to approve expenditures on new projects. In our example, 60 rockets would meet approval in a referendum since more voters prefer 60 to any alternative number of rockets. In Canada, the Alberta Taxpayer Protection Act (1994) requires a referendum to introduce a sales tax. Referendums are also used in municipal finance. For example, school boards in Alberta may impose special education levies approved by referendum (Treff and Perry, 2007: ch. 10).

[7] We assume the absence of externalities or any other considerations that would make private costs and benefits unequal to their social counterparts.

TABLE 7.5

		Voter		
Project	Melanie	Rhett	Scarlet	Total Net Benefits

Logrolling Can Also Lower Welfare

Project	Melanie	Rhett	Scarlet	Total Net Benefits
Hospital	200	−110	−105	−15
Library	−40	150	−120	−10
Pool	−270	−140	400	−10

is positive, but Rhett and Scarlet would vote against it because their benefits are negative. The hospital would therefore lose. Similarly, the library and the swimming pool would go down in defeat.

Vote trading can remedy this situation. Suppose Melanie agrees to vote for the library if Rhett consents to vote for the hospital. Melanie comes out ahead by 160 (= 200 − 40) with such a trade; Rhett comes out ahead by 100 (= 150 − 50). They therefore strike the deal, and the hospital and library pass. In the same way, Melanie and Scarlet can make a deal in which Melanie's support for the pool is given in return for Scarlet's vote for the hospital. Thus, logrolling allows all three measures to pass, a desirable outcome.

Opponents of logrolling stress it is likely to result in special interest gains not sufficient to outweigh general losses. Large amounts of waste can be incurred. For example, Allan MacEachen was able to get an oil refinery and a heavy water plant located in his home province of Nova Scotia through collecting political IOUs during his time as House Leader for the Trudeau government (Savoie, 1990: 200). An examination of two major federal transfer programs over the period 1988–2000 provides some evidence that electoral districts represented by senior members of the governing party receive more government transfers per resident (Milligan and Smart, 2005).

Table 7.5 illustrates a situation in which logrolling leads to such undesirable outcomes. Here we have the same three voters and three projects under consideration as in Table 7.4, but with a different set of net benefits. Every project has a negative net benefit. Each should therefore be rejected, as would be the case if the projects were voted on one at a time.

However, with logrolling, some or all of these inefficient projects could pass. Suppose Melanie offers to support the library in return for Rhett's vote for the hospital. The deal is consummated because both of them come out ahead: Melanie by 160 (= 200 − 40) and Rhett by 40 (= 150 − 110). With the support of Melanie and Rhett together, both projects pass. In the same way, Rhett and Scarlet can trade votes for the pool and the library, so both of those projects are adopted.

To understand the source of this outcome, consider again Melanie and Rhett's vote trading over the hospital and the library. Note that Scarlet comes out behind on both projects. This demonstrates how, with logrolling, a majority of voters can form a coalition to vote for projects that serve their interests but whose costs are borne mainly by the minority. Hence, despite the fact that the benefits of the projects to the majority exceed the costs, this is not true for society as a whole. We conclude that although logrolling can sometimes improve on the results from simple majority voting, this is not necessarily the case.

Arrow's Impossibility Theorem

We have shown that neither simple majority voting nor logrolling has entirely desirable properties. Many other voting schemes have also been considered, and they, too, are flawed.[8] An important question is whether *any* ethically acceptable method for translating individual preferences into collective preferences escapes these problems. It depends on what is meant by "ethically acceptable." Nobel laureate Kenneth Arrow (1951) proposed that in a democratic society, a collective decision-making rule should satisfy the following criteria:[9]

1. It can produce a decision whatever the configuration of voters' preferences. Thus, for example, the procedure must not fall apart if some people have multipeaked preferences.

---

[8] These include point voting (each person is given a fixed number of points that are cast for the different alternatives), plurality voting (the alternative with the most votes wins), Borda counts (each alternative is ranked by each voter, and the ranks are totalled to choose), Condorcet elections (the alternative that defeats the rest in paired elections wins), and exhaustive voting (the proposal favoured least by the largest number of voters is repeatedly removed until only one remains). See Levin and Nalebuff (1995) for further details.

[9] Arrow's requirements have been stated in a number of different ways. This treatment follows Blair and Pollak (1983).

2. It must be able to rank all possible outcomes.

3. It must be responsive to individuals' preferences. Specifically, if every individual prefers A to B, then society's ranking must prefer A to B.

4. It must be consistent in the sense that if A is preferred to B and B is preferred to C, then A is preferred to C.[10]

5. Society's ranking of A and B depends only on individuals' rankings of A and B. Thus, the collective ranking of defence expenditures and foreign aid does not depend on how individuals rank either of them relative to research on a cure for AIDS. This assumption is known as the **independence of irrelevant alternatives**.

6. Dictatorship is ruled out. Social preferences must not reflect the preferences of only a single individual.

Taken together, these criteria seem quite reasonable. They say that society's choice mechanism should be logical and respect individuals' preferences. Unfortunately, the stunning conclusion of Arrow's analysis is that in general it is *impossible* to find a rule that satisfies all these criteria.[11] A democratic society cannot be expected to be able to make consistent decisions.

This result, called Arrow's Impossibility Theorem, thus casts doubt on the very ability of democracies to function. Naturally, the theorem has generated debate, much of which has focused on whether other sets of criteria might allow formation of a social decision-making rule. It turns out that if any of the six criteria is dropped, a decision-making rule that satisfies the other five *can* be constructed. But whether or not it is permissible to drop any of the criteria depends on one's views of their ethical validity.

Arrow's theorem does not state that it is *necessarily* impossible to find a consistent decision-making rule. Rather, the theorem only says that it cannot be guaranteed that society will be able to do so. For certain patterns of individual preferences, no problems arise. An obvious example is when members of society have identical preferences. Some radical theorists have suggested that the real significance of Arrow's theorem is that it shows the need for a virtual uniformity of tastes if a democracy is to work. They then argue that many institutions have the express purpose of molding people's tastes to make sure that uniformity emerges. An example is mandatory public education. This observation is consistent with the view of the British statesman Benjamin Disraeli: "Whenever is found what is called a paternal government, there is found state education. It has been discovered that the best way to ensure implicit obedience is to commence tyranny in the nursery." Lott (1999) analyzed the pattern of expenditures on education across countries and found a result similar in spirit to Disraeli's assertion—more totalitarian governments tend to make greater investments in public education, other things being the same.

A very different view is that Arrow's theorem does not really have much to say about the viability of democratic processes. Another Nobel Prize winner, James Buchanan (1960: 83), views the inconsistencies of majority voting as having beneficial aspects:

> Majority rule is acceptable in a free society precisely because it allows a sort of jockeying back and forth among alternatives, upon none of which relative unanimity can be obtained. . . . It serves to insure that competing alternatives may be experimentally and provisionally adopted, tested, and replaced by new compromise alternatives approved by a majority group of ever-changing composition. This is [the] democratic choice process.

Another important question raised by Arrow's theorem concerns the use of a social welfare function in economic analysis. Recall from Chapter 2 that a social welfare function is a rule that evaluates the desirability of any given set of individuals' utilities. In a democratic society, the social welfare function must be chosen collectively. But Arrow's theorem says that it may be impossible to make such decisions, and hence we cannot assume that a social welfare function really exists. However, if it does not exist, how can economists use the social welfare function to rank alternative states? Some economists have therefore rejected the function's use. They argue that it is merely a way of introducing value judgments and not a representation of "society's" preferences. Thus, a social welfare function does not isolate the correct allocation of resources. However, most economists believe that the function is an important tool. It may not provide "the" answer, but it can be used to draw out the implications of alternative sets of value judgments. With this interpretation, the social welfare function provides valuable insights.

---

[10] More precisely, in this context *preferred to* means *better than* or *just as good as*.

[11] The proof involves fairly sophisticated mathematics. The procedure of proof is to show that if all six conditions are imposed, phenomena like the voting paradox can arise.

REPRESENTATIVE DEMOCRACY

Although the discussion of public decision-making thus far sheds light on some important questions, it is based on an unrealistic view of government. It is essentially a big computer that elicits from citizens their preferences and uses this information to produce social decisions. The state has no interests of its own; it is neutral and benign.

In fact, of course, government is done by people—politicians, judges, bureaucrats, and others. To understand the realities of public choice, one must study the goals and behaviour of the people who govern. This section discusses some models of government action based on these individuals' motivations and behaviour. These models assume that people in government attempt to maximize their self-interest.

Elected Politicians

Our earlier discussion of direct democracy led to the median voter theorem: if individual preferences are single peaked and can be represented along a single dimension, the outcome of majority voting reflects the preferences of the median voter. In reality, direct referendums on fiscal matters are most unusual. More commonly, citizens elect representatives who make decisions on their behalf. Nevertheless, under certain assumptions the median voter theory can help explain how these representatives set their positions.

Consider an election between two candidates, Smith and Jones. Assume voters have single-peaked preferences along the spectrum of political views. Voters cast ballots to maximize their own utility, and candidates seek to maximize the number of votes received.

What happens? Under these conditions, a vote-maximizing politician adopts the preferred program of the median voter—the voter whose preferences are exactly in the middle of the distribution of preferences. To see this, assume voters rank all positions on the basis of whether they are "conservative" or "liberal." Figure 7.4 shows a hypothetical distribution of voters who most prefer each point in the political spectrum. Suppose that Candidate Jones adopts position M, at the median, and Candidate Smith chooses position S to the right of centre. Because all voters have single-peaked preferences and want to maximize utility, each supports the candidate whose views lie closest to his or her own. Smith will win all the votes to the right of S, as well as some of the votes between S and M. Because M is the median, one-half of the voters lie to the left of M. Jones will receive all of these votes and some of those to the right of M, guaranteeing him a majority. The only way for Smith to prevent himself from being "outflanked" is to move to position M himself. Therefore, it pays both candidates to place themselves as close as possible to the position of the median voter.

This model has two striking implications. First, successful political parties offer policies that are in the "centre" of the political spectrum. The wisdom of this strategy was reflected in the words of retiring B.C. premier

FIGURE 7.4

MEDIAN VOTER THEOREM FOR ELECTIONS

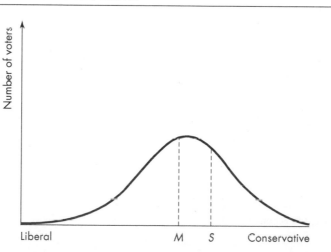

Bill Bennett to his successor, Bill Vander Zalm: "Bill, I got a piece of advice for you. Please. Stay in the middle! Don't go too far to the right. Stay in the middle."[12] Or in the words of Pierre Elliott Trudeau, one of Canada's longest-serving prime ministers and, in that sense, one of our most successful politicians—"We are in the extreme centre, the radical middle. That is our position."[13] It appears that party platforms that are perceived as too far from the middle of the road fare poorly with the electorate. After the 2004 federal election, when the new Conservative Party led by Stephen Harper ran on a right-wing agenda and fell short of its expectations, a commentator remarked that the voters' message was "go mainstream or go home."[14]

Second, the replacement of direct referendums by a representative system will have *no* effect on the outcome. Both simply mirror the preferences of the median voter. Thus, government spending cannot be "excessive" because political competition for votes leads to an expenditure level that is exactly in accordance with the median voter's wishes.

Before taking these rather optimistic results too much to heart, however, several aspects of the analysis require careful examination.

Single-dimensional rankings. If all political beliefs cannot be ranked along a single spectrum, the median voter theorem falls apart because the identity of the median voter depends on the issue being considered. The median voter with respect to affirmative action questions may not be the same person as the median voter on atomic energy issues. Similarly, just as in the case of direct referendums, if preferences are not single peaked, there may not be a stable voting equilibrium at all.

Two-party system. The median voter model assumes that there are two political parties competing for votes. Canada, like Great Britain and the United States, is often regarded as a two-party country, based on the historical rivalry between two dominant federal parties, but strong third and even fourth parties often exist. If there are more than two parties, their platforms will tend to disperse and voters can have incentives to choose strategically. That is, citizens may cast their votes in ways that do not always reflect their first choice, and the winning party does not necessarily win the majority of the votes.[15]

Ideology. The model assumes that politicians are simple vote maximizers, but they may care about more than just winning elections. The tension between maintaining ideological purity and winning power by adopting a less doctrinaire platform with a broad electoral appeal was a constant source of conflict in the Co-operative Commonwealth Federation (CCF), the forerunner of the New Democratic Party. One proponent of ideological purity was Carlyle King, a professor of English and president of the CCF in Saskatchewan, who argued,

> The trouble is that socialist parties have gone a-whoring after the Bitch Goddess. They have wanted Success, Victory, Power; forgetting that the main business of socialist parties is not to form governments but to change minds. When people begin to concentrate on success at the polls, they become careful and cautious; and when they become careful and cautious, the virtue goes out of them.[16]

Personality. The assumption that voters' decisions depend only on issues may be unrealistic. Personalities may sometimes be more important. Prime Minister Brian Mulroney's low popularity at the end of his time in office was due largely to perceived arrogance.

Leadership. In the model, politicians passively respond to voters' preferences. But these preferences may be influenced by the politicians themselves. This is just another way of saying that politicians provide leadership. Indeed, at times in history rational calculations of voter self-interest have apparently given way altogether to the appeal of charismatic politicians. "Politics is magic. He who knows how to summon forces from the deep, him they will follow."[17]

---

[12] Quoted in Olive (1993: 100).

[13] Quoted in Olive (1993: 115).

[14] Peterson (2004).

[15] For an analysis of majority rule with three parties, see Breyer (1987).

[16] Quoted in Walter Young (1969: 127).

[17] Hugo von Hofmannsthal, quoted in Schorske (1981: 172).

Decision to vote. The analysis assumes every eligible citizen chooses to exercise his or her franchise. If the candidates' positions are too close, however, some people may become too apathetic to vote. Individuals with extreme views may feel too alienated to vote. The model also ignores the costs of acquiring information and voting. A fully informed voter makes a determination on the suitability of a candidate's platform, the probability that the candidate will be able and willing to keep his or her promises, and so forth. The fact that these costs may be high, together with the perception that a single vote will not influence the outcome anyway, may induce a self-interested citizen to abstain from voting. A free-rider problem emerges—each individual has an incentive not to vote, but unless a sizable number of people do so, a democracy cannot function. Although lower voter participation rates are often bemoaned (for example, in the 2011 federal election, 61 percent of electors voted, down from 75 percent in the 1988 election), the real puzzle may be why the percentage is so *high*. Part of the answer may be the success with which the educational system instills the idea that the citizen's obligation to vote transcends narrow self-interest.

Public Employees

The next group we consider is public employees, also referred to as bureaucrats. To understand their role, note that the legislation enacted by elected politicians is often vague. The precise way a program is implemented is largely in the hands of public employees. For example, the Environmental Protection Act stipulates that the government must "take preventive and remedial measures to protect, enhance and restore the environment" [Canadian Environmental Protection Act, 1999, Section 2(1)(a.1)]. What is the scientific standard to be used to determine the requirement for "enhancing" and "restoring" the environment? The law is silent on these issues. The task of filling these gaps falls to the bureaucrats at Environment Canada, giving them enormous latitude and power.

Bureaucrats have been the target of much bitter criticism. They are blamed for being unresponsive, creating excessive red tape, and intruding too much into the private affairs of citizens. A senior minister in the Liberal government of Prime Minister Paul Martin called bureaucrats "the enemy."[18] Remember, however, that a modern government simply cannot function without bureaucracy. Bureaucrats provide valuable technical expertise in the design and execution of programs. The fact that their tenures in office often exceed those of elected officials provides a vital "institutional memory." Another important function of bureaucrats is to provide accurate documentation of public sector transactions to ensure that all eligible citizens receive equal treatment from a particular publicly provided service, and to prevent various forms of corruption.

On the other hand, it would be naive to assume a bureaucrat's only aim is to interpret and passively fulfill the wishes of the electorate and its representatives. Bureaucrats might instead be interested in increasing their perquisites of office, public reputation, power, and patronage.[19] Niskanen (1971) suggested that power, status, and so on are positively correlated with the size of the bureaucrat's budget and concluded that the bureaucrat's objective is to maximize his or her budget. Applying this logic to ineffective reforms of the federal public service in Canada, which grew by 34 percent between 2001 and 2011, Donald Savoie (2013: 241) argues that "Managers took advantage of their new-found authority to move funds between votes and activities to add to their salary and operations budgets." Savoie also notes that there are episodes of retrenchment in the size of the public service, such as the period of program reviews in the Paul Martin government and the more recent cutbacks in 2011 by the government of Stephen Harper.

Thus, the widespread suspicion that bureaucrats' main concern is empire building is hard to confirm or deny. After surveying studies of the determinants of bureaucrats' salaries in Canada, the United States, and the United Kingdom, Robert Young (1991: 52) concluded that "there exists little relationship between the growth of bureaus and the career prospects of bureaucrats. There is no strong empirical support for the view that civil servants obtain higher salary increases and faster promotions when they are in bureaucracies that are growing faster than normal."

---

[18] Savoie (2013).

[19] Obviously, this distinction is blurred in the real world. Firm executives care about power and job perks as well as money. Nevertheless, the distinction is useful for analytical purposes.

THE GREEK BAILOUT REFERENDUM

Few recent political events have dominated the news like the July 5, 2015 referendum in Greece. Greek voters were asked whether to accept or reject the fiscal austerity measures, consisting of spending cuts and tax hikes, imposed by the country's international debt holders, as conditions for providing additional bailout funds. The newly elected government campaigned for a 'no' vote. Leading up to the referendum, many news commentators interpreted a 'no' vote as leading inevitably to Greece exiting the euro currency zone, and possibly even leaving the European Union. Some economists, such as Paul Krugman, supported a 'no' vote, arguing that the austerity measures would cause a contraction in the country's GDP and hence render it even less capable of meeting its debt obligations. Other observers predicted an economic catastrophe for Greece and potentially further exists from the Eurozone by other highly indebted countries, if voters refused the terms of bailout. A decisive majority (61 percent) of Greek citizens cast their votes for the 'no' side. Referenda are relatively seldom-used political mechanisms in which the entire electorate is asked to vote directly on a particular, usually crucial, policy issue. Scotland held a referendum in 2014 on whether to become an independent country. Quebec held two referenda in 1980 and 1995 on whether to separate from Canada. In announcing the referendum in Greece, the Greek Prime Minister declared, "Greece, the birthplace of democracy will send a resounding democratic response to Europe and the world."

Based on Krugman (2015), Menton (2015), Papadimas and Malzezou (2015), Tsipras (2015), and "How Alexis Tsipras's Greek Referendum Call Came After Creditors Covered His Proposals in Red Ink." *The Wall Street Journal*, June 28, 2015.

Complete references for this feature can be found in the References section on page 477.

Special Interests

We have been assuming so far that citizens who seek to influence government policy can act only as individual voters. In fact, people with common interests can exercise disproportionate power by acting together. The source of the group's power might be that its members tend to have higher voter participation rates than the population as a whole. Alternatively, members might be willing to use their incomes to make campaign contributions and/or pay bribes. For example, in 2014, registered political parties received $48.8 million in contributions.[20] On what bases are these interest groups established? There are many possibilities.

Source of income: Capital or labour. According to orthodox Marxism, people's political interests are determined by whether they are capitalists or labourers. This view is too simple to explain interest-group formation in contemporary Canadian society. Even though there is a tendency for those with high incomes to receive a disproportionate share of their income from capital, much of the income of the rich is also derived from labour. Thus, it is difficult even to identify who the capitalists are and who the labourers are. Indeed, studies of the distribution of income in Western nations indicate that the driving force behind inequality in total income is the inequality in labour income (Lee, 2008).

Size of income. On many economic policy issues, the rich and the poor have different views, independent of the sources of their incomes. The poor favour redistributive spending programs and the rich oppose them. Similarly, each group supports implicit or explicit subsidies for goods they tend to consume intensively. Hence, the rich support tax-deductible retirement savings whereas the poor favour noncontributory public pensions.

Source of income: Industry of employment. Both workers and owners have a common interest in government support for their industry. A good example is the automobile industry, where both the Canadian

---

[20] Calculations based on data from the Elections Canada website, www.elections.ca.

auto workers union and the Big Three auto producers lobby for limits on the importation of automobiles from Japan and South Korea (Brennan, 2007).

Region. Residents of geographical regions often share common interests. Albertans want favourable tax treatment for the oil and gas industry, Quebecers want protection for the dairy industry, and the residents of Atlantic Canada want enhanced unemployment insurance benefits. "Given Canada's vast geography, its uneven economic development, and the lack of strong ideologies or even policy preferences in our political parties, the regional factor is perhaps more important in Canadian politics than in any other country" (Savoie, 1990: 195).

Demographic and personal characteristics. The elderly favour public health care and generous public pensions; young married couples are interested in good schools and low payroll taxes. Religious beliefs play a major role in debates over the funding of abortion and provincial funding of private schools. Ethnic groups differ on the propriety of government expenditure for minority language education. Gender is an important basis for interest-group formation (Erickson and O'Neill, 2002); in the 2006 federal election, women voted in disproportionately large numbers for the NDP (Gidengil et al., 2006).

The list could go on indefinitely. Given the numerous bases on which interest groups can be established, it is no surprise that people who are in opposition on one issue may be in agreement on another; "politics makes strange bedfellows" is more or less the order of the day.

This discussion has ignored the question of how individuals with common interests actually manage to organize themselves. Belonging to a group may require membership fees, donation of time, and so forth. Each individual has an incentive to let others do the work while he or she reaps the benefits, becoming a free rider. The probability that a group will actually form increases when the number of individuals is small and it is possible to levy sanctions against non-joiners. But in some cases, financial self-interest is probably not the explanation. It is only necessary to observe the debate over the impact of human activity on global warming to realize the influence of ideology and emotion on the decision to join a group.

Rent seeking. Advocacy groups can be used to manipulate the political system to redistribute income to specific groups of citizens. Generically, such activity is called **rent seeking**: using the government to obtain higher than normal returns ("rents"). An important variant is when a group of producers induces the government to restrict the output of their industry. Restricting output leads to higher prices for producers, allowing them to earn rents. For example, lobbying by Canadian dairy farmers kept tariff levels high enough to restrict imports after the 1994 General Agreement on Tariffs and Trade (GATT) mandated the removal of import quotas (Baylis and Furtan, 2003). While tariffs are used to limit the imports of cheeses, butter, and other dairy products, domestic quotas control the supply of dairy production within Canada.

To analyze rent seeking, consider Figure 7.5, which depicts the market for milk. The demand curve is D. For simplicity, we assume that the supply of milk, S, is horizontal. In the absence of government intervention, the equilibrium is at the intersection of supply and demand, where output is Q_c and price is P_c. (The subscript c reminds us that it is the competitive outcome.) It would be in the milk producers' interest if they could all agree to reduce their respective outputs and thereby force up the market price. More precisely, they would be better off if they jointly acted to maximize industry profits and split them up—in effect to form a **cartel**, an arrangement under which suppliers band together to restrict output and raise price.

Why don't they just do it? Because even though collectively they would benefit by being a part of a cartel, this does not mean that it is in any producer's self-interest. When the cartel raises its price, any individual farm has an incentive to cheat; that is, to increase its production beyond the agreed-upon quota. But all farms face this incentive, and as they all increase their outputs, the price falls back to the competitive equilibrium. This is where the government comes in. If the producers can get the government to enforce the cartel, then they can maintain the high price without having to worry about cheating. In the case of the milk industry, the government has a simple way to enforce the cartel; any farmer wishing to produce milk must be licensed and have a quota—and the total amount of milk produced is controlled by the number of quotas available. The program has been very successful from the farmers' point of view. Canadian milk prices are nearly twice as high as prices in the United States where dairy production is deregulated, leading to huge rents for the owners of quotas. In Alberta, a quota is valued at about $38,000 for, essentially, one dairy cow (Stephenson, 2013).

What is the best price from the cartel's standpoint? To maximize industry profits, the cartel needs to produce the output at which industry marginal cost (the incremental cost of producing a hectolitre of milk) equals industry

FIGURE 7.5

RENT SEEKING

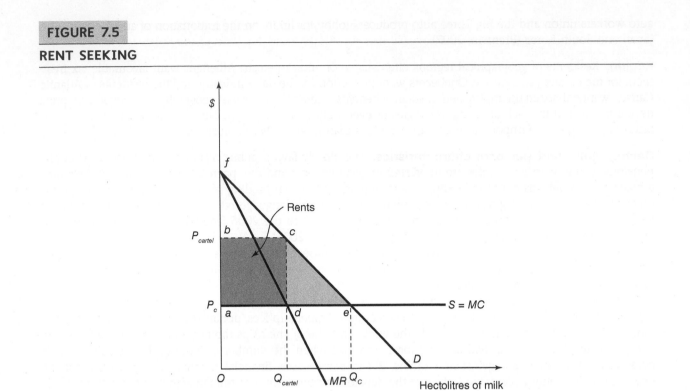

marginal revenue (the incremental revenue from selling a hectolitre of milk). The supply curve represents the marginal cost (MC) of production, and the marginal revenue is depicted as MR. The cartel output, Q_{cartel}, is determined by their intersection, and the associated price is P_{cartel}. By virtue of the higher price they receive per hectolitre (distance ab) on each of the ad units they sell, the dairy farmers can earn rents equal to area abcd.

It costs money for the producers to maintain the system of quotas. Presumably, they have to hire lobbyists and make campaign contributions to key members of Parliament, and so on. What is the maximum amount they are willing to pay to maintain the system? Because rents are a payment above the ordinary return, the *most* that the firms would be willing to pay for their favoured position is the total amount of the rents, area abcd.

So far, it would seem that the rent-seeking behaviour simply leads to a transfer from consumers (who pay a higher price) to the producers (who receive rents). But more is at stake. Recall that consumer surplus is the area above the price and below the demand curve (see the appendix to Chapter 3). Prior to the quotas, therefore, consumer surplus was the area *fae*. After the quotas are put in place, the consumer surplus is area *fbc*. Hence, consumers are worse off by the difference between the two areas, or area *abce*. Recall that, of this, area *abcd* goes to the producers. Who gets the rest of the lost surplus, area *dce*? The answer is nobody—it is the **deadweight loss** to society, a pure waste with no accompanying gain. The deadweight loss occurs because the increase in milk prices distort consumers' choices between dairy and all other goods, leading to less milk being produced than is efficient.

In the standard treatments of monopoly, area *dce* is the only deadweight loss. But in our rent-seeking model, the deadweight loss might actually be larger. As already suggested, rent seeking can use up resources—lobbyists spend their time influencing legislators and bureaucrats, consultants testify before regulatory panels, and advertisers conduct public relations campaigns. Resources that could have been used to produce new goods and services are instead consumed in a struggle over existing goods and services. Hence, area *abcd* does not represent a mere lump-sum transfer; it is a measure of real resources used up to maintain a position of market power. In short, according to this view, the deadweight loss associated with rent seeking is the sum of *abcd* and *dce*, or *abce*. The resource cost associated with rent seeking can be substantial. A survey of pay levels for lobbyists in Washington, D.C., found that 89 executives earned more than $1 million, with the head of a drug industry lobby earning nearly $4.5 million and the leader of a business lobbying group earning over $5.5 million (*Wall Street Journal*, 2010).

We cannot conclude that area *abcd* is always the loss, however. In many cases, this area may overstate the efficiency cost of rent seeking. For example, some rent seeking takes the form of campaign contributions and bribes, and these are simply transfers–they do not "use up" real resources. An important contribution of the rent-seeking model is that it focuses our attention on the potential size of the waste generated by the government's power to create rents.

An obvious question is why bills that benefit only the members of a special interest group receive majority support in the House of Commons. After all, Figure 7.5 shows that the losses to consumers are greater than the gains to the producers. Why don't the consumers prevent the introduction of such licensing and quotas?

One reason is that interest groups and bureaucrats may be well organized and armed with information, whereas those who will bear the costs are not organized and may not even be aware of what is going on. Even if those citizens who will bear the costs are well informed, it may not be worth their while to fight back. Since the costs of the program are spread over the population as a whole, any given citizen's share is low, and it would not be worth the time and effort to organize an opposition. In contrast, the benefits are relatively concentrated, making political organization attractive for potential beneficiaries.

Other Actors

Without attempting to be exhaustive, we list a few other parties who affect government fiscal decisions.

The judiciary. Court decisions on the legality of various taxes have major effects on government finance. For example, in Canada the judiciary has interpreted provincial retail sales taxes as "direct taxes" and therefore the provincial governments have been allowed to levy them. In contrast, in Australia retail sales taxes were ruled to be indirect taxes and therefore the state governments were prohibited from levying them. The judiciary also affects the expenditure side of the budget. For example, the courts have ruled that governments must provide the same benefits to same-sex couples that they provide to heterosexual couples.

Journalists. The ability to bring certain issues to public attention gives the press considerable influence. For example, the widespread publicity given to crumbling bridges and roads has induced a number of jurisdictions to increase spending on infrastructure. Politicians, bureaucrats, and special interest groups often try to use the media to influence the outcome of debates on fiscal issues. For example, in recent years, concerns expressed about population aging created pressure to improve public pension programs in Canada. This attention contributed to an enhancement of the Guaranteed Income Supplement paid by the federal government to low-income seniors.

Experts. Information is potentially an important source of power. Legislative aides who gain expertise on certain programs often play important roles in drafting statutes. They can also affect outcomes by virtue of their ability to influence which items are put on the legislative agenda. Of course, there are also experts outside the government. Many academic social scientists have sought to use their expertise to influence economic policy. Economists love to quote John Maynard Keynes's (1965/1936: 383) famous dictum that "the ideas of economists and political philosophers, both when they are right and when they are wrong, are more powerful than is commonly understood. Indeed, the world is ruled by little else." However, it is extremely difficult to determine whether social science research influences policy, and if so, through what channels this influence operates.

EXPLAINING GOVERNMENT GROWTH

Much of the concern about whether government operates efficiently has been stimulated by the rate of growth in government. As documented in Chapter 1, over the long run, government expenditures in Canada have grown enormously, both in absolute terms and proportionately. A growing public sector is not a uniquely Canadian experience, as the figures for a few other Western countries in Table 7.6 indicate. Thus, as we search for explanations for the growth in government, care must be taken not to rely too heavily on events and institutions that are peculiar to Canada. Also, the various explanations are not necessarily mutually exclusive. No single theory accounts for the whole phenomenon. Indeed, even taken together, they still leave much unexplained. Some of the most prominent theories follow.

TABLE 7.6

	Government Expenditure as a Percent of GDP in Selected Countries						
	Post-World War I (About 1920)	Pre-World War II (About 1937)	Post-World War II (About 1960)	(1980)	(1990)	(2000)	(2015)
Canada	13.3	18.6	28.6	38.8	46.0	40.5	39.5
France	27.6	29.0	34.6	46.1	49.8	51.1	56.9
Germany	25.0	42.4	32.4	47.9	45.1	44.7	43.7
Italy	22.5	24.5	30.1	41.9	53.2	45.4	50.6
Japan	14.8	25.4	17.5	32.0	31.7	38.7	41.6
Netherlands	13.5	19.0	33.7	55.2	54.0	41.7	45.7
Spain	9.3	18.4	18.8	32.2	42.0	39.1	41.9
Sweden	8.1	10.4	31.0	60.1	59.1	53.6	52.2
United Kingdom	26.2	30.0	32.2	43.0	39.9	33.6	43.1
United States	7.0	8.6	27.0	31.8	33.3	33.9	37.7

Source: Table 1, in Vito Tanzi and Ludger Schuknecht, "Reforming Government: An Overview of Recent Experience," *European Journal of Political Economy,* Vol. 13 (September 1997); and Organisation for Economic Cooperation and Development, *OECD Economic Outlook Volume 2015, Iss. 1* (Paris: OECD Publishing, June 2015), Annex table 25.

Citizen preferences. Growth in government expenditure is an expression of the preferences of the citizenry. Suppose the median voter's demand for public sector goods and services (G) is some function (f) of the relative price of public sector goods and services (P) and income (I):

$$G = f(P, I) \qquad (7.1)$$

There are many different ways such a demand function can lead to an increasing proportion of income spent on public sector goods and services. Suppose that when income increases by a given percentage, the quantity demanded of public goods and services increases by a greater percentage—the income elasticity of demand is greater than one. If so, the process of income growth by itself leads to an ever-increasing share of income going to the public sector, other things being the same.[21] Similarly, if the price elasticity of demand for G is less than one and P increases over time, an increase in government's share of income may also occur.

The important point is that the relative increase in the size of the public sector does not necessarily imply something is "wrong" with the political process. Government growth could well be a consequence of the wishes of voters, who rationally take into account its opportunity cost in forgone consumption in the private sector. The question then becomes whether the actual changes in P and I over time can account for the actual historical changes in G. To answer this question, a natural approach is to begin by computing the actual percentage changes in P and I that have occurred over time; then multiply the percentage change in P by an econometric estimate of the elasticity of G with respect to P, and the percentage change in I by the elasticity with respect to I. This calculation yields the percentage change in G attributable solely to changes in P and I. The figure can then be compared to the actual change in G. One estimate is that only about 40 percent of the growth in U.S. public budgets can be explained by Equation (7.1).

Landon, McMillan, Muralidharan, and Parsons (2006) used data from 1989 to 2004 to estimate the demand functions of the median voter for Canadian provincial government expenditures on health, social services, education, and a residual spending category.[22] The explanatory variables included real per capita income,

---

[21] The hypothesis that government services rise at a faster rate than income is often called **Wagner's Law**, after Adolph Wagner, the nineteenth-century economist who formulated it.

[22] Standard data sources do not reveal the identity of the voter with median preferences for the public good; hence, we do not know his or her income. The typical procedure is to assume that either the median income or the average income in the community is also the income of the median voter.

federal government transfers, demographic variables, and the relative price of government services. Their model explained a large proportion of the variation in expenditure levels across provinces and over time. Paul Boothe (1995: 83) analyzed the determinants of the growth of eleven categories of provincial government spending in Alberta between 1968 and 1991 and found that they were "reasonably well explained by economic variables such as real per capita income, the tax price of government services, and the unemployment rate."[23] He also found that political variables such as the government's share of the popular vote and the size of its legislative majority seemed to affect the level of some kinds of government spending. This suggests that more is going on than a simple median-voter story can explain.

A variant of the citizen-preferences approach is based on the observation that most of the growth in government spending in the second half of the twentieth century is attributable to social insurance programs, such as unemployment insurance, health insurance, and pensions. Popular support for the introduction and expansion of these programs stems from the belief that private markets deliver inadequate protection against risks (see Chapter 9 for an analysis of private insurance markets). From this perspective, the growth of government reflects its role for overcoming certain market failures. Federal insurance against unemployment was introduced in Canada in 1940, hospital insurance in 1957, and public pension programs in 1952 and 1966. The fact that social insurance programs arose gradually may reflect learning-by-doing in administering programs and gradual improvements in record-keeping technologies, such as computerization.[24]

Marxist view. Some Marxist theories view the rise of state expenditure as inherent in the political-economic system. In the Marxist model, the private sector tends to overproduce, so the capitalist-controlled government must expand expenditures to absorb this production. Typically, this is accomplished by augmenting military spending. At the same time, the state attempts to decrease worker discontent by increasing spending for social services. Eventually, rising expenditures outpace tax revenue capacity, and the government collapses.

The historical facts seem to contradict this analysis. For example, it is noteworthy that in Western Europe the enormous increase in the size and scope of government in the post–World War II era has been accompanied by anything but a resurgence in militarism. The main contribution of this Marxist analysis is its explicit recognition of the links between the economic and political systems as sources of government growth.

Chance events. In contrast to the theories that view government growth as inevitable are those that consider it as the consequence of chance events. In "normal" periods there is only moderate growth in public expenditure. Occasionally, however, external shocks to the economic and social system "require" higher levels of government expenditure and novel methods of financing. Even after the shock disappears, higher levels continue to prevail because of inertia. Peacock and Wiseman (1967) call this the *displacement effect*. Examples of shocks are the Great Depression, World War II, the war in Afghanistan, and the recession brought on by the financial crisis of 2008.

Income redistribution. As George Bernard Shaw observed, "A Government which robs Peter to pay Paul can always depend on the support of Paul."[25] It has been hypothesized that government grows because low-income individuals use the political system to redistribute income toward themselves (see Meltzer and Richard, 1981). The idea is that politicians can attract voters whose incomes are at or below the median by offering benefits that impose a net cost on those whose incomes are above the median. As long as average income exceeds the median, and the mechanisms used to bring about redistribution are not too detrimental to incentives, politicians have an incentive to increase the scope of government sponsored income distribution. Suppose, for example, that there are five voters whose incomes are $5,000, $10,000, $15,000, $25,000, and $40,000. The median income is $15,000 and the average income is $19,000. A politician who supports government programs that transfer income to those with less than $25,000 will win in majority voting.

If this is the case, it must still be explained why the share of public expenditures increases gradually (as in Table 7.6). Why not a huge once-and-for-all transfer, as the poor confiscate the incomes of the rich? One reason

---

[23] The tax price of government spending was defined as the proportion of spending that Albertans would finance through taxes. Interest income from the Alberta Heritage Saving Trust Fund and natural resource revenue were assumed to reduce the price of government spending for Albertans.

[24] Moene and Wallerstein (2001) use a median voter model to explain political support for insurance against unemployment, while Gonzalez and Wen (2015) view the provision of social insurance programs as a cost-effective way for the government to satisfy demands for redistribution away from the top of the income distribution.

[25] Quoted in Smith (1993: 14).

is because, in Western countries, property and/or status requirements for voting have gradually been abolished during the last century. Extension of the right to vote to those at the bottom of the income scale increases the proportion of voters likely to support politicians promising redistribution. Hence, the gradual extension of the franchise leads to continuous growth in government rather than a once-and-for-all increase.

One limitation of this theory is that it fails to explain the methods used by government to redistribute income. If it is correct, most income transfers should go to the poor and should take the form that would maximize their welfare; that is, direct cash transfers. Instead, many transfers in Canada are in-kind transfers, such as subsidized tuition at universities, which mainly benefit the middle- and upper-income classes.

Government programs that benefit different income classes can exist simultaneously, so various views of government redistribution are not necessarily mutually exclusive. The important point here is their common theme. Politicians, rent-seeking special interest groups, and bureaucrats vote themselves programs of ever-increasing size.

Controlling Government Growth

As already noted, substantial growth in the public sector need not imply that anything is wrong with the budgetary process. For those who believe that public sector fiscal behaviour is more or less dictated by the preferences of the median voter, bringing government under control is a non-issue. On the other hand, for those who perceive growth in government as a symptom of flaws in the political process, bringing government under control is very much a problem.

Two types of argument are made in the controllability debate. One view is that the basic problem results from commitments made by government in the past, so there is very little current politicians can do to change the rate of growth or composition of government expenditures. Entitlement programs that provide benefits to the retired, disabled, unemployed, sick, and others are the largest category of uncontrollable expenses. When we add other items, such as payments on the national debt, farm support programs, and certain defence expenditures, about 75 percent of the federal budget is uncontrollable.[26]

Are these expenditures really uncontrollable? If legislation created entitlement programs, it can take them away. In theory, then, many of the programs can be reduced or even removed. In reality, both moral and political considerations work against reneging on past promises to various groups in the population. Any serious reductions are likely to be scheduled sufficiently far into the future so that people who have made commitments based on current programs will not be affected.

According to the second argument, our political institutions are fundamentally flawed, and bringing things under control is more than just a matter of changing the entitlement programs. Most of the focus on bringing government spending under control has been on the budget-making process. Over the years, critics of the process have argued that public sector budget-making is undisciplined and that strict budgetary rules are required.

Beginning in the 1990s, six provinces passed legislation whose goal was to impose some discipline by requiring balanced budgets or spending limitations.[27] For example, by Manitoba law (S.M. 1995, c. 7) the remuneration of the members of the Executive Council is reduced by 40 percent if provincial expenditures exceed revenues. The federal government introduced similar legislation in its 2015 Balanced Budget Act (Bill C-59). Critics of balanced budget statutes argue that the laws simply encourage "ingenious politicians and bureaucrats to spend time looking for ways to get around the rules through accounting hocus-pocus and subterfuges of various kinds."[28] Subversion of deficit control is facilitated by the fact that most provincial balanced budget rules contain "escape" clauses in the case of adverse events or significant reductions in revenues. Given such anecdotes, it is natural to ask whether fiscal institutions matter at all.

One way to address the question is to investigate whether governments with strict budgetary rules have smaller deficits and react more quickly to unanticipated shortfalls in revenue than those with lenient rules. There is some evidence from the fiscal behaviour of U.S. states that, in fact, this is what happens. It is a bit tricky to

---

[26] Major federal transfers to persons, federal transfers to provinces in support of health and social programs, federal debt charges, and direct program expenses for national defence, farm income support, student financial support, and Crown corporations summed to $177.5 billion out of the total federal expenses of $238.8 billion in 2008–09 (Treff and Ort, 2011: Tables 2.1, 2.2, and 12.1).

[27] See Philipps (1997) for a history and a critical assessment of balanced budget acts in Canada.

[28] Finance Minister Paul Martin quoted in R. Carrick, "Balanced Budget Legislation Draws Criticism from Martin" *The [Windsor] Star* (2 September 1995) H8.

interpret this evidence, because we do not know if the outcomes in the states with strict rules really are due to the rules themselves. It could be, for example, that strict rules are passed by fiscally conservative legislators, who would deal aggressively with deficits even without legal compulsion. Several econometric studies have concluded that, even after taking such complications into account, fiscal institutions matter. In an analysis of federal budget rules, economist Alan Auerbach found that "rules did have some effects, rather than simply being statements of policy intentions. The rules may also have had some success at deficit control" (Auerbach, 2008).

Some analysts argue that legislating balanced budget rules is unnecessary because financial markets exert pressure on heavily indebted governments through higher interest rates and credit rating downgrades on government bonds (Kneebone, 1994). The Canadian experience of the 1990s is remarkable in this regard. The federal net public debt to GDP ratio reached 73 percent in 1994–95, compared with less than 19 percent twenty years earlier. One-third of federal tax revenues in 1994 went to finance interest on public debt alone and the deficit equalled almost six percent of GDP. In the wake of rising real interest rates and a weak currency, the government harnessed popular support for anti-deficit action and cut federal spending by 20 percent, spread over three years, to achieve consecutive budget surpluses from 1997 to 2007.

The sovereign debt crisis currently gripping a number of European countries has led to renewed attention to Canada's federal expenditure cuts in the 1990s. Paul Martin (1996) described three principles in the federal government's *political* strategy for controlling government spending during his tenure as finance minister from 1993 to 2002. (1) *Establish short-term targets with prudent fiscal assumptions.* This forces politicians to deal with budgetary balance on a continual basis, rather than postponing decisions to later years. (2) *Use program reviews to allocate the cuts.* Instead of unilateral spending cuts across department, ministers are obliged to prioritize programs. (3) *Engage in public consultation.* An open process increases public input, confidence, and understanding. In the context of institutional change, implementation of Paul Martin's principles can be seen as a change in the political culture behind the budget-making process. This transformation toward more disciplined public spending appears to have been facilitated by the public perception of an economic crisis during the 1990s.

CONCLUSIONS

Public decision-making is complicated and not well understood. Contrary to simple models of democracy, there appear to be forces pulling government expenditures away from levels that would be preferred by the median voter. However, critics of the current budgetary process have not come up with a satisfactory alternative. The formulation of meaningful rules and constraints for the budgetary process, either at the constitutional or statutory level, is an important item on both the academic and political agendas for the years ahead.

It should be stressed that the judgment that currently government may be inequitable or inefficient does not necessarily imply that government as an institution is "bad." People who like market oriented approaches to resource allocation can nevertheless seek to improve markets. The same goes for government.

SUMMARY

- Political economy applies economic principles to the analysis of political decision-making.
- Economists have studied several methods for choosing levels of public goods in a direct democracy:
  - Lindahl pricing results in a unanimous decision to provide an efficient quantity of public goods, but relies on honest revelation of preferences.
  - Majority voting may lead to inconsistent decisions regarding public goods if some people's preferences are not single peaked.
  - Logrolling allows voters to express the intensity of their preferences by trading votes. However, minority gains may come at the expense of greater general losses.
- Arrow's Impossibility Theorem states that, in general, it is impossible to find a decision-making rule that simultaneously satisfies a number of apparently reasonable criteria. The implication is that democracies are inherently prone to inconsistency regarding public goods and other decisions.

- Explanations of government behaviour require studying the interaction of elected officials, public employees, and special interest groups.
- Under restrictive assumptions, the actions of elected officials mimic the wishes of the median voter.
- Public employees have an important impact on the development and implementation of economic policy. One theory predicts that bureaucrats attempt to maximize the size of their agencies' budgets, resulting in oversupply of the service.
- Rent-seeking private citizens form groups to influence government activity. Special interests can form on the basis of income source, income size, industry, region, or personal characteristics.
- The growth of government has been rapid by any measure. Explanations of this phenomenon include:
  - Citizens simply want a larger government.
  - The public sector must expand to absorb private excess production.
  - Random events (such as wars) increase the growth of government, while inertia prevents a return to previous levels.
  - Certain groups in the population use the government to redistribute income to themselves.
- Proposals to control the growth in government focus on the imposition of strict budgetary rules.

EXERCISES

1. Yasser and Hikaru are video game fans and they agree to jointly sponsor the prize fund for a tournament. They wish to attract marquee players to the event and they recognize that the larger is the prize fund, the more marquee players they will attract. Suppose Yasser's demand for marquee players is $Q = 100 - 60S_Y$, while Hikaru's demand is $Q = 60 - 40S_H$, where Q is the number of marquee players who will participate in the event and S_Y and $S_H = 1 - S_Y$ are Yasser's and Hikaru's shares of the cost of sponsoring the prize fund.

   a. Sketch the demand functions of Yasser and Hikaru in a diagram like Figure 7.1. Identify the Lindahl equilibrium point.

   b. What proportion of the prize fund is paid by Yasser at the equilibrium? What proportion is paid by Hikaru? How many marquee players will participate in the tournament?

   c. Suppose the total prize fund must be increased by $100 to attract each additional marquee player to the tournament. What is the total size of the prize fund in the equilibrium?

2. Suppose there are five people—1, 2, 3, 4, and 5—who rank projects A, B, C, and D as follows:

1	2	3	4	5
A	A	D	C	B
D	C	B	B	C
C	B	C	D	D
B	D	A	A	A

   a. Sketch the preferences, as in Figure 7.2.

   b. Will any project be chosen by a majority vote rule? If so, which one? If not, explain why.

3. Consider a society with three people (John, Eleanor, and Abigail) who use majority rule to decide how much money to spend on a public park. There are three options for spending: *H* (high), *M* (medium), and *L* (low). These individuals rank the three options in the following way:

Rank	John	Eleanor	Abigail
1	M	L	H
2	L	M	M
3	H	H	L

a. Consider all possible pairwise elections: *M* versus *H*, *H* versus *L*, and *L* versus *M*. What is the outcome of each election? Does it appear, in this case, that majority rule would lead to a stable outcome on spending on the public park? If so, what is the choice? Would giving one person the ability to set the agenda affect the outcome? Explain.

b. Now suppose that Eleanor's preference ordering changed to the following: first choice = *L*, second choice = *H*, and third choice = *M*. Would majority rule lead to a stable outcome? If so, what is the choice? Would giving one person the ability to control the agenda affect the outcome? Explain.

4. Return to Exercise 5 in Chapter 4, where Moe, Larry, and Curly are hiring the services of an acting coach. Suppose the coach's fee is $15 per hour.

a. If the trio share the hourly cost equally, and they use majority voting to determine the number of hours of coaching to hire, how many hours will they choose? Is this close to the efficient quantity?

b. Suppose that the cost of hiring the coach is divided in the following way: Moe and Curly each pay $1 per hour, and Larry pays $13 per hour. Show that in this case majority voting leads to excessive spending on the acting coach.

5. Three voters, A, B, and C, will decide by majority rule whether to pass bills on issues X and Y. *Each of the two issues will be voted on separately.* The change in net benefits (in dollars) that would result from the passage of each bill is as follows:

	Issue	
Voter	**X**	**Y**
A	+6	−3
B	−1	+4
C	−2	−3

a. Which issues (if any) would pass if decided by majority rule? Is this the efficient outcome?

b. Which issues (if any) would pass if logrolling were allowed? Would logrolling improve efficiency? Would it result in the efficient outcome?

c. Suppose that it were legal for one voter to pay another voter to vote in a certain way. Would allowing such side payments improve efficiency in part b? Would it result in the efficient outcome?

d. What amount of side payments would take place if paying for votes were allowed?

6. Industries in the country of Technologia invest in new equipment that annually increases productivity of private workers by 3 percent. Government employees do not benefit from similar technical advances.

a. If wages in the private sector are set equal to the value of the marginal product, how much will they rise yearly?

b. Government workers annually receive increases so that wages remain comparable to those in the private sector. What happens to the price of public services relative to privately produced goods?

c. If the same quantity of public services is produced each year, what happens to the size of the government (measured by spending)?

7. In 1998, the people of Puerto Rico held a referendum in which there were five choices: retain commonwealth status, become a state, become independent, adopt "free association" (a type of independence that would delegate certain powers to the United States), and "none of the above." Discuss the problems that can arise when people vote over five options.

8. In 2005, Kuwait women won the right to vote in parliamentary elections. Indeed, women voters now outnumber men voters in Kuwait because women are automatically registered

while men have to register on their own. One woman noted, "The Ministers of Parliament used to vote against us; now they are wooing us to vote for them" (Fattah, 2006). What does this tell us about the validity of the prediction of the median voter theorem?

9. Assume that the demand curve for milk is given by $Q = 100 - 10P$, where P is the price per 2-litre carton and Q is the quantity demanded per year. The supply curve is horizontal at a price of $2.

   a. If the market is competitive, what is the price per carton of milk and the number of cartons sold?

   b. With the connivance of some politicians, the dairy farmers are able to form and maintain a cartel. What is the cartel price, and how many cartons of milk are purchased? (*Hint*: The marginal revenue curve (*MR*) is given by $MR = 10 - Q/5$. Also, remember that the supply curve shows the marginal cost associated with each level of output.)

   c. What are the rents associated with the cartel?

   d. Suppose that to maintain the cartel the dairy farmers simply give lump-sum campaign contributions to the relevant politicians. What is the maximum contribution they are willing to make? What is the deadweight loss of the cartel?

   e. Suppose that instead of lump-sum contributions to politicians, the dairy farmers hire lobbyists and lawyers to make their case to Members of Parliament. How does this change your estimate of the deadweight loss associated with this rent-seeking activity?

10. Why do you think firms lobby the government to enact policies that restrict production in their industry, rather than simply agreeing to restrict production on their own?

CHAPTER 8

Fiscal Federalism

Canadian federalism is more than a form of government. It's also a system of values that allows different people in diverse communities to live and work together in harmony for the good of all.

—Jean Chretien

AFTER READING THIS CHAPTER, THE STUDENT SHOULD BE ABLE TO:

LO1 Define fiscal federalism.

LO2 Outline what the expenditure decentralization ratio and the revenue decentralization ratio measure.

LO3 Summarize how expenditure and revenue shares for the different level of governments in Canada have changed over time.

LO4 Describe the process of community formation using club theory and identify the key factors that influence community size.

LO5 Outline the main result of the Tiebout model and identify the key conditions needed for the result to occur.

LO6 Discuss the advantages and disadvantages of greater decentralization.

LO7 Use theory to explain how conditional and unconditional grants can potentially influence a recipient government's spending decisions.

LO8 Briefly outline how each of the three major federal cash transfer programs in Canada work.

In the spring of 1997, Glen Clark, the premier of British Columbia, declared "war" . . . on the United States Navy. He announced the decision to cancel the provincial lease that allowed U.S. and Canadian naval vessels to conduct military exercises in the Georgia Strait between the mainland and Vancouver Island. Clark's announcement followed the breakdown of talks between Canada and the United States on sharing the salmon fishery north of Vancouver Island.

The reason the B.C. salmon wars received so much attention was the incongruity of a provincial government in effect making foreign policy. International relations "belong" to the federal government. On the other hand, decisions regarding the management of public lands "belong" to provinces. Is this decentralized decision-making desirable?

We have so far examined an efficiency role for government in correcting market failures associated with public goods and externalities. We have also discussed the government's role in redistributing income to address fairness or equity concerns. In Canada, there are various levels of government. Which level of government should do what? These are important issues in Canada where, as noted earlier, there are different levels of government, each operating with considerable autonomy. The appropriate division of power among them has been a matter of controversy since the founding of the nation. This chapter examines the normative and positive aspects of public finance in a federal system.

BACKGROUND

A federal system consists of different levels of government that provide public goods and services and have some scope for making decisions. The subject of **fiscal federalism** examines the functions undertaken by different levels of government and the ways in which they relate with each other. A federal system is character-ized as being more centralized (or less decentralized) than another when more of its decision-making powers are in the hands of authorities with a larger jurisdiction. A common measure of the extent to which a system is decentralized is the **expenditure decentralization ratio**, defined as the share of total government expenditures made by subnational governments, exclusive of grants received from the central government. Table 8.1 shows the subnational (provincial plus local) governments' share of the combined expenditures of central, state/provin-cial, and local governments for Canada and a number of other countries. With the exception of France, all the countries shown have federal systems. The degree of decentralization differs quite a bit even among the federal countries. For the countries shown, the decentralization ratio is very low for France and highest for Canada.

The expenditure decentralization ratio is by no means a foolproof indicator. Fiscal arrangements between different levels of government can, for example, make it difficult to determine the degree of decentralized decision-making using such ratios. Suppose that provinces make expenditures for social assistance, but a portion of the money comes in the form of grants from the federal government. Ottawa decides that no province will receive these grants unless it mandates that there will be no residency requirement placed on social assistance recipients. Every province complies. Who is really in charge? The point is that if provincial govern-ment spending behaviour is constrained by the federal government, the decentralization ratio over-estimates the true extent of decentralization in the system. Conversely, if provinces effectively lobby the federal govern-ment to achieve their own ends, the decentralization ratio may underestimate the degree of decentralized economic power.

Another common measure of the extent to which decision-making authority is decentralized is revenue decentralization, typically measured as the ratio of subnational (provincial and local) government revenues to total government revenues. This measure may also misrepresent the extent to which decision-making author-ity is decentralized, if for example a provincial government receives a large share of a particular type of tax revenue but does not have the power to determine the tax rate or tax base. Such problems have led research-ers to develop new measures that better reflect the degree of decision-making autonomy that subnational governments actually have.

Keeping in mind these limitations, we examine government spending and revenue shares for different levels of government over time in Table 8.2. The long-run trend has been for provincial governments to increase their share of spending at the expense of local government. With respect to revenue, there has been a major shift toward the provinces, with the provinces increasing their revenue share at the expense of both federal and local governments, particularly from 1950 to 1980. These changes are consistent with the evidence in Table 8.1, which shows an increase in expenditure decentralization in Canada over the period 1970–1975 to 1996–2001. Despite these changes, there are persistent gaps in the revenue and expenditure shares for the different levels of government.

TABLE 8.1

Subnational Governments' Share of Total Government Expenditures, Six Year Averages (in percent)		
Country	1970–1975	1996–2001
Canada	48.3	53.2
United States	35.7	39.5
Germany	39.7	33.4
Australia	27.4	31.6
France	10.8	12.1

Source: Stegarescu (2009), Table 1.

TABLE 8.2

Distribution of Canadian Government Revenue* and Expenditure** by Level of Government, 1926-2009 (in percent)

	Federal		Provincial		Local	
	Revenue	Expenditure	Revenue	Expenditure	Revenue	Expenditure
1926	44.9	37.8	18.0	20.2	37.1	42.0
1939	41.4	33.5	26.8	36.2	31.8	30.3
1950	65.2	51.9	20.8	26.0	14.0	22.1
1960	60.8	50.5	21.8	24.8	17.3	24.7
1970	48.7	35.3	36.2	38.0	15.1	26.7
1980	44.7	37.8	41.8	40.3	13.4	21.9
1990	45.4	41.0	41.7	40.1	13.0	19.0
2000	47.4	38.4	41.5	42.7	11.2	18.8
2009	53.3	33.2	40.3	46.2	6.4	20.6

* Revenues are net of grants received from other levels of government.
** Expenditures are net of grants made to other levels of government.

Source: Data are from Karin Treff and Deborah Ort, *Finances of the Nation*, 2010 (Toronto: Canadian Tax Foundation, 2011), tables B3 and B5. The data found in tables B3 and B5 are, in turn, based on Statistics Canada's system of national accounts.

A number of important spending activities are mostly in the hands of provincial and local governments. This is partly the result of the explicit constitutional division of powers and responsibilities between the federal and provincial governments that we discussed in Chapter 1. Table 8.3 shows that the subnational government level accounted for more than 75 percent of government spending in the areas of health, education, transportation and communications, and the environment in 2008-09. The federal government, on the other hand, accounted for over 70 percent of spending in labour, employment, and immigration, while expenditure shares for protection of persons and property and for social services were more balanced between the two government levels.

TABLE 8.3

Expenditure Shares by Level of Government, 2008-09[a] (in percent)

	Federal Government	Local, Provincial, and Territorial Governments
Health	21.4	78.6
Education	6.0	94.0
Social Services	58.5	41.5
Protection of Persons and Property	57.0	43.0
Environment	15.9	84.1
Transportation and Communications	11.0	89.0
Labour, Employment, and Immigration	71.6	28.4
Other	69.3	30.7
Total	40.9	59.2

[a] This is the final year of FMS data available. Statistics Canada has adopted a new accounting standard, the Canadian Government Finance Statistics (CGFS), but data allowing a comparison of government revenues and expenditures by level of government and across time are not yet available.

Source: Authors' calculation based on Financial Management System (FMS) data obtained from Statistics Canada's CANSIM II database http://cansim2.statcan.ca Table 385-0001.

Tables 8.2 and 8.3 leave us with a critical question: does the division of powers as laid out in the Constitution Act 1982 and interpreted by the courts make sense according to some economic criteria? Before we can provide an answer, we need to discuss the special features associated with subnational government.

COMMUNITY FORMATION

To understand the appropriate fiscal roles for local jurisdictions, we consider why communities are formed. It is helpful to think of a community as a club—a voluntary association of people who band together to share some kind of benefit. This section develops a theory of clubs and uses that theory to explain how the size of a community and its provision of public goods are determined.

Consider a group of people who wish to band together to purchase land for a public park. To keep things simple, assume that all members of the group have identical tastes and that they intend to share the use of the park and its costs equally. The "community" can costlessly exclude all nonmembers, and it operates with no transaction costs. Given the assumption of identical tastes, we need to consider only the desires of a representative member. Two decisions must be made: how large a park to acquire and how many members to have in the community.

Assuming that it wants to maximize the welfare of its citizens, how does the community make these decisions? Consider first the relationship between the total cost per member and the number of members, given that a certain size of park is selected. Clearly, the larger the community, the more people there are to shoulder the expense of the park, and the smaller the required contribution per member. But if the per capita cost continually decreases with membership size, why not simply invite an infinite number of people to join? The problem is that as more people join the community, the park becomes congested. The **marginal congestion cost** measures the dollar cost of the incremental congestion created by each new member. We assume that the marginal congestion cost increases with the number of members. *The community should expand its membership until the marginal decrease in the membership fee just equals the per person marginal increase in congestion cost.*

Now turn to the flip side of the problem; for any given number of members in the community, how big should the park be? A bigger park yields greater benefits, although like most goods we assume it is subject to diminishing marginal utility. The marginal cost of increased park acreage is just the price of the extra land divided by the number of members sharing its cost. *The size of the park, measured in acres, should be increased to the point where each member's marginal benefit just equals the per member marginal cost.*

We can now put together these two pieces of the picture to describe an optimal community or club. The optimal community is one in which the number of members and the level of services simultaneously satisfy the condition that the marginal cost equal the corresponding marginal benefit. Although this club model is very simple, it highlights the crucial aspects of the community formation process. Specifically, it suggests how community size depends on the types of public goods the people want to consume, the extent to which these goods are subject to crowding, and the costs of obtaining them, among other things. Viewing communities as clubs does leave unanswered several important questions that are relevant for understanding subnational public finance:

1. How are the public services to be financed? A country club can charge a membership fee, but a community normally levies taxes to pay for public goods.
2. A club can exclude nonmembers and so eliminate the free-rider problem. How can communities achieve this end?
3. When people throughout the country organize themselves into many different clubs (communities), will the overall allocation of public goods prove to be equitable and efficient?

These questions are taken up in the next section.

THE TIEBOUT MODEL

"Love it or leave it." When people who oppose government policy are given this advice, it is generally as constructive as telling them to "drop dead." Only in extreme cases do we expect people to leave their country because of government policy. Because of the large monetary and psychic costs of emigrating, a more realistic option is to stay home and to try to change the policy. On the other hand, most citizens are not as strongly attached to their local communities. If you dislike the policies being followed in Surrey, B.C., perhaps the easiest (but not necessarily costless) thing to do is move a few kilometres away to Richmond, B.C. This section discusses the relationship among intercommunity mobility, voluntary community formation, and the efficient provision of public goods.

Chapter 4 examined the idea that markets generally fail to provide public goods efficiently. The root of the problem is that the market does not force individuals to reveal their true preferences for public goods. Everyone has an incentive to be a free rider. The usual conclusion is that some kind of government intervention is required.

In an important article, Tiebout (1956) (rhymes with "me too") argued that the ability of individuals to move among jurisdictions produces a market-like solution to the local public goods problem. Individuals vote with their feet and locate in the community that offers the bundle of public services and taxes they like best. Much as citizens satisfy their demands for private goods by purchasing them on the market, they satisfy their demands for public services by the appropriate selection of a community in which to live and pay taxes. In equilibrium, people distribute themselves across communities on the basis of their demands for public services. Each individual receives his or her desired level of public services and cannot be made better off by moving (or else he or she would). Hence, the equilibrium is Pareto efficient, and government action is not required to achieve efficiency.

TIEBOUT'S ASSUMPTIONS

Tiebout's provocative assertion that a quasi-market process can solve the public goods problem has stimulated a large amount of research. Much of that research has been directed toward finding a precise set of sufficient conditions under which the ability of citizens to vote with their feet leads to efficient public goods provision. Some of the conditions are as follows:[1]

1. *No externalities arise from local government behaviour.* As noted later, to the extent that there are spillover effects among communities, the allocation of resources is inefficient.
2. *Individuals are completely mobile.* Each person can travel costlessly to a jurisdiction whose public services are best for him or her. The location of a place of employment puts no restriction on where individuals live and does not affect their income.
3. *People have perfect information with respect to each community's public services and taxes.*
4. *There are enough different communities so that each individual can find one with public services meeting his or her demands.*
5. *The cost per unit of public services is constant, so that if the quantity of public services doubles, the total cost also doubles.* In addition, the technology of public service provision is such that if the number of residents doubles, the quantity of the public service provided must double.

To see why these conditions are required for a Tiebout equilibrium to be efficient, imagine instead that the cost per unit of public services fell as the scale of provision increased. In that case, there would be scale economies of which independently operating communities might fail to take advantage.

This assumption makes the public service essentially a publicly provided private good. "Pure" public goods (such as national defence) do not satisfy this assumption. However, many local services, such as education and garbage collection, appear to fit this description to a reasonable extent.

6. *Public services are financed by a proportional property tax.* The tax rate can vary across communities.[2]
7. *Communities can enact exclusionary zoning laws—statutes that prohibit certain uses of land.* Specifically, they can require that all houses be of some minimum size. To see why this assumption is crucial, recall that in a Tiebout equilibrium, communities are segregated on the basis of their members' demands for public goods. If income is positively correlated with the demand for public services, community segregation by income results. In high-income communities, the level of property values tends to be high, and hence the community can finance a given amount of public spending with a relatively low property tax rate. Low-income families have an incentive to move into rich communities and build relatively small houses. Because of the

---

[1] Not all of these conditions were included in Tiebout's original article.

[2] Tiebout (1956) assumed finance by head taxes. The more realistic assumption of property taxation is from Hamilton (1975).

low tax rate, low-income families have relatively small tax liabilities, but nevertheless enjoy the high level of public service provision. As more low-income families get the idea and move in, the tax base per family in the community falls. Tax rates must be increased to finance the expanded level of public services required to serve the increased population.

Since we assume perfect mobility, the rich have no reason to put up with this. They can just move to another community. But what stops the poor from following them? In the absence of constraints on mobility, nothing stops them. Clearly, it is possible for a game of musical suburbs to develop in a Tiebout model. Exclusionary zoning prevents this phenomenon and thus maintains a stable Pareto efficient equilibrium.

TIEBOUT AND THE REAL WORLD

The Tiebout model is clearly not a perfect description of the real world. People are not perfectly mobile, there are probably not enough communities so that each family can find one with a bundle of services that suits it perfectly, and so on. Moreover, contrary to the model's implication, we observe many communities within which there are massive income differences and, hence, presumably different desired levels of public service provision. Just consider any major city. However, we should not dismiss the Tiebout mechanism too hastily. There is a lot of mobility in the Canadian economy. For example, in 2013-14 about 320,000 people (just under 1 percent of the total population) changed their province of residence. And in Canada's major urban areas, residents often have a choice among several communities in which they may wish to live. Looking at Toronto, Montreal, and Vancouver, Turcotte and Vézina (2010) find that about 14 percent of the population aged 25 to 44 years had moved from the central municipality to a surrounding municipality and about 5 percent moved in the opposite direction between 2001 and 2006.

There have been a number of empirical tests of the Tiebout hypothesis. One type of study looks at whether the values of local public services and taxes are capitalized (i.e., translated into higher local property or housing values). The idea is that if people move in response to local packages of taxes and public services, differences in these packages should be reflected in property values. A community with better public services should have higher property values, other things (including taxes) being the same. Studies suggest that capitalization is a fairly widespread phenomenon.[3] Other studies examine whether changes in the levels of local public goods (or bads) lead to migration across jurisdictions. For example, Banzhaf and Walsh (2008) find that people migrate as local pollution levels change, evidence that people do indeed "vote with their feet." These results suggest that, at least in some settings, the Tiebout model is a good depiction of reality.

INTERPROVINCIAL FISCALLY INDUCED MIGRATION

In Canada, economists have paid a good deal of attention to the implications of Tiebout's theory for migration between provinces. In the absence of government, economic theory suggests that the people will move from one province when they expect to earn a higher income and thus a higher standard of living. In Figure 8.1 (adapted from Day and Winer, 1997) we consider two provinces, M (Mountainia) and A (Atlantica). Downward-sloping curves MPL_M and MPL_A represent the marginal product of labour (demand) curves for each region. Thus, the vertical axes measure wage rates (dollars per hour) and the horizontal axis measures numbers of workers in the two provinces. Suppose the initial distribution of workers among the two provinces is found at point B. At this point, wages are higher in province M than in province A and we would expect some workers to migrate from A to M seeking the higher wages. The increased (reduced) supply of labour in province M (A) will cause wages to fall (rise) until equilibrium is reached at point C. At this point the supply of labour in province M is measured by the distance $0_M C$ and the supply of labour in province A is measured by the distance $0_A C$. At point C, marginal products of labour are equalized in both provinces and an efficient distribution of labour is achieved.

Tiebout's theory applies when, in addition to wage differentials, there are also higher **net fiscal benefits** (NFBs) in one of the two provinces. NFBs are simply the value of publicly provided services minus their cost to the recipient of those services. According to a theory proposed by Boadway and Flatters (1982), higher NFBs in

---

[3] See Chapter 20 for a discussion of capitalization in the context of property taxes.

FIGURE 8.I

ANALYSIS OF THE EFFECT OF NET FISCAL BENEFITS ON MIGRATION

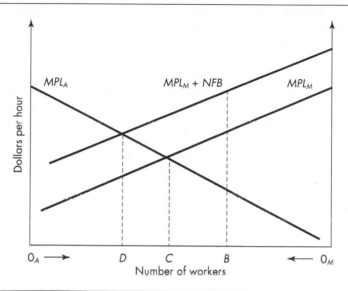

Source: Adapted from Day and Winer (1997).

province *M* may provide an incentive for too many people to migrate. The parallel line above MPL_M adds the NFB that might come as a result of a greater endowment of natural resources to province *M*. In this case (again starting at point *B*), too many workers will migrate from *A* to *M* to achieve an efficient distribution of labour. The difference in migration caused by the NFB is measured by the segment *DC*. This migration response to differences in NFBs is called *fiscally induced migration*. One proposal for correcting this inefficiency is to use intergovernmental grants to equalize NFBs across provinces. This reasoning has often been used to provide an efficiency justification for the Canadian federal government's extensive equalization program, discussed later in this chapter.

A number of important questions arise. First, is there compelling evidence that migration responds to differences in NFBs? Second, are there positive net gains from using equalization to restore the efficient distribution of labour across provinces? Third, does Canada's equalization program achieve these net gains or does the program introduce its own inefficiencies?

There is some evidence to suggest that migration is sensitive to NFBs. Day and Winer (1994) found some evidence of migration responding to differences in the levels of expenditure, transfers, and taxation across provinces, although the magnitude of these responses would likely be empirically fairly small in the short term and would take long periods of time to have a significant effect. They also found that migration responded to regional differences in unemployment insurance benefits.[4]

The evidence on the second question is mixed. Watson (1986) used estimates from Winer and Gauthier (1982) to calculate the efficiency gains that would accrue to Canada if an equalization program were able to close the gap in incomes that arises from differences in NFBs between provinces. He finds that the cost of the program far outweighed its benefits in terms of increased labour market efficiency. Wilson (2003) argues that Watson's approach underestimates the potential efficiency gains from equalization because it focuses only on annual migration responses. Migration adjustment can, however, take much longer than one year. Recalculating Watson's results, taking into account the full migration responses, Wilson finds that the efficiency case for equalization is much stronger.

Evidence for the third question suggests that for Canada equalization (or, more generally, intergovernmental grants) may in practice actually worsen migration inefficiencies.[5] Courchene (1970) and others have argued that intergovernmental transfers may make the distribution of labour across provinces worse rather than better by inhibiting migration that should come about as a result of wage differentials. Recent work by Albouy (2012)

[4] This conclusion is disputed in work by Lin (1995).

[5] There are other potential distortions. See, for example, Smart (1998) (2007).

showing that federal transfers in Canada increase inefficiency costs by about $4.3 billion per year provides some strong evidence in support of this argument. Using Canadian data, he estimates NFBs by province for 2001. NFBs, expressed in per capita terms and as a deviation from the national average, range from a high of $2,171 in Newfoundland to a low of –$1,083 in Ontario. Albouy finds that reductions in NFBs offset 76 percent of the income gain associated with moving to a province where the wage level is one dollar higher—a powerful disincentive to labour mobility in response to wage differentials.

This debate highlights an important issue. Equalization may, in practice, be designed with several objectives in mind (including addressing concerns about fiscally induced migration, equity, and affordability) and may have unintended consequences. For instance, Smart (1998) shows that equalization transfers can distort recipient governments' tax policies by giving them an incentive to increase distortionary taxes. Empirically, the tax-raising effect is not insignificant (see Smart (2007)). In the case of mobile capital, the tax-raising effect associated with equalization may actually help to offset the downward pressure on corporate tax rates resulting from tax competition. Boadway (2004b) offers a useful guide to the theory and practice of equalization.

OPTIMAL FEDERALISM

Now that we have an idea of how to characterize subnational governments, we return to our earlier question. Based on economic criteria, what is the optimal allocation of responsibilities among levels of government in a federal system? The goal of the theory of optimal federalism is to determine the proper division of activities among the levels of government; see Breton and Scott (1978). Let us first briefly consider macroeconomic functions.

While textbook treatments of fiscal policy portray governments as actively adjusting taxation and spending levels to smooth out slumps and booms in economic activity, the reality for most federations is that almost all macroeconomic stabilization comes from so-called automatic stabilizers; see Boothe and Petchey (1996). Taxes, like income or sales taxes, are automatic stabilizers in that tax revenues automatically rise when the economy is strong and decline when it is weak. On the spending side, automatic stabilizers include government programs, such as employment insurance and social assistance, that rise when the economy is weak and fall when it is strong. As long as a government's budget includes automatic stabilizers, it will contribute to macroeconomic stabilization regardless of whether it is at the national or subnational level.[6]

With respect to the microeconomic activities of enhancing efficiency and equity, there is considerably more controversy. Posed within the framework of welfare economics, the question is whether a centralized or decentralized system is more likely to maximize social welfare.[7] To keep things simple, most of our discussion assumes just two levels of government: central and "regional." No important insights are lost with this assumption.

ADVANTAGES OF A DECENTRALIZED SYSTEM

Tailoring government to local tastes. Some people want expensive computers used in the education of their children; others believe this is unnecessary. Some people enjoy parks; others do not. Some people believe government should be financed by income taxes; others think user fees are best. A central government tends to provide the same level of public services throughout the country, regardless of the fact that people's tastes differ. As de Tocqueville observed, "In great centralized nations the legislator is obliged to give a character of uniformity to the laws, which does not always suit the diversity of customs and of districts" (Oates, 1972: 31). Clearly, it is inefficient to provide individuals with more or less of a public good than they desire if the quantity they receive can be more closely tailored to their preferences. Under a decentralized system, individuals with similar tastes for public goods group together, so communities provide the types and quantities of public goods desired by their inhabitants. (Remember the "club" view of communities.) A closely related notion is that a regional government's greater proximity to the people makes it more responsive to citizens' preferences than

---

[6] While this is true for fiscal policy, it is not true for monetary policy. Federations with a common currency and integrated financial markets can have only a single interest rate or exchange rate policy, even if that policy has different impacts in different regions of the country.

[7] Of course, this assumes that we can even define a consistent social welfare function and, further, that there is agreement over which population—regional or national—citizens wish to redistribute income.

a central government. This is especially likely to be the case in a large country where the costs of obtaining and processing information on everybody's tastes are substantial.

This logic suggests that the more preferences vary in an area, the greater the benefits to decentralized decision-making in that area. To test the predictive power of this notion, Strumpf and Oberholzer-Gee (2002) examine how U.S. states differ with respect to the level of government that regulates the sale of liquor. People from different religious backgrounds are observed to differ in their beliefs as to whether the sale of liquor should be prohibited. The theory of federalism implies that states with greater religious diversity should be more likely to decentralize control over regulatory policy toward alcohol, everything else being the same. They found support for this hypothesis; local control increases with variation in preferences within the state.

The logic of federalism also suggests that economic regulations enacted at the national level may not make sense in every community. In Canada, regulations for workplace health and safety are set by provincial governments. Should a single set of regulations be set in Ottawa if the nature of work varies greatly across provinces? Should a single standard be set by the federal government when educational circumstances and resources vary from city to city and province to province? In the past, standards for student–teacher ratios were generally set by individual school boards. More recently, many provincial governments have moved to province-wide standards for class size. Finally, regulations regarding Sunday shopping are set by provinces (or municipalities). Will local wishes and needs be considered if a single rule is imposed by Parliament for the entire country?

Fostering intergovernmental competition. Many theories of government behaviour focus on the fact that government managers may lack incentives to produce at minimum feasible cost (see Chapter 7). Managers of private firms who fail to minimize costs are eventually driven out of business. In contrast, politicians and government managers can continue to muddle along. However, if citizens are aware of other jurisdictions where programs are better managed, then substantial mismanagement may cause citizens to use their vote to support political parties that promise change. This threat may create incentives for politicians and government managers to produce more efficiently and be more responsive to their citizens.

Experimentation and innovation in regionally provided goods and services. For many policy questions, no one is certain what the right answer is, or even whether there is a single solution that is best in all situations. One way to find out is to let each region choose its own way, and then compare the results. A system of diverse governments enhances the chances that new solutions to problems will be sought.[8] As U.S. Supreme Court Justice Louis Brandeis once observed, "It is one of the happy incidents of the Federal system that a single courageous state may, if its citizens choose, serve as a laboratory, and try moral, social, and economic experiments without risk to the rest of the country."

From all appearances, Brandeis's laboratories are busily at work in Canada as well. Examples include:

- In 1962, the province of Saskatchewan instituted a program of health insurance in which the government eliminated private payment for doctors' services. Doctors were thereafter paid their fees from the provincial fund. After an initial bitter strike by Saskatchewan doctors, the program became a model that was adopted by provinces across the country.

- With rapid growth in the number of two-income families and working mothers, provision of public and private childcare services is much more important. Quebec and British Columbia now provide substantial subsidies for childcare with the expectation that long-run social and economic benefits flow from such policies. Provinces will learn from one another.

- There are increasing differences in tuition at provincial universities across Canada, as well as "experiments" in varying tuition from program to program. Tuition differences among programs may reflect differences in the social and private benefits of programs, as well as differing costs. University leaders, and others, are carefully watching these experiences.

- Some provinces are "experimenting" with different climate policies aimed at reducing GHG emissions. B.C. has introduced a tax on carbon emissions. Quebec has adopted, and Ontario has promised to introduce, a cap and trade scheme. Alberta uses a regulatory approach where large emitters are required to achieve specific emissions intensity reduction targets (emissions intensity refers to emissions per unit of output) but has announced a plan to introduce a broad-based carbon tax.

---

[8] See Oates (2008) for a brief but interesting discussion of "laboratory federalism."

In the past, some programs that began as experiments at the provincial level eventually became federal policy. After the Great Depression, for example, the designers of the federal unemployment insurance program took advantage of the experience of several provinces that had earlier instituted programs for unemployment relief. Due to fiscal and other pressures, we will see increasing experimentation in the delivery of health care.

DISADVANTAGES OF A DECENTRALIZED SYSTEM

Consider a country composed of a group of small communities. Each community government makes decisions to maximize a social welfare function depending only on the utilities of its members—outsiders do not count.[9] How do the results compare with those that would emerge from maximizing a national social welfare function that attempts to take into account all citizens' utilities? We consider efficiency, then equity issues.

Efficiency Issues

Several reasons why a system of decentralized governments might lead to an inefficient allocation of resources are outlined below.

Externalities. We define a public good with benefits that accrue only to members of a particular community as a *local public good*. For example, the public library in Brandon, Manitoba, has little effect on the welfare of people in Sherbrooke, Quebec. However, in many situations, the activities undertaken by one community can affect the utility levels of people in other communities. If one town provides good public education for its children and some of them eventually emigrate, then other communities may benefit from having a better-educated work force. Towns can affect each other negatively as well. If Edmonton, Alberta, does not properly clean the water it returns to the North Saskatchewan River, some of the waste makes its way to Prince Albert, Saskatchewan. In short, communities impose externalities (both positive and negative) on each other. If each community cares only about its own members, these externalities are overlooked. Hence, according to the standard argument, resources are allocated inefficiently.

Scale economies in provision of public goods. For certain public services, the cost per person may fall as the number of users increases. If several communities coordinate their use of such services, the members of all participating communities are better off because each person pays less for the service. Thus, for example, it might make sense for neighbouring communities to run their police departments jointly and so avoid the costs of acquiring duplicate communications equipment. Communities that operate with complete independence lose such opportunities for cost savings.

Of course, various activities are subject to different scale economies. The optimal scale for library services might differ from that for fire protection. And both surely differ from the optimal scale for national defence. This observation, incidentally, helps rationalize a system of overlapping jurisdictions—each jurisdiction can handle those services with scale economies that are appropriate for the jurisdiction's size.

On the other hand, consolidation is not the only way for communities to take advantage of scale economies. A town might contract out to other governments or to the private sector for the provision of certain public goods and services. For example, the city of Ottawa has privately provided garbage collection.

Inefficient tax systems. Roughly speaking, efficient taxation requires that inelastically demanded or supplied goods be taxed at relatively high rates, and vice versa.[10] Suppose that the supply of capital to the entire country is fixed, but capital is highly mobile across subfederal jurisdictions. Each jurisdiction realizes that if it levies a substantial tax on capital, the capital will simply move elsewhere, thus making the jurisdiction worse off. In such a situation, a rational jurisdiction taxes capital very lightly, or even subsidizes it. Tax competition may lead to underprovision of public goods. (Tax collusion leading to overprovision of public goods, while probably less common, may also occur.)

In reality, of course, the total capital stock is not fixed in supply. Nor is it known just how responsive firms' locational decisions are to differences in local tax rates. For example, there is some statistical evidence from

---

[9] Recall that we are ignoring, for now, the questions of how the social welfare function is determined and whether the people who run the government actually try to maximize it. See Chapter 7.

[10] See Chapter 16.

the United States that employment growth in a jurisdiction is inversely correlated with its tax rates on businesses (Mark, McGuire, and Papke, 2000). For France, Rathelot and Sillard (2008) find that increasing the differential in local business taxes across municipalities had a significant and positive effect on the probability that a firm will set up in the lower-taxed municipality. In any case, the basic point remains: taxes levied by decentralized communities may not be efficient from a national point of view. Instead, communities may select taxes on the basis of whether they can be exported or shifted to outsiders. For example, Saskatchewan rebates a portion of the gasoline tax paid by residents, thus imposing the full tax only on visitors.[11]

An implication of tax shifting is that communities may purchase too many local public goods. Efficiency requires that local public goods be purchased up to the point where their social marginal benefit equals social marginal cost. If communities can shift some of the tax burden to other jurisdictions, the community's perceived marginal cost is less than social marginal cost. This induces them to increase their purchases of local public goods until the social marginal benefit equals the perceived marginal cost rather than the social marginal cost. The result is an inefficiently large amount of local public goods.

Scale economies in tax collection. Individual communities may not be able to take advantage of scale economies in the collection of taxes. Each community has to devote resources to tax administration, and savings may be obtained by having a joint taxing authority. Why not split the costs of a single computer to keep track of tax returns, rather than having each community purchase its own? Of course, some of these economies might be achieved just by cooperation among the jurisdictions, without actual consolidation taking place. In several provinces, provincial sales taxes are harmonized with the federal Goods and Services tax and are collected by the Canada Revenue Agency.

Equity Issues

In a utilitarian philosophical framework, the maximization of social welfare may require income transfers to the poor. Suppose that the pattern of taxes and expenditures in a particular community is favourable to its low-income members. If there are no barriers to movement between communities, we might expect an "in-migration" of the poor from the rest of the country. As the poor population increases, so does the cost of the redistributive fiscal policy. At the same time, the town's upper-income people may decide to exit. Why should they pay high taxes for the poor when they can move to another community where the expenditure pattern is to their own benefit? Thus, the demands on the community's tax base increase while its size decreases. Eventually, the redistributive program has to be abandoned.

This argument relies heavily on the notion that people's decisions to locate in a given community are influenced by the available tax-welfare package. Some evidence along these lines is provided by Glaeser (2012), who argues that "if a locality tries to heavily redistribute, then wealthier citizens and businesses have an incentive to flee." The interpretation of this finding is a bit tricky; it might be the case that causation runs in the other direction—states whose citizens have experienced wage increases vote for more progressive tax systems. In any case, the result suggests that caution is required when decentralized jurisdictions attempt to undertake income redistribution.

IMPLICATIONS

The foregoing discussion makes it clear that a purely decentralized system cannot be expected to maximize utilitarian social welfare.[12] Efficiency requires that those commodities with spillovers that affect the entire country—*national public goods*—be provided at the national level. Defence is a classic example. On the other hand, it seems appropriate that local public goods be provided locally. This leaves us with the in-between case of community activities that create spillover effects that are not national in scope. One possible solution is to put all the communities that affect each other under a single regional government. In theory, this government would take into account the welfare of all its citizens, and so internalize the externalities. However, a larger governmental jurisdiction carries the cost of less responsiveness to local differences in tastes.

---

[11] As usual, a precise answer to the tax incidence question requires information on market structure, elasticity of demand, and the structure of costs. See Chapter 14.

[12] Oates (2008) gives a useful summary of the evolution of the fiscal federalism literature, including the contributions of two relatively new strands, the second generation approach to, and the political economy/institutional models of, fiscal federalism.

An alternative method for dealing with externalities is a system of Pigouvian taxes and subsidies. Chapter 5 shows that efficiency can be enhanced when the government taxes activities that create negative externalities and subsidizes activities that create positive externalities. We can imagine the central government using similar devices to influence the decisions of regional governments. For example, if primary and secondary education create benefits that go beyond the boundaries of a jurisdiction, the central government can provide regions with educational subsidies. Regional autonomy is maintained, yet the externality is corrected. As we will see in Chapter 13, this is exactly the rationale used in Canada for federal grants to support post-secondary education, a provincial responsibility.

Our theory suggests a fairly clean division of responsibility for public good provision. In practice, there is considerable interplay between levels of government. For example, although provinces have primary responsibility for environmental regulation, citizens and firms must also obey numerous federal regulations. Given that regions might ignore the externalities created by their actions in the absence of such regulations, the presence of regulations may improve welfare. However, some believe that the system of federal, in addition to provincial, government regulation has become so complicated that it may be difficult to determine which government has responsibility for what.

THE ROLE OF THE CONSTITUTION

Although economic theory provides some guidance regarding the division of spending responsibilities and taxation in federal systems, generally speaking the actual division of powers is dictated by the country's constitution and its interpretation by the courts. Canada is no exception to this general rule. Canada's original Constitution of 1867 (the British North America Act) was an agreement among four British colonies: New Brunswick, Nova Scotia, Ontario (Upper Canada), and Quebec (Lower Canada). The British North America Act (BNA Act) laid out specific responsibilities for both the federal (Section 91) and the provincial (Section 92) governments. Federal powers include such matters as public debt, the regulation of trade and commerce, the postal service, defence, currency and coinage, and Native Peoples and lands reserved for Native Peoples. Provincial powers include such matters as provincial borrowing, the management and sale of public lands, hospitals and asylums, and generally all matters of a local or private nature within the province. Section 93 also gives powers over education to the provinces.

Over time, the Constitution has been interpreted by the courts—first by the Judicial Committee of the Privy Council in London, and later by the Supreme Court of Canada. These interpretations have resulted in an actual division of responsibilities that differs in some respects from the written Constitution. An important theme in judicial interpretation has been the affirmation of the federal government's right to act in areas of provincial responsibility through its use of the "spending power" under the general provision of Section 91 for the federal government "to make laws for the Peace, Order and Good Government of Canada." Thus, today we observe the federal government involved in funding such activities as health care and education, which constitutionally are the exclusive responsibility of the provinces.

Chapter 1 discusses the tremendous growth in government during the twentieth century. Although the Constitution provides an important element of stability in a changing environment, the changing role of government and differing interpretations of the Constitution have created pressures and disagreements between the federal and provincial levels. The result has been a continual process of adjustment within the federation. The ability of Canadian federalism to adjust to changing needs has been and continues to be an essential attribute.[13]

In 1982, the federal government and all provinces except Quebec agreed to a major revision of the Constitution (Constitution Act, 1982). Although many important new provisions were added, one of the most interesting for students of fiscal federalism was related to regional disparities. In Section 36, the federal government and the provinces committed to reducing regional economic disparities. Further, in Section 36(2) the federal government committed to the principle of "making equalization payments to ensure that provincial governments have sufficient revenues to provide reasonably comparable levels of public services at reasonably comparable levels of taxation." This brings us to the matter of intergovernmental grants.

---

[13] For an extensive review of the first 60 years of federal–provincial relations that provides insights into Canada's federation that are often as pertinent today as in the 1930s, see the *Report of the Royal Commission on Dominion-Provincial Relations* (Canada, 1940). See, in particular, Book II, Section G: "Abstract of the Leading Recommendations."

INTERGOVERNMENTAL GRANTS

Table 8.2 showed that while the federal government's share of total government revenue exceeded its share of total government expenditure, the opposite was true for provincial and local governments. Intergovernmental grants from one level of government to another are the main method for changing fiscal resources within a federal system and helping to "close" the gaps between revenue and expenditure shares at the different government levels. Table 8.4 presents data on federal transfers to lower-level governments in Canada. Between 1926 and 2009, grants from the federal government to provinces and local governments have ranged from 4.7 percent to 25 percent of total federal outlays. Grants, as a percentage of total federal outlays, grew rapidly in the postwar period until the mid-1970s and then declined gradually, reaching 18 percent in 2000. By 2009, the share of federal spending on grants had risen to 25 percent. As shown in the last column in Table 8.4, about 22 percent of combined provincial and local government revenue came from federal grants in 2009.

Grants help finance activities that run practically the entire gamut of government functions. More than half of federal grant outlays go for programs relating to post-secondary education, health, and social assistance. Grants are also used for general fiscal assistance, development of infrastructure, and other purposes.

Why are intergovernmental transfers such an important source of finance for provincial programs? One explanation emphasizes that over the last several decades the demand for the types of services traditionally provided by provincial and local governments—health, education, and social assistance—has been growing rapidly. However, provincial and local revenue structures, which depend heavily on sales and property taxes, have not provided the means to keep pace with the growth of desired expenditures. In contrast, federal tax revenues have tended to grow automatically over time, largely due to the substantial federal share of the personal income tax. Hence, there is a "mismatch" between where tax money is collected and where it is

TABLE 8.4

Federal Transfers to Lower Levels of Government, Selected Measures[a,b], Various Years

	Total Federal Transfers (millions of 2002 dollars)	As a Percentage of Federal Expenditures	As a Percentage of Provincial and Local Expenditures	As a Percentage of Provincial and Local Total Revenue
1926	190	4.7	2.9	3.0
1939	1,113	16.4	9.8	10.3
1950	2,145	10.6	12.7	13.4
1960	6,413	14.7	17.6	19.2
1970	16,995	23.4	16.5	17.3
1980	26,508	21.5	15.7	16.3
1990	34,546	18.4	14.1	14.7
2000	32,964	17.6	11.4	11.1
2009	54,780	25.2	13.9	21.7

[a] Federal expenditures do not include CPP and QPP payments. Provincial and local government expenditures include provincial expenditures net of transfers to local government in order to avoid double counting the transfers between these two levels of government. Provincial and local government total revenue is calculated using local government revenue net of transfers also to avoid double counting.

[b] These figures do not include the "tax point" transfers to the provinces. Such transfers occur when there is an agreement that the federal government will reduce its tax rates, enabling the provinces to simultaneously raise their rates by an equivalent amount. For 2011–12, the estimated cash transfer (as part of the Canada Health Transfer and the Canada Social Transfer) was about $38.5 billion. The "tax point" transfer attached to these grants was worth an additional $21.9 billion in current dollars.

Source: The numbers are calculated using data from Karen Treff and Deborah Ort, *Finances of the Nation, 2010* (Toronto: Canadian Tax Foundation, 2011), Tables B3 and B.5; Statistics Canada, *Canadian Economic Observer, Historical Statistical Supplement, 1995/96*, Cat. No. 11-210-XPB (Ottawa, July 1996); and Statistics Canada, *Canadian Economic Observer, Historical Statistical Supplement, 2009/10*, Cat. No. 11-210-XPB (Ottawa, August 2010).

INTERGOVERNMENTAL GRANTS AND ACCOUNTABILITY

In Canada, provinces do relatively more of the spending while the federal government collects a greater share of revenue and transfers some of that revenue back to the provinces. Intergovernmental transfers are a key feature of fiscal federalism in Canada. These grants are considerable—around $65 billion for 2014–15. While there are certainly benefits to this system, some argue there is a serious downside to large intergovernmental grants.

In the lead-up to the federal government's 2015 budget, William Robson, president and CEO of the C. D. Howe Institute, argued that the federal government should just say no when the provinces come asking for more cash. Robson claims the problem is the lack of accountability. When the spending of provincial governments is financed (or partly financed) by taxes raised by the federal government, the accountability of provincial governments to their voters is weakened. And because provincial government spending is not clearly linked to provincial taxes, there is less pressure by the public for spending restraint. In the past, escalating federal cash to the provinces led to more provincial spending, not less. Robson argues that provincial governments need to increase taxes to obtain the revenue they need so that they can be held accountable for their successes and failures to deliver what they promised to voters. Another option might be to alter the structure of intergovernmental grants; for example, using earmarked grants, as discussed in Smart and Bird (2009). Both options may offer potential for improving accountability and, possibly, controlling government spending, but neither option appears to be high on any politician's agenda.

Based on Smart and Bird (2009) and Robson, "More Money for Provinces? Just Say No, Mr. Harper," *The Globe and Mail.* October 7, 2014.

Complete references for this feature can be found in the References section on page 479.

demanded.[14] Grants from the federal government to provinces, and from provinces to municipalities, provide a way of correcting this mismatch.

The mismatch theory is unsatisfying because it fails to explain why provinces and municipalities cannot raise their tax rates to keep up with increases in the demand for local public goods and services. One possible explanation is that tax competition limits the extent to which provinces can raise taxes. This argument may apply in the case of taxes on highly mobile factors like capital but is less convincing when considering all the taxes that are available to provincial governments. As noted in the next section, we probably have to turn to political considerations to explain the pattern of intergovernmental grants.

THE THEORY OF INTERGOVERNMENTAL GRANTS

A grant's structure can influence its economic impact. There are basically two types of grants, conditional and unconditional, which we discuss in turn.

Conditional Grants

Conditional grants are sometimes called categorical grants. The donor specifies, to some extent, the purposes for which the recipient can use the funds. The ways in which conditional grant money must be spent are often spelled out in minute detail. There are several types of conditional grants.

Matching grant. For every dollar given by the donor to support a particular activity, a certain sum must be expended by the recipient. For example, a grant might indicate that whenever a province spends a dollar on an approved infrastructure project, the federal government will contribute a dollar as well.

---

[14] This mismatch is also referred to as a "fiscal imbalance" or a vertical fiscal gap. See Boadway (2004a), Council of the Federation (2006), and Bird and Tarasov (2004) for a discussion on the optimal size of the fiscal imbalance.

FIGURE 8.2

ANALYSIS OF A MATCHING GRANT

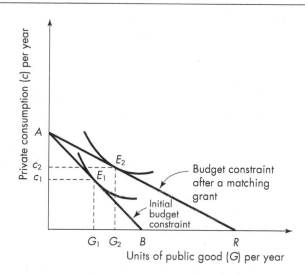

The standard theory of rational choice can help us understand the effects of a matching grant. In Figure 8.2, the horizontal axis measures the quantity of provincial government output, G, consumed by the residents of the Province of Atlantica. The vertical axis measures the amount of private good, c, consumed by the province. To keep things simple, assume that units of G and c are defined so the price of one unit of each is \$1. Hence, assuming no saving, c is equal to after-tax income. With these assumptions, Atlantica's budget constraint between c and G is a straight line whose slope in absolute value is one. The unitary slope indicates that for each dollar Atlantica is willing to spend, it can obtain one unit of public good. The budget constraint is denoted as AB in Figure 8.2.

Suppose that Atlantica's preferences for G and c can be represented by a set of conventionally shaped indifference curves.[15] Then, if the province seeks to maximize its utility subject to the budget constraint, it chooses point E_1, where public good consumption is G_1 and private goods consumption is c_1.

Now suppose that a matching grant regime of the sort just described is instituted. The federal government matches every dollar that Atlantica spends. When Atlantica gives up \$1 of income, it can obtain \$2 worth of G—one of its own dollars and one from the federal government. The slope (in absolute value) of Atlantica's budget line therefore becomes one-half. In effect, the matching grant halves the price of G. It is an *ad valorem* subsidy on consumption of the public good. The new budget line is drawn in Figure 8.2 as AR.[16]

At the new equilibrium, Atlantica consumes G_2 public goods and has c_2 available for private consumption. Note that not only is G_2 greater than G_1, but c_2 is also greater than c_1. Atlantica uses part of the grant to buy more of the public good and part to reduce its tax burden. It would be possible, of course, to draw the indifference curves so that c_2 equals c_1, or even so that c_2 is less than c_1. Nevertheless, there is a distinct possibility that part of the grant meant to stimulate public consumption will be used not to buy more G, but to obtain tax relief. In an extreme case, the province's indifference curves might be such that $G_2 = G_1$. In this case, the province consumes the same amount of the public good and uses the entire grant to reduce taxes. Thus, theory alone cannot indicate how a matching grant affects a province's expenditure on a public good. It depends on the responsiveness of demand to changes in price.

A matching grant is a sensible way to correct for the presence of a positive externality. As explained in Chapter 5, when an individual or a firm generates a positive externality at the margin, an appropriate subsidy can enhance efficiency. The same logic applies to a province. A province may underprovide goods, such as

---

[15] Of course, this supposition ignores all the problems—and perhaps the impossibility—of preference aggregation, considered in Chapter 7.

[16] It is worth noting that in this partial analysis, the budget line does not take into account the federal taxes required to finance the matching grant.

education or highway infrastructure, that potentially generate benefits which spill over into other provinces. Of course, all the problems that arise in implementing the efficient subsidy scheme are still present. In particular, the federal government has to be able to measure the actual size of the externality.

Closed-ended matching grant. With a matching grant, the cost to the donor ultimately depends on the recipient's behaviour. If Atlantica's consumption of G is very stimulated by the program, the federal government's contributions will be quite large, and vice versa. To put a ceiling on the cost, the donor may specify some maximum amount that it will contribute. Such a closed-ended matching grant is illustrated in Figure 8.3. As before, prior to the grant, Atlantica's budget line is AB, and the equilibrium is at point E_1. With the closed-ended matching grant, the budget constraint is the kinked line segment ADF. Segment AD has a slope of minus one-half, reflecting the one-for-one matching provision. But after point D, the donor no longer matches dollar for dollar. Atlantica's opportunity cost of a unit of government spending again becomes \$1, which is reflected in the slope of segment DF.

The new equilibrium at E_3 involves more consumption of G than under the status quo, but less than under the open-ended matching grant. The fact that the grant runs out limits its ability to stimulate expenditure on the public good. Note, however, that in some cases the closed-endedness can be irrelevant. If desired provincial consumption of G involves expenditure below the ceiling, the presence of the ceiling simply does not matter. In graphical terms, if the new tangency had been along segment AD of Figure 8.3, it would be irrelevant that points along DR were not available.[17]

Nonmatching grant. Here the donor gives a fixed sum of money with the stipulation that it be spent on the public good. Figure 8.4 depicts a nonmatching grant to buy AH units of G. At each level of provincial income, Atlantica can now buy AH more units of the public good than it could before. Thus, the new budget constraint is found by adding a horizontal distance AH to the original budget constraint AB. The result is the kinked line AHM.[18]

Atlantica maximizes utility at point E_4. Note that although public good consumption goes up from G_1 to G_4, the difference between the two is less than the amount of the grant, AH. Atlantica has followed the stipulation that it spend the entire grant on G, but at the same time it has reduced its own expenditures for

FIGURE 8.3

ANALYSIS OF A CLOSED-ENDED MATCHING GRANT

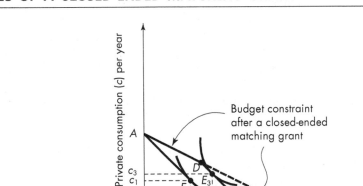

---

[17] Between 1966 and the early 1990s, the federal government made matching grants to the provinces in support of social assistance expenditures. By "capping" growth in these grants to three provinces in 1990–91 through 1994–95 while imposing no such cap for the other seven provinces, the federal government converted this grant to a closed-ended matching grant for these three provinces. Baker, Payne, and Smart (1999) estimated that the cap caused expenditure growth rates to be significantly lower than would be predicted in the absence of the cap. So, in this case, the closed-ended nature of the grant does appear to restrict the stimulative effect of the matching grant.

[18] Diagrammatically, the analysis of the conditional, nonmatching grant as illustrated in Figure 8.4 is identical to the analysis of an in-kind transfer shown in Figure 6.7 in Chapter 6.

FIGURE 8.4

ANALYSIS OF A NONMATCHING GRANT

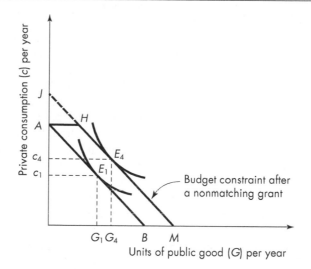

the public good. If the donor expected expenditures to be increased by exactly *AH*, then Atlantica's reaction has frustrated these hopes. It turns out that the situation depicted in Figure 8.4 is a good description of reality.

Unconditional Grants

Observe from Figure 8.4 that budget line *AHM* looks almost as if it were created by giving the province an unrestricted lump-sum grant of *AH* dollars. An unconditional grant would have led to a budget line *JM*, which is just segment *MH* extended to the vertical axis. Atlantica happens to behave exactly the same way facing constraint *AHM* as it would have if it had faced *JM*. In this particular case, then, the conditional grant could just as well have been an unrestricted lump-sum grant. Intuitively, as long as the province wants to consume at least an amount of the public good equal to the grant, the fact that the grant is conditional is not relevant. In contrast, if the province wanted to consume less of the public good than *AH* (if the indifference curves were such that the optimum along *JM* is to the left of *H*), then the conditional nature of the grant actually affects behaviour.

Why should the federal government be in the business of giving unconditional grants to provinces? One reason may be an imbalance or mismatch between revenue-raising capabilities and expenditure responsibilities. There may be a problem of tax competition among the provinces with the result that revenues are sub-optimally low. Uniform tax rates levied by the federal government, with revenues distributed to the provinces, can help to reduce this problem. A third reason is that such grants can equalize the income distribution. It is not clear that this argument stands up under scrutiny. Even if a goal of public policy is to help poor people, it does not follow that the best way to do so is to help poor provinces. After all, the chances are that even a province with a low average income will probably have some relatively rich members, and vice versa. If the goal is to help the poor, why not give them the money directly?

One possible explanation is that the federal government is particularly concerned that the poor consume a greater quantity of the publicly provided good. An important example is education. However, as we just demonstrated, with unconditional grants we cannot know for sure that all the money will ultimately be spent on the favoured good. Indeed, the same is generally true for conditional grants as well.

Measuring need. In any case, an unconditional grant program requires that the donor determine which provinces "need" money and in what amounts.[19] Allocations are often based on complicated formulas established by the donor government. The amount of grant money received by a recipient government could depend on such factors as the size of its tax bases, per capita income, demographics, and unemployment relative to the national average.

---

[19] In some cases, eligibility for conditional grants is also based on need.

In Canada (and in other federal systems, such as Germany and Australia) an important factor in determining how much a subnational government receives from the federal government is its **tax effort**, normally defined as the ratio of tax collections to tax capacity. The idea is that provinces that try hard to raise taxes but still cannot finance a very high level of public services are worthy of receiving a grant. Unfortunately, it is quite possible that this and related measures yield little or no information about a province's true effort. Suppose that Atlantica is in a position to export its tax burden in the sense that the incidence of any taxes it levies falls on outsiders. A high tax rate then tells us nothing about how much the residents of the province are sacrificing.

More fundamentally, the tax effort approach may be rendered totally meaningless because of the phenomenon of capitalization. Consider two towns, Brookville and Welland. They are identical except for the fact that Brookville has a brook providing water at essentially zero cost. In Welland, on the other hand, it is necessary to dig a well and pump the water. Welland levies a property tax to finance the water pump. If there is a tax in Welland and none in Brookville, and the communities are otherwise identical, why should anyone live in Welland? As people migrate to Brookville, property values increase there (and decrease in Welland) until there is no net advantage to living in either community. In short, property values are higher in Brookville to reflect the presence of the brook.

For reasons discussed previously, we do not expect the advantage to be necessarily 100 percent capitalized into Brookville's property values. Nevertheless, capitalization compensates at least partially for the differences between the towns. Just because Welland levies a tax does not mean it is "trying harder" than Brookville, because the Brookville residents have already paid for their water in the higher price paid for living there. We conclude that conventional measures of tax effort may not be very meaningful.

INTERGOVERNMENTAL GRANTS IN CANADA

As we saw earlier in the chapter, intergovernmental transfers are an important source of revenue for provincial and municipal governments, and an important expenditure item for the federal government. Constitutionally, both federal and provincial governments are sovereign within their spheres of influence. Municipalities have no special constitutional status; their expenditure responsibilities and revenue sources are determined by the provincial governments. This section focuses mainly on intergovernmental grants from the federal government to the provinces. Some attention is also given to recent innovations in federal transfers to local governments.

Most federal–provincial transfers come under three major programs: the Canada Health Transfer (CHT), the Canada Social Transfer (CST), and Equalization. Table 8.5 shows the share of provincial revenues accounted for by major federal transfers in 2013–14. The share of provincial revenue coming from federal cash grants ranges from a high of about 34 percent for Nova Scotia to a low of 8.8 percent in Alberta.[20] The table also shows aggregate payments for each of the three major transfers. Cash transfers to the provinces in support of health account for just over half of all major cash transfers. In per capita terms, PEI received the largest per capita transfer of over $3,500 while Alberta's per capita transfer was the lowest at $996.

Below, we provide a brief description of Canada's major transfer programs.

The CHT and CST. Provincial programs in health care are supported by the Canada Health Transfer (CHT), while the Canada Social Transfer (CST) supports provincial spending in the areas of post-secondary education and social assistance. Both the CHT and the CST are technically nonmatching conditional grants. However, few conditions are actually attached to the use of funds. Important conditions are the prohibition of residency requirements to determine eligibility for social assistance and an adherence to the five principles of the Canada Health Act (discussed in Chapter 9). In the past, grants in support of health, social assistance, and post-secondary education took the form of matching grants. Over time, however, these matching grants have been replaced by nonmatching grants.

Currently, CHT transfers consist of a cash component and a tax point component and are allocated to provinces on an equal per capita basis.[21] The total amount of funds available for the CHT cash component grows at a rate of 6 percent per year, as determined by legislation. Beginning in 2014–15, the CHT will be

---

[20] Canada's three territories also receive CHT and CST grants as well as transfers from the Territorial Formula Financing (TFF) program. The TFF, similar in nature to equalization, is designed to allow the three territories to provide public services comparable to those available in the provinces. For 2013–14, about 75 percent of all territorial revenues came from federal cash grants.

[21] For a detailed explanation of tax point transfers and the history of grants in support of health, post-secondary education, and social services; see http://www.fin.gc.ca/fedprov/his-eng.asp.

TABLE 8.5

Major Federal Transfers to Provinces and Territories: Share of Provincial Revenues, Aggregate and per Capita Amounts, 2013–14

	Federal Transfers as a Share of Provincial Revenue (%)	Canada Health Transfer (millions)	Canada Social Transfer (millions)	Equalization (millions)	Major Cash Transfers[b] (millions)	Cash Transfers per Capita ($)
Newfoundland and Labrador	9.3%	$492	$184	$0	$676	$1,280
Prince Edward Island	32.7%	$129	$51	$340	$520	$3,574
Nova Scotia	33.8%	$835	$328	$1,458	$2,971	$3,151
New Brunswick	32.1%	$669	$263	$1,513	$2,494	$3,301
Quebec	19.1%	$7,211	$2,834	$7,833	$17,878	$2,193
Ontario	17.1%	$11,980	$4,709	$3,169	$19,858	$1,465
Manitoba	23.2%	$1,119	$440	$1,792	$3,358	$2,654
Saskatchewan	11.8%	$967	$384	$0	$1,351	$1,221
Alberta	8.8%	$2,601	$1,390	$0	$3,991	$996
British Columbia	13.2%	$4,187	$1,593	$0	$5,780	$1,261
CANADA[a]	*16.8%*	*$30,190*	*$12,176*	*$16,105*	*$58,877*	*$1,675*

[a] The territories are excluded from this table.
[b] Major cash transfers include other payments, such as offshore offset payments and transfer protection payments, if applicable.

Source: Data on major cash transfers are taken from the Federal Department of Finance's website "Federal Support to Provinces and Territories," http://www.fin.gc.ca/access/fedprov-eng.asp. Revenue data used to calculate the share of provincial revenues from major cash transfers were taken from the Fiscal Reference Tables October 2014, http://www.fin.gc.ca/frt-trf/2014/frt-trf-14-eng.asp. Per capita amounts calculated using population data for 2013 taken from CANSIM @CHASS database, Table 051-0001 (all data accessed June 22, 2015).

allocated on an equal per capita *cash* basis and, in 2017–18, the annual growth in total CHT cash will be calculated based on a three-year moving average of the annual growth in nominal GDP, with a floor of 3 percent per year. CST transfers are allocated to provinces on an equal per capita cash basis; total CST cash is also legislated to grow at a fixed rate—in this case, 3 percent per year. The details of these transfer programs, including the total amounts available, how monies are allocated to provinces, and whether the conditions of each program are being met, are determined solely by the federal government and are often a source of tension between the federal and provincial governments.[22]

Equalization. This program is the main vehicle for addressing fiscal disparities across provincial governments. For 2014–15, equalization payments to provinces will total $16.7 billion, with six of 10 provinces receiving a grant. These grants are unconditional and the total amount available for equalization payments currently grows in line with GDP (growth rate is set equal to the three-year moving average in the annual growth in nominal GDP).

---

[22] The federal government's decision to move from the equal per capita allocation (which includes cash plus value of tax points) to an allocation based on equal per capita cash for CHT is one such example. See Smart (2010) for a discussion of some the issues resulting from this change.

The program has evolved substantially since it was formally introduced in 1957. Prior to 2004, equalization grants were unconditional and open-ended. Payments from the federal government to provinces were determined by comparing the fiscal capacity of each province with a given standard. Provinces with fiscal capacities below the standard received a payment while above-standard provinces did not. The open-ended nature of the grant meant that the total cost to the federal government in any given year was determined by the deficiencies in provincial fiscal capacities relative to the chosen standard. Changes introduced in 2007 and in 2009 fundamentally changed the way equalization operated and, at the same time, made entitlement calculations arguably more complex. It is, however, relatively straightforward to see how deficiencies in fiscal capacities are calculated (and how a province's equalization grant would be determined, ignoring some of the complications associated with the program's added bells and whistles).

The federal government begins by measuring provincial fiscal capacities for five tax bases: personal income tax, business income tax, consumption tax, property tax, and natural resources. The system is known as the representative tax system. The next step is to determine how much revenue a province would generate, in per capita terms, if it levied the national average tax rate on its tax base. For equalization purposes, *national* refers to the 10 provinces only and does not include the territories. Revenues are then compared to the per capita revenues that could have been generated by levying the same tax rate on the *standard* base, where the standard is defined as the national average. The province's per capita deficiency is added up for all five tax bases and multiplied by the province's population to arrive at its equalization entitlement before adjustments.

Formally, E_{ij} measures the per capita revenue deficiency (or surplus) for tax base j in province i and is calculated as:

$$E_{ij} = t_j(b_{Sj} - b_{ij})$$ (8.1)

where

b_{Sj} is the *standard* per capita tax base for revenue source j (national tax base divided by national population);
b_{ij} is the *actual* per capita tax base for revenue source j in province i; and
t_j is the national average tax rate for base j (national revenues divided by the national tax base).

Aggregating over the five tax bases yields the province's per capita equalization payment:

$$E_i = \sum_{j=1}^{5} t_j(b_{Sj} - b_{ij})$$ (8.2)

The province's aggregate payment before adjustments (TE_i) is found by multiplying E_i by the province's population, N_i:

$$TE_i = E_i N_i$$ (8.3)

With some manipulation, it is possible to rewrite Equation (8.3) in the following form:

$$TE_i = \sum_{j=1}^{5} R_j\left(\frac{N_i}{N} - \frac{B_{ij}}{B_j}\right)$$ (8.4)

where R_j is national revenues from tax base j, N_i/N is province i's share of national population, and B_{ij}/B_j is province i's share of the national tax base, j. In this form, province i's deficiency for revenue source j is calculated as the difference in the province's share of population and its share of the tax base for j. If the population share exceeds the tax base share, the province has a deficiency in this base. Multiplying this deficiency with total revenues to be equalized and summing over all five tax bases, we find TE_i.

Let's see how equalization is calculated using Equation (8.4). Illustrative data on national revenues, population shares, and tax-base shares for three provinces—Prince Edward Island, Quebec, and Ontario—are shown in Table 8.6. Consider the personal income tax base. National revenues for this base, R_j, equal $74.7 billion. Both PEI and Quebec have population shares that exceed their respective shares of this tax base so they have a deficiency in generating revenue from this source. Multiplying this deficiency by total personal income tax revenues generates a positive equalization entitlement in this revenue category for both provinces. Ontario's share of the personal income tax base (about 41 percent) *exceeds* its share of the population (38.9 percent). So it has a surplus in this tax base. Multiplying this surplus by $74.7 billion generates a negative equalization entitlement for this

TABLE 8.6

Equalization: Illustrative Calculations for Selected Provinces

	Total Revenues by Tax Base (millions of dollars)	PEI				Quebec				Ontario			
		Population Share	Tax Base Share	Base Deficiency	Equalization Entitlement (millions of dollars)	Population Share	Tax Base Share	Base Deficiency	Equalization Entitlement (millions of dollars)	Population Share	Tax Base Share	Base Deficiency	Equalization Entitlement (millions of dollars)
1. Personal Income Taxes	74,677	0.0042	0.0027	0.0015	115	0.2329	0.1905	0.0425	3,172	0.3887	0.4116	−0.0229	−1,711
2. Business Income Taxes	16,216		0.0014	0.0028	45		0.1775	0.0555	899		0.3079	0.0808	1,310
3. Consumption Taxes	72,344		0.0036	0.0006	42		0.2198	0.0131	951		0.3731	0.0156	1,129
4. Natural Resources	8,757		0.0000	0.0042	37		0.1728	0.0602	527		0.0142	0.3745	3,280
5. Property Taxes and Miscellaneous	59,160		0.0028	0.0014	82		0.1824	0.0506	2,992		0.3937	−0.0050	−294
Total Equalization by Province					$322				$8,541				$3,713

Source: This table has been prepared using data for 2009–10 supplied by the Department of Finance, March 2011. The equalization calculations assume the 2007 equalization formula is in place and do not take into account various adjustments that would be made.

tax base for Ontario. Ontario also has a surplus with respect to the property tax base but is deficient in the business income, consumption, and natural resources tax bases. By summing a province's entitlements over the five tax bases we arrive at total equalization entitlements for the three provinces before any adjustments. In our example, all three provinces have positive entitlements before adjustments (i.e., TE_i is positive).[23]

What are some of these adjustments? In Budget 2007, the federal government introduced a fiscal capacity cap to ensure that equalization payments would not lift a province's total fiscal capacity above that of any non-receiving province.[24] The federal government also announced that only 50 percent of natural resource revenues would now be included for equalization purposes.[25] The fiscal capacity cap was redefined in 2009 so that equalization would not lift the fiscal capacity of any one receiving province higher than the average of all receiving provinces. Finally, a ceiling was imposed on the annual growth in total payments. This was an important change since it has the effect of converting equalization from an open-ended to a close-ended grant. These changes were motivated in part by the federal government's concerns about the cost of equalization when Ontario became an equalization recipient for the first time in 2009.

To see how a province's actual equalization payment is affected by the fiscal capacity cap and the fixed annual growth rate in total payments, we modify Equation (8.2)[26]:

$$\hat{E}_i = \left(\sum_{j=1}^{5} t_j (b_{Sj} - b_{ij}) \right) - A - G \qquad (8.5)$$

$\hat{E}_i$, province i's actual per capita equalization payment, will differ from its per capita entitlement, E_i, if adjustments are made for the fiscal cap, the fixed growth rule, or both. A is the value of any reduction in province i's per capita entitlement due to the 2009 fiscal capacity cap. G reflects the adjustment needed if the actual growth in total equalization payments (after taking into account the fiscal capacity cap) exceeds that allowed by the fixed growth rate. If total equalization entitlements do exceed that allowed by the fixed growth rule, the federal government determines how much total payments need to be reduced to achieve the budget limit. Dividing that amount by total population yields G, the equal per capita reduction to per capita payments needed to hit the target.

The fixed growth rule has been criticized by a number of economists. Feehan (2014), for example, argues that it interferes with the basic principle that equalization payments rise (or fall) when fiscal disparities across provinces worsen (or improve). He estimates that the growth rule has generated substantial cost savings for the federal government. In 2010–11, the growth rule saved the federal government $4.5 billion, the largest annual savings to date. More modest costs savings (less than $0.5 billion) are estimated for 2013–14.[27]

Other. There are a number of smaller grant programs not included in Table 8.5. For example, the federal government estimated in its 2010 budget that it would transfer about $4.2 billion in infrastructure grants to provincial, territorial, and municipal governments. Infrastructure grants in Canada generally take the form of a closed-ended matching grant. Included as infrastructure grants are the federal government's $2 billion in gas tax sharing grants to municipal governments. Introduced in 2005, these funds are allocated across provinces on an equal, per capita basis. The grants flow through provincial governments to municipal governments to help fund longer-term infrastructure projects. Federal revenue sharing with municipal governments is a new feature of Canada's major fiscal transfers, at least since the 1940s. Unlike other infrastructure grants (made for specific programs with specific end dates), the federal government has plans to make these grants permanent.[28]

---

[23] If the sum of a province's entitlements over the five tax bases is negative ($TE_i < 0$), then the province is not eligible for equalization.

[24] See the federal government's Budget Plans for 2007 and 2009 for details. Many aspects of the 2007 equalization program were recommended in *Achieving a National Purpose: Putting Equalization Back on Track*, a report prepared by the Expert Panel on Equalization and Territorial Formula Financing (known as the O'Brien Report) in May 2006.

[25] The treatment of natural resource revenues for equalization purposes has been the subject of a long-standing debate in Canada. See Exercises 7 and 8 at the end of this chapter.

[26] We have partly adopted the approach used in Feehan (2014) to illustrate how the fiscal capacity cap and fixed growth rule can cause a discrepancy in a province's actual per capita payment and its per capita before adjustments. Feehan (2014) and Smart (2010) provide a useful discussion of the impact of these adjustments.

[27] Feehan (2014), pages 10–11.

[28] Snoddon and Hobson (2010) discuss infrastructure grants in the context of fiscal federalism and intergovernmental grants in Canada.

Also included in this category are federal grants in lieu of taxes (a replacement for property tax on federal buildings and lands since the Crown cannot be taxed), transportation grants, and other items.

GRANTS AND SPENDING BEHAVIOUR

Our provincial indifference curve analysis in Figures 8.2 to 8.4 begs a fundamental question: whose indifference curves are they? According to median voter theory (Chapter 7), the preferences are those of the province's median voter. Bureaucrats and elected officials play a passive role in implementing the median voter's wishes.

A straightforward implication of the median voter rule is that a $1 increase in individual income has exactly the same impact on public spending as receipt of a $1 unconditional grant. In terms of Figure 8.4, both events generate identical parallel outward shifts of the initial budget line. If the budget line changes are identical, the changes in public spending must also be identical.[29]

A considerable amount of empirical work has been done on the determinants of local public spending. Contrary to what one might expect, virtually all studies conclude that a dollar received by the community in the form of a grant results in *greater* public spending than a dollar increase in community income. Roughly speaking, the estimates suggest that a dollar received as a grant generates 40 cents of public spending, while an additional dollar of private income increases public spending by only 10 cents. This phenomenon has been dubbed the **flypaper effect** because the money seems to stick in the sector where it initially hits.

Some explanations of the flypaper effect focus on data and econometric issues while others focus on the role of bureaucrats and politics. In the model of Filimon, Romer, and Rosenthal (1982), bureaucrats seek to maximize the size of their budgets. As budget maximizers, the bureaucrats have no incentive to inform citizens about the community's true level of grant funding. By concealing this information, the bureaucrats may trick citizens into voting for a higher level of funding than would otherwise have been the case. According to this view, the flypaper effect occurs because citizens are unaware of the true budget constraint. To support their theory, Filimon, Romer, and Rosenthal noted that in states with direct referendums on spending questions, ballots often contain information about the tax base but rarely have data on grants.

An alternative explanation of the flypaper effect is that it is a result of incomplete political contracting between governments and citizens. Chernick (1979) and Knight (2002) explore models where grants are viewed as a type of political contract between the donor and recipient governments and grants are allocated based on an auction. However, even after controlling for the problems of incomplete political contracting, Knight (2002) still finds evidence of a flypaper effect.

Understanding the flypaper effect is important if we wish to appropriately design transfers to lower levels of government. Designing grants so that they achieve their desired purposes depends critically on knowing how grants will be spent and why they will be spent in a particular way (Inman (2008)).

OVERVIEW

At the beginning of this chapter, we posed some questions concerning federal systems. Is decentralized decision-making desirable? How should responsibilities be allocated? How should local governments finance themselves? We have seen that economic reasoning suggests federalism is a sensible system. Allowing local communities to make their own decisions very likely enhances efficiency in the provision of local public goods. However, efficiency and equity considerations are also likely to require a significant economic role for a federal government. In particular, a system in which only local resources are used to finance local public goods is viewed by many as inequitable.

Although our focus has naturally been on economic issues, questions of power and politics are never far beneath the surface in discussions of federalism. The dispersion of economic power is generally associated with the dispersion of political power. How should power be allocated? Do you view your provincial premier as a warrior fighting for recognition of regional concerns in national decision-making, or as an agent of big business, ignoring environmental concerns in favour of economic development? When you think of the federal government, do you picture an uncaring and remote bureaucrat imposing bothersome regulations, or a strong

---

[29] This result does not necessarily hold if subnational governments use distortionary taxes to finance their expenditures. See Dahlby (2011).

prime minister standing up for Canada's national interests? The different images coexist in our minds, creating conflicting feelings about the proper distribution of governmental power.

SUMMARY

- In a federal system, different governments provide different services to overlapping jurisdictions. The Canadian federal system includes the federal government, provinces, and municipalities.

- Community formation may be analyzed using the club model. The club model indicates that community size and the quantity of public goods depend on tastes for public goods, costs of providing public services, and the costs of congestion.

- The Tiebout model emphasizes the key roles of mobility, property tax finance, and zoning rules in local public finance. Under certain conditions, "voting with the feet"—moving to one's preferred community—results in a Pareto efficient allocation of public goods.

- The advantages of decentralization are the ability to alter the mix of public services to suit local tastes, the beneficial effects of competition among local governments, and the potential for low-cost experimentation at the subnational level.

- Disadvantages of decentralization are intercommunity externalities, forgone scale economies in the provision of public goods, inefficient taxation, and loss of scale economies in tax collection. In Canada, the Constitution and its subsequent interpretation by the courts plays an important role in the division of expenditure responsibilities between Ottawa and the provinces.

- Grants may be either conditional or unconditional. Each type of grant embodies different incentives for local and provincial governments. The final mix of increased expenditure versus lower taxes depends on the preferences dictating local and provincial choices.

- Historically, the federal government relied on both open-ended matching grants and unconditional grants to transfer cash to the provinces. Today, federal transfers to provinces are predominantly nonmatching.

- Empirical studies of intergovernmental grants indicate a flypaper effect—an increase in grant money induces greater spending on public goods than does an equivalent increase in local income. One possible explanation is that bureaucrats exploit citizens' incomplete information about the community budget constraint.

EXERCISES

1. For each of the following, decide whether the activity should be under the control of the federal, provincial, or municipal government, and explain why.
   a. Auto air pollution control regulations.
   b. Regulations governing whether physicians infected with HIV should be allowed to perform invasive surgery.
   c. Provision of weather satellites.
   d. Public refuse collection.
2. Illustrate the following circumstances using community indifference curves and the provincial government budget constraint:
   a. An unconditional grant increases both the quantity of public goods purchased and local taxes.
   b. A matching grant leaves provision of the public good unchanged.
   c. A closed-ended matching grant has the same impact as a conditional nonmatching grant.
   d. A closed-ended matching grant leaves local taxes unchanged.

3. The federal government drastically cut transfers to provinces and replaced some conditional grants for social assistance with unconditional ones. Discuss the effects of these changes on the following:

   a. The level of spending by provincial governments.

   b. The composition of spending by provincial governments.

   c. The quality of social assistance programs.

4. An econometric study found that the more ethnically diverse a country, the more decentralized its public sector is likely to be, other things being the same (Panizza, 1999). Is this finding consistent with our theory of federalism?

5. Assume that two municipalities (in the same province) have different demand curves for firefighters and can hire firefighters at the same constant marginal cost.

   a. Draw diagrams illustrating the demand curves and how many firefighters would be hired by each of the two municipalities.

   b. As a result of amalgamation, assume that each of the two municipalities is required to hire the same number of firefighters, and that the number hired in each municipality is the average of the number hired before amalgamation. Show the loss in welfare resulting from the requirement that the two municipalities hire the same number of firefighters.

   c. Show how the magnitude of the welfare loss may be affected by the elasticity of the demand curves in the two municipalities.

6. Consider the case where the federal government is willing to spend $X in the form of a grant to provinces. Using diagrams such as those in Figures 8.2 and 8.4, show that with normally shaped indifference curves the increase in welfare will be greater if a nonmatching grant, rather than a matching grant, is used.

7. When the federal government announced its changes to equalization in 2007, it provoked an immediate and negative response from the premier of Newfoundland. He argued that the federal government had broken its promise to exclude all nonrenewable-resource revenues. If the purpose of equalization is to equalize disparities in fiscal capacities, what reasons would the premier of Newfoundland have for wanting nonrenewable resources excluded from the formula? What arguments could you make for increasing the inclusion rate from the 50 percent under the former system to the 100 percent under the new system?

8.* This problem uses equalization data provided in an Excel spreadsheet available on the Online Learning Centre at www.mcgrawhill.ca/olc/rosen.

   a. Using the template and data provided in the spreadsheet, calculate the tax base deficiency and equalization entitlement for each tax base for Newfoundland, Nova Scotia, New Brunswick, Manitoba, Saskatchewan, Alberta, and B.C. Use the calculations for Ontario, Quebec, and PEI as a guide. Which provinces have a deficiency in all five tax bases? Which provinces have a surplus in all five bases?

   b. Based on these illustrative calculations, what is the total amount of equalization required? What provinces are equalization recipients? Note that if a province has a negative entitlement overall, it receives a zero transfer. Also note that in practice, several other adjustments are made to arrive at final equalization entitlement entitlements. We abstract from these adjustments for the purposes of this example.

   c. Suppose that included natural resource revenues increase by $1 billion and assume that provincial tax base shares are unchanged. What happens to aggregate equalization payments? Which recipient province receives the largest share of the increase in total equalization? Can you explain why?

---

* Difficult

PART FOUR
Public Expenditures in Canada

We have analyzed the circumstances in which market outcomes are either inefficient or unfair. In the next five chapters, we use the framework provided by welfare economics to study some of the major expenditure programs of Canadian governments.

The first three of these chapters focus on programs that provide insurance against different types of risks. These programs include health care, employment insurance, and public pensions and are collectively referred to as social insurance. Social insurance represents a large and growing share of government spending in Canada. We begin in Chapter 9 with a discussion of risk and insurance using health care as the example. We examine how insurance markets work and why they may fail to provide efficient and fair outcomes. We also examine the role the government plays in the health insurance market. In Chapter 10 we review the provision of employment insurance which provides workers with insurance to protect against temporary income losses from unemployment. The Canada and Quebec Pension Plans and the Old Age Security program are examined in Chapter 11. These programs provide retirees with insurance against the possibility that people may use up their resources before they die.

Social welfare and education programs, the other major spending areas of government, are discussed in Chapters 12 and 13. Social welfare programs are an important part of Canada's social safety net, providing income support to individuals with low or no income. We review these programs and their effects on work incentives in Chapter 12. Finally, in Chapter 13 we use the framework of welfare economics to understand the role of government in education.

It is helpful to keep in mind some complications that arise when analyzing the major expenditure programs in Canada. Some programs are motivated by the desire to redistribute income *and* by the need to provide insurance coverage for income losses that may not be provided by the private insurance market. Important interactions sometimes exist between programs. For example, the duration of employment insurance benefits affects the number of individuals who have to apply for welfare programs if they are unemployed for a long period of time and exhaust their unemployment insurance benefits. Finally, federal and provincial responsibilities in the provision of health, welfare, and education sometimes overlap, resulting in a need for federal–provincial coordination and intergovernmental grants.

CHAPTER 9

Health Care

That any sane nation, having observed that you could provide for the supply of bread by giving bakers a pecuniary interest in baking for you, should go on to give a surgeon a pecuniary interest in cutting off your leg, is enough to make one despair of political humanity.

—George Bernard Shaw

Moving toward alternatives, including those provided by the private sector, is a natural development of our health care system.

—Stephen Harper

AFTER READING THIS CHAPTER, THE STUDENT SHOULD BE ABLE TO:

LO1 Describe the function of health insurance.

LO2 Calculate the actuarially fair insurance premium.

LO3 Using a diagram, illustrate the conditions under which an individual would purchase insurance.

LO4 Describe the role of insurance firms in pooling risks.

LO5 Explain how adverse selection can lead to a market failure in the market for health insurance.

LO6 Outline how government intervention can address the adverse selection problem.

LO7 Demonstrate how the problem of moral hazard can lead to inefficient levels of health services.

LO8 Outline how information, externality, and equity concerns can give rise to problems in privatized health care markets.

LO9 Discuss the current challenges facing Canada's health care system and the difficulties encountered when attempting to measure its performance.

Many Canadians believe that our health system, often referred to as Medicare, is one of the best in the world, but they are concerned that it may not be one of the best for much longer. While there are constant pressures to increase spending on health care, provincial governments are seeking ways to reform our health care system. In this chapter we begin by asking what makes health care different from other goods and services. We then describe Medicare and the role played by the Canada Health Act. Next, we compare the Canadian system to health systems in other parts of the world. Finally, we focus on some key challenges and future directions for health care in Canada.

WHAT IS SPECIAL ABOUT HEALTH CARE?

Health care figures prominently in Canadian public policy debates. This is partly due to the belief that health care is unique and that private markets alone cannot be trusted to determine health care outcomes. Health care, of course, is different from goods like digital cameras and iPods because receiving it can be a matter of life and death. But food and shelter are also crucial for survival, and the country is not debating whether private markets are a good way to provide these commodities.

Another reason why health care commands so much public attention is that we spend so much on it, and the amounts are increasing rapidly. Health expenditures were less than 6 percent of gross domestic product in 1960, and they are now over 10 percent. In itself, the fact that people are spending proportionately more on a commodity is neither unique nor alarming. Expenditures on personal computers and game consoles have also been going up dramatically in recent years, but no one seems terribly upset about it.

When economists consider what is special about the health care market, they ask why that market is unlikely to provide health care in socially optimal amounts. The reasons include those outlined below.

The Role of Insurance

Health care costs can be unpredictable and very large. In such a situation, people will want insurance. Their insurance coverage in turn affects the amount of health care they receive when they are sick. Health insurance is mainly publicly provided in Canada, whereas in the United States health insurance for most workers is provided through private plans.

To understand the unique aspects of the market for health insurance, we must first understand the general role of insurance. Understanding the theory of insurance will help us both to understand health care issues and to analyze a number of government programs that protect people against a variety of adverse events. These programs, several of which are discussed in subsequent chapters, are collectively referred to as **social insurance**.

Basically, the way that health insurance works is that buyers pay money, called an insurance premium, to providers of insurance, who in turn agree to disburse some money to the insured person should an adverse health event such as illness occur. Other things being the same, the greater the insurance premium, the more compensation the buyer receives in case of illness.

To think about why people are willing to pay for insurance, it helps to analyze a specific numerical example. Consider Emily, whose income is $50,000 per year. Suppose that there is a 1 in 10 chance that she will get sick in a given year and that the cost of the illness (in terms of medical bills and lost time at work) is $30,000, thus leaving her with only $20,000 in income for that year.

In order to evaluate the options available to Emily, we need to understand the statistical concept of **expected value**, which is the amount of money an individual can expect to receive "on average" when she faces uncertain outcomes. The expected value is computed by taking the weighted sum of each of the uncertain outcomes, with the weights being the probabilities of the respective outcomes. Algebraically,

$$\text{Expected value } (EV) = (\text{Probability of outcome 1} \times \text{Payout in outcome 1})$$
$$+ (\text{Probability of outcome 2} \times \text{Payout in outcome 2}) \qquad (9.1)$$

For example, suppose that you will receive $12 if a heart is drawn from a deck of cards, and that you will lose $4 if a spade, diamond, or club is drawn. The probability of drawing a heart is ¼ and the probability of drawing some other suit is ¾. Therefore, the expected value to you of this uncertain event is computed as $EV = (¼)(\$12) + (¾)(-\$4) = \$0$. For this uncertain situation, the expected value is zero—on average, you would neither gain nor lose money.

Now let's turn to the problem confronting Emily. Table 9.1 examines two options available to her each year. In option 1, she does not buy insurance. Thus, she keeps earning $50,000 and risks losing $30,000 if the illness happens. Emily faces two possible outcomes with option 1: either she does not get sick and has an income of $50,000 (column A), or she gets sick and has an income of $20,000 (column B). The probability of the first outcome is 9 in 10, and the probability of the second outcome is 1 in 10. Using Equation (9.1) we compute in column C the expected value (also known as her expected income) of this option as follows:

$$EV(\text{Option 1}) = (9/10)(\$50,000) + (1/10)(\$20,000) = 47,000 \qquad (9.2)$$

TABLE 9.I

				Lost	(A)	(B)	(C)
				Income If	Income If	Income If	
Insurance		Probability of Staying	Probability of Getting	Income If She Gets	Income If She Stays	Income If She Gets	Expected
Options	Income	Healthy	Sick	Sick	Healthy	Sick	Value
Option 1: No Insurance	$50,000	9 in 10	1 in 10	$30,000	$50,000	$20,000	$47,000
Option 2: Full Insurance	$50,000	9 in 10	1 in 10	$30,000	$47,000	$47,000	$47,000

Why people buy insurance. Now consider option 2. Rather than accepting the risk of having only $20,000 if she becomes ill, Emily can instead pay an insurer an annual premium that will cover her expenses in case of illness. How much would this insurance policy cost? An **actuarially fair insurance premium** would charge just enough to cover the expected compensation for the expenses. In other words, an actuarially fair insurance premium would charge the expected value of the loss so that, on average, the insurance company neither loses nor gains any money. (The insurance company would need to charge above the actuarially fair insurance premium in order to cover any overhead costs. But to keep things simple, for now we assume that there are no such costs.) Given that there is a 9 in 10 chance of no loss in income and a 1 in 10 chance of a $30,000 loss, the expected value of the loss is (9/10)($0) + (1/10)($30,000) = $3,000. So the actuarially fair insurance premium would be $3,000 each year. Think of this from the insurer's point of view. By charging $3,000 to each of 10 people with a 1 in 10 risk of losing $30,000, the insurer can receive $30,000 each year, which is just enough to cover the insurer's expected payouts for the year. When the risk of the adverse event increases, so does the premium that the company must charge in order to break even.

Buying a full insurance policy at the actuarially fair premium yields the same expected value for Emily as buying no insurance at all. However, if she is risk averse, having the insurance policy makes her better off.

In option 2, Emily pays the annual $3,000 premium whether she is sick or not. If she turns out to be healthy (column A), her income is therefore $47,000. If she gets sick (column B), she still pays the $3,000 insurance premium, yet the $30,000 in lost income due to illness is fully compensated by her insurer. Therefore, her income is still $47,000. In short, with option 2 Emily receives $47,000 whether she is sick or healthy.

Given that options 1 and 2 both provide the same expected income, one might guess that Emily would be indifferent between them. However, such reasoning ignores the fact that option 2 gives Emily $47,000 with *certainty* (whether she is sick or not), whereas option 1 gives her $47,000 *on average*. We can show that in general, Emily prefers option 2, which provides the same expected income, but with certainty.

To see why, recall that a standard assumption of economic theory is that people prefer more income to less, but that each additional unit of consumption contributes smaller and smaller gains in utility. Such "diminishing marginal utility" means that the pain of losing an incremental dollar is greater than the pleasure of gaining an additional dollar.

Emily's problem is illustrated by Figure 9.1, which shows her utility measured on the vertical axis and her income on the horizontal axis. This function, labelled U, has a concave curvature, which reflects the assumption of diminishing marginal utility. If she is sick, then she is at point A, with utility U_A. If she turns out to be healthy this year, then she is at point B, with utility U_B. One reasonable view of how a person behaves when confronted with such risk is that she uses the strategy that maximizes her utility on average, or her **expected utility**. To compute expected utility, we use the same logic behind the expected value formula and weight the utility level associated with each outcome by the probability of that outcome occurring. Thus,

$$\text{Expected utility } (EU) \text{ for Emily} = (9/10)U(\$50,000) + (1/10)U(\$20,000) \tag{9.3}$$

where $U(\$50,000)$ is the utility of $50,000 and $U(\$20,000)$ is defined analogously.

FIGURE 9.1

WHY PEOPLE BUY INSURANCE

Emily's expected income is the same whether she buys full insurance at the actuarially fair premium (point D) or does not buy insurance (point C). However, because she has diminishing marginal utility of income, she is better off with the full insurance option.

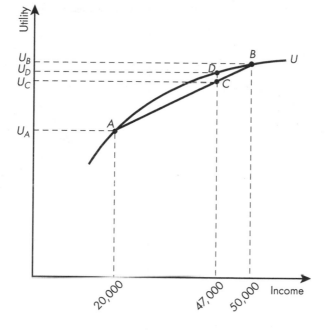

Diagrammatically, Equation (9.3) is equivalent to moving 90 percent up from U_A to U_B along the vertical axis and 90 percent from $20,000 to $50,000 along the horizontal axis, which corresponds to point C that is located on the line that connects points A and B in Figure 9.1. So if Emily chooses option 1 and does not buy insurance, she is at point C, with utility U_C. But if Emily instead buys insurance so that she receives $47,000 for sure, then she is at point D, with utility U_D, which is higher than the utility she receives with no insurance. So while both options give the same expected income, the option with certainty gives her higher expected utility. Thus, because people have diminishing marginal utility, they have a preference for **risk smoothing**, which entails reducing income in high-earning years in order to protect themselves against major drops in consumption in low earning years.

Do people buy insurance if premiums are not actuarially fair? This example illustrates a fundamental result; under the standard assumption of diminishing marginal utility of income, when an individual is offered actuarially fair insurance, she insures fully against the possible loss of income from illness.

But what if the insurance company does not offer an actuarially fair premium? Let's consider again the example in Figure 9.1, where we showed that the actuarially fair premium is $3,000. Suppose instead the insurance company charges more than that to cover the same loss, say $4,000 per year in premiums. Will Emily stop buying insurance? Not necessarily.

Figure 9.2 shows that the answer depends on the shape of her utility function. If she has the utility function shown in panel A, then she would rather not purchase this insurance. To see why, recall that if she did not buy insurance, her expected income is $47,000 (point C). Notice that she is indifferent between point C and point E on this diagram, because they both give the same expected utility. Point E corresponds to her receiving $46,500 with certainty; that is, it is achieved if she fully insures against the risk at a premium of $3,500. Therefore, she is willing to pay up to $3,500 for insurance rather than going without insurance. If the insurance company charges $4,000, she won't buy the plan.

If, instead, Emily has the utility function shown in panel B, then she is willing to pay up to $10,000 for insurance (which puts her at point E'). Because the insurance company only charges $4,000, she buys coverage and achieves higher utility than if she goes uninsured.

FIGURE 9.2

DO PEOPLE BUY INSURANCE IF PREMIUMS ARE NOT ACTUARIALLY FAIR?

The more risk averse Emily is, the more she is willing to pay for full insurance. In panel A, she is only willing to pay up to $3,500 for full insurance, while in panel B she is willing to pay up to $10,000 for full insurance.

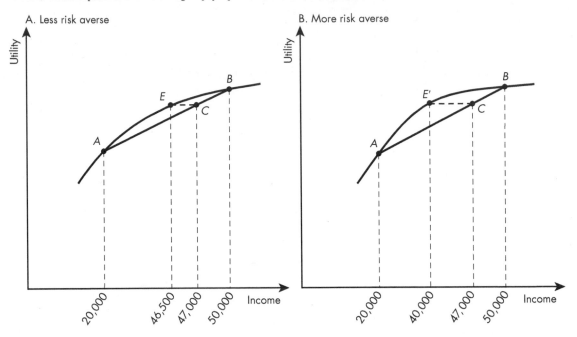

The difference between panels A and B is that the utility function in panel B has more curvature. This demonstrates a general result; the demand for insurance depends on the curvature of the utility function, also known as the level of **risk aversion**. Someone who is relatively more risk averse (for example, the utility function in panel B rather than the utility function in panel A) is willing to pay a greater amount above the actuarially fair premium. This difference is called the **risk premium**. Intuitively, this makes sense—the greater the curvature, the more rapid the diminishing marginal utility of income. That is, greater risk aversion means a greater relative loss of utility from losing income, and therefore a greater willingness to pay to insure against the loss.

The fact that insurance companies can charge higher premiums than the actuarially fair rate suggests that people are in fact risk averse. Even in a competitive market, insurance companies charge higher than the actuarially fair premiums to allow them to cover such items as administrative costs and taxes. The difference between the premium an insurance company charges and the actuarially fair premium is called the **loading fee**. One simple way to measure the loading fee is the ratio of market insurance premiums divided by benefits paid out. Today the average loading ratio for private insurance in companies in the United States is about 1.20 (Phelps, 2010).

The administration of private health insurance is expensive, due to the complexity of insurance contracts and billing procedures, along with the cost of marketing. One estimate is that 31 percent of total health care expenditures in the United States are for administration costs, in contrast to 16.7 percent in Canada (Woolhandler, Campbell, and Himmelstein, 2003). A lower administration cost is one of the principal arguments given by the 1964 Royal Commission on Health Services in advocating for publicly provided health insurance in Canada.

The Role of Risk Pooling

The previous example leads us to consider the highly important role that insurance companies play in pooling together people who face risks. To begin, consider the very unrealistic situation in which the insurance company insures only Emily, and no one else. By purchasing a policy from this company, Emily can eliminate the financial risks associated with illness. But now the insurance company is stuck with the risk. From a societal point of view, risk has not been reduced; it has simply been transferred from the individual to the insurance company.

Now suppose that the company has 10 customers instead of one. If it charges an actuarially fair premium to each of them, and each faces a 1 in 10 chance of getting sick, then this would be enough to cover expenses should one of the 10 people get sick, as expected. No one knows which of the people will get sick, but the insurance company has a pretty good idea of what its payments will be. Risk has been substantially reduced. Still, it's conceivable that two people would get sick, leaving the insurance company with the risk of being 50 percent short on funds. If instead the insurance company covered 100,000 people instead of just 10, then the likelihood of having to deal with more than 1 in 10 sick people would decrease dramatically. Think of a roulette wheel in which the odds of landing on black versus red are 50 percent. You may get lucky and land on black two or three times in a row, but as the number of spins increases, the proportion of times one lands on black will converge to 50 percent. The same is true of the insurance company—the more people in its insurance pool, the more predictable its outlays. This greater predictability allows the insurance company to charge a premium that with some assurance will cover its costs and thus lower the risk it faces. In effect, then, by *pooling* the risk across individuals, the insurance company has actually lowered risk from a social point of view.[1]

Asymmetric Information in the Health Insurance Market

With the basics of the health insurance market in hand, we are ready to return to the key question—what is special about it? After all, given that there is an incentive to provide health insurance (in a competitive market, loading fees allow insurers to make a normal profit), why is government intervention needed?

One problem stems from a market failure phenomenon that we first encountered in Chapter 2—**asymmetric information**. Asymmetric information exists when one party in a transaction has information that is not available to another party in the transaction, and it is especially problematic in the market for health insurance. Asymmetric information can give rise to an adverse selection problem and a moral hazard problem. In the health insurance context, the **adverse selection** problem arises because the buyer of insurance often has more information about the *probability of incurring a loss* than does the seller. A **moral hazard** problem can occur because the insured individual has more information about *actions* undertaken that affect the probability of incurring a loss than does the insurance company.

How Adverse Selection Can Cause Failure in the Insurance Market

To illustrate the problem of adverse selection, let's return to our previous example, where we showed that an insurance policy costing $3,000 would fully insure Emily.

Now assume that there are nine other people in addition to Emily, each of whom also faces a risk of losing $30,000 due to illness. However, while some of them face a 1 in 10 chance of illness like Emily, others face a 1 in 5 risk. Further, assume that only each individual knows whether he or she is at high or low risk for illness. (The individual has information about family medical history, health habits, stress at work, and so on, that the insurance company lacks.) We examine this situation in Table 9.2, which assumes that one-half of the 10 people face a 1 in 5 risk. As shown in column C of the table, the high-risk people have an expected income loss of $6,000, and the low-risk people have an expected income loss of $3,000. Now, if the insurance company knew who the high-risk individuals were, it could charge them a higher premium and cover its costs (column D). The problem is that it does not know—individuals in this example have more information about their health status than the company. Therefore, the insurer has no choice other than to charge everyone the same premium. If the insurer charges a $3,000 premium (column E), it is a great deal to the buyers who have a 1 in 5 risk of getting sick, because their expected compensation is $6,000, yet they pay only a $3,000 premium. However, the company would have expected annual *losses* of $15,000, since it would not make enough in premiums to cover the expected payouts. An insurance company with expected annual losses would not stay in business for long.

In the presence of these losses, the insurer might instead decide to charge each of the 10 people a premium of $4,500, which is the average expected income loss across all 10 people (column F). These 10 people would pay a total of $45,000 in premiums, and the expected payout would also be $45,000. Thus the insurer could stay in business (ignoring, to keep things simple, the administrative costs).

---

[1] While a larger insurance pool helps to eliminate the risk, it only works if the risk is independent across the insured people. For example, the risk of an earthquake is not independent across residents of south western British Columbia. If one home in the area gets destroyed, then others in the area will likely get destroyed as well, and the insurance company won't have enough money to compensate everyone. With the important exception of contagious diseases, for the most part this isn't a problem with health insurance.

TABLE 9.2

How Adverse Selection Can Cause Failure in the Insurance Market

Insurance Buyer	(A) Probability of Getting Sick	(B) Lost Income if Sick	(C) Expected Lost Income	(D) Expected Benefit Minus Premium (Differential Premiums)	(E) Expected Benefit Minus Premium (Premium = $3,000)	(F) Expected Benefit Minus Premium (Premium = $4,500)
Emily	1 in 10 (low risk)	$30,000	$3,000	$0	$0	$−1,500
Jacob	1 in 10 (low risk)	30,000	3,000	0	0	−1,500
Emma	1 in 10 (low risk)	30,000	3,000	0	0	−1,500
Michael	1 in 10 (low risk)	30,000	3,000	0	0	−1,500
Madison	1 in 10 (low risk)	30,000	3,000	0	0	−1,500
Joshua	1 in 5 (high risk)	30,000	6,000	0	3,000	1,500
Olivia	1 in 5 (high risk)	30,000	6,000	0	3,000	1,500
Matthew	1 in 5 (high risk)	30,000	6,000	0	3,000	1,500
Hannah	1 in 5 (high risk)	30,000	6,000	0	3,000	1,500
Ethan	1 in 5 (high risk)	30,000	6,000	0	3,000	1,500
Insurer's net profits				0	−15,000	0

But there is a problem here as well. With a $4,500 premium, the insurance plan remains a good deal for the high-risk people. They each expect to receive $6,000 in health care compensation, although they only pay $4,500 in premiums. However, the $4,500 premium is a bad deal for the low-risk people. Their expected health care compensation is $3,000, while they must pay $4,500 in premiums. Consequently, the high-risk people are attracted to this insurance plan while the healthier people may not purchase it. In short, because of the information asymmetry, the insurer gets customers who are, from its point of view, the wrong people. This phenomenon is known as **adverse selection**. More generally, adverse selection occurs when an insurance provider sets a premium based on the average risk of the population, but the low-risk people do not purchase the insurance policy, leaving the insurer to lose money.

But the story is not over. If the five healthier people decide not to buy insurance, the $4,500 premium is no longer enough for the insurance company to recover its expected payouts to the remaining five people. The insurance company must raise its premium. If the risk of illness had differed among the remaining customers, the company would again expect to lose the relatively low-risk people. In short, if an insurance company has less information on the health risks faced by its customers than do the customers, any premium set to cover the average risk level may induce the lower-risk people to leave the market. People who could have benefited from insurance at an actuarially fair rate go without insurance, and indeed, the market may stop functioning altogether as more and more participants opt out. This phenomenon is sometimes described by the colourful term "death spiral."

We have shown that adverse selection *can* kill off a market, not that it necessarily *will*. Recall from our discussion of Figure 9.2 that the more risk averse a person is, the more likely that person is to purchase an insurance policy that is not actuarially fair. If an insurance company charged a uniform premium, which was actuarially fair for the high-risk people, this would be a bad deal for the low-risk people. However, given that most people are risk averse, the low-risk people might still want to buy the insurance coverage. In such a case, the market for insurance would not collapse, although it might underprovide coverage for some low-risk people.[2] Ultimately, it is an empirical question whether adverse selection is present in a given market, and if so, whether it actually leads to market failure.[3]

---

[2] Insurance companies often sell partial coverage policies, which expose the individual to some risk. See Pauly (1974) and Rothschild and Stiglitz (1976).

[3] See Cohen and Siegelman (2010) for a survey of the empirical literature on adverse selection in insurance markets.

Empirical evidence: A death spiral at Harvard? In the presence of adverse selection, relatively healthy people may decline insurance coverage if the premium is set based on the community's average health risk. This would lead to higher premiums and healthy people opting out. Such a "death spiral" could lead to a collapse of the market. But is this important as a real-world phenomenon?

Cutler and Reber (1998) examined a change in Harvard University's employee health insurance coverage. Before the change, Harvard employees could enroll in a more generous insurance plan for only a slightly larger premium than if they enrolled in a less generous plan. Thus, Harvard gave a large subsidy for the generous insurance plan. Motivated by budget problems, in 1995 Harvard changed to a system in which the university would contribute an equal amount to each insurance plan, regardless of which one an employee chose. Each employee would get an amount that could be used for any of the insurance options. As a consequence, a person in the generous plan had to pay out about $700 more per year than someone in a less generous plan.

Thus, suddenly, people at Harvard had to pay more if they wanted the more generous insurance plan. As expected from standard economic theory, many people left the generous plan to enroll in a less generous plan. But the people who switched plans were not a random subsample from the original enrollees. Specifically, those who left the generous plan were younger (and presumably healthier) than those who decided to stay. This indicates sorting by health status as predicted by the theory of adverse selection. Sure enough, the premium for the generous plan increased substantially (it doubled!) one year later in order to cover the increased costs of insuring an older (and presumably less healthy) population. This again led to the relatively younger people leaving the generous plan. Rather than raise premiums even higher, the plan was dropped the following year. So within two years of the change, adverse selection eliminated the generous plan.

Does adverse selection justify government intervention? Before determining whether government intervention is warranted when there is adverse selection in an insurance market, we will consider some private market responses to adverse selection. One market response is to provide insurance coverage to all members of a particular group, such as the employees of a firm. Group coverage circumvents the adverse selection problem because all members of the group are covered, and not just those who think that they have a high probability of a loss. Thus, group health insurance can be provided to all of the employees of a firm at premiums that are lower than in the open market, which is subject to an adverse selection process.[4] The problem with group coverage is that it is only available to individuals who are members of large groups. The employees of a small firm or the self-employed cannot obtain group coverage, and this may distort individuals' decisions concerning whether to work for a large or a small firm. It also means that individuals risk losing their insurance coverage if they are laid off by their employer.

Another response to the adverse selection problem is that insurance companies may categorize individuals according to some observable characteristic—such as age, sex, or marital status—which is an imperfect indicator of an individual's risk type. For example, automobile insurers charge a 20-year-old male a higher premium than a 20-year-old female because, on average, young males have a higher claim frequency than young females. This does not mean that all 20-year-old males are high-risk drivers and all 20-year-old females are low-risk drivers. Each group contains high and low risks, but there is a higher proportion of high-risk drivers among the 20-year-old male population than among the 20-year-old female population. While an insurance company may not be able to distinguish who is a high or low risk, it can tell males from females, and it may decide to use these imperfect indicators of loss probabilities to charge different premiums to males and females. The use of these imperfect indicators helps to create more homogeneous risk groups, but it raises ethical issues regarding discrimination. The Supreme Court has ruled that sex-based automobile insurance premiums do not contravene the Canadian Charter of Rights and Freedoms because the insurance industry has demonstrated that its use of these categories is based on statistical evidence that young males have higher loss probabilities than young females. However, many people feel uncomfortable with such rationalizations and wonder whether discrimination on the basis of race or religion would also be accepted if it were supported by statistical evidence. It is well known that the elderly, on average, incur higher health expenditures than the rest of the population. Private health insurers would charge higher premiums to the elderly and, indeed, anyone with a history of illness. Insurance companies' use of information obtained from genetic testing to predict individuals' likeliness of contracting hereditary diseases

---

[4] Employer-provided plans are commonly used in the United States. In Canada, such group plans are common for supplementary coverage beyond provincial health insurance (e.g., Blue Cross, Sun Life).

raises many important ethical and economic issues. Those who are genetically inclined toward sickness would have to pay significantly more for insurance, and perhaps even be priced out of the market.

In summary, categorizing people into risk classes and charging them different premiums can improve efficiency, but would reduce the scope for insurance coverage for many groups. Citizens may prefer a social insurance scheme that does not discriminate among individuals according to some observable characteristics that are correlated with expected losses.

A primary characteristic of social insurance programs is that they are *compulsory*. This means that they are not subject to the adverse selection process that arises when individuals can use their private information regarding their loss probability to choose their insurance coverage. The welfare implications of adopting compulsory social insurance in order to overcome an adverse selection problem can be assessed using, once again, the example in Table 9.2. Suppose that the private market provides full coverage to high-risk individuals at an actuarially fair premium equal to $6,000, and that low-risk individuals do not purchase any insurance coverage. When the social insurance program is introduced, it provides full coverage for the entire population. All individuals will have to contribute, either in premiums or in taxes, an amount equal to $4,500 per person to cover the expected cost of the claims. (We'll ignore any administrative cost to keep things simple.) High-risk individuals, who previously purchased full coverage from the private sector, will be better off with the social insurance scheme because their premium or their contribution will decline from $6,000 to $4,500. However, low-risk individuals might prefer zero coverage to paying $4,500 for full coverage. Such a situation is illustrated in Figure 9.3, which uses the utility function for Emily depicted previously in panel A of Figure 9.2.

Low-risk individuals prefer zero coverage to social insurance. In Figure 9.3, the maximum premium that Emily would pay for full coverage (P_{MAX}) is $3,500, which is less than the social insurance premium of $4,500. Emily's utility from full social insurance coverage is U_F whereas her expected utility when uninsured is higher at U_C. If, however, Emily were more risk averse than depicted in Figure 9.3, she might prefer full social insurance coverage rather than remaining uninsured.

We can conclude that a compulsory full insurance program may not be a Pareto improvement over the private market outcome. It will make high-risk individuals better off, but it will possibly make low-risk individuals worse off.[5] A trade-off of this sort might be acceptable on equity grounds. Furthermore, it can be shown that with the compulsory full-coverage policy, the high-risk individuals gain more than the low-risk

---

FIGURE 9.3

LOW-RISK INDIVIDUALS PREFER ZERO COVERAGE TO SOCIAL INSURANCE

The maximum Emily is willing to pay for social insurance is $3,500, which is less than the insurance premium of $4,500.

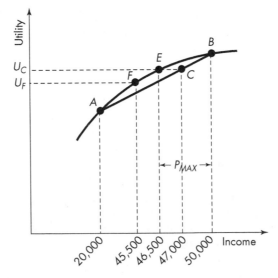

---

[5] Compulsory *partial* insurance coverage may still be Pareto improving in this case (Dahlby, 1981).

individuals lose.[6] Hence, compulsory full insurance can be justified on a cost–benefit basis when the private market is afflicted with an adverse selection problem.

Obamacare and adverse selection. In an effort to increase the proportion of Americans covered by health insurance, the United States government passed the Patient Protection and Affordable Care Act (2010), commonly referred to as Obamacare. Certain features of the law deal with the problem of adverse selection. The centrepiece of the Act is the requirement for insurers to accept anyone who wants insurance at the same price for the given level of coverage. To prevent the death spiral that might result if sicker individuals purchase health insurance while healthier individuals do not, it was mandated that all individuals who can afford health insurance must purchase some minimally comprehensive policy or face a financial penalty. Being able to afford insurance was defined as not having to pay more than 8 percent of monthly income and earning more than the official poverty line amount. To make sure that insurance plans provide adequate quality, the government outlined four levels of acceptable coverage.

Moral Hazard and Market Failure

Even in the absence of adverse selection, public or private health insurance may distort people's incentives. First, if people know that they have insurance, they may take less care to avoid risks. Thus, people with insurance may adopt more unhealthy lifestyles (eating a lot of junk food and not exercising much) because the negative consequences of doing so are reduced by insurance. Second, people have incentives to over-consume health care services (such as visits to the doctor), because the insurance pays for some or all of the cost. These incentive problems are referred to as **moral hazard**.

Moral hazard can be analyzed using a conventional supply-and-demand diagram. In Figure 9.4, the market demand curve for medical services in the absence of insurance is labelled D_m. To keep things simple, assume that the marginal cost of producing medical services is a constant, P_0. Hence, the supply curve, S_m, is a horizontal line at P_0. As usual, equilibrium is at the intersection of supply and demand; the equilibrium price

FIGURE 9.4

MARKET FOR MEDICAL SERVICES

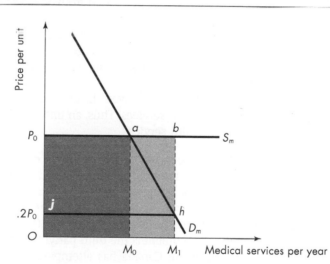

---

[6] Using the example in Table 9.2, the per capita net gain is ($6,000 − $4,500) + ($P_{MAX}$ − $4,500$), where P_{MAX} is the maximum amount each low-risk individual is willing to pay for full insurance. The first term is the per capita gain to the high-risk individuals from the reduction in their premiums. The second term is negative and represents the per capita loss to the low risks from being forced to contribute to a full coverage policy. Their loss is the difference between the value that they place on full insurance, P_{MAX}, and the $4,500 they have to contribute. The expression above simplifies to (P_{MAX} − $3,000$). Recall that the actuarially fair premium for the low risks is precisely $3,000. The maximum premium that a low-risk individual would pay for full insurance must exceed his or her actuarially fair premium; in Figure 9.3, for example, P_{MAX} equals $3,500. Hence, there is a net social gain from compulsory full insurance. Although we have shown this with an example, the proposition holds true in general.

and quantity are P_0 and M_0, respectively. Total expenditure in the market is the product of the price per unit times the number of units; that is, OP_0 times OM_0, or rectangle P_0OM_0a (the darker-shaded area in the diagram).

Before proceeding, we should note one possible objection to Figure 9.4—the downward sloping demand curve. When people are sick, don't they just follow the doctor's orders, regardless of price? Would you haggle with your surgeon in the midst of an appendicitis attack? The implication of this view is that the demand curve for medical services is perfectly vertical, not downward sloping. Such reasoning ignores the fact that many medical procedures are discretionary. Patients make the initial decision about whether to seek health care. And despite the conflict-of-interest issue referred to above, patients do not always comply with their doctor's advice. Pauly (1986) surveyed a number of empirical studies suggesting that when the price of medical services goes down, the quantity demanded increases.

How does the introduction of insurance affect the market? To keep things simple, assume that the policy pays for 80 percent of the health care costs, leaving the patient to pay for 20 percent. Even with Canadian Medicare, some health services, such as drugs, are not fully insured. The proportion not covered is called the **coinsurance rate**. The key to analyzing the impact of insurance is to realize that a 20 percent coinsurance rate is equivalent to an 80 percent reduction in the price facing the patient—if the incremental cost to the hospital for a day's stay is $800, the patient pays only $160. In Figure 9.4, the price confronted by the patient is no longer P_0, but only 0.2 times P_0. Given this lower price, the quantity demanded increases to M_1, and the patient spends area $OjhM_1$ on medical services.

Note that at the new equilibrium, although the patient is paying $0.2P_0$ per unit, the marginal cost of providing health services is still P_0; the difference $(0.8P_0)$ is paid by the insurance. Hence, total expenditures are OP_0 times OM_1, or the rectangle P_0OM_1b, with the insurance company paying P_0bhj. Thus, as a consequence of the insurance, health care expenditures increase from P_0OM_0a to P_0OM_1b, or the grey area aM_0M_1b.

The problem here is that the individual consumes medical services past the point where the marginal benefit to the individual equals the marginal cost. This is inefficient, because for each medical service consumed beyond M_0, the additional cost (measured by marginal cost) outweighs the additional benefit (measured by the individual's marginal willingness to pay, which is the vertical distance to the demand curve).[7] We can measure the size of the inefficiency, known as the **deadweight loss**, by summing the differences between the marginal cost and marginal benefit for each unit of medical services purchased from M_0 to M_1. The deadweight loss is therefore the triangle abh.

Of course, the actual amount by which expenditures increase depends on the shape of the demand curve, the precise provisions of the insurance policy, and so on.[8] But the general point is clear—with insurance, consumers do not confront the full marginal costs of their health care, which leads to an increase in both the quantity demanded and total expenditure.

In summary, whereas adverse selection creates gaps in private health insurance coverage, moral hazard leads to excessive spending for certain types of medical services. Thus, an unregulated market for health insurance is unlikely to deliver efficient quantities of health services.

Does moral hazard justify government intervention? In the presence of moral hazard, we can expect inefficiently high health care spending if patients do not confront the cost of the services they purchase. The efficiency problems caused by moral hazard are not unique to private health insurance markets. They arise whenever a third party pays for all or part of the marginal cost of medical services. In the preceding example of private insurance, the insurance company was the third party, covering 80 percent of the marginal cost. When insurance, is provided publicly, then the government is the third party, but the analysis of moral hazard is exactly the same. The public health care system in Canada has attempted to contain costs by imposing budget caps on Medicare spending and rationing medical services. This has led to controversies over waiting times for medical treatments. We discuss waiting times later in the chapter.

---

[7] See the discussion of consumer surplus in the appendix of Chapter 2.

[8] A famous experiment was conducted in the United States by the RAND Corporation in the 1970s. People were randomly assigned into insurance plans with different coinsurance rates to see how their spending on health care would be affected. The results suggest that a 10 percent increase in the price of medical services reduces the quantity of health care by about 2 percent (Newhouse et al., 1993).

Other Problems in the Health Care Market

We have dwelt at length on the topic of insurance because it is central to understanding various social insurance programs in Canada. However, there are other important concerns about private health care markets.

Poor information. We normally assume that consumers are fairly well informed about the commodities they purchase—when you buy an apple, you have a pretty good idea of how it will taste and how much satisfaction it will give you. In contrast, when you are ill, you may not have a very good sense of what medical procedures are appropriate. To make things more complicated, the person on whom you are likely to rely for advice in such a situation, your physician, is also the person who is selling you the commodity. Patients' lack of information is the rationale for a number of government regulations, such as the licensing of doctors for quality assurance.[9]

Paternalism. People may not understand how insurance works, or they may lack the foresight to purchase it. Paternalistic arguments suggest that people should be forced into a medical insurance system for their own good. Krugman (2006), for example, argues that, "people who are forced to pay for medical care out of pocket don't have the ability to make good decisions about what care to purchase." A related concern is that children may bear a cost from a lack of health care when a family head chooses not to purchase insurance.

Income redistribution. There does, indeed, appear to be a strong societal consensus in Canada that everyone should have equal access to necessary medical services, regardless of their ability to pay. The public health system is an important vehicle for redistributing income from higher- to lower-income groups (Van Doorslaer, 2008). Nevertheless, recent evidence suggests that the poor are less likely than the rich to have a family doctor or to receive specialist medical care in Canada (Curtis and MacMinn, 2008). These are sources of inequity in the delivery of health care. In the United States, the poor and elderly are covered by public programs. Even so, 16 percent of the U.S. population (about 49 million people) were without either private or public health insurance (DeNavas-Walt et al., 2012). It is typically workers in low-paying jobs, workers without regular employment, and self-employed workers who are uninsured. With key provisions of the Affordable Care Act taking effect in 2014, the number of uninsured Americans declined to 32 million people (Smith and Medalia, 2015).

Externalities. Health services received by an individual may also improve the health of others by reducing the spread of infectious diseases. For example, if you get a flu vaccination there is a positive externality, because it reduces the probability that others will become infected by the flu. Not properly accounting for these externalities may cause individuals to under consume certain health services if they are privately provided. In many instances, however, health care confers no externalities. Getting treated for a broken arm improves your welfare but does not increase the utility of others.

NATIONAL MEDICARE IN CANADA

Medicare refers to Canada's national health insurance program, which covers the full cost of all medically necessary hospital and physician services. It is a single-payer system in that medical care providers directly bill the government for the cost of service. Fees for each type of medical service are set by the government of each province. In reality, Canada's national program consists of 13 provincial and territorial health insurance plans, which are all framed by the principles of the Canada Health Act.

The Canada Health Act

The Canada Health Act was passed by Parliament in 1984. The act lays out five conditions or principles that provincial health plans must follow to be eligible for federal grants. The five conditions are as follows:

1. *Universality.* All residents are entitled to health insurance coverage.
2. *Accessibility.* There can be no financial or other barriers to receiving medically necessary hospital and physician services. Reasonable compensation for physicians and hospitals must be paid, and extra billing (beyond payments made by the provincial plans) is prohibited.

---

[9] Exercise 9 considers a specific example.

3. *Comprehensiveness.* All medically necessary services must be insured. However, the definition of medically necessary services is left to the provinces.

4. *Portability.* Coverage must be maintained when a resident moves within Canada or travels outside the country. Out-of-country coverage is limited to payment at existing provincial rates.

5. *Public administration.* The administration of the health insurance plan must be on a non-profit basis by a public authority.

An important implication of the Canada Health Act is that it prohibits private health insurance for all medically necessary treatments. Private insurance is permitted for services not covered by Medicare. Private health care *delivery* is not illegal in Canada; indeed, physicians are private practitioners. However, most provinces require physicians to either "opt in" or "opt out" of the public insurance system. If they opt out, they are ineligible to bill the government for patient fees and they are required to use the same fee-for-service schedule as the public system.[10]

All provinces have affirmed their support of the conditions of the Canada Health Act on numerous occasions, and public support for the Act is very strong. Despite the Act, however, per capita health spending and the range of services insured varies across the provinces. To illustrate, Figure 9.5 shows public sector health spending by province as well as the national average in 2014 in per capita terms. Per capita expenditures in Quebec were about 7.5 percent below the national average of $3,960 in 2014, whereas Newfoundland spent about 28 percent more than the national average. These variations reflect, in part, differences in the demographic profiles of the provinces, differences in remuneration for medical personnel, and different population densities.

Some advocates for a strong federal role in health care have argued that maintaining the federal government's ability to levy financial penalties on provinces is critical to enforcing adherence to the five principles of the Canada Health Act. However, when they have been invoked by the federal government, financial penalties have been small relative to the size of provincial health spending. Boothe and Johnston (1993) have argued that the Canada Health Act is not really much of a financial constraint to provinces—rather, it is the broad public support for the five principles that maintains adherence to the Act.

The History of Canadian Health Care Financing

Until the 1940s, hospital and medical care in Canada was largely privately funded. Individual patients paid doctors for their services, and many hospitals were run by religious or voluntary organizations, where ability

---

FIGURE 9.5

PER CAPITA HEALTH EXPENDITURE BY PROVINCIAL GOVERNMENTS IN 2014*

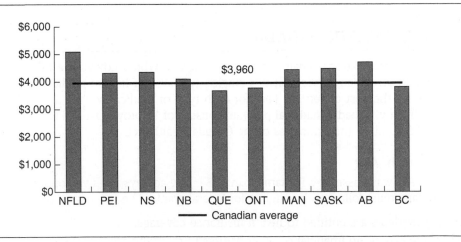

*Forecast.

Source: Canadian Institute for Health Information, *National Health Expenditure Trends, 1975 to 2014*, Table B.4.2.

---

[10] See Flood and Archibald (2001) for a survey of health insurance legislation in each province.

to pay was taken into account. Constitutionally, the public provision of health care is the responsibility of the provinces. In 1947, the government of Saskatchewan became the first province to introduce a program of provincial hospital insurance. The federal government offered health grants to the provinces in 1948 to help pay for hospital services. With the introduction of the Hospital Insurance and Diagnostic Services Act in 1957, the federal government shared the cost of hospital services with the provinces. By 1961, all provinces had hospital insurance plans, with the federal government contributing about 50 percent of the cost on average.

While provinces were developing insurance schemes to cover the cost of hospital services, payments to physicians were still largely private. Saskatchewan once again took the lead by introducing a provincial Medicare scheme that included payments to doctors. Opposition by doctors led to a bitter strike in 1962 but the Saskatchewan approach was soon adopted by other provinces, in part because the federal government again offered to share the cost through the Medical Care Act of 1966. By 1971, all provinces had programs, with the federal government contributing about one-half the cost. Provincial shares were paid from general tax revenues and, in some cases, health care premium charges.

In 1977, the federal government combined its support for Medicare and post-secondary education into a single grant, which was converted from a shared-cost to a "block" grant. The new grant, known as Established Program Financing (EPF)[11] was no longer designed to pay one-half of the cost of provincial health programs, but it would provide equal per capita grants to provinces, scheduled to grow at the same rate as Canadian GDP. A few years later, the federal government introduced measures to limit the growth in these grants. EPF grants were replaced in 1996 with a block grant to support health, education, and post-secondary education–the Canadian Health and Social Transfer (CHST). In 2004, the CHST was separated into the Canada Social Transfer (CST) to support provincial social programs and the Canada Health Transfer (CHT).[12] Between 2004 and 2016, total CHT cash was legislated to grow at a rate of 6 percent per year. Starting in 2017–18, growth in CHT cash transfers will be tied to the rate of growth in nominal GDP. CHT cash transfers, estimated at $34 billion for 2015–16, represent the largest of the federal transfer programs, accounting for about one-half of total transfers to provinces.

Trends in Health Expenditures

Federal transfers for health play an important role in provincial and territorial government spending on health care. Figure 9.6 shows provincial (and territorial) government per capita spending on health in constant 2002

FIGURE 9.6

PROVINCIAL AND TERRITORIAL GOVERNMENT PER CAPITA HEALTH EXPENDITURES, 1975 TO 2014 (CONSTANT 2002 DOLLARS)

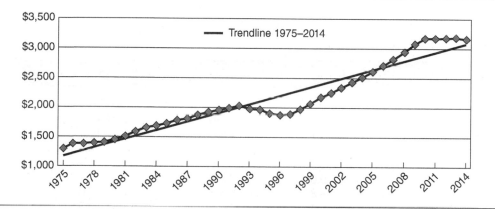

Source: Authors' construction using data from Canadian Institute for Health Information, *National Health Expenditure Trends,* 1975 to 2014, Table B.4.2 and Statistics Canada's CANSIM II database http://cansim2.statcan.ca, series V41693271.

---

[11] Thus, the federal government used a shared-cost grant to encourage provinces to adopt programs, and then moved to a block grant once the programs were "established." See Chapter 8 for a discussion of these grants.

[12] The CHST and the CHT both retained the conditions of the Canada Health Act.

FIGURE 9.7

TOTAL HEALTH EXPENDITURES AS A PERCENT OF GDP

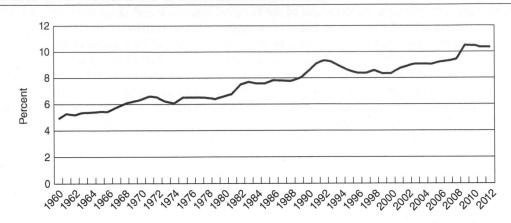

Note: Total health expenditures include both private and public spending.

Source: OECD (2014), "OECD Health Data: Health expenditure and financing: Health expenditure indicators,", OECD Health Statistics (database). doi: http://dx.doi.org/10.1787/data-00349-en (Accessed on May 13, 2015.)

dollars. The early 1990s was the period of greatest federal restraint. During this period real per capita provincial government spending on health fell compared with the periods of growth before and after.

Figure 9.7 shows that total spending on health as a percentage of GDP increased from 4.9 percent in 1960 to 10.4 percent in 2014. Total spending includes both public and private spending on health. Several periods of rapidly increasing expenditures can be identified. The first period, from 1966 to 1971, coincides with the establishment of Medicare, when health care expenditures increased from 5.5 to 6.6 percent of GDP. The year 2000 marks the start of the most recent period of significant growth; health spending accounted for 8.3 percent of GDP in 2000, and by 2012 its share had increased to 10.4 percent. The period of restraint in health spending in the early 1990s is also evident in Figure 9.7.

Another important trend is the change in the pattern of health spending. Table 9.3 compares the expenditure shares of eight major categories of health spending in 1975 and 2014. Over this period, there has been a

TABLE 9.3

Percent Shares of Health Care Expenditures by Category			
	1975	**2014**	**Percentage Point Change**
Hospitals	44.7	29.6	−15.1
Other Institutions	9.2	10.3	0.6
Physicians	15.1	15.5	0.4
Other Professionals	9.0	10.1	1.1
Drugs	8.8	15.8	7.0
Capital	4.4	4.1	−0.3
Health Administration	2.8	3.1	0.3
Other Health Spending	4.6	11.5	6.9

Note: Total health expenditures include both private and public spending.

Source: Canadian Institute for Health Information, *National Health Expenditure Trends*, 1975 to 2014, Table A.3.1.2.

substantial drop in the share spent on hospitals, reflecting the trend to deliver more services in the community and in the home. The other notable change is the increased share of spending on drugs. In addition to the increasing cost of drugs, this trend probably reflects scientific advances in the development of drugs to treat more illnesses more effectively, and also the aging population, since seniors are relatively large consumers of pharmaceuticals. The share of spending on physician services has remained relatively stable. The share of "other health spending" has almost tripled. About a third of this increase reflects increases in spending on public health services. Overall, the government sector's share of total health spending declined somewhat from 76.2 percent in 1975 to about 70 percent in 2014 mainly because of the rapid increase in expenditures on drugs, which are largely privately financed.

COMPARING HEALTH SYSTEMS AROUND THE WORLD

How does the Canadian health system look in comparison with other countries? A good place to start is to examine the data provided in Table 9.4. In this table we present selected health statistics from nine OECD countries. In the first column we look at an important characteristic of each country—the proportion of seniors in the population (defined as persons 65 years of age and over). Since seniors are the biggest consumers of health care services, this statistic gives us an indication of the demand for health services in each country. We see that, of the nine countries considered, Canada has a relatively young population compared to countries like Germany and Japan.

The second column reports the number of practising doctors per 1,000 residents. This statistic gives us an indication of the supply of health services by country.[13] Canada, along with Japan, has the lowest figure, with 2.4 doctors per 1,000 residents. Germany and Sweden have substantially more.

The next two columns provide some information on the output of the health care system—measures of the health of the population. The first statistic is average life expectancy. Among the nine countries considered, Canada's average life expectancy of 81.5 years ranks below that of Japan, Sweden, Australia, and France.

TABLE 9.4

	Selected Health Statistics for OECD Countries, 2011				
	Percent of Population Over 65	Physicians per 1,000 Population	Life Expectancy at Birth	Infant Mortality Deaths per 1,000 Live Births	Total Health Expenditures as a Percent of GDP
Australia	13.8	3.5	82.0	3.8	8.6
Canada	14.5	2.4	81.5	4.8	10.4
France	16.9	3.3	82.2	3.5	11.1
Germany	20.6	4.2	80.8	3.6	10.9
Japan	23.3	2.3*	82.7	2.3	10.0
New Zealand	13.3	2.7	81.2	5.2	10.0
Sweden	18.4	4.1	81.9	2.1	9.0
United Kingdom	16.4	2.6	81.0	4.3	8.9
United States	13.3	2.7	78.7	6.1	16.3

* Data are for 2010.

Source: OECD (2014), OECD. Stat, (database). doi: http://dx.doi.org/10.1787/data-00285-en. (Accessed on 15 May 2015.)

---

[13] Clearly there are other indicators one would include in a more in-depth treatment of this issue. Physicians are only one of many different health care providers, and different countries could well have the same services delivered by different providers.

Of the countries ranked below Canada, the United States has the lowest average life expectancy of 78.7 years. The second statistic is infant mortality. Here Canada ranks close to the bottom, along with the United States and New Zealand. Japan and Sweden, on the other hand, both have infant mortality rates significantly lower than either Canada or the United States.

The fifth column compares the expenditures on health services across countries. Of the nine countries included in Table 9.4, Canada's share of GDP devoted to health care is the fourth highest. Among all OECD countries, Canada ranks seventh after the United States, France, Switzerland, Germany, Australia, and Denmark. Although the United States devotes a substantially larger percentage of GDP to health care, life expectancy and infant mortality are significantly worse than in Canada.[14] However, Swedish health outcomes are substantially better than in Canada, despite the greater proportion of seniors in the Swedish population and a smaller percentage of GDP devoted to health care. Consistent with these data, research has shown that many factors unrelated to the health care system, such as the income support system, are important determinants of health outcomes.

CHALLENGES AND FUTURE DIRECTIONS

As we noted at the beginning of the chapter, Canadians value their health system highly, but they are concerned about whether it will survive in the future because of rapidly rising costs and the need for fiscal balance. In 2014, governments in Canada spent about $151 billion to finance health care, while private expenditure on health care cost a further $63.4 billion. Between 1975 and 2014, inflation-adjusted health care expenditures in Canada more than tripled.[15] As Thomas Courchene (2002) has warned, "rising health care costs are cutting into primary, secondary, and university education, into welfare expenditures, into policing, into environmental protection and, progressively, into provincial and municipal infrastructure."[16] If other government services deteriorate because of rising health care costs, then the quality of life, and ultimately the health status of Canadians, will also deteriorate. In this section we look at the current state of the health system and consider some challenges and directions for the health system in the future.

Over the period from 1980 to 1993, the number of acute-care beds in hospitals declined from 4.6 to 3.7 per 1,000 population. The decline has continued; by the mid 2000s there were 2.5 acute-care beds per 1,000. The average length of stay for acute-care hospitals in Canada has also declined, falling from 10 days in 1980 to 7.6 days in 2011.[17] Does this suggest that the Canadian health system is in decline?

If one focuses on the ultimate goal of any health system—to maintain and enhance the health of the population—the answer seems to be no. Consider the following statistics:[18]

1. Canadians' rating of their own health has remained virtually unchanged over the past 10 years.
2. Life expectancy is increasing for both men and women. For males, life expectancy increased from 71.7 years in 1980 to 79.3 years in 2011. Life expectancy for females increased from 78.9 to 83.6 over the same period.
3. The proportion of the population reporting that health problems limit their daily activities is declining, especially among older Canadians.
4. There is a declining trend in work-related injuries.
5. The rate of low-birthweight babies has been stable since the 1980s.
6. Death rates from most major causes, particularly deaths due to heart disease and injuries, have declined since the 1970s.

[14] O'Neill and O'Neill (2008) argue that differences in infant mortality and life expectancy between the United States in Canada have more to do with differences in behaviour than with the health care systems. For Canada, a contributing factor is the relatively high infant mortality rate for those living in isolated areas and in some of Canada's First Nations communities (see Luo et al., 2010).

[15] See Canadian Institute for Health Information, *National Health Expenditure Trends, 1975–2014*, Table A.2.1.

[16] This crowding-out effect is not supported by the results found in Landon et al. (2006).

[17] Data on hospital beds and average length of stay are taken from OECD (2014), "OECD Health Data: Health care utilisation," OECD Health Statistics (database). doi: http://dx.doi.org/10.1787/data-00542-en. (Accessed on 19 May 2015.)

[18] These statistics are based on data obtained from OECD (2014), "OECD Health Data: Health status," OECD Health Statistics (database). doi: http://dx.doi.org/10.1787/data-00540-en. (Accessed on 19 May 2015) and Health and Welfare Canada (1996: ch. 2).

Thus, considering the impact of the health care system on health outcomes (and recognizing that many other factors are important determinants of health), there seems to be little evidence to support the view that the Canadian health system is in decline.

Despite these generally promising signs, the Canadian health system is facing important cost pressures. The aging population is expected to increase the demand for health care services substantially over the next three decades. Changes in diets and reduced physical activity levels since the 1980s have contributed to a steady increase in the prevalence of obesity among Canadians. Obesity is estimated to have contributed $2 billion in additional health care costs (and a total economic burden of $4.6 billion) in 2008.[19] Improving technology has reduced the cost of some health services (allowing, for example, shorter hospital stays), but has also increased the range of available services (some of which are costly). Technological innovation has been especially apparent in the area of drugs. While new drugs can contribute greatly to treatment, many of them are also very costly. Coupled with the trend toward publicly funded drug plans, especially for seniors, we can understand both the growth in drugs as a share of total health spending and the increasing role played by the public sector in those expenditures.

There are also challenges with respect to access and waiting times for health services. Table 9.5 compares wait-time indicators relating to access to specialists, surgery, and doctors for Canada and a number of other countries. These data suggest that wait times in Canada are high relative to these other countries. For example, 29 percent of those who needed to see a specialist waited more than two months in Canada as compared with 10 percent in Germany and 6 percent in the U.S. In Canada, 51 percent of those individuals seeking medical attention saw a doctor or nurse the same day or next day, compared to 63 percent in Australia and 79 percent

TABLE 9.5

Wait Times Compared for Selected Countries, 2013 (in percent)						
	Canada	Australia	Germay	New Zealand	UK	US
Last time needed medical attention, was able to see a doctor or nurse the same or next day*	51	63	59	75	79	59
Waiting time for emergency care was 2 hours or more[a]	48	25	23	14	16	28
Waiting time to see a specialist was 2 months or more[b]	29	18	10	19	7	6
Waiting time of 4 months or more for elective/ nonemergency surgery[c]	18	10	3	15	n/a	7

* These data are for 2011. All other data are for 2013.
[a] Based on those who used an emergency room in the past two years.
[b] Based on those who saw, or needed to see, a specialist in past two years.
[c] Based on those those needing elective surgery in past year.

Source: Davis, K. et al. (2014), Exhibit 5.

---

[19] Public Health Agency of Canada and Canadian Institute of Health Information (2011). Economic costs include health care costs plus indirect costs associated with lost productivity from premature death and disability.

in the UK. The percentage of those in Canada needing emergency care who waited two hours of more was three times higher than in the UK.

Concerns surrounding increasing waiting times for medical treatments and the financial sustainability of Medicare resulted in three major government reports on health care by the end of 2002: the Mazankowski Report (Alberta, 2001), the Kirby Report (Senate, 2002), and the Romanow Report (Canada, 2002).[20] Although the specific recommendations in the reports differ, all stress the importance of achieving cost reductions and quality improvements through better management and accountability in the system. Recommendations to achieve operating efficiencies include the development of performance indicators, a better use of information technologies, a greater emphasis on preventive care, decentralizing health care management, and going beyond the family physician and nurse by developing genuinely interdisciplinary teams of health professionals. Both the Romanow Report and the Kirby Report argue for significant expansions in Medicare coverage (to include, for example, palliative care and drugs) and a higher level of federal financing. The three reports combined made more than 100 recommendations and stimulated debate on health care reform in Canada.

What will the Canadian health care system look like in the future? A number of important issues continue to be discussed:

Changing incentives. The question here is, does the current fee-for-service method of paying physicians (especially for primary care) provide the best incentive to deliver the right amount of health care at the lowest cost? Fee-for-service remuneration rewards fast "through-put" of patients and discourages physician referrals to nurses and other health professionals for services they are qualified to do. The Kirby Report recommends that fee-for-service for family practitioners should be replaced by a system based mainly on capitation. Under this system, patients would enroll in a group practice of primary care givers. The group would receive an annual payment based on the number of patients on its list, adjusted for such factors as age and gender. Currently, some provinces are experimenting with alternative remuneration schemes for physicians to compare both the health and cost outcomes.

Defining medically necessary services. The Canada Health Act leaves the definition of medically necessary services to the individual provincial health insurance schemes. We observe significant variations in per capita spending on health and the range of insured services across provinces. Some provinces are examining the idea of developing an explicit list of medically necessary services (and thus a corresponding list of services that could be provided privately outside of the Canada Health Act). Currently, only non-insured services are explicitly defined.[21]

A national pharmacare program. As we saw earlier, the trend in Canada has been to spend more on drugs overall, and to increase the public share of that spending. Both the Kirby Report and the Romanow Report recommend that drugs be included as part of the publicly funded health system. Critics of pharmacare argue that the plan is too expensive and that private insurance for drugs is available. An estimated 41.6 percent of prescribed drug expenditures in 2013 were financed by the public sector while 34.5 and 23.9 percent were covered by private insurers and households, respectively.[22]

Privatization. In a landmark decision by the Supreme Court of Canada in 2005 (*Chaoulli v. Quebec*), the Court ruled that in the presence of long waiting times for medical treatment under Medicare, the restrictions on private medical insurance coverage in Quebec violate citizens' rights to life and security of person. Most provinces have similar laws that discourage the private financing of health care, consistent with the public administration principle of the Canada Health Act.

The government of Quebec issued a consultation document in 2006 recommending a lifting of the ban on private insurance for certain procedures that are included in a provincial guarantee of timely

---

[20] See also the Fyke Report (Saskatchewan, 2001).

[21] The National Forum on Health (1997) argues that pressure to develop such lists be resisted, because medical necessity of a given service will vary across individual patients.

[22] Canadian Institute for Health Information (2014).

PHARMACARE—TOO COSTLY TO CONTEMPLATE?

Spending on prescription drugs in Canada is attracting an increasing amount of attention for at least two reasons. It is one of the fastest growing components of health spending, accounting for 8.8 percent of total spending in 1975 and rising to 15.8 percent today. And unlike hospital and medical services where more than 90 percent of the funding is public, only about 42 percent of the spending on prescription drugs is public. According to a recent C.D. Howe Institute study, "Canada has the distinction of being the only country in the world with a universal public health insurance program that excludes coverage for prescription drugs." This gives rise to concerns over equitable access to drugs and, if financial obstacles prevent some individuals from filling their prescriptions, the health improvements and possible cost savings elsewhere in the system will not be fully realized.

Media reports suggest that pressure for universal drug coverage in Canada is mounting, but is it too costly to contemplate? A 2015 study published in the *Canadian Medical Association Journal* finds that a public and universal system would *reduce* rather than increase spending on prescription drugs, estimating a 32 percent reduction relative to 2012–13 levels. The main source of savings is lower brand-name and generic drug prices from increased buyer power and economies of scale.

While health is a provincial responsibility, the federal government is involved in drug safety, patents, and regulation. So despite potential cost savings, equity arguments, and growing enthusiasm in favour of a national universal drug plan, one is unlikely to emerge without the federal government as a willing partner. So far, that partnership has failed to materialize.

Based on Morgan et al. (2013), Goodman (2015), Gagnon (2013), Morgan et al. (2015), and "Two New Reports Call for National Prescription Drug Plan," *The Globe and Mail*, December 3, 2014.

Complete references for this feature can be found in the References section on page 479.

access.[23] Proponents of expanding the role of the private sector in health financing and care believe that costs and waiting times will be reduced. Opponents of privatization fear that it will lead to a gradual dismantling of Medicare.

The Romanow Report discusses some key issues in regard to the timely access to services and wait times in a mixed environment with both public and private provision. Wait times for diagnostic tests such as MRIs (magnetic resonance imaging) can, for example, be lengthy. Some individuals may purchase these tests privately and then may use their tests to re-enter the public system and get treatment, potentially jumping ahead in the queue. The report recommended targeted funding in support of reducing wait times for diagnostic services and better management of wait lists, including the development of comparable information and common indicators.

As part of the 2004 *10-Year Plan to Strengthen Health Care*, the provinces made a commitment to take steps to reduce wait times for five key areas (cancer, heart, diagnostic imaging, joint replacements, and sight restoration) by March 31, 2007, and to develop comparable indicators of access and benchmarks for medically acceptable wait times. In addition, the federal government committed $5.5 billion over 10 years to wait-time reduction funding for the provinces. Progress on achieving these goals has been slow. Selected data are presented in Table 9.6.

More data are needed before any firm conclusions on reductions in wait times can be made. However, Table 9.6 does show that the percentage of patients receiving these services within the medically acceptable wait times varies significantly by province.

User charges. Canada is the only industrialized country that prohibits user charges for publicly insured health services (Senate, 2002: 15.7). User charges can take the form of deductibles from insurance claims, nominal fees for services (e.g., $5), or coinsurance, where patients pay a fixed percentage of the cost of services. User charges may discourage overuse of the health care system and are advocated in the Mazankowski Report.

---

[23] See Quebec (2006: 8).

TABLE 9.6

Percent of Patients Receiving Care Within Benchmark Wait Times

	Hip Replacement Percent within 182 days		Knee Replacement Percent within 182 days		Radiation Therapy Percent within 28 days	
	2010	2014	2010	2014	2010	2014
NFLD	75	96	67	92	94	98
PEI	90	87	73	78	97	90
NS	57	58	42	44	85	88
NB	79	74	67	56	87	97
QUE	88	84	83	81	98	99
ONT	91	88	89	86	97	99
MAN	63	71	57	71	100	100
SASK	69	93	61	89	97	97
AB	78	87	69	81	94	97
BC	85	67	76	57	92	95

Source: Data are taken from the Canadian Institute for Health Information's annual reports on wait times, https://secure.cihi.ca/estore/productSeries.htm?locale=en&pc=PCC395 (Accessed May 21, 2015).

The Kirby Report counters that most health care spending is beyond patient control and that such fees are unfair to the sick and the poor.

SUMMARY

- For a risk-averse person, an insurance plan that charges an actuarially fair premium increases expected utility because it allows risk smoothing.
- The more risk averse an individual is, the more he or she is willing to pay for an insurance policy.
- By pooling individuals into one insurance program, an insurance company can lower risk from a societal point of view.
- Health care services may be different from other commodities and services for a number of reasons, including adverse selection, moral hazard, and society's desire to act paternalistically, to redistribute income, or to internalize externalities.
- Adverse selection arises when those being insured know more about their risk than the insurance company does. This prevents the insurance company from charging premiums that are in line with each individual's expected losses. If the insurance company instead charges an average premium across all customers, the low-risk people will tend to drop out of the plan, leaving the insurer to lose money.
- The more information insurance companies can obtain about their customers' health risk the more they can overcome the inefficiencies of adverse selection. Yet sorting by health risk would generate inequities.
- Government can address adverse selection by providing universal health insurance coverage.
- Moral hazard arises when obtaining insurance leads to changes in behaviour that increase the likelihood of the adverse outcome. In the case of medical care, insured individuals may consume medical services beyond the point where the marginal benefit equals the marginal cost.
- Government provision of health insurance faces the same moral hazard problem as private insurance, because it too reduces the price of medical services faced by patients.
- Health care insurance is a provincial government responsibility. The federal government contributes transfers to support health care services.

- The Canada Health Act lays out five conditions that must be met for provincial health insurance schemes to qualify for federal transfers. The federal government may unilaterally reduce transfers if it decides that a provincial scheme is not meeting the conditions of the Canada Health Act.

- Compared with health systems in selected OECD countries, Canada's health system produces average or above-average outcomes at above-average cost.

- As we look to the future of the Canadian health care system, we note that the health of Canadians is generally improving over time.

- Health experts agree that better management is needed to adapt the Canadian health system to future needs.

- Significant future public cost pressures will come as a result of the aging population; technical advances in health sciences, which will expand the range of health problems that can be treated; and the increasing reliance on public funding for drugs.

- Current debates about future directions for the Canadian health care system centre on changing incentives faced by physicians and other health care providers, defining a list of medically necessary services, the value of a national pharmacare program, and the role of the private sector in health care financing.

EXERCISES

1. Why is the demand for health care services different from the demand for other kinds of services?

2. Judging from media reports, the Canadian health system is operating under tremendous financial pressure, and is in danger of collapse. As an economist advising the federal Minister of Health, what evidence would you collect to determine if the concerns reported in the media were justified?

3. What role has the Canada Health Act played in shaping the evolution of the Canadian health system?

4. Suppose that an individual's demand curve for doctor visits per year is given by the equation $P = 100 - 25Q$, where Q is the number of doctor visits per year and P is the price per visit under a private medical system. Suppose also that the marginal cost of each doctor visit is $50.

   a. How many visits per year would be efficient? What is the total cost of the efficient number of visits?

   b. Suppose the government introduces medical insurance. There is no deductible, but suppose there is a coinsurance rate of 50 percent. How many visits to the doctor will occur now? What are the individual's out-of-pocket costs? How much does the government pay for these individual doctor visits?

5. Can you think of reasons why the problem of adverse selection in the market for health care insurance might become more severe among the older cohorts in the population?

6. In Germany and the Netherlands, public health care insurance is voluntary for people with relatively high annual incomes (while public coverage is mandatory for those with middle and lower incomes). However, the private insurers must accept all those who apply for coverage. Explain how this regulation can help deal with the problem of adverse selection in the health insurance market.

7. To work out this problem, you'll need a calculator that can take logarithms or a spreadsheet program. Suppose that your utility function is $U = \ln(4I)$, where I is the amount of income you make in a given year. Suppose that you typically make $30,000 per year, but there is a 5 percent chance that, in the next year, you will get sick and lose $20,000 in income due to medical costs.

   a. What is your expected utility if you do not have insurance to protect against this adverse event?

b. Suppose you can buy insurance that will cover your losses if you get sick. What would be the actuarially fair premium? What is your expected utility if you buy the insurance policy?

c. What is the most that you would be willing to pay for this policy?

8. Nathan's income in a typical year is $75,000. There is a 10 percent chance that Nathan will be seriously ill next year, incurring $15,000 in medical expenses. Samantha also earns $75,000 in a typical year. Her chance of becoming seriously ill next year and incurring $15,000 in medical expenses is 20 percent.

a. Calculate the actuarially fair premium for full insurance for (i) Nathan and (ii) Samantha.

b. Suppose that a private insurance firm cannot distinguish between Nathan and Samantha in terms of their risk and assumes the risk of being seriously ill in the general population is 10%. In this context, discuss the adverse selection problem the firm might face.

c. Can a compulsory, government-run health insurance program avoid the problem of adverse selection? Explain why or why not.

9. Suppose that a lack of information leads individuals to underestimate the true benefits of "early detection" medical procedures, like screening for colon cancer. This leads to a discrepancy in the informed demand (which captures the true private marginal benefits from screening tests) and the uninformed demand.

a. Use a supply and demand diagram to illustrate how this lack of information could lead to an inefficiently low level of colon cancer screening tests being undertaken. Be sure to indicate the size of the inefficiency resulting from poor information on your graph.

b. How might the government intervene to address this source of market failure?

CHAPTER 10

Employment Insurance

The UI program is designed to provide workers with earnings-related benefits in the event of unemployment; it is not designed to provide all Canadians with a minimum level of income; nor is UI designed to redistribute incomes on a vertical basis.

–Canadian Labour Congress

For us, Unemployment Insurance is a federal social assistance program, whose purpose is to protect against temporary interruption of earnings.

–Fédération des femmes du Québec

I don't see UI as a problem. I see that $1 million a week coming into the Miramichi economy as a God-send, as a matter of fact. UI is not the problem. It is one of the strengths of the economy.

–Miramichi Regional Development Corporation

AFTER READING THIS CHAPTER, THE STUDENT SHOULD BE ABLE TO:

LO1 Define the main labour market indicators used to describe labour market conditions.

LO2 Identify labour market trends from data presented in tables and graphs.

LO3 Explain the market failure rationale for government provision of employment insurance.

LO4 Outline the distributional rationale for government provision of employment insurance.

LO5 Summarize the key design features of Canada's Employment Insurance program.

LO6 Discuss how the Employment Insurance program may affect the unemployment rate through its impact on the labour market, including the effect on layoffs, quits, duration of unemployment, and labour mobility.

LO7 Outline the distributional impacts of the employment insurance program and explain why its redistribution effects are limited.

Employment insurance plays a central role in Canada's income security system. It is one of the largest and most complex programs of the federal government, providing income protection for just over 15 million Canadians in 2013–14.[1] Expenditures included $9.9 billion on regular benefits, $3.4 billion on family benefits (maternity and parental leave), $1.3 billion on sickness benefits, and $248 million on fishing benefits.

---

[1] Prior to 1996, the Employment Insurance program was called the Unemployment Insurance program. We will use "employment insurance" as a generic term for programs that provide temporary financial assistance or benefits to unemployed individuals. The term "Unemployment Insurance" or UI is used to refer to the pre-1996 program, while "Employment Insurance" or EI refers to the post-1996 program.

An additional $468 million was spent on self-employment assistance, wage subsidies, and various training-related benefits. Overall, 711,042 individuals received a total of $15.4 billion in benefits in 2013–14.

Employment insurance is also one of the most controversial government programs. Part of the reason for the controversy, and the continual search for reforms, is that there are very different views about the role of employment insurance in the Canadian income security system. The lead quotes for this chapter were drawn from submissions to the Forget Commission of Inquiry on Unemployment Insurance in the mid-1980s, and they express different views about the role of the program (Forget, 1986). The Canadian Labour Congress emphasized the insurance role of the UI program; the Fédération des femmes du Quebec emphasized the fact that it was a *federal* (as opposed to a provincial) social assistance program, albeit for temporary income losses; and the Miramichi Regional Development Corporation emphasized the importance of employment insurance as a support for the Miramichi region. Given these diverse views, it is little wonder that there has been an ongoing debate about the Employment Insurance program.

This chapter begins with a look at the nature of and trends in unemployment in Canada, followed by a discussion of why the government provides employment insurance. We then provide a brief history of employment insurance in Canada and examine the effects of employment insurance on individuals' and firms' labour market behaviour. Finally, we consider the distributional implications of employment insurance.

UNEMPLOYMENT IN CANADA

Unemployment is measured by Statistics Canada's Labour Force Survey. Households are contacted by the survey each month, and individuals over 15 years of age are asked a variety of questions about their labour market behaviour.[2] Individuals are considered to be **unemployed** if they did not have a job at the time of the survey but were available for work and made an effort to find a job during the previous four weeks. They are also counted as unemployed if they were available for work and were waiting to be recalled to a job from which they had been laid off within the last twenty-six weeks or were waiting to report to a new job within four weeks. Individuals who had a job—regardless of the number of hours worked—or who were off work because of illness, vacation time, or an industrial dispute are considered to be employed. The **labour force** is defined as the total number of individuals who are employed and unemployed. The **unemployment rate** is the percentage of the labour force that is unemployed. Those who did not have a job and did not actively search for employment, such as full-time students, are classified as **not in the labour force**.

Table 10.1 provides a snapshot of Canada's labour market in 2014. There were 19.1 million people in the labour force; 17.8 million of these individuals were employed while the number of unemployed was about 1.3 million. The unemployment rate was 6.9 percent and the **labour force participation rate**, (measured as the percentage of the working-age population in the labour force), was 66 percent. The **employment rate**, which measures total employment as a percentage of the working-age population, was 61.4 percent. The **working-age population** consists of individuals between the ages of 15 and 64.

These data provide information on the number (stock) of people in each labour market state—employed, unemployed, and not in the labour force. Flows between different labour market states are also important. For instance, the level of unemployment at a particular point in time depends on the rate at which

- individuals are laid off or quit their jobs, but continue to search for new jobs;
- unemployed individuals find acceptable job offers and become employed;
- unemployed individuals drop out of the labour force; and
- individuals enter or re-enter the labour force and look for employment.

The flow of individuals between categories of labour market activity can actually be quite large relative to the stock of the employed, the unemployed, and those not in the labour force. So, even if the number of unemployed has changed little from one month to the next, this does not mean that the pool of unemployed comprises the same individuals. Some of the unemployed have become employed, some employed have lost their jobs and become unemployed, some have quit the labour force altogether, and so on. Understanding

---

[2] The labour force survey also excludes persons living on reserves, members of the military, and people living in institutions, such as prisons.

TABLE 10.1	
Labour Market Data, 2014	
	2014
Population 15 years and over	29.0 million
Labour force	19.1 million
–Employed	17.8 million
–Unemployed	1.3 million
Labour force participation rate (%)	66.0
Employment rate (%)	61.4
Unemployment rate (%)	6.9
• Job losers (as % of labour force)	3.0
• Job leavers (as % of labour force)	1.3
• Not in the labour force (as % of the labour force)	1.8

Source: Statistics Canada's CANSIM II database (http://cansim2.statcan.ca), Table 282-0002 and Table 282-0216.

these labour market flows is important for understanding the causes of unemployment and for designing policies aimed at reducing unemployment. Later in the chapter, we present a simple model that describes the relationship between the unemployment rate, the **separation rate** (the rate at which individuals are laid off or quit their jobs), and the **job-finding rate**. Table 10.1 also shows unemployment rates for different categories of unemployed. Note that while 44 percent of the unemployed were job losers, about 26.4 percent of the unemployed were new entrants or re-entrants to the labour force.[3]

Defining and measuring the "true" unemployment rate is very difficult. Some individuals are interested in gaining employment but may think that their chances of getting employment are so low that they no longer think it worthwhile to search for a job. These **discouraged workers** are not counted as unemployed because they stop looking for work and drop out of the labour market. There may be other "unemployed" individuals who, in practice, make very little effort to find a job and yet still report that they are looking for employment. Individuals differ in how they describe their effort or their aspirations to find a job, and this means that the measured unemployment rate may understate or overstate the "actual" level of unemployment. Because of these differences in self-reporting, some economists feel that the employment rate is a better measure of the state of the labour market. One difficulty with both the employment rate and the unemployment rate is that individuals with a job are considered to be employed even if they would like to work more hours. Part-time employment has become increasingly common, and many individuals with part-time jobs report that they would like to work more hours, but are not able to do so. Such individuals can be viewed as partially unemployed, but this aspect of unemployment is not reflected in the official unemployment rate.[4] Because of the significant conceptual problems in defining unemployment and the practical difficulties in measuring it, a good deal of caution has to be exercised when interpreting labour market statistics.

Figure 10.1 shows trends in key labour market indicators since 1946. There has been an upward trend in the labour force participation rate, from 54.4 percent in 1965 to 66 percent in 2014. The increase in labour force participation over this period has been due to the dramatic increase in the participation rate of married females. Also evident are the larger fluctuations in the employment rate as a result of expansions and contractions in the economy. These are mirrored by fluctuations in the unemployment rate. Although there has been an upward trend in the employment rate between 1946 and 2014, the unemployment rate has also been trending up. During the 1950s, the average unemployment rate was 4.2 percent, in the 1970s it was 6.7 percent,

---

[3] To see this, let the number of job losers be equal to J. Solve for J by taking 3.0 percent of the 19.1 million in the labour force (0.03 × 19.1 million = 573,000). Job losers as a percentage of total unemployed equals 573,000 divided by 1.3 million, or 44 percent.

[4] According to a recent CIBC report, the share of non-student workers aged 20 to 24 working part time has increased from about 8% in the late 1990s to just under 12% in 2012 (see Tal, 2013).

FIGURE 10.1

LABOUR MARKET TRENDS, 1946–2014

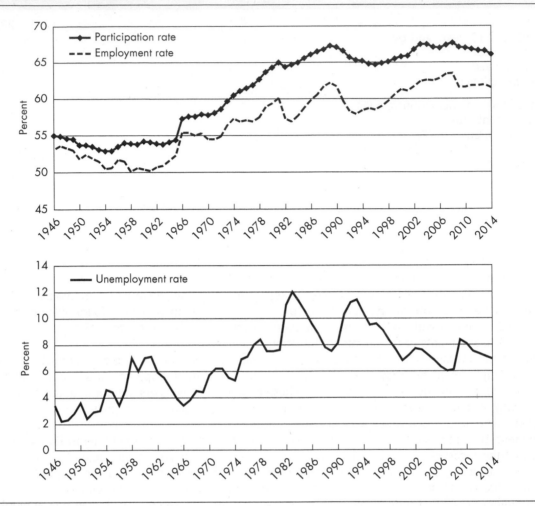

Note: These data are for both sexes, aged 15 years and over.

Sources: Adapted from Statistics Canada, *The Labour Force, November 1995* (Ottawa: 1995), 71–001 for 1946 to 1975. For 1976 and beyond, the above data are taken from the Statistics Canada, CANSIM II database (http://cansim2.statcan.ca), Table 282-0002.

and in the 1990s it was 9.5 percent. This upward trend has been a major concern for Canadians. Since 1995, the unemployment rate has been trending down. Over the period from 2000 to 2014, the average unemployment rate was 7.1 percent.

In evaluating the severity of a country's unemployment, economists often focus on duration, because long periods of unemployment may be particularly damaging to a worker's skills and self-esteem. While in recent years Canada's overall unemployment rate has been comparable to those of a number of Western European countries, long-term unemployment has been less of a problem. In Canada, 12.9 percent of the unemployed were without a job for more than a year in 2014. In France, the rate was 42.7 percent and in the United States it was just over 23 percent.[5]

---

[5] See OECD. (2015). "Labour Market Statistics: Unemployment by duration: incidence," *OECD Employment and Labour Market Statistics* (database). DOI: http://dx.doi.org.libproxy.wlu.ca/10.1787/data-00322-en (Accessed on 11 August 2015).

TABLE 10.2

Unemployment: Rates and Duration by Province, 2014		
	Unemployment Rate (percent)	Average Duration of Unemployment (weeks)
Newfoundland	11.9	16.4
Prince Edward Island	10.6	16.5
Nova Scotia	9.0	18.9
New Brunswick	9.9	19.6
Quebec	7.7	22.9
Ontario	7.3	22.4
Manitoba	5.4	16.0
Saskatchewan	3.8	13.5
Alberta	4.7	14.5
British Columbia	6.1	19.3
Canada	6.9	20.8

Source: Adapted from the Statistics Canada, CANSIM II database, http://cansim2.statcan.ca/, Tables 282-0002 and 282-0048.

Table 10.2 shows that there is substantial variation in unemployment rates and unemployment duration across provinces. In 2014, Newfoundland experienced the highest rate of unemployment at 11.9 percent, significantly above the Canadian rate of 6.9 percent. Saskatchewan's unemployment rate was the lowest, at 3.8 percent. More generally, the Atlantic provinces have experienced above-average unemployment rates, while provinces west of Ontario have generally experienced below-average unemployment rates. The average duration of an unemployment spell was 20.8 weeks in 2014. As we shall see, regional unemployment differences have influenced the design of Employment Insurance in Canada. Unemployment rates also vary according to individuals' demographic characteristics. Table 10.3 indicates that in 2014 males had a slightly higher average unemployment rate than females. Young people, on average, had higher unemployment rates than older workers, but the average duration of unemployment was higher for older workers. And unemployment rates were lower for workers with more education and training.

TABLE 10.3

Demographic Characteristics and Unemployment, 2014		
Demographic Characteristics	Unemployment Rate (percent)	Average Duration of Unemployment (weeks)
SEX:		
Male	7.4	21.4
Female	6.4	20.0
AGE:		
15–24 years	13.4	12.2
25–44 years	6.0	20.7
45 years and older	5.5	28.5
EDUCATIONAL ATTAINMENT:		
Some high school	14.1	
High school graduate	7.6	
University degree	4.9	

Source: Adapted from the Statistics Canada, CANSIM II database (http://cansim2.statcan.ca), Tables 282-0002, 282-0003, and 282-0048.

THE RATIONALE FOR PUBLIC EMPLOYMENT INSURANCE

Why should the government provide employment insurance? First, we examine the possibility of market failure, and then we consider the role of employment insurance as an income redistribution program.

Market Failure in the Provision of Employment Insurance

As aggregate demand fluctuates over the business cycle, and as the economy adjusts to changes in technology, international competitiveness, and consumer spending patterns, workers face the risk of temporary income losses and unemployment. As a consequence, risk-averse workers may want to purchase insurance to protect against this risk. As we discussed in Chapter 9, private markets may fail to provide adequate amounts of insurance in situations where **adverse selection** and **moral hazard** are important.

Consider the problem of adverse selection. Individuals face different probabilities of being unemployed for different lengths of time, and those workers with the highest probability of becoming unemployed for long periods of time will have the highest demand for employment insurance. Private insurance firms would have to charge relatively high premiums to make a profit, which would make private employment insurance unattractive for many low-risk individuals. Employment insurance is also subject to a moral hazard problem because workers and their employers can influence, to some extent, the probability and the magnitude of a loss. A firm can affect the probability that its workers will be unemployed by deciding whether to lay off workers or reduce hours during a recession. Workers can affect the duration of a spell of unemployment (the magnitude of the loss) by deciding how much effort to put into searching for a new job or deciding whether to accept a new job at a lower rate of pay or in a new region. Because it is difficult for the insurer to determine whether, or to what extent, an unemployment spell is the fault of a firm or a worker, a private employment insurance company would have to pay out large amounts of money for a "full coverage" policy. To reduce the incentive to collect employment insurance, a private firm could offer "partial coverage" policies where only part of the lost wages of an unemployed worker would be covered. It might also charge higher premiums to workers who made more frequent claims.

A compulsory government insurance program can avoid the adverse selection problem. Premiums can be based on the average expected loss for the entire labour force. This is especially beneficial for those who face an above-average risk of unemployment. However, government provision does not eliminate the moral hazard problem. Government-run employment insurance systems may include features designed to reduce the incentives for layoffs and lengthy spells of unemployment. For example, employment insurance systems often do not cover the first few weeks of unemployment, and the benefit or replacement rate is typically less than 100 percent, covering only a fraction of the worker's lost employment earnings. These features are equivalent to deductibles and coinsurance clauses in more conventional insurance policies.

In addition to overcoming the adverse selection problem, a compulsory government insurance program reduces job search costs. This may improve job search efficiency and may also lead to improved matching between job seekers and employers.

Another reason why the private sector may not be able to provide employment insurance is because employment insurance claims increase dramatically during recessions and decline during economic expansions. The cyclical nature of unemployment means that the risk-pooling mechanism cannot eliminate the risk from the cost of providing employment insurance. A national government has a greater capacity to borrow than a private corporation in order to finance employment insurance claims during a recession, and therefore it has an important advantage in the provision of employment insurance.

Employment Insurance as an Income Redistribution Program

Many think that employment insurance is primarily an income support or redistribution program. Conflicting views over the purpose of social insurance programs have been a recurring element in the debate over the design of these programs in Canada, as the following quote from the 1943 *Report on Social Security for Canada* (the Marsh Report) indicates:

> The understanding of social insurance . . . is still confused because too much emphasis is placed on the second word and too little on the first word of the phrase. Social insurance brings in the resources of the state, i.e., the resources of the community as a whole, or in a particular case that part of the

resources which may be garnered together through taxes or contributions. It does not mean . . . that there must be a precise actuarial adjustment of premiums to risk in each individual case.[6]

Redistribution occurs when an individual's contribution, or premium, differs from his or her expected payout from the insurance coverage. The expected payout from an insurance policy is called the actuarially fair premium. To illustrate, if Sam faces a 20 percent probability of being unemployed for 10 weeks each year, during which time he would collect $4,000 in employment insurance benefits, then the actuarially fair premium for this employment insurance coverage is $800. If Sam's premium is less than $800, then he is in effect receiving a subsidy. If his premium is more than $800, then Sam is making a net contribution. Competition among private insurance companies means that this type of redistribution among their policy holders does not occur. If an identifiable group were charged more than the expected cost of their insurance coverage, another company could offer them a lower premium. In contrast, a social insurance program, such as employment insurance, can involve redistribution because such programs are usually compulsory, and there is no competitive pressure from alternative suppliers to force premiums in line with expected benefits. Thus, employment insurance can be considered an income redistribution program if it leads to this type of redistribution. The employment insurance program may also lead to redistribution if the total contributions from the insured do not cover the benefits that are paid out and the deficiency is financed from other government revenues. Consequently, both the way that employment insurance benefits are structured and the way that they are financed will determine whether the employment insurance system involves redistribution.

Later in this chapter we consider whether the Canadian Employment Insurance program has resulted in redistribution. For now, we consider whether it is desirable to redistribute through employment insurance. Those who think that employment insurance should function as an income redistribution program argue that social insurance programs help to supplement social assistance programs. Proponents argue that all taxpayers should subsidize employment insurance benefits because the provision of these benefits reduces the amount that governments would otherwise have to spend on social assistance. Employment insurance also allows governments to provide income support linked to labour market activity. The disincentives to return to work are not as great as they might be under welfare programs where the implicit tax rate on earnings is often very high. Having an income support system with two different programs—employment insurance for those who normally have full-time employment and social assistance for those with only limited ability to be self-supporting—means that each program can be geared to a different segment of the population. This allows the social assistance system to be more generous than it otherwise would be if it were the only income support program.

Critics of the notion that the employment insurance system is primarily an income redistribution program argue that, in practice, the employment insurance program does a poor job of redistributing income to the poor, it violates the goals of horizontal and vertical equity, and it has caused major distortions in labour market decisions of firms and workers because it lacks an insurance orientation.

Before considering these criticisms further, we review the main features of Canada's Employment Insurance program.

THE HISTORY OF THE CANADIAN EMPLOYMENT INSURANCE SYSTEM

The Creation of the UI Program

The unprecedented increase in unemployment during the 1930s inflicted enormous suffering on Canadian workers and their families. In 1933, approximately 25 percent of the labour force was unemployed, and 15 percent of the population was "on relief," which was largely funded by the provincial and municipal governments. These events convinced many Canadians that the federal government should be involved in the provision of social insurance programs. However, the social insurance program enacted by Prime Minister R. B. Bennett's Conservative government in 1935 was ruled *ultra vires;* that is, outside the jurisdiction of the federal government. With the agreement of the provinces, the BNA Act (now the Constitution Act, 1982) was amended to give the federal government exclusive jurisdiction over the provision of unemployment insurance,

---

[6] Marsh (1975: 10–11).

and Prime Minister William Lyon Mackenzie King's Liberal government passed the 1940 Unemployment Insurance Act, which established a program of unemployment benefits.

The program was the largest social insurance program enacted by a Canadian government up to that time. It was based on insurance principles, with coverage limited to those in jobs for which there was a moderate risk of unemployment, about 42 percent of the labour force. Higher-risk jobs in agriculture, forestry, and fishing, and lower-risk jobs in the police, the armed forces, and government employment were excluded. The program was largely financed by contributions from employers and employees, with the federal government paying 20 percent of the total contributions plus the administration costs out of general revenue. By focusing on the group with a moderate risk of unemployment, and with a heavy reliance on premiums from employers and employees in this group, the extent of redistribution under the program was limited.

Benefits for the eligible unemployed were about 50 percent of the wage rate with a supplement for a married claimant.[7] There was a maximum duration of benefits; the maximum was lower if benefits were received in the previous three years. This feature was intended to curtail the use of the program by the seasonally unemployed. In the 1950s, coverage was expanded to provide some seasonal unemployment benefits, and in 1956, Unemployment Insurance benefits were extended to "self-employed" fishermen. These amendments represented important departures from the insurance principles upon which the original program had been based and introduced greater scope for redistribution.

The 1971 Reforms

The Unemployment Insurance Act (Bill C-229) made significant changes to the program in 1971. Changes included expanding UI coverage to 93 percent of the labour force (excluding the self-employed), more-generous benefits, and a reduction in the minimum number of weeks required for eligibility. Special benefits (sickness, maternity, and retirement) were also introduced.[8] The duration of benefits was linked to the number of weeks worked in the qualifying period, and increased when the national unemployment rate exceeded 4 percent and when the unemployment rate in the worker's region exceeded the national average by one to three percentage points. This feature was known as **regional extended benefits**. Regular and special benefits and the administration costs of the system were financed by contributions collected from employers and employees. The federal government paid for the unemployment insurance benefits that were attributable to a national unemployment rate in excess of 4 percent, the regional extended benefits, the training benefits, and the benefits for self-employed fishermen out of general revenues.

The increased share of GNP going to UI benefits (0.9 percent of GNP in 1971 to 1.9 percent of GNP in 1975) prompted a number of reforms aimed at reducing the generosity of the system and curtailing abuse.[9] These reforms included an increase in the disqualification period for those who had quit their job without just cause or were fired for misconduct, and a reduction in the benefit rate from two-thirds of insurable earnings to 60 percent.

UI: 1980 to 1994

The economy suffered through two recessions during the period 1980 to 1994. The unemployment rate increased from 7.6 to 12 percent from 1981 to 1983, and from 7.5 to 11.4 percent from 1989 to 1993. Each recession was accompanied by a sharp increase in UI claims that, combined with changes to how UI was financed, resulted in a large deficit in the UI account.[10] The federal government responded by increasing contribution rates and taking measures to reduce benefits.[11] The benefit rate was reduced from 60 to 55 percent

---

[7] Guest (1980: 108).

[8] See Phipps (2006) for an overview of the evolution of maternity and parental employment insurance benefits in Canada. She notes that the opinion on whether such benefits should in fact be part of employment insurance is not unanimous.

[9] GNP data are taken from Statistics Canada, *Canadian Economic Observer, Historical Statistical Supplement, 2009/10*, Cat. No. 11-210-XPB (Ottawa, August 2010). Data on total unemployment benefits come from Statistics Canada's *Historical Statistics of Canada: Section E Wages and Working Conditions;* http://www.statcan.gc.ca/pub/11-516-x/pdf/5500095-eng.pdf.

[10] An important change in how unemployment insurance was financed was introduced in 1989. Beginning in 1991–92, the federal government's contributions toward the financing of unemployment insurance would stop and the system would become entirely financed by employer and employee contributions.

[11] The employee contribution rate rose from $2.25 in 1990 to $3.07 in 1994. Over the same period, the contribution rate for employers increased from to $3.15 to $4.30.

of insurable earnings (with some exceptions). Those who voluntarily quit their jobs without just cause were no longer eligible for UI benefits and the minimum requirement for UI eligibility in high unemployment regions (unemployment in excess of 13 percent) increased from 10 to 12 weeks (as compared to 20 weeks in a region with unemployment at 6 percent or less). Implementing these changes, particularly the relatively large increase in the employer contribution rate, during the recession may have exacerbated the unemployment problem.

Over the same period, UI reform was discussed in two major reports—the Macdonald Royal Commission on the Economic Union and Development Prospects for Canada, released in 1985, and the Forget Commission of Inquiry on Unemployment Insurance in 1986. The Macdonald Commission recommended that the system be re-established on insurance principles and that the income redistribution component of UI be met through a negative income tax (NIT) system, which would provide all Canadians with a guaranteed annual income. The Forget Commission recommended that the regional extended benefits be abolished and that they be replaced with an earnings supplementation program similar to a NIT. Both reports met with considerable opposition, especially from Atlantic Canada and from representatives of the labour movement, and, as a result, their recommendations were largely ignored.

Employment Insurance Today

In the aftermath of the 1990–92 recession, the federal government launched a major review of Canadian social security programs, including Unemployment Insurance. This review culminated in the implementation of the 1996 Employment Insurance Act (Bill C-12), which lay the foundation of the program we see operating today. Additional reforms were subsequently introduced in 2012. We outline some of key features of today's employment insurance program below.[12]

Eligibility. The 1996 reform introduced eligibility based on the number of hours, rather than weeks, worked during the previous 52 weeks and on the regional unemployment rate. Since part-time employment was becoming increasingly more important, and many workers did not have a "standard" 35 to 40 hour workweek, "hours worked" was argued to be a better measure of time spent working. For regular EI benefits, the minimum number of hours needed to be eligible for benefits ranges from 420 (if the regional unemployment rate exceeds 13.1 percent) to 700 (the regional unemployment rate is 6 percent or less). This feature is referred to as the variable entrance requirements. A higher number of hours is required for new entrants and for those re-entering the labour market after an absence of two years. To qualify for special benefits (sickness, maternity, or parental), workers need to have accumulated 600 hours in the previous 52 weeks.

EI benefits. The EI benefit rate, for most claimants, is now 55 percent of insurable earnings. The 1996 reform reduced the annual maximum insurable earnings (MIE) from $42,380 in 1995 to $39,000 in 1996. It remained at that level until 2006. Since then, the MIE has been increasing. For 2015, the MIE is set at $49,500 with a maximum amount per week of $524. Low-income claimants with children can receive more generous benefits. If their family income is less than $25,921 per year they are eligible for the Family Supplement, which can increase their benefit rate to 80 percent of insurable earnings. Approximately, 4.8 percent of all EI claimants received this supplement in 2013–14. There is also a clawback provision for high-income claimants.

Duration of benefits. After the two-week waiting period, the maximum length of a claim is 45 weeks (reduced from 50 weeks in the 1996 reform). A maximum of 15 weeks of maternity or sickness benefits is available. For parental benefits, the maximum duration of benefits was initially 10 weeks but this was extended to 35 weeks in 2000. On occasion, the federal government has introduced temporary measures that have extended the duration of benefits. For example, the maximum benefit duration for regular benefits was extended by five weeks for claims in the period between March 2009 and September 2010 as part of the government's plan to support a recovering economy.

Experience rating. The 1996 reform included an intensity rule to introduce some **experience rating** into the program. Under the rule, the benefit rate was to be reduced by one percentage point, up to a maximum

---

[12] Mowat Centre (2012) provides a discussion of the 2012 EI changes; Gray (2006) reviews the EI program in the 2000s and changes made since 1996.

ELIGIBILITY REQUIREMENTS FOR EMPLOYMENT INSURANCE: UNFAIR AND INEFFICIENT

The most recent recession in 2008 set off a new round of debate about Canada's employment insurance program. EI eligibility is one feature in particular that attracts attention. Controversy arises in part because the hours you need to work to qualify for benefits (and the duration of benefits you receive) are dependent on where you live. Bédard and Fortin provide an example to show how EI currently works. Consider a worker who earns $560 a week. If this worker lives in Cape Breton, Nova Scotia, they need only 420 hours of work to qualify for EI benefits. If this worker is laid off, he or she could receive $264 a week in EI benefits for 30 weeks. If this same worker lived in Saskatoon, he or she would need to have worked 700 hours to qualify for EI. And if this worker was laid off, they would be eligible for $280 a week in benefits for 14 weeks. Many argue that different benefits based solely on where you live is unfair and interferes with the efficient operation of the national labour market.

Eligibility for new labour market entrants, particularly young people, is also a growing concern. New entrants to the labour force need to accumulate 910 hours of work to qualify for EI benefits as compared to the 420 to 700 hours needed for other workers. Since young people often work part-time jobs or only part of the year, they have difficulty collecting EI benefits but are required to paid EI premiums on their earnings. Economist Frances Woolley describes this approach to EI and young people as an "EI as crack cocaine" mentality. Given a concern that using EI at a young age may cause a dependence on EI, tougher eligibility requirements are needed. While this might be the case, Woolley argues that it is unfair that young people pay into a system that is "stacked" against them. She argues that young workers who contribute to EI but fail to qualify for benefits should get their premiums refunded.

Despite widespread criticism, reforming the variable entrance requirements for employment insurance does not appear to be a priority for the federal government.

Based on Bédard and Fortin (2015), MacEwen (2015), McKenna (2011), and "Canada's shame: EI is stealing from the young." *The Globe and Mail,* June 7, 2012.

Complete references for this feature can be found in the References section on page 480.

of 5, for every 20 weeks of regular or fishing benefits. The rule was intended to discourage repeated EI use but it was eliminated in 2000. In 2012, a different form of experience rating was introduced. Three categories of claimants were created (long-tenured workers, occasional claimants, and frequent claimants) and the definition of what constitutes suitable employment now differs depending on the type of claimant. Frequent claimants are required to begin looking for work immediately, and after seven weeks of benefits are required to accept any work they are qualified for, as long as it pays a minimum of 70 percent of their previous wage. Long-tenured claimants are required, after 18 weeks of benefits, to accept any similar job paying a minimum of 80 percent of their previous wage.

Financing. Benefits are financed by premiums that are collected from employees and employers. In 2015, the employee and employer contribution rates were $1.88 and $2.63, respectively, for every $100 of insurable earnings up to the maximum of $49,500. The employer rate is set at 1.4 times the employee rate. The maximum annual contribution was $930.60 for an employee and $1,302.84 for an employer. Note that the employment insurance premiums are not related to the employee's history of claims or the past layoffs of the firm and therefore need not correspond in any way to the insured's actuarially fair premium. The uniformity and compulsory nature of the premiums means that they are essentially payroll taxes that are "earmarked" to finance a particular program.

In summary, insurance and distributional features are both evident in our current system of employment insurance. Insurance elements include the premium financing and the receipt of benefits in the event of unemployment. Distributional aspects include the clawback of benefits for high-income users, the variable entrance requirements, the family supplement, and the benefits for self-employed fisherman.

TABLE 10.4

The Labour Market Effects of the Canadian Employment Insurance System

DIRECT EFFECTS
· Layoffs
· Quits
· Duration of unemployment
· Labour force participation and labour supply

SYSTEMIC EFFECTS
· Industrial mix
· Labour mobility
· Education, training, and occupational choices

MACROECONOMIC EFFECTS
· Automatic stabilizing effects

THE LABOUR MARKET EFFECTS OF EMPLOYMENT INSURANCE

The complexity of the EI system in part reflects the challenges of designing a system to achieve insurance and distributional objectives and, at the same time, reduce some of the disincentive effects associated with the moral hazard problem. Individuals and employers may both have an incentive to change their labour market behaviour in the presence of employment insurance so that the expected loss from unemployment increases.[13] Significant research effort has been devoted to trying to understand how the employment insurance system affects labour market behaviour. Studies have focused on the effects of EI on the duration of unemployment, job search behaviour, layoffs, the unemployment rate, labour mobility, and seasonal unemployment. We briefly discuss some of these effects below.

To help organize the discussion, we will use the schema shown in Table 10.4. The effects can be divided into direct effects, systemic effects, and macroeconomic effects. The direct effects of the employment insurance system are the effects on labour market dynamics (i.e., the flows between the unemployed, the employed, and the not-in-the-labour-force categories). The systemic effects refer to changes in the economic environment that determine employment patterns in the economy. The macroeconomic effects refer to the way that the employment insurance system affects the transmission of economic shocks to the economy and their impact on the unemployment rate.

Results from studies in the mid-1970s that focused on the effects of the employment insurance system on the level of unemployment in the wake of the 1971 reforms are inconclusive.[14] There are a number of reasons why it is has been difficult to reach a consensus on the effects of the 1971 reforms. First, employment insurance programs are extremely complicated, with many different provisions that affect the "generosity" of the system. Generosity is affected by the benefit rate, the maximum insurable earnings amount, the number of weeks of work that are required for UI eligibility, and the maximum duration of benefits. It is therefore quite difficult to measure the generosity of the employment insurance system using a single variable. Shannon and Kidd (2000) show that these institutional details, depending on how they are accounted for, influence the estimated impacts of employment insurance. A second problem is that other factors, such as the oil price increases in the 1970s and high real interest rates since the early 1980s, may have contributed to the rise in the unemployment rate. It is difficult to disentangle the effects of the changes in the employment insurance system on the unemployment rate from the effects of these shocks to the economy and the other, more subtle long-term trends, such as changes in labour force participation behaviour and technological change.

---

[13] Note that moral hazard refers to the changes in the behaviour of individuals and firms, operating within the rules of the system, that increase expected payouts. Moral hazard is not primarily concerned with agents who break the rules for personal gain. Cheating the employment insurance system is undoubtedly a problem, just as tax evasion is a problem. (See Chapter 16 for an analysis of tax evasion.) Investigation and enforcement measures can help to reduce the amount of cheating that takes place.

[14] See Corak (1994) for a review of this early literature.

Direct Effects

Employment and unemployment are affected by the rate at which firms lay off workers and employees voluntarily quit their jobs, and the rate at which unemployed workers are hired by firms. Layoffs and hiring occur because of (a) seasonal variations in the demand for labour, (b) fluctuations in aggregate demand over the business cycle, and (c) long-term secular changes in the economy, as some industries expand and others contract due to changes in technology, international competitiveness, and consumer spending patterns. Even under "normal" economic conditions, some firms will be downsizing and laying off workers while other firms are expanding and hiring more labour. The reallocation of labour among firms, perhaps in different industries and in different regions, is neither instantaneous nor costless, and unemployment will occur in even a well-functioning labour market.

Of the three sources of labour demand fluctuations, an insurance-based employment insurance system is primarily intended to deal with unemployment caused by the business cycle. Seasonal layoffs, insofar as they are highly predictable, do not represent an insurable risk. The long-term secular changes in the economy often mean that workers have to acquire new skills. Insurance is not the issue here. Rather, it is the need for training. And where retraining or relocation is not possible, the unemployed may require longer-term financial assistance. Our current EI system is not solely an insurance-based system; it also provides benefits for seasonal unemployment and sometimes for retraining.

Our discussion of the direct effects of employment insurance on unemployment can be considered with simple equations that capture the relationships between the unemployment rate, the separation rate (layoffs and quits), the job-finding rate, and the average duration of unemployment.

Let f denote the probability that an unemployed workers finds an *acceptable* job over a given week—the **job-finding rate**. By acceptable, we mean that the worker prefers to take the job offer rather than continue to search for a better one. This probability depends on the frequency of receiving a job offer and the quality of the job offer, in terms of the wage rate and the characteristics of the job. Thus, you should think of the probability f as being determined partly by luck and partly by the unemployed worker's job search strategy. Given f, the probability that the worker is hired in week T, after having not found an acceptable job for the previous T-1 weeks, is given by:[15]

$$\text{Probability of a job in week T} = f(1 - f)^{T-1} \tag{10.1}$$

The worker's average duration of unemployment (denoted by du) is the expected number of weeks of unemployment before finding an acceptable job. Using the probability expression in Equation (10.1), average duration is equal to:[16]

$$du = (1 \text{ week}) \times f(1 - f)^0 + (2 \text{ weeks}) \times f(1 - f)^1 + (3 \text{ weeks}) \times f(1 - f)^2 + \cdots \tag{10.2}$$

$$= 1/f$$

This result is intuitive. If an unemployed person has, say, a one-in-four chance of finding a job over a given period of time ($f = 1/4$), then on average it will take the person 4 months ($4 = 1/f$) to find a job.

Now let s denote the probability that an employed worker is laid off or quits—the job **separation rate**. Then the change in the unemployment rate between any pair of weeks, Δur, is given by:

$$\Delta ur = s \times (1 - ur) - f \times ur \tag{10.3}$$

Equation (10.3) states that the change in the unemployment rate equals the separation rate, s, times the proportion of the labour force that is not unemployed, minus the job-finding rate, f, times the proportion of the labour force

---

[15] To see this, think of flipping a coin. The probability of flipping a "heads" on the Tth turn after T-1 consecutive "tails" is $(1/2)(1/2)^{T-1}$. Now generalize this to the case where the coin is not a fair coin, such that the probability of flipping "heads" is f, rather than one-half. In Eq. 10.1 we assume that the probability of finding a job does not change during the worker's unemployment spell. Furthermore, to keep things simple, we will assume that the probability f is identical for all workers.

[16] The result uses the properties of infinite sums:

$$du = (1)f + (2)(1 - f)f + (3)(1 - f)^2 f + \cdots$$

$$= \frac{f}{1 - f}\sum_{n=1}^{\infty} n(1 - f)^n = \frac{f}{1 - f} \times \frac{1 - f}{f^2} = \frac{1}{f}$$

that is unemployed. When the unemployment rate is unchanging, which can be regarded as an equilibrium situation in which the flows in and out of unemployment are balanced, $\Delta ur = 0$, and hence, $ur = s/(s + f)$. Finally, noting the relationship between average duration, du, and the job-finding rate in Equation (10.2), the equilibrium unemployment rate can be re-expressed as a function of the separation rate and the average duration of unemployment:

$$ur = \frac{s}{s + 1/du} = \frac{s \times du}{1 + s \times du} \qquad (10.4)$$

Equation (10.4) can be used to consider how employment insurance affects the equilibrium unemployment rate through the incentive effects the program has on the separation rate and on the length of time an unemployed worker spends unemployed, which in turn depends in part on the worker's incentives to accept a job offer.[17]

We are now ready to discuss the effect of employment insurance on the layoff and quit rates, and on the duration of unemployment spells.

Layoffs. Job separations are classified as permanent, temporary, or voluntary (quits). The layoff rate (calculated as the number of workers permanently or temporarily laid off divided by the number of employed workers) in the most recent recession was estimated at 1.95, compared to a layoff rate of 2.94 and 2.66 for the recessions occurring in the 1980s and 1990s respectively.[18] Depending on its design, employment insurance can distort a firm's decision with respect to layoffs, especially temporary layoffs.

During a downturn in the demand for its products, a firm will generally cut back production and reduce its use of inputs, including labour. A reduction in the demand for labour can be achieved through a reduction in the number of hours worked by each worker or by reducing the number of workers. If employment insurance provides workers with replacement income in the event of a layoff but not when hours of work are reduced, laying off workers becomes more attractive than cutting hours of work. Since 1982, Canada's Employment Insurance system has included the Work-Sharing program. Under a work-sharing agreement, employees work a reduced workweek and, under certain conditions, receive EI benefits. Normally, the arrangements are between 6 and 26 weeks, but in 2009 the federal government introduced temporary changes that increased the maximum duration to 52 weeks and eased the application process. The incentive to choose layoffs over a reduction in hours to deal with reduced demand may be muted by the Work-Sharing program.[19]

Some workers and firms may find it in their interest to create jobs that last just long enough to qualify the workers for employment insurance benefits. In regions with high unemployment, only 12 weeks of employment were required in 1996 to qualify a worker for 32 weeks of benefits. The effect of the variable entrance requirement on length of jobs has been studied by Christofidies and McKenna (1995) and Green and Riddell (1995). The former study found that 5 to 6 percent of all jobs ended when the entrance requirement was satisfied, and that the reduced entrance requirements in the high unemployment regions reduced the length of these jobs by about 20 percent. Green and Riddell (1995) found that the increase in the entrance requirement from 10 weeks to 14, which occurred in the high unemployment areas of Canada in 1990, resulted in a reduction in the unemployment rate and an increase in the average length of employment. Thus, the entrance requirements of the employment insurance system seem to affect the length of employment spells.

Quits. The effect of the employment insurance system on the behaviour of job quitters can be discerned to some extent by comparing the duration of unemployment in Canada with that of the United States. Prior to 1993, Canadians who quit their jobs were eligible for employment insurance, whereas Americans who quit their jobs were not. Over the period 1980 to 1988, Baker, Corak, and Heisz (1996: Table 3) found that, while job quits represent about the same proportion of total job separations in Canada as in the United States, the average duration of unemployment for a quitter was 20.6 weeks in Canada but 11.2 weeks in the United States. Thus, extending employment insurance coverage to job quitters tends to increase the unemployment rate through its effect on the job search behaviour of those who quit, rather than increasing the number of quits.

---

[17] TD Economics (2014) reported a job separation rate of 2.5 percent and a job-finding rate of 30 percent for Canada in September 2014.

[18] The layoff rate was calculated over the period from 2008 to 2011. See Chan, Morissette and Frenette (2011).

[19] The number of work-sharing agreements fluctuates over the business cycle. According to a recent study by the Mowat Centre, an estimated 20,128 layoffs were averted in 2008–09 as a result of the work-sharing arrangements (Mowat Centre Employment Insurance Task Force, 2011). The unemployment rate in 2008 was 6.1 percent. Had all averted layoffs actually been layoffs (joining the pool of unemployed) the unemployment rate would have been about 6.25 percent.

Duration of unemployment. Employment insurance can influence the length of time unemployed workers search for a job. The intensity of job search may also be affected. The higher the employment insurance benefit rate, the lower the opportunity cost of turning down a low-paying job in the hope of eventually finding a better-paying job. Thus, one prediction of labour market search models is that an increase in the employment insurance benefit rate will increase the expected duration of a worker's unemployment spell. A similar incentive effect occurs when the *duration* of EI benefits increase. However, for the unemployed worker who is *not* eligible for employment insurance or who has exhausted their benefits, an increase in EI benefits may reduce the duration of unemployment. The increase in benefits associated with a future job (and subsequent unemployment spell) makes getting a job more attractive to this particular group of unemployed.[20]

The consensus from the empirical literature is that the EI benefit rate and the duration of EI benefits have sizeable effects on the duration of unemployment.[21] It is important to note that if employment insurance-induced increases in the duration of unemployment lead to an increase in the length of time that workers spend searching for a job, labour market performance can be improved. The overall unemployment rate may fall if a longer period of search generates a better "match" or "fit" between the worker and the firm. If workers are under pressure to accept the first available job, many workers will accept jobs that do not fully use their skills. Krueger and Mueller (2010) use U.S. data to test this hypothesis. They find that time devoted to job search actually decreased with increases in the maximum weekly employment insurance benefit.

Labour force participation and labour supply. The employment insurance system can influence the choices an individual makes about participating in the labour force. Since all workers pay the same employment insurance premium, the decision to work is effectively subsidized if the marginal entrant has an above-average probability of becoming unemployed and collecting EI benefits. Holding the number of jobs constant, an increase in the labour force participation rate means that the unemployment rate will increase. Green and Riddell (1993), for example, found that the 1975 amendments to the employment insurance program, which reduced the eligibility age for employment insurance from 75 to 65, significantly reduced the labour force participation rate of workers over the age of 65.

Employment insurance can also influence an individual's decision on how much labour to supply once in the labour force. Kuhn and Riddell (2010) examine the effects of Canada's Employment Insurance system on labour supply decisions using microdata for New Brunswick and Maine from 1970 to 1990. The authors exploited longstanding differences in the generosity in employment insurance in Maine (which has a state-run program) and in New Brunswick (which is part of the federal government's program). They found that changes in employment insurance resulted in only a modest overall effect on labour supply but caused a significant shift in the *distribution* of weeks worked in New Brunswick. Workers were pulled from the zero weeks worked and the 40 to 52 weeks-worked categories into the 1 to 39 weeks-worked category, the one most subsidized by employment insurance during that period. Counterfactual simulation results suggest that the 1971 UI reform can explain all of the reduction in full-year work for males in New Brunswick between 1970 and 1990—a striking result.

Systemic Effects

The employment insurance system can also increase the unemployment rate by altering the mix of industries in the economy, by affecting workers' incentives to move from high unemployment regions or industries to regions or industries with low unemployment rates, and by changing the training, education, and occupational choices that workers make.

Industrial mix. Since the EI premium is the same for all workers and firms and is independent of the expected employment insurance benefits for individual workers or the likelihood that a firm will lay off its workers, the system can be viewed as subsidizing employment in the seasonal and more volatile sectors of the economy and taxing employment in sectors that provide more stable employment. Figure 10.2b shows the ratios of the employment insurance benefits received to employment insurance premiums paid by industry in Canada in 2012. A ratio greater than 1 implies that an industry (or region) received relatively more regular benefits than it contributed in premiums as compared to the national average. The industries with a high benefit-to-tax ratio,

[20] See Mortensen's (1977) model of job search and unemployment insurance.

[21] See Tatsiramos and van Ours (2014) for a recent survey.

FIGURE 10.2

RELATIVE BENEFIT–TAX RATIOS BY INDUSTRY AND PROVINCE, 2012

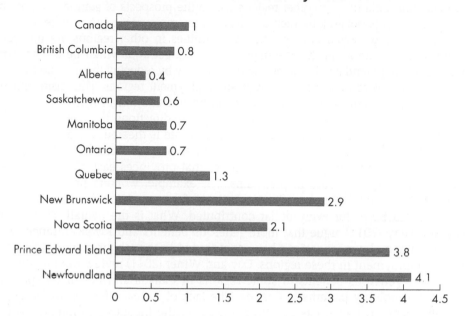

A. Relative Benefit–Tax Ratios by Province

B. Relative Benefit–Tax Ratios by Industry

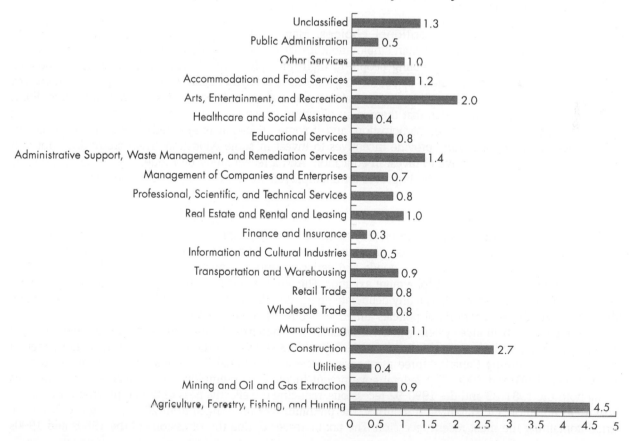

Source: Human Resources and Skills Development Canada (2014), Annex 2:19.

such as agriculture, forestry, fishing, and construction, tend to be seasonal industries or industries that are subject to volatile swings in market demand. This pattern of implicit taxes and subsidies increases the overall unemployment rate in the economy.

Labour mobility. Employment insurance can potentially encourage greater labour mobility as benefits help unemployed workers finance a move to other regions where the prospects of getting a job are better. If some of these unemployed migrants obtain jobs, then the national unemployment rate may be reduced. The system may also encourage migration when employment opportunities in other regions are uncertain, because it provides income support in the event that the migrant does not get a job when he or she moves. However, employment insurance can potentially discourage labour mobility by reducing the income gain from migration, therefore reducing the incentive to move out of high unemployment regions. This disincentive is reinforced when EI benefits are more generous (lower entrance requirements and longer benefit periods) in high unemployment regions. Since these incentive effects work in opposite directions, the overall effect of employment insurance on labour mobility and the national unemployment rate is theoretically ambiguous.

Employment insurance does provide greater support to some provinces, in particular those that tend to have higher unemployment rates. Figure 10.2a shows that provinces east of Ontario receive relatively more in benefits than they contribute in premiums. For example, workers in Newfoundland and New Brunswick received $4.10 and $2.90 in benefits, respectively, for every dollar that they contributed, whereas in Ontario they received $0.70 for every dollar contributed. What is the overall effect of this on labour mobility? Busby and Gray (2011) argue that more-generous benefits and lower entrance requirements for unemployed in high unemployment regions have contributed to the labour market rigidities and the persistence of high unemployment in these regions. Day and Winer (2011) review the literature and conclude that, on balance, more-generous benefits in some regions in Canada and not in others have not significantly altered regional mobility patterns in Canada. The lack of a clear effect on mobility may be due to the fact that employment insurance has offsetting effects on the incentive to migrate to find work. The program's complexity may also make it difficult to empirically distinguish the contribution of the different incentive effects on migration.

Education, training, and occupational choices. May and Hollett (1995) have argued that one of the most detrimental aspects of the Canadian employment insurance system is that it has discouraged the acquisition of education and training by young people in high unemployment–rate areas, such as Newfoundland. They claimed that a generous system, by subsidizing seasonal employment and "make work" projects, increases the opportunity cost of acquiring education or training and makes the "pogey" lifestyle more attractive. Kuhn and Riddell (2010) argue, however, that there is an offsetting incentive effect. To the extent that employment insurance encourages labour force participation, and if some education is required to engage in the labour market, then EI could, in theory, provide incentives to invest in some education. Their study does not find evidence of a strong disincentive to invest in education. And a recent study by Riddell and Song (2011) finds evidence that education significantly improves an unemployed worker's re-employment success.

Macroeconomic Effects

Automatic stabilizing effects. The employment insurance system can act as an automatic stabilizer, if total benefit payments increase and total premiums decrease during a recession, thereby helping the unemployed maintain their expenditures on goods and services. During a boom, total benefits decline and total premiums collected increase as employment expands. This helps reduce inflationary pressures. The stabilizing effect of the EI system occurs without any deliberate policy decisions by governments and, therefore, has many advantages over discretionary fiscal policies aimed at stabilizing the economy.

An employment insurance system will act as an automatic stabilizer if annual expenditures exceed revenues during a recession, and vice versa during a boom. Figure 10.3 shows that the Employment Insurance program incurred a deficit during Canada's three most recent recessions. Annual EI surpluses were recorded in each year between 1994 and 2008. The federal government increased the employment insurance premium rates during both the 1981–83 and the 1990–92 recessions, reducing the effectiveness of the Employment Insurance program as an automatic stabilizer. In contrast, the premium was unchanged from 2008 through to 2010, the period containing the most recent recession. The tax increases during the recessions of the 1980s and 1990s

FIGURE 10.3

ANNUAL REVENUE MINUS EXPENDITURE ON EMPLOYMENT INSURANCE

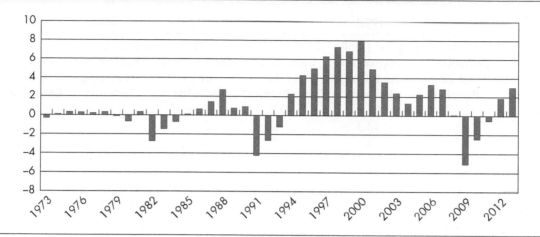

Note: The data for 2009 reflect the difference between EI revenues and expenditures after taking into account the federal government's funding enhancements associated with its 2009 budget.

Sources: Based on data from Statistics Canada. *Unemployment Insurance Statistics, 1995,* Table 21 (Ottawa: Statistics Canada, 1995), 73-202S; *Chief Actuary's Outlook on the Employment Insurance Account for 2005,* http://www.hrsdc.gc.ca/en/ei/reports/pr2005.pdf; *EI Monitoring and Assessment Report,* various years; and *Public Accounts,* various years.

increased the cost of hiring labour when the demand for labour was declining and reduced the net incomes of those who continued to have employment. Allowing larger deficits during recessions would help to improve the performance of employment insurance as an automatic stabilizer.

Figure 10.3 shows that the revenues from employment insurance premiums have exceeded expenditures by a substantial margin since 1994. By 2009, the Employment Insurance program had a cumulative surplus of about $57 billion. The chief actuary for the EI program concluded that a reserve fund of $10 to $15 billion would be enough to prevent higher premiums during a recession.[22] With the cumulative surplus well in excess of the recommended reserve fund, the question of what to do about the "EI surplus" arose. Recent federal legislation was introduced partly to address this issue. The EI Account was closed as of December 2008, replaced by the newly created Employment Insurance Operating Account. This account is managed by the Canada Employment Insurance Financing Board (also new). These changes were implemented to improve the premium rate-setting mechanism and to ensure that EI revenues and expenditures balance over time (beginning in 2011). This new approach to EI premium rate setting has not really taken hold as the federal government intervened by introducing a three-year freeze to EI premiums in 2013.

THE DISTRIBUTIONAL EFFECTS OF EMPLOYMENT INSURANCE

The extent to which employment insurance alleviates poverty and redistributes income from the affluent to the less well-off depends on how the benefits are distributed and how the program is financed. We will begin by considering the effect of employment insurance benefits and then examine employment insurance financing.

The Distribution of Employment Insurance Benefits

There are numerous elements in the employment insurance program that contribute to its redistributive effects. These include premiums that do not depend on expected losses, the clawback of benefits for higher income earners, and the supplementary benefits for low-income families. Finnie and Irvine (2011) consider the

---

[22] Human Resources Development Canada, "Chief Actuary's Report on Employment Insurance Premium Rates for 2001," Ottawa.

TABLE 10.5

Distributional Impacts of Employment Insurance, 1992 and 2002

	1992			2002		
	% Distribution of EI Benefits	% of Decile Population Receiving Benefits	% Distribution of EI Contributions*	% Distribution of EI Benefits	% of Decile Population Receiving Benefits	% Distribution of EI Contributions*
Decile 1	25.2	51.4	0.7	22.6	27.5	1.2
Decile 2	18.7	43.3	2.0	20.5	29	2.7
Decile 3	17.9	44.7	3.9	17.9	28.3	5.0
Decile 4	14.2	38.3	6.2	13.9	24	7.5
Decile 5	9.9	29.5	9.0	9.6	18.2	10.1
Decile 6	6.1	19.9	11.7	6.2	12.6	12.6
Decile 7	3.9	14.3	14.3	4.4	9.4	15.2
Decile 8	2.4	10	17.1	2.7	6.9	15.7
Decile 9	1.2	6.2	18.1	1.4	4.8	15.8
Decile 10	0.3	2.1	17.1	0.6	2	14.3
Total	100	26	100	100	16.3	100

* Contributions include only those made by employees.

Source: The data in this table are taken from Finnie and Irvine (2011), Table 2.

distributional impact of the employment insurance program in 1992, 1996, and 2002. Some of their results are displayed in Table 10.5. The table shows the distribution of EI benefits by income decile, the percentage of each decile receiving EI benefits, and the share of total employee premiums paid by each decile, for 1992 and 2002. EI's redistributive impact is evident. In 2002, the lowest two income deciles received 43 percent of EI benefits while their share of total employee EI premiums was only 3.9 percent. In contrast, the top two deciles received 2.0 percent of EI benefits but accounted for just over 30 percent of employee premiums.

Between 1992 and 2002, there were several changes to EI, including an increase in the eligibility requirements, a reduction in the benefit rate, and a reduction in the maximum duration of EI benefits. The effects of these reforms are also evident in the table. Finnie and Irvine note that the shares of EI benefits going to the lowest decile is virtually unchanged between 1992 and 2002 but the percentage of individuals in this group receiving benefits fell from 51.4 percent in 1992 to 27.5 percent in 2002. A similar pattern is observed for almost all the other deciles.

Using employment insurance benefits as a tool for redistributing income can be problematic. First, the employment insurance program provides relatively few benefits to those individuals with very low or no income, because these individuals often have little attachment to the labour market due to disability, age, or other responsibilities (e.g., single mothers with small children). And those who have accumulated less than the required number of hours during the qualifying period are not eligible for EI benefits. Second, it is clear from Table 10.5 that employment insurance benefits do go to individuals who are not poor. In this respect, EI is not a particularly efficient mechanism for redistributing income. Third, there are significant horizontal inequities—unequal treatment of equals—in the distribution of employment insurance benefits. For example, two individuals who earn the same wage rate and make the same contributions to employment insurance but live in regions with different unemployment rates receive different expected benefits because the qualifying and benefit periods are based on the regional unemployment rate.

The redistribution from employment insurance may not always be desirable or equitable. Because of these shortcomings, many feel that employment insurance should be structured primarily on insurance principles. Other social insurance programs (to alleviate poverty and to address low or no income for those not eligible for employment insurance) are perhaps better suited to income redistribution.

The Burden of EI Financing

Table 10.5 shows that the lowest income decile's share of employee EI premiums is quite low relative their share of EI benefits, while higher income deciles pay a larger share. Typically, a tax is considered **progressive** (and more redistributive) if the tax burden, as a percentage of income, increases as income increases. Since the contribution shares are quite similar for deciles 7 to 10, the extent of redistribution achieved via Employment Insurance contributions is limited. There are several reasons for this. EI premiums are payable on each $100 of insurable earnings up to a maximum (set at $49,500 for 2015). So, individuals with incomes in excess of the maximum insurable earnings pay the same amount in premiums regardless of how much income they earn. As well, the richest households receive a substantial proportion of their income from self-employment and investment income that is not taxed to finance employment insurance. For these reasons, redistribution from the highest-income groups is limited. Additionally, the lowest income households often have little attachment to the labour market (so do not pay EI premiums and do not receive EI benefits) and are receiving a high proportion of their income from government transfers (such as social assistance and Old Age Security). As a result, employment insurance financing does little to redistribute income to the lowest income groups.

Unfortunately, the data presented in Table 10.5 may not tell the whole story in regards to the redistributive effects of EI premiums for two reasons. First, the data presented do not include the burden associated with EI premiums paid by employers. Second, the degree to which employment insurance redistributes income depends, in part, on who actually bears the burden of the EI premiums, or payroll taxes, after accounting for any tax-induced changes in wages. Chapter 14 provides a more detailed discussion of tax incidence. Here, we provide a very brief overview of why tax-induced wage changes matter. An employee payroll tax, like the EI premium, will be borne by workers unless there is an increase in their wage rates. Most workers do not have the power to increase their own wage rates to offset the effect of a tax increase. Therefore, economists have generally concluded that employees will bear the burden of an employee payroll tax. We can consider the burden of the employer payroll tax using the same framework. An increase in an employer payroll tax will push up the cost of hiring workers and potentially reduce the number of workers employed by firms. In a competitive labour market, the reduced demand for labour will put downward pressure on wage rates. If the supply of labour is completely inelastic, the wage rate will decline by the full amount of the employer payroll tax, and the entire burden of the employer payroll tax will be shifted to workers.

In some situations, the burden of an employer payroll tax may not be shifted to *all* workers. Low income workers who earn the minimum wage rate may not bear the burden of the employer payroll tax because employers are unable to reduce wage rates below the minimum. These low-wage workers may, however, bear part of the burden through reduced employment opportunities. At the other extreme, high-income workers who are represented by strong unions may be able to prevent employers from shifting the burden of the employer payroll tax to them. Overall, the theoretical and empirical studies tend to support the notion that most of the burden of the employer payroll tax is shifted to workers.[23]

Regional Redistribution Through Employment Insurance

The data in Figure 10.2 suggest that the distributional effects of employment insurance by region and industry are significant. Attempts to reform EI have frequently been opposed by the provincial governments of eastern Canada because, in spite of its potentially harmful effects on resource allocation and its inequitable treatment of individuals, it has become an important source of income for individuals living in Quebec and the Atlantic provinces. Employment insurance also potentially redistributes income to workers in the primary industries (agriculture, forestry, fishing, and trapping) and construction, which are more seasonal in nature, from workers in other sectors of the economy. While average weekly earnings in some primary industries are low, mining and construction workers, for example, have average weekly earnings that exceed the average over all industries. This means that a low-wage clerk in the finance or utilities sector subsidizes a high-wage carpenter in the construction sector.

Experience-Rated Premiums

Some of these cross-subsidies would be eliminated if employment insurance were financed through a system of experience-rated premiums. Under this system, which is used to finance employment insurance in the

---

[23] See Dahlby (1993) for a review of the evidence regarding the shifting of payroll taxes.

United States, employers pay higher premiums the more frequently they lay off workers. This premium structure is similar to private automobile insurance where those who make more frequent claims have to pay higher premiums. Adopting experience-rated premiums in Canada would mean that premiums would go up in industries such as construction, where layoffs are common, and workers' after-tax wage rates in these industries would probably decline, at least to some degree. In other industries where layoffs are less common, premiums would decline and workers' after-tax wage rates would tend to increase. To the extent that high-wage industries, such as construction, have high layoff rates and are subsidized by low-wage and low-layoff industries, the switch to experience-rated employment insurance premiums would increase the fairness of the employment insurance system. However, many of the sectors with high layoff rates are also low-wage industries, and a switch to experience-rated premiums would impose significant burdens on many low-wage workers in these industries.

Experience-rated premiums might also help to reduce the overall unemployment rate through changes in firms' incentives to lay off workers and through changes in the distribution of the cost of employment insurance across industries. Experience-rated premiums would provide firms with an incentive to reduce layoffs during a recession or off-season. Industries where firms continued to have high layoff rates would face higher costs than those with low layoff rates, and over time the high-layoff industries would contract and the low-layoff industries would expand. More employment would occur in the stable, nonseasonal sectors of the economy, and the overall unemployment rate would be expected to decline. Even if experience rating does not have a significant effect on firms' layoff behaviour, the change in the distribution of the costs under experience rating would improve the allocation of labour in the long run, but this policy option would increase the unemployment rate in the short term because it would take time for workers displaced from the current high-benefit–tax ratio industries to be absorbed by the current low-benefit–tax ratio industries. Experience rating would have a detrimental effect in Quebec and the Atlantic provinces because the high-benefit–tax ratio industries are concentrated in these provinces, and therefore there may be considerable opposition to any reforms that would increase premiums and reduce job opportunities in these regions.

CONCLUSION

The Employment Insurance program, like its predecessor, is a compromise between an insurance program and an income redistribution program. As an insurance program, only contributors are covered, and the benefits are larger for those who have higher earnings because they suffer larger losses when they are unemployed. As an income redistribution program, the benefits for lower-income households are enhanced through the Family Supplement, and the payouts to high-income claimants are reduced through the clawback. Consequently, EI benefits are based on both the insured's loss and the household's need. EI financing also contains elements of the insurance and income redistribution concepts. Premiums are collected from the insured, but they do not vary with the size of the insured's risk or history of claims. This results in some pro-poor redistribution, but the amount of redistribution is limited because there is an upper limit on the contributions by high-income earners.

The dual nature of the EI program means that it may not perform either of its functions very well. Ongoing debate has focused on the merits of separating the insurance and redistribution functions, with EI run on strict insurance principles to provide all workers with coverage against income losses due to unemployment, and with the income redistribution function performed by a negative income tax program or other social assistance programs. While the separation of functions would have many advantages from the perspective of equity and efficiency, there are serious obstacles to this type of reform. First, there would always be interactions between the insurance program and the redistribution program—people who received more insurance benefits would receive less from the redistribution program—and the terms and conditions of one program would likely influence the design of the other program. Thus, it is unlikely that EI could ever be a "pure" insurance program. The second problem is that any negative income tax program would have to be coordinated with provincial welfare programs. The provinces might object to the federal government establishing a negative income tax program and prefer federal grants to enhance their own welfare programs. Consequently, it is very difficult for the federal government to divide the EI program into separate insurance and income support programs. While many of the EI reforms, such as the move to hours-based eligibility, are significant improvements in the design of the program, the major issues and tensions that have been present in the employment insurance system for more than twenty-five years remain.

SUMMARY

- Between the 1950s and the mid-1990s, there was a steady upward trend in the rate of unemployment, with year-to-year fluctuations caused by the business cycle.

- The rise in the unemployment rate has meant that employment insurance plays a central role in the provision of income security in Canada. Indeed, Employment Insurance is the largest program in the collection of programs that provide social insurance in Canada.

- The rise in the unemployment rate and increased role of employment insurance has also raised questions. Has employment insurance contributed to the high unemployment rates? Does employment insurance provide income security in an effective and equitable manner?

- Public provision of employment insurance can be justified on the basis of market failure due to adverse selection. The public sector can also provide employment insurance more effectively than the private sector because of its greater ability to borrow to finance benefits in the event of a major recession. Moral hazard issues mean that employment insurance should be designed so that firms and workers have some incentive to reduce the number of layoffs and the duration of unemployment spells.

- There may also be efficiency gains associated with employment insurance if it allows for better job search effort and improved matching between employees and employers.

- Employment insurance may affect the unemployment rate through its effects on layoffs, quits, the duration of unemployment spells, the labour force participation rate, the industrial mix, labour mobility, education and training choices, and its automatic stabilizing effects.

- Employment insurance redistributes income to the extent that a worker's expected benefits exceed the premium. In Canada, premiums are not experience rated, and there are significant net transfers to the primary industries—agriculture, forestry, and fishing—and to the construction industry and the small business sector. There are substantial net transfers to workers in Quebec and the Atlantic region.

- Since the early 1990s, several reforms have been introduced: eligibility now depends on hours of work and the unemployment rate in the region in which the claimant resides, the maximum duration of benefits is higher for claimants in high unemployment regions, claimants are categorized based on their previous experience with collecting EI benefits, and the requirements for what constitutes suitable work depend on the claimant's category (and therefore the claimant's experience with collecting EI in the past).

EXERCISES

1. **a.** Show that the unemployment rate, *ur*, is related to the employment rate, *er*, and labour force participation rate, *pr*, as follows:

$$ur = \left(1 - \frac{er}{pr}\right)$$

b. Suppose the labour market is in equilibrium when the labour force participation rate is 0.60 and the employment rate is 0.55. What is the unemployment rate in this economy?

c. Suppose that an increase in employment insurance benefits causes the participation rate to increase to 0.61. What would be the effect on the unemployment rate? Use a diagram to illustrate your answer and explain your assumptions.

2. **a.** Suppose the layoff rate is 0.02 and the average duration of a spell of unemployment is four and one-half months. Using Equation 10.4, what is the equilibrium unemployment rate in this economy?

   b. Suppose that an increase in employment insurance benefits causes the separation rate to increase to 0.021. What would be the effect on the unemployment rate and why would it change?

   c. Suppose that an increase in employment insurance benefits causes the average duration of a spell of unemployment to increase by one week. What would be the effect on the unemployment rate and why would it change?

3. What problems would arise in setting experience-rated employment insurance premiums with regard to the following?

   a. Distinguishing between quits and layoffs.

   b. Setting rates for new businesses.

   c. Setting rates for small businesses with only a couple of employees.

   d. Firms declaring bankruptcy.

4. Consider an individual whose earnings are taxed at a rate of 25 percent under the personal income tax and at a combined rate of 10 percent under the Canada Pension Plan and Employment Insurance payroll taxes. Suppose that if the individual becomes unemployed, EI replaces 50 percent of his or her before-tax earnings. (Note that EI benefits are subject to income tax, but not payroll taxes.) What percentage of the individual's after-tax income is replaced by EI? What are the implications for the effects of EI on unemployment?

5. Consider the following situation. A couple, who recently had twins, makes two claims for parental leave. The husband makes a claim for the birth of one twin. The wife makes her claim for the birth of the other twin. As the head of Employment Insurance in Canada, would you allow either or both of these claims? Discuss your reasoning.

6. Two individuals, Harry and Ron, are both working. Harry faces a 10 percent chance of becoming unemployed for three months and losing $12,000 in income. Ron's probability of becoming unemployed is lower, at 8 percent, but he too would be unemployed for three months and would lose $12,000 in income.

   a. Suppose the employment insurance benefit rate is 55 percent so that 55 percent of lost earnings are replaced. Calculate the expected payout for Harry and Ron.

   b. Suppose that participating in the national employment insurance program is compulsory and that the annual premium of $594 is paid by both individuals. Does this scheme involve redistribution? If so, who gains and who loses?

   c. If an actuarially fair premium was to be charged, what annual premium would each worker be charged?

7. Briefly discuss the effects of a higher benefit rate on the duration of unemployment. How are the incentive effects altered if the change in the benefit rate is expected to be temporary rather than permanent?

CHAPTER 11

Public Pensions

Will you still need me, will you still feed me, when I'm sixty-four?

—John Lennon and Paul McCartney

All societies have to provide for the elderly who can no longer earn income. In traditional societies, a few individuals could accumulate enough assets during their working lives to finance their consumption in their declining years. For most individuals who managed to survive to old age, the family provided the income support and other services, such as nursing care. In the twentieth century, with the decline in the extended family and the increase in life expectancy, the public sector has emerged as the most important source for retirement income for most Canadians.

The Canadian retirement income system rests on three "pillars": the Old Age Security program, the Canada and Quebec Pension Plans, and tax-assisted private savings and pensions. The Old Age Security program, which consists of the Old Age Security (OAS) pension, the Guaranteed Income Supplement (GIS), and the Allowance provided $41.8 billion in benefits in 2013–14. These federal programs are financed out of general revenues and provide basic income support for the elderly. The second pillar consists of the Canada Pension Plan (CPP) and Quebec Pension Plan (QPP), which are compulsory, earnings-related pension schemes that also provide other benefits, such as payments for disability. They are financed by earmarked payroll taxes that are levied on employers and employees. These programs provided approximately $49.0 billion in benefits in 2013–14. The third pillar consists of the Registered Pension Plan (RPP) and the Registered Retirement Savings Plan (RRSP), which receive special tax treatment under the Canadian income tax system. These programs supported about $89 billion in private pension and retirement income in 2012.[1] This chapter focuses on the first two pillars of the retirement income system. (The third pillar, RPPs and RRSPs, is discussed in Chapter 17.)

---

[1] The Tax-Free Savings Account (TFSA) was introduced in the February 26, 2008, federal budget. Although seniors are expected to receive about one-half of the total benefits provided by the TFSA, the stated purpose of the program is to assist all families in saving for major purchases in life. The TFSA is discussed in Chapter 17.

Recent opinion polls suggest that many Canadians support some form of expansion of the CPP/QPP program. At the same time, they are concerned about the expected rapid increase in pension and health care expenditures as the baby boom generation retires.[2] The cost of the OAS program, for example, was projected by the Office of the Chief Actuary to rise from 2.3 percent of GDP in 2010 to 3.1 percent in 2030.[3] This tension between the desire for greater financial security after retirement and the question of affordability is central to discussions on pension reforms. The 1998 changes to the CPP that increased contribution rates and reduced some benefits were a major response to the unsustainable features of public pensions, as was the announcement in the federal budget of 2012 of a gradual increase in the age of eligibility for OAS benefits from 65 to 67 years old.

This chapter examines public pension policy issues in Canada. We begin by considering the following questions. Why should the public sector intervene in the provision of retirement income? If there are legitimate reasons for intervening, what type of intervention is warranted? We shall then consider the effects of public pensions on savings behaviour and retirement decisions. The final part of the chapter describes in more detail the history and structure of the OAS and CPP, and considers the issue of intergenerational equity in the design of public pensions.

PUBLIC INTERVENTION IN THE PROVISION OF RETIREMENT INCOMES

Among the "usual suspects" for market failure, adverse selection, paternalism, and redistribution are the most prominent issues as far as the provision of retirement income is concerned. There are also other features of the pension market such as decision-making costs, the Samaritan's dilemma, the absence of inflation indexation in private pensions and annuities, and the possibility that the public sector can provide a higher rate of return than the private sector—that have to be considered.

Adverse selection in the market for annuities. Everyone realizes that there is a chance of dying too young and thus leaving one's family with inadequate income. But, perhaps less obviously, there is also a risk of living too long. Consider the story about Marge, a 69-year-old Toronto dweller, who stated her worries about outliving her savings: "I will be in trouble if I live more than 10 years or so."[4] How might Marge have been able to protect herself from these financial problems? By purchasing a type of insurance policy called a life annuity, individuals can ensure that they will always receive some income for the rest of their lives. An **annuity** is acquired by paying a financial institution a price upfront in return for a specified annual income.[5] Notice the symmetry between a life annuity and life insurance. With life insurance, you pay the insurance company a given annual amount for as long as you live, and, in return, the company pays a lump sum when you die. With a life annuity, you pay the company a lump sum and it provides you with a fixed annual amount for as long as you live. Life insurance policies and annuities serve the same basic function: they enable **consumption smoothing**, whereby people reduce consumption in high-earning years in order to increase consumption in low-earning years.

A risk-averse person is willing to reduce her consumption by buying an annuity in return for a guaranteed income throughout her retirement. The market for annuities is, however, subject to an **adverse selection** process. Individuals probably know more about their health status than an insurance company does (see Chapter 9). Those individuals who expect to live for a long period of time are willing to pay a higher price for an annuity than individuals who expect to live only a short length of time. Thus, those who have the longest life expectancy are the ones who are most likely to demand annuities. Because the price of an annuity must reflect the life expectancy of the average annuity purchaser, the adverse selection process drives up the price that must be charged, and as a result individuals will reduce the amount of their retirement fund that they convert to annuities, exposing themselves to a greater risk of outliving their savings. A compulsory contributory public pension scheme overcomes the adverse selection problem if everyone is forced to participate, and the pension payouts can be based on the life expectancy of the entire population and not just those who anticipate living a long life. Therefore, a compulsory contributory pension scheme

---

[2] The baby boom lasted about 20 years in Canada, with cohorts born from 1946 to 1965 (Statistics Canada, 2012). Thus, the first generation of baby boomers retired in 2011.

[3] OSFIC (2011).

[4] Schlesinger (2014).

[5] In general, the insurer makes guaranteed regular payments, though not all types of annuities provide payments for the rest of a lifetime. In our discussion of annuities, we are referring to life annuities.

has the potential of offering individuals a higher rate of return on their contributions than they could get in the private market when the purchase of annuities is voluntary.

Private annuity markets will try to use observable information on individuals' life expectancies in setting annuity prices. Women are charged higher prices for an annuity than men because the life expectancy of a woman at age 65 is 21 years, whereas it is 18 years for a 65-year-old man.[6] Many view this form of statistical discrimination as offensive, especially because women generally have lower retirement incomes and are more likely to be impoverished in their old age. A public sector pension plan in which contributions and benefits are the same for both sexes can overcome this problem.

Paternalism. Some individuals are myopic and will not save enough for their retirement. They will live to regret the excessive consumption spending of their youth. This argument raises two issues. First, is it true that people would fail to provide adequately for their retirement years? To find out requires estimating how people would behave in the absence of the public pension programs. This is very difficult to do. Second, even if it is true, it does not necessarily follow that the government should step in. Those with a highly individualistic philosophical framework believe that people should be left to make their own decisions, even if this occasionally results in mistakes.

Redistribution. The preceding discussion assumed that individuals can earn enough during their working lives to be able to save for an adequate level of consumption during their retirement. However, some individuals' incomes are so low during their working lives that they are unable to save for their retirement. These individuals will be destitute when they retire, and society has an obligation to prevent them from falling into abject poverty. A noncontributory pension scheme, such as Old Age Security, ensures that all seniors have a basic level of income. One might question whether the elderly need a special income redistribution program, aside from the fact that Old Age Security is a federal program and therefore the cost of providing income support for the elderly is borne by all Canadians, whereas welfare programs are funded by the provinces.

A separate income redistribution program for the elderly may be desirable for three reasons. First, the elderly have characteristics, such as their inability to work, that set them apart from younger welfare recipients. Therefore, an income redistribution program for the elderly can be designed with their special needs and characteristics in mind. Second, providing income support in the form of a "pension" may reduce the stigma that is often associated with welfare. Third, a society may want to engage in intergenerational redistribution if incomes are rising and society wants the elderly to share in the benefits of economic growth and prosperity. Thus, the income redistribution motive can justify the financing of pension benefits out of current tax revenues.

Miscalculation and decision-making costs. Even if individuals are not myopic, they may underestimate how much they must save in order to have a reasonable level of consumption in their retirement years. For example, if an individual's earnings increase at 2 percent a year and if she wants her consumption level in retirement to be two-thirds of her pre-retirement consumption level, then, over a 30 year period she will have to save 17 percent of her annual disposable income if the real rate of return on her savings is 3 percent and she lives for 15 years after retirement.[7] If the individual underestimates the required savings rate, she may not be aware of her mistake until it is too late to correct it. Hiring a professional adviser may be costly. If public decision makers select an appropriate retirement program for everyone, individuals do not have to waste resources making their own decisions. A clear criticism here is that there is no reason to believe the government would necessarily choose the right kind of policy. After all, different people have different needs, so it might be better to promote public education and retirement counselling and to let people choose their own retirement scheme.

The Samaritan's dilemma. Given that a society has income redistribution programs for the poor and the elderly, some young people may decide not to save for their old age, gambling that they will be supported by the public sector when they retire. This is an example of **moral hazard**, which occurs when the existence (or expectation) of insurance increases the likelihood of the adverse outcome (see Chapter 9). Society may frown on such behaviour, but be unwilling to withhold benefits from those who have taken advantage of the system if it would mean that they would fall into abject poverty. To prevent individuals from planning to take advantage of the retirement income support system, society may force individuals to save for their retirement by introducing a compulsory contributory pension scheme. Individuals' contributions during their working lives

---

[6] Statistics Canada (2010: 16).

[7] See Diamond (1977: 288).

could either be included in a common pension fund, which would be invested by the public sector's fund managers, or they could be segregated in a private fund, similar to an RRSP. The individual, when he reaches the age of retirement, would then use the accumulated fund to finance consumption during retirement.

Inflation indexation. Another problem with annuity contracts and private employer-sponsored pension plans is that they do not provide benefits that are indexed to the cost of living. Even a relatively modest annual inflation rate of 3 percent will reduce the purchasing power of a fixed annual income by one-third in 13.5 years. Thus, the elderly face the risk that the purchasing power of their pensions and annuities will be eroded through inflation. The public sector has less difficulty than the private sector in providing inflation-indexed pensions because tax revenues normally increase as rapidly as the inflation rate, and perhaps even more rapidly if the income tax system is not indexed. It is often argued that the public sector can help the private sector in providing inflation-indexed pensions if the public sector issues inflation-indexed bonds (called *real return bonds*). The private pension funds can purchase these bonds and use the income from them to provide inflation-indexed pensions. The Government of Canada issues inflation-indexed bonds, but the demand for these bonds has been rather modest, perhaps because the rate of inflation has declined in recent years and other investments have offered more attractive real rates of return.

Pay-as-you-go financing versus fully funded pensions. Public sector pensions can be financed on a pay-as-you-go basis, which means that the benefits paid to current retirees come from payments made by those who are currently working. There is no need to accumulate a fund in order to pay the public pension benefits. In contrast, with private sector pension schemes, workers' contributions are accumulated in a fund, and a worker's expected benefits when he retires are equal to his accumulated contributions and investment income from the fund. The private sector can only offer funded pensions because it cannot force the current generation of workers to pay for the pensions of those who are currently retired. The public sector can use pay-as-you-go financing because the state can make contributions to its pension scheme compulsory.

The implicit rate of return on a pure pay-as-you-go system is strictly determined by the growth rate of the contribution base, consisting of wages and salaries. The growth rate of the contribution base is determined by growth of the wage rate (reflecting productivity improvements) and population growth. To see this, recall that the benefits received by retirees in a given year equal the payments made by workers in the same year. If N_b is the number of beneficiaries and B is the average benefit per retiree, then the total benefits are $N_b \times B$. The taxes paid by workers in a given year are the product of the public pension payroll tax rate (t), the number of covered workers (N_w), and the average covered wage per worker (w): $t \times N_w \times w$. Hence, equality between total benefits received in a year and total taxes paid in a year requires that

$$N_b \times B = t \times N_w \times w \qquad (11.1)$$

By rearranging terms, we see that the average benefit per retiree in a given year is

$$B = t \times \frac{N_w}{N_b} \times w \qquad (11.2)$$

Equation (11.2) has several important implications. First, if we assume that the tax rate is constant over time, then average benefits can increase only if wages increase or if the number of workers relative to retirees increases (that is, the population grows). If neither of these happens, then each year retirees receive an average benefit equal to exactly what they paid in taxes, so they earn an implicit rate of return of zero. (We refer to the return from a pay-as-you-go system as "implicit," to distinguish it from returns that accrue from investing in capital goods.) If, however, wages and population both increase at a constant rate, then retirees receive a positive return on the taxes they contributed to the public pension, with the return equal to the sum of wage growth and population growth. Thus, for example, if wages are increasing at 1.5 percent annually and the population is growing at 1 percent annually, then the return on taxes paid is 2.5 percent.[8]

Pay-as-you-go financing can be an attractive method of financing pensions if the economy's total wages and salaries (the contribution base) is growing faster than the rate of return on investments that are held by pension funds. Under these conditions, if the contribution rate is the same for each generation, then the ratio of a

---

[8] More precisely, the return on taxes paid is 2.515 percent, computed as $100 \times (1.015 \times 1.01) - 1$.

FIGURE 11.1

GROWTH OF TOTAL WAGES AND SALARIES AND REAL INTEREST RATES

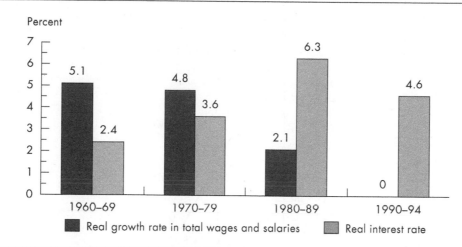

Source: Federal, Provincial, and Territorial Governments of Canada, *"An Information Paper for Consultations on the Canada Pension Plan,"* February 1996, p. 23. Reproduced with the permission of the Minister of Public Works and Government Services Canada, 1997.

generation's pension benefit to its contributions will be higher under the pay-as-you-go financing scheme than it would be with the same contribution rate under a fully funded pension scheme. The superiority of the pay-as-you-go financed pension was proclaimed by Nobel laureate Paul Samuelson:

> The beauty of social insurance is that it is actuarially unsound. Everyone who reaches retirement age is given benefit privileges that far exceed anything he has paid in. . . . How is this possible? It stems from the fact that the national product is growing at compound interest and can be expected to do so for as far ahead as the eye can see. Always there are more youths than old folks in a growing population. More important, with real incomes growing at some three percent a year, the taxable base upon which benefits rest in any period are much greater than the taxes paid historically by the generation now retired. . . . A growing nation is the greatest Ponzi game ever contrived.[9]

In the 1960s, when Samuelson wrote these words and when the CPP and QPP were established, the real growth rate of wages and salaries exceeded the real interest rate, and pay-as-you-go seemed to be the best way to finance these programs (see Figure 11.1). In the 1970s, the gap between the growth rate of wages and salaries and real interest rates declined. Since the 1980s the real interest rate has exceeded the growth rate of wages and salaries, mainly because of much lower rates of productivity growth and slower growth in employment. With hindsight, the choice of pay-as-you-go financing for the CPP and QPP was not wise, and the decline in productivity growth and employment growth forced major changes in these programs in 1998. These changes will be discussed later in this chapter.

Most countries with public pension schemes use pay-as-you-go financing because it is politically attractive, when the pension scheme is initiated, to offer the first generation of pensioners benefits that greatly exceed their contributions. In some cases, this intergenerational transfer may be justified if that generation had low retirement income prospects because of a war or an economic depression. In other cases, it may not be justified on equity grounds, but giving a large net benefit to one group of voters while imposing potential burdens on future generations who are not yet born, let alone voters, has been irresistible to politicians. The potential effects of pay-as-you-go public pensions on individuals' economic decisions are assessed in the next section.

---

[9] Quoted in Oreopoulos (1996: 6); reprinted by permission of the publisher. A Ponzi game is an illegal pyramid investment scheme where the returns to the initial investors are financed by the capital contributed by later investors. Such schemes may produce high rates of return for early investors, but they inevitably collapse because there is nothing to guarantee that later investors will get their investment back, let alone receive a return.

FIGURE 11.2

BUDGET CONSTRAINT FOR PRESENT AND FUTURE CONSUMPTION

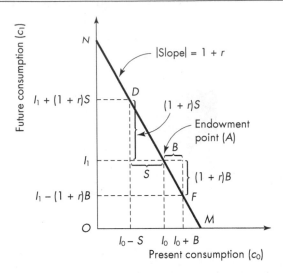

EFFECTS OF PUBLIC PENSIONS ON ECONOMIC BEHAVIOUR

Some economists argue that a public pension influences people's behaviour in ways that impair economic efficiency. Most of the discussion has focused on saving behaviour and labour supply decisions. The impact of public pensions on behaviour is difficult to estimate, and remains controversial. Nonetheless, the theoretical and empirical research in this area has provided a number of valuable insights.

Saving Behaviour

The starting point for most work on public pensions and saving is the **life-cycle model**, which states that consumption and saving decisions are based on lifetime considerations. A person with diminishing marginal utility prefers to smooth consumption over time, and saving provides a mechanism to achieve this goal. Hence, during their working lives, individuals save some portion of their incomes to accumulate wealth from which they can finance consumption during retirement.[10] Such funds can be invested until they are needed, thus increasing the economy's capital stock or its net holding of foreign assets.

The introduction of a public pension system can substantially alter the amount of lifetime saving. Such changes are the consequences of three effects: (1) the wealth substitution effect, (2) the retirement effect, and (3) the bequest effect.

Wealth substitution effect. Workers realize that in exchange for their public pension contributions they will receive a guaranteed retirement income. The present value of future public pension benefits is an important part of a family's assets and is often referred to as **public pension wealth**.[11] If workers view the taxes levied to finance the public pension as a means of "saving" for these future benefits, they will tend to save less on their own. This phenomenon is referred to as the **wealth substitution effect**. As emphasized earlier, with pay-as-you-go financing the contributions are not all saved—almost all is paid out immediately to the current beneficiaries. Thus, there is no increase in public saving to offset the decrease in private saving, which means a reduction in the total amount of saving and capital accumulation.

Figure 11.2 analyzes the wealth substitution effect within the framework of the life-cycle model. Consider Bingley, who expects to live for two periods: "now" (period 0) and the "future" (period 1). Bingley has an income of I_0 dollars now and knows that his income will be I_1 dollars in the future. (Think of "now" as working years,

---

[10] Of course, savings are also accumulated for other reasons as well: to finance the purchase of durables, to use in case of a rainy day, and so forth. For a more complete discussion of the life-cycle theory, see Modigliani (1986).

[11] The concept of present value is explained in Chapter 3.

FIGURE 11.3

UTILITY MAXIMIZING CHOICE OF PRESENT AND FUTURE CONSUMPTION

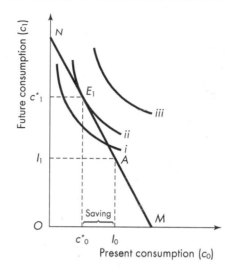

when I_0 is labour earnings, and the "future" as retirement years, when I_1 is fixed pension income.) His problem is to decide how much to consume in each period. When Bingley decides how much to consume, he simultaneously decides how much to save or borrow. If his consumption is less than current income, he saves.

The first step in analyzing the saving decision is to depict the possible combinations of present and future consumption available to Bingley—his budget constraint. In Figure 11.2, the amount of current consumption, c_0, is measured on the horizontal axis, and future consumption, c_1, is measured on the vertical axis. One option available to Bingley is to consume all his income just as it comes in—to consume I_0 in the present and I_1 in the future. This bundle, called the endowment point, is denoted by A in Figure 11.2. At the **endowment point**, Bingley neither saves nor borrows.

Another option is to save out of current income in order to consume more in the future. Suppose Bingley decides to save S dollars this period. If he invests his savings in an asset with a rate of return of r, he can increase his future consumption by $(1 + r)S$—the principal, S, plus the interest, rS. Thus, by decreasing present consumption by S, Bingley can increase his future consumption by $(1 + r)S$. Graphically, this possibility is represented by moving S dollars to the left of point A, and $(1 + r)S$ dollars above it—point D in Figure 11.2.

Alternatively, Bingley can consume more than I_0 in the present if he can borrow against his future income. Assume that Bingley can borrow money at the same rate of interest, r, at which he can lend. If he borrows B dollars to add to his present consumption, Bingley must pay back B *plus* interest of rB. Hence, Bingley can increase present consumption by B only if he is willing to reduce future consumption by $B + rB = (1 + r)B$. Graphically, this process involves moving B dollars to the right of the endowment point, and then $(1 + r)B$ below it—point F in Figure 11.2.

By repeating this procedure for various values of S and B, we can trace out the budget line MN, which passes through the endowment point A and has a slope in absolute value of $1 + r$. As always, the slope of a budget line represents the opportunity cost of one good in terms of the other. Its slope of $1 + r$ indicates that the cost of \$1 of consumption in the present is $1 + r$ dollars of forgone consumption in the future.[12] Because MN shows the tradeoff between consumption across time, it is called the **intertemporal budget constraint**.

To determine the choice along MN, we introduce Bingley's preferences between future and present consumption, which are represented by conventionally shaped indifference curves in Figure 11.3. In this figure, we reproduce Bingley's budget constraint, MN, and superimpose a few indifference curves labelled *i*, *ii*, and *iii*.

---

[12] To represent the budget line algebraically, note that the fundamental constraint facing Bingley is that the present value of his consumption equals the present value of his income. The present value of his consumption is $c_0 + c_1/(1 + r)$, while the present value of his income stream is $I_0 + I_1/(1 + r)$. Thus, his selection of c_0 and c_1 must satisfy $c_0 + c_1/(1 + r) = I_0 + I_1/(1 + r)$. The reader can verify that viewed as a function of c_0 and c_1 this is a straight line whose slope is $-(1 + r)$ and that passes through the point (I_0, I_1).

FIGURE 11.4

CROWDING OUT OF PRIVATE SAVING DUE TO PUBLIC PENSION

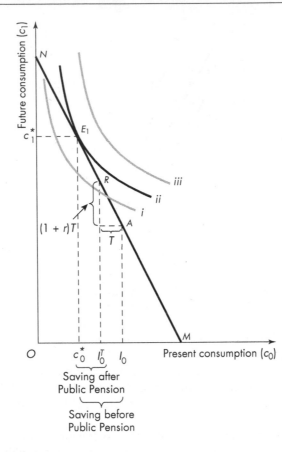

Subject to the budget constraint MN, Bingley maximizes utility at point E_1, where he consumes c_0^* in the present and c_1^* in the future. How much does Bingley save? Because present income, I_0, exceeds present consumption, c_0^*, the difference, $I_0 - c_0^*$, is savings.[13]

We now consider how the introduction of a public pension might affect the saving decision. To simplify the analysis, we'll assume that the implicit return from the public pension just equals the market interest rate. That is, if Bingley paid $\$T$ in public pension premiums during his working years, then his pension benefit when he retires is $\$(1 + r)T$.[14] (An interesting and related analysis—which we provide as an exercise at the end of the chapter—examines the consequences when the implicit rate of return from a public pension differs from the rate of return from private saving.)

How does the introduction of a public pension program change Bingley's saving behaviour? Figure 11.4 reproduces budget constraint MN from Figure 11.3. Starting at point A, the public pension premium, or tax, moves Bingley T dollars to the left—present consumption is reduced by the tax. But at the same time, the program moves him up a distance of $(1 + r)T$, because his future consumption is increased by that amount. In short, the combination of the tax now, together with the benefit in the future, places Bingley on the point R of the original budget constraint MN. In effect, R has replaced A as the endowment point. Therefore, as long as Bingley can continue to save and borrow at the market rate of interest, the budget constraint is still MN, and Bingley's optimal bundle remains at E_1. However, even though his ultimate lifetime consumption pattern is the same, there is a critical difference in Bingley's behaviour. In order to attain E_1, Bingley now only needs

---

[13] The utility maximizing point could occur to the right of point A, in which case Bingley borrows rather than saves.

[14] In this simple case, Bingley's pension *wealth* is also $\$T$, which is the present value of his pension benefit.

to save $I_0^T - c_0^*$, which is less than he was saving before the public pension program. In other words, Bingley views his pension plan contributions as a part of his savings, and therefore he saves less on his own. Thus, the public pension program crowds out private saving. This is the wealth substitution effect. Since a pay-as-you-go system does not channel the contributions into capital accumulation, public saving does not compensate for this reduction in private saving.

Retirement effect. A public pension may induce people to retire earlier than they would have, if they have to reduce their participation in the labour force to receive benefits. However, if the length of retirement increases, the individual has more nonworking years during which consumption must be financed, but fewer working years to accumulate funds. This **retirement effect** tends to increase saving.

Bequest effect. Suppose an important reason for saving is the bequest motive—people want to leave inheritances for their children. Suppose, in addition, people realize that a public pension system tends to shift income from children (worker/taxpayers) to parents (retiree/benefit recipients). Then parents may save more to increase bequests to their children and, hence, offset the distributional effect of public pensions. In essence, people increase their saving to undo the impact of public pensions on their children's incomes. This is referred to as the **bequest effect**.

Empirical Evidence on Savings

Given that the three effects work in different directions, theory alone cannot tell us how public pensions affect saving. It is difficult to investigate this issue empirically because the CPP/QPP program was started nationwide at the same time. One could examine changing patterns in private savings over time as the level of generosity of the program changed, but this would leave the concern that other factors changing over time might be causing the changes in savings patterns.

An alternative tack is to rely on cross-sectional data to estimate personal savings as a function of public pension wealth. Most of these studies find a negative statistical relationship between public pension wealth and saving, but a minority finds a positive effect. It is not too surprising that the cross-sectional estimates vary substantially, since public pension wealth depends on individual characteristics such as gender and marital status. However, these same characteristics could themselves affect saving behaviour. It is therefore difficult to sort out the independent effect of public pensions.

Some recent studies have relied on quasi-experiments that took place in some countries when they introduced reforms to their programs that led to sharp changes in expected net benefits for some people, but not for others. For example, Attanasio and Brugiavini (2003) studied the impact of major reforms to Italy's public pension system in 1992. The reforms substantially reduced retirement benefits; however, the size of the reductions varied across households. This allowed them to compare the changes in savings behaviour for those greatly affected by the reforms with those who were not. They found that public pension wealth has a substantial effect on private saving–every $100 of public pension wealth crowds out about $40 of private saving.[15] Vaillancourt, Lammam, Herzog, and Ebrahimi (2015) exploited the variation in the CPP contribution rate between 1996 and 2004 to examine whether Canadian households substitute between public and private savings. Their results associate a 0.895 percentage point drop in the private savings rate of the average Canadian household with each percentage point increase in the CPP contribution rate (the average private savings rate for all households was 7.1 percent in 1996, the year before the CPP reforms). Taking all empirical research together, it seems likely that the public pension system has reduced saving, though the magnitude of the effect is unclear.

Retirement Decisions

A public pension plan can create an incentive for early retirement through its effect on a worker's public pension wealth—the expected present value of future benefits to which an individual is entitled. Suppose, for example, that Kitty, a 60-year-old, is deciding whether or not to work another year. By continuing to work and delaying public pension benefits, she will receive higher monthly benefits when she does retire, under the rules of the Canada (and Quebec) Pension Plan, as we explain later. Hence, there is a tradeoff in the determination of Kitty's public pension wealth between forgoing pension benefits for another year and receiving

---

[15] Attanasio and Rohwedder's (2003) similar analysis of public pension reform in the United Kingdom finds an even larger effect on private saving.

ONTARIO AND FEDS SCRAP OVER PENSION PLAN

The Ontario Retirement Pension Act, Bill 56, was enacted in 2015 and requires the province to establish its own mandatory public pension plan before January 1, 2017. Under the new plan, pension contributions would be invested in a trust fund and would not form part of general government revenues. Ontario has invited other provinces to participate. In announcing the new plan, Ontario's finance minister said, "the CPP, which provides payments averaging $6,900 a year, isn't enough to provide for Ontarians in their retirement years unless they have decent pension plans at work—which 65 percent don't." However, the federal government under PM Stephen Harper opposed expanding CPP benefits and is openly critical of the provincial plan. In reply to Ontario's suggestion that costs could be kept down if Canada Revenue Agency helps to administer the plan, the federal employment minister declared, "We're not going to facilitate this new tax." The political hostilities highlight different ideological perspectives on the role of government in pensions. From the standpoint of the federal Conservatives, private savings should play a large role in retirement planning, while the Ontario Liberals see a role for government in using tax revenues to protect those individuals most at risk from under-saving. Another consideration in the public pension debate is the trend in the private sector to move away from defined benefit plans to defined contribution plans. The latter form of private pensions leave retirees with the risk of weak financial returns on their pension contributions. In contrast, public pensions resemble defined benefit plans in paying guaranteed benefits. The scrap over pension reforms is likely to take centre stage in upcoming federal and provincial elections.

Based on Ferguson (2015), Geddes (2013), McFarland (2014), and "Province scrap over Ontario pension plan." *The Toronto Sun,* July 30, 2015.

Complete references for this feature can be found in the References section on page 481.

a permanent increase in future benefits. If the net effect of delaying retirement is to increase her public pension wealth, then she has an incentive to work at least another year. If the net effect on her public pension wealth is negative, her incentive is to retire immediately. The net benefits associated with waiting a year to claim benefits also depend on how long Kitty expects to live—the longer her life expectancy, the greater the incentive to wait and receive higher monthly benefits.

Another factor affecting the timing of retirement is the reduction, or "claw back," of pension benefits as a result of a pensioner's income exceeding certain levels. If, by working an additional year, Kitty can accumulate more private wealth as well as qualify for larger CPP benefits, then her retirement income will be higher than if she had stopped working immediately at age 60. Under the rules of the Guaranteed Income Supplement and Old Age Security programs, Kitty's GIS and OAS benefits might be clawed back, depending on the size of her retirement income. This tends to make working an additional year less attractive.

The public pension wealth created by the CPP and QPP and the rules concerning early retirement, along with the clawback of GIS and OAS benefits, may have induced some workers to take early retirement.[16] From 1960 to 1999, the proportion of men aged 55–64 participating in the labour force fell from 87 percent to 61 percent.[17] Many investigators believe that changes to the Canadian public pension system have played an important role in the dramatic change in retirement patterns, but other factors, such as rising incomes, changing life expectancies, changes in the demand for different occupations, inflation, and the amount of wealth accumulated in private pensions, have been at least as important.

---

[16] Up until the mid-1980s, however, the CPP may have induced workers to delay retirement because the phasing-in of benefits meant that postponing retirement led to significantly higher pensions.

[17] See Baker, Gruber, and Milligan (2003: 262). The researchers attribute about 20 percent of the decline to the incentive effects of Canada's income security programs. See also Fougère et al. (2009) for simulations of the incentive effects of early retirement rules and benefit clawbacks. However, employment rates for men in the 55 to 64 age group have been rising since 1999.

Implications

Some economists believe that the public pension system depresses both work effort and saving. However, the evidence is murky, and many others are unconvinced. Even if the system does distort economic decisions, this does not necessarily make public pensions a bad thing. If society wants to achieve some level of income security for its members, then presumably it should be willing to pay for that security in terms of some loss of efficiency. On the other hand, efforts should be made to structure the system so that work and saving incentives are adversely affected as little as possible.

THE OLD AGE SECURITY PROGRAM

The federal government's involvement in the provision of public pensions began with the Old Age Pension Act of 1927 in which the federal government agreed to pay half (and in 1931, three-quarters) of the cost of means-tested pensions administered by the provinces. In 1952, the federal government introduced a universal pension of $40 per month to all Canadians over the age of 70 under the Old Age Security Act. The maximum annual OAS benefit (in 2014 dollars) was about $4,200 at that time. Benefits increased sharply from 1957 to 1967. Real benefits declined somewhat after 1967 due to the fact that benefits were only partially indexed to inflation. The age of eligibility was gradually reduced to 65 in 1970. Full indexation to the consumer price index (CPI) was introduced in 1973, and benefit levels have been relatively constant in real terms since then. In particular, since 1992 the annual maximum real benefit has been about $6,700 (in 2014 dollars) every year.[18] OAS pensions are taxed under the personal income tax, and for an individual with annual income in excess of an inflation-indexed threshold ($72,809 in 2015) there is an additional clawback of $15 for each additional $100 earned above this threshold. The full pension, which is provided to those who have lived in Canada for at least 40 years after age 18, was $565 per month in September 2015.

The Guaranteed Income Supplement, which was introduced in 1967, operates like a negative income tax program (see Chapter 12). Single individuals with no income other than the OAS pension received $766 per month, and a married couple each received $508 a month in September 2015. Benefits are reduced by 50 cents for each dollar of income (other than OAS pension) that the individual or couple receives. Thus, the combination of OAS and GIS ensured that a single senior had a minimum monthly income of $1,331 in September 2015, and the GIS benefit was reduced to zero when the individual had other non-OAS income equal to $18,382 per year. GIS benefits are nontaxable and indexed to the CPI.

The Allowance (formerly Spouse's Allowance), which was introduced in 1975, is an income-tested benefit that is paid to the spouse or the common-law partner of an OAS pensioner, or to a widow or widower. The recipient must be 60 to 64 years of age and have lived in Canada for at least 10 years after the age of 18. The maximum monthly Allowance was $1,073 in September 2015, and the benefit is reduced by 75 cents for each dollar of non-OAS income received by the recipient or the couple. Benefits are not taxable and are indexed to the CPI.

In 2013–14, 5.3 million individuals received OAS, 1.7 million received GIS, and 83,000 received the Allowance. Of the approximately $41.8 billion in payments, OAS pensions accounted for 76 percent of the total, GIS was about 22 percent, and the Allowance was less than 2 percent of the total.[19]

The Old Age Security program, in conjunction with the CPP and QPP and the provincial income support programs for seniors, has helped to lower the incidence of poverty among those over age 65. The poverty rate among families headed by someone over age 65 has fallen from 41.1 percent in 1969 to 7.1 percent in 1994. For single seniors, the poverty rate has declined from 69.1 percent in 1969 to 47.6 percent in 1994.[20] The dramatic decline in the incidence of poverty among the elderly must be counted as one of the most remarkable successes of the Canadian public pension system.

---

[18] The calculation of maximum real benefits uses information from Human Resources and Social Development Canada (1994), Tables 1-A and 1-E; Human Resources and Skills Development Canada (2011), Table 26; and *Quarterly Report of the Canada Pension Plan and Old Age Security* (Ottawa: Service Canada), *various issues*. The Consumer Price Index is used as the deflator.

[19] Figures on program expenditures and numbers of recipients are available from the following source: Human Resources and Skills Development Canada, *Canada Pension Plan, Old Age Security: Statistical Bulletin, June 2015* (Ottawa: Service Canada). Program features are described in Canada, *Quarterly Report of the Canada Pension Plan and Old Age Security, July-September* 2015, Cat. ISPB-258-04-13E (Ottawa: Service Canada).

[20] Battle (1996: 152). Refer also to Figure 6.4 in Chapter 6 to see the downward trend in the incidence of poverty among the elderly.

The Old Age Security program has also been beset by two interrelated problems—targeting the OAS pension to those who need income assistance and reducing the generosity of the system in view of the projected increase in OAS benefits because of population aging.

Universal versus Targeted Income Transfers

If one views the OAS program as primarily an income redistribution program for the elderly, then the question arises whether the benefit should be provided as a universal flat-rate payment to all recipients regardless of their income, or whether the benefit should be targeted to the elderly who are poor. When the OAS was established in 1952, it was a universal benefit for seniors. This type of transfer has its supporters. For example, Monica Townsend (1995: 3) has argued the following:

> The rationale for Old Age Security as a universal, flat-rate benefit paid to all seniors, was that seniors had made a contribution to society and that society as a whole would acknowledge that by paying them benefits in their older years. It is widely recognized that such programs promote social solidarity and are far less vulnerable to cutbacks than social assistance type benefits which are income or means tested. Because everyone benefits from them, they usually have wide public support.

Critics of universal transfer programs point to the inequity of providing transfers to everyone, including middle- and upper-income groups, that have to be financed by general taxes, some of which are borne by those with low incomes. The critics argue that a negative income tax scheme, such as GIS, is a fairer and more efficient transfer mechanism than a lump-sum transfer, such as OAS, when it has to be financed by distortionary taxation. They note that if universal transfers are to achieve widespread support they must be financed by highly progressive taxes that fall mainly on the rich so that the median voter, who is probably in the middle-income range, is a net beneficiary. The problem is that highly progressive taxes are also very distortionary and may not raise enough revenue to finance a large transfer program. If a society decides that it is not willing or able to impose highly progressive taxes, then the median voter will be a net contributor, and the alternative of providing a targeted transfer to those with low incomes will be more attractive. (This assumes that the transfer program is motivated by altruism toward the elderly poor as well as self-interest.) A clawback of OAS benefits and Family Allowance was introduced in 1989, and Ken Battle (1996: 147) views this as "a milestone in the history of Canadian social policy. It appeared to spell the end of the universal foundation of the child and elderly benefit systems, one of the sacred principles of the universalist welfare state."[21]

The introduction of the OAS clawback in 1989 was more symbolic than real. The OAS pension is reduced by 15 cents for each dollar that an individual's income exceeds $72,809 in 2015.[22] Thus, a single senior with $80,000 of income in 2015 would have his or her OAS pension reduced by about $1,078, but would still receive a net pension of over $5,686 per year. A couple where each received $50,000 of income would still be entitled to the full OAS pension. Furthermore, since 2007, a pensioner is permitted to split up to 50 percent of his or her eligible pension income with a spouse or common-law partner.[23] Income splitting can be used by a couple to avoid the OAS clawback. Less than 5 percent of seniors are subject to the clawback and only 2 percent lose their entire OAS benefit through the clawback. Many commentators believe the 1989 clawback of OAS pensions did not go far enough in targeting the pension to low-income seniors.

Population Aging

The second problem confronting the OAS program is the projected increase in expenditures as the baby boom generation reached age 65 starting in 2011. Figure 11.5 shows the percentage of the population over age 65 from 1946 to 2031. From 1946 to 1966, the percentage of the population over age 65 increased only modestly because

---

[21] In 1993, the Mulroney government replaced the Family Allowance and child tax credit with the income-tested Child Tax Benefit. However, in 2006, the Harper government introduced a universal child care benefit (UCCB) and the program was expanded in 2015 to include a new benefit for children aged six through 17, and the payments that parents receive for children under the age of six were increased. The UCCB is discussed in Chapter 17.

[22] However, income earned through a Tax-Free Savings Account is not subject to the clawback.

[23] Ineligible pension income includes OAS and CPP benefits, as well as earnings from a Registered Retirement Income Fund (RRIF) if the transferor is under the age of 65.

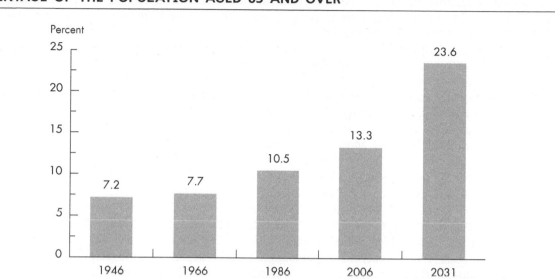

FIGURE 11.5

PERCENTAGE OF THE POPULATION AGED 65 AND OVER

Source: Statistics Canada, Demography Division (for 1946); Statistics Canada, 1966 Census; Statistics Canada, Demography Division, Population Projections for Canada, Provinces and Territories 2009–2036 (2010), Table 10.1, Catalogue no. 91-520-X.

the increase in the life expectancy of the elderly was offset by the very high birth rate that occurred in Canada during those years. The "baby bust," which followed the baby boom, will have a major repercussion on the age composition of the population in the twenty-first century—the percentage of the population over age 65 is projected to almost double between 2006 and 2031 when the last of the baby boomers turns 65. The number of working-age Canadians for every person aged 65 and over will decrease from 4.90 in 2010 to 2.61 in 2031. The projected increase in the number of seniors, from 3.9 million in 2001 to 9.3 million in 2031, could more than triple the total OAS/GIS program expenditures in just three decades.[24] To cope with population aging, the age of eligibility for OAS/GIS will gradually increase from 65 to 67, starting in 2023, with full implementation by 2029.

THE CANADA PENSION PLAN

The Canada Pension Plan and the Quebec Pension Plan (CPP/QPP) were established in 1966 as compulsory earnings-related pension programs financed on a pay-as-you-go basis. Changes to the CPP require the approval of the federal government and two-thirds of the provinces with two-thirds of the population. CPP/QPP benefits consist of retirement benefits, disability benefits, and survivor benefits.[25] About 8.2 million Canadians received over $49.0 billion CPP/QPP benefits in 2013–14.

Retirement benefits. A contributor at age 65 is entitled to a pension, which is based on the following formula:

$$\text{CPP pension} = 0.25 \times (\text{average YMPE for the previous five years})$$

$$\times (\text{average ratio of pensionable earnings to YMPE}) \qquad (11.1)$$

where YMPE is the yearly maximum pensionable earnings. Since the mid-1980s, the YMPE has equalled the average industrial wage. If a contributor's pensionable earnings in any year exceed the YMPE, then the ratio is

---

[24] Government of Canada (1996: 34).

[25] QPP and CPP provide equivalent retirement and disability benefits, but there are differences in survivor benefits (Service Canada, 2015). CPP expenditures are from *CPP and OAS Annual Statistics Tables* (Ottawa: Government of Canada); QPP expenditures are from *Régime de rentes du Québec Statistiques de l'année 2014* (Québec: La Régie des rentes du Québec). QPP figures have been adjusted from calendar year to fiscal year.

set equal to one. In computing the average ratio of pensionable earnings to YMPE, an individual may eliminate from the calculation up to 17 percent of years with the lowest earnings and years in which the individual was providing care for children under the age of 7 years. An individual who turned 65 in 2015 and who earned the YMPE or higher over his or her entire working life would be entitled to receive 25 percent of the average YMPE from 2011 to 2015, and thus $12,780 a year or about $1,065 per month. Subsequent payments are indexed to the CPI and fully taxable under the personal income tax. Individuals may elect to receive their pension as early as age 60 or as late as age 70. The annual pension is permanently reduced by 6 percent for each year that it is received before age 65, and it is increased by 7 percent for each year that it is postponed after age 65. This means that, if contributors start receiving their CPP pensions at the age of 60, their pension amounts will be 36 percent less than if taken at age 65. If contributors start receiving their CPP pension at the age of 70, their pension amounts will be 42 percent more than if taken at age 65. Historically, the adjustment rates were 0.5 percent for each month before or after one's 65th birthday, but they were changed between 2012 and 2016 to restore actuarial fairness to the taking of early or late retirement, in view of increasing life expectancy. The average age at which CPP pension benefits begin is 62.5 years. In 2013–14, $37.2 billion in CPP/QPP retirement benefits were paid to 6.0 million Canadians, representing 76 percent of total CPP/QPP expenditures.

Recipients of CPP pensions who choose to work can continue to make CPP contributions, which will increase their benefits through the Post-Retirement Benefit (PRB). The program was created in 2012 and paid its first benefits in 2013. The PRB is added to an individual's CPP retirement pension, even if the maximum pension amount is already being received. The amount of the PRB depends on the recipient's age and earnings. The maximum annual PRB amount is 1/40th of the maximum CPP retirement benefit, or $320 in 2015.

Disability benefits. Individuals who are unable to work because of physical or mental disability are entitled to disability benefits until age 65, at which point they receive their retirement benefits. The disability benefit is a flat rate, equal to $466 per month in 2015, plus 75 percent of the CPP retirement pension that the individual would have been entitled to at age 65. Additional benefits are also paid if the disabled individual has children under the age of 18 or who are 18 to 25 and attending an educational establishment. In 2013–14, disability benefits were $5.1 billion, or 10 percent of total CPP/QPP expenditures.

Survivor benefits. At the death of the CPP contributor, there is a one-time payment of a death benefit to the estate of the deceased. The maximum death benefit is $2,500. The surviving spouse of a deceased contributor who is between the ages of 45 and 65, or less than 45 with dependent children, is entitled to a pension, which is a fixed rate plus 37.5 percent of the CPP retirement pension that the deceased would have received. The maximum benefit in 2015 was $581 per month. At age 65, the surviving spouse is entitled to a pension equal to 60 percent of the pension entitlement of the deceased. An orphan's benefit is also paid to the children of a deceased CPP contributor if the child is less than 18 years old or between 18 and 25 years and attending an educational institution full-time. In 2013–14, total survivor benefits represented $6.6 billion, or 13 percent of total CPP/QPP expenditures.

Contributions. A self-employed individual whose pensionable earnings are less than YMPE makes contributions to the CPP according to the following formula:

$$\text{CPP contribution} = \text{contribution rate} \times (\text{pensionable earnings} - \text{YBE}) \tag{11.2}$$

where YBE is the year's basic exemption, which is equal to $3,500. In 2015, the YMPE was $53,600 and the contribution rate was 9.9 percent.[26] An individual whose pensionable earnings exceeded the YMPE in 2015 paid the maximum contribution of 0.099 ($53,600 − $3,500), or $4,960. An employed individual paid half of this amount, and his or her employer paid the other half.[27]

Analysis of the CPP Contribution Increases

From 1966 to 1982, the contribution rate of 3.6 percent exceeded the rate that would have been required to fund the CPP benefits in each year (i.e., the pay-as-you-go contribution rate), and the surplus of revenue over

---

[26] The QPP contribution rate was identical to the CPP rate before 2012. It is 10.50 percent in 2015 and is scheduled to increase by 0.15 percentage points per year until it reaches 10.80 percent in 2017.

[27] The CPP contributions are payroll taxes (see Chapter 14).

TABLE 11.1

Breakdown of the Pay-as-you-go Rate Increase for the Canada Pension Plan	
	Pay-as-you-go Contribution Rate
Rate in 2030 as projected when the CPP started	5.5
Change in demographics	2.6
Change in economics	2.2
Enrichment of benefits	2.4
Increase in disability claims	1.5
Rate in 2030 as projected by the chief actuary in 1995	14.2

Source: Federal, Provincial, and Territorial Governments of Canada, *"An Information Paper for Consultations on the Canada Pension Plan,"* February 1996, p. 20. Reproduced with the permission of the Minister of Public Works and Government Services Canada.

expenditures was used to establish the Canada Pension Plan reserve fund, which was invested in provincial government bonds. The CPP was not intended to be a funded pension plan. The CPP reserve fund, which by the mid-1990s had reached $40 billion or about two years' worth of benefits, provided a cushion so that the contribution rate would not fluctuate wildly from year to year in the event of economic fluctuations. After 1983, the 3.6 percent contribution rate was less than the pay-as-you-go contribution rate and the shortfall was financed out of the investment earnings of the reserve fund. From 1987 to 1996, the CPP contribution rate was increased by 0.2 percentage points a year, but the 1996 contribution rate of 5.6 percent was still below the pay-as-you-go contribution rate of 7.85 percent.

When the CPP was established in 1966, it was predicted that contribution rates would never have to rise higher than to 5.6 percent. But by 1995, in his *Fifteenth Actuarial Report*, the chief actuary of the CPP anticipated that the contribution rate would have to rise to 14.2 percent in the future in order to pay for benefits in 2030, in the absence of pension reforms.[28] This led to major reforms to the CPP program in 1998. The lessons learned from the history of CPP financing are central to the current policy debates on potential expansions of the program.

Why has the contribution rate increased from the 3.6 percent rate in 1966 when the CPP was established? The reasons include the initial decision to fund the CPP on a pay-as-you-go basis, errors in forecasting future demographic and economic trends, enhancements to regular and disability benefits, and delays in adjusting the contribution rates once these trends were recognized. Table 11.1 shows the four main factors that were responsible for the increase in the pay-as-you-go rate from 5.5 percent (the expected future rate when the CPP was started) to the projected rate of 14.2 percent. The first was the change in demographics. When the CPP was established in 1966, the birth rate had just started to decline, and the implication of this for the age composition of the population in the twenty-first century was not foreseen. CPP pensions are financed by the contributions of the current working population. The decline in the average number of workers per pensioner from 6.7 in the 1960s to 2.4 in 2030 means that the contribution rate that has to be levied on the earnings of the working generation would be higher than anticipated. In addition, the elderly are living longer. When the CPP was established, life expectancy at age 65 was 15.3 years. The chief actuary projected that life expectancy at age 65 would increase to 19.8 years in 2030. Therefore, pensions would have to be paid for 4.5 years longer than anticipated. These demographic changes increase the pay-as-you-go rate by 2.6 percentage points in 2030 and account for about 30 percent of the total increase in the pay-as-you-go rate.

The second factor was the change in economics. As we have seen, pay-as-you-go financing is attractive when the total wages and salaries (the contribution base of the working generation) is growing faster than the rate of return on assets that are normally held by pension plans. As Figure 11.1 indicated, total wages and salaries were increasing rapidly in the 1960s, and these trends were extrapolated into the future, implying that future contribution rates would be relatively modest. Since the mid-1970s, productivity growth rates have plunged, and the chief actuary, in forecasting the pay-as-you-go rate for 2030, assumed that productivity will

---

[28] See OSFIC (1995).

grow by 1 percent per year. The slower than anticipated productivity growth rate means that the pay-as-you-go rate in 2030 was projected to be 2.2 percentage points higher than anticipated, accounting for about 25 percent of the total increase in the pay-as-you-go rate.

The third factor was the enhancement of CPP benefits since its inception. These enhancements include:[29]

- full indexation of benefits in 1975,
- provision of survivor benefits to widowers in 1975,
- dropping retirement and earnings tests in 1975,[30]
- allowing the child-rearing drop-out provision in calculating contributions in 1978,
- enhanced benefits and reduced contribution requirements for disability claims, and
- allowing recipients of survivor benefits to retain benefits upon remarriage.

All of these changes increased the generosity of the CPP system. They added 2.4 percentage points to the pay-as-you-go rate in 2030 and accounted for 28 percent of the total increase in the pay-as-you-go rate.

The fourth factor was the unanticipated increase in disability claims. Between 1989 and 1994 the incidence of new disability cases increased from 4.28 to 6.34 per thousand for males and from 2.99 to 5.79 per thousand for females. Part of the reason for the increase in the number of claims was the administrative guidelines that were issued in 1989, which allowed adjudicators to take into account the unemployment rate in the applicant's region, the availability of jobs, and the person's skills in determining eligibility for disability benefits. The recession of the early 1990s increased the number of applicants who could qualify on the basis of labour market conditions. In addition, the Canada Pension Plan Advisory Board noted that private insurers and the provincial governments increased their efforts to get individuals to apply for CPP disability benefits. For a provincial government, shifting the disabled from provincial social welfare and worker's compensation to the CPP is attractive because it means that the cost of supporting the disabled is borne by all Canadian workers (outside Quebec) and not just the province's own taxpayers.

In summary, demographic and economic changes were responsible for just over half of the increase in the projected cost of the CPP. These factors were beyond the control of the designers of the CPP, but the implications of these changes for the CPP were clear from at least 1980 on. However, the federal and provincial governments were very reluctant to reform the CPP and some of the changes that they implemented in the 1970s and 1980s, such as making it easier to collect disability benefits, contributed to the problem.

The 1998 Reforms to the CPP

In an attempt to restore public confidence in the Canada and Quebec Pension Plans and reduce contribution rates in the twenty-first century, the federal government and eight of the ten provinces agreed on a series of reforms to the Canada and Quebec Pension Plans. Table 11.2 contains a summary of the changes in 1998 and their impacts anticipated at the time of the reform. Changes to the financing and investment policies of the CPP account for about three-quarters of the four-percentage-point reduction in the previously projected 14.2 percent contribution rate in the year 2030. Benefit reductions are responsible for a one-percentage-point reduction in the contribution rate in 2030.

Financing and investment changes. The contribution rate rose from 5.85 in 1997 to 9.9 percent in 2003, where it was projected to remain for the rest of the twenty-first century. With the contribution rate now exceeding the pay-as-you-go rate, the ratio of the reserve fund to expenditures was forecasted to increase steadily from 2.0 percent in 1997 to 6.9 percent in 2075. The larger fund would be invested in a diversified portfolio of securities, including stocks, in order to achieve a higher real rate of return (projected at 3.8 percent) than was previously attained by investing in provincial government bonds (2.5 percent). Another measure to increase total contributions was the freezing of the year's basic exemption at $3,500 instead of setting it at 10 percent of the year's maximum pensionable earnings as was the previous policy.

---

[29] See Federal, Provincial, and Territorial Governments of Canada, *"An Information Paper for Consultations on the Canada Pension Plan,"* February 1996, pp. 23–24.

[30] "Originally, contributors aged 65 to 69 could only receive their retirement benefits if they passed a retirement test, and their subsequent benefit up to age 70 was reduced if they earned more than a set amount." Ibid., p. 23.

TABLE 11.2

1998 Reforms to Canada Pension Plan	
Change **Financing and Investment:**	**Impact** **On Stable Contribution Rate:**
Acceleration of contribution rate increases from 5.6 percent in 1996 to a stable level of 9.9 percent in 2003.	Reduces the stable contribution rate by 0.5 percentage points.
Higher rate of return to be earned on a diversified market portfolio for CPP Investment Board.	Reduces the stable contribution rate by 1.0 percentage points.
Freezing the year's basic exemption at $3,500.	Reduces the stable contribution rate by 1.4 percentage points.
Benefits:	**On Pay-as-you-go Contribution Rate:**
More stringent entitlement rules for disability benefits.	Reduces the pay-as-you-go contribution rate by 0.44 percentage points in 2030.
Pensions based on YMPE over the previous five years.	Reduces the pay-as-you-go contribution rate by 0.44 percentage points in 2030.
Limits on combined survivor/retirement and survivor/disability pensions.	Reduces the pay-as-you-go contribution rate by 0.15 percentage points in 2030.
Limits on death benefits.	Reduces the pay-as-you-go contribution rate by 0.14 percentage points in 2030.

All financing and benefit changes combined have the impact of reducing the legislated contribution rate in 2030 from 14.2 percent to 9.9 percent (the stable contribution rate of 9.9 percent is reached in 2003).

Source: OSFIC (1997).

Benefit changes. New retirement pensions would be based on the average year's maximum pensionable earnings (YMPE) over the last five years instead of the last three years. Averaging the YMPE over five years instead of three years reduces pension benefits if, as seems likely, the YMPE increases over time due to inflation and productivity growth. If the YMPE increases by 4.5 percent a year due to inflation and productivity growth (as was assumed by the chief actuary), then the shift from three-year averaging to five-year averaging is equivalent to cutting the benefit rate from 25 percent to 24 percent of the YMPE over the last three years of a career. The magnitude of the effective reduction in the CPP retirement benefit is larger the higher the rate of inflation. The administration of the disability benefits was also tightened and the retirement pensions of disability beneficiaries were reduced. Finally, the maximum death benefit was reduced from $3,580 to $2,500. In summary, under the 1998 reforms, a rapid increase in the contribution rate was combined with some limited benefit reductions in an effort to keep the contribution rate below 10 percent in the twenty-first century.

Assessment. The 1998 reforms marked a shift in the financing of the CPP from its original pay-as-you-go foundation to a significantly funded one. Funding can ease the strain of population aging by raising the level of national saving, and thus, ultimately, increasing the economic output required to supply goods and services to future retirees. This process is reflected by returns on capital investment that are expected to remain higher than total wage growth during the next half-century.[31]

The chief actuary of Canada reaffirmed the long-term sustainability of the CPP at a contribution rate of 9.9 percent in his *26th Annual Report on the Canada Pension Plan* (2013).[32] Taking into account recent amendments to the CPP, the updated forecast of the reserve fund-to-expenditures ratio shows a steady increase from 4.7 in 2013 to 5.4 in 2025. Investment income is now projected to represent 30 percent of CPP revenues in

---

[31] See OSFIC (2010).

[32] Ibid.

2050, compared to 15 percent in 2013. If, however, the 9.9 percent contribution rate proves to be inadequate in the future, due to unforeseen demographic and economic changes, then raising the age of entitlement for CPP benefits should be considered as an alternative to further contribution increases. As mentioned earlier, when the CPP was established, the average life expectancy at age 65 was 15.3 years. It is currently 20.3 years and is expected to increase further. Individuals are living longer and choosing to retire at a younger age. As we have seen, the provision of a public pension system may have contributed to the trend in early retirement. The longer life expectancy and improved health of today's 65-year-olds suggests that they should be able to work for a longer period and enjoy the same length of retirement as previous generations. Gradually increasing the retirement age to 67, as the United States has done, would reduce the steady state contribution rate by just over half a percentage point. It is sometimes argued that delaying the age of entitlement would increase unemployment because older workers would postpone retirement and retain the jobs that would otherwise be filled by younger workers. However, the Canadian economy may have less difficulty in providing jobs for workers of all ages as the ratio of workers to the retired population sharply declines with the retirement of the baby boomers. In any case, increasing the age of entitlement needs to be done gradually so that workers can revise their savings and retirement plans well in advance of the changes. In the view of many, the failure to increase the age of entitlement in 1998 was a missed opportunity and a major shortcoming of those reforms.

Intergenerational Redistribution through the CPP

A generation of retirees can receive extraordinarily high returns from a pay-as-you-go system when the system is just starting up. Specifically, when the system is launched, retirees receive an average benefit equal to the right-hand side of Equation (11.2), yet they never had to pay any payroll taxes during their working years. This amounts to an infinite return, which is indeed very generous.[33] Just as retirees at the time the system was started received a windfall, if we were to end the pay-as-you-go system at some particular time, then the newly retired would be in a bad position–they would have paid into the system during their working years but would receive no retirement benefits in return.

The entitlement to a CPP pension despite having contributed for only a few years and the relatively low contribution rates in the early years of the CPP have resulted in a substantial intergenerational income transfer.[34] The generation that was born in 1915 and turned 65 in 1980 received, on average, about $5.50 in benefits for every dollar that it contributed to the CPP, while those born after 1975 were expected to receive less than 50 cents for every dollar contributed to the CPP in the absence of the 1998 CPP reforms.[35] The 1998 reforms, which increased the contribution rate to 9.9 percent, further eroded the net benefits from the CPP to workers born between 1945 and 1995. However, the reforms also reduced the expected burden on future generations and make it less politically attractive for future governments to arbitrarily reduce or even terminate the CPP. Higher contributions now are the price that current generations have to pay in order to ensure the political viability of the CPP when they retire.

One way to gauge the intergenerational equity of the CPP is to compare the internal rate of return (IRR) from participation in the CPP across age cohorts.[36] Contributions are paid during a person's career, while benefits are paid later in retirement, so the IRR represents the implicit return on a worker's contributions. A higher rate of return indicates better value from the CPP. The real (inflation-adjusted) IRR for generations born between 1940 and 2010, as projected by the chief actuary of Canada in 2013, are shown in Figure 11.6. The differences in rates across cohorts provide an indication of the degree of intergenerational transfer present in the CPP. The return for individuals born in 1940 is almost triple the return of those born after 1980. However, the rates stabilize for cohorts born after 1970 at about 2.3 percent, which can be regarded as a competitive real rate of return in the current low-interest rate environment.[37]

---

[33] This exaggerates the sizes of the actual expected lifetime net benefits enjoyed by the "early" beneficiaries of the CPP program, as benefit levels were phased in over the first decade of the program.

[34] Godbout, Trudel, and St. Cerny (2014) identify these two aspects of CPP as the most important for explaining the differential returns from CPP across the generations of cohorts.

[35] See Oreopoulos (1996).

[36] The IRR is the rate of interest that equates the present value of an individual's expected benefits with the present value of the individual's expected contributions (see Chapter 3).

[37] For comparison, the real IRR for the generations born in 1911 and 1929 was 22.5 percent and 10.2 percent, respectively (OSFIC, 1997: 14).

FIGURE 11.6

INTERGENERATIONAL REDISTRIBUTION: REAL INTERNAL RATES OF RETURN FROM THE CPP

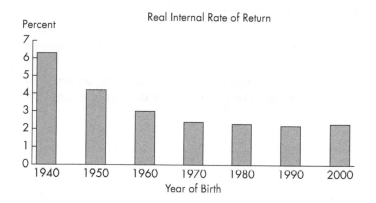

Source: Table 34 in OSFIC (2010) *and* Table 21 in OSFIC (2013).

CONCLUSION

In this chapter, we have considered two of the pillars of Canada's retirement income system. The OAS program is primarily an income redistribution program for the elderly. The CPP/QPP is primarily an earnings-related public pension scheme. Its existence (but not its pay-as-you-go financing) can be justified on the basis of market failure—adverse selection in the market for annuities, paternalism, the Samaritan's dilemma, and inflation indexation. The introduction of these programs in the 1950s and 1960s resulted in a significant decline in poverty among the elderly, but it may have had adverse effects on savings rates and retirement decisions. The massive intergenerational wealth transfers that are inherent in these programs have called into question their long-term viability, although the 1998 reforms restored a sense of sustainability to CPP/QPP.

The history of CPP/QPP reforms reminds us that governments often have a very short time horizon. A week is a long time in politics, but the decisions made in that week may have profound effects on public sector pensions, and the contributions required to finance them, in 70 years' time. The temptation to put off unpopular decisions, or to consider only those reforms that make a majority of the current voting population better off, pushes the problems and the costs onto future generations. Finally, it is worth noting that pensioners are a potent interest group. They have high voter turnout rates, and they are often portrayed in the media as a particularly deserving group.

SUMMARY

- Canada's retirement income system consists of three pillars: Old Age Security, the Canada and Quebec Pension Plans, and tax-assisted private savings and pensions.

- Public provision of pensions can be justified on the basis of market failure. The causes of market failure include adverse selection in the market for annuities, paternalism, redistribution, decision-making costs, the Samaritan's dilemma, and the absence of inflation indexation with private pensions.

- With pay-as-you-go financing, the current working generation pays the pension of the retired generation. There is no need for a pension fund. Pay-as-you-go financing is superior to a funded pension scheme when the growth rate of total real wages and salaries exceeds the real interest rate on assets held in pension funds.

- Pay-as-you-go pensions may reduce private saving, the wealth substitution effect, or increase saving, the retirement and bequest effects. A reasonable conclusion on the basis of the econometric results is that saving has been reduced, but by how much is not clear.

- The percentage of retired older workers has increased dramatically since the 1950s, and the introduction of the public pension programs may have contributed to this trend.

- CPP contribution rates increased sharply with the 1998 reforms because of population aging, the slow-down in the growth rate of real wages, the enhancement of benefits that occurred in the 1970s and 1980s, and increases in disability claims.

- The CPP has resulted in a large intergenerational transfer of income, because the age cohorts that were born before 1950 will receive benefits that are far in excess of their contributions.

EXERCISES

1. "Public pensions improve economic welfare. Because the system distributes current earnings of the young (which they would save anyway) to the old, the old are better off and the young are unaffected." Discuss carefully.

2. Will an increase in the Canada Pension Plan contribution rate increase the national savings rate?

3. Why do we have two public pension systems, OAS/GIS/SA and CPP/QPP? Discuss the rationale for having two pension systems and the relationship between them.

4. In her novel *Sense and Sensibility* Jane Austen wrote, "If you observe, people always live forever when there is any annuity to be paid them." Relate this quotation to the issue of adverse selection in annuity markets.

5. Consider a model in which an individual lives only two periods. The individual has diminishing marginal utility of consumption and receives an income of $20,000 in period 1 and an income of $5,000 in period 2. The private interest rate is 10 percent per period, and the person can borrow or lend money at this rate. Assume also that the person intends to consume all of his income over his lifetime (that is, he won't leave any money for his heirs).

   a. If there is no public pension program, what is the individual's optimal consumption in each period?

   b. Now assume there is a public pension program that takes $3,000 from the individual in the first period and pays him this amount with interest in the second period. What is the impact of this system on the person's saving?

6. Figure 11.4 assumed that the implicit rate of return from the public pension was the same as the private rate of return available to Bingley from private savings. Assume now that the public pension has a lower rate of return than the private return. How would the introduction of this public pension system affect the budget constraint in Figure 11.4? What do you expect to happen to the amount Bingley saves?

7. Use Equation (11.1) to discuss the problem that arises if the goal of policy is to keep the replacement ratio, B/w, constant over time if the dependency ratio, N_b/N_w, is growing. Now suppose that instead of keeping the replacement ratio constant over time, the goal of policy is to maintain a constant level of benefits B. Explain how this changes one's view of the consequences of an increasing dependency ratio, especially if wages are increasing over time due to productivity gains.

8. Discuss: "Over the long term, the rate of return to stocks is greater than the rate of return to government bonds. Therefore, it would be easier to care for future generations of retirees if the CPP reserve fund were invested in stocks rather than government bonds."

9. In 1990, the ratio of people age 65 or older to people ages 20 to 64 in the United Kingdom was 26.7 percent. In the year 2050, this ratio is expected to be 45.8 percent. Assuming a pay-as-you-go public pension system, what change in the payroll tax rate between 1990 and 2050 would be needed to maintain the 1990 ratio of benefits to wages? If the tax rate were kept constant, what would happen to the ratio if benefits to wages?

10. In a test for asymmetric information in the French auto insurance market, Chiappori and Salanié (2000) look at the relationship between the comprehensiveness of an individual's policy and the cost per unit of coverage. Their argument is that, in the presence of asymmetric information, the more comprehensive the coverage, the greater the cost per franc of coverage. Explain the reasoning behind this argument. (By the way, they find no evidence for asymmetric information on this basis.)

CHAPTER 12
Social Welfare Programs

As for me, welfare has been a beautiful gift from my county. It permitted me to escape from a nightmarish situation and to survive even when in poor health. Perhaps even more important, it gave my children a full-time parent when they needed one most. While I expect that many people will always be rigid and judgmental about welfare, I hope that at least some facts can be made clear. Welfare recipients do not have great bundles of money to live on each month. A welfare cheque is, believe me, barely adequate for survival and is well below the poverty lines. Furthermore, it is a system which seems to be designed to keep you down once you are down. It would help if people could remember that most welfare recipients do not want to be in that position and would gladly change places with anyone who is not.

–Anonymous welfare recipient, quoted in National Council of Welfare, Welfare in Canada (1987)

AFTER READING THIS CHAPTER, THE STUDENT SHOULD BE ABLE TO:

LO1 Outline the rationale for social assistance.

LO2 Explain how social assistance differs from social insurance.

LO3 Summarize the recent trends in the incidence of low income in Canada.

LO4 List the basic steps to calculating social assistance benefits.

LO5 Outline how one might evaluate the adequacy of welfare incomes.

LO6 Explain how the basic parameters of social assistance, *W* and *t*, affect a recipient's utility-maximizing choice of leisure and work effort, using Equation (12.1) and indifference curve analysis.

LO7 Explain how an earning exemption affects social assistance benefits and the income gain associated with working while on social assistance.

LO8 Describe the term "welfare wall," and discuss the implications of the welfare wall for the design of social assistance.

LO9 Outline how a negative income tax (or guaranteed minimum income scheme) works and some of its advantages and disadvantages.

There is a consensus in our society that no Canadian should live in abject poverty. While there may be disagreements as to what constitutes a basic standard of living or how income support for the poor should be provided, most Canadians agree that the provision of a social safety net is an essential activity of government.[1] Our welfare

---

[1] Public opinion research supports the view that income redistribution and addressing poverty are important issues to Canadians. About 81 percent of Canadians agree that the government should do something to reduce the gap between rich and poor, although there is some evidence that the strength of this belief has declined in the last two decades. In terms of where the federal government should increase

programs express in a concrete way the fundamental values of Canadian society. The strengths and weaknesses of the welfare system are eloquently expressed by an anonymous welfare recipient in the above quotation.

In this chapter, we describe how social assistance programs in Canada operate, the characteristics of welfare recipients, and the factors that lead individuals to turn to social assistance for income support. We also discuss the effects that welfare programs have on work and the empirical evidence for the disincentive effects of social welfare programs. Finally, we examine two widely discussed alternatives to welfare, a negative income tax and workfare, and highlight some ongoing challenges.

Before turning to this discussion, it is important to distinguish between social assistance, or welfare, and social insurance. Social insurance offers insurance against certain adverse events, such as losing a job or incurring health care expenses. Participation is compulsory and benefits are paid out to the individual when the adverse event occurs, regardless of the participant's level of income. As a result, social insurance is not intended to redistribute income from rich to poor.[2] Social assistance, or welfare, provides benefits to those with little or no income who are deemed to be in need. Benefits are means-tested, meaning that they are paid out to individuals whose incomes are below some benchmark. So while social assistance protects individuals against the risk of living in poverty, it operates quite differently from social insurance. It is intended to redistribute income to those individuals with little or no income.

This chapter examines the social welfare programs that are a basic component of our social safety net. These programs have been under pressure because of the rapid expansion in the number of welfare recipients since the 1970s. An increasing number of welfare recipients are classified as unemployed employable persons, causing some to question whether the receipt of welfare should be conditional on participation in job training and/or community employment programs. Some think that welfare benefits are "too high," making welfare more attractive than work. These concerns may have motivated the highly controversial reductions in welfare rates in Alberta in 1993 and in Ontario in 1995. Others have blamed tight monetary policy, public expenditure cuts, and free trade for the decline in the real earnings of low-skilled workers, resulting in the increased reliance on social assistance programs.

WELFARE PROGRAMS: DESCRIPTIONS AND TRENDS

There is no single welfare system for Canada. Under the Constitution, provincial governments are responsible for the provision of social assistance programs. As we shall see, social assistance can and does vary quite a bit across the provinces and territories and there are significant differences in the benefit levels and administration of welfare across provinces.

Although welfare is a provincial responsibility, the federal government plays a role. The federal government transfers cash to low-income individuals directly through the tax system using a refundable tax credit known as the Working Income Tax Benefit (WITB). This credit aims to provide support to working individuals with low income and to encourage labour force participation. As well, the federal government delivers cash support to low-income families with children, using the Canada Child Tax Benefit (CCTB) and, in partnership with provincial governments, the National Child Benefit Supplement (NCBS). These are briefly discussed below and in more detail in Chapter 17. The federal government also has an indirect role in that it transfers revenues to the provinces in support of their social welfare expenditures. In 1966, the federal government introduced the Canada Assistance Plan (CAP). Under this program, the federal government provided open-ended matching grants to the provinces, covering 50 percent of their eligible expenditures on social welfare. Eligible expenditures had to meet certain federal guidelines, the most important of which were that the provinces could not impose residency requirements and that provincial welfare benefits were to be provided on the basis of need. These matching grants were eventually replaced with block grants in 1996. Today, the federal government indirectly supports provincial spending on social programs and post-secondary education with the Canada Social Transfer (CST). Under the CST, provinces receive an equal per capita cash grant. Technically, these transfers are nonmatching, conditional grants. However, the only

---

spending, reducing child poverty and social services for the elderly are supported by 78 and 69 percent of respondents, respectively. Support for more spending on social services for the poor has varied over time—from a low of 41 percent in 1994 to a high of 81 percent in 2006. In 2010, 51 percent indicated that this was a high priority area for more federal spending. See the results of recent public opinion poll research released by Environics Institute in 2011. This research is available at www.environicsinstitute.org/PDF-FocusCanada2010.pdf.

[2] Of course, as we have seen, a social insurance program can include elements that are intended to be redistributive. This was the case with Employment Insurance. In such circumstances, the program is not a pure social insurance program.

FIGURE 12.1

TRENDS IN THE PERCENTAGE OF THE POPULATION RECEIVING SOCIAL ASSISTANCE AND THE UNEMPLOYMENT RATE

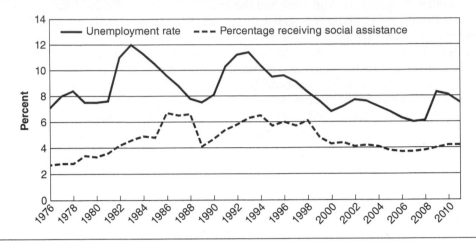

Sources: Statistics Canada's CANSIM II database http://cansim2.statcan.ca, series V466668, V21161027, and V2461224.

condition is the prohibition of residency requirements to determine eligibility for social assistance. For 2013–14, CST cash transfers totalled $12.2 billion.

Who Needs Social Assistance?

To determine who needs social assistance, we must first determine which individuals are living in poverty. In Chapter 6, we defined the low income rate as the percentage of the population with income below a threshold level, commonly referred to as the poverty line. The low income rate (based on income before taxes and transfers) was 12.9 percent in 2011.[3] The incidence of low income is significantly higher for some groups. For example, persons under the age of 18 in female lone-parent families and unattached individuals have poverty rates in excess of 30 percent, considerably higher than the average rate of 12.9 percent.[4]

The need for social assistance is generally higher when the unemployment rate is higher. For instance, some individuals may need social assistance if they have been unemployed for a long time and have exhausted their Employment Insurance (EI) benefits. Others may require social assistance because they are ineligible for EI benefits. As Figure 12.1 indicates, the percentage of the population receiving social assistance increased during the recessions of the early 1980s and 1990s.[5] Falling unemployment rates do not, however, necessarily lead to a decline in the welfare case load. In the latter half of the 1980s and again in the years following Canada's most recent recession, from 2009 to 2011, the percentage of population on social assistance persisted despite steady declines in the unemployment rate. Obviously, other factors besides the unemployment rate have had an important influence on the number of social assistance recipients.[6]

[3] Figure 6.4 shows a low income rate (based on income *after* taxes and transfers) of 8.8 percent in 2011. A comparison of the low income rates based on before and after taxes and transfers is an indicator of the extent to which government tax and transfer policies have reduced poverty.

[4] See Statistics Canada, CANSIM Table 202-0802.

[5] Kneebone and White (2014) construct an alternative historical series on the number of non-elderly social assistance recipients by province and nationally from 1969 to 2012. Their data show a more dramatic decline in the social assistance rate for Canada from 1990 to 2012. According to their data, the percentage of the non-elderly population receiving social assistance fell from a high of about 12 percent in the early 1990s to a low of just over 6 percent in 2012.

[6] For example, changes in eligibility requirements (a tightening or loosening of rules and processes) can have a significant impact on caseloads. See Boessenkool (1997) and Kneebone and White (2009).

TABLE 12.1

	British Columbia	Ontario
Single	–	33.0
–Men	29.0	–
–Women	16.7	–
Couples	2.6	20.7[b]
Two-Parent Families	8.0	
Single-Parent Families	43.7	46.3

Distribution of Social Assistance Benefits by Family Type, British Columbia and Ontario, 2014[a] (in percent)

[a] Data includes beneficiaries under each province's basic program (Temporary Assistance Program in BC and Ontario's Ontario Works Program) and does not include beneficiaries under disability support programs.

[b] Data for Two-Parent Families and Couples are reported together in Ontario.

Source: Based on data taken from http://www.sd.gov.bc.ca/research/ and http://www.mcss.gov.on.ca/en/mcss/programs/social/reports/ow_quarterly.aspx.

Who Receives Welfare?

It is quite challenging to find Canada-wide data on the characteristics of social assistance recipients, especially after 2008. Table 12.1 provides some data on social assistance beneficiaries by family type for British Columbia and Ontario, for 2014. Single individuals and single-parent families account for the bulk of assistance in both provinces.

The Level of Social Assistance Benefits

How are benefits determined and how much do social assistance recipients receive?

Although the specifics vary from province to province, social assistance benefits are calculated in three steps. One common characteristic of provincial welfare programs is that social assistance payments are made to individuals or families on the basis of their needs. So the first step is to assess an individual's basic needs for food, shelter, clothing, household supplies, and personal care, as well as any special needs, such as medications or dental care. Second, the financial resources of the family—income from employment or other sources, such as employment insurance or worker's compensation—are determined. The assets of potential recipients are also taken into account, with exemptions for household furniture, automobiles, homes, and tools of employment, as well as exemptions for earnings and for liquid financial assets, such as funds in savings accounts, below certain limits. In the final step, social assistance payments are calculated as the difference between assessed needs and available resources, up to a set maximum.[7]

Figure 12.2 shows the annual welfare incomes by province for four types of households in 2013. These welfare incomes include the maximum regular social assistance benefits available in each province, as well as federal and provincial child benefits, the GST tax credit, and other provincial tax credits. The calculations do not include any payments for special needs, such as dental care, and are based on the assumption that the individual or family has no other financial resources.

Figure 12.2 indicates that there is considerable variation in the social assistance benefits that are available to a given type of household in different provinces. For example, the welfare income of a single employable person in 2013 ranged across provinces from a low of $6,807 per year in New Brunswick to a high of $10,876 in Newfoundland. Welfare income for a single parent with one child also varied, ranging from $15,117 in Manitoba to $20,986 in Newfoundland. The level of benefits is generally higher in the Yukon and the Northwest Territories compared to Nunavut and the provinces. Differences in social assistance rates across provinces and territories reflect variations in the cost of living and fiscal capacities across jurisdictions, differences in preferences for welfare programs, as expressed through the political process, and the structure of the welfare programs themselves.

[7] We focus the discussion in this chapter on the main program delivering social assistance to individuals. However, there are a number of other provincial programs and benefits that individuals might have access to. These include childcare subsidies, housing, programs that provide other benefits to children, employment and training services, health benefits, etc.

FIGURE I2.2

ANNUAL WELFARE INCOMES IN 2013

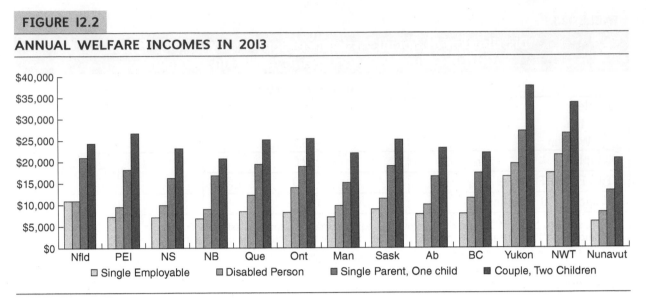

☐ Single Employable   ▨ Disabled Person   ▨ Single Parent, One child   ■ Couple, Two Children

Source: Data taken from Appendix A, Tweedle, Battle, and Torjman (2014).

Differences in how earnings and liquid assets are treated in the calculations of available resources can also generate differences in welfare income across provinces that are not apparent in Figure 12.2. To see how, consider a simple example. Harry is a single, employable individual who has been receiving the maximum monthly social assistance benefits for four months. He recently landed a job earning $300 a month. Will these wage earnings affect Harry's monthly welfare benefit? The answer depends on what province Harry lives in and the earnings exemption provided by the social assistance program.[8]

To illustrate how different earnings exemptions work, let W be the maximum monthly welfare benefit for a single employable individual (with no wage earnings), E denotes monthly wage earnings, and B is the actual monthly welfare benefit received. Suppose Harry lives in British Columbia where the earnings exemption is a flat amount equal to $200. In this case, Harry's actual monthly welfare benefit would be calculated as $B = W - (E - 200)$. By earning $300 in wages, Harry would see his welfare benefit reduced by $100. As a result, his overall monthly income (welfare benefit plus earnings) would increase by $200 if he took the job. If Harry, on the other hand, lived in PEI, the first $75 in wage earnings would be exempt and 10 percent of the amount in excess of this would also be exempt. The monthly welfare benefit for Harry living in PEI would be calculated as $B = W - 0.9(E - 75)$. So, if Harry earns $300 in wage earnings, his welfare cheque would be reduced by $202.5 and his overall income would increase by $97.5 if he took the job. Figure 12.3 illustrates how Harry's overall income would change based on the earnings exemptions in effect in 2013 in each of the 10 provinces. We also show the change in income if a lone parent (Hermione) with one child landed the job with $300 in wage earnings. The earnings exemptions are clearly more generous in some provinces (Alberta, Manitoba, and British Columbia) than in others. Note that, generally speaking, a single parent is considered employable if the dependent children are healthy and have reached a certain age. As well, the maximum benefit (W) payable to a single, employable individual and to a lone parent with children will differ, since benefit rates are usually adjusted to take into account the number of dependents in the household and their ages. In addition, there is often a supplement for lone parents. While the maximum benefit may differ between Harry and the lone parent with one child in the above example, the earnings exemption, and therefore the amount of the $300 in earnings they get to keep, are often the same. Figure 12.3 shows that, while this is generally true, there are some exceptions. In Newfoundland, New Brunswick, Saskatchewan, and Prince Edward Island the lone parent keeps more of the $300 than does the single, employable person.

The implications of the earnings exemption for work incentives are discussed later in the chapter.

The welfare incomes reported in Figure 12.2 include not only basic social assistance benefits but also a variety of federal and provincial tax benefits. Such tax benefits make up an increasingly important component of income

---

[8] Employable means that the individual is capable of working. Factors that may restrict a single individual's employability include medical conditions, physical limitations, learning disabilities, and certain personal circumstances.

FIGURE 12.3

HOW OVERALL INCOME CHANGES WHEN A WELFARE RECIPIENT RECEIVES $300 IN EARNED INCOME, BY PROVINCE

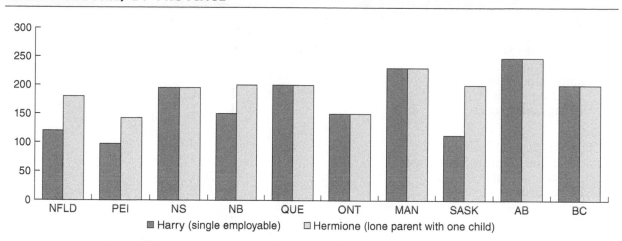

Notes: Calculated assuming $300 in earnings and the different provincial earnings exemptions in effect in 2013. Information on earnings exemptions by province obtained from Tweedle, Battle, and Torjman (2014).

Source: Authors' tabulations.

security in Canada. The federal government's Canada Child Tax Benefit (CCTB) provides a payment to low-income families with children delivered through the personal income tax system. In 2015, the maximum annual payment was $1,470.96 per child under 18 years of age for the first and second child, plus an additional $102.96 for the third and each additional child. Benefits are reduced or "clawed back" as family income increases.[9] The National Child Benefit program delivers another federal benefit, the National Child Benefit Supplement (NCBS), to low income families with children. The program is a joint federal-provincial initiative. The supplement pays $2,278.92 for the first child, $2,016 for the second, and $1,917.96 for each additional child in 2015, with reductions depending on family income. Under the National Child Benefit program, provinces have the option to reduce the welfare benefits they pay to families with children by the amount of the supplement and to instead use the funds for other provincial programs and child benefits. This has allowed the provinces to provide additional support for low income families that are not on welfare without reducing the level of support for families who are on welfare.

Tax credits represent a significant contribution to income for some social assistance recipients. Table 12.2 considers the income supports available to a lone-parent family with one child under the age of six years with no earned income, living in Ontario. The family could receive $4,068 in basic social assistance plus an additional $7,224 in shelter allowance from the Ontario Works program. The Ontario Child Benefit and the Ontario Trillium benefit (which includes the Ontario sales, energy, and property tax credits) add another $2,877 in income, while federal tax credits (including the Child Tax Benefit, National Child Benefit Supplement, the Universal Child Care Benefit, and the GST Tax credit) contribute a further $6,347 in income support.

Are Welfare Incomes Adequate?

Do social welfare programs in Canada prevent welfare recipients from being impoverished? The answer to this question depends, of course, on where we draw the poverty line.[10] If we use Statistics Canada's low income cut-off lines (LICO), then the 2013 welfare incomes for the three family types shown in Figure 12.2—single employable, lone parent with one child, and couple with two children—were all below the poverty line (with one exception). For example, in Nova Scotia, the welfare income of a single employable person was only 42.3 percent of the LICO, and the welfare income of a lone parent with one child was 80 percent of the LICO.[11]

---

[9] Chapter 17 provides details on the Canada Child Tax Benefit clawback and the implications of this for the marginal tax rate.

[10] See Chapter 6 for a discussion of the measurement of poverty lines.

[11] Tweedle, Battle, and Torjman (2014), table 3.

TABLE 12.2

Income Support for a Lone Parent With One Child Under 6 Years of Age, Living in Ontario, With No Earned Income (2015)*	
Ontario:	
Ontario Works Basic Allowance	$ 4,068
Ontario Works Shelter Allowance	$ 7,224
Ontario Child Benefit	$ 1,310
Ontario Trillium Benefit	
–Sales tax credit	$ 574
–Energy and property tax credit	$ 993
Federal:	
Child Tax Benefit	$ 1,471
National Child Benefit Supplement	$ 2,279
Universal Child Care Benefit	$ 1,920
GST Tax Credit	$ 677
Total	*$20,516*

* The amounts shown are based on maximum amounts for a lone-parent family with one child under the age of six.

Source: Adapted from Ontario Social Assistance Review Advisory Council (2010), Table 5, page 10.

However, if one measures poverty using an absolute deprivation concept, then a somewhat different picture of the adequacy of welfare incomes may emerge, since basic-needs poverty lines are typically lower than the LICO. Clearly, the adequacy of a welfare income depends on whether one thinks that welfare income should only protect against extreme deprivation, or that it should provide a reasonable standard of living in line with prevailing norms of Canadian society.

WELFARE PROGRAMS AND WORK INCENTIVES

The questions of whether welfare reduces work effort and the incentive to participate in the labour force and whether more-generous benefits can lead to a dependence on social assistance have dominated discussions of welfare policy for years. In the next section, we use a simple model to help understand these incentive effects.

The Basic Tradeoffs

To understand the effects of social assistance on work effort, we need to abstract from the complex rules and interactions that characterize social welfare programs in reality, and instead characterize welfare policy in terms of only two policy parameters. The first is the basic welfare entitlement that an individual receives if they are not working, W. The second is t, the rate at which the basic entitlement is reduced when the social assistance recipient earns $\$E$ in income. Suppose that the basic welfare entitlement is $500 but this is reduced by 50 cents for every dollar the individual earns. The individual's monthly welfare benefit, B, is calculated as:

$$B = W - tE \tag{12.1}$$

Recall Harry from our example above. If Harry is receiving social assistance and starts earning $300 a month, according to Equation (12.1), his welfare benefit falls from $500 to $350. His benefit is reduced by $150, or $t \times E$. This benefit reduction rate, t, is in effect a tax on earnings. If Harry was to earn $1,000 a month, his welfare benefit would be reduced to zero.[12]

Equation (12.1) highlights the fundamental dilemma in designing a social welfare program. For a given W, increasing the tax (also referred to as the benefit reduction, or clawback, rate) discourages work effort, since

---

[12] Once $B = 0$, the individual is no longer on social assistance.

ONTARIO'S DEPRIVATION INDEX

In 2009, the Ontario government implemented a new measure of poverty—the Ontario Deprivation Index. The index consists of a list of 10 items considered necessary for a reasonable standard of living, including fresh fruit and vegetables daily, appropriate clothing for a job interview, a place to live free of pests, ability to have friends or family over for a meal once a month, and access to transportation. A household is considered to be poor if it cannot afford two items on the list. Defining poverty based on whether a set of activities or items are available differs from defining poverty based on a level of income, such as the definitions produced by Statistics Canada. Statistics Canada calculates threshold levels of income (known as low income cut offs, or LICOs) by determining the income level at which an individual (or family) with that income is spending 20 percentage points more of after-tax income on food, shelter, and clothing than the average individual (or family). An individual with income below this level is deemed to have low income. The LICO is not without problems. It is a relative measure, so the benchmark is always moving. Observers note that it is almost impossible to explain how the LICO is constructed. Even Statistics Canada discourages its use as a poverty line. Statistics Canada produces two other measures—the low income measure (LIM) and the market basket measure (MBM). The LIM, calculated as 50 percent of median household income with adjustments for household size, is easier to understand. The MBM, similar in spirit to Ontario's Deprivation Index, is based on the cost of a basket of goods and services, including food, footwear, and shelter, representing a modest, basic standard of living for a family of two adults and two children, adjusted for different regions.

At the time, the introduction of the Deprivation Index was celebrated as a valuable step forward in measuring poverty, because it emphasized not only the need for basic necessities but also the necessity of social interaction. Although other countries have used deprivation indices to monitor poverty, Ontario was the first jurisdiction in North America to do so. The Ontario government intended to use the index as a tool for evaluating its success in reducing poverty but this is no longer possible as changes made by Statistics Canada in 2012 eliminated the survey that carried the Ontario Deprivation Index.

Based on Matern, Mendelson, and Oliphant (2009), Coyne (2013), Monsebraaten (2009), and "Defining Necessities." *The Globe and Mail*, December 4, 2009.

Complete references for this feature can be found in the References section on page 482.

social assistance recipients do not get to keep much of the income generated from that effort. Lowering t provides a greater incentive to earn income but also increases the costs of the social welfare program.

Analysis of Work Incentives

We will use indifference curve analysis to help understand how welfare affects an individual's choice of how much time to devote each month to work and how much to non-market activity, which we call leisure. For economists, "leisure" means "time not spent in paid work." Watching *Hockey Night in Canada* is leisure, but so is time spent mowing your lawn or doing your laundry. Consider Jane Doe. Even if Doe does not work, there is an upper limit to the amount of leisure she can consume, because there are just so many hours in a month. This number of hours is referred to as the time endowment. We illustrate this in Figure 12.4 where the horizontal axis measures the number of hours of leisure. The time endowment is measured as distance TO. We assume that all time not spent on leisure is devoted to work in the market. Any point on the horizontal axis, therefore, simultaneously indicates hours of leisure and hours of work. For example, at point a, Oa hours are devoted to leisure, and the difference between that and the time endowment, TO, represents time spent at work, aT.

Our first problem is to illustrate how Doe's income, which is measured on the vertical axis, varies with her hours of work. Assume that she can earn a wage of $\$w$ per hour. Also, for the moment, assume that no welfare is available and her income for any number of hours worked is just the product of $\$w$ and the number of hours. Suppose, for example, Doe does not work at all. If labour is her only source of income, her income is simply zero. This option of zero work and zero income is represented by point T.

FIGURE 12.4

BUDGET CONSTRAINT FOR THE LEISURE/INCOME CHOICE

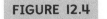

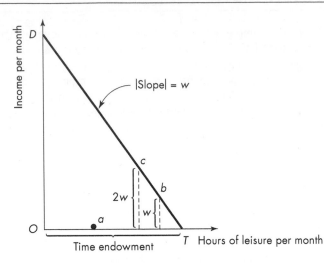

If Doe works one hour each week, her consumption of leisure equals her time endowment minus one hour. This point is one hour to the left of T on the horizontal axis. Working one hour gives her a total of w. The combination of one hour of work with a total income of w is labelled point b. If Doe works two hours—moves two hours to the left of T—her total income is $2 \times w$, which is labelled point c. Continuing to compute the income associated with each number of hours of work, we trace out all the leisure/income combinations available to Doe—straight line TD, whose slope, in absolute value, is the wage rate. TD is the analog of the budget constraint in the usual analysis of the choice between two goods. Here, however, the goods are income and leisure. The price of an hour of leisure is its opportunity cost (the income forgone by not working that hour), which is just the wage.

To know which point on TD Doe chooses, we need information on her tastes or preferences. In Figure 12.5 we reproduce the budget constraint TD. Assume that preferences for leisure and income can be represented by normal, convex-to-the-origin indifference curves. Three such curves are labelled i, ii, and iii in Figure 12.5. Utility is maximized at point E_1, where Doe devotes OF hours to leisure, works FT hours, and earns income OG.

FIGURE 12.5

UTILITY MAXIMIZING CHOICE OF LEISURE AND INCOME

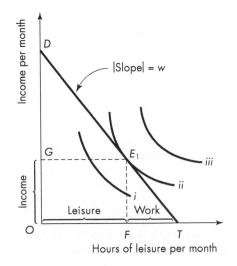

FIGURE 12.6

BUDGET CONSTRAINT UNDER A WELFARE SYSTEM WITH A 50 PERCENT TAX RATE ON ADDITIONAL EARNINGS

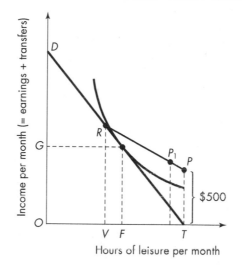

Hours of leisure per month

Suppose now that Doe becomes eligible to receive a basic social assistance benefit (*W*) of $500 per month. However, her benefits are reduced by $0.50 for each dollar she earns. How does the social assistance program modify her budget constraint? In Figure 12.6, clearly one option that social assistance makes available to Doe is point *P*, which is associated with zero hours of work and an income of $500 from welfare. Now suppose that Doe works one hour. Graphically, she moves one hour to the left from *P*. When Doe works one hour, she receives the wage $*w* from her employer, but simultaneously her welfare benefit is reduced by 0.5 × $*w*. The hour of work has netted her only half the hourly wage. This is shown by point P_1, where there is one hour of work and total income is $500 + 0.5*w*. In effect, Doe's earnings are being taxed at a rate of 50 percent. Additional hours of work produce a net gain in income but at a rate lower than the wage rate.

Jane continues to earn an effective wage of *0.5w* until she works *VT* hours, at which point her income from working is high enough that her welfare benefit is reduced to zero. Thus, there is a kink in the budget constraint at point *R*. Beyond that point, each hour of work raises her income by $*w*.[13] Thus, the budget constraint is the kinked line *PRD*. Segment *PR* has a flatter slope (equal to *0.5w* in absolute value) than segment *RD* (with a slope equal to *w* in absolute value).

How will Doe respond to such incentives? As usual, the outcome depends on the shape of the individual's indifference curves. Figure 12.7 shows one distinct possibility: she maximizes utility at point *S*, reducing the hours she works from *VT* to *KT*.

Although it is no longer the case, in the past some provinces did not have any earnings exemption, implying a 100 percent tax on the earnings of social welfare recipients. We start with an analysis of the budget constraint and work incentives in this case. Figure 12.8 replicates Jane Doe's budget constraint (given as *DT*) in the absence of a welfare program. Suppose, like before, that Jane becomes eligible to receive a basic welfare entitlement of $500. As was the case above, point *P*, which is associated with zero hours of work and an income of $500 from welfare, is an option for Jane. Now suppose Jane works one hour. Graphically, she moves one hour to the left from *P*. When Doe works one hour, she receives a wage of $*w* from her employer, but simultaneously her welfare benefit is reduced $*w*. The hour of work has netted nothing as her income is still $500. Additional hours of work in this case continue to produce no net gain in income, so the budget constraint is flat. This continues until point *R*, above which point Doe's earnings exceed $500 and she is out of the welfare system altogether. Beyond this point, an additional hour of work raises her income by $*w*. Jane's budget constraint given this welfare system is represented by *PRD*.

---

[13] If Doe becomes subject to the income tax, her take-home wage will be less than $*w*. This consideration is unimportant in the current context and is discussed in Chapter 18 under "Labour Supply."

FIGURE 12.7

FIGURE 12.7

WORK DECISION UNDER A WELFARE SYSTEM WITH A 50 PERCENT TAX RATE ON ADDITIONAL EARNINGS

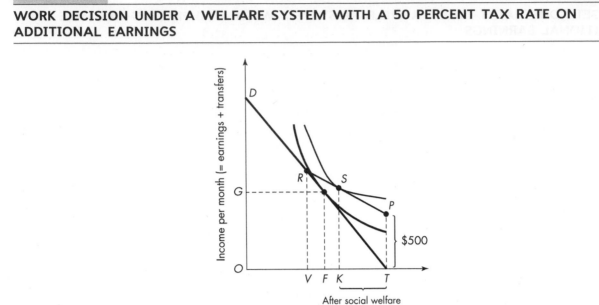

How does Jane respond? One possibility is to choose point *P* and supply no labour. In no case will a rational person work between zero and *PR* hours. This should come as no surprise. Why should someone work if she can receive the same income by not working?[14]

FIGURE 12.8

WORK DECISION UNDER A WELFARE SYSTEM WITH A 100 PERCENT TAX RATE ON ADDITIONAL EARNINGS

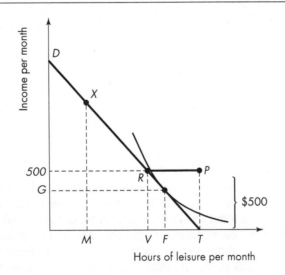

---

[14] In a more complicated model, an individual might select a point along segment RD to develop her skills or to signal her quality to future employers by maintaining a continuous work history. A choice along RD might also reflect a strong preference for income or a social norm that discourages the consumption of leisure.

Of course, a welfare system with a 100 percent tax on earnings does not necessarily induce an individual to stop working. Suppose that an individual chose a point like X along segment RD in Figure 12.8 before the welfare system is introduced (that is, the indifference curve is tangent at X rather than as illustrated in Figure 12.8). This individual will either continue to choose X or instead will choose P, depending on the shape of the indifference curves, If X is chosen, the individual works MT hours per month and if the resulting income falls below the poverty line, then this individual is a member of the working poor.

Empirical Evidence on Disincentive Effects

Figure 12.8 depicts a classic welfare system in which the implicit tax rate on additional earnings is 100 percent. For social assistance recipients not in the labour force, this may represent a significant disincentive to entering the labour force and earning income. This situation is often referred to as a welfare wall. Having recognized this, most provincial governments generally allow welfare recipients to keep all of their earnings below some exemption level. Welfare benefits are then reduced by less than a dollar for each additional dollar earned. For example, in Manitoba the exempt earnings level is $200 per month for singles and the benefit reduction rate on earnings above this threshold is 70 percent. In Alberta, the first $230 in earnings is exempt, with a benefit reduction or tax rate of 75 percent on earnings in excess of this amount.

Benefits, like the National Child Benefit Supplement, delivered through the income tax system and phased out as income increases, also contribute to high marginal tax rates (MTR), especially for those with low incomes. The increasing marginal tax rates at low levels of income are a strong disincentive to working and discourage social assistance recipients from joining the labour force.[15] Laurin and Poschmann (2011) calculate marginal tax rates for Quebec for different family situations in 1999 and 2011. Figure 12.9 shows the effective marginal tax

FIGURE 12.9

EFFECTIVE MARGINAL TAX RATES FOR A TYPICAL DUAL-EARNER FAMILY OF FOUR (TWO PARENTS, TWO CHILDREN), QUEBEC, 1999 AND 2011.

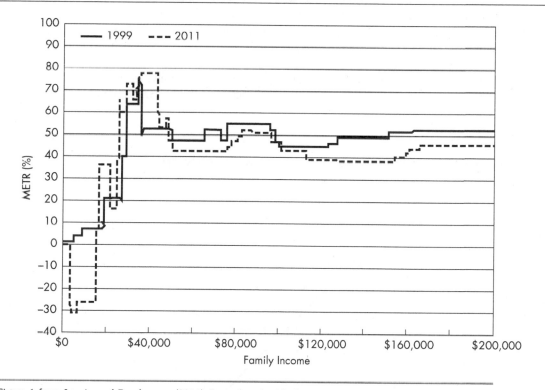

Source: Figure 1 from Laurin and Poschmann (2011). Reproduced with the permission of the C. D. Howe Institute.

---

[15] For a more detailed discussion of marginal effective tax rates see Chapter 17.

rates for a typical family of four with two earners and two children. Note that the figure does not include the contribution of Quebec's social assistance (and its earnings exemption and clawback) to the marginal tax rate. It does, however, nicely illustrate the marginal tax rates associated with the federal plus provincial personal income tax system, including the effects of federal and Quebec tax credits/benefits delivered through the tax system—such as the child tax benefit, NCBS, GST credit, and various other credits that are phased out as income rises.

The marginal tax rate increases from about 10 percent, given a family income of $20,000, to 60 to 70 percent, given a family income in the range of $30,000 to $40,000. In contrast, for family income above $50,000, the marginal tax rate ranges between 40 to 50 percent. This pattern is not unique to Quebec. The marginal tax rates for families with children are calculated for all provinces in Poschmann (2008). He shows that the marginal tax rates for families with children and income in the range of $20,000 to $40,000 are quite high in all provinces, reaching close to 60 percent at the upper bound of this income range.

How big are these incentive effects in reality? Empirical analysis generally supports the theoretical predictions that more generous benefits increase the number of those on welfare as well as the duration of a welfare spell, especially for certain groups. As well, there is evidence that the incentive effects for labour force participation and hours of work are as theory predicts.

Using data for the late 1980s, Allen (1993) and Charette and Meng (1994) find that higher welfare rates increased the probability of welfare participation by women. Fortin, Lacroix, and Drolet (2004) examine the effect of benefit levels on the length of welfare spells in Quebec. Their results indicate that higher social assistance benefits for individuals under age 30 increased the average duration of a welfare spell for men aged 22 to 29 by 3.8 months. The impact for single women in the same age category was greater, increasing the average welfare spell duration by 5.9 months. The results in Lemieux and Milligan (2008) provide further evidence of the negative effects of higher welfare benefits on employment.

Reductions in the welfare wall (as measured by the marginal tax rate) are found by Milligan and Stabile (2007) to have strong labour participation effects for social assistance recipients. The authors estimate the impact of the National Child Benefit Supplement on labour participation and on the receipt of social assistance for single mothers. When the National Child Benefit (NCB) was introduced, some provinces, like Ontario and Alberta, decided to integrate the NCB with their social assistance programs. Since integrating provinces chose to subtract the NCB benefit from the social assistance payment, the welfare wall was essentially lowered in those provinces. Other provinces, like B.C. and Quebec, did not integrate the federal government benefit with their own programs. Differences in provincial government responses created differences in work incentives across provinces.

To illustrate how integration affects work incentives, Figure 12.8 is redrawn in Figure 12.10. In the absence of the NCB, Doe's budget constraint, given the province's social assistance (SA) program, is *PRD*. Suppose the

FIGURE 12.10

WORK DECISION AND WELFARE IN AN INTEGRATED PROVINCE

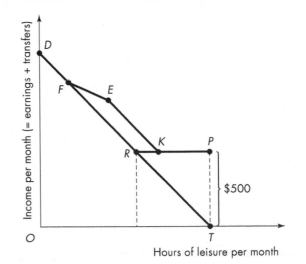

federal government introduces a $100 NCB for which Doe is eligible. How does this affect Doe's budget constraint? Assuming Doe lives in an integrated province and works zero hours, she receives $400 in social assistance and a $100 NCB payment. Integration means that the original $500 social assistance benefit is reduced by the amount of the NCB. Note that since the provincial SA benefit is $400 rather than $500, it takes fewer hours of work to fully exhaust the payment (i.e., reduce it to zero). This is illustrated by the shorter flat segment *PK* (as compared to *PR*). Since the range of hours of work over which Doe faces a 100 percent marginal tax rate is smaller, the welfare wall and the work disincentive effect are therefore reduced.

Note that along the portion *EK*, as income rises there is no reduction in the NCB—Doe gets the full $100. However, once income rises above a certain level the NCB is reduced until eventually it reaches zero (i.e., at point F in Figure 12.10). Doe's new budget constraint is given as *PKEFD*.

What happens if Doe lives in a non-integrated province? Figure 12.11 illustrates this case. As before, the maximum SA benefit is $500. If Doe chooses to work zero hours, she is entitled to $500 in SA plus the $100 NCB. To exhaust the SA benefit, Doe needs to work at least *BT* hours—the same amount of hours as was the case before the NCB was introduced (i.e., as in Figure 12.8). Thus, in this province, the welfare wall and the work disincentive have not been reduced. Doe's new budget constraint is *QMLND*. Along the portion *LN*, the NCB is reduced as income increases, as was the case in Figure 12.10. Along segment *ND*, the individual receives neither the SA nor the NCB benefits.

Exploiting this cross-province variation in work incentive effects, Milligan and Stabile (2007) estimate the impact of the NCB on (i) labour participation and (ii) the receipt of social assistance for single mothers. They find that a reduction in social assistance benefits of $1,000 is associated with a 3.3 to 4.7 percentage point increase in the labour force participation of single mothers. During the period from 1997 to 2000, the number of single women on social assistance declined from 49 to 33 percent. Using their estimates, the authors calculate that social assistance integration with the NCB (as illustrated in Figure 12.10) could account for 19 to 27 percent of the overall reduction in the take-up of social assistance among single women during that period. Using a similar econometric technique, Milligan and Stabile (2009) provide some additional evidence consistent with their earlier findings; the decision to integrate or not with the NCB affects labour force participation in a manner consistent with what theory predicts.

Finally, Scarth and Tang (2008) use a simulation approach to investigate the effects of the federal government's Working Income Tax Benefit (WITB). They find that a WITB lowers the unemployment rate and improves the average incomes of the poor targeted by such a program. The effects are bigger if the program is financed by spending cuts (or from the fiscal dividend associated with debt reduction) rather than a tax on high income individuals.

FIGURE 12.11

WORK DECISION IN A NON-INTEGRATED PROVINCE

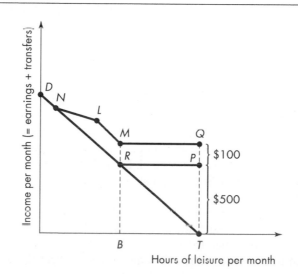

Putting work incentives in perspective. Public concern over how much welfare recipients work may be somewhat misplaced. True, an important aspect of any welfare system is the incentive structure it creates. But if the goal of welfare policy were only to maximize work effort, the government could simply force the poor into workhouses, as was done under the English Poor Law of 1834. Using the tax-transfer system to provide a social safety net inevitably means that individuals' economic decisions are distorted. Designing a good transfer system means that there should be a careful balancing of incentive and equity considerations.

Welfare Dependence

The public concern over the welfare system has encompassed broader issues than just those of hours of work per month or the incentive to join the labour force. One such issue is whether receipt of social assistance reduces the chances that a recipient will ever become self-supporting. In terms of the economist's standard framework for analyzing work decisions, the question is whether the receipt of welfare changes the slopes of an individual's leisure/income indifference curves—that is, people become "lazier" if they are on welfare for an extended period of time—or whether their labour market skills atrophy when they are not employed. Barrett and Cragg (1995) examined the length of time that individuals were on welfare in British Columbia over the period 1980 to 1992. Their results suggest that only a small proportion of welfare recipients were continuously dependent on welfare. Fortin, Lacroix, and Roberge (1995) found that the rate at which 25- to 30-year-old individuals leave the welfare system declined after the individual had been on welfare for four months, but the exit rate for younger individuals (18–24 years) was not affected by the length of time on welfare. They also found that individuals who had previously been on welfare had higher exit rates from welfare. Thus, the evidence from the Fortin, Lacroix, and Roberge study indicated that, at least for young people, contact with the welfare system does not generate increasing welfare dependency.

Another way that social assistance might create long-term welfare dependence is through its effects on family structure. The impact of welfare on family structure has been fiercely debated in the United States because the most important welfare program over the period from 1935 to 1996, Aid to Families with Dependent Children (AFDC), was generally available only for one-parent families. It was argued that this induced fathers to leave their families. Mothers left to fend for themselves could neither earn enough money to bring the family out of poverty nor provide a proper environment for raising children. In Canada, the impact of welfare on family structure is perceived to be less of a problem because a two-parent family is eligible for welfare if it satisfies the needs test. There are concerns that the Canadian welfare system affects the incentives for a single parent to marry and also the divorce rate among low income families, but this subject has not been extensively studied in Canada. The welfare system's effect on family structure does not, however, seem to have played a major role in the increase in the welfare case load, because most of the growth has been in unattached individuals and married couples. More studies are required to understand the complex forces that are changing the nature of the family in Canada before we can assess the impact of the welfare system on family structure.

WELFARE ALTERNATIVES AND ONGOING CHALLENGES

Concerns about the current welfare system are sufficiently serious that a number of alternative approaches have been considered. We discuss two of these: the negative income tax and workfare.

Negative Income Tax

A negative income tax (NIT) is an income support program in which all individuals or families are guaranteed a basic annual income, even if they have zero earnings. If they have positive earnings their grants are reduced only by some fraction of their earnings. A NIT scheme differs from a classical welfare scheme in that the implicit marginal tax rate on earnings is less than 100 percent, and benefits are determined on the basis of income deficiency rather than on the assessment of need. Because NIT schemes contain an implicit guarantee that an individual's or a family's income will not fall below a certain level, such schemes are also known as Guaranteed Annual Income (GAI) schemes.

A NIT scheme would operate as follows. Suppose that the basic monthly grant is $500, and the system has a tax rate on additional earnings of 50 percent. If Doe earns $180, her grant is reduced by $90 (= .50 × $180) to $410. Doe's total monthly income is then the sum of $410 (from grant) plus $180 (from earnings), or $590. Figure 12.7 can be used again to show how this NIT scheme would affect Doe's budget constraint.

Recall that the benefit received (*B*) is related to the basic grant (*W*), tax rate (*t*), and level of earnings (*E*) by $B = W - tE$. It follows that the benefit is zero ($B = 0$) when $E = W/t$ or is at any higher level of *E*. The earnings level, W/t, is referred to as the break-even earnings under a NIT scheme. The Canadian income security system has some components that operate like a NIT scheme. The Guaranteed Income Supplement (GIS) program, which is described in Chapter 11, is a NIT scheme for those over 65 years of age, and the Child Tax Benefit (and the NCB Supplement) and GST tax credit have the characteristics of a NIT as do some provincial benefits and tax credits.

A universal NIT was proposed for Canada in the 1971 Senate "Report on Poverty" and by the 1985 Macdonald Royal Commission. A more recent proposal was made in Duclos (2007). The proponents of a universal NIT stress the following benefits:

* Welfare recipients would have more incentive to work because the marginal tax rate on their earnings would be lower.
* The working poor would receive some income support if they earn less than the break-even earnings.
* The administration of the welfare system could be simplified by eliminating the assessment of needs under the current social assistance programs and by eliminating the duplication and overlap with other income security programs such as the GST credit, the GIS, the Child Tax Benefit, housing subsidies, and possibly employment insurance.

There are, however, a number of perceived problems with a universal NIT system. The NIT may prove to be more costly than means-tested social assistance, since all individuals whose income falls below the break-even level (not just those who would pass the means test required for social assistance) get a cheque. The calculation of the break-even earnings level reflects the tradeoff between the size of the basic grant and the tax rate on additional earnings. A system that has low tax rates and high guaranteed incomes will have a high break-even earnings level, which means that a substantial portion of the population will qualify for benefits. This means that the rest of the population will have to pay higher taxes in order to finance it. The findings presented in Clavet, Duclos, and Lacroix (2013) suggest these concerns warrant serious consideration. They undertake an ex-ante evaluation of a 2009 proposal by a Quebec government advisory committee that recommends a form of a guaranteed minimum income scheme. The proposal makes two important recommendations: it sets a baseline for financial support equal to 80 percent of Statistics Canada's market basket measure for disposable income in municipalities with populations under 30,000 (about \$32,777 in 2011), and that individuals working at least an average of 16 hours a week at minimum wage receive 100 percent of this amount.[16] Clavet, Duclos, and Lacroix (2013) find that the proposal has strong negative labour force participation effects and entails a significant budgetary cost to the government in terms of transfer outlays and provincial taxes forgone. The authors note that costs would be even higher if the analysis also included the labour market effects from raising taxes to fund the program.

A second problem with a NIT scheme is that, while it could increase the work incentive for current welfare recipients, it would likely reduce the work incentive for the working poor who would become eligible for benefits. The working poor would face higher marginal tax rates on their earnings than under the current system, generating a substitution effect in favour of leisure, and the guaranteed income would generate an income effect that would also favour increased consumption of leisure.

Finally, like a conventional welfare scheme, the NIT is a passive income support scheme. Financial support is provided so that basic material needs are met, but recipients are not provided with the opportunities to improve their skills through formal training or on-the-job work experience, which would allow them to become self-sufficient. There is no reciprocal responsibility for the welfare/NIT recipient to try to become a more productive member of society. Dissatisfaction with passive income support programs has led to increased interest in workfare programs.

Workfare

Conventional welfare and negative income tax programs allow welfare recipients to choose their hours of work. If the receipt of the benefit lowers hours of work, so be it. An alternative scheme is workfare. Able-bodied

---

[16] Statistics Canada's market-based measure is based on the cost of a basket of goods and services representing a modest, basic standard of living. It includes the costs of food, clothing, footwear, transportation, shelter, and other expenses for a reference family of two adults and two children. Market-based measure threshold amounts for different regions and provinces are available at www.statcan.gc.ca/pub/75f0002m/2013002/tbl/tbl04-eng.htm.

individuals receive transfer payments only if they agree to participate in a work-related activity and accept employment, if offered. Proponents of workfare argue that it has a number of advantages: (1) requiring welfare recipients to work may make the program more popular politically and, hence, lead to more-generous benefits; (2) by making it harder to collect welfare, it will reduce the number of welfare recipients and lower the costs of welfare; and (3) it gives people the opportunity to gain work experience and skills, allowing them ultimately to escape from poverty. A study by Fortin, Truchon, and Beausejour (1993), which simulated labour supply responses to changes in Quebec's tax-transfer system, indicated that there are workfare programs that are potentially superior to the existing welfare system.

A number of skeptical questions have been raised about workfare. Is such a system an affront to the dignity of the poor? Can useful jobs be found for recipients? In light of the huge case loads that welfare administrators have to handle, can they differentiate between people who are able-bodied and those who are not? Are the costs of administering workfare prohibitive? Obviously, there is great deal of controversy about the effectiveness and the morality of workfare programs.[17] A review of the U.S. experience with workfare by Gueron (1993: 171) concludes that, "(1) implementing participation mandates is feasible but difficult, and (2) such programs result in positive and cost-effective—although modest—gains but do not lift large numbers of people out of poverty."

Since the mid 1990s, provincial social assistance programs have moved in the direction of pure welfare to welfare-to-work and workfare, where eligibility for social assistance requires participation in some employment-related activities, such as training or job search. In addition, several provinces have introduced some form of earned income tax credits or working income benefits to help with the transition from welfare to work.

For example, Ontario introduced the Ontario Works program in 1998. The program requires social assistance recipients (excluding seniors, persons with disabilities, and single parents with young children) to participate in community projects or job training. In June 2000, the government of Ontario reported that it had created over 30,000 workfare placements. During the early 1990s, new applicants to Alberta's social assistance program were directed to training and work projects. Between 1993 and 1996, "more than 35,000 former and potential welfare clients went through various work, training, and education programs" (Boessenkool, 1997: 16). Most of the reduction in the caseload during this period was achieved by reducing the inflow of new cases (especially of young, single, employable individuals) and not by increasing the rate at which existing recipients left the welfare rolls. Welfare became a program of last resort, and applicants had to demonstrate that they had exhausted all other avenues of income support before they were provided with assistance. A recent study by Finnie, Irvine, and Sceviour (2005) on exit and entry trends for social assistance in the 1990s reinforces Boessenkool's assessment.

Ongoing Challenges

We briefly highlight some ongoing challenges for social assistance in Canada:

- *Complexity.* Existing welfare systems deliver benefits to low income individuals through a variety of sources at both the federal and provincial government levels. Table 12.2 shows the numerous channels through which benefits are available for a lone parent with one child under the age of six living in Ontario. While the income delivered through the various welfare benefits is substantial, there are a large number of different programs, each with its own exemptions and clawback rates. This makes it difficult to determine the marginal tax rate (and the height of the welfare wall) for a given individual. It also makes social assistance program incredibly complex. Sheikh (2015) notes that Ontario's social assistance program has over 800 rules with more than 240 benefit rates, contributing to high administration costs.

- *Childcare hurdle.* For a single parent, the costs of childcare can represent a significant hurdle to joining the labour market. Some provinces offer programs, such as subsidized childcare, to assist with childcare expenses. As well, the federal government's Universal Child Care Benefit pays families $160 per month per child under six (which are treated as taxable benefits). But as a recent report from the Ontario Social Assistance Advisory Council in 2010 argues, even if a fully subsidized child care spot is available, child-care costs will exceed the amount received from the Universal Child Care Benefit.[18] How high is this hurdle and do current policies adequately address it?

---

[17] The pros and cons of workfare are contained in Krashinsky (1995) and Lightman (1995). See also the National Welfare to Work Study funded by Human Resources Development Canada at http://publish.uwo.ca/~pomfret/ wtw/ and the Self-Sufficiency project at http://www.srdc.org.

[18] Ontario Social Assistance Review Advisory Council (2010), page 10.

- *Treatment of assets.* Some have argued that the treatment of assets (a problem referred to as asset stripping) in determining eligibility for social assistance contributes a significant barrier to leaving welfare once people are receiving it. (See, for example, Battle, Mendelson, and Torjman (2005) and National Council on Welfare (2010)). Clearly a tradeoff exists. Allowing welfare recipients to retain more of their assets will potentially increase caseloads and program costs. On the other hand, having some assets can help promote transitions back to self-sufficiency. Some assets, such as Registered Education Savings Plans, have recently been exempted but there is ongoing debate about what the appropriate level of asset exemptions should be.

SUMMARY

- Welfare programs are the responsibility of the provincial governments, but the federal government has played a significant role in the financing and design of programs through intergovernmental transfer programs, like the Canada Social Transfer, and through a number of benefits delivered through the personal income tax system.

- Eligibility for social assistance has been based on need. The level of social assistance benefits varies widely from province to province.

- Children and single parents represent a significant percentage of welfare cases.

- Welfare programs impose high marginal tax rates (the welfare wall) on the earnings of welfare recipients. Economic theory suggests that this may discourage work and participation in the labour force. This hypothesis is confirmed by empirical research.

- In response to concerns over the work incentives created by social assistance, a number of federal and provincial initiatives have been introduced to encourage labour force participation and ease the transition from social assistance to work. These initiatives include the federal government's Working Income Tax Benefit, reforms in provincial social assistance programs that have reduced clawback rates and increased earnings exemptions, and the creation of earned income tax benefits in some provinces.

- A negative income tax is an income support program in which individuals or families are guaranteed a basic annual income. Benefits are reduced as earnings increase. The main problem in designing a negative income tax is the tradeoff between providing adequate support and, at the same time, providing good work incentives.

- Under workfare, able-bodied individuals receive benefits only if they work or enrol in a training program. Preliminary evidence on these programs is mixed.

EXERCISES

I. Elizabeth's wage rate is $5 per hour. She faces a welfare system that pays a monthly benefit of $150. The benefit is reduced by 25 cents for each dollar of earnings.

   a. Sketch the budget constraint in a leisure/income diagram. How many hours does she have to work before her benefit is reduced to zero?

   b. Sketch a set of indifference curves consistent with Elizabeth's participation in the labour market and her 60 hours of work. What is her monthly welfare benefit?

   c. Draw your diagram for part (a) again, and now sketch a set of indifference curves consistent with Elizabeth not participating in the market.

   d. Suppose the government introduces a workfare program that requires welfare recipients to work 100 hours per month. If welfare recipients work 100 hours they keep their earnings and receive $100 in benefits. The welfare benefits are reduced by 25 cents for each dollar of earnings after the recipient works 100 hours. Draw Elizabeth's budget constraint with the workfare program.

e. Is Elizabeth better off under the workfare program than she was under the welfare program?

2. Suppose you wanted to conduct an econometric study of the impact of job training programs on future earnings. What data would you need? Suggest a specific estimating equation.

3. Discuss: "Workfare is an efficient way to transfer income if the quantity of leisure consumed by the recipient appears in the utility function of the donor."

4. One factor thought to contribute to the increase in social assistance recipients is an increase in the ratio of social assistance benefits to earnings for low income individuals. Using a graph like the one in Figure 12.8, discuss how a decline in the wage rate can result in an individual, initially working and not receiving welfare, deciding to quit their job and take up social assistance.

5. Hermione, without a job or job prospects, has been on social assistance for the past four months. Social assistance pays a basic benefit of $600 a month with a benefit reduction rate of 75 percent for earned income. Her welfare benefit is given as $B = 600 - 0.75E$, where E represents monthly earnings.

a. Hermione has just been offered a part-time job working 5 hours a day, 5 days a week, earning an hourly wage of $11. Sketch a budget constraint for Hermione given the social assistance scheme in place and the wage rate available for part time work. How much income would she earn if she accepted the job? Would Hermione still be on social assistance if she took the job?

b. Illustrate these two possibilities:

(i) Hermione is better off (i.e., is on a higher indifference curve) when she takes the job, and

(ii) Hermione is better off not taking the job and remaining on social assistance.

c. Suppose that the province decides to exempt the first $400 in earned income so that now the basic welfare entitlement is reduced by $0.75 for every dollar of earned income in excess of $400. Draw a new diagram to illustrate how this exemption affects Hermione's budget constraint. Suppose that before the policy change Hermoine decided not to take the job. Might Hermione have made a different decision in regard to accepting the part-time job if the new policy had been in place? Explain.

d. Suppose that Hermione is actually a single parent with one child under the age of six. Discuss how the requirement of daycare can influence Hermione's decision to take the part-time job, given (i) the original welfare policy and (ii) the reformed welfare policy is in place? What other policy changes could help address the problems that Hermione faces?

6. There is a growing concern with the incidence of poverty among unattached, non-elderly individuals. Feng, Dubey, and Brooks (2007) find that being a high school leaver is an important risk factor for being in low income for this group. Provincial welfare and workfare programs often require recipients to participate in some job/employment related activities. Discuss the strengths and weaknesses of this approach compared with an approach that stressed investments in human capital and education.

CHAPTER 13

Education

The enormous investment in education over the years has paid dividends. . . . But our past commitment to education cannot guarantee our nation's continuing economic success.

—Government of Canada (1994: 57–58)

There are few areas of public finance—and certainly few within the sphere of "social expenditures"—which seem more ripe for application of the benefit principle than postsecondary education.

—Richard M. Bird (1976: 225)

AFTER READING THIS CHAPTER, THE STUDENT SHOULD BE ABLE TO:

LO1 Explain how the existence of positive externalities can provide an efficiency rationale for government involvement in education.

LO2 Describe three different information problems related to education and explain how these problems can justify government involvement in education.

LO3 Outline why the public goods and market power arguments for government intervention do not generally apply to education.

LO4 Describe how (i) distributional concerns and (ii) a belief in commodity equalitarianism can motivate government involvement in education.

LO5 Summarize the roles of local, provincial, and federal governments in the control and funding of education at the elementary and secondary as well as post-secondary levels.

LO6 Summarize the issues involved in measuring the effects of government spending on educational outcomes.

LO7 Briefly describe the private and social rates of return to education and discuss why their estimates might vary by level of education, sex, and field of study.

LO8 Outline how a voucher system works to increase competition between public schools.

Education is one of the most important public sector expenditure items, accounting for 16.1 percent of all government spending in Canada and 6.3 percent of the country's GDP in 2009 (see Table 13.1). At the elementary and secondary education level, over 93 percent of education spending is public spending, reflecting the fact that about 95 percent of all students at this level participate in the public system.[1] At the post-secondary level, about two-thirds of total spending is public; private expenditures, including tuition fees, represent

---

[1] Data on elementary/secondary education expenditures are for 2012 and are taken from CANSIM Table 478-0014. Data on the percentage of students enrolled in the public elementary/secondary system is for 2010/2011 and is based on data from Table 1.1 of Statistics Canada (2013).

TABLE 13.1

Public Expenditures on Education as a Share of Total Public Expenditure and GDP, Selected Years

Year	Government Expenditures	GDP
1950	11.0	2.1
1970	22.9	7.7
1990	14.0	6.2
2000	15.1	5.6
2009	16.1	6.3

Sources: Adapted from Canadian Economic Observer. *Historical Statistical Supplement 1995/96,* 11-210 (Ottawa: July 1996); Canadian Economic Observer. *Historical Statistical Supplement, 2009/10,* 11-210 (Ottawa: August 2010); and "Historical Statistics of Canada," 1983, Catalogue 11-516, Released July 29, 1999, series W47-60; and Statistics Canada's CANSIM II database, Series V156311, V156287, and V646925.

32.4 percent of spending at this level.[2] At first glance, education seems to be a *private* good, improving students' welfare by enhancing their abilities and contributing to higher incomes. Why then is the government so extensively involved in education, rather than leaving its provision to the market?

This chapter begins by considering the various efficiency and equity rationales that might justify government's involvement in education. As we shall see, all three levels of government in Canada are involved in some way in education, even though education, like health and social assistance, is a provincial responsibility. The chapter also examines some funding and control challenges that arise when different levels of government are involved in education. Following this, we explore some of the issues that dominate public debate over education, including the impact of education spending on education outcomes, the quality of education, and the relationship between education and earnings. In the final section, we explore some options for addressing existing and future challenges in public education in Canada.

JUSTIFYING GOVERNMENT INTERVENTION IN EDUCATION

Government might intervene in markets for efficiency reasons, distributional considerations, or both. As we have seen in earlier chapters, markets sometimes fail to provide goods efficiently when those goods are public goods, when they give rise to externalities, when they are provided by a monopoly, or when there is asymmetric information. Let's examine how these efficiency arguments might apply to education. Then we'll turn to distributional considerations.

Is Education a Public Good?

Recall that a public good is non-rival and nonexcludable. Education doesn't fit either of these criteria. It is rival in consumption, at least to some extent, because as the number of students in the classroom increases past some point, each student receives less individualized attention, the classroom becomes congested, and additional strains on education resources arise. Unlike a non-rival good, adding one more "consumer" of education imposes a cost on other consumers. Education is excludable because one can easily prevent a student from obtaining the services provided by a school. Thus, education is primarily a private good, improving students' welfare by enhancing their ability to earn a living.[3]

Does Education Generate Positive Externalities?

That primary, secondary, and post-secondary education increase productivity may be true, but *as long as individuals' earnings reflect their higher productivity, there is no externality*. It might be the case, however, that a

---

[2] See Table B.2.6, Statistics Canada and Council of Education Ministers. *Education Indicators in Canada: Report of the Pan-Canadian Education Indicators Program.* (No 81-582-XIE). http://www.statcan.gc.ca/pub/81-582-x/2015002/sectionb-eng.htm#b2

[3] One possible exception to this is post-secondary education spending on research, which we discuss later in the chapter.

FIGURE 13.1

EXTERNALITIES AND THE DEMAND FOR EDUCATION

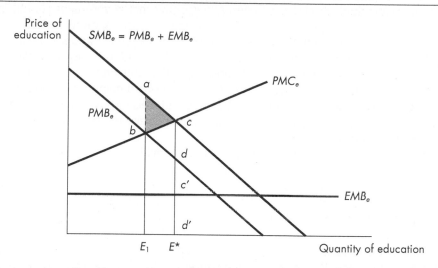

person's education generates benefits to others in society. One possible externality is that education contributes to a literate and well-informed populace, supporting a smoothly functioning modern democracy and contributing to political stability. For example, Glaeser, Ponzetto, and Shleifer (2006) find a positive correlation between the levels of education and democratic government across countries. Acemoglu et al. (2005) also find evidence of a positive correlation but argue that it could be misleading to ascribe a causal relationship because countries vary so much in terms of their cultures, histories, and social institutions. They focus instead on how changes in years of education within a country change an index of democracy. They find that once you look within countries, the positive correlation between education and democracy disappears. These studies remind us that many seemingly obvious propositions can be very difficult to verify empirically.

Another argument is that public schools are a powerful socialization force in a society with large numbers of recent immigrants and a diverse ethnic mix. Education may also facilitate the adoption of new technologies and contribute to lower crime rates through higher levels of employment and income. Each of these proposed rationales points to externalities associated with education, and an argument that, if left to private decisions alone, too little education is produced and consumed.[4]

Figure 13.1 illustrates the private market for education. PMB_e is the private marginal benefit from education, and PMC_e is the private marginal cost of education. The amount of education provided in a year will be E_1, assuming no government involvement. EMB_e is the external marginal benefit from education that is due to externalities associated with education. SMB_e reflects the social marginal benefit from education—the sum of the private benefit (PMB_e) and the marginal externality (EMB_e). EMB_e may either increase or decrease as education expenditures increase. It is assumed to remain constant in Figure 13.1. In this example, SMC_e is equal to PMC_e. The efficient amount of education equals E^*, the level of education that equates SMC_e with SMB_e. The private market outcome, E_1, results in too little education. One way to achieve E^* is for the government to provide a subsidy equal to the external marginal benefit at E^*, in this case cd (or $c'd'$) in Figure 13.1. The additional cost of moving from E_1 to E^* is equal to the area E_1E^*cb, while the additional benefit equals E_1E^*ca, with a net gain in welfare of abc.

In practice, it is difficult to determine the size of the subsidy required to achieve efficiency.[5] In any case, government involvement is justified only if the benefits outweigh the costs, where the costs include

---

[4] For a brief review of these arguments, see Poterba (1994) and Hanushek, Leung, and Yilmaz (2003).

[5] Recent empirical studies provide some evidence on the size and significance of these externalities. Milligan, Moretti, and Oreopoulos (2004) find a sizeable effect of education on civic behaviour, as measured by increases in the probability that the individual will vote. They use their results to calculate that the voter turnout rate in the 2000 US national election would have been 10.4 to 12.3 percentage points lower if the high school completion rate remained fixed at the 1964 rate instead of increasing by 36.1 percentage points as it did between 1964 and 2000. Dee (2004) also finds evidence of a large and significant effect of education on various measures of the level and quality of civic engagement.

the excess burdens associated with taxes required for financing the subsidies, should the public sector become involved.

It is likely that the external benefits to education vary by education level. For example, the socialization benefits to education may exhibit diminishing returns, suggesting that government should intervene less in higher education than in earlier levels. In Canada, public involvement is more limited for post-secondary education, where students pay substantial tuition, as compared to elementary and secondary education which are free. At the same time, it is interesting to note that preschool education is largely left to the private sector and to families.[6] Public subsidies to education for those aged five and under occur through tax credits for childcare, but the level of public involvement is modest compared with elementary and secondary education. We lack clear measures of externalities that explain the differing levels of public involvement in the early and later years. It may be the case that patterns of public involvement have more to do with political and historical factors than with externalities.

Note that the quantity of education in Figure 13.1 may be provided by the private sector, and subsidized by a grant to the producer or with a voucher for students to be used for education. In reality, education funding goes far beyond subsidization; public elementary and secondary education are both free (taxpayer financed) and compulsory. Furthermore, we stressed in Chapter 4 the distinction between government provision (i.e., financing) of a good and government production of that good. The externality argument doesn't fully explain why governments not only fund this level of education but produce it as well.

One theory is that public education produces human capital while simultaneously inculcating belief in the existing political system (see, for example, Friedman et al., 2011). Because individuals care about their human capital but receive no private gains from belief in the political system, private schools in competition for students would devote all their resources to producing human capital. According to this view, the development of a common commitment to established democratic processes is more easily carried out in a system of public schools protected from competition. Indoctrination that has occurred through public schools in totalitarian states must not be lost sight of in considering whether this is a positive reason for government involvement.

On-the-job training is also an area where externalities are cited as reason for public sector involvement. Here, it is a case of "third-party effects"—a private company financing the training realizes only part of the benefits. Where portable skills are provided, employees may either "walk" or be "poached" by competitors. Employers, unable to internalize all of the benefit, will underinvest in training. The inability to internalize benefits from on-the-job training has led to the suggestion that public policies should encourage private companies to spend more on training. Figure 13.1 can be used to represent this situation, where $c'd'$ is the subsidy required to get the right amount of private spending. Such a subsidy can be delivered through the tax system or through direct expenditures.

Is There a Market Power Problem?

Where transportation costs are high, local schools have an element of monopoly power that could potentially lead to market failure. This argument is, however, not very persuasive, except perhaps in rural areas. In small communities or rural settings, economies of scale may create a natural monopoly, and public control may be required to obtain schooling of an acceptable quality at a reasonable price. In a highly urbanized country such as Canada, most schooling is provided in settings where the potential for competition exists. Thus, fear of monopoly power does not provide a strong argument for public provision of education in many Canadian settings.

Is There an Asymmetric Information Problem?

Here we consider three information-related rationales that might justify government involvement in education: insufficient information for informed decisions, asymmetric information and imperfections in the market for loans, and asymmetric information about innate ability.

Insufficient information for informed decisions. Education, if based entirely on decisions by parents, will depend on information available to parents and on parental values. Parents who are unaware of high private returns to education may choose to spend little on education, limiting future opportunities available

---

[6] This is less so in Quebec, where public expenditures per child are higher than elsewhere through significant subsidizing of childcare activity. Ontario has also recently introduced public funding for universal full-day kindergarten.

to their children. Decisions become more complex when there is a diversity of schooling opportunities. Only parents who possess the interest, ability, and capacity to assimilate the required information will benefit from increased choice. Government involvement, greater uniformity in schools, and compulsory schooling to a certain age protect students (to some extent) against uninformed, short-sighted, or self-serving decisions by parents.[7]

Imperfect capital markets. If students are unable to finance their education from cash flows or savings, they may require a loan. However, students are unable to borrow against the prospect of future earnings since it is impossible to use these future earnings as collateral against the loan. Should the student default on the loan, the lender is unable to claim their human capital as collateral. Information asymmetry also makes it difficult for lenders to determine who the good risks are. These problems create imperfections in the capital market (limits may be imposed on borrowing, lending rates may rise). Depending on the severity of the problem, the market for student loans may even fail to materialize. This may lead some individuals to underinvest in education even though the benefits of additional education exceed the costs.

As an argument for public involvement, the imperfect capital market argument has some merit. One possible remedy for this market failure is for government loan programs to ensure that loans are available to students, or to their parents, at the going rate of interest. This approach may be more effective at the post-secondary level as compared to the elementary and secondary level. In the case of elementary and secondary students, parents would have to assume substantial debt with no assurance that the children—those who realize the higher income resulting from education—will assist in the repayment. As well, those who benefit from education and need a loan to finance it may not have the legal authority to take out the loan, and underspending may still occur. To overcome this problem, elementary and secondary education could be subsidized by the government or publicly provided. In the case of post-secondary students, where it is likely that the benefiting student has the authority to assume the obligation of repayment, government loan programs are a viable option.

Note that the government may run its own loan program or work through private lending institutions. The imperfect capital market problem does not by itself provide an efficiency basis for providing loans at below market interest rates. Below market interest rates could be motivated by the presence of positive education externalities (and the efficiency rationale for subsidizing education). Without the presence of such externalities, below market interest rates (or modified repayment schedules) may encourage students and society to invest unwisely in some forms of education. In this case, such subsidies would be inefficient.[8]

Education as a signal. The acquisition of detailed information about a potential employee's abilities is often costly, and educational qualifications may provide a useful signal to potential employers. Innate ability is required to move through the educational system, with the result that the correlation between the level of formal education and innate ability is likely to be relatively strong. Consequently, some companies consider only applicants who possess certain academic qualifications for a job, because those who have the qualifications have succeeded in highly competitive environments and have a higher innate ability than those who do not.

To see the signalling role of education, consider the following simple model.[9] There are two types of individuals—a high productivity type (H) and a low productivity type (L). Employers are willing to pay each type a wage equal to their respective marginal products—w_H for the high type and w_L for the low type. Employers are unable to distinguish a worker's type but can observe an individual's level of education. Since the acquisition of education is less costly to the high productivity type (because of higher innate ability), high productivity types can signal their type by investing in education.

---

[7] Oreopoulos (2007) finds evidence that one extra year of compulsory schooling has a significant and positive effect on lifetime wealth. Given these lifetime gains, he argues that the education-as-investment model cannot fully explain the decision of some high school students to drop out. One possible explanation is that students are myopic and do not have sufficient information to make an efficient decision on how much education to invest in. Compulsory education until some minimum age can help address this issue.

[8] Under the Canada Student Loans program, students pay the market rate of interest but do not make any payments (and no interest accumulates) for the first six months following graduation. This holiday from payments and interest represents a significant subsidy.

[9] This is Spence's (1973) model of education as a signal, as summarized in Löfgren, Persson, and Weibull (2002).

FIGURE 13.2

INDIFFERENCE CURVES FOR LOW AND HIGH PRODUCTIVITY WORKERS

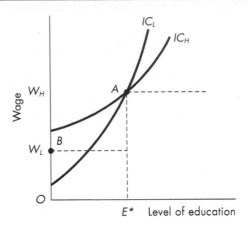

We can illustrate the basic problem using Figure 13.2. Education (E) is measured as a continuous variable on the horizontal axis and the wage rate is measured on the vertical axis. To focus on the problem of asymmetric information, education is assumed to have no effect on productivity. Thus, the wages that employers are willing to pay the high and low types (w_H and w_L) are fixed. Thus, in a world with perfect information, no one would invest in education. With asymmetric information, suppose employers are willing to pay individuals w_H if they have a level of education equal to at least E^*, and w_L if they do not. Note that since education confers no productivity benefits and is costly to obtain, workers make a choice to invest nothing in education ($E = 0$) or choose E^*. There is no benefit to investing above E^* since the wage will not increase. Nor is there any benefit to education levels between 0 and E^* since the low wage is fixed and education is costly. Does this strategy ensure that low productivity types get paid the low wage and only the high productivity types invest in education and get paid the higher wage?

The dotted lines in Figure 13.2 illustrate the wage schedule that employers will pay based on education level. To determine what level of education is chosen by each type, let's consider preferences over wages and education for the two types. Note that for both types utility is increasing as we move in the northwest direction (i.e., less education and higher wages) since education involves a cost and has no consumption or productivity-enhancing value. Consider point A. The indifference curve for the high type, IC_H, running through this point is flatter than the low type's indifference curve (IC_L) at point A. Why? The indifference curve illustrates the combinations of wages and education that the high type finds equally satisfying. If either type has an education level one unit above E^*, they both require a higher wage to be equally satisfied. However, the low type requires a bigger increase in the wage since they face higher costs of obtaining that extra unit of education.

How does each type rank the wage–education combination at B relative to that at A? Notice that for the high type, a move from A to B would lower their utility because B lies below the indifference curve IC_H. For the low productivity type, combination B lies above IC_L, indicating that the loss in utility from the lower wage they receive is more than compensated for by the cost savings that result from not having to invest in education. So, in this simple model, and given the employers' strategy, high productivity workers will invest in education, choosing E^*, and receive wage w_H. Low productivity workers do not invest in education and receive w_L. Thus, each worker receives their true marginal product.

This simple model raises an interesting problem. Students pursue further education not because it will enhance their performance in a certain job, but because it gives them access to the job. The higher salary in this case is due to innate ability. If those with high innate ability are highly productive, whether or not they have received an education, there will be a tendency to overinvest in education. Education as a signal suggests that the market may devote too many resources to education when signalling does not enhance productivity. Of course, the model's assumption that education does not enhance productivity is extreme. Part of the higher income associated with more education may be due to enhanced productivity and part may be due to the fact that education is a screening device that identifies individuals with high innate ability for prospective employers. Signals may have social value if they enhance society's productivity by, for example, preventing "round pegs from being put in square holes."[10]

Distributional Considerations

Welfare economics suggests that equity must also be considered, and, here too, arguments can be made for government involvement in education. We first consider the equity argument for intervening at the elementary and secondary school level and then examine the distributional considerations at the post-secondary level.

Elementary and secondary education. Because access to education is an important source of social mobility, it is an important good to be made available to all citizens. Differences in parental resources would lead to differences in education if education were left to the private sector. This would lead to unequal job and income opportunities over a lifetime. Fairness requires that some goods, like education, be available to everyone. Recall from Chapter 6 the notion of **commodity egalitarianism**. Because of the value placed on equal opportunity, and society's view of the role of education, citizens value education beyond any monetary return it yields to them as individuals.

The government could support education in a number of ways. It could transfer funds directly to parents with children, allowing them to choose how much to spend on education. It could provide vouchers or funds to be used for no other purpose than to pay for a child's education; parents may be allowed to choose a public or private school. Or the government could fund only public schools and require students to attend up to a certain age. Mandating public education or providing vouchers reflect a wish to guarantee that public funds are used to the benefit of children, that redistribution occurs from the old to the young, and that a particular target population benefits. They ensure that all students have reasonably uniform opportunities that are not dependent on family resources and, in doing so, promote *equality of opportunity*.

Post-secondary education. Public support for post-secondary education in Canada takes the form of subsidized tuition fees and government intervention in the market for student loans. Subsidies for university students represent a transfer from taxpayers as a whole to university students. Proponents of these subsidies argue that if they were removed fewer people would pursue post-secondary education.[11] This may be true, because removing the subsidies would increase private costs for individuals. But this by itself does not justify subsidizing post-secondary education and redistributing income from taxpayers to university students. If there were subsidies for young people who wanted to open auto repair shops and these were cut, then the number of auto repair shops would also decline. Why should a potential car mechanic be treated differently from a potential classicist or physician?

Views on the appropriateness of such a transfer are likely to be affected by whether one looks at *lifetime* income or annual income. Students, to the extent that they have withdrawn from the labour force, are likely to have temporarily low incomes. On this basis the transfer may seem appropriate. However, university students in Canada continue to be disproportionately from families with above-average incomes, and university graduates have higher lifetime incomes. Thus, when one looks at the family incomes of students, or expected lifetime incomes, the argument for transfers through heavily subsidized tuition fees or subsidized loans is much weakened.

Some argue that this reasoning ignores imperfections in the private market for loans. As we discussed above, it is difficult to provide collateral for loans used to finance investments in human capital—investments that people make in themselves to increase their productivity. The resulting capital market imperfections can also give rise to equity concerns. Since families with low income and students without family support may find it

---

[10] While there is a sizeable literature on education and signalling, it is empirically challenging to separately identify the effects of signalling from the investment aspects of education. Some studies try to overcome this by looking at differences between groups where signalling or screening is less likely. See for example Heywood and Wei (2004), and Ferrer and Riddell (2008).

[11] The Canadian evidence suggests that higher tuition fees have a small, negative effect on the decision to attend university. Neill (2009) finds that a $1,000 increase in tuition leads to a reduction in demand for university enrolment of between 2.5 and 5 percentage points. Johnson (2008), however, finds that for those already enrolled in university, higher tuition fees have no impact on the decision to continue or quit.

especially difficult to obtain loans from the private sector, they may underinvest in education. Government-supplied loans may allow students from lower income families (who are qualified for, and who would have otherwise gone to, university but could not obtain a loan to do so) to go to university. These loans may help to reduce income inequality. There is, however, some evidence to suggest that financial constraints do not explain much of the gap in post-secondary attendance rates at the lower end of the income distribution.[12]

THE CONTROL AND FUNDING OF EDUCATION IN CANADA

There are both efficiency and equity rationales that help to justify government involvement in education. But what level of government should intervene? Here, we discuss some issues relating to the control and funding of education.

We begin by looking at some summary data on education spending in Canada. Since education is primarily a provincial responsibility, data are usually presented at the provincial level. However, as we shall see, all three levels of government are involved to some extent in education, so education data are sometimes presented by level of government. And since the motivations for government involvement may depend on the level of education being considered, education statistics are sometimes presented separately for (i) elementary and secondary education and (ii) post-secondary education.

Elementary and Secondary Education

Figure 13.3 shows public spending per student at the elementary and secondary level by province. Spending at this level varies quite significantly across provinces. In Alberta, per student spending was 108 percent of the all-province average in 2010–11. B.C. had the lowest per student spending relative to the average, about 91.8 percent. Provincial differences in spending may reflect differences in the cost of living, fiscal capacities, or political preferences.

FIGURE 13.3

PUBLIC EXPENDITURES PER ELEMENTARY/SECONDARY STUDENT, 2010–11

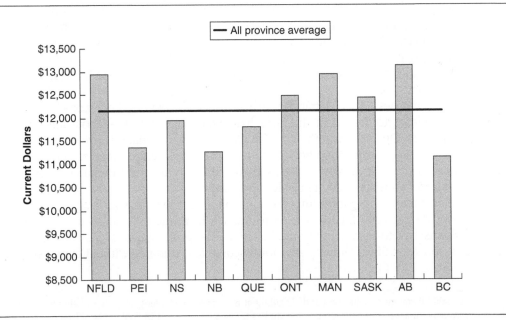

Note: Public expenditures include both operating and capital expenditures. The territories are not included in the provincial average.

Source: Data was taken from Statistics Canada (2013).

---

[12] See Frenette (2008).

At this level of education, the federal government plays only a minor role, with a spending share of about 6 percent.[13] The main players are provincial governments and local governments (and local school boards). Historically, local school boards have overseen the management of the local elementary and secondary system. They also had a significant role in setting local property taxes for education purposes and in deciding how those funds were spent. In recent decades, however, there has been a trend to centralize authority and responsibility for elementary and secondary school funding with the provincial government. Today, in provinces where local property taxes for education still exist, local school boards have a significantly diminished (or nonexistent) role in setting the rates or spending the local funds raised from these taxes (Saskatchewan and Ontario, for instance).[14] In other provinces, there are provincial (but not local) property tax levies specific to education (Alberta, for instance) and, in some cases, there is no local or provincial education property tax (Newfoundland and New Brunswick). The result has been a decline in the share of education funding coming from local property taxes and a corresponding increase in the share of funding from provincial grants to local school boards.[15]

Figure 13.4 shows the share of local school board revenues derived from provincial, local, and other sources in 2012. The provincial government in New Brunswick, for example, has assumed all the responsibilities for education—this is reflected in Figure 13.4 by the near 100 percent share of funds coming from provincial sources. In Alberta, 29 percent of funds come from local sources as compared to 42 percent in 1989.[16]

There are other differences among the provinces. In some provinces—Quebec, Ontario, Saskatchewan, and Alberta—local and provincial taxes support public *and* separate (religiously affiliated) school systems, while in

FIGURE 13.4

SCHOOL BOARD REVENUES BY SOURCE OF FUNDS, 2012

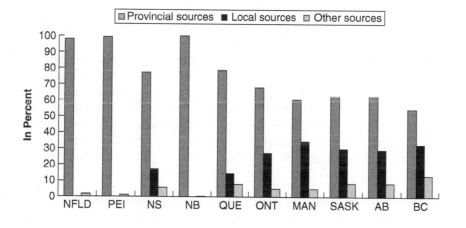

Note: "Other" includes the federal government, student and other school fees, and other private sector sources.

Source: Data are from CANSIM II Table 4780010 (accessed September 16, 2015).

[13] The federal government has responsibility for elementary and secondary education of children of armed forces personnel, for inmates of federal institutions, and for Aboriginals and Inuit.

[14] Manitoba is the exception. For a summary of provincial education systems and education financing, see Garcea and Munroe (2014), Auld and Kitchen (2006), and Treff and Ort (2012). Details about the Manitoba system are available at http://www.edu.gov.mb.ca/k12/finance/schfund/.

[15] There are some exceptions. For example, in B.C. and Alberta, local school boards may levy a local school property tax to fund new programs and capital expenditures if approved by a local referendum or plebiscite. In Alberta, separate school boards can opt out of the provincial property tax and set their rates locally. However, the province adjusts its grants to these local boards to ensure that all school boards have the same funding per student.

[16] Garcea and Munroe (2014).

others, such as Nova Scotia and Prince Edward Island, public funds are used *only* for public schools. School boards are elected in most provinces. No provincial support is provided to *private* elementary and secondary schools in Newfoundland, the Maritime provinces, or Ontario, while Manitoba provides some support for private secondary but not private elementary schools. In contrast, Quebec, Saskatchewan, Alberta, and British Columbia partially fund private schools that meet government standards.

Does the allocation of education funding and control responsibilities in the provinces make economic sense? How do we explain the trend toward greater centralization of funding and control at the provincial level?

Advantages of local control. One argument in favour of the decentralized provision of a good is that it can be tailored to local tastes (see Chapter 8). Because many parents hold strong views about the education of their children and these views differ across communities, this is an important argument for a leading role played by local governments and school boards in providing education at the elementary and secondary level.

In this framework, local governments raise money for education primarily through local property taxation. Individuals living within a school district are the ones who benefit most from spending on local schools. To the extent that the benefits are localized, as with other goods and services, it is reasonable to levy taxes and fees on those who benefit. Efficient allocation of resources occurs where the marginal benefit equals the marginal cost. Some of those benefiting from the education system may not have children—local citizens benefit from well-educated neighbours, and a homeowner without children may see an increase in house value as the quality of nearby schools improves (Fischel, 1998).

Accountability is likely to be enhanced when there exists a strong link between those who pay and those who benefit; in other words, when decisions regarding tax-financed education are made by those expected to benefit. This link is strongest for the consumption of private goods, but local taxes paid for local benefits can be a close approximation. A link between local property taxes and education costs may lead to greater scrutiny of increasing costs, and increased accountability.

Disadvantages of local control. Local control and funding for education may give rise to potential problems. Huge variations in the property tax base across municipalities can result in large differences in funding for local school districts. This may be viewed as inequitable and may conflict with a desire to use education as a means of improving the distribution of income. There is also the possibility that tax competition between local jurisdictions may lead to underspending on education and other services relative to the efficient level. Lower taxes, which are needed to attract new businesses and jobs, bring immediate political payoffs but result in lower spending on education, which does not reflect returns to individuals and society over the longer run. As well, the benefits of education are not all private. To the extent that the benefits of education spill over local boundaries, the local government, failing to take into account these spillovers or externalities, will underprovide education. These considerations suggest a role for provincial governments.

The role of education grants from the province to local school boards. If local taxes on property or other local tax bases were heavily relied on for school finance, disparities in income and property wealth across school districts would likely lead to disparate school quality. Provincial governments have responded to this problem by assuming a greater role in funding education (from general tax revenue, from property tax revenues for school purposes, or a combination of both). Local school boards receive grants from the province to achieve (more or less) equal funding per student.[17] This is consistent with commodity egalitarianism and with externalities associated with education. Note that not all provinces make grants to *private* schools, although these schools are likely to have some of the same positive externalities that exist for public schools.

[17] For example, Ontario uses a series of grants. The Ontario Pupil Foundation Grant accounts for over 50 percent of all grants made to local school boards. It funds various expenditures, including teachers' salaries, educational assistants, guidance counsellors, textbooks, classroom supplies, and classroom computers. The grant is calculated on a per-pupil basis. Grants are sometimes adjusted or supplemented, as in British Columbia and Manitoba, to take into account specific cost factors such as teachers' salaries, student composition, and a dispersed student population. In Manitoba, where local school boards retain some authority over setting and spending local education property taxes, some grants are adjusted to reflect varying abilities to fund expenditures from the local tax base.

Some economists (e.g., Bird and Slack, 1983) see complete provincial takeover as "an eminently logical extension of the apparent trend of educational policy in Canada since the Second World War" (p. 95). This view is supported by those who believe that public education of a well-defined quality should be available to all, that **wealth neutrality** should exist in the provision of education, and that benefits from local control and variation are likely to be modest. Wealth neutrality is a situation where ability to pay, defined by factors such as the property tax base or income levels, has no effect on the quality of education in local jurisdictions. So long as local governments are free to raise local taxes to enhance their public education system, wealth neutrality cannot exist. All provinces have adopted policies that contribute to wealth neutrality (within the province) and have a major impact on local school expenditures.

The separation (in part or in full) of funding from control may come with problems as well. It may be difficult to maintain meaningful local control of the schools if the financing comes from a higher level of government—he who pays the piper, calls the tune. Separation may also have implications for accountability at both the local and provincial government levels. There is some evidence suggesting that when provincial standardization occurs across local jurisdictions, higher levels of spending and higher costs may result.[18] Rather than moving high spending areas down to the average, the tendency is to move the average up. Likewise, standardization of cost factors, such as teacher salaries, may also raise averages.

Post-Secondary Education

At the post-secondary level, per student spending is higher and more variable across provinces, as compared to spending at the elementary and secondary level. Figure 13.5 shows per student spending by publicly funded universities and colleges, regardless of the source of funds (government grants, tuition fees, donations, etc.). Newfoundland had the highest spending per student, about 135 percent of the all-province average, while per student spending was lowest in Quebec at about 67 percent of the average.

The provincial government has the most prominent role in post-secondary education funding and control; local governments are not involved. Although post-secondary education is a provincial responsibility, the federal government provides financial support for post-secondary education through three distinct

FIGURE 13.5

POST-SECONDARY EXPENDITURES PER STUDENT, 2012

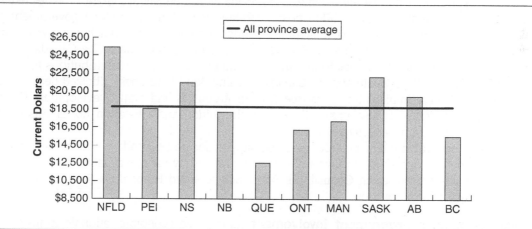

Note: Includes spending by publicly funded universities and colleges. The territories are not included in the all-province average.

Source: Data was taken from CANSIM II, Tables 477-0059 and 477-0019 (accessed September 16, 2015).

---

[18] Easton (1988: 55–56). A recent U.S. study adds support to this argument. Hoxby (1995, no page numbers) found that "increases in states' shares of school funding have been associated with significant increases in per-pupil schooling costs," and that "a higher state share of school funding not only does not appear to improve educational attainment, but worsens it by a small but statistically significant amount."

TABLE 13.2

Federal Support for Post-Secondary Education, 2013 (in $ millions)	
Support for Research[a]	
–Canadian Institutes of Health Research (CIHR)	$ 836
–Natural Science and Engineering Research Council (NSERC)	775
–Social Science and Humanities Research Council (SSHRC)	252
Canada Student Loan Program[b] (2012–13)	2,576
Canadian Foundation for Innovation[a]	404
Other[a]	757
TOTAL[c]	*$5,600*

[a] Data from CANSIM II, Table 477-0058 (accessed September 16, 2015).
[b] Includes loans to both full-time and part-time students. See Table 1.2 in Employment and Social Development Canada (2014). *Canadian Student Loans Program Statistical Review, 2012-13.* Available at http://www12.hrsdc.gc.ca.
[c] The total does not take into account indirect support for post-secondary education from the federal government that comes from the Canada Social Transfers to provinces or federal measures that promote savings for educational purposes, like the Canada Education Savings Plan.

channels–grants to provinces, financial assistance to students, and research funding. Table 13.2 provides partial detail on federal programs that provide support for post-secondary education.

Federal grants to provinces for post-secondary education have a long history, beginning in as early as 1885 when a land grant established the University of Manitoba. The form of grants for post-secondary education purposes has changed over time–ranging from per student grants to provinces (based initially on the number of enrolled veterans and then on the population of the provinces) to 50 percent cost-sharing grants. Currently, provincial spending on post-secondary education and other social programs is supported by the Canada Social Transfer.

The federal government offers financial assistance for students pursuing post-secondary education through a variety of programs. Under the Canada Student Loans program (which is jointly administered with the provinces), the federal government offers guaranteed loans to eligible students, and in some cases provides assistance with loan repayments.[19] The Canada Student Grant program is aimed at students from lower income families. Under this program, eligible recipients can receive a grant of $100 to $250 per month of study in 2014, depending on the level of family income. The Canada Education Savings Grant provides federal support to assist and encourage saving for a child's post-secondary education. The federal government provides a closed-ended matching grant (with a matching rate dependent on net family income) with a yearly and lifetime maximum. The funds must be paid into a Registered Education Savings Plan. The Canada Learning Bond provides additional financial incentives to low income families to encourage contributions to an RESP. Both the Canada Education Savings Grant and the Canada Learning Bond have been criticized because of their low take-up rates and high administration costs (see Human Resources and Skills Development Canada, 2009). Indirect financial assistance is also provided through the tuition and education tax credits in the federal personal income tax system (see Chapter 17).

Finally, the federal government provides research support for post-secondary education through research grants and scholarships that support university students, awarded by various agencies including the National Sciences and Engineering Research Council, the Social Sciences and Humanities Research Council, and the Canadian Foundation for Innovation.

Rationale for federal government involvement. Is there an economic rationale to justify the federal government's involvement in post-secondary education?

Strong post-secondary systems in the Atlantic provinces and in Saskatchewan have for years exported their graduates to rapidly growing parts of the country such as Toronto, Vancouver, and Calgary. During industrial booms, education has facilitated successful moves to Ontario; with the resource boom of the 1970s, and again

---

[19] See Canadian Council on Learning (2010) for a recent overview of the Canada Student Loans program, with a particular focus on issues relating to the repayment of these loans.

more recently, talented professionals and tradespeople moved to Alberta. Provinces do not capture part of the return to higher education—future income streams and taxes that flow from the education—and underspending on post-secondary education may occur if left to the provinces alone.[20] Ease of transferability among post-secondary institutions also contributes to labour force flexibility. This is important when part-time studies are common, extend over a lengthy period, and may be interrupted by job changes. High levels of education and national standards facilitate mobility and contribute to social and economic development, and to a sense of nationhood. Thus, since benefits of higher education extend beyond provincial borders, important externalities accompany provincial spending. The federal government can play a role in helping to address these externalities.

The federal government's support of post-secondary education can also be justified based on the public good aspect of knowledge generated from research. The benefits of this public good certainly spill over provincial borders and are more likely to be national in scope. Sole reliance on provincial provision then would result in too little of this good being provided. This provides an additional rationale for federal government involvement.

WHAT DOES GOVERNMENT INTERVENTION IN EDUCATION ACCOMPLISH?

Government involvement in education finance and, in the case of elementary and secondary education, in the production of education, is extensive and generates a great deal of public debate. We consider three questions that are crucial to informing this debate. First, we consider the question of whether education spending is high enough and, relatedly, the question of whether more spending improves educational outcomes. The second question focuses on how to measure the quality of education and educational outcomes. And, finally, the third question asks how spending on education affects earnings.

More Spending, Better Performance?

Suppose we accept the arguments in favour of government-produced (and tax-financed) education at the elementary and secondary level. An important question is whether higher expenditures on education actually lead to better education. This question is inherently difficult to answer because it is not exactly clear what better education is. Education has many goals, including improving students' cognitive skills, teaching them responsibility and how to get along with others, and improving the quality of their lives, both economically and socially. It is hard to quantify these things, let alone summarize them all in a single measure. Most studies focus on a narrow set of outcomes that at least have the virtue of being measureable. These include test scores, attendance records, drop-out rates, continuation rates, and earnings.

Hanushek (2002) surveyed 376 statistical estimates of the relationship between input usage and various measures of educational attainment taken from 89 different publications. The inputs considered are the teacher/pupil ratio, teacher education, teacher experience, teacher salary, and expenditures per pupil. He reached the startling conclusion that the data support almost no correspondence between student expenditure and student performance.

What are we to make of these results? We do not conclude schooling is unimportant; clearly, there are effective and ineffective schools. However, the research indicates that we cannot predict which schools will be effective simply by looking at data on their purchased inputs. The same is true of teachers; data on degrees held or years of teaching experience do not usefully discriminate between effective and ineffective teachers. A recent study for Ontario supports the view that hard-to-measure inputs, like leadership and teamwork, may play an important role in education outcomes. Using Ontario's elementary school test scores, Johnson (2005)

---

[20] Dickson, Milne, and Murrell (1996: 322) estimate the internal rate of return to the New Brunswick government for its 1990 expenditures on universities at 2.6 percent for males and 1.4 percent for females. This reflects that 36 percent of alumni no longer reside in the province. The province's return is in the form of higher income tax and sales tax revenues due to the higher incomes of graduates. However, the complete picture of the return on public spending must include the higher income taxes and sales taxes that flow to the federal government, the combined return to the provincial and federal governments is estimated at about 7 percent for both men and women. What are the implications of these estimates? If funding were left to the province alone, the low returns would encourage reduced provincial spending on universities. The significant returns beyond provincial borders provide reason for federal support for higher education.

conducted a study to identify good schools—those that outperform schools with similar socioeconomic characteristics. Johnson also interviewed principals, teachers, and parents associated with good performers.[21] Some of the characteristics noted were teamwork, strong extracurricular programs, and effective use of volunteers.[22]

Education Spending and the Quality of Education

Obviously, the goal of education policy is not to increase education expenditures per se, but rather it is to improve students' academic performance. Therefore, it is useful to evaluate the efficacy of various kinds of spending. For example, is it more effective to reduce the student–teacher ratio, hire teachers with greater levels of experience and education, increase teachers' salaries, or provide newer books and facilities?

A popular option is to reduce class size. Reducing class size has been a policy priority in a number of provinces. Ontario launched a smaller class size initiative in 2003, with hard caps on class size in primary grades introduced in 2012. In 2003–04, 31 percent of primary classes had 20 students or less compared to 90 percent of classes in 2013–14.[23] British Columbia has also reduced class size at the elementary level using caps. Manitoba launched a smaller class size initiative in 2011 with the goal of implementing a cap of 20 in the primary grades by 2017. In contrast, Saskatchewan and Alberta do not have hard caps in place.

Reducing class size generates costs and benefits. Additional costs arise because more teachers must be hired and more classroom space is needed. The benefits, potential improvements in educational outcomes, are more challenging to measure. One approach is to use test scores. Hoxby (2000), for example, finds no effect on test scores from smaller kindergarten classes. Angrist and Lavy (1999) find that smaller class size had a positive impact on tests scores but not for all elementary grades. Dynarski et al. (2011) use data from the Tennessee Student/Teacher Achievement Ratio experiment (known as Project STAR) to investigate the longer-run impact of class size on post-secondary educational outcomes.[24] They find that students in smaller classes tested higher than students in larger classes, but the test score effects faded out by middle school. Even though being in a smaller class did not have a long-term impact on test scores, the study finds that it did increase the probability of attending and graduating from college.

The results from the STAR Project have reinforced policy-makers' beliefs that smaller classes are a good thing. But one must be careful about assuming the results will apply in other settings. California provides an example of the dangers of ignoring this possibility. In 1996, California introduced a law effectively mandating a state-wide reduction in class size. In order to substantially increase the number of teachers, teachers with less experience and fewer credentials were hired. Remarkably, Jepson and Rivkin (2002) found that the benefits of the smaller class size were offset by the costs associated with the deterioration in teacher quality. Thus, reducing class size in California did not improve the quality of education.

This does not mean all expenditures are futile. For example, there is evidence that, while classes of 20 are not measurably better than classes of 30, classes with fewer students may be better, especially if the students are in the early grades and performing at below-average levels. Targeted class size reductions rather than province-wide reductions may generate benefits at the same time as avoiding some of the costs associated with universal reductions.

Education Spending and Earnings

Although the relationship between education spending and test scores is an interesting and important question, it tells us little about how education spending affects future earnings. Education is an investment in human capital, and as such, we expect the investment to generate a reasonable rate of return in the form of higher earnings. If higher education spending at lower levels of education does not increase test scores, we may not

---

[21] Johnson defines good performers as schools with test results (averaged over a four-year period) that were ". . . usually better than 90 percent of schools with similar socioeconomic community characteristics" (Johnson, 2005: 211).

[22] Holding schools accountable for performance as measured by standardized tests results may have unintended consequences. Jacob and Levitt (2003), for example, found evidence that school accountability led some teachers in Chicago to cheat by changing answers to their students' standardized tests. Another study, Figlio (2005), found evidence that schools assign long suspensions to low-performing students subject to disciplinary action near the test-taking period.

[23] See http://www.edu.gov.on.ca/eng/cst/provinceResults.html.

[24] Project STAR randomly assigned kindergarten students to smaller (13 to 17 students) and larger classes (22 to 25 students).

ARE TEACHERS' SALARIES TOO HIGH?

The Ontario government, faced with a $10.9 billion deficit in 2015, is looking for ways to cut costs. One of the options under consideration is to limit increases in teachers' compensation. According to a *National Post* commentator, the shockingly high salaries paid to teachers in this province is "the elephant in the classroom." The commentator argues that the province should implement hard salary caps and buy-outs to encourage the "top-heavy glut" of high earners to retire. The government is not advocating extreme measures, but proposals to limit pay increases for teachers is certainly a contributing factor in the ongoing conflict between the Ontario government and the unions.

If the government limits the growth in teachers' salaries, will the quality of education decline? Not necessarily, according to a 2015 C.D. Howe report by David Johnson on teacher salaries and student outcomes. Focusing on Canada's six largest provinces, the report finds that teachers' salaries, relative to other, similar workers in the province, are highest in Ontario and lowest in B.C. The analysis also finds no clear relationship between province-wide student assessment results and relative teacher compensation. The results suggest that in provinces like Ontario, where teachers' salaries are relatively high, there is scope to limit the growth in government expenditures by limiting the growth in teachers' salaries without negatively affecting the quality of education. Johnson suggests that relative compensation could be reduced slowly over time by agreement on a series of wage settlements where wage growth is less than the rate of inflation.

Has the government opted for this approach? Although a tentative agreement between the Ontario government and the Ontario Secondary School Teachers Federation promises 2.5 percent growth in teacher salaries over the next two years, not all teachers' unions have an agreement. We will have to wait and see what kind of wage increases are included in these agreements and what inflation looks like over the next few years to determine the answer that question.

Based on Johnson (2015), Ross (2015) and "Ontario's teachers are overpaid." *National Post*, August 25, 2015.

Complete references for this feature can be found in the References section on page 484.

be very concerned if these expenditures increase people's earnings as adults. Likewise, if higher education expenditures increase test scores but have no effect on earnings, then we might ask whether this spending is a good investment. If public sector investment in education does not yield a reasonable return (referred to as the social rate of return), spending should be reallocated to other public services or taxes should be cut in order to increase resources available for private use.

Estimating private and social returns to education expenditures is understandably complex. The private rate of return reflects income gains to the individual net of private resource costs. The social rate of return incorporates private and external benefits and costs associated with education. Measuring rates of return requires the researcher to distinguish between returns to innate abilities and those to formal education, and (usually arbitrary) values must be assigned to externalities.

A number of studies have estimated the rate of return to education in Canada.[25] Consider the decision to invest in a master's degree as compared with stopping your education once you have obtained an undergraduate degree. The private benefits of this investment capture the impact of a master's degree on after-tax earnings as compared with what your after-tax income would be with only an undergraduate degree. The higher income generates additional tax revenue for the government, which counts as a social benefit. The social benefits are measured as the difference in before-tax earnings from having a master's versus having an

---

[25] See, for example, Burbidge, Magee, and Robb (2003); Emery (2005); and Boudaret, Lemieux, and Riddell (2010). Constantatos and West (1991) offer a dated but illuminating exercise for Canada. This study attempts to estimate the private and social returns to education for Canada under different assumptions about (i) the efficiency costs associated with tax financed education and (ii) the portion of the earnings differential due to innate ability differentials.

TABLE 13.3

Private and Social Internal Rates of Return to Education by Sex, Level of Education, and Selected Undergraduate Fields of Study, 2000

Type of Degree	Private Rates of Return (%)		Social Rates of Return (%)	
	Men	Women	Men	Women
Undergraduate	11.5	14.1	8.6	9.2
Master's	2.9	5	less than 0	2.1
PhD	less than 0	3.6	less than 0	4.1
Education	9	14	8.2	11.9
Engineering	9	14.2	4.7	5.9
Commerce	9	19.3	8.2	16.4
Health Sciences	18.1	17.7	9.7	7.6

Source: Moussaly-Sergieh and Vaillancourt (2009), Table 2.

undergraduate degree. Your private costs include tuition fees, the cost of textbooks, and other related expenses as well as the after-tax earnings that you give up while in school acquiring the higher degree. Social costs include the forgone pre-tax earnings, university spending, and book and related expenses. An internal rate of return (IRR) is calculated as the discount rate that equates the stream of monetary benefits to the stream of monetary costs. Education is an attractive investment if the internal rate of return is higher than the rate of return on alternative investment opportunities.[26]

Moussaly-Sergieh and Vaillancourt (2009) use 2001 census data to estimate earnings profiles for individuals based on the highest degree obtained. These earnings profiles are then used to determine the private and social benefits to acquiring a certain level of education. Note that the social benefits associated with addressing the externality and asymmetric information problems are not included here. Table 13.3 shows a selection of the private and social rates of return, as calculated by Moussaly-Sergieh and Vaillancourt. In general, the rates of return for education are higher for women as compared to men. This is because the forgone income associated with time spent acquiring education is generally lower for women than for men. The rates of return are consistent with the principle of diminishing returns. And note that social rates of return are lower than private rates of return. The private and social rates of return also vary quite significantly by field of study.

The authors recommend that governments should take into account the differential social rates of return when making decisions on tuition fees, noting that "subsidizing a higher share of the costs of education in fields with low social IRRs may encourage over-investment in certain types of human capital" (Moussaly-Sergieh and Vaillancourt, 2009, p. 5). In Canada, the government sector subsidizes education at all levels using tax revenues. These public expenditures are included as a cost in the calculation of the social rate of return. Recall from Chapter 4 that the social cost of raising an additional dollar of tax revenue to fund education (the marginal cost of public funds) may be more than $1 because of the excess burden associated with the tax. Most studies, including the one discussed above, do not account for this in their calculations. Given the low social rates of return found by Moussaly-Sergieh and Vaillancourt (2009), especially at higher levels of education, it is difficult to argue in favour of more tax-financed expenditures on higher education.

Challenges and New Directions

Canadians value their education system highly. According to a recent poll, when asked about where the government should be spending more, 70 percent of Canadians noted education as a priority area.[27] In a poll focused on elementary and secondary education, 87 percent supported increased government funding for public elementary schools and, if more money was spent, reducing class size received the most support of the

---

[26] See Chapter 3 for a discussion of the internal rate of return. Recall that there can be problems using the internal rate of return to compare projects that are different in size or scale.

[27] See the results of recent public opinion poll research released by Environics Institute in 2011. This research is available at http://www.environicsinstitute.org/PDF-FocusCanada2010.pdf.

eight options surveyed. Two-thirds of Canadians believed student achievement was best measured by teachers; only one-third preferred standardized, province-wide tests.[28] Quality of education is an ongoing issue, as reflected in concern over class size, standardized testing, and the level of education spending. At the post-secondary level, concerns over rising tuition fees and access dominate the debate. There are also concerns about participation trends for post-secondary education.

Many argue that major structural changes are needed in public education. We discuss a few options below.

Increased competition. Economists are often quick to consider whether any market in trouble might not benefit from an infusion of competition. This is true in the debate over what to do about Canada's elementary and secondary schools, as well as its colleges and universities. The essence of competition is that consumers can choose among suppliers. In contrast, the elementary and secondary public school system has often operated on a take-it-or-leave-it basis: the only public school available to a student is the one assigned to the student's neighbourhood. Important exceptions are school systems where there is open enrolment, which permits (usually to a limited degree) students to choose the school they wish to attend. In these cases, schools may develop and advertise strengths that appeal to particular students. For example, the province of British Columbia introduced legislation in 2002–03 that gave parents the right to send children to a public school of their choice, as long as the receiving school had space.

The basic approach is to provide financial support to students rather than directly to schools. Each student could be given a tuition voucher, for example, that could be redeemed at whatever qualified school the student's family liked best. Proponents of school vouchers believe that the effects of competition would be as salutary in the education market as they are in other markets. Terrible schools that do not reform would lose enrollees and be forced to close. According to this view, parents and students' perceptions of teacher quality, which is more or less ignored by the public school system, would become the basis for punishing bad teachers and poorly run schools.

Critics of market-oriented schemes offer a number of objections:

- Consumers in the education market may not be well-informed, so the competitive outcome would be far from satisfactory.

- Moving children to private schools might reduce the positive externalities of education. Greater competition among schools could lead them to focus on improving the private benefits to the students (such as increasing their wage earnings potential) while ignoring aspects of education that yield societal benefits (such as building a shared sense of national identity).

- Relatively good students might use vouchers to escape poorly performing schools, leaving the weaker students behind. Because the quality of a student's education depends, in part, on the quality of his or her peers, the result would be an even worse education for the poor students than before the introduction of the voucher system. When Chile introduced a voucher system several years ago, it appears that the higher-ability students did in fact opt out of the public schools in disproportionately high numbers (Ladd, 2002, p. 19).

- A voucher system may be inequitable. The goal of the voucher system is to provide the opportunity for families to choose a private school should they wish. However, some families would opt for a private school even without a voucher, so providing them with a voucher would serve only to increase their income. To the extent that such families have higher average incomes, the end result would be to accentuate inequalities in the distribution of income.

Many issues are involved in designing a voucher system. How much latitude can schools have in designing their curricula? Can schools hire teachers who lack professional credentials? Who establishes the appropriate credentials for teachers? How will students' families be informed about the different schooling choices available to them? Who has responsibility for accepting and integrating disruptive children into the classroom? If a government provides vouchers to students, the government must also decide if the vouchers can be used for both public and private schooling. Where use is limited to public schools, this is similar to existing situations where students choose their school and funding is based on the number of students enrolling. However, where

---

[28] See the CTF National Issues in Education poll 2010 at http://www.ctf-fce.ca/Documents/FinalPollhighlights E.pdf.

public authorities are reluctant to close existing physical facilities and have limited ability to hire and fire, efficiency will not be achieved.

A number of communities have experimented with voucher programs, and studies have shown a range of effects. Deming et al. (2011), for example, found that students who were able to choose among public schools within a district were more likely to graduate high school. The results of Hoxby (2003) and Figlio and Hart (2014) suggest that competition generated by voucher programs leads to improvements in test scores in nearby public schools.

The willingness of some provinces (but not others) to partially fund private schools, with funding based on student enrolment, is a move to increase the choice of parents and to increase competition. Providing tax credits, particularly refundable credits, for parents using private schools would have a similar effect. But as long as funding for private schools is substantially below that for public schools, competitive forces will be limited. Competitive forces may also be reduced if lobbying by strong interest groups, such as teachers' unions, that benefit from limited competition leads to an over-reliance on publicly provided education.

School accountability. Most provinces conduct some form of standardized testing to monitor academic performance. There is significant debate over how to interpret and use these test results. Johnson (2005) argues convincingly that the school rankings produced by some are flawed because they fail to control for the effects of differences in socioeconomic conditions across schools.

Proponents of school accountability believe that it provides an incentive for school administrators and teachers to reduce bureaucracy and to focus on providing core educational skills to students. Hanushek and Raymond (2005) found that the introduction of school accountability in various U.S. states led to an improvement in student achievement only if the schools received sanctions or rewards that were tied to their performance. Issuing of report cards on school performance by itself did not provide sufficient incentive for improvement.

The most common criticism of standardized testing is that detrimental effects arise from focusing too much on the tests. The concern is that teachers don't have any incentive to foster creativity, problem-solving, and socialization skills and instead focus on teaching to the test. Jacob (2005) finds evidence to support this. Another concern is that school accountability leads to strategic gaming (Jacob and Levitt, 2003).

The economic literature demonstrates the clear tradeoffs involved with designing a policy of school accountability using standardized testing. Tying rewards and sanctions to explicit performance standards provides incentives for schools to change; however, it also provides incentives for unintended behaviour, such as gaming the system. This illustrates a more general proposition that arises again and again in public finance: people respond to incentives, and unless this fact is taken into account, even well-intentioned public policies may have unintended negative consequences.

SUMMARY

- Although education is generally publicly provided, it is not a public good. One exception to this is education spending on research that produces general knowledge (which can be jointly consumed and is non-excludable). Government intervention does not appear to be justifiable based on a market power problem. The existence of positive externalities associated with education and problems of asymmetric information do, however, provide efficiency rationales for government involvement in education.

- Distributional concerns arising from capital market imperfections and a belief in commodity egalitarianism provide equity rationales for government involvement in education.

- Education is a provincial responsibility but all three levels of government are involved to some extent. There is significant variation across provinces in real per student spending at both the elementary/secondary and post-secondary education levels. There is also considerable provincial variation in how education is funded (especially at the elementary and secondary level) and the extent to which local school boards rely on local property taxes versus provincial grants.

- Local responsibility for education can be justified on the basis of different tastes across communities, and because externalities from education primarily affect the local community. However, equity considerations and inefficiencies that may result from tax competition justify provincial involvement in the distribution of resources available for elementary and secondary education. Externalities associated with university research and a highly skilled and mobile work force justify federal involvement in post-secondary education.

- With some exceptions, provinces provide equal per pupil grants to local public school boards. This contributes to greater *wealth neutrality* in the provision of education.

- The evidence on whether increasing public spending on education improves educational outcomes, as measured by test scores, is mixed.

- Although generally publicly provided, much of the return to education is in the form of privately realized higher incomes. Estimates of social returns to education in Canada may justify current levels of spending on elementary and secondary education. Evidence is less clear for post-secondary education where the social rates of return are marginal.

- Much of the benefit from post-secondary education is in the form of higher incomes for individuals. These private returns, coupled with questionable distributional effects of existing public subsidies, are arguments for higher tuition, more effective loan programs, and possibly lower public funding. Signalling also provides an argument for possibly lower public funding.

- Research suggests that the link between spending and educational outcomes is, at best, very weak. This has led to demand for new ways to deliver education and enhance student performance, including the introduction of standardized testing, increased competition using vouchers, and the possibility of tying rewards and sanctions to school performance.

EXERCISES

1. What are the different rationales given to explain government involvement in education? Explain whether the rationales have different implications for government involvement in post-secondary education versus elementary and secondary education.

2. Many studies find that higher levels of education quality (as measured by test scores) increase the rate of growth in national income. Discuss whether this finding is sufficient to support the argument that government should subsidize education.

3. Suppose a family with only one child earns $50,000 per year and lives in a community without publicly provided education.
   a. Draw the family's budget constraint showing the tradeoff between the quantity of education for the child and all other goods.
   b. Suppose the option of free public education worth $8,000 per student is introduced. The family has the option of either spending its money on private education OR participating in the free public system that provides $8,000 worth of education. Show how this changes the family's spending (consumption) possibilities.
   c. Suppose that after the introduction of the free public education system the family reduces its consumption of education. Draw a set of indifference curves that is consistent with this outcome.
   d. Now suppose a voucher system is introduced. The voucher is redeemable for $8,000 worth of education. How does the voucher change the family's budget constraint? What happens to the amount of education the family purchases for the child (as compared to the case where no publicly provided education is available)?

4. Hanson (2006) provides evidence that the private rate of return to university education differs substantially depending on the area of study. Tuition fees that differ substantially from

program to program would result in more equal private rates of return from area to area. Explain why. Would you support a policy change in this direction? Explain your reasoning.

5. In David Johnson's *Signposts of Success*, elementary schools are identified as "good" schools when they outperform other schools with similar socioeconomic characteristics. For example, if two schools have the same predicted test results based on having the same socioeconomic characteristics (such as percentage of students living in single-parent families, percentage of recent immigrants among students, and average household income), but one has higher actual test results, this school could be defined as a good school. What problems would arise if schools were ranked against all other schools based on actual test results without taking into account the socioeconomic characteristics of the school community?

6. Consider the social rates of return provided in Table 13.3. The social rates of return for graduate degrees appear to be very low (or negative). Based on these estimates, an analyst recommends that government support for graduate education be reduced. Discuss the merits of this recommendation. Is there any reason to think the "true" social rate of return to graduate education might be higher or lower than reported?

PART FIVE
A Framework for Tax Analysis

Both politicians and economists have long searched for a set of principles to guide tax policy. Several centuries ago, the French statesman Jean-Baptiste Colbert suggested, "The art of taxation is the art of plucking the goose so as to get the largest possible amount of feathers with the least possible squealing."* Modern economics takes a somewhat less cynical approach, emphasizing how taxes should be levied to enhance economic efficiency and to promote a "fair" distribution of income. These are the topics of the next three chapters. Our goal is to construct a theoretical framework for thinking about tax policy. A thorough discussion of actual Canadian tax institutions is deferred to Part 6.

*George Armitage-Smith, *Principles and Methods of Taxation* (London: John Murray, 1907), p. 36.

CHAPTER 14

Taxation and Income Distribution

Struggle and contrive as you will, lay your taxes as you please, the traders will shift it off from their own gain.

—John Locke

AFTER READING THIS CHAPTER, THE STUDENT SHOULD BE ABLE TO:

LO1 Distinguish between the statutory incidence and the economic incidence of a tax.

LO2 Illustrate the difference between a marginal tax rate and an average tax rate.

LO3 Describe two ways of measuring tax progressiveness.

LO4 Relate the incidence of a tax to the elasticities of supply and demand.

LO4 Explain why a tax on economic profits cannot be shifted onto consumers.

LO5 Explain how a tax on land becomes capitalized in the price of land.

LO6 Give examples of tax equivalence relations in general equilibrium models.

LO7 Analyze the output effect and the substitution effect of a partial factor tax.

Canadian policy debates about the tax system are dominated by the question of whether its burden is distributed fairly. A sensible discussion of this issue requires some understanding of how taxes affect the distribution of income. A simple way to determine how taxes change the income distribution would be to conduct a survey in which each person is asked how many dollars he or she pays to the tax collector each year. Simple—but usually wrong. An example demonstrates that correctly assessing the burden of taxation is much more complicated.

Suppose the price of a bottle of wine is $10. The government imposes a tax of $1 per bottle, to be collected in the following way. Every time a bottle is purchased, the tax collector (who is lurking about the store) takes a dollar out of the wine seller's hand before the money is put into the cash register. A casual observer might conclude that the wine seller is paying the tax.

However, suppose that a few weeks after its imposition, the tax induces a price rise to $11 per bottle. Clearly, the proprietor receives the same amount per bottle as he did before the tax. The tax has apparently made him no worse off. The entire amount of the tax is being paid by consumers in the form of higher prices. On the other hand, suppose that after the tax the price increases to only $10.30. In this case, the proprietor keeps only $9.30 for each bottle sold; he is worse off by 70 cents per bottle. Consumers are also worse off, however, because they have to pay 30 cents more per bottle.[1] In this case, producers and consumers share the burden of the tax. Yet another possibility is that after the tax is imposed, the price stays at $10. If this happens, the consumer is no worse off, while the seller bears the full burden of the tax.

The **statutory incidence** of a tax indicates who is legally responsible for paying the tax. All three cases in the preceding paragraph are identical in the sense that the statutory incidence is on the seller. But the situations

---

[1] Actually, the change in the prices faced by consumers and producers is only part of the story. There is also a burden due to the tax-induced distortion of choice. See Chapter 15.

differ drastically with respect to who really bears the burden. Because prices may change in response to the tax, knowledge of statutory incidence tells us *essentially nothing* about who is really paying the tax. In contrast, the **economic incidence** of a tax is the change in the distribution of private real income brought about by a tax. Our focus in this chapter is on the forces that determine the extent to which statutory and economic incidence differ—the amount of **tax shifting**.

TAX INCIDENCE: GENERAL REMARKS

Several observations should be kept in mind in any discussion of how taxes affect the distribution of income.

Only People Can Bear Taxes

The Canadian legal system treats certain institutions as if they were people. The most prominent example is the corporation. Although for many purposes this is a convenient fiction, it sometimes creates confusion. From an economist's point of view, people—shareholders, workers, landlords, consumers—bear taxes. A corporation cannot. Thus, when some politicians declare "business must pay its fair share of taxes," it is not clear what, if anything, this means.

Given that only people can bear taxes, how should they be classified for purposes of incidence analysis? Often their role in production—what inputs they supply to the production process—is used. (Inputs are often referred to as *factors of production*.) The focus is on how the tax system changes the distribution of income among capitalists, labourers, and landlords. This is referred to as the **functional distribution of income**.

Framing the analysis this way may seem a bit old-fashioned. In eighteenth-century England, it may have been the case that property owners never worked and workers owned no property. But in contemporary Canada, many people who derive most of their income from labour also have savings accounts and/or common stocks. (Often, these assets are held for individuals in pensions.) Similarly, some people own huge amounts of capital and also work full-time. Thus, it seems more relevant to study how taxes affect the way in which total income is distributed among people: the **size distribution of income**. Given information on what proportion of people's income is from capital, land, and labour, changes in the factor distribution can be translated into changes in the size distribution. For example, a tax that lowers the relative return on capital tends to hurt those at the top of the income distribution because a relatively high proportion of the incomes of the rich is from capital.[2]

Other classification schemes might be interesting for particular problems. When the Trudeau government enacted the National Energy Program in October 1980, the incidence by region received a great deal of attention. (The shift in income from Alberta to central Canada involved tens of billions of dollars.) Alternatively, when proposals are made to change the taxation of income from pensions, analysts often look at incidence by age. It is easy to think of further examples based on sex, ethnicity, and so forth.

Both Sources and Uses of Income Should be Considered

In the previous wine tax example, it is natural to assume that the distributional effects of the tax depend crucially on people's spending patterns. To the extent that the price of wine increases, the people who tend to consume a lot of wine are made worse off. However, if the tax reduces the demand for wine, the factors employed in wine production may suffer income losses. Thus, the tax may also change the income distribution by affecting the *sources* of income. Suppose that poor people spend a relatively large proportion of their incomes on wine, but that vineyards tend to be owned by the rich. On the uses-of-income side then, the tax redistributes income away from the poor, but on the sources side it redistributes income away from the rich. The overall incidence depends on how both the sources and uses of income are affected. This distinction plays an important role in the debate over hotel room taxes and other taxes on "tourism." Proponents focus on the uses side, arguing that relatively well-to-do "tourists" bear the tax, while opponents may point to the lower-income wage earners and small business people adversely affected on the sources side.

---

[2] However, some low-income retirees also derive the bulk of their income from capital.

In practice, economists commonly ignore effects on the sources side when considering a tax on a commodity, and ignore the uses side when analyzing a tax on an input. This procedure is appropriate if the most systematic effects of a commodity tax are on the uses of income, and those of a factor tax are on the sources of income. The assumption simplifies analyses, but its correctness must be considered for each case. (See Fullerton and Rogers, 1997.)

Incidence Depends on How Prices are Determined

We have emphasized that the incidence problem is fundamentally one of determining how taxes change prices. Clearly, different models of price determination may give quite different answers to the question of who really bears a tax. This chapter considers several different models and compares the results.

A closely related issue is the time dimension of the analysis. Incidence depends on changes in prices, but change takes time. In most cases, one expects responses to be larger in the long run than the short run. Thus, the short- and long-run incidence of a tax may differ, and the time frame that is relevant for a given policy question must be specified.

Incidence Depends on the Disposition of Tax Revenues

Balanced-budget incidence computes the combined effects of levying taxes and government spending financed by those taxes. In general, the distributional effect of a tax depends on how the government spends the money. Expenditures on Alzheimer's research have a very different distributional impact than spending on hot lunches for school children. Some studies assume the government spends the tax revenue exactly as the consumers would if they had received the money. This is equivalent to returning the revenue as a lump sum and letting consumers spend it.

Tax revenues are usually not earmarked for particular expenditures. It is then desirable to be able to abstract from the question of how the government spends the money. The idea is to examine how incidence differs when one tax is replaced with another, holding the government budget constant. This is called **differential tax incidence**. Because differential incidence looks at changes in taxes, it is useful to have a reference point. The hypothetical "other tax" used as the basis of comparison is often assumed to be a **lump-sum tax**—a tax for which the individual's liability does not depend upon behaviour. (For example, a 10 percent income tax is *not* a lump-sum tax because it depends on how much the individual earns. But a head tax of $500 independent of earnings is a lump-sum tax.)

Finally, **absolute tax incidence** examines the effects of a tax when there is no change in either other taxes or government expenditure. Absolute incidence is of most interest for macroeconomic models in which tax levels are changed to achieve some stabilization goal.

Tax Progressiveness Can be Measured in Several Ways

Suppose that an investigator has managed to calculate every person's real share of a particular tax—the economic incidence as defined above. The purpose of such an exercise is often a characterization of the tax as proportional, progressive, or regressive.

The definition of **proportional** is straightforward; it describes a situation in which the ratio of taxes paid to income is constant regardless of income level.[3] Defining progressive and regressive is not easy, and unfortunately, ambiguities in definition sometimes confuse public debate. A natural way to define these words is in terms of the **average tax rate**, the ratio of taxes paid to income. If the average tax rate increases with income, the system is **progressive**; if it falls, the tax is **regressive**.[4]

Confusion arises because some people think of progressiveness in terms of the **marginal tax rate**—the *change* in taxes paid with respect to a change in income. To illustrate the distinction, consider the following very simple income tax structure. Each individual computes his or her tax bill by subtracting $3,000 from income and paying an amount equal to 20 percent of the remainder. (If the difference is negative, the individual gets a subsidy equal to 20 percent of the figure.) Table 14.1 shows the amount of tax paid, the average tax rate, and

---

[3] However, the definition of income is not straightforward; see Chapter 17.

[4] As a matter of convention, taxes are generally referred to as progressive, regressive, or proportional in relation to income. Alternatively, they might be viewed in relation to consumption or wealth.

TABLE 14.1

Tax Liabilities Under a Hypothetical Tax System			
Income	Tax Liability	Average Tax Rate	Marginal Tax Rate
$ 2,000	$ −200	−0.10	0.2
3,000	0	0	0.2
5,000	400	0.08	0.2
10,000	1,400	0.14	0.2
30,000	5,400	0.18	0.2

the marginal tax rate for each of several income levels. The average rates increase with income. However, the marginal tax rate is constant at 0.2 because for each additional dollar earned, the individual pays an additional 20 cents, regardless of income level. People could disagree about the progressiveness of this tax system and each could be right according to their own definitions.[5] It is, therefore, very important to make the definition clear when using the terms *regressive* and *progressive*. In the remainder of this book, we assume that they are defined in terms of average tax rates.

Measuring the *degree* of progressiveness of a tax system is more difficult and controversial than defining progressiveness. Many reasonable alternatives have been proposed. We consider two simple ones. The first says that the greater the increase in average tax rates as income increases, the more progressive the system. Algebraically, let T_0 and T_1 be the true (as opposed to statutory) tax liabilities at income levels I_0 and I_1, respectively (I_1 is greater than I_0). The measurement of progressiveness, v_1, is

$$v_1 = \frac{\frac{T_1}{I_1} - \frac{T_0}{I_0}}{I_1 - I_0} \tag{14.1}$$

Once the analyst computes the values of T_0 and T_1 and substitutes into Equation (14.1), the tax system with the higher value of v_1 is said to be more progressive.

The second possibility is to say that one tax system is more progressive than another if its elasticity of tax liabilities with respect to income (i.e., the percentage change in tax liabilities divided by the percentage change in income) is higher. Here the expression to be evaluated is v_2, defined as

$$v_2 = \frac{T_1 - T_0}{T_0} \div \frac{I_1 - I_0}{I_0} \tag{14.2}$$

Now consider the following proposal. Everyone's tax liability is to be increased by 20 percent of the amount of the tax he or she currently pays. This proposal would increase the tax liability of a person who formerly paid T_0 to $1.2 \times T_0$, and the liability that was formerly T_1 to $1.2 \times T_1$. Does the proposal make the tax system more progressive? It depends on which measure is used. Substituting the expressions $1.2 \times T_0$ and $1.2 \times T_1$ for T_0 and T_1, respectively, in Equation (14.1), v_1 increases by 20 percent. The proposal thus increases progressiveness. But if the same substitution is done in Equation (14.2), the value of v_2 is unchanged. (Both the numerator and denominator are multiplied by 1.2, which cancels out the effect.) The lesson here is that even very intuitively appealing measures of progressiveness can give different answers.[6] Intelligent public debate requires that people make their definitions clear.

---

[5] With a basic exemption exceeding $18,000, Alberta would argue that its single rate tax of 10 percent, from 2001 to 2015, was more progressive than the previous multi-rate income tax.

[6] Note also that v_1 and v_2, in general, depend on the level of income. That is, even a single tax system does not usually have a constant v_1 and v_2. This further complicates discussions of the degree of progressiveness.

PARTIAL EQUILIBRIUM MODELS

With preliminaries out of the way, we turn now to the fundamental issue of this chapter: how taxes affect the income distribution. We have argued that the essence of the problem is that taxes induce changes in relative prices. Knowing how prices are determined is therefore a key ingredient in the analysis. In this section we analyze **partial equilibrium models** of price determination–models that look only at the market in which the tax is imposed and ignore the ramifications in other markets. This kind of analysis is most appropriate when the market for the taxed commodity is relatively small compared with the economy as a whole. The vehicle for our analysis is the supply and demand model of perfect competition.

Unit Taxes on Commodities

We study first the incidence of a **unit tax**, so named because it is levied as a fixed amount per unit of a commodity sold. For example, the federal government imposes a tax on wine of \$0.62 per litre and a tax on cigarettes of \$2.63 per pack. Suppose that the price and quantity of wine are determined competitively by supply (S_w) and demand (D_w) as in Figure 14.1. Before imposition of the tax, the quantity demanded and price are Q_0 and P_0, respectively.

Now suppose that a unit tax of \$u per litre is imposed on each purchase, and the statutory incidence is on buyers. A key step in incidence analysis is to recognize that in the presence of a tax the price paid by consumers and the price received by suppliers differ. Previously, we could use a supply–demand analysis to determine the *single* market price. Now, this analysis must be modified to accommodate two different prices, one for buyers and one for sellers.

We begin by determining how the tax affects the demand schedule. Consider an arbitrary point a on the demand curve. Recall that this point indicates that the *maximum* price per litre that people would be willing to pay for Q_a litres is P_a. After the unit tax of u is imposed, the most that people would be willing to spend for Q_a is still P_a. There is no reason to believe that the tax affects the underlying valuation people place on wine. However, when people pay P_a per litre, producers no longer receive the whole amount. Instead, they receive only ($P_a - u$), an amount that is indicated as point b in Figure 14.1. In other words, after the unit tax is imposed, a is no longer a point on the demand curve *as perceived by suppliers*. Point b is on the demand curve as perceived by suppliers, because they realize that if Q_a is supplied, they receive only ($P_a - u$) per litre. It is irrelevant to the suppliers how much consumers pay per litre; all that matters to suppliers is the amount they receive per litre.

FIGURE 14.1

PRICE AND QUANTITY BEFORE TAXATION

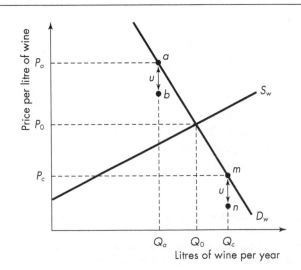

FIGURE 14.2

INCIDENCE OF A UNIT TAX IMPOSED ON THE DEMAND SIDE

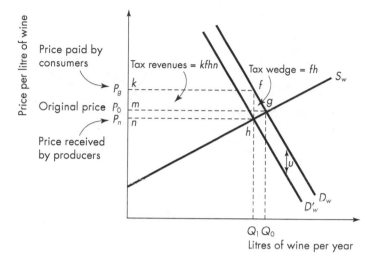

Of course, point a was chosen arbitrarily. At any other point on the demand curve, the story is the same. Thus, for example, after the tax is imposed, the price received by suppliers for output Q_c is at point n, which is found by subtracting the distance u from point m. Repeating this process at every point along the demand curve, we generate a new demand curve located exactly u dollars below the old one. In Figure 14.2, the demand curve so constructed is labelled D'_w. Schedule D'_w is relevant to suppliers because it shows how much they receive for each unit sold.

We are now in a position to find the equilibrium quantity of wine after the unit tax is imposed. The equilibrium is where the supply equals demand as perceived by suppliers. In Figure 14.2, this occurs at output Q_1. Thus, the tax lowers the quantity sold from Q_0 to Q_1.

The next step is to find the new equilibrium price. As noted earlier, there are really two prices at the new equilibrium: the price received by producers, and the price paid by consumers. The price received by producers is at the intersection of their effective demand and supply curves, which occurs at P_n. The price paid by consumers is P_n *plus u*, the unit tax. To find this price geometrically, we must go up from P_n a vertical distance exactly equal to u. But by construction, the distance between schedules D_w and D'_w is equal to u. Hence, to find the price paid by consumers, we simply go up from the intersection of D'_w and S_w to the original demand curve D_w. The price so determined is P_g. Because P_g includes the tax, it is often referred to as the price gross of tax. On the other hand, P_n is the price net of tax.

Consumers are made worse off by the tax because P_g, the new price they face, is higher than the original price P_0. But the consumers' price does not increase by the full amount of the tax: $(P_g - P_0)$ is less than u. Producers also pay part of the tax in the form of a lower price received per litre. Producers now receive only P_n, whereas before the tax they received P_0. Thus, both producers and consumers are made worse off by the tax.[7] Notice that consumers and producers "split" the tax in the sense that the increase in the consumer price $(P_g - P_0)$ and the decrease in the producer price $(P_0 - P_n)$ just add up to $\$u$.

By definition, revenues collected are the product of the number of units purchased, Q_1, and the tax per unit, u. Geometrically, Q_1 is the width of rectangle $kfhn$ and u is its height, so tax revenues are the area of this rectangle.

---

[7] In terms of surplus measures, consumers are worse off by area $mkfg$ and producers are worse off by $mghn$. The loss of total surplus exceeds the tax revenues by triangle fhg; this is the excess burden of the tax, as explained in Chapter 15. Area $mghn$ is the loss in producer surplus. Just as consumer surplus is the area between the demand curve and a horizontal line at the going price, producer surplus is the area between the supply curve and a horizontal line at the going price. For a review of consumer surplus, see the Appendix to Chapter 3.

FIGURE 14.3

INCIDENCE OF A UNIT TAX IMPOSED ON THE SUPPLY SIDE

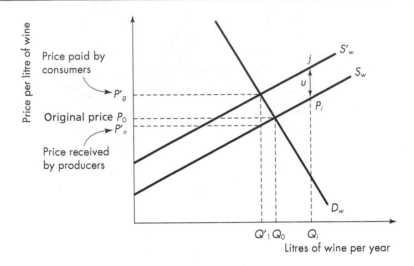

This analysis has two important implications:

1. *The incidence of a unit tax is independent of whether it is levied on consumers or producers.* Suppose the same tax, u, had been levied on the suppliers of wine instead of the consumers. Consider an arbitrary price, P_i, on the original supply curve in Figure 14.3. The supply curve indicates that for suppliers to produce Q_i units, they must receive at least P_i per unit. After the unit tax, suppliers must still receive P_i per unit. For them to do so, however, consumers must pay price $P_i + u$ per unit, which is shown geometrically as point j. It should now be clear where the argument is heading. To find the supply curve as it is perceived by consumers, S_w must be shifted up by the amount of the unit tax. This new supply curve is labelled S'_w. The post-tax equilibrium is at Q'_1, where the schedules S'_w and D_w intersect. The price at the intersection, P'_g, is the price paid by consumers. To find the price received by producers, we must subtract u from P'_g, giving us P'_n. A glance at Figure 14.2 indicates that $Q'_1 = Q_1$, $P'_g = P_g$, and $P'_n = P_n$. Thus, the incidence of the unit tax is independent of the side of the market on which it is levied.

   This is the same as our statement that the statutory incidence of a tax tells us nothing of the economic incidence of the tax. It is irrelevant whether the tax collector stands (figuratively) next to consumers and takes u dollars every time they pay for a litre of wine or stands next to sellers and collects u dollars from them whenever they sell a litre. Figures 14.2 and 14.3 prove that what matters is the size of the disparity the tax introduces between the price paid by consumers and the price received by producers, and not on which side of the market the disparity is introduced. The tax-induced difference between the price paid by consumers and the price received by producers is referred to as the **tax wedge** (the distance between P'_n and P'_g in Figure 14.3).

2. *The incidence of a unit tax depends on the elasticities of supply and demand.* In Figure 14.2, consumers bear the brunt of the tax—the amount they pay goes up much more than the amount received by producers goes down. This result is strictly determined by the shapes of the demand and supply curves. In general, the more elastic the demand curve, the less the tax borne by consumers, *ceteris paribus*. Similarly, the more elastic the supply curve, the less the tax borne by producers, *ceteris paribus*. Intuitively, elasticity provides a rough measure of an economic agent's ability to escape the tax. The more elastic the demand, the easier it is for consumers to turn to other products when the price goes up, and therefore, more of the tax must be borne by suppliers. Conversely, if consumers purchase the same amount regardless of price, the whole burden can be shifted to them. Similar considerations apply to the supply side.

FIGURE 14.4

TAX INCIDENCE WHEN SUPPLY IS PERFECTLY INELASTIC

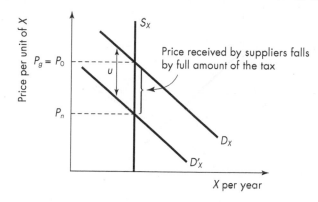

Illustrations of extreme cases are provided in Figures 14.4 and 14.5. In Figure 14.4, commodity X is supplied perfectly inelastically. When a unit tax is imposed, the effective demand curve becomes D'_X. As before, the price received by producers (P_n) is at the intersection of S_X and D'_X. Note that P_n is exactly u less than P_0. Thus, the price received by producers falls by exactly the amount of the tax. At the same time, the price paid by consumers, $P_g (= P_n + u)$, remains at P_0. When supply is perfectly inelastic, producers bear the entire burden. Figure 14.5 represents an opposite extreme. The supply of commodity Z is perfectly elastic. Imposition of a unit tax leads to demand curve D'_Z. At the new equilibrium, quantity demanded is Z_1 and the price received by producers, P_n, is still P_0. The price paid by consumers, P_g, is therefore $P_0 + u$. In this case, consumers bear the entire burden of the tax.[8]

Ad Valorem Taxes

We now turn to the incidence of an **ad valorem tax**, a tax with a rate given as a *proportion* of the price. For example, clothing in Toronto is taxed at 13 percent of its price, via the Harmonized Sales Tax (HST).

Luckily, the analysis of ad valorem taxes is very similar to that of unit taxes. The basic strategy is still to find out how the tax changes the effective demand curve and to compute the new equilibrium. However,

FIGURE 14.5

TAX INCIDENCE WHEN SUPPLY IS PERFECTLY ELASTIC

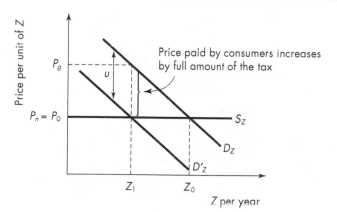

---

[8] Note that as long as input costs are constant, the long-run supply curve for a competitive market is horizontal as in Figure 14.5. Hence, under these conditions, in the long run consumers bear the entire burden of the tax.

FIGURE 14.6

INTRODUCING AN AD VALOREM TAX

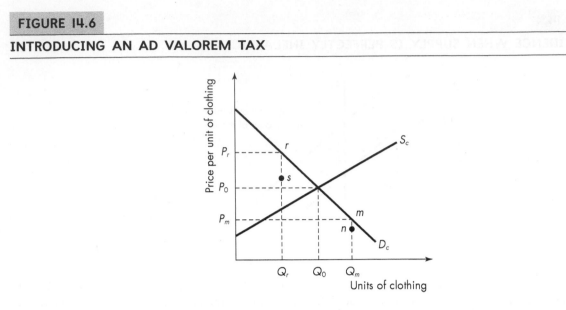

instead of moving the curve down by the same absolute amount for each quantity, the ad valorem tax lowers it in the same *proportion*. To show this, consider the demand (D_c) and supply (S_c) curves for clothing in Figure 14.6. In the absence of taxation, the equilibrium price and quantity are P_0 and Q_0, respectively. Now suppose that a tax of 25 percent of the gross price is levied on the consumption of clothing.[9] Consider point m on D_c. After the tax is imposed, P_m is still the most that consumers will pay for Q_m of clothing; the amount producers will receive is 75 percent of the vertical distance between point m and the horizontal axis, which is labelled point n. Hence, point n is one point on the demand curve perceived by producers. Similarly, the price at point r migrates down one-quarter of the way between it and the horizontal axis to point s. When this exercise is repeated for every point on D_c, the effective demand curve facing suppliers is determined as D_c' in Figure 14.7. From here, the analysis proceeds exactly as for a unit tax. The equilibrium is at the intersection

FIGURE 14.7

INCIDENCE OF AN AD VALOREM TAX

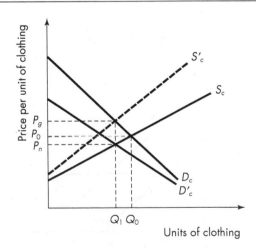

---

[9] A fundamental ambiguity is involved in measuring ad valorem tax rates. Is the tax measured as a percentage of the net or gross price? In this example, the tax is 25 percent of the gross price, which is equivalent to a rate of 33 percent of net price. To see this, note that if the price paid by the consumer were $1, the tax paid would be 25 cents, and the price received by producers would be 75 cents. Expressing the 25 cent tax bill as a fraction of 75 cents gives us a 33 percent rate as a proportion of the net price.

of S_c and D'_c with the quantity exchanged Q_1, the price received by clothing producers P_n, and the price paid by consumers P_g. As before, the incidence of the tax is determined by the elasticities of supply and demand. (An ad valorem tax can also be analyzed with a shift in the supply curve, as from S_c to S'_c.)

Taxes on Factors

So far we have discussed taxes on goods, but the analysis can also be applied to factors of production.

The payroll tax. Consider the payroll tax used to finance the Canada Pension Plan (CPP). As noted in Chapter 11, in 2015 a tax equal to 4.45 percent of workers' pensionable earnings was paid by their employers and a tax at the same rate paid by the workers themselves—a total of 9.9 percent.[10] This division has a long history and is a consequence of our lawmakers' feeling that the payroll tax should be shared by employers and employees. It is important to realize that the *statutory distinction between workers and bosses is irrelevant.* As suggested earlier, the incidence of this labour tax is determined only by the wedge the tax puts between what employees receive and employers pay.

This point is illustrated in Figure 14.8, where D_L is the demand for labour and S_L is the supply of labour. For purposes of illustration, assume S_L to be perfectly inelastic. Before taxation, the wage is w_0. The ad valorem tax on labour moves the effective demand curve to D'_L. As usual, the distance between D'_L and D_L is the wedge between what is paid for an item and what is received by those who supply it. After the tax is imposed, the wage received by workers falls to w_n. On the other hand, w_g, the price paid by employers, stays at w_0. In this example, despite the statutory division of the tax, the wage rate received by workers falls by exactly the amount of the tax—they bear the entire burden.

Of course, we could have gotten just the opposite result by drawing the supply curve as perfectly elastic. The key point to remember is that nothing about the incidence of a tax can be known without information on the relevant behavioural elasticities. In fact, there is some evidence that the elasticity of the total supply of hours of work is about zero (Fuchs et al., 1998).[11] At least in the short run, labour probably bears most of the payroll tax, despite the continuing debates on the "fair" distribution of the burden.

FIGURE 14.8

INCIDENCE OF A PAYROLL TAX WITH AN INELASTIC SUPPLY OF LABOUR

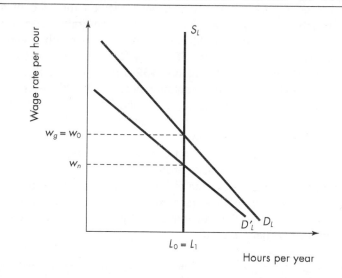

---

[10] After earnings exceed a certain level, the payroll tax rate falls. Employment Insurance (EI) premiums of 1.88 percent on employees and 2.63 percent on employers in 2015 makes the total federal payroll tax 14.41 percent over a range of earnings. See Chapters 10 and 11.

[11] See also the cross-country study by Hassett and Mathur (2006), which finds that manufacturing wages are unresponsive to average income tax rates.

Capital taxation in a global economy. The strategy for analyzing a tax on capital is essentially the same as that for analyzing a tax on labour—draw the supply and demand curves, shift or pivot the relevant curve by an amount depending on the size of the tax, and see how the after-tax equilibrium compares with the original one. In an economy that is closed to trade, it is reasonable to assume that the demand curve will slope downward (firms demand less capital when its price goes up), and that the supply of capital will slope upward (people supply more capital [i.e., save more] when the return to saving increases).[12] In this case, the owners of capital will bear some of the burden of the tax, the precise amount depending on the supply and demand elasticities.

Suppose now that the economy is open and capital is perfectly mobile across countries. In effect, there is a single world market for capital, and if suppliers of capital cannot earn the going world rate of return in a particular country, they will take it out of that country and put it in another. In terms of a supply and demand diagram, the supply of capital to a particular country is perfectly elastic—its citizens can purchase all the capital they want at the going rate of return, but none whatsoever at a lower rate. The implications for the incidence of a tax on capital are striking. As in Figure 14.5, the before-tax price paid by the users of capital rises by exactly the amount of the tax, and the suppliers of capital bear no burden whatsoever. Intuitively, capital will simply move abroad if it has to bear any of the tax; hence, the rate of return has to rise.

Now, even in today's highly integrated world economy, capital is not perfectly mobile across countries. However, for a country like Canada whose capital market is small relative to the world market, the supply curve is much more horizontal than for the United States. Policy-makers who ignore world trade and capital flows will tend to overestimate their ability to place the burden of taxation on owners of capital. To the extent

---

IN THE NEWS

EUROPEAN FOOTBALLERS RUN FROM SUPERTAXES

In 2013, France introduced a controversial "supertax" of 75 percent on salaries above a 1 million euro threshold, aiming to reduce the country's large public deficit and symbolizing fairness for the middle class. French soccer clubs were horrified. "This new tax will cost first-division teams 82 million euros," France's Football League said in a statement. "With these crazy labor costs, France will lose its best players." Clubs threatened to strike, although polls indicated little sympathy for the multi-millionaires at clubs like Paris Saint-Germain, where more than 10 players qualified for the tax. Meanwhile, a 2014 change in the French league statutes, which would have allowed the club of Monaco (on France's border) to play in the French league while preserving its tax-free status, was quashed by legal action from rival teams that feared losing marquee players to Monaco. These observations beg the question: do the world's best paid athletes select club teams to play for with their eyes on countries' tax rates? (David Beckham and Lionel Messi earned $50.6 and $39.3 million in 2013, according to Forbes' list of highest paid players.) A report by Deloitte consultants noted that a 10 percentage point tax increase on high earners in Britain in 2010 would make players in the English Premier League "likely to request pay increases" and clubs face "an increase in their wage bill or potentially losing the player to an overseas rival." A recent study by Henrik Kleven, Camille Landais, and Emmanuel Saez on 14 European nations, shows that soccer players do indeed tend to locate in countries that have comparatively low income tax rates, and the elasticity is especially pronounced for the most-able and well-paid athletes. The authors are addressing the broader question of how tax rates affect taxpayer behaviour: "[F]ootball players are likely to be a particularly mobile segment of the labor market, and our study therefore provides an upper bound on the migration response for the labor market as a whole." And France's supertax was abandoned on February 1, 2015.

Based on Love (2015), Henry (2013), NBER Digest (2015), Smith (2009), Viscusi (2013), and "France's 75% millionaire tax approved by country's high court." *Financial Post*, December 30, 2013.

Complete references for this feature can be found in the References section on page 485.

---

[12] However, saving need not increase with the rate of return. See Chapter 18.

that capital is internationally mobile, taxes on capitalists are shifted to others and the apparent progressivity of taxes on capital proves to be illusory. Capital escapes the tax by migrating to other jurisdictions, and, having less capital with which to work, less-mobile factors such as labour are less productive and bear the burden of the tax on capital.

Commodity Taxation with Monopoly

The assumption of competitive markets has played a major role in our analysis. We now discuss how the results might change under the polar opposite assumption of monopoly—one seller.[13] Figure 14.9 depicts a monopolist that produces commodity X. Before any taxation, the demand curve facing the monopolist is D_X, and the associated marginal revenue curve is MR_X. The marginal cost curve for the production of X is MC_X, and the average total cost curve, ATC_X. As usual, the condition for profit maximization is that production be carried to the point where marginal revenue equals marginal cost, at output X_0 where the price charged is P_0. Economic profit per unit is the difference between average revenue and average total cost, distance ab. The number of units sold is db. Hence, total profit is ab times db, which is the area of rectangle $abdc$.

Now suppose that a unit tax of u is levied on X. For exactly the same reasons as before, the effective demand curve facing the producer shifts down by a vertical distance equal to u.[14] In Figure 14.10, this demand curve is labelled D'_X. At the same time, the marginal revenue curve facing the firm also shifts down by distance u because the firm's incremental revenue for each unit sold is reduced by the amount of the tax. The new effective marginal revenue curve is labelled MR'_X.

The profit-maximizing output, X_1, is found at the intersection of MR'_X and MC_X. Using output X_1, we find the price received by the monopolist by going up to D'_X, the demand curve facing him, and locate price P_n. The price paid by consumers is determined by adding u to P_n, which is shown as price P_g on the diagram. After-tax profit per unit is the difference between the price *received by the monopolist* and average total cost, distance fg. The number of units sold is if. Therefore, monopoly economic profits after tax are measured by area $fghi$.

What are the effects of the tax? Quantity demanded goes down ($X_1 < X_0$); the price paid by consumers goes up ($P_g > P_0$); and the price received by the monopolist may go either up or down, depending on the shapes of the marginal revenue and marginal cost curves. In Figure 14.10, the price received by the monopolist goes down ($P_n < P_0$). Note that monopoly profits are lower under the tax—area $fghi$ in Figure 14.10 is smaller than

FIGURE 14.9

EQUILIBRIUM OF A MONOPOLIST

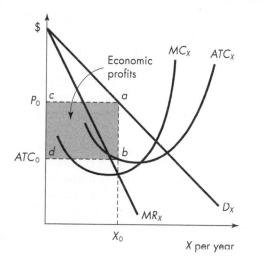

[13] See Eaton, Eaton, and Allen (2012: Ch. 10) for a review of price and output determination under monopoly.

[14] Alternatively, we could shift the marginal cost curve up by u. The final outcomes are identical.

FIGURE 14.10

IMPOSITION OF A UNIT TAX ON A MONOPOLIST

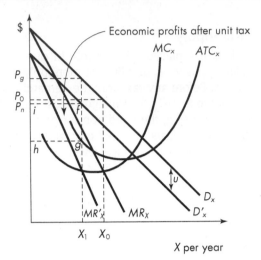

area *abdc* in Figure 14.9. Despite its market power, a monopolist is in general made worse off by a unit tax on the product it sells. In public debate it is often assumed that a firm with market power can simply pass on all taxes to consumers. This analysis shows that even a completely greedy and grasping monopolist must bear some of the burden. As before, the precise share of the burden borne by consumers depends on the elasticity of the demand schedule.

It is straightforward to repeat the exercise for an ad valorem tax on the monopolist (D_X and MR_X pivot instead of moving down in a parallel fashion); this is left as an exercise for the reader.

Taxes on Profits

So far we have been discussing taxes based on sales. Firms can also be taxed on their **economic profits**, defined as the return to owners of the firm in excess of the opportunity costs of the factors used in production. (Economic profits are also referred to as *supranormal* or *excess profits*.) We now show that as long as firms are profit maximizing, a tax on economic profits cannot be shifted—it is borne only by the owners of the firm.

Consider first a perfectly competitive firm in short-run equilibrium. The firm's output is determined by the intersection of its marginal cost and marginal revenue schedules. A tax of a given rate on economic profits changes neither marginal cost nor marginal revenue. Therefore, no firm has the incentive to change its output decision. Because output does not change, neither does the price paid by consumers, so they are no worse off. The tax is completely absorbed by the firms. Another way to get to the same result is this—if the tax rate on economic profits is t_p, the firm's objective is to maximize after-tax profits, $(1 - t_p)\pi$, where π is the pretax level of economic profits. But it is just a matter of arithmetic that whatever strategy maximizes π is identical to the one that maximizes $(1 - t_p)\pi$. Hence, output and price faced by consumers stay the same, and the firm bears the whole tax.

In long-run competitive equilibrium, a tax on economic profits has no yield, because economic profits are zero—they are all competed away. For a monopolist, there may be economic profits even in the long run. But for the same reasons given in the preceding paragraph, the tax is borne by the owners of the monopoly. If a firm is maximizing profits before the profits tax is imposed, the tax cannot be shifted.[15]

Because they distort no economic decisions, taxes on economic profits might appear to be very attractive policy alternatives. However, profits taxes have received very little support from public finance specialists. The

---

[15] On the other hand, if the firm is following some other goal, it may raise the price in response to a profits tax. One alternative to profit maximization is revenue maximization; firms try to make their sales as large as possible, subject to the constraint that they earn a "reasonable" rate of return.

main reason is the tremendous problems in making the theoretical notion of economic profits operational. For example, excess profits are often computed by examining the rate of return that a firm makes on its capital stock and comparing it with some "basic" rate of return set by the government. Clearly, how the capital stock is measured is important. Should the original cost be used, or the cost of replacing it? And what if the rate of return is high, not because of excess profits, but because the enterprise is very risky and investors have to be compensated for this risk? Considerations such as these lead to major difficulties in administration and compliance.[16]

Tax Incidence and Capitalization

"An old tax is a good tax" is a familiar adage to economists. The reason is that the burden of the tax will have been borne by a previous owner or generation. For example, if a tax was imposed on land or buildings before purchase by the existing owner, he or she would have paid less because of the tax's effect on the after-tax income from the property. To eliminate or lower the tax unexpectedly now would lead to a "windfall gain," and an unexpected increase in the tax would cause a "windfall loss."[17] Let's now look more closely at a tax on land.

Early in the twentieth century, several western Canadian provinces taxed only land, and not the buildings and other improvements on the land. Since then there has been continuing discussion of whether tax rates on the value of land should be higher than those on the value of improvements. In other words, should taxes on land be raised and those on improvements lowered?

This question leads us to consider the special issues that arise when land is taxed. For these purposes, the distinctive characteristics of land are that it is fixed in supply and it is durable. Suppose the annual rental rate on land is $\$R_0$ this year. It is known that the rental will be $\$R_1$ next year, $\$R_2$ two years from now, and so on. How much should someone be willing to pay for the land? If the market for land is competitive, the price of land is just equal to the present discounted value of the stream of the rents. Thus, if the interest rate is r, the price of land (P_R) is

$$P_R = \$R_0 + \frac{\$R_1}{1 + r} + \frac{\$R_2}{(1 + r)^2} + \cdots + \frac{\$R_T}{(1 + r)^T} \qquad (14.3)$$

where T is the last year the land yields its services (possibly infinity).

Assume it is announced that a tax of $\$u_0$ will be imposed on land now, $\$u_1$ next year, $\$u_2$ two years from now, and so forth. From Figure 14.4 we know that because land is fixed in supply, the annual rental received by the owner falls by the full amount of the tax. That means that the landlord's return initially falls to $\$(R_0 - u_0)$, in year 1 to $\$(R_1 - u_1)$, and in year 2 to $\$(R_2 - u_2)$. Prospective purchasers of the land take into account the fact that if they purchase the land, they buy a future stream of tax liabilities as well as a future stream of returns. Therefore, the most a purchaser is willing to pay for the land after the tax is announced (P'_R) is

$$P'_R = \$(R_0 - u_0) + \frac{\$(R_1 - u_1)}{1 + r} + \frac{\$(R_2 - u_2)}{(1 + r)^2} + \cdots + \frac{\$(R_T - u_T)}{(1 + r)^T} \qquad (14.4)$$

Comparing Equations (14.4) and (14.3), we see that, as a consequence of the tax, the price of land falls by

$$u_0 + \frac{u_1}{1 + r} + \frac{u_2}{(1 + r)^2} + \cdots + \frac{u_T}{(1 + r)^T}$$

Thus, at the time the tax is imposed, the price of the land falls by the present value of all *future tax payments*. This process by which a stream of taxes becomes incorporated into the price of an asset is referred to as **capitalization**.

Because of capitalization, the person who bears the full burden of the tax forever is the landlord at the time the tax is levied. To be sure, future landlords make payments to the tax authorities, but such payments are not really a "burden" because they just balance the lower price paid at purchase. Capitalization complicates attempts

---

[16] See Gillis and McLure (1979) for further details.

[17] This concept is developed further in the discussion of horizontal equity in Chapter 16.

to assess the incidence of a tax on a durable item that is fixed in supply. Knowing the identities of current owners is not sufficient—one must know who the landlords were at the time the tax was imposed. In light of this analysis, it's no wonder that significant changes in taxes on real property, and land in particular, lead to strong taxpayer resistance.[18]

GENERAL EQUILIBRIUM MODELS

A great attraction of partial equilibrium models is their simplicity—examining only one market at a time is a relatively uncomplicated affair. In some cases, however, ignoring feedback into other markets leads to an incomplete picture of a tax's incidence. Suppose, for example, that a tax is levied on all capital used in the construction of housing. Partial equilibrium analysis of this tax would involve analyzing only the supply and demand curves for housing capital. But suppose that the tax induces some people who formerly invested in housing to invest their capital in factories instead. As new capital flows into the manufacturing sector, the rate of return to capital employed there falls. Thus, capitalists in the manufacturing sector may end up bearing part of the burden of a tax imposed on the housing sector.

More generally, when a tax is imposed on a sector that is "large" relative to the economy, looking only at that particular market may not be enough. **General equilibrium analysis** takes into account the ways in which various markets are interrelated.

Another problem with partial equilibrium analysis is that it gives insufficient attention to the question of just who the "producers" of a taxed commodity are. The "producer" is a composite of entrepreneurs, capitalists, and workers. In many cases, the division of the tax burden among these groups is important. General equilibrium analysis provides a framework for investigating it.

Before turning to the specifics of general equilibrium analysis, note that the fundamental lesson from partial equilibrium models still holds—because of relative price adjustments, the statutory incidence of a tax generally tells nothing about who really bears its burden.

Tax Equivalence Relations

The idea of dealing with tax incidence in a general equilibrium framework at first appears daunting. After all, thousands of different commodities and inputs are traded in the economy. How can we keep track of all their complicated interrelations? Luckily, for many purposes, useful general equilibrium results can be obtained from models in which there are only two commodities, two factors of production, and no savings. For illustration, call the two commodities food (F) and manufactures (M), and the two factors capital (K) and labour (L). There are nine possible ad valorem taxes in such a model:

$$t_{KF} = \text{a tax on capital used in the production of food}$$
$$t_{KM} = \text{a tax on capital used in the production of manufactures}$$
$$t_{LF} = \text{a tax on labour used in the production of food}$$
$$t_{LM} = \text{a tax on labour used in the production of manufactures}$$
$$t_F = \text{a tax on the consumption of food}$$
$$t_M = \text{a tax on consumption of manufactures}$$
$$t_K = \text{a tax on capital in both sectors}$$
$$t_L = \text{a tax on labour in both sectors}$$
$$t = \text{a general income tax}$$

Each of the first four taxes, which are levied on a factor in only some of its uses, is referred to as a **partial factor tax**.

Certain combinations of these taxes are equivalent to others. One of these equivalences is already familiar from the theory of the consumer. Taxes on food (t_F) and manufactures (t_M) at the same rate are equivalent to

---

[18] If a land tax is anticipated before it is levied, then presumably it is borne at least in part by the owner at the time the anticipation becomes widespread. In theory, then, even finding out the identity of the landowner at the time the tax was imposed may not be enough. Further, at the fringes of urban areas that are adjacent to farmland, the supply of urban land can be extended, so the incidence is not entirely on landlords.

TABLE 14.2					
Tax Equivalence Relations					
t_{KF} and	and	t_{LF} and	are equivalent to		t_F and
t_{KM} are equivalent to	and	t_{LM} are equivalent to	are equivalent to		t_M are equivalent to
t_K	and	t_L	are equivalent to		t

Source: Charles E. McLure, Jr., "The Theory of Tax Incidence with Imperfect Factor Mobility," *Finanzarchiv* 30 (1971): 29.

an income tax (t).[19] To see this, just note that equiproportional taxes on all commodities have the same effect on the consumer's budget constraint as a proportional income tax. Both create a parallel shift inward.

Now consider a proportional tax on both capital (t_K) and labour (t_L). Because in this model all income is derived from capital or labour, it is a simple matter of arithmetic that taxing both factors at the same rate is also equivalent to an income tax (t).

Perhaps not so obvious is the fact that partial taxes on both capital and labour in the food sector at a given rate $(t_{KF} = t_{LF})$ are equivalent to a tax on food (t_F) at the same rate. Because capital and labour are the only inputs to the production of food, making each of them more expensive by a certain proportion is equivalent to making the food itself more expensive in the same proportion.

More generally, any two sets of taxes that generate the same changes in relative prices have equivalent incidence effects. All the equivalence relations that can be derived using similar logic are summarized in Table 14.2. For a given ad valorem tax rate, the equivalences are shown by reading across the rows or down the columns. To determine the incidence of all three taxes in any row or column, only two have to be analyzed in detail. The third can be determined by addition or subtraction. For example, from the third row, if we know the incidence of taxes on capital and labour then we also know the incidence of a tax on income.

In the next section, we discuss the incidence of four taxes: a food tax (t_F), an income tax (t), a general tax on labour (t_L), and a partial tax on capital in manufacturing (t_{KM}). With results on these four taxes in hand, the incidence of the other five can be determined by using Table 14.2.

The Harberger Model

The pioneering work in applying general equilibrium models to tax incidence is by Harberger (1974). The principal assumptions of his model are as follows:

1. *Technology.* Firms in each sector use capital and labour to produce their outputs. The technologies in each sector are such that a simultaneous doubling of both inputs leads to a doubling of output—constant returns to scale.[20] However, the production technologies may differ across sectors. In general, the production technologies differ with respect to the ease with which capital can be substituted for labour (the **elasticity of substitution**) and the ratios in which capital and labour are employed. For example, it has been calculated that the capital–labour ratio in the production of food is about twice that used in the production of textiles.[21] The industry in which the capital–labour ratio is relatively high is characterized as **capital intensive**; the other is **labour intensive**.

2. *Behaviour of factor suppliers.* Suppliers of both capital and labour maximize total returns. Moreover, capital and labour are perfectly mobile—they can freely move across sectors according to the wishes of their owners. Consequently, the net marginal return to capital must be the same in each sector, and so must the net

---

[19] Note that, given the assumption that all income is consumed, an income tax is also equivalent to a tax on consumption expenditure.

[20] It is also assumed that the production function is homogeneous, a technical condition meaning that each ratio of factor prices is uniquely associated with a given ratio of capital to labour.

[21] See Congressional Budget Office (1997).

marginal return to labour. Otherwise, it would be possible to reallocate capital and labour in such a way that total net returns could be increased.

3. *Market structure.* Firms are competitive and maximize profits, and all prices (including the wage rate) are perfectly flexible. Therefore, factors are fully employed, and the return paid to each factor of production is the value of its marginal product—the value to the firm of the output produced by the last unit of the input.

4. *Total factor supplies.* The total amounts of capital and labour available to the economy are fixed. But, as already suggested, both factors are perfectly free to move between sectors.

5. *Consumer preferences.* All consumers have identical preferences. A tax, therefore, cannot generate any distributional effects by affecting people's uses of income. This assumption allows us to concentrate on the effect of taxes on the sources of income.

6. *Tax incidence framework.* The framework for the analysis is differential tax incidence. We consider the substitution of one tax for another. Therefore, approximately the same amount of income is available before and after the tax, so it is unnecessary to consider how changes in aggregate income may change demand and factor prices.

Clearly, these assumptions are somewhat restrictive, but they serve to simplify the analysis considerably. Later in this chapter, we consider the consequences of dropping some of them. We now employ Harberger's model to analyze several different taxes.

Analysis of Various Taxes

A commodity tax (t_F). When a tax on food is imposed, its relative price increases (although not necessarily by the amount of the tax). Consumers are thereby induced to substitute manufactures for food. Consequently, less food and more manufactures are produced. As food production falls, some of the capital and labour formerly used in food production are forced to find employment in manufacturing. Because the capital–labour ratios differ between the two sectors, the relative prices of capital and labour have to change for manufacturing to be willing to absorb the unemployed factors from food production. For example, assume that food is the capital-intensive sector. (Canadian agriculture does, in fact, use relatively more capital equipment—tractors, combines, and so forth—than many types of manufacturing.) Therefore, relatively large amounts of capital must be absorbed in manufacturing. The only way for all this capital to find employment in the manufacturing sector is for the relative price of capital to fall—including capital already in use in the manufacturing sector. In the new equilibrium, then, *all* capital is relatively worse off, not just capital in the food sector. More generally, a tax on the *output* of a particular sector induces a decline in the relative price of the *input* used intensively in that sector.

To go beyond such qualitative statements, additional information is needed. The greater the elasticity of demand for food, the more dramatic will be the change in consumption from food to manufactures, which ultimately induces a greater decline in the return to capital. The greater the difference in factor proportions between food and manufactures, the greater must be the decrease in capital's price for it to be absorbed into the manufacturing sector. (If the capital–labour ratios for food and manufactured goods were identical, neither factor would suffer relative to the other.) Finally, the harder it is to substitute capital for labour in the production of manufactures, the greater the decline in the rate of return to capital needed to absorb the additional capital.

Thus, on the sources side of the budget, the food tax tends to hurt people who receive a proportionately large share of their incomes from capital. Given that all individuals are identical (assumption 5), there are no interesting effects on the uses side. However, were we to drop this assumption, then clearly those people who consumed proportionately large amounts of food would tend to bear relatively larger burdens. The total incidence of the food tax then depends on both the sources and uses sides. For example, a capitalist who eats a lot of food is worse off on both counts. On the other hand, a labourer who eats a lot of food is better off from the point of view of the sources of income, but worse off on the uses side.

An income tax (t). As already noted, an income tax is equivalent to a set of taxes on capital and labour at the same rate. Since factor supplies are completely fixed (assumption 4), this tax cannot be shifted. It is borne in proportion to people's initial incomes. The intuition behind this result is similar to the analogous case in the partial equilibrium model; since the factors cannot "escape" the tax (by opting out of production), they bear the full burden.

A general tax on labour (t_L). A general tax on labour is a tax on labour in all its uses in the production of both food and manufactures. As a result, there are no incentives to switch labour use between sectors. Further, the assumption of fixed factor supplies implies labour must bear the entire burden.

A partial factor tax (t_{KM}). When capital used in the manufacturing sector only is taxed, there are two initial effects:

1. *Output effect.* The price of manufactures tends to rise, which decreases the quantity demanded by consumers.
2. *Factor substitution effect.* As capital becomes more expensive in the manufacturing sector, producers there use less capital and more labour.

A flowchart for tracing the implications of these two effects is presented in Figure 14.11. The output effect is described on the left side. As its name suggests, the output effect is a consequence of reductions in the production of manufactures. When the price of manufactures increases and less is demanded, capital and labour are released from manufacturing and must find employment in the production of food. If the manufacturing sector is labour intensive, then (relatively) large amounts of labour have to be absorbed in the food sector, and the relative price of capital increases. If, on the other hand, the manufacturing sector is capital intensive, the relative price of capital falls. Thus, the output effect is ambiguous with respect to the final effect on the relative prices of capital and labour.

This ambiguity is not present with the factor substitution effect, as depicted in the righthand side of Figure 14.11. As long as substitution between capital and labour is possible, an increase in the price of capital induces manufacturers to use less capital and more labour, tending to decrease the demand for capital and its relative price.

Putting the two effects together, we see that if manufacturing is capital intensive, both effects work in the same direction, and the relative price of capital must fall. But if the manufacturing sector is labour intensive, the final outcome is theoretically ambiguous. Even though the tax is levied on capital, it can make labour worse off! More generally, as long as factors are mobile between uses, a tax on a given factor in *one* sector ultimately affects the return to *both* factors in *both* sectors. Such insights cannot be obtained with the partial equilibrium models discussed earlier in this chapter.

FIGURE 14.11

INCIDENCE OF A PARTIAL FACTOR TAX (t_{KM}) IN A GENERAL EQUILIBRIUM MODEL

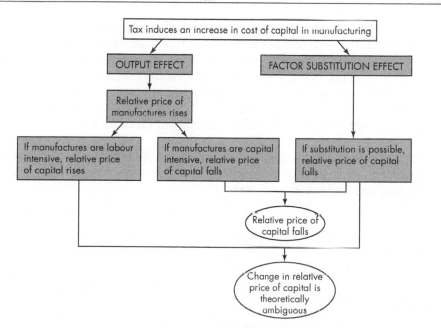

Much of the applied research on incidence in general equilibrium models has focused on the corporation income tax. Such work assumes that the two sectors are "corporate" and "noncorporate," and that the corporation income tax is an ad valorem tax on capital only on its use in the corporate sector.[22] Given the theoretical ambiguity of the effect of a partial factor tax on the demand for capital, empirical work is required to find its incidence. Although different studies have reached different conclusions, in an open economy such as Canada's it is unlikely that the corporate income tax results in a fall in the after-tax return to capital owners. Capital can easily be moved to other locations, and the tax is likely to fall on workers who will have less capital to work with, or on consumers where producers are able to raise prices on goods not subject to international competition.[23]

Some Qualifications

Changes in the assumptions underlying the general equilibrium model can modify its implications for tax incidence in the following ways.

Differences in individuals' tastes. By assumption 5, all consumers have the same preferences for the two goods. When they do not, tax-induced changes in the distribution of income change aggregate spending decisions and, hence, relative prices and incomes. Consider a general tax on labour. As noted, in the model with fixed factor supplies, this is borne entirely by labourers. However, if labourers consume different commodities than capitalists, those commodities favoured by labourers face a decrease in demand. Resources are then allocated away from these commodities, and the factor used intensively in their production receives a lower return. If labourers tend to consume capital-intensive goods disproportionately, capital can end up bearing part of the burden of a general tax on labour.

Immobile factors. By assumption 2, resources are free to flow between sectors, seeking the highest rate of return possible. However, for institutional or technological reasons, some factors may be immobile. For example, if certain land is zoned for residential use, it cannot be used in manufacturing, no matter what the rate of return. Abandoning perfect mobility can dramatically affect the incidence implications of a tax. For example, earlier we showed that if factors are mobile, the incidence of a partial factor tax is ambiguous, depending on the outcome of several conflicting effects. If the factor is immobile, however, the incidence result is clear-cut— the taxed factor bears the whole burden. Intuitively, this is because the factor cannot "escape" taxation by migrating to the other sector. Note also that because the return to the taxed immobile factor falls by just the amount of the tax, the prices of capital and labour in the untaxed sectors are unchanged, as is the price of the good in the taxed sector.

Variable factor supplies. By assumption 4, the total supplies of both factors are fixed. In the long run, however, the supplies of both capital and labour to the economy are variable. Allowing for growth can turn conclusions from the static model completely on their heads. Consider a general factor tax on capital. When the capital stock is fixed, this tax is borne entirely by the capital's owners. In the long run, however, less capital may be supplied due to the tax.[24] To the extent this occurs, the economy's capital–labour ratio decreases, and the return to labour falls. (The wage falls because labour has less capital with which to work, and, hence, is less productive, *ceteris paribus*.) Thus, labour can be made worse off as a result of a general tax on capital.

Because the amount of calendar time that must elapse before the long run is reached may be substantial, short-run effects should not be regarded as inconsequential. On the other hand, intelligent policy also requires consideration of the long-run consequences of taxation.

---

[22] Specifically, it is assumed the capital is financed by selling shares of stock as opposed to borrowing. As we see in Chapter 21, this is a somewhat controversial view.

[23] The most typical finding for a large economy such as the United States is that much of the tax is shifted to the owners of all capital, not just owners of capital in the corporate sector (Congressional Budget Office, 2012). The effect of the tax may be quite different in Canada where higher taxes may cause capital to relocate to the large U.S. market, causing less-mobile factors to bear a significant part of the burden (McKenzie and Mintz, 1992).

[24] However, the supply of capital does not necessarily decrease. See Chapter 18.

APPLIED INCIDENCE STUDIES

Partial Equilibrium Analysis

Lee (2007) uses a partial equilibrium model of tax incidence as a framework to estimate how the Canadian system of federal and provincial taxation affected the distribution of income from 1990 to 2005.[25] During this 15-year period, there were numerous important tax reforms, including the introduction of the Goods and Services Tax (GST), changes in payroll taxes, and cuts to federal and provincial income tax rates on corporations and individuals. Using a "broad income" concept that includes transfer payments and imputed income, and measuring incidence based on annual income, Lee employs the following set of shifting assumptions:

- personal income taxes borne by the taxpayer with no shifting
- corporate income taxes borne totally by owners of corporations
- sales and excise taxes borne by consumers in proportion to consumption expenditures
- payroll taxes borne by labour, whether paid by employer or employee, and in proportion to wages and salaries that are subject to tax
- property taxes on land borne by landowners, and taxes on structures borne by consumers of services from structures (e.g., a retailer is assumed to pass any property tax on the structure on to consumers of goods or services)

The shifting assumptions are combined with information generated by Statistics Canada on the income sources and expenditures of families at different income levels to determine the incidence of the various taxes—personal income tax, corporate income tax, sales and excise taxes, payroll taxes, property taxes, and other taxes. Figure 14.12 shows the results for the tax system as a whole. The average tax rates are depicted across income deciles, whereby families are divided into ten equal-sized groups, ranked from lowest to highest incomes. Deciles are appropriate for comparisons over time to control for the effects of inflation on nominal incomes. Table 14.3 gives the income cut-offs corresponding to each decile for 1990 and 2005 (in constant 2010 dollars). The top decile is split further into percentiles. Lee summarizes his overall findings as follows:

> By 2005, the Canadian tax system was much less fair than it was in 1990. Overall, the Canadian tax system in 2005 has become flatter, with total tax rates ranging from 30.7% of income at the bottom of the income spectrum, some modest progressivity up to the middle of the income distribution, peaking at 36.5%, then modestly regressive thereafter, falling back to 30.5% for the top 1% of families.

The incidence of the different types of taxes are illustrated for 2005 in Figure 14.13. Each curve in Figure 14.13 shows the tax incidence as a percentage of broad income. For example, for a household in the bottom decile, 17 percent of its broad income is taken by commodity taxes. The personal income tax is progressive over all but the highest incomes, while commodity taxes, property taxes, and other taxes are regressive across the income spectrum. Payroll taxes, initially progressive, turn regressive around the sixth decile. The corporate income tax adds a progressive element at the highest income levels.

Figure 14.14 gives the results for federal and provincial taxes in 2005.[26] While federal taxes are progressive up to the middle decile, provincial taxes are regressive across all deciles. The regressiveness of provincial taxes is due to property taxes and commodity (or sales) taxes.

---

[25] The pioneering work in this field was done by the Canadian economist Irwin Gillespie in the 1960s. The study by Marc Lee follows closely the approach of Vermaeten et al. (1994). In another paper, Vermaeten et al. (1995) examine changes in Canadian tax incidence for the period 1951 to 1988, comparing tax incidence for the years 1951, 1961, 1969, and 1988. See also Kesselman and Cheung (2004) for a survey of incidence studies for Canada.

[26] Local property taxes are included in provincial taxes, since municipalities are constitutionally within the purview of their provincial governments.

FIGURE 14.12

AVERAGE TAX RATE, TOTAL TAXES, BY BROAD INCOME, CANADA, 1990 TO 2005

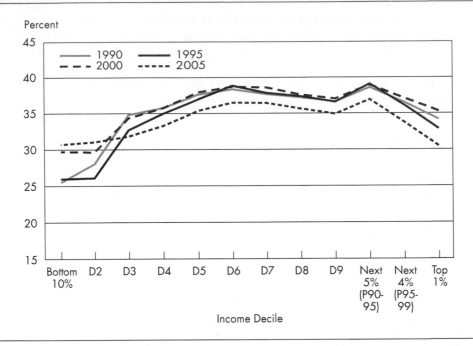

Source: Reproduced with the permission of the Canadian Centre for Policy Alternatives from Marc Lee, "Eroding Tax Fairness: Tax Incidence in Canada, 1990 to 2005," November 2007, figure 1.

It should be clear by now that all incidence results depend crucially on the underlying models. The income definition and the various shifting assumptions all affect the outcome. For example, if capital flows freely between sectors, corporate capital will not bear the entire burden of the corporation income tax; where imperfect competition exists, corporations may pass on corporate income taxes to consumers through higher prices;

TABLE 14.3

Decile Cut-Offs, 1990 and 2005 (in constant 2010 dollars)		
	1990	**2005**
D1	$1–13,129	$1–14,723
D2	13,130–19,319	14,724–20,695
D3	19,320–27,874	20,696–29,136
D4	27,875–36,345	29,137–38,834
D5	36,346–46,466	38,835–49,570
D6	46,467–58,457	49,571–62,561
D7	58,458–72,631	62,562–78,718
D8	72,632–90,790	78,719–98,600
D9	90,791–120,622	98,601–131,081
P90–95	120,623–152,789	131,082–165,000
P95–99	152,790–282,712	165,001–289,389
P99–100	282,713–Max	289,390–Max

Source: Table A2 in Lee (2007), adjusted for inflation using the CPI. Incomes in the table correspond to Statistics Canada's "total income" concept, which is the sum of market income and transfers.

FIGURE 14.13

AVERAGE TAX RATE, BY REVENUE SOURCE, BROAD INCOME, STANDARD CASE, CANADA, 2005

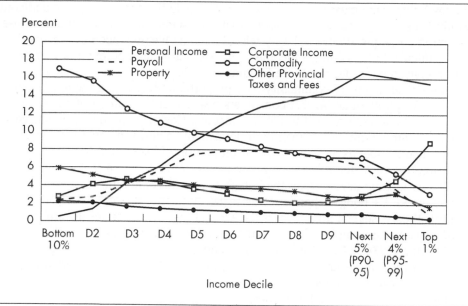

Source: Reproduced with the permission of the Canadian Centre for Policy Alternatives from Marc Lee, "Eroding Tax Fairness: Tax Incidence in Canada, 1990 to 2005," November 2007, figure 5.

FIGURE 14.14

EFFECTIVE TAX RATE, BY LEVEL OF GOVERNMENT, BROAD INCOME, CANADA, 2005

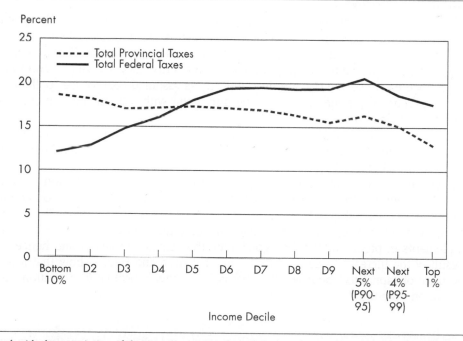

Source: Reproduced with the permission of the Canadian Centre for Policy Alternatives from Marc Lee, "Eroding Tax Fairness: Tax Incidence in Canada, 1990 to 2005," November 2007, using table 1.

union power may prevent employers from fully shifting payroll taxes onto employees; and where capital is less than perfectly mobile, capital owners may bear part of the tax on structures. Changing assumptions may lead to sharply different outcomes than the ones shown in Figures 14.12 to 14.14.

Another problem with placing too much reliance on an analysis such as the above is the use of "annual" incomes of families. Using some measure of lifetime income would be more appropriate and could change the results importantly. To see why, we begin by noting that a substantial amount of empirical research suggests people's consumption decisions are more closely related to some lifetime income measure than to the value of income in any particular year. A family's income being *temporarily* high or low in a year does not have that great an impact on consumption decisions (see Friedman, 1957).

Assume that the consumption of commodity X is proportional to lifetime income. Assume further that the supply curve for X is horizontal, so that consumers bear the entire burden of any tax on X. Then a tax on X would be proportional with respect to lifetime income. However, in any particular year some people have incomes that are temporarily higher than their permanent values, and some have lower. A person with a temporarily high income spends a relatively small proportion of his annual income on X as he does not increase his consumption of X due to the temporary nature of the increase in income. Similarly, a person with a temporarily low income devotes a relatively high proportion of her income to good X. In short, based on annual income, good X's budget share appears to fall with income, and a tax on X looks regressive. Consistent with this theory, several investigators have found that incidence results are sensitive to whether *lifetime* or *annual* measures are employed. For example, in their analysis of Canadian tax incidence, Davies, St-Hilaire, and Whalley (1984: 643) found that sales and excise taxes were 27.2 percent of the annual incomes in the lowest income decile, and 8.5 percent in the highest decile—a decidedly regressive pattern. Using lifetime income, however, the regressivity is substantially reduced, with sales and excise taxes taking 15.0 percent of lifetime income in the lowest decile, and 12.4 percent in the highest decile. We conclude that even though empirical work of the sort done by Lee is suggestive, the results must be viewed with caution (see Davies, 1992).

The foregoing discussion has focused entirely on the incidence of taxes. It has ignored the incidence of government expenditures. The negative effect of taxes on those with low incomes may be much more than offset by the positive effect of government transfer payments and benefits from other government programs. The reverse may be true for those with high incomes.[27]

General Equilibrium Analysis

Public concern over environmental degradation and global warming has prompted calls for governments to impose new regulations and taxes on the emission of pollutants. A study by Fullerton and Heutel (2007) examines the incidence of a pollution tax in a general equilibrium framework. They reinterpret the two sectors in the Harberger model as representing a "clean" industry and a "dirty" industry. In addition to the capital and labour used to produce each commodity, the dirty industry is assumed also to use "pollution" as an input. That is, in order to produce the same quantity of the dirty good with less pollution, more capital or labour must be shifted from the clean industry to the dirty industry.

The researchers theoretically analyze the incidence arising from a per-unit tax on pollution in the presence of proportional taxes on capital and labour. The aim is to determine the effects of a pollution tax on the price of the dirty good and on labour and capital incomes.

The pollution tax generates an output effect and substitution effects between pollution and the other inputs. Fullerton and Heutel show that the net effect is very complicated and may generate counterintuitive results. Suppose, for example, that capital is a *better* substitute for pollution than is labour. Thus, the pollution tax would tend to raise the demand for capital and, hence, increase the return to capital. However, if capital and labour are complements in producing the dirty good, then the demand for labour and hence wages will also increase as a result of the increase in demand for capital. Fullerton and Heutel show that it is even possible that the relative price of capital to labour will fall—that is, "the better substitute for pollution can bear *more* of the burden of a tax on pollution."

---

[27] Studies of the overall incidence of tax and expenditure systems are complex and quite rare. One Canadian study found the combined incidence of government taxes and expenditures to be progressive (see Gillespie, 1976).

The elasticities of substitution among capital, labour, and pollution are crucial for evaluating the incidence of a pollution tax. Lacking solid empirical estimates for these, the distributional effects of a pollution tax in general equilibrium remain largely hypothetical and is an active area of current research.

A study by Fullerton and Heutel (2011) applies their two-sector general equilibrium model to estimate the tax incidence of a proposed carbon tax in the United States.[28] The authors classify three industries—petroleum refining, electricity, and transportation—as the "dirty" sector of the economy and all other industries as the "clean" sector.[29] Using the best available estimates for the parameters of the model, together with data on the sources of income and expenditure patterns of households across income deciles in the United States, Fullerton and Heutel find (in their base case) that the incidence of the carbon tax is regressive on both the uses side of income and the sources side of income.

On the uses side, the carbon tax is regressive because lower-income households spend a relatively higher fraction of their incomes on carbon-intensive goods, whose prices rise as a result of the tax.[30] On the sources side, the substitution effect places more of the burden on labour (labour is an inferior substitute for pollution compared with capital), while the output effect places more of the burden on capital (the dirty industry is capital intensive). As the output effect is found to dominate the substitution effect in the model, households that receive a greater than average fraction of their incomes from wage earnings bear relatively less of the carbon tax burden. It turns out that the fraction of income from wages in the United States is increasing across all deciles, due to the decreasing fraction of income from government transfers across deciles.[31] Hence, the overall burden of a carbon tax is expected to be regressive. It remains to be seen whether future research, using models with more than two sectors and more reliable estimates of the factor substitution elasticities, will confirm the results of these early studies on the incidence of a carbon tax.

CONCLUSIONS

We began this chapter with an innocent question: who bears the burden of a tax? It led us to an analysis of the sometimes complicated relationships among various markets. We have seen that price changes are the key to finding the burden of a tax, but that price changes depend on a lot of things: market structure, elasticities of supply and demand, movements of factors of production, and so on. At this stage, an obvious question is, what do we really know?

For taxes that may reasonably be analyzed in isolation, the answer is, "Quite a bit." To do a partial equilibrium incidence analysis, one needs only to know the market structure and the shapes of the supply and demand curves. In cases other than a clear-cut monopoly, the competitive market paradigm has proved to be a sensible choice of market structure. Incidence analysis is on firm ground.

Even in general equilibrium models, incidence analysis is straightforward for a tax on an immobile factor—the incidence is entirely on the taxed factor. More generally, though, if a tax affects many markets, incidence depends on the reactions of numerous supply and demand curves for goods and inputs. The answers are correspondingly less clear.

---

[28] On October 1, 2007, Quebec became the first province to introduce a carbon tax, in order to help the province reach its Kyoto Protocol target for greenhouse gas emissions by 2012. A revenue-neutral carbon tax was also implemented in British Columbia on July 1, 2008, and the final scheduled rate increase took effect on July 1, 2012. The rates are based on $30 per tonne of CO_2 equivalent emissions, which translates to a tax rate of 6.67 cents per litre of gasoline, for example. This "green tax" is a proxy for a tax on pollution. See Beck, Rivers, Wigle, and Yonezawa (2015) for an analysis of the incidence of the B.C. carbon tax using a computable general equilibrium model. The authors find that the B.C. carbon tax is highly progressive.

[29] The outputs of these industries correspond approximately to consumption goods involving the combustion of fossil fuels. Hence, Fullerton and Heutel classify consumer expenditures on electricity, natural gas, fuel oil and other fuels, and gasoline as the "dirty" sector when assessing the uses-side of the carbon tax incidence.

[30] The uses-side result is corroborated by other recent studies. See, for example, Hassett, Mathur, and Metcalf (2009) and Burtraw, Sweeney, and Walls (2009).

[31] This is the case even though the fraction of income from capital is highest at the top deciles.

Unfortunately, it seems that many important taxes, such as the corporate tax, fall into the last category. Why is this? It may be for the very reason that the incidence is hard to find. (What are the political chances of a tax that clearly hurts some important group in the population?) Complicated taxes may actually be simpler for a politician because no one is sure who actually ends up paying them.

In any case, the models in this chapter tell us exactly what information is needed to understand the incidence even of very complex taxes. To the extent that this information is currently unavailable, the models serve as a measure of our ignorance. This is not altogether undesirable. As St. Jerome noted, "It is worse still to be ignorant of your ignorance."

SUMMARY

- Statutory incidence refers to the legal liability for a tax, while economic incidence shows the actual sacrifice of income due to the tax. Knowledge of the legal incidence usually tells us little about economic incidence.

- Economic incidence is determined by the way price changes when a tax is imposed. The incidence of a tax ultimately falls on individuals via both their sources and uses of income.

- Depending on the policy being considered, it may be appropriate to examine balanced budget, differential, or absolute incidence.

- In partial equilibrium competitive models, tax incidence depends on the elasticities of supply and demand. The same general approach can be used to study incidence in a monopolized market.

- Due to capitalization, the burden of future taxes may be borne by current owners of an inelastically supplied durable commodity, such as land.

- General equilibrium incidence analysis is often conducted using a two-sector, two-factor model. This framework allows for nine possible taxes. Certain combinations of these taxes are equivalent to others.

- Taxing a single factor in its use only in a particular sector changes relative factor prices and, hence, the distribution of income. The particular outcome depends on factor intensities, ease of substitution in production, mobility of factors, and elasticities of demand for outputs.

- Applied incidence studies indicate that the Canadian tax system is progressive up to the middle of the income distribution, then modestly regressive thereafter.

- Finally, on a cautionary note, it is essential to keep in mind that income distribution is affected more by government expenditures and regulations than by taxation. The incidence of these activities, as well as taxation, must be examined to gain a fuller understanding of the government's impact on income distribution.

EXERCISES

1. In the province of Alberta, the tax on hotel rooms is 5 percent. Supporters of this tax argue that the tax benefits the province because its victims are largely out-of-province tourists. Use the theory of tax incidence to analyze this claim.

2. Higher payroll taxes may be required to finance the Canada Pension Plan as the population ages. If employers are asked to pay all of any such increase, rather than sharing the increase equally between employers and employees, how would this affect wages and employment? Would businesses likely end up paying for the increase in CPP premiums?

3. For commodity X, average cost is equal to marginal cost at every level of output. Assuming that the market for X is competitive, analyze the effects when a unit tax of u dollars is imposed. Now analyze the effects of the same tax assuming that the market for X is a monopoly. Discuss the differences.

4. Assume that the capital-labour ratios are identical in all sectors of the economy. What determines the incidence of a tax on the output of any single sector?

5. Internet purchases are thought to be highly sensitive to tax rates, and applying sales taxes to all such purchases substantially reduces the number of online buyers and the amount of online spending. What are the implications for the incidence of sales taxes that include Internet (as well as other) sales?

6. Suppose that the demand for cigarettes in a hypothetical country is given by $Q_C^D = 2,000 - 200\, P_C$, where Q_C^D is the number of packs demanded and P_c is the price per pack. The supply of cigarettes is $Q_C^D = P_C \times 200$.

   a. Find the price and quantity of cigarettes, assuming the market is competitive.

   b. In an effort to reduce smoking, the government levies a tax of $2 per pack. Compute the quantity of cigarettes after the tax, the price paid by consumers, and the price received by producers. How much revenue does the tax raise for the government? How much revenue comes from consumers, and how much from producers?

7. Suppose that the demand curve for a particular commodity is $Q^D = a - bP$, where Q^D is the quantity demanded, P is the price, and a and b are constants. The supply curve for the commodity is $Q^S = c + dP$, where Q^S is the quantity supplied and c and d are constants. Find the equilibrium price and output as functions of the constants a, b, c, and d.

   Suppose that a unit tax of u dollars is imposed on the commodity. Show that the new equilibrium quantity, producer price, and consumer price are the same regardless of whether the tax is imposed on producers or buyers of the good.

   Now express the incidence on producers and on buyers as proportions of the tax revenue and comment on how the incidence depends on the slopes of the demand curve $(-b)$ and the supply curve (d).

8. In 2004, the city of Cologne, Germany, instituted a "pleasure tax." Among other things, the tax applied to massage parlours, table-dancing clubs, and brothels. Many sex workers complained that the tax was unjust because it was levied on them rather than the men who patronize their services. One sex worker said, "I can't increase what I charge" to make up for the tax increase.

   a. Implicit in the sex worker's assertion is an assumption about the elasticity of demand for her services. What is that assumption, and do you think it is realistic?

   b. What would be the economic implications for sex workers if the tax were instead levied on their patrons?

9. Suppose that the income tax in a certain nation is computed as a flat rate of 5 percent, but no tax is levied above $50,000 in taxable income. Taxable income, in turn, is computed as the individual's income minus $10,000; that is, everyone gets a $10,000 deduction. What are the marginal and average tax rates for each of the following workers? (Evaluate the marginal tax rate at each person's current income level.)

   a. A part-time worker with annual income of $9,000.

   b. A retail salesperson with annual income of $45,000.

   c. An advertising executive with annual income of $600,000.

   Is the tax progressive, proportional, or regressive with respect to income?

10. Arnie has an income of Y and spends it only on food and music. Let P_F and P_M denote the price of food and music, respectively, and denote the quantities by Q_F and Q_M. In the absence of taxes, Arnie's budget constraint is $Y = P_F Q_F + P_M Q_M$. Now suppose an ad valorem tax of 25 percent is imposed on both food and music. What income tax rate is equivalent to this commodity tax?

11. Petroleum products manufacturing is one of the most capital-intensive industries in Canada. Use a general equilibrium framework to discuss the possible incidence of a tax on petroleum products.

12. The applied incidence study by Lee (2007), discussed in this chapter, assumes that personal income taxes are fully borne by the taxpayer with no shifting. However, there is some evidence provided by Schaafsma (1992) that Canadian dentists shift a portion of personal income taxes onto dental patients in the form of higher dental fees. Suppose that all high-end professional labour (e.g., lawyers, doctors) is able to fully shift forward personal income taxes onto consumers. Discuss how this might affect the pattern of tax incidence represented in Figure 14.12.

13. According to the study by Kleven, Landais, and Saez (2015), the international migration decisions of top-earning European soccer players is very sensitive to income tax rates—when the tax rates they face in their own country increase substantially, they move to another country. What are the implications of this finding for the incidence of income taxes on such players? Support your answer with a graph.

CHAPTER 15

Taxation and Efficiency

Waste always makes me angry.

—Rhett Butler in *Gone With the Wind*

AFTER READING THIS CHAPTER, THE STUDENT SHOULD BE ABLE TO:

LO1 ▸ Define the equivalent variation of a tax and depict it graphically.

LO2 ▸ Define the excess burden of a tax and illustrate it with indifference curves and budget constraints.

LO3 ▸ Use results from welfare economics to explain why an income tax entails an excess burden.

LO4 ▸ Explain why a lump-sum tax is efficient but not widely used.

LO5 ▸ Identify the excess burden of a tax and a subsidy on a graph with demand and supply curves.

LO6 ▸ Estimate the excess burden in a market using price elasticities and expenditure data.

LO7 ▸ Illustrate the excess burden resulting from the differential taxation of inputs.

Taxes impose a cost on the taxpayer. It is tempting to view the cost as simply the amount of money that he or she hands over to the tax collector. However, an example indicates that this is just part of the story.

Consider Breyer Dove, a citizen who typically consumes ten ice cream cones each week, at a price of $1 per cone. The government levies a 25 percent tax on his consumption of ice cream cones, so now Dove faces a price of $1.25.[1] In response to the price hike, Dove reduces his ice cream cone consumption to zero, and he spends the $10 per week on other goods and services. Obviously, because Dove consumes no ice cream cones, the ice cream tax yields zero revenue. Do we want to say that Dove is unaffected by the tax? The answer is no. Dove is worse off because the tax has induced him to consume a less-desirable bundle of goods than previously. We know that the after-tax bundle is less desirable because, before tax, Dove had the option of consuming no ice cream cones. Since he chose to buy ten cones weekly, this must have been preferred to spending the money on other items. Thus, despite the fact that the tax raised zero revenue, it made Dove worse off.

This example is a bit extreme. Normally, we expect that an increase in price diminishes the quantity demanded but does not drive it all the way to zero. Nevertheless, the basic result holds—because a tax distorts economic decisions, it brings about an **excess burden**—a loss of welfare above and beyond the tax revenues collected. Excess burden is sometimes referred to as *welfare cost*, or *deadweight loss*. In this chapter we discuss the theory and measurement of excess burden, and explain why it is an important concept for evaluating actual tax systems.

---

[1] As emphasized in Chapter 14, the price paid by the consumer generally does not rise by the full amount of the tax. This assumption, which is correct if the supply curve is horizontal, is made here only for convenience.

FIGURE 15.1

EFFECT OF A TAX ON THE BUDGET CONSTRAINT

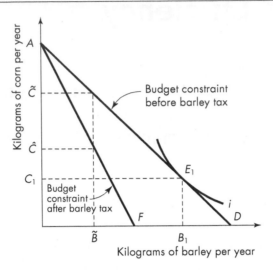

EXCESS BURDEN

Ruth has a fixed income of I dollars, which she spends on only two commodities: barley and corn. The price per pound of barley is P_b and the price per pound of corn is P_c. There are no taxes or "distortions," such as externalities or monopoly in the economy, so the prices of the goods reflect their social marginal costs. For convenience, these social marginal costs are assumed to be constant with respect to output. In Figure 15.1, Ruth's consumption of barley is measured on the horizontal axis and her consumption of corn on the vertical. Her budget constraint is the line AD, which has slope $-P_b/P_c$ and horizontal intercept I/P_b. Assuming Ruth wants to maximize her utility, she chooses a point like E_1 on indifference curve i, where she consumes B_1 kilograms of barley and C_1 kilograms of corn.

Now suppose the government levies a tax at a percentage rate of t_b on barley so the price Ruth faces becomes $(1 + t_b)P_b$. (The before-tax price is unchanged because of our assumption of constant social marginal costs.) Imposition of the tax changes Ruth's budget constraint. It now has a slope of $-[(1 + t_b)P_b/P_c]$ and horizontal intercept $I/[(1 + t_b)P_b]$. This is represented in Figure 15.1 as line AF. (Because the price of corn is still P_c, lines AF and AD have the same vertical intercept.)

Note that for any given consumption level of barley, the vertical distance between AD and AF shows Ruth's tax payments measured in corn. To see this, consider an arbitrary quantity of barley $\widetilde{B}$ on the horizontal axis. Before the tax was imposed, Ruth could have both $\widetilde{B}$ kilograms of barley and $\widetilde{C}$ kilograms of corn. After the tax, however, if she consumed $\widetilde{B}$ kilograms of barley, the most corn she could afford would be $\hat{C}$ kilograms. The difference (distance) between $\widetilde{C}$ and $\hat{C}$ must therefore represent the amount of tax collected by the government measured in kilograms of corn. If we choose, we can convert tax receipts to dollars by multiplying the distance $\widetilde{C}\hat{C}$ by the price per kilogram of corn, P_c. For convenience, we can choose to measure corn in units such that $P_c = 1$. In this case, the distance $\widetilde{C}\hat{C}$ measures tax receipts in corn *or* dollars.

So far, we have not indicated which point Ruth chooses on her new budget constraint, AF. Figure 15.2 shows that her most preferred bundle is at E_2 on indifference curve ii, where her consumption of barley is B_2, her consumption of corn is C_2, and her tax bill is the associated vertical distance between AD and AF, GE_2. Clearly, Ruth is worse off at E_2 than she was at E_1. However, *any* tax would have put her on a lower indifference curve.[2] The important question is whether the barley tax inflicts on Ruth a greater utility loss than is necessary to raise revenue GE_2. Alternatively, is there some other way of raising revenue GE_2 that would cause a smaller utility loss to Ruth? If so, the barley tax has an excess burden.

---

[2] This ignores benefits that might be obtained from the expenditures financed by the tax.

FIGURE 15.2

EFFECT OF A TAX ON THE CONSUMPTION BUNDLE

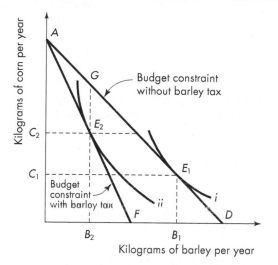

To investigate this issue, we need to find a dollar equivalent of the loss that Ruth suffers by having to move from indifference curve *i* to *ii*. One way to measure this is the **equivalent variation**—the amount of income we would have to take away from Ruth (before the barley tax was levied) to induce her to move from *i* to *ii*. The equivalent variation measures the loss inflicted by the tax as the size of the reduction in income that would cause the same decrease in utility as the tax.

To depict the equivalent variation graphically, recall that taking away income from an individual is represented by a parallel movement inward of her budget line. Hence, to find the equivalent variation, all we have to do is shift *AD* inward, until it is tangent to indifference curve *ii*. The amount by which we have to shift *AD* is the equivalent variation. In Figure 15.3, budget line *HI* is parallel to *AD* and tangent to indifference curve *ii*. Hence, the vertical distance between *AD* and *HI*, ME_3, is the equivalent variation. Ruth is indifferent between losing ME_3 dollars and facing the barley tax.

FIGURE 15.3

EXCESS BURDEN OF THE BARLEY TAX

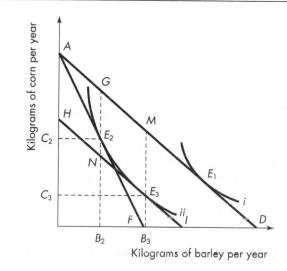

Note that the equivalent variation ME_3 exceeds the barley tax revenues of GE_2. To see why, just observe that ME_3 equals GN, because both measure the distance between the parallel lines AD and HI. Hence, ME_3 exceeds GE_2 by distance E_2N. This is really quite a remarkable result. It means that the barley tax makes Ruth worse off by an amount that actually exceeds the revenues it generates. In Figure 15.3, the amount by which the loss in welfare (measured by the equivalent variation) exceeds the taxes collected—the excess burden—is distance E_2N.

Does *every* tax entail an excess burden? Define a **lump-sum tax** as a certain amount that must be paid regardless of the taxpayer's behaviour. If the government levies a $100 lump-sum tax on Ruth, there is nothing she can do to avoid paying the $100, other than to leave the country or die. In contrast, the barley tax is not a lump-sum tax, because the revenue yield depends on Ruth's barley consumption.

Let us analyze a lump-sum tax that leaves Ruth as well off as the barley tax. To begin, we must sketch the associated budget line. It must have two characteristics. First, it must be parallel to AD. (Because a lump-sum tax simply takes away money from Ruth, it does not change the relative prices of barley and corn; two budget lines embodying the same price ratio must be parallel.) Second, because of the stipulation that Ruth attain the same utility level as under the barley tax, the budget line must be tangent to indifference curve *ii*.

Budget line HI in Figure 15.3, which is tangent to indifference curve *ii* at point E_3, satisfies both these criteria. If confronted with this budget line, Ruth would consume B_3 kilograms of barley and C_3 kilograms of corn. The revenue yield of the lump-sum tax is the vertical distance between E_3 and the before-tax budget constraint, or distance ME_3. But we showed earlier that ME_3 is also the equivalent variation of the move from indifference curve *i* to *ii*. This comes as no surprise, since a lump-sum tax is just a parallel shift of the budget line. Because the revenue yield of a lump-sum tax equals its equivalent variation, *a lump-sum tax has no excess burden*.

In short, a lump-sum tax that leaves Ruth on the *same indifference curve* as the barley tax generates more revenue for the government. Alternatively, if we compared a lump-sum tax and a barley tax that raised the *same revenue*, the lump-sum tax would leave Ruth on a higher indifference curve. The skeptical reader may suspect that this result is merely an artifact of the particular way the indifference curves are drawn in Figure 15.3. This is not the case. It can be shown that as long as the indifference curves have the usual shape, a tax that changes relative prices generates an excess burden.[3] Alternatively, a tax that changes relative prices is inefficient in the sense that it lowers individual utility more than is necessary to raise a given amount of revenue.

EXCESS BURDEN: QUESTIONS AND ANSWERS

The previous section's discussion of excess burden raises some important questions.

If lump-sum taxes are so efficient, why aren't they widely used? Lump-sum taxation is an unattractive policy tool for several reasons. Suppose the government announced that every person's tax liability was $2,000 per year. This is a lump-sum tax, but most people would consider it unfair for everyone to pay the same tax regardless of their economic circumstances. In 1990, the government of British Prime Minister Margaret Thatcher implemented a tax that in some ways resembled a lump-sum tax. The property tax that had financed local government was replaced by a head tax; in each local jurisdiction the amount depended on that jurisdiction's per capita revenue needs. The tax was a lump sum in the sense that a person's tax liability did not vary with the amount of income earned or property owned; it did vary, however, with a person's choice of where to live. The perceived unfairness of that tax was one of the factors that led to Mrs. Thatcher's downfall in 1990. The tax was repealed in 1991 by her successor, John Major.

As a way of producing more equitable results, one might consider making people pay different lump-sum taxes based on their incomes. A rich person might be required to pay $20,000 annually, independent of his or her economic decisions, while a poor person would pay only $500. The problem with this proposal is that people entering the work force would soon realize that their eventual tax burden depended on their incomes. They would then adjust their work and savings decisions accordingly. In short, because the amount of income individuals earn is at least in part under their control, the income-based tax is not a lump-sum tax.

---

[3] As noted, this assumes there are no other distortions in the economy. For proof, see Kaplow (2008).

Ultimately, to achieve an equitable system of lump-sum taxes, it would be necessary to base the tax on some underlying "ability" characteristic that measured individuals' *potential* to earn income. In this way, high- and low-potential people could be taxed differently. Because the base is potential, an individual's tax burden would not depend on behaviour. Even if such an ability measure existed, however, it would be difficult for it to be observed by the taxing authority. Individual lump-sum taxes are thus best viewed as standards of efficiency, but not as major policy options in a modern economy.[4]

Are there any results from welfare economics that would help us understand why excess burdens arise? Recall from Chapter 2 that a necessary condition for a Pareto efficient allocation of resources is that the marginal rate of substitution of barley for corn in consumption (MRS_{bc}) equals the marginal rate of transformation of barley for corn in production (MRT_{bc}). Under the barley tax, consumers face a price of barley of $(1 + t_b)P_b$. Therefore, they set

$$MRS_{bc} = \frac{(1 + t_b)P_b}{P_c} \qquad (15.1)$$

Equation (15.1) is the algebraic representation of the equilibrium point E_2 in Figure 15.3.

Producers make their decisions by setting the marginal rate of transformation equal to the ratio of the prices *they receive*. Even though Ruth pays $(1 + t_b)P_b$ per kilogram of barley, the barley producers receive only P_b–the difference goes to the tax collector. Hence, profit-maximizing producers set

$$MRS_{bc} = \frac{P_b}{P_c} \qquad (15.2)$$

Clearly, as long as t_b is not zero, MRS_{bc} exceeds MRT_{bc}, and the necessary condition for an efficient allocation of resources is violated.

Intuitively, when MRS_{bc} is greater than MRT_{bc}, the marginal utility of substituting barley consumption for corn consumption exceeds the change in production costs necessary to do so. Thus, utility would be raised if such an adjustment were made. However, in the presence of the barley tax there is no *financial* incentive to do so. The excess burden is just a measure of the utility loss. The loss arises because the barley tax creates a wedge between what the consumer pays and what the producer receives. In contrast, under a lump-sum tax, the price ratios faced by consumers and producers are equal. There is no wedge, so the necessary conditions for Pareto efficiency are satisfied.

Does an income tax entail an excess burden? The answer is generally yes, but it takes a little thinking to see why. Figure 15.3 showed the imposition of a lump-sum tax as a downward parallel movement from *AD* to *HI*. This movement could just as well have arisen via a tax that took some proportion of Ruth's income. Like the lump-sum tax, an income reduction moves the intercepts of the budget constraint closer to the origin but leaves its slope unchanged. Perhaps, then, lump-sum taxation and income taxation are equivalent. In fact, if income were fixed, an income tax *would* be a lump-sum tax. However, when people's choices affect their incomes, an income tax is *not* generally equivalent to a lump-sum tax.

Think of Ruth as consuming *three* commodities, barley, corn, and leisure time, *l*. Ruth gives up leisure (that is, she supplies labour) to earn income that she spends on barley and corn. In the production sector, Ruth's leisure is an input to the production of the two goods. The rate at which her leisure time can be transformed into barley is MRT_{lb} and into corn, MRT_{lc}. Just as a utility maximizing individual sets the marginal rate of substitution between two commodities equal to their price ratio, the *MRS* between leisure and a given commodity is set equal to the ratio of the wage (the price of leisure) and the price of that commodity.

Again, appealing to the theory of welfare economics, the necessary conditions for a Pareto efficient allocation of resources in this three-commodity case are

$$MRS_{lb} = MRT_{lb}$$

$$MRS_{lc} = MRT_{lc}$$

$$MRS_{bc} = MRT_{bc}$$

---

[4] Interestingly, one observable characteristic that has a surprisingly high correlation with income is height–taller people tend to have greater incomes. See Mankiw and Weinzierl (2010) for the implications of this fact for optimal tax design.

A proportional income tax, which is equivalent to a tax at the same rate on barley and corn, leaves the third equality unchanged, because producers and consumers still face the same *relative* prices for barley and corn. (The tax increases both prices by the same proportion, so their ratio is unchanged.) However, it introduces a tax wedge in the first two conditions. To see why, suppose that Ruth's employer pays her a before-tax wage of w, and the income tax rate is t. Ruth's decisions depend on her after-tax wage, $(1 - t)w$. Hence, she sets $MRS_{lb} = (1 - t)w/P_b$. On the other hand, the producer's decisions are based on the wage rate he or she pays— the before-tax wage, w. Hence, the producer sets $MRT_{lb} = w/P_b$. Consequently, $MRS_{lb} \neq MRT_{lb}$. Similarly, $MRS_{lc} \neq MRT_{lc}$. In contrast, a lump-sum tax leaves all three equalities intact. Thus, income and lump-sum taxation are generally not equivalent.

The fact that the income tax breaks up two equalities whereas taxes on barley and corn at different rates break up all three is in itself irrelevant for determining which system is more efficient. Once *any* of the equalities fails to hold, a loss of efficiency results, and the sizes of the welfare losses cannot be compared merely by counting wedges. Rather, the excess burdens associated with each tax regime must be computed and then compared. There is no presumption that income taxation is more efficient than a system of commodity taxes at different rates, which is referred to as *differential commodity taxation*. It *may* be true, but this is an empirical question that cannot be answered on the basis of theory alone.[5]

If the demand for a commodity does not change when it is taxed, does this mean that there is no excess burden? The intuition behind excess burden is that it results from distorted decisions. If there is no change in the demand for the good being taxed, one might conclude there is no excess burden. This conjecture is examined in Figure 15.4. Naomi, the individual under consideration, begins with the same income as Ruth and faces the same prices and taxes. Hence, her initial budget constraint is AD, and after the barley tax it is AF. However, unlike Ruth, Naomi does not change her barley consumption after the barley tax; that is, $B_1 = B_2$. The barley tax revenues are $E_1 E_2$. Is there an excess burden? The equivalent variation of the barley tax is RE_3. This exceeds the barley tax revenues of $E_1 E_2$ by $E_2 S$. Hence, even though Naomi's barley consumption is unchanged by the barley tax, it still creates an excess burden of $E_2 S$.

The explanation of this paradox begins with the observation that even though Naomi's barley consumption doesn't change, her corn consumption does (from C_1 to C_2). When the barley tax changes barley's relative price, the marginal rate of substitution is affected, and the composition of the commodity *bundle* is distorted.

EXCESS BURDEN OF A TAX ON A COMMODITY WHOSE ORDINARY DEMAND CURVE IS PERFECTLY INELASTIC

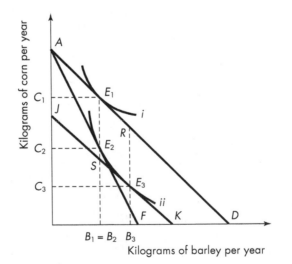

---

[5] Income taxation is necessarily more efficient than differential commodity taxation only when the underlying structure of consumer preferences has a very particular property. See Sandmo (1976).

A more rigorous explanation requires that we distinguish between two types of responses to the barley tax. The movement from E_1 to E_2 is the *uncompensated response*. It shows how consumption changes because of the tax, and incorporates effects due to both losing income and the tax-induced change in relative prices. Now, we can imagine decomposing the move from E_1 to E_2 into a move from E_1 to E_3, and then from E_3 to E_2. The movement from E_1 to E_3 shows the effect on consumption of a lump-sum tax. This change, called the **income effect**, is due solely to the loss of income because relative prices are unaffected. In effect, then, the movement from E_3 to E_2 is strictly due to the change in relative prices. It is generated by giving Naomi enough income to remain on indifference curve *ii* even as barley's price rises due to the tax. Because Naomi is being compensated for the rising price of barley with additional income, the movement from E_3 to E_2 is called the *compensated response*, also sometimes referred to as the **substitution effect**.

The compensated response is the important one for calculating excess burden. Why? By construction, the computation of excess burden involves comparison of tax collections at points E_2 and E_3 on indifference curve *ii*. But the movement from E_3 to E_2 along indifference curve *ii* is precisely the compensated response. Note also that it is only in moving from E_3 to E_2 that the marginal rate of substitution is affected. As shown earlier, this change violates the necessary conditions for a Pareto efficient allocation of commodities.

An ordinary demand curve depicts the uncompensated change in the quantity of a commodity demanded when price changes. A **compensated demand curve** shows how the quantity demanded changes when price changes *and* simultaneously income is compensated so that the individual's commodity bundle stays on the same indifference curve. A way of summarizing this discussion is to say that excess burden depends on movements along the compensated rather than the ordinary demand curve.

Although these observations may seem like theoretical nit-picking, they are actually quite important. In many policy discussions, attention is focused on whether or not a given tax influences observed behaviour, with the assumption that if it does not, no serious efficiency problem is present. For example, some would argue that if hours of work do not change when an income tax is imposed, then the tax has no adverse efficiency consequences. We have shown that such a notion is fallacious. A substantial excess burden may be incurred even if the uncompensated response of the taxed commodity is zero.

EXCESS BURDEN MEASUREMENT WITH DEMAND CURVES

The concept of excess burden can be reinterpreted using (compensated) demand curves. This interpretation relies heavily on the notion of consumer surplus—the difference between what people would be *willing* to pay for a commodity and the amount they actually have to pay. As shown in the appendix to Chapter 3, consumer surplus is measured by the area between the demand curve and the horizontal line at the market price. Assume that the compensated demand curve for barley is the straight line D_b in Figure 15.5. For convenience, we continue to assume that the social marginal cost of barley is constant at P_b, so that the supply curve is the horizontal line marked S_b.[6] In equilibrium, q_1 kilograms of barley are consumed. Consumer surplus, the area between the price and the demand curve, is *aih*.

Again, suppose that a tax at percentage rate t_b is levied on barley, so the new price, $(1 + t_b)P_b$, is associated with supply curve S_b'. Supply and demand now intersect at output q_2. Observe the following characteristics of the new equilibrium:

1. Consumer surplus falls to the area between the demand curve and S_b', *agf*.

2. The revenue yield of the barley tax is rectangle *gfdh*. This is because tax revenues are equal to the product of the number of units purchased (*hd*) and the tax paid on each unit: $(1 + t_b)P_b - P_b = gh$. But *hd* and *gh* are just the base and height, respectively, of rectangle *gfdh*, and hence, their product is its area.

3. The sum of post-tax consumer surplus and tax revenues collected (area *hafd*) is less than the original consumer surplus (*ahi*) by area *fid*. In effect, even if we returned the tax revenues to barley consumers as a lump sum, they would still be worse off by triangle *fid*. The triangle, then, is the excess burden of the tax.

---

[6] The analysis is easily generalized to the case when the supply curve slopes upward. See footnote 7. Hines (1999) provides a thorough and readable review of the origin and use of "Harberger triangles" for measuring excess burden, and the potential problems and limitations in using such measures.

EXCESS BURDEN OF A COMMODITY TAX

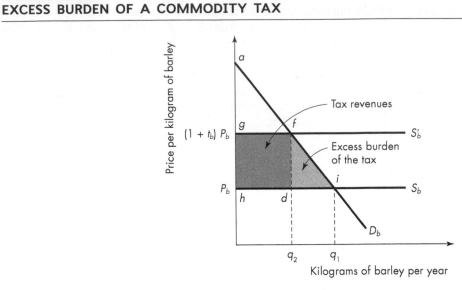

This analysis provides a convenient framework for computing an actual dollar measure of excess burden. The area of triangle *fid* is one-half the product of its base (the tax-induced change in the quantity of barley) and height (the tax per kilogram). Some simple algebra leads to the conclusion that this product, which estimates the excess burden (*EB*), can be written

$$EB = \frac{1}{2}\eta P_b q_1 t_b^2 \qquad (15.3)$$

where η (Greek *eta*) is the absolute value of the compensated price elasticity of demand for barley.[7] (A proof is provided in Appendix A at the end of this chapter.)

A high (absolute) value of η indicates that the compensated quantity demanded is quite sensitive to changes in price. Thus, the presence of η in Equation (15.3) makes intuitive sense—the more the tax distorts the (compensated) consumption decision, the higher the excess burden. $P_b \times q_1$ is the total revenue expended on barley, initially. Its inclusion in the formula shows that the greater the initial expenditure on the taxed commodity, the greater the excess burden.

Finally, the presence of t_b^2 suggests that as the tax rate increases, excess burden goes up with its square. Doubling a tax quadruples its excess burden, other things being the same. Therefore, two relatively small taxes will have a smaller excess burden than one large tax that raises the same amount of revenue, other things being the same. In other words, a broader tax has less excess burden than a narrow tax.

Because excess burden increases with the square of the tax rate, the *marginal* excess burden from raising one more dollar of revenue exceeds the *average excess* burden. That is, the incremental excess burden of raising one *more* dollar of revenue exceeds the ratio of total excess burden to total revenues. This fact has important implications for cost–benefit analysis. Suppose, for example, that the average excess burden per

---

[7] The formula is an approximation that holds strictly only for an infinitesimally small tax levied in the absence of any other distortions. When the supply curve is upward sloping rather than horizontal, the excess-burden triangle contains some producer surplus as well as consumer surplus. The formula for excess burden then depends on the elasticity of supply as well as the elasticity of demand. Bishop (1968) shows that in this case, the excess burden is

$$\frac{1}{2}\frac{P_b q}{\dfrac{1}{\eta} + \dfrac{1}{\varepsilon}}t_b^2$$

where ε is the elasticity of supply. Note that as ε approaches infinity, this expression collapses to Equation (15.3). This is because an ε of infinity corresponds to a horizontal supply curve as in Figure 15.5.

NEWFOUNDLAND'S "DINOSAUR TAX"

Britain under Margaret Thatcher experienced mass riots when the government levied a "Community Charge" that resembled a lump-sum tax. Perhaps less known is that, as late as 1962, seven Canadian provinces used the Poll Tax, and today it is still an important source of revenues for about a dozen municipalities in Newfoundland and Labrador. The Poll Tax is a fixed levy on the adult residents of a municipality, if they don't own real estate there and, hence, don't pay property taxes. The amounts vary by community; in 2015 it was $200 per year in Corner Brook and $325 in Clarenville, for example. Critics of the tax point to its regressive nature: "When you target individuals who don't own property, by definition you are generally pre-disposed to taxing lower income individuals," said a town councillor of Grand Falls-Windsor. "It is essentially a dinosaur tax," he continued. However, proponents observe that the Poll Tax is a simple way for each individual to contribute toward the cost of local public services and that the tax is more neutral than property taxes. "Some people invest heavily in their properties and as a result they pay a lot of property tax," said the mayor of Clarendon. "Some people invest very little in their property but have all kinds of toys and spend their money on other things that doesn't drive their value up and they don't pay as much taxes." The Poll Tax broadens the municipal tax base, reducing the need to raise more revenue from property taxes. "It's a source of revenue the town of Clarenville depends upon and they're not prepared to change at this point in time," said the mayor. In fact, in Corner Brook the residential and commercial property tax rates were lowered in 2013, even while the Poll Tax was raised by $25.

Based on Bennett (2012), CBC News (2013), and "Poll Tax Remains." *The Packet*, December 31, 2013.

Complete references for this feature can be found in the References section on page 485.

---

dollar of tax revenue is 20 cents, but the marginal excess burden (MEB) per additional dollar of tax revenue is 40 cents. These are plausible figures for Canada (Dahlby, 2006). The social cost of each dollar raised for a given public project is the dollar *plus* the incremental excess burden of 40 cents. Thus, a public project must produce marginal benefits of more than $1.40 per dollar of explicit cost if it is to improve welfare.

Concern over excess burden was one major reason that the federal government replaced the manufacturers' sales tax (MST) with the GST in 1991. Many goods and services were excluded from the MST tax base, resulting in a narrow base and high tax rates. Whalley and Fretz (1990) estimated the MEB to be 35 cents for the MST, while that for a more broadly based sales tax such as the GST was 7.3 cents.[8]

Pre-existing Distortions

This analysis has assumed no distortions in the economy other than the tax under consideration. In reality, when a new tax is introduced, there are already other distortions: monopolies, externalities, and pre-existing taxes. This complicates the analysis of excess burden.

Suppose that consumers regard gin and rum as substitutes. Suppose further that rum is currently being taxed, creating an excess burden "triangle" like that in Figure 15.5. Now the government decides to impose a tax on gin. What is the excess burden of the gin tax? In the gin market, the gin tax creates a wedge between what gin consumers pay and what gin producers receive. As usual, this creates an excess burden. But the story is not over. If gin and rum are substitutes, the rise in the consumers' price of gin induced by the gin tax increases the demand for rum. Consequently, the quantity of rum demanded increases.

---

[8] Whalley and Fretz (1990: 49) estimated that an efficiency gain of $849 million (1980 dollars), or $30 per capita, would accompany the replacement of the MST by a broadly based sales tax. Another real-world example is the 10 percent tax on airline tickets in the United States. If the price elasticity of demand is 1.0 (Oum, Waters, and Yong, 1992) and airline revenues (price times the number of tickets) is $107 billion annually (U.S. Bureau of the Census, 2009, p. 658), Equation (15.3) tells us that the airline ticket tax imposes an annual excess burden of $1/2 \times 107 \times (0.10)^2$ billion, or $535 million.

Now, because rum was taxed under the status quo, "too little" of it was being consumed. The increase in rum consumption induced by the gin tax helps move rum consumption back toward its efficient level. There is, thus, an efficiency gain in the rum market that helps offset the excess burden imposed in the gin market. In theory, the gin tax could actually lower the overall excess burden. This is an example of the **theory of the second best**: in the presence of existing distortions, policies that in isolation would increase efficiency can decrease it, and vice versa. (A graphical demonstration of this phenomenon is contained in Appendix B at the end of this chapter.)

Thus, the efficiency impact of a given tax or subsidy cannot be considered in isolation. To the extent that there are other markets with distortions, and the goods in these markets are related (either substitutes or complements), then the overall efficiency impact depends on what is going on in all the markets. To compute the overall efficiency impact of a set of taxes and subsidies, it is generally incorrect to calculate separately the excess burdens in each market and then add them up. The aggregate efficiency loss is not equal to the "sum of its parts."

This result can be quite discomfiting because, strictly speaking, it means that *every* market in the economy must be studied to assess the efficiency implications of *any* tax or subsidy. In most cases, practitioners simply assume that the amount of interrelatedness between the market they are concerned with and other markets is sufficiently small that cross-effects can safely be ignored. Although this is clearly a convenient assumption, its reasonableness must be evaluated in each particular case.

A controversy from the field of environmental economics provides an instance where accounting for pre-existing distortions is important. Recall from Chapter 5 that, in the presence of an externality, a tax can enhance efficiency. A tax set equal to the marginal external cost (a "Pigouvian tax") in effect forces a polluter to take into account the costs that he imposes on other people and induces him to reduce output. Now, recall also that the Canadian income tax system is highly inefficient. By distorting labour supply and other decisions, the income tax creates large excess burdens. Linking these two observations together, some have proposed that we increase reliance on environmental taxes and use the revenues to reduce income taxes. This idea is called the *double-dividend hypothesis* because the scheme increases efficiency both in the market with the polluter and in the markets that are distorted by the income tax.

However, there is a possible flaw in this logic. To see why, note that the pollution taxes drive up the prices of the goods that are produced using polluting technology. But when commodity prices go up, in effect this is a decrease in the real wage rate—a given dollar amount of wages buys you fewer goods and services. Put another way, the environmental taxes are, to some extent, also taxes on earnings. So if the labour market is already distorted because of an income tax, the environmental tax exacerbates the problem. It turns out that the added excess burden in the labour market can actually outweigh the efficiency gains from correcting the externality (Parry and Oates, 2000). In other words, the efficient pollution tax can be lower than in a situation in which there is not a pre-existing income tax. This is not to say that Pigouvian taxation is a bad idea, only that its consequences for efficiency depend on the extent to which existing taxes already distort the labour market.

The Excess Burden of a Subsidy

Commodity subsidies are important components of the fiscal systems of many countries. In effect, a subsidy is just a negative tax, and like a tax, it is associated with an excess burden. To illustrate the calculation of the excess burden of a subsidy, we consider a subsidy for owner-occupied housing.

Assume that the demand for owner-occupied housing services is the straight line D_h in Figure 15.6. Supply is horizontal at price P_h, which measures the social marginal cost of producing housing services. Initially, the equilibrium quantity is h_1. Now suppose that the government provides a subsidy of s percent to housing producers. The new price for housing services is then $(1 - s)P_h$ and the associated supply curve is S_h'. The subsidy increases the quantity of housing services consumed, to h_2. If the purpose of the subsidy was to increase housing consumption, then it has succeeded. But if its goal was to maximize social welfare, is it an appropriate policy?

Before the subsidy, consumer surplus was area *mno*. After the subsidy, consumer surplus is *mqu*. The benefit to housing consumers is the increase in their surplus, area *nouq*. But at what cost is this benefit obtained? The cost of the subsidy program is the quantity of housing services consumed, *qu*, times the subsidy per unit, *nq*, or rectangle *nvuq*. Thus, the cost of the subsidy actually exceeds the benefit—there is an excess burden equal to the difference between areas *nvuq* and *nouq*, which is the shaded area *ovu*.

FIGURE 15.6

EXCESS BURDEN OF A HOUSING SUBSIDY

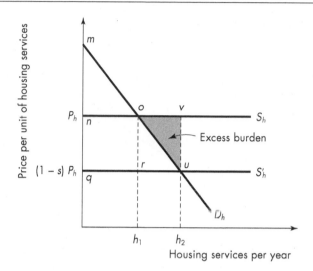

How can subsidizing a good thing like housing be inefficient? Recall that any point on the demand curve for housing services measures how much people value that particular level of consumption. To the right of h_1, although individuals do derive utility from consuming more housing, its value is less than P_h, the marginal cost to society of providing it. In other words, the subsidy induces people to consume housing services that are valued at less than their cost—hence, the inefficiency.[9]

A very important policy implication follows from this analysis. One often hears proposals to help some group of people by subsidizing a commodity that they consume heavily. We have shown that this is an inefficient way to aid people. Less money could make them just as well off if it were given to them as a direct grant. In Figure 15.6, people would be indifferent between a housing subsidy program costing *nvuq* and a direct grant of *nouq*, even though the subsidy program costs the government more money.[10] This is one of the reasons why many economists prefer direct income transfers to commodity subsidies.

The Excess Burden of Income Taxation

The theory of excess burden that we have developed for taxing commodities applies just as well to factors of production. In Figure 15.7, Jacob's hours of work are plotted on the horizontal axis and his hourly wage on the vertical. Jacob's compensated labour supply curve, which shows the smallest wage that would be required to induce him to work each additional hour, is labelled S_L. Initially, Jacob's wage is w and the associated hours of work L_1. In the same way that consumer surplus is the area between the demand curve and the market price, worker surplus is the area between the supply curve and the market wage rate. When the wage is w, Jacob's surplus is therefore area *adf*.

Now assume that an income tax at a rate t is imposed. The after-tax wage is then $(1 - t)w$, and given supply curve S_L, the quantity of labour supplied falls to L_2 hours. Jacob's surplus after the tax is *agh*, and the government collects revenues equal to *fihg*. The excess burden due to the tax-induced distortion of the work choice is the amount by which Jacob's loss of welfare (*fdhg*) exceeds the tax collected: area *hid* (= *fdhg* − *fihg*). In analogy to Equation (15.3), area *hid* is approximately

$$EB = \tfrac{1}{2}\varepsilon w L_1 t^2 \qquad\qquad (15.4)$$

where ε is the compensated elasticity of hours of work with respect to the wage.

---

[9] Alternatively, after the subsidy, the marginal rate of substitution in consumption depends on $(1 - s)P_h$, while the marginal rate of transformation in production depends on P_h. Hence, the marginal rate of transformation is not equal to the marginal rate of substitution, and the allocation of resources cannot be efficient.

[10] This result is very similar to that obtained when we examined in-kind subsidy programs in Chapter 6. That chapter also discusses why commodity subsidies nevertheless remain politically popular.

FIGURE 15.7

EXCESS BURDEN OF A TAX ON LABOUR

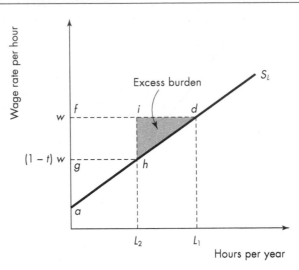

A reasonable estimate of ε for a Canadian male is about 0.2. Suppose that before taxation Jacob works 2,000 hours per year at a wage of $20 per hour. A tax on earnings of 40 percent is then imposed. Substituting these figures into Equation (15.4), the excess burden of the tax is about $640 annually. One way to put this figure into perspective is to note that it is approximately 4 percent of tax revenues. Thus, in this example, each dollar of tax collected would create an excess burden of 4 cents.

Of course, wage rates, tax rates, and elasticities vary across members of the population, so different people are subject to different excess burdens. Moreover, the excess burden of taxing labour also depends on tax rates levied on other factors of production. Jorgenson and Yun (2001) estimated that, for plausible values of the relevant elasticities, the excess burden of labour-income taxation in the United States is about 27 percent of the revenues raised. As we show in Chapter 18, however, there is considerable uncertainty about the values of some of the key elasticities. Hence, this particular estimate must be regarded with caution. Still, evidence indicates that the excess burden of labour-income taxation, relative to revenues raised, may be higher in Canada than in the United States. Dahlby and Ferede (2011) reported that the excess burden of one more dollar from the personal income tax averaged $1.28 for the provinces and was $0.17 for the federal income tax in 2006.[11]

DIFFERENTIAL TAXATION OF INPUTS

In the income tax example just discussed, we assumed that labour income was taxed at the same rate regardless of where the labour was supplied. But sometimes the tax levied on a factor of production depends on where it is employed. For instance, because of the corporate income tax, some argue that capital employed in the corporate sector faces a higher rate than capital in the noncorporate sector. Another example is the differential taxation of labour in the household and market sectors. If an individual does housework, valuable services are produced but not taxed.[12] On the other hand, if the same individual works in the market, the services are subject to the income and payroll taxes. The fact that labour is taxed in one sector and untaxed in another distorts

---

[11] Fortin and Lacroix (1994) estimated the cost of raising an additional dollar in Quebec through the personal income tax to be from $1.39 to $1.53, indicating an excess burden of 39 to 53 percent for the marginal dollar.

[12] The value of housework was expressed nicely by a biblical author who wrote during an era in which it was assumed homes were managed only by females. In Proverbs, he discusses in detail the many tasks performed by the woman who "looketh well to the ways of her household" (Prov. 31:27). His general conclusion is that "her price is far above rubies" (Prov. 31:10). Unfortunately, price data on rubies during the biblical era are unavailable. Chandler (1994) estimates the value of household work in Canada, using opportunity cost and replacement cost methods, at between 31 and 46 percent of GDP in 1992.

FIGURE 15.8

THE ALLOCATION OF TIME BETWEEN HOUSEWORK AND MARKET WORK

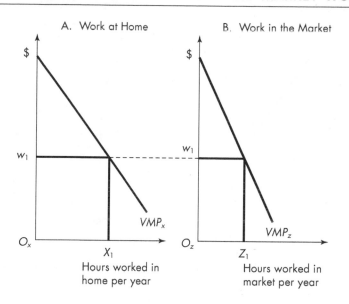

A. Work at Home
B. Work in the Market

X_1
Hours worked in home per year

Z_1
Hours worked in market per year

people's decisions on how much time to spend on each. The efficiency cost can be measured using Figure 15.8.[13] In Figure 15.8A, hours of work in the household sector are measured on the horizontal axis, and dollars are measured on the vertical. Now define the **value of the marginal product (VMP)** of hours worked in the household sector as the dollar value of the *additional* output produced for each hour worked. The schedule VMP_x in Figure 15.8A represents the value of the marginal product of household work. It is drawn sloping downward, reflecting the reasonable assumption that as more hours are spent in the home, the incremental value of those hours decreases. This is just an example of the law of diminishing marginal returns.

Similarly, schedule VMP_z in Figure 15.8B shows the value of the marginal product of hours worked in the market sector. Although we also expect VMP_z to slope downward, there is no reason to expect that its shape should be identical to that of VMP_x.

For simplicity, assume that the total number of hours of work available is fixed, so that the only question is how to divide the work between the market and household sectors. Assume further that individuals allocate their time between housework and market work to maximize their total incomes. As a result of this allocation process, the value of the marginal product of labour is the same in both sectors. If it were not, it would be possible for people to reallocate labour between the sectors to increase their incomes. In Figure 15.8, the initial equilibrium occurs where X_1 hours are devoted to housework and Z_1 hours to market work. The value of the marginal product of labour in both sectors is w_1 dollars. Competitive pricing ensures that the wage in the market sector is equal to the value of the marginal product.

Now assume that a tax of t is levied on income from market work, but the return to housework is untaxed. Immediately after the tax is levied, the net return to market work declines to $(1 - t)w_1$. The original allocation is no longer desirable to individuals because the return to the last hour of work in the household (w_1) exceeds the comparable rate in the market, $(1 - t)w_1$. As a result, people begin working less in the market and more at home. As individuals devote less time to the market sector, VMP_z begins to rise; as they enter the household sector, VMP_x falls. Equilibrium is reached when the *after-tax* value of marginal product in the market sector equals the value of marginal product in the household sector. In Figure 15.9, this occurs when people work X_2 hours in the home and Z_2 hours in the market. Because the total hours of work are fixed, the increase in hours in the household sector exactly equals the decrease in the market sector—distance X_1X_2 equals distance Z_2Z_1.

At the new equilibrium, the after-tax VMP_s in the two sectors are both equal to $(1 - t)w_2$. However, the *before tax VMP* in the market sector, w_2, is greater than the VMP in the household sector, $(1 - t)w_2$. This means that

---

[13] The model was developed by Harberger (1974) and Boskin (1975).

FIGURE 15.9

DIFFERENTIAL FACTOR TAXATION

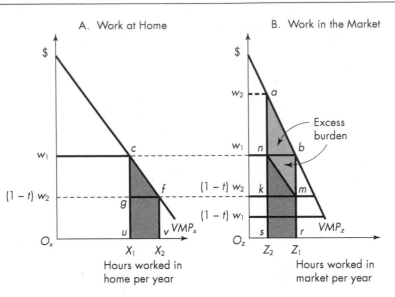

if more labour were supplied to the market sector, the increase in income there (w_2) would exceed the loss of income in the household sector, $(1 - t)w_2$. But there is no incentive for this reallocation to occur, because individuals are sensitive to the returns they receive *after tax*, and these are already equal. The tax, thus, creates a situation in which there is "too much" housework being done and "not enough" work in the market. In short, the tax leads to an inefficient allocation of resources in the sense that it distorts incentives to employ inputs in their most productive uses. The resulting decrease in real income is the excess burden of the tax.

To measure the excess burden, we must analyze Figure 15.9 closely. Begin by observing that as a result of the exodus of labour from the market; the value of output there goes down by *abrs*, the area under VMP_z between Z_1 and Z_2.[14] On the other hand, as labour enters the household sector, the value of output increases by *cfvu*, the area under the VMP_x curve between X_1 and X_2. Therefore, the excess burden is area *abrs* minus area *cfvu*. Because $X_1X_2 = Z_2Z_1$ (remember, the total supply of hours is fixed), it follows that area *cfvu* equals area *nmrs*. Hence, the difference between *abrs* and *cfvu* is simply *abmn*. This area, which is the excess burden of the tax, has a convenient algebraic representation:

$$EB = \tfrac{1}{2}(\Delta Z)tw_2 \qquad\qquad (15.5)$$

where ΔZ is the change in hours worked in the market sector.[15] The greater the change in the allocation of labour (ΔZ) and the greater the tax wedge (tw_2), the greater the excess burden. In general, whenever a factor is fixed in total supply and is taxed differently in different uses, a misallocation of factors between sectors, and hence an efficiency loss, is generated.

DOES EFFICIENT TAXATION MATTER?

Every year dozens of documents relating to the details of government spending and taxation are published. You would look in vain, however, for an "excess burden budget" documenting the distortionary impact of government fiscal policies. The reason for this is not hard to understand. Excess burden does not appear in

---

[14] The vertical distance between *VMP* and the horizontal axis at any level of input gives the value of marginal prod-uct for that level of input. Adding up all these distances gives the value of the total product. Thus, the area under *VMP* gives the value of total product.

[15] Proof: Area *abmn* is the sum of two triangles *abn* and *nbm*. Triangle $abn = (1/2)(nb)(an) = (1/2)\Delta Z(an)$. Triangle $nbm = (1/2)(nb)(bm) = (1/2)(\Delta Z)(bm)$. Their sum is $(1/2)(\Delta Z)(an + bm) = (1/2)(\Delta Z)tw_2$.

anyone's bookkeeping system. Conceptually, it is a rather subtle notion and not easy to make operational. Nevertheless, although the losses in real income associated with tax-induced changes in behaviour are hidden, they are real, and according to some estimates, very large. We have emphasized repeatedly that efficiency considerations alone are never enough to determine policy. Still, it is unfortunate that policy makers often seem to ignore efficiency altogether.

The fact that a tax generates an excess burden does not mean that the tax is bad. One hopes, after all, that it will be used to obtain something beneficial for society, either in terms of public goods or income redistribution. But to determine whether or not the supposed benefits are large enough to justify the costs, intelligent policy requires that excess burden be included in the calculation as a social cost Moreover, as we see in the next chapter, excess burden is extremely useful in comparing alternative tax systems. Providing estimates of excess burden is an important role for economists.

SUMMARY

- Taxes generally impose an excess burden—a cost beyond the tax revenue collected.
- Excess burden is caused by tax-induced distortions in behaviour. It may be examined using either indifference curves or compensated demand curves.
- Lump-sum taxes do not cause distortions, but are unattractive as policy tools. Nevertheless, they are an important standard against which the excess burdens of other taxes can be compared.
- Excess burden may result even if observed behaviour is unaffected, because it is the compensated response to a tax that determines its excess burden.
- When a single tax is imposed, the excess burden is proportional to the compensated elasticity of demand, and to the square of the tax rate.
- In cost–benefit analysis, the marginal excess burden of raising funds by taxation should be included as a cost.
- Excess-burden calculations typically assume no other distortions. If other distortions exist, the incremental excess burden of a new tax depends on its effects in other markets.
- Subsidies also create excess burdens because they encourage people to consume goods valued less than the marginal social cost of production.
- The differential taxation of inputs creates an excess burden. Such inputs are used "too little" in taxed activities and "too much" in untaxed activities.

EXERCISES

1. Which of the following is likely to impose a large excess burden?
   a. A tax on land.
   b. A subsidy for personal computers.
   c. A tax of $75 on iPods, MP3 payers, and smart-phones. (An "iPod Tax" was proposed in 2010 in a private member's bill to Parliament in Canada.)
   d. A subsidy for investment in "high-tech" companies.
   e. A 5 cent tax on bottled water. (Such a tax exists in Chicago.)
   f. A 10 percent tax on all computer software.
2. The combined federal and provincial taxes on a carton of 200 cigarettes were reduced from $24 to $10 in Ontario in February 1994. (a) Describe how you would compute the reduction in excess burden that results from this lowering of the tax. (b) Or might such a tax reduction worsen efficiency? Explain.

3. "In the formula for excess burden given in Equation (15.3), the tax is less than one. When it is squared, the result is smaller, not bigger. Thus, having t^2 instead of t in the formula makes the tax less important." Comment.

4. Under the Canadian tax system, capital that is employed in the corporate sector is taxed at a higher rate than capital in the noncorporate sector. This problem will analyze the excess burden of the differential taxation of capital.

    Assume that there are two sectors, corporate and noncorporate. The value of marginal product of capital in the corporate sector is given by $VMP_c = 100 - K_c$, where K_c is the amount of capital in the corporate sector; the value of marginal product of capital in the noncorporate sector is given by $VMP_n = 80 - 2K_n$, where K_n is the amount of capital in the noncorporate sector. In total, there are 50 units of capital in society.

    a. In the absence of any taxes, how much capital is used in each sector? (*Hint:* Draw a diagram along the lines of Figure 15.9 to organize your thoughts.)

    b. Suppose that a unit tax of 6 is levied on capital employed in the corporate sector. After the tax, how much capital is employed in each sector? What is the excess burden of the tax?

5. In 2012, the Nigerian government removed a subsidy on fuel. One critic of the removal of the subsidy argued that the government was unable to articulate how this would benefit Nigerians, stating, "They made economic arguments that were abstract at best and non-sensical at worst" (Adichie, 2012). See if you can do a better job at explaining the rationale for removing such a subsidy.

6. Setting a price ceiling for a good (below the normal market price) results in an excess burden. Demonstrate this, by using supply and demand curves. In addition, show how the imposition of a tax on a substitute good, by affecting the demand for the good with a price ceiling, increases the excess burden (Hines, 1999: 180).

7. Suppose the market demand curve for beer is described by the equation $Q_b^D = 600 - 15P_b$, where Q_b^D is the number of cases of beer and P_b is the price. The supply curve is given by $Q_b^D = 10P_b$.

    a. Calculate the elasticities of demand and supply at the equilibrium quantity.

    b. Suppose the government introduces an excise tax of 15 percent per case of beer. Determine the excess burden of this tax using the formula in footnote 7 and the elasticities found in part (a).

    c. Calculate the tax revenues and the average excess burden.

8. Suppose a 10 percent tax is imposed on airplane tickets.

    a. Use Equation (15.3) to calculate the excess burden of this tax when the price elasticity of compensated demand is −1.1 and airplane ticket revenues are $91 billion annually.

    b. In the short run, the supply of flights is relatively inelastic, since flights have been scheduled and customers have purchased their tickets, while supply is very elastic in the long run, because airlines are free to cancel flights and adjust their routes. Use the expression for excess burden in footnote 7 to contrast the excess burden from the airplane ticket tax from a short-run perspective with the excess burden in the long run.

    c. Air travel contributes to greenhouse gas emissions. Discuss how this consideration may alter the size of the excess burden from the tax on airplane tickets.

APPENDIX A

Formula for Excess Burden

This appendix shows how the excess burden triangle *fdi* of Figure 15.5 may be written in terms of the compensated demand elasticity. The triangle's area, A, is given by the formula

$$A = 1/2 \times base \times height$$

$$= 1/2 \times (di) \times (fd). \qquad (15A.1)$$

fd is just the difference between the gross and net prices (ΔP_b):

$$fd = \Delta P_b = (1 + t_b) \times P_b - P_b = t_b \times P_b \qquad (15A.2)$$

di is the change in the quantity (Δq) as a result of the price rise:

$$di = \Delta q \qquad (15A.3)$$

Now, note that the definition of the price elasticity, η, is

$$\eta = \frac{\Delta q P_b}{\Delta P_b q}$$

so that

$$\Delta q = \eta \left(\frac{q}{P_b}\right) \Delta P_b \qquad (15A.4)$$

We saw in Equation (15A.2) that $\Delta P_b = t_b \times P_b$, so that Equation (15A.4) yields

$$\Delta q = \eta \times \frac{q}{P_b} \times (t_b P_b) = \eta \times q \times t_b \qquad (15A.5)$$

Finally, recall that $di = \Delta q$ and substitute both Equation (15A.5) and (15A.2) into Equation (15A.1) to obtain

$$A = \tfrac{1}{2}(di)(fd)$$

$$= \tfrac{1}{2}(\eta q t_b) \times (t_b P_b)$$

$$= \tfrac{1}{2} \times \eta \times P_b \times q \times (t_b)^2$$

as in the text.

APPENDIX B

Multiple Taxes and the Theory of the Second Best

This appendix discusses the measurement of excess burden when a tax is imposed in the presence of a pre-existing distortion.

In Figure 15.10, we consider two goods, gin and rum, whose demand schedules are D_g and D_r, and whose before-tax prices are P_g and P_r, respectively. (The prices represent social marginal costs and are assumed to be constant.) Rum is currently being taxed at a percentage rate t_r so its price is $(1 + t_r)P_r$. This creates an excess burden in the rum market, triangle *abc*. Now suppose that a tax on gin at rate t_g is introduced, creating a wedge between what gin consumers pay and gin producers receive. This creates an excess burden in the gin market of *efd*. But this is not the end of the story. If gin and rum are substitutes, the increase in the consumers' price of gin induced by the gin tax shifts the demand curve for rum to the right, say to D_r'. As a consequence, the quantity of rum demanded increases from r_2 to r_3, distance *cg*. For each bottle of rum purchased between r_2 and r_3, the amount that people pay [$(1 + t_r)P_r$] exceeds the social cost (P_r) by distance *cb*. It can be shown that consumer surplus in the rum market is unchanged, but there is an increase in tax revenue. Hence, there is a social gain of *cb* per bottle of rum times *cg* bottles, or area *cbhg*.

To summarize: given that the tax on rum was already in place, the tax on gin creates an excess burden of *efd* in the gin market *and* simultaneously decreases excess burden by *cbhg* in the rum market. If *cbhg* is sufficiently large, the tax can actually reduce overall excess burden. This is an example of the theory of the second best, which states that in the presence of existing distortions policies that in isolation would increase efficiency can decrease it, and vice versa.

FIGURE 15.10

EXCESS BURDEN OF A TAX IN THE PRESENCE OF AN EXISTING TAX

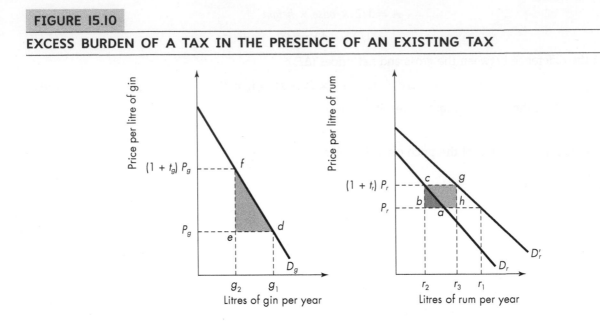

This discussion is a special case of the result that the excess burden of a *set* of taxes generally depends on the whole set of tax rates, as well as on the degree of substitutability and complementarity among the various commodities. Specifically, suppose that n commodities are subject to taxation. Let P_i be the before-tax price of the ith commodity, t_i the ad valorem tax on the ith commodity, and S_{ij} the compensated response in the demand of the ith good with respect to a change in the price of the jth good. Then the overall excess burden is

$$-1/2 \sum_{i=1}^{n} \sum_{i=1}^{n} t_i P_i t_j P_j S_{ij}$$

For example, in the two-good case just discussed, where the goods are g and r, the overall excess burden is

$$-1/2 \left(t_r^2 P_r^2 S_{rr} + 2 t_r t_g P_g S_{rg} + t_g^2 P_g^2 S_{gg} \right).$$

CHAPTER 16

Efficient and Equitable Taxation

A nation may fall into decay through taxation in two ways. In the first case, when the amount of the taxes exceeds the powers of the nation and is not proportioned to the general wealth. In the second case, when an amount of taxation, proportioned on the whole to the powers of the nation, is viciously distributed.

—Pietro Verri

AFTER READING THIS CHAPTER, THE STUDENT SHOULD BE ABLE TO:

LO1 Derive the Ramsey rule for optimal commodity taxation.

LO2 State the inverse elasticity rule and the Corlett-Hague rule.

LO3 Explain the Ramsey solution to the problem of optimal user fees.

LO5 Summarize Edgeworth's model of optimal income taxation.

LO6 Explain how modern studies address the problems with Edgeworth's model.

LO7 Explain why the "time inconsistency of optimal policy" induces inefficiency.

LO8 Compare and contrast three definitions of horizontal equity.

LO9 Provide a graphical analysis of a model of optimal tax evasion.

Critics of the Canadian revenue system argue that high marginal tax rates cause inefficiencies. Others counter that the proposed tax reforms are unfair. How are we to choose among alternative policies? Our goal in this chapter is to establish a set of criteria for evaluating real-world tax systems. We begin by looking at efficiency and distributional considerations that fit squarely within the framework of conventional welfare economics. We then turn to other criteria that do not fit so neatly, but have considerable importance and appeal.

OPTIMAL COMMODITY TAXATION

The premier of your province has asked you for advice on how to design a tax system. At what rates should various goods be taxed? The purpose of the theory of optimal commodity taxation is to provide a framework for answering this question. Of course, before going to work, it would be fair for you to ask the premier a question in return—what goal do you seek? At the outset, we assume that the premier's only goal is to finance the province's given expenditure level with a minimum of excess burden and without using any lump-sum taxes. We return later to issues that arise when there are concerns about distribution as well as efficiency.

To begin, consider the situation of Stella, a representative citizen who consumes only two commodities, X and Y, as well as leisure, l. The price of X is P_x, the price of Y is P_y, and the wage rate (which is the price of leisure) is w. The maximum number of hours per year that Stella can work—her **time endowment**—is fixed at T.

(Think of T as the amount of time left over after sleep.) It follows that hours of work are $(T - l)$; all time not spent on leisure is devoted to work. Income is the product of the wage rate and hours of work: $w(T - l)$. Assuming that Stella spends her entire income on commodities X and Y (there is no saving), her budget constraint is

$$w(T - l) = P_xX + P_yY \tag{16.1}$$

The left-hand side gives total earnings, and the right-hand side shows how the earnings are spent. Equation (16.1) can be rewritten as

$$wT = P_xX + P_yY + wl \tag{16.2}$$

The left-hand side of Equation (16.2) is the value of the time endowment. It shows the income that Stella could earn if she worked every waking hour.

Now, suppose that it is possible to tax X, Y, and l at the same ad valorem rate, t. The tax raises the effective price of X to $(1 + t)P_x$, of Y to $(1 + t)P_y$, and of l to $(1 + t)w$. Thus, Stella's after-tax budget constraint is

$$wT = (1 + t)P_xX + (1 + t)P_yY + (1 + t)wl \tag{16.3}$$

Dividing through Equation (16.3) by $(1 + t)$, we have

$$\frac{wT}{1 + t} = P_xX + P_yY + wl \tag{16.4}$$

Comparison of Equations (16.3) and (16.4) points out the following fact: a tax on all commodities, including leisure, at the same percentage rate, t, is equivalent to reducing the value of the time endowment from wT to $[1/(1 + t)] \times wT$. For example, a 25 percent tax on X, Y, and l is equivalent to a reduction of the value of the time endowment by 20 percent. However, because w and T are fixed, their product, wT, is also fixed; for any value of the wage rate, an individual cannot change the value of his or her time endowment. Therefore, a tax that reduces the value of the time endowment is in effect a lump-sum tax. We know from Chapter 15 that lump-sum taxes have no excess burden. We conclude that a tax at the same rate on all commodities, *including leisure*, is equivalent to a lump-sum tax and has no excess burden.

In practice, putting a tax on leisure time is impossible. The only available tax instruments are taxes on commodities X and Y. Therefore, some excess burden generally is inevitable. The goal of optimal commodity taxation is to select tax rates on X and Y in such a way that the excess burden of raising the required tax revenue is as low as possible. It is popular to suggest that the solution to this problem is to tax X and Y at the same rate—so-called **neutral taxation**. We will see that, in general, neutral taxation is *not* efficient.

The Ramsey Rule

To raise the revenue with the least excess burden possible, how should the tax rates on X and Y be set? To minimize *overall* excess burden, the *marginal* excess burden of the last dollar of revenue raised from each commodity must be the same. Otherwise, it would be possible to lower overall excess burden by raising the rate on the commodity with the smaller marginal excess burden, and lowering the rate on the commodity with the larger marginal excess burden.

To explore the consequences of this typical example of marginal analysis in economics, suppose for simplicity that, for our representative consumer, X and Y are unrelated commodities—they are neither substitutes nor complements for each other. Hence, a change in the price of either commodity affects its own demand and not the demand for the other. Figure 16.1 shows Stella's compensated demand for X, D_x. Assume that she can buy all the X she wants at the price P_0, so the supply curve of X is horizontal.

Suppose that a small unit tax of u_x is levied on X, which lowers quantity demanded from X_0 to X_1, ΔX in the figure. As proven in the last chapter, the excess burden of the tax is the area of triangle *abc*. Now, suppose we raise the tax by 1, so it becomes $(u_x + 1)$. The total price is $P_0 + (u_x + 1)$; quantity demanded falls by Δx to X_2; and the associated excess burden is triangle *fec*. The marginal excess burden is the difference between the two triangles, trapezoid *fbae*. The area of the trapezoid is one-half its height (Δx) times the sum of its bases $[u_x + (u_x + 1)]$. Thus, the marginal excess burden is $1/2 \, \Delta x \, [u_x + (u_x + 1)]$.

FIGURE 16.1

MARGINAL EXCESS BURDEN

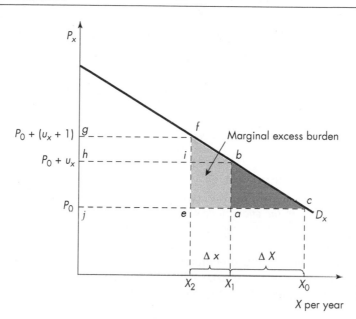

With a bit of algebra,[1] we can simplify this expression to obtain that the marginal excess burden is approximately ΔX:

$$\Delta X = \text{marginal excess burden} \qquad (16.5)$$

Recall that excess burden minimization requires information on the marginal excess burden on the *last dollar* of revenue collected. Now that we know the marginal excess burden induced by the tax increase, we must compute the associated increase in revenues. Then all we have to do is divide the marginal excess burden by the change in revenues. By definition, this quotient is the marginal excess burden per incremental dollar of revenue collected.

To compute the change in tax revenues associated with raising the rate from u_x to $(u_x + 1)$, note that when the tax rate is u_x, tax revenues are $u_x X_1$ (the tax per unit times the number of units sold). In Figure 16.1, this is the rectangle *hbaj*. Similarly, when the tax rate is $(u_x + 1)$, tax revenues are *gfej*. Comparing these two rectangles, we see that when the tax goes up, the government gains area *gfih* but loses *ibae*. Thus, the change in revenues is *gfih* − *ibae*. Using algebra, this is $X_2 - (X_1 - X_2)u_x$. A bit of mathematical manipulation[2] leads us to the following approximation to the change in tax revenue:

$$X_1 - \Delta X = \text{marginal tax revenue} \qquad (16.6)$$

Marginal excess burden per additional dollar of tax revenue is Equation (16.5) divided by Equation (16.6), or

$$\frac{\Delta X}{X_1 - \Delta X}$$

---

[1] The area of the trapezoid is $(1/2)\,\Delta x(2u_x + 1)$ or $\Delta x u_x + (1/2)\,\Delta x$, which we can approximate as $\Delta x u_x$ because the second term, which corresponds to triangle *fib*, is relatively small and can be ignored. Now note that $1/\Delta x$ and $u_x/\Delta X$ are equal because both measure the slope (in absolute value) of D_x. Hence, $\Delta x u_x = \Delta X$, which is the marginal excess burden.

[2] Note that the expression for marginal tax revenue is equivalent to $X_2(u_x + 1) - X_1 u_x = X_2 + u_x(X_2 - X_1)$. From Figure 16.1, $X_2 = X_1 - \Delta x$. Substituting gives us $X_1 - \Delta x - u_x \Delta x$. But $\Delta x = \Delta X/u_x$ (see footnote 1), giving us $X_1 - \Delta X(1 + u_x)/u_x$. Provided that u_x is large relative to 1, this can be approximated as $X_1 - \Delta X$, the expression in the text for marginal tax revenue.

Exactly the same reasoning indicates that if a unit tax of u_y is levied on Y, the marginal excess burden per last dollar of revenue is

$$\frac{\Delta Y}{Y_1 - \Delta Y}$$

Because the condition for minimizing overall excess burden is that the marginal excess burden per last dollar of revenue be the same for each commodity, we must set

$$\frac{\Delta X}{X_1 - \Delta X} = \frac{\Delta Y}{Y_1 - \Delta Y}$$

This implies

$$\frac{\Delta X}{X_1} = \frac{\Delta Y}{Y_1} \qquad (16.7)$$

To interpret Equation (16.7), note that the change in a variable divided by its total value is just the percentage change in the variable. Hence, Equation (16.7) says that *to minimize total excess burden, tax rates should be set so that the percentage reduction in the quantity demanded of each commodity is the same*. This result, called the **Ramsey rule**, after its discoverer Frank Ramsey (1927), also holds even for cases when X, Y, and l are related goods–substitutes or complements.

But why should efficient taxation induce equiproportional changes in quantities demanded rather than equiproportional changes in prices? Because excess burden is a consequence of distortions in *quantities*. To minimize total excess burden requires that all these changes be in the same proportion.

A reinterpretation of the Ramsey rule. It is useful to explore the relationship between the Ramsey rule and demand elasticities. Let η_x be the compensated elasticity of demand for X. Let t_x be the tax rate on X, this time expressed as an ad valorem rate rather than a unit tax.[3] Now, by definition of an ad valorem tax, t_x is the percentage increase in the price induced by the tax. Hence, $t_x \eta_x$ is the percentage change in the price times the percentage change in quantity demanded when the price increases by 1 percent. This is just the percentage reduction in the demand for X induced by the tax. Defining t_y and η_y analogously, $t_y \eta_y$ is the proportional reduction in Y. The Ramsey rule says that to minimize excess burden, these percentage reductions in quantity demanded must be equal:

$$t_x \eta_x = t_y \eta_y \qquad (16.8)$$

Now divide both sides of the equation by $t_y \eta_x$ to obtain

$$\frac{t_x}{t_y} = \frac{\eta_y}{\eta_x} \qquad (16.9)$$

Equation (16.9) is the **inverse elasticity rule**: as long as goods are unrelated in consumption, tax rates should be inversely proportional to elasticities. That is, the higher is η_y relative to η_x, the lower should be t_y relative to t_x.[4] Efficiency does not require that all rates be set uniformly.

The intuition behind the inverse elasticity rule is straightforward. An efficient set of taxes should distort decisions as little as possible. The potential for distortion is greater the more elastic the demand for a commodity. Therefore, efficient taxation requires that relatively high rates of taxation be levied on relatively inelastic goods.

---

[3] In a competitive market, any unit tax can be represented by a suitably chosen ad valorem tax, and vice versa. For example, suppose a commodity is subject to a unit tax of 5 cents, and the price paid by consumers is 50 cents. Then the resulting excess burden is the same as that which would be induced by an ad valorem tax at a rate of 10 percent of the after-tax price.

[4] A more careful demonstration requires a little calculus. Recall from Equation (15.3) in Chapter 15 that the excess burden on commodity X is $\frac{1}{2}\eta_x P_x X t_x^2$. Similarly, the excess burden on Y is $\frac{1}{2}\eta_y P_y Y t_y^2$. Then the total excess burden is $\frac{1}{2}\eta_x P_x X t_x^2 + \frac{1}{2}\eta_y P_y Y t_y^2$. (We can just add up the two expressions because, by assumption, X and Y are unrelated.) Now, suppose the required tax revenue is R. Then t_x and t_y must satisfy the relation $P_x X t_x + P_y Y t_y = R$. Our problem is to choose t_x and t_y to minimize $\frac{1}{2}\eta_x P_x X t_x^2 + \frac{1}{2}\eta_y P_y Y t_y^2$ subject to $R - P_x X t_x - P_y Y t_y = 0$. Set up the Lagrangian expression $\mathcal{L} = \frac{1}{2}\eta_x P_x X t_x^2 + \frac{1}{2}\eta_y P_y Y t_y^2 + \lambda[R - P_x X t_x - P_y Y t_y]$ where λ is the Lagrange multiplier. Taking $\partial \mathcal{L}/\partial t_x$ yields $\eta_x t_x = \lambda$ and $\partial \mathcal{L}/\partial t_y$ yields $\eta_y t_y = \lambda$. Hence, $\eta_x t_x = \eta_y t_y$, and Equation (16.9) follows immediately.

The Corlett–Hague rule. Corlett and Hague (1953) proved an interesting implication of the Ramsey rule; when there are two commodities, efficient taxation requires taxing the commodity that is complementary to leisure at a relatively high rate. To understand this result intuitively, recall that *if* it were possible to tax leisure, a "first-best" result would be obtainable—revenues could be raised with no excess burden. Although the tax authorities cannot tax leisure, they *can* tax goods that tend to be consumed jointly *with* leisure, indirectly lowering the demand for leisure. If yachts are taxed at a very high rate, people consume fewer yachts and spend less time at leisure. In effect, then, taxing complements to leisure at high rates provides an indirect way to "get at" leisure and, hence, move closer to the perfectly efficient outcome that would be possible if leisure were taxable.[5]

Vertical Equity

At this point you may suspect that efficient tax theory has unpleasant policy implications. For example, the inverse elasticity rule says inelastically demanded goods should be taxed at relatively high rates. Is this fair? Do we really want a tax system that collects the bulk of its revenue from taxes on insulin?

Of course not. Efficiency is only one criterion for evaluating a tax system; fairness is also important. In particular, it is widely agreed that a tax system should have **vertical equity**; that is, it should distribute burdens fairly across people with different abilities to pay. The Ramsey rule has been modified to consider the distributional consequences of taxation. Suppose, for example, that the poor spend a greater proportion of their income on commodity X than do the rich, and vice versa for commodity Y. X might be bread, and Y caviar. Suppose further that the social welfare function puts a higher weight on the utilities of the poor than on those of the rich. Then even if X is more inelastically demanded than Y, optimal taxation may require a higher rate of tax on Y than X (Diamond, 1975). True, a high tax rate on Y creates a relatively large excess burden, but it also tends to redistribute income toward the poor. Society may be willing to pay the price of a higher excess burden in return for a more equal distribution of income. In general, the extent to which it makes sense to depart from the Ramsey rule depends on the following:

1. The strength of society's egalitarian preferences. If society cares only about efficiency—a dollar to one person is the same as a dollar to another, rich or poor—then it may as well strictly follow the Ramsey rule.
2. The extent to which the consumption patterns of the rich and poor differ. If the rich and the poor consume both goods in the same proportion, taxing the goods at different rates cannot affect the distribution of income. Even if society has a distributional goal, it cannot be achieved by differential taxation of X and Y.

Summary

If lump-sum taxation were available, taxes could be raised without any excess burden at all. Optimal taxation would need to focus only on distributional issues. Lump-sum taxes are not available, however, so the problem becomes how to collect a given amount of tax revenue with as small an excess burden as possible. In general, minimizing excess burden requires that taxes be set so that the (compensated) demands for all commodities are reduced in the same proportion. For unrelated goods, this implies that tax rates should be set in inverse proportion to the demand elasticities. However, if society has distributional goals, departures from efficient taxation may be appropriate.

OPTIMAL USER FEES

So far we have assumed that all production occurs in the private sector. The government's only problem is to set the tax rates that determine consumer prices. Sometimes, the government itself is the producer of a good or service. In such cases, the government must directly choose a **user fee**—a price paid by users of a good or service provided by the government. As usual, we would like to determine the "best" possible user fee. Analytically, the optimal tax and user-fee problems are closely related. In both cases, the government sets the final

---

[5] Several European countries have recently reduced their tax rates on a number of labour-intensive services that are easily substitutable for home-produced services. The logic is similar to the Cortlett–Hague insight. In this case, home production is untaxable. Hence, the tax on market supplied labour services distorts the consumer's choice in favour of home production. To reduce this distortion, the tax rates on labour services have now been lowered, relative to other goods and services. See Sørensen (2007).

FIGURE 16.2

A NATURAL MONOPOLY

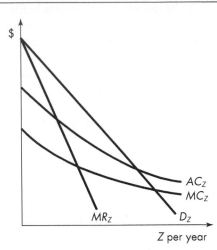

price paid by consumers. In the optimal tax problem, this is done indirectly by choice of the tax rate, while in the optimal user-fee problem it is done directly.

When does the government choose to produce a good instead of purchasing it from the private sector? Government production is likely when the production of some good or service is subject to continually decreasing average costs—the greater the level of output, the lower the cost per unit. Under such circumstances, it is unlikely that the market for the service is competitive. A single firm can take advantage of economies of scale and supply the entire industry output, at least for a sizable region. This phenomenon is often called **natural monopoly.** Examples are highways, bridges, electricity, and cable television. In some cases, these commodities are produced by the private sector and regulated by the government (electricity); in others they are produced by the public sector (highways). Although we study public production here, many of the important insights apply to regulation of private monopolies.

Figure 16.2 measures the output of the natural monopoly, Z, on the horizontal axis, and dollars on the vertical. The average cost schedule is denoted AC_Z. By assumption, it decreases continuously over all relevant ranges of output. Because average cost is decreasing, marginal cost must be less than average. Therefore, the marginal cost (MC_Z) curve, which shows the incremental cost of providing each unit of Z, lies below AC_Z. The demand curve for Z is represented by D_Z. The associated marginal revenue curve is MR_Z. It shows the incremental revenue associated with each level of output of Z.

To illustrate why decreasing average costs often lead to public sector production or regulated private sector production, consider what would happen if Z were produced by an unregulated monopolist. The monopolist seeking to maximize profits produces up to the point that marginal revenue equals marginal cost, output level Z_m in Figure 16.3. The associated price, P_m, is found by going up to the demand curve, D_Z. Monopoly profits are equal to the product of number of units sold times the profit per unit and are represented geometrically by the light-shaded rectangle.

Is output Z_m efficient? According to the theory of welfare economics, efficiency requires that price equal marginal cost—the value that people place on the good must equal the incremental cost to society of producing it. At Z_m, price is greater than marginal cost. Hence, Z_m is inefficient. This inefficiency, plus the fact that society may not approve of the existence of the monopoly profits, provides a possible justification for government taking over the production of Z.

The obvious policy prescription seems to be for the government to produce up to the point where price equals marginal cost. In Figure 16.3, the output at which $P = MC$ is denoted Z^*, and the associated price is P^*. There is a problem, however: at output Z^*, the price is less than the average cost. Price P^* is so low that the operation cannot cover its costs, and it continually suffers losses. The total loss is equal to the product of

FIGURE 16.3

ALTERNATIVE PRICING SCHEMES FOR A NATURAL MONOPOLY

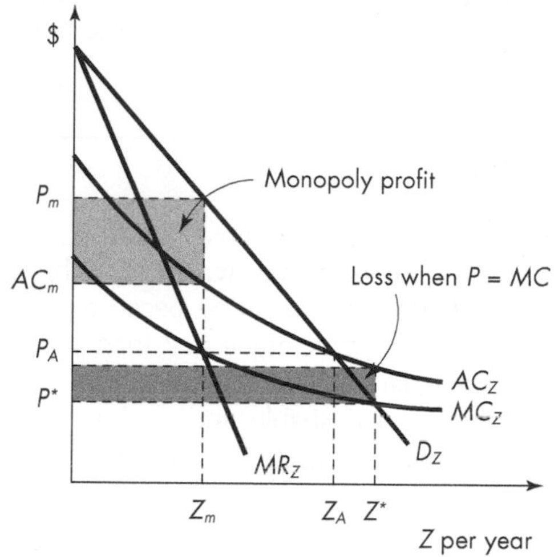

the number of units sold, Z^*, times the loss per unit, measured as the vertical distance between the demand curve and AC_Z at Z^*. Geometrically, the loss is the darker-shaded rectangle in Figure 16.3.

How should the government confront this dilemma? Several solutions have been proposed.

Average cost pricing. By definition, when price equals average cost, there are neither profits nor losses—the enterprise just breaks even. The operation no longer has to worry about a deficit. Geometrically, this corresponds to the intersection of the demand and average cost schedules in Figure 16.3, where output is Z_A and price is P_A. However, note that Z_A is less than Z^*. Although average cost pricing leads to more output than at the profit-maximizing level, it still falls short of the efficient amount.

Marginal cost pricing with lump-sum taxes. Charge $P = MC$, and make up the deficit by levying lump-sum taxes. Charging $P = MC$ ensures efficiency in the market for Z; financing the deficit with lump-sum taxes on the rest of society guarantees that no new inefficiencies are generated by meeting the deficit. However, there are two problems with this solution.

First, as previously noted, lump-sum taxes are generally unavailable. It is more likely that the deficit will have to be financed by distorting taxes, such as income or commodity taxes. If so, the distortion in the market where the tax is levied may more than outweigh the efficiency gain in the market for Z.

Second, there is also a widespread belief that fairness requires consumers of a publicly provided service to pay for it—the so-called **benefits-received principle**. If this principle is taken seriously, it is unfair to make up the deficit by general taxation. If the Canadian Coast Guard rescues me from a stormy sea, why should you pay for it?

A Ramsey solution. So far we have been looking at one government enterprise in isolation. Suppose that the government is running *several* companies, and as a group they cannot lose money but any individual enterprise can. Suppose further that the government wants the financing to come from users of the services produced by the enterprises. By how much should the user fee for each service exceed its marginal cost?

Does this question sound familiar? It should, because it is essentially the same as the optimal tax problem. In effect, the difference between the user fee and the marginal cost is just the "tax" that the government levies on the commodity. And just as in the optimal tax problem, the government has to raise a certain amount of revenue in this case, enough for the group of enterprises to break even. The Ramsey rule gives the answer: set the user fees so that demands for each commodity are reduced proportionately. This analysis, by the way, illustrates one of the nice features of economic theory. Often a framework that is designed to study one problem can be fruitfully applied to another problem that seems to be quite different.

Summary

Of the various possibilities for dealing with decreasing costs, which has Canada chosen? In many cases, average cost pricing has been selected both for publicly owned and regulated private enterprises. Although average cost pricing is inefficient, it is probably a reasonable compromise. It has the virtue of being fairly simple and adheres to the popular benefits-received principle. Some economists, however, argue that more reliance on Ramsey pricing would be desirable.

OPTIMAL INCOME TAXATION

Thus far, we have assumed that a government can levy taxes on all commodities and factors of production. We now turn to the question of how to design systems in which tax liabilities are based on people's incomes. Income taxation is an obvious candidate for special attention because of its importance in the revenue structures of most developed countries. In addition, some argue that income is an especially appropriate tax base because it is the best measure of an individual's ability to pay. For the moment, we merely assume that society has somehow decided that an income tax is desirable, and ask how to structure it. In subsequent chapters, we discuss whether income really is a particularly desirable tax base.

Edgeworth's Model

At the end of the nineteenth century, Edgeworth (1959/1897) examined the question of optimal income taxation using a simple model based on the following assumptions:

1. Subject to the revenues required, the goal is to make the sum of individuals' utilities as high as possible. Algebraically, if U_i is the utility of the ith individual and W is social welfare, the tax system should maximize

$$W = U_1 + U_2 + \cdots + U_n, \qquad (16.10)$$

   where n is the number of people in the society.

2. Individuals have identical utility functions that depend only on their incomes. These utility functions exhibit diminishing marginal utility of income; as income increases, an individual becomes better off, but at a decreasing rate.

3. The total amount of income available is fixed.

Edgeworth's assumptions are virtually identical to the assumptions behind the optimal income distribution model presented in Chapter 6 under "Rationales for Income Redistribution." There we showed that, with these assumptions, maximization of social welfare requires that each person's marginal utility of income be the same. When utility functions are identical, equal marginal utilities of income occur only at equal levels of income. The implications for tax policy are clear—taxes should be set in such a way that the after-tax distribution of income is as equal as possible. In particular, income should be taken first from the rich because the marginal utility lost is smaller than that of the poor. If the government requires more revenue even after complete equality has been reached, the additional tax burden should be evenly distributed.

Edgeworth's model, then, implies a radically progressive tax structure—incomes are levelled off from the top until complete equality is reached. In effect, marginal tax rates on high-income individuals are 100 percent. However, as stressed in Chapter 6, each of the assumptions underlying this analysis is subject to question. Beginning in the 1970s, economists began investigating how Edgeworth's results change when certain assumptions are relaxed.

Modern Studies

One of the most vexing problems with Edgeworth's analysis is the assumption that the total amount of income available to society is fixed. Confiscatory tax rates are assumed to have no effect on the amount of output produced. More realistically, suppose that individuals' utilities depend not only on income, but on leisure as well. Then income taxes distort work decisions and create excess burdens (see Chapter 15). A society with an additive social welfare function thus faces an inescapable dilemma. On the one hand, it wants to allocate the tax burden to equalize the after-tax distribution of income. However, in the process of doing so, it reduces the

FIGURE 16.4

A LINEAR INCOME TAX

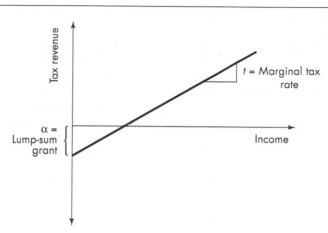

total amount of real income available. Designing an optimal income tax system—one that maximizes social welfare—must consider the costs (in excess burden) of achieving more equality. In Edgeworth's model, the cost of obtaining more equality is zero, which explains the prescription for a perfectly egalitarian outcome.

How does Edgeworth's result change when work incentives are taken into account? Modern studies use a model similar to Edgeworth's, except that individuals choose between income and leisure. To simplify the analysis, suppose that the amount of tax revenues collected from a person is given by

$$Revenues = -\alpha + t \times Income \qquad (16.11)$$

where α and t are positive numbers. For example, suppose that $\alpha = \$3,000$ and $t = .25$. Then a person with income of $20,000 would have a tax liability of $2,000 (= $-\$3,000 + .25 \times \$20,000$). A person with an income of $6,000 would have a tax liability of *minus* $1,500 (= $-\$3,000 + .25 \times \$6,000$). Such a person would receive a $1,500 grant from the government.

In Figure 16.4, we graph Equation (16.11) in a diagram with income measured on the horizontal axis and tax revenues on the vertical. When income is zero, the tax burden is negative—the individual receives a lump-sum grant from the government of α dollars. Then, for each dollar of income, the individual must pay t dollars to the government. Thus, t is the marginal tax rate, the proportion of an additional dollar that must be paid in tax. Because the geometric interpretation of Equation (16.11) is a straight line, it is referred to as a **linear income tax schedule**. In popular discussions, a linear income tax schedule is often referred to as a **flat tax**. Note that even though the marginal tax rate for a linear tax schedule is constant, the schedule is *progressive* in the sense that the higher an individual's income, the higher the proportion of income paid in taxes (see Chapter 14). Just how progressive depends on the precise values of α and t. Greater values of t are associated with more progressive tax systems. However, at the same time that high values of t lead to more progressiveness, they create larger excess burdens. The optimal linear income tax problem is to find the "best" combination of α and t—the values that maximize social welfare (Equation (16.10)) subject to the constraint that a given amount of revenue be collected.

Some countries have a single marginal tax rate (Russia is an example), but most countries have several marginal tax rates, which kick in at different income thresholds (see Chapter 17). However, even when allowing for multiple marginal tax rates, Mankiw, Weinzierl, and Yagan (2009) show that the solution to the optimal non-linear income tax problem is well approximated by an optimal linear income tax schedule.[6] Their study finds that the optimal marginal tax rate is between 48 and 50 percent. This is considerably less than the value

---

[6] They find that the optimal non-linear income tax schedule departs from a nearly constant marginal tax rate only at the low and high tails of the income distribution.

of 100 percent implied by Edgeworth's analysis. Thus, even quite modest incentive effects appear to have important implications for optimal marginal tax rates. They also find that the optimal lump-sum grant to low-ability workers (the α in our model) is just over 60 percent of the average income per worker.

In general, the more elastic the supply of labour, the lower the optimal value of t, other things being the same. Intuitively, the cost of redistribution is the excess burden it creates. The more elastic the supply of labour, the greater the excess burden from taxing it (see Equation (15.4) in Chapter 15). More elastic labour supply, therefore, means a higher cost to redistribution, so that less should be done. Researchers have also investigated how alternative social welfare functions affect the results, focusing on the impact of giving different social weights to the utilities of the rich and the poor. In Equation (16.10), more egalitarian preferences are represented by assigning the utilities of poor people higher weights than utilities of the rich. An interesting extreme case is the maximin criterion, according to which the only individual who receives any weight in the social welfare function is the person with the minimum utility (see Chapter 6). Stern (1976) found that the maximin criterion calls for a marginal tax rate of about 80 percent. Not surprisingly, if society has extremely egalitarian objectives, high tax rates are called for. Even here, though, the rates fall short of 100 percent.

Another interesting result of optimal income taxation concerns the marginal tax rate on the highest earners and the lowest earners when the tax schedule can have multiple tax rates. Gruber and Saez (2002) investigated a model that allowed for four marginal tax rates. Their analysis indicates that people in the highest income bracket should face *lower* marginal tax rates than people in the lowest bracket. In contrast, in most real-world income tax systems, marginal tax rates increase with income. For example, in Canada, the marginal tax rate on the lowest income bracket is zero, and on the highest it is 54.75 percent, in 2015 (in New Brunswick).[7] The intuition behind the result is that, by lowering the marginal tax rate on high-income people, they are induced to supply more labour, and the increased tax revenue can be used to lower the tax burdens on low-income individuals. Importantly, although marginal tax rates fall with income, average tax rates rise with income, so the optimal tax system is still progressive. A canton (state) in Switzerland actually implemented a tax system that imposes lower marginal tax rates on higher earners (Rabushka, 2003).

This cataloguing of results may convey a somewhat false sense of precision as to what economists really know about the optimal tax system. After all, there are many controversial value judgments behind the additive social welfare that the optimal tax system seeks to maximize. Moreover, as explained in Chapter 18, there is substantial uncertainty about the behavioural elasticities that are crucial to analyzing the tradeoff between efficiency and equity. Nevertheless, it is extremely informative to have explicit calculations of what the optimal tax rates would be under alternative sets of assumptions. These reveal the implications of different ethical and behavioural assumptions, and thus foster coherent discussions of tax policy.

POLITICS AND THE TIME INCONSISTENCY PROBLEM

Optimal taxation is a purely normative theory. It does not purport to predict what real-world tax systems look like, or to explain how these tax systems emerge. The theory pays little attention to the institutional and political setting in which tax policy is made. Holcombe (2002) argues that in the presence of real-world political institutions, policy recommendations based on optimal tax logic may actually reduce welfare.

Assume that in a certain society, there are three commodities, X, Y, and leisure. Labour is totally fixed in supply, and therefore income is fixed. Currently, this society levies a tax on X, but its constitution forbids taxing Y. Viewing this situation, a student of optimal tax theory might say something like this: "You are running an inefficient tax system. Because labour is totally fixed in supply, you could have no excess burden if you taxed X and Y at equal rates—an income tax. I recommend that you lower the tax on X and impose a tax at the same rate on Y. Set the rates so that the same amount of revenue is collected as before."

Suppose, however, that the citizens suspect that if they allow Y to be taxed, their politicians and bureaucrats will *not* lower the tax rate on X. Rather, they will simply take advantage of the opportunity to tax something new to make tax revenues as large as possible. As we saw in Chapter 7 under "Explaining Government Growth," certain theories of the public sector suggest that those who run the government can and will maximize tax revenues

---

[7] However, the clawing back of government transfers for social assistance, child benefits, and other tax credits significantly raises the effective marginal tax rate at lower incomes in Canada (see Chapter 17).

QUEBEC'S "GOOD NEWS BUDGET"

In a province struggling with high tax rates and a string of budget deficits since the 2008–09 recession, Quebec's finance minister promised citizens that his March 26, 2015, budget would contain "good news." There would be zero deficit in 2015–16, some tax relief, and improvements in the design of means-tested cash transfers. There was also a pledge to consider overhauling the tax system in the future, after public consultations. A week before the budget was delivered, the government released the report of its Quebec taxation review committee, which recommended a wholesale reduction in income taxes, financed by new sources of revenue, such higher electricity rates, higher water taxes, and charges on various goods as well as an increase in the Quebec sales tax. All told, this represented a $4.4 billion package of corporate and personal income tax cuts with no net impact on the government's revenues. The budget plan indicated that the idea of a higher sales tax was "under review," and a few days after his budget speech, the finance minister said in a TV interview, "the worst tax you can have is an income tax, while the one that causes the least distortion is a consumption tax." The declaration was interpreted as tacit endorsement of the tax committee's argument that taxing income discourages savings, investment, and employment, while taxing consumption is less damaging to economic growth. Opposition parties were unimpressed; the PQ finance critic said, "We've already got the highest sales taxes in North America and raising those will hurt business and consumers." Others were disappointed by spending cuts to education and health. Whether the government decides to continue down the road of structural reforms to Quebec's tax system is something to watch for.

Based on Gordon (2015), CTV News Montreal (2015), and "Quebec must follow through on tax reform." *The Gazette*, June 17, 2015.

Complete references for this feature can be found in the References section on page 486.

despite the wishes of the citizenry. Therefore, by constitutionally precluding the taxation of *Y*, the citizens may be rationally protecting themselves against an inefficiently large public sector. In other words, if citizens do not trust the government, what looks inefficient from the point of view of optimal commodity taxation may be efficient in a larger setting.[8] There is, in fact, some evidence that governments with tax systems that generate large excess burdens tend to grow more slowly than governments with efficient tax systems (Becker and Mulligan, 2003).

Issue relating to these considerations may help explain, in part, the current controversy over the tax treatment of purchases made on the Internet. Proponents of Internet taxation argue that a good purchased in a store is essentially the same commodity as the same good purchased on the Internet. Taxing the former but not the latter distorts consumers' choices between the two modes of purchase, and, hence, creates an excess burden. Opponents argue that taxing Internet sales would simply fuel increases in the size of the public sector, which is already inefficiently large.

This situation is related to a more general phenomenon called the **time inconsistency of optimal policy**, which occurs when the government cannot implement an optimal tax policy because the stated policy is inconsistent with the government's incentives over time. Consider a proposal made by the deputy prime minister of the United Kingdom in 2012. In order to help reduce the country's deficit, he proposed a tax on the wealth of the rich British citizens (Frank, 2012). Importantly, the tax was to be imposed only one time; it would not be repeated in the future. While wealthy Britons presumably would not be pleased to pay the tax, it would appear to have no impact on their current incentives to save for the future. Such a tax is, in effect, a lump-sum levy and, therefore, fully efficient.

There is a problem, however. The British government would have an incentive to renege on its promise that the tax would be levied only once and pull exactly the same trick next year, raising yet more revenue without an excess burden. Thus, the stated tax policy will be inconsistent with the government's incentives

---

[8] Winer and Hettich (2004) provide further comparisons between optimal tax theory and an approach that takes politics into account.

over time. Even worse, the capitalists realize the government has an incentive to renege. They will change their saving behaviour to reflect the expectation that the more they save now, the more they will be taxed next year. Because the expected tax changes behaviour, it introduces an inefficiency.

In short, unless the government can *credibly* promise not to renege, it cannot conduct the fully efficient tax policy. To avoid this time-inconsistency problem, the government must be able to commit itself to behave in certain ways in the future. How can this be done? One possible approach is to enact constitutional provisions that would forbid the government to go back on its promises. However, as long as the government has an underlying incentive to renege, suspicions will remain, frustrating attempts to run an efficient policy. These considerations suggest that the credibility of the political system must be considered before making recommendations based on optimal tax theory.[9]

OTHER CRITERIA FOR TAX DESIGN

As we have seen, optimal taxation depends on the trade off between "efficiency" and "fairness." However, the use of these concepts in optimal tax theory does not always correspond closely to lay usage. In the context of optimal tax theory, a fair tax is one that guarantees a socially desirable distribution of the tax burden; an efficient tax is one with a small excess burden. In public discussion, on the other hand, a fair tax is often one that imposes equal liabilities on people who have the same ability to pay, and an efficient tax system is one that keeps down administrative and compliance expenses. These alternative notions of fairness and efficiency in taxation are the subject of this section.

Horizontal Equity

The American humorist Will Rogers once said, "People want *just* taxes more than they want *lower* taxes. They want to know that every man is paying his proportionate share according to his wealth." This criterion for evaluating a tax system is embodied in the economist's notion of **horizontal equity**: people in equal positions should be treated equally. To make horizontal equity an operational idea, one must define "equal positions." Customarily, some observable index of ability to pay, such as income, expenditure, or wealth, defines equal position.

Unfortunately, these measures represent the *outcomes* of people's decisions and are not really suitable measures of equal position. Consider two individuals, both of whom can earn $10 per hour. Mr. *A* chooses to work 1,500 hours each year, while Ms. *B* works 2,200 hours each year. *A*'s income is $15,000 and *B*'s is $22,000, so that, in terms of income, *A* and *B* are not in "equal positions." In an important sense, however, *A* and *B* are the same, because their earning capacities are identical—*B* just happens to work harder. Thus, because work effort is at least to some extent under people's control, two individuals with different incomes may actually be in equal positions. Similar criticism would apply to expenditure or wealth as a criterion for measuring equal positions.

These arguments suggest that the individual's wage *rate* rather than income be considered as a candidate for measuring equal positions, but this idea has problems too. First, investments in human capital—education, on-the-job training, and health care—can influence the wage rate. If Mr. *A* had to go to university to earn the same wage that Ms. *B* is able to earn with only a high school diploma, is it fair to treat them the same? Second, computation of the wage rate requires division of total earnings by hours of work, but the latter is not easy to measure. (How should time spent on coffee breaks be counted?) Indeed, for a given income, it would be worthwhile for a worker to exaggerate hours of work to be able to report a lower wage rate and pay fewer taxes. Presumably, bosses could be induced to collaborate with their employees in return for a share of the tax savings.

As an alternative to measuring equal position either in incomes or wage rates, Feldstein (1976) suggests it be defined in utilities. Hence, the **utility definition of horizontal equity**: (a) if two individuals would be equally well off (have the same utility level) in the absence of taxation, they should also be equally well off if there is taxation; and (b) taxes should not alter the utility ordering—if *A* is better off than *B* before taxation, he should be better off after.

---

[9] See Boadway, Marceau, and Marchand (1996) for a rationalization of publicly provided education as a solution to a problem of time-inconsistent taxation of income from human capital.

To assess the implications of Feldstein's definition, first assume all individuals have the same preferences; that is, identical utility functions. In this case, individuals who consume the same commodities (including leisure) should pay the same tax, or, equivalently, all individuals should face the same tax schedule. Otherwise, individuals with equal before-tax utility levels would have different after-tax utilities.

Now assume that people have diverse tastes. For example, let there be two types of individuals, Gourmets and Sunbathers. Both groups consume food (which is purchased using income) and leisure, but Gourmets put a relatively high value on food, as do Sunbathers on leisure time. Assume further that before any taxation, Gourmets and Sunbathers have identical utility levels. If the same proportional income tax is imposed on everybody, Gourmets are necessarily made worse off than Sunbathers, because the former need relatively large amounts of income to support their food habits. Thus, even though this income tax is perfectly fair, judged by the traditional definition of horizontal equity, it is not fair according to the utility definition. Indeed, as long as tastes for leisure differ, *any* income tax violates the utility definition of horizontal equity.

Of course, the practical difficulties involved in measuring individuals' utilities preclude the possibility of having a utility tax. Nevertheless, the utility definition of horizontal equity has some provocative policy implications. Assume again that all individuals have the same preferences. Then it can be shown that *any* existing tax structure does not violate the utility definition of horizontal equity *if* individuals are free to choose their activities and expenditures.

To see why, suppose that in one type of job a large part of compensation is in the form of amenities that are not taxable. These might include pleasant offices, access to a swimming pool, and so forth. In another occupation, compensation is exclusively monetary, all of which is subject to income tax. According to the traditional definition, this situation is a violation of horizontal equity, because a person in the job with a lot of amenities has too small a tax burden. But, if both arrangements coexist and individuals are free to choose, then the net after-tax rewards (including amenities) must be the same in both jobs. Why? Suppose that the net after-tax reward is greater in the jobs with amenities. Then individuals migrate to these jobs to take advantage of them. But the increased supply of workers in these jobs depresses their wages. The process continues until the net returns are equal. In short, although people in the different occupations pay unequal taxes, there is no horizontal inequity because of adjustments in the *before-tax* wage.

Some suggest that certain tax advantages available only to the rich are sources of horizontal inequity. According to the utility definition, this notion is wrong. If these advantages are open to everyone with high income, and all high-income people have identical tastes, then the advantages may indeed reduce tax progressiveness, but they have no effect whatsoever on horizontal equity.

We are led to a striking conclusion. Given common tastes, a pre-existing tax structure cannot involve horizontal inequity. Rather, all horizontal inequities arise from *changes* in tax laws. This is because individuals make commitments based on the existing tax laws that are difficult or impossible to reverse. For example, people may buy larger houses because of the preferred tax treatment for owner-occupied housing.[10] When the tax laws are changed, their welfare goes down, and horizontal equity is violated. Many of the initiatives to broaden the tax base in Finance Minister Allan MacEachen's 1981 tax reform were attacked on the basis that "desirable incentives" had suddenly become "unattractive loopholes." These observations give new meaning to the dictum, "The only good tax is an old tax."[11]

The fact that tax changes may generate horizontal inequities does not necessarily imply that they should not be undertaken. After all, tax changes may lead to improvements from the points of view of efficiency and/ or vertical equity. However, the arguments suggest that it might be appropriate, somehow, to ease the transition to the new tax system. For example, if it is announced that a given tax reform is not to go into effect until a few years subsequent to its passage, people who have based their behaviour on the old tax structure will be able to make at least some adjustments to the new regime. The problem of finding fair processes for changing tax regimes (known as **transitional equity**) is very difficult, and not many results are available on the subject.

The very conservative implications of the utility definition of horizontal equity should come as no great surprise, because implicit in the definition is the notion that the pretax status quo has special ethical validity. (Otherwise, why be concerned about changes in the ordering of utilities?) However, it is not at all obvious why

---

[10] See Chapter 18.

[11] See the discussion of tax capitalization in Chapter 14.

the status quo deserves to be defended. A more general feature of the utility definition is its focus on the *outcomes* of taxation. In contrast, some have suggested that the essence of horizontal equity is to put constraints on the *rules* that govern the selection of taxes, rather than to provide criteria for judging their effects. Thus, horizontal equity excludes capricious taxes, or taxes based on irrelevant characteristics. For example, we can imagine the government levying special lump-sum taxes on people with red hair, or putting very different taxes on angel food and chocolate cakes. The **rule definition of horizontal equity** would presumably exclude such taxes from consideration, even if they somehow had desirable efficiency or distributional effects.

However, identifying the permissible set of characteristics on which to base taxation is a problem. Most people would agree that religion and race should be irrelevant for purposes of determining tax liability. On the other hand, there is continuing disagreement as to whether or not marital status should influence tax burdens (see Chapter 17 under "Choice of Tax Unit"). And even once there is agreement that certain characteristics are legitimate bases for discrimination, the problem of how much discrimination is appropriate still remains. Everyone agrees that serious physical impairment should be taken into account in determining personal tax liability. But how much must your vision be impaired before you are eligible for special tax treatment as blind? And by what amount should your tax bill be reduced?

We are forced to conclude that horizontal equity, however defined, is a rather amorphous concept. Yet it continues to have enormous appeal as a principle of tax design. Notions of fairness among equals, regardless of their vagueness, will continue to play an important role in the development of tax policy.

Costs of Running the Tax System

An implicit assumption in the models we have been studying is that collecting taxes involves no costs. However, contrary to this assumption, tax administration is not a costless activity. Tax authorities require resources to do their job. At the same time, taxpayers incur costs in complying with the tax system. These include outlays for accountants and tax lawyers, as well as the value of taxpayers' time spent filling out tax returns and keeping records.

The costs of administering the personal income and payroll taxes in Canada are fairly low. For example, Vaillancourt (1989) found that the government spends only about $1 to raise each $100 in tax revenues.[12] However, the compliance costs of personal income taxes are quite substantial. According to estimates reported by Speer, Palacios, Lugo, and Vaillancourt (2014), the average Canadian taxpayer devotes about five hours to preparing his or her own return and an additional two hours are spent on appeals and planning, while those paying to have their tax returns prepared spent an average of $108 for professional assistance. The average taxpayer cost (value in dollars of time spent plus spending) is estimated by these researchers to be at least $190 for direct tax compliance and $235 including appeals and tax planning, in 2012. Multiplying the latter figure by 26.9 million taxpaying units in 2012 gives a total compliance cost of $6.3 billion, which is 2.9 percent of personal income taxes collected, or 0.3 percent of GDP. To this we must add the substantial compliance costs of employers.[13] Total administrative and compliance costs faced by governments, individuals, and businesses for the gamut of federal, provincial, and municipal taxes paid in Canada—personal and corporation income taxes, payroll taxes, Goods and Services Tax (GST), sales and excise taxes, and property taxes—are estimated by Vaillancourt, Roy-César, and Barros (2013) to be between 1.5 and 1.8 percent of GDP, which amounts to each Canadian incurring a cost of between $754 and $917 in 2012 dollars.[14]

Clearly, the choice of tax and subsidy systems should take account of administrative and compliance costs. Even systems that appear fair and efficient (in the excess burden sense) might be undesirable because they are excessively complicated and expensive to administer. Consider the possibility of taxing output produced in the home—housecleaning, childcare, and so on. As suggested in Chapter 15, the fact that market work is taxed but housework is not creates a sizable distortion in the allocation of labour. Moreover, taxing

---

[12] These cost estimates are for the personal income tax, and for Employment Insurance and Canada Pension Plan premiums collected from employees and employers.

[13] Employer compliance costs were estimated by Vaillancourt (1989) to be 3.5 percent of the personal income and payroll taxes collected in 1986.

[14] The estimate of the total administrative and compliance cost is given by Vaillancourt, Roy-César, and Barros for 2011. We convert the figure to per capita 2012 dollars for comparability with the previous discussion of the compliance cost of personal income taxes.

differentially on the basis of choice of workplace violates some notions of horizontal equity. Nevertheless, the difficulties involved in valuing household production would create such huge administrative costs that the idea is infeasible.

Unfortunately, in many cases, administrative problems receive insufficient attention. A classic case is that of the combined federal and provincial excise taxes on tobacco products at the end of 1993 and into 1994.[15] Early in 1994, taxes on cigarettes had reached a level (between $2.75 and $3 per pack of 25) at which smuggling across the Canada–U.S. border was rampant. Perhaps two-thirds of all cigarettes in Quebec were purchased illegally. The smuggling problem was also serious in Ontario and other eastern provinces. Cigarette taxes were subsequently cut by as much as 60 percent in Quebec and Ontario, with lesser reductions in other provinces, to reduce the incentive to evade the taxes. An additional 350 customs inspectors were hired, and the number of RCMP anti-smuggling agents was doubled. In 2015, excise taxes on cigarettes in Ontario and Quebec remained well below those in other provinces.

The GST has also proved to have higher than anticipated compliance and administrative costs. One study found GST *compliance* costs to be 17 percent of tax collected for businesses with annual sales of $100,000 or less, and 2.65 percent for those with yearly sales over $1 million. Revenue Canada estimated *administrative* costs at 3 percent of the revenues, much higher than for similar taxes in other countries (House of Commons, 1994).

Obviously, no tax system is costless to administer; the trick is to think carefully about whether or not the administrative costs are worth the benefits. In some cases, it may be necessary to trade off excess burden against administrative costs. For example, it might be very cumbersome to administer a sales tax system in which each commodity has its own rate, despite the fact that this is the general tack prescribed by the Ramsey rule. Any reductions in excess burden that arise from differentiating the tax rates must be compared to the incremental administrative costs.

Tax Evasion

We now turn to one of the most important problems facing any tax administration—cheating. First, it is important to distinguish between tax avoidance and tax evasion. **Tax avoidance** is changing your behaviour so as to reduce your legal tax liability. There is nothing illegal about tax avoidance:

> Over and over again courts have said that there is nothing sinister in so arranging one's affairs so as to keep taxes as low as possible. Everybody does so, rich or poor; and all do right, for nobody owes any public duty to pay more than the law demands. . . . To demand more in the name of morals is mere cant. (Judge Learned Hand, *Commissioner v. Newman*, 1947)

In contrast, **tax evasion** is failing to pay legally due taxes. If a tax on mushrooms is levied and you sell fewer mushrooms, it is tax avoidance. If you fail to report your sales of mushrooms to the government, it is tax evasion. Tax evasion is not a new problem. Over two thousand years ago Plato observed, "When there is an income tax, the just man will pay more and the unjust less on the same amount of income." In recent years, however, the phenomenon of tax evasion has received a large amount of public attention.

Tax cheating is extremely difficult to measure. Although the Canada Revenue Agency has not published estimates on tax cheating, the government has publicly acknowledged it as an important issue.

There are several common ways to commit tax fraud:

1. *Keeping two sets of books to record business transactions.* One records the actual business and the other is shown to the tax authorities. Some evaders use two cash registers. Underreporting income is especially prevalent among people who own their own businesses. Schuetze (2002) estimates that 12 to 21 percent of self-employment income in Canada goes unreported.
2. *Moonlighting for cash.* Of course, there is nothing illegal in working an extra job. In many cases, however, the income received on such jobs is paid in cash rather than by cheque. Hence, there is no legal record, and the income is not reported to the tax authorities.

---

[15] This discussion is based on information found on pages 8:5 to 8:7 in *The National Finances, 1994*.

3. *Bartering.* "I'll fix your car if you bake me five loaves of bread." When you receive payment in kind instead of money, it is legally a taxable transaction. However, such income is seldom reported.

4. *Dealing in cash.* Paying for goods and services with cash and cheques made out to "cash" makes it very difficult for the Canada Revenue Agency to trace transactions.

At one time, tax evasion was associated with millionaires who hid their capital in Swiss bank accounts. Now the current image of a tax evader may well be a repairer whose income comes from "unofficial" work not reported for tax purposes, or a small business where cash transactions are common. We first discuss the positive theory of tax evasion, and then turn to the normative question of how public policy should deal with it.

Positive analysis of tax evasion. Assume Al cares only about maximizing his expected income.[16] He has a given amount of earnings and is trying to choose R, the amount that he hides from the tax authorities. Suppose Al's marginal income tax rate is 0.3; for each dollar shielded from taxable income, his tax bill falls by 30 cents. This is the marginal benefit to him of hiding a dollar of income from the tax authorities. More generally, when Al faces a marginal income tax rate t, the marginal benefit of each dollar shielded from taxation is t.

The tax authority does not know Al's true income, but it randomly audits all taxpayers' returns. As a result, there is some probability, ρ, that Al will be audited. If he is caught cheating, Al pays a penalty that increases with R at an increasing rate. Note that if it were costless to monitor Al every second of every day, there would be no opportunities for evasion. The fact that such monitoring is infeasible is the fundamental source of the problem.

Assuming that Al knows the value of ρ and the penalty schedule, he makes his decision by comparing the marginal costs and benefits of cheating. In Figure 16.5, the amount of income not reported is measured on the horizontal axis, and dollars on the vertical. The marginal benefit (MB) for each dollar not reported is t, the amount of tax saved. The expected marginal cost (MC) is the amount by which the penalty goes up for each dollar of cheating (the marginal penalty) times the probability of detection. For example, if the additional penalty for hiding the 1,000th dollar is $1.50 and the probability of detection is 1 in 3, then the *expected* marginal penalty is 50 cents. The "optimal" amount of cheating is where the two schedules cross, at R^*. R^* is optimal in the sense that on *average* it is the policy that maximizes Al's income. In a world of uncertainty, finding the best policy in this "expected value" sense is a reasonable way to proceed. It is possible, of course, that it will be

---

FIGURE 16.5

OPTIMAL TAX EVASION IS POSITIVE

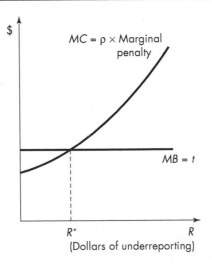

---

[16] This model is similar in structure to those that have been used to describe criminal behaviour in general. See Becker (1968) and Cowell (1990).

FIGURE 16.6

OPTIMAL TAX EVASION IS ZERO

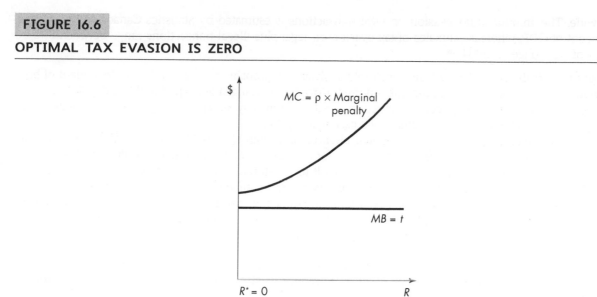

optimal not to cheat at all. For the individual in Figure 16.6, the marginal cost of cheating exceeds the marginal benefit for all positive values of R, so the optimum is equal to zero.

The model implies that cheating increases when marginal tax rates go up. This is because a higher value of t increases the marginal benefit of evasion, shifting up the marginal benefit schedule so the intersection with marginal cost occurs at a higher value of R.[17] On the basis of such reasoning, many people thought the increase in marginal tax rates on average Canadians that occurred from 1950 through the early 1980s contributed to an increase in tax cheating, and that the reductions in marginal rates in the budgets of 1987 and 2000 would help address the problem. A further implication of the model is that cheating decreases when the probability of detection goes up and when the marginal penalty rate increases. Both of these steps raise the expected marginal cost of cheating.

Although this model yields useful insights, it ignores some potentially important considerations.

Psychic costs of cheating. Simply put, tax evasion may make people feel guilty. One way to model this phenomenon is by adding psychic costs to the marginal cost schedule. For some very honest people, the psychic costs are so high they would not cheat even if the expected marginal penalty were zero.

Risk aversion. Figures 16.5 and 16.6 assume people care only about expected income, and that risk, per se, does not bother them. To the extent that individuals are risk averse, their decisions to engage in what is essentially a gamble may be modified.

Work choices. The model assumes the only decision is how much income to report. The type of job and the amount of before-tax income are taken as given. In reality, the tax system may affect hours of work and job choices. For example, high marginal tax rates might induce people to choose occupations that provide substantial opportunities for evading taxation, the so-called **underground economy**. This includes economic activities that are legal but easy to hide from the tax authorities (home repairs) as well as work that is criminal, per se (prostitution, selling drugs). Based on a random survey carried out in the region of Quebec City, Lemieux, Fortin, and Frechette (1994) found that when marginal tax rates increase, so does the probability of participating in the underground sector. The range of estimates on the size of the underground economy in Canada is

---

[17] This prediction is borne out by the econometric work of Clotfelter (1983), who estimated for the United States that the elasticity of underreported income with respect to the marginal tax rate is about 0.84. This means that for a 10 percent increase in the marginal tax rate, say from 30 to 33 percent, unreported income increases by 8.4 percent.

quite wide. The amount of tax evasion on legal transactions is estimated by Statistics Canada to be, at most, 5.2 percent of GDP, whereas estimates of tax evasion on legal plus illegal transactions range between 8 to 16 percent of GDP (Pigeon, 2004).[18]

Changing probabilities of audit. In our simple analysis, the probability of an audit is independent of both the amount evaded and the size of income reported. However, in Canada audit probabilities depend on occupation and the size of reported income. Tax returns filed electronically are also more likely to be audited. This complicates the model, but does not change its essential aspects.

It is clear that cheating is a more complicated phenomenon than Figures 16.5 and 16.6 suggest. Nevertheless, the model provides us with a useful framework for thinking about the factors that influence the decision to evade. Unfortunately, by its very nature, it is difficult to do empirical work on tax evasion. Consequently, it is not known whether high fines or frequent audits are more effective ways of deterring cheating. One tentative result that emerges from several econometric studies is that, for most groups, audits do increase the probability of subsequent compliance, but the magnitude of the effect is small (Blumenthal, Christian, and Slemrod, 2001).

Normative analysis of tax evasion. Most public discussions of the underground economy assume that it is a bad thing and that policy should be designed to reduce its size. Although possibly correct, this proposition is worth scrutiny.

An important question in this context is whether or not we care about the welfare of tax evaders. In the jargon of welfare economics, do the utilities of participants in the underground economy belong in the social welfare function? Assume for the moment that they do. Then under certain conditions, the existence of an underground economy raises social welfare. For example, if the supply of labour is more elastic to the underground economy than to the regular economy, optimal tax theory suggests that the former be taxed at a relatively low rate. This is simply an application of the inverse elasticity rule, Equation (16.9). Alternatively, suppose that participants in the underground economy tend to be poorer than those in the regular economy, and that the underground economy permits employment of individuals who would be unemployed if normal taxes and other regulations (e.g., minimum wages) applied. Then to the extent society has egalitarian income redistribution objectives, leaving the underground economy intact might be desirable.

Consider now the policy implications when evaders are not given any weight in the social welfare function, and the goal is simply to eliminate cheating at the lowest administrative cost possible. Figure 16.5 suggests a fairly straightforward way to accomplish this objective. The expected marginal cost of cheating is the product of the penalty rate and the probability of detection. The probability of detection depends on the amount of resources devoted to tax administration; if the Canada Revenue Agency has a big budget, it can catch a lot of cheaters. However, even if the tax authorities have a small budget so that the probability of detection is low, the marginal cost of cheating can still be made arbitrarily high if the penalty is large enough. If only one tax evader were caught each year, but he or she were publicly hanged for the crime, the *expected* cost of tax evasion would deter many people. The fact that such a draconian policy has never been seriously proposed in Canada indicates that existing penalty systems try to incorporate *just retribution*.[19] Contrary to the assumptions of the utilitarian framework, society cares not only about the end result (getting rid of cheaters), but also the processes by which the result is achieved.

Amnesty. In their search for a socially acceptable way to deal with tax evaders, state governments in the United States have declared periods of **tax amnesty**. During a tax amnesty, people can pay delinquent taxes without facing criminal charges for their previous tax evasion. It is difficult to assess the likely impact on tax collections of a tax amnesty. Tax amnesties in the United States have often been accompanied by an announced intention to increase enforcement efforts, and the success of many "tax amnesty programs" may be due partly to increased enforcement. A further problem in assessing the success of tax amnesty programs lies in the

---

[18] A wide variety of methods have been used to estimate the underground economy in Canada. See Smith (1994), Mirus et al. (1994), Spiro (1994), and Giles and Tedds (2001).

[19] Other nations have not been so constrained in enforcing economic honesty. In China, for example, embezzlement can be a capital offence.

long-term effects of tax amnesties on tax compliance. When tax amnesties are declared repeatedly, the knowledge that an amnesty is forthcoming can lower taxpayers' perceived chances of being prosecuted for future tax evasion. By lowering the expected costs of future tax evasion, an amnesty program that brings with it an expectation of future amnesties may actually *increase* tax evasion.

OVERVIEW

Traditional analysis of tax systems elucidated several "principles" of tax design: taxes should have horizontal and vertical equity, be "neutral" with respect to economic incentives, be administratively easy, and so on. In recent years, public finance economists have integrated these somewhat ad hoc guidelines with the principles of welfare economics. The optimal tax literature *derives* the criteria for a good tax using an underlying social welfare function.

On some occasions, optimal tax analysis has corrected previous errors. For example, it may *not* be efficient for all tax rates to be the same (neutral)–taxing tobacco products more heavily than other goods may be efficient. Furthermore, optimal tax theory has clarified the tradeoffs between efficiency and equity in tax design. As a by-product, the various definitions of "equity" have been scrutinized.

The result of this work is not a blueprint for building a tax system, if for no other reason than the economic theory forming the basis for optimal tax theory has its own problems. In this context two comments are cogent. First, optimal tax theory generally ignores political and social institutions. An "optimal" tax may easily be ruined by politicians or be overly costly to administer.[20] Second, while the optimal tax approach points out that the concept of horizontal equity is difficult to make operational, the fact remains that *equal treatment of equals* is an appealing ethical concept. Horizontal equity is difficult to integrate with optimal tax theory because of the latter's focus on outcomes rather than processes.

Thus, optimal tax theory has used the tools of welfare economics to add analytical strength to the traditional discussion of the goals of tax design. Nevertheless, it is wedded to the utilitarian welfare approach in economics and therefore it is open to criticisms concerning the adequacy of this ethical system.

SUMMARY

- Efficient commodity tax theory studies how to raise a given amount of revenue with a minimum of excess burden.

- The Ramsey rule stipulates that to minimize excess burden, tax rates should be set so that the proportional reduction in the quantity demanded of each good is the same.

- When goods are unrelated in consumption, the Ramsey rule implies that relative tax rates should be inversely related to compensated demand elasticities.

- Choosing optimal user fees for government-produced services is quite similar to choosing optimal taxes.

- Income taxation is a major source of revenue in developed countries. Edgeworth's early study of optimal income taxes stipulated that after-tax incomes be equal. However, when the excess burden of distorting the leisure–income tradeoff is included, marginal tax rates of far less than 100 percent are optimal. A surprising result of optimal income tax theory is that if marginal tax rates are allowed to vary, in general, the marginal tax rate on the highest income should be zero.

- Tax systems may be evaluated by standards other than those of optimal tax theory. Horizontal equity, the costs of administration, incentives for tax evasion, and political constraints all affect the design of tax systems.

- Traditional definitions of horizontal equity rely on income as a measure of "equal position" in society. However, it is not clear that income as conventionally measured does an adequate job.

---

[20] For an assessment of the influence of economic theory in guiding tax reforms in Canada, see Bird and Smart (2001).

The utility definition is more precise, but leads to radically different policy provisions and contains an inherent bias toward the pretax status quo. Other definitions of horizontal equity focus on the rules by which taxes are chosen.

- The costs of running a tax system are ignored in most theoretical analyses. However, administrative and compliance costs affect the choice of tax base, tax rates, and the amount of tax evasion.

EXERCISES

1. "If the compensated demand for a single commodity is completely inelastic, the most socially desirable ad valorem tax rate on this commodity will be higher than the tax rates on other commodities." Comment.

2. Indicate which of the following statements is true, false, or uncertain, and explain why:

   a. A proportional tax on all commodities, including leisure, is equivalent to a lump-sum tax.

   b. Efficiency is maximized when all commodities are taxed at the same rate.

   c. Average cost pricing for a natural monopoly allows the enterprise to break even, but the outcome is inefficient.

   d. Tom's workplace provides free access to a fitness room; Jerry's does not. Horizontal equity requires that Tom be taxed on the value of having access to the fitness room.

3. Prior to 1988, Canada's tax authorities permitted business meals and entertainment expenses to be fully deducted in calculating taxable income. Since then, the allowed deduction has been reduced to 50 percent of the expense. This affects those who incur such expenses as part of normal business activity. Evaluate this change in tax policy using the alternative criteria for horizontal equity.

4. In Thailand, where commodity taxes account for almost 60 percent of tax revenues, the price elasticities for food, alcohol, and telecommunications are estimated to be −0.10, −0.84, and −0.25, respectively (Chandoevwit and Dahlby, 2007). If the goal of policy is to raise tax revenue with the least excess burden possible, what tax rates should be applied to alcohol and telecommunications, when the tax rate on food is fixed at 1.6 percent? (Suppose the commodities are neither substitutes nor complements.) What implications for setting the tax rates arise if combating alcohol addiction is a policy goal?

5. "Peter the Great at one time levied a tax upon beards. He held that the beard was a superfluous and useless ornament. The tax is said to have been proportional according to the length of the beard and progressive according to the social position of the possessor" (Groves, 1946: 51). Evaluate Peter's beard tax from the standpoint of optimal tax theory and from the standpoint of horizontal equity.

6. According to estimates by Goolsbee and Petrin (2004), the elasticity of demand for basic cable service is −0.51, and the elasticity of demand for direct broadcast satellites is −7.40. Suppose that a community wants to raise a given amount of revenue by taxing cable service and the use of direct broadcasting satellites. If the community's goal is to raise the money as efficiently as possible, what should be the ratio of the cable tax to the satellite tax? Discuss briefly the assumptions behind your calculation.

7. Suppose that Sharlene faces a marginal income tax rate of 35 percent, and if she cheats on her taxes, there is a 2 percent chance that she will be caught. Suppose also that the marginal penalty of tax evasion is $10R$, where R is the amount of unreported income (in thousands of dollars). How much income will Sharlene fail to report?

8. In Canada, a husband and wife are taxed separately on their incomes. In contrast, in the United States the fundamental unit of taxation is the family; regardless of whether the husband or the wife earns an extra dollar, it is taxed at the same rate. Imagine that family

utility increases with family consumption, but decreases with each spouse's hours of work. Each spouse's hours of work depend on his or her wage. A tax on earnings distorts the work decision of each spouse, creating an excess burden. How should taxes be set so the family's excess burden is as small as possible?

9. A study by Dahlby and Ferede (2015) provides estimates of the marginal excess burden per additional dollar of revenue in the Canadian provinces (in 2013). For Manitoba, it is 2.07 for the corporate income tax and 0.36 for the general sales tax. Based on these estimates, use the Ramsey rule to propose a direction for tax reform that would reduce the total excess burden from taxation in the province without reducing revenues. Explain your reasoning.

10. A study by Judge and Cable (2004) finds that taller people have higher incomes; every extra inch in height amounts to a predicted salary increase of nearly $800 per year. On the basis of optimal tax theory, does it make sense to tax individuals based on their height rather than their income? Why? What objections might be raised against using height as a basis for taxation?

11. The demand for X is given by $X = 100 - 2P_x$, and its supply is perfectly elastic at $P_x = 14$. The demand for Y is given by $Y = 350 - 3P_y$, and its supply is perfectly elastic at $P_y = 18$. The government aims to raise R dollars by imposing ad valorem taxes t_x and t_y on the consumption of X and Y. What is the optimal ratio of taxes t_x/t_y according to the inverse elasticity rule? If $R = \$1,000$, what are the optimal solutions for t_x and t_y?

12.* Jack and Jill live alone on an island. Their labour supply schedules are identical and given by $L = (1 - t)w$, where t is the income tax rate and w denotes the wage. Jill's wage is 6 and Jack's is 2. The tax paid by an individual is twL and each receives a transfer equal to half the total revenues. Jack and Jill have identical utility functions given by $U = C - (1/2)L^2$, where C denotes consumption (the individual's income after tax and transfer). If the social welfare function is $W = 3U_{Jack} + U_{Jill}$, what is the optimal tax rate? [*Hint:* Write W as a function of the tax rate t.] Why is the optimal tax rate not 0? Why is it not 1?

13. In Adam Smith's *The Wealth of Nations*, he describes a "window tax" that was imposed on dwellings in England. The tax per window increased with the number of windows.

a. Evaluate this tax in terms of the likely cost of administering it.

b. Evaluate it in terms of vertical equity.

c. Describe a simple way by which people with already existing dwellings could avoid tax.

d. Relate such avoidance behaviour to the concept of excess burden.

---

* Difficult

PART SIX

The Canadian Revenue System

The next five chapters describe and analyze the major sources of revenue in the Canadian fiscal system. This involves some bad news and some good news. The bad news is that it is hard to know just how long the descriptive material will be correct. For example, federal government tax changes since 2011 include a reduced corporate income tax rate, the Family Tax Cut and an enhancement of the Universal Childcare Benefit, an increase in the tax rate on dividends received from Canadian-controlled private corporations, and new rules for income splitting for calculating personal income taxes. Many additional changes are likely to be made by provincial governments each year. Significant changes to our tax system are continually under consideration, and adjustments will continue to be made even if major change does not occur in the next few years. The good news is that after seeing the tools of public finance applied to the existing tax institutions, the reader will be in a position to analyze new taxes and tax changes that may arise. Moreover, we discuss some major proposed modifications for each of the existing taxes.

Describing each tax individually seems to be the only feasible expositional technique. Nevertheless, keep in mind that the various taxes do interact. For example, the property tax on a building used for business purposes is tax deductible in the calculation of income tax. More generally, failure to consider more than one tax at a time gives a misleading picture of the overall magnitude, as well as the allocation, of the tax burden.

CHAPTER 17

The Personal Income Tax

It was true as taxes is. And nothing's truer than them.

—Charles Dickens, David Copperfield

AFTER READING THIS CHAPTER, THE STUDENT SHOULD BE ABLE TO:

LO1 Describe the steps for calculating personal income tax liability.

LO2 Define and evaluate the Haig-Simons concept of comprehensive income.

LO3 Identify sources of money income that are excluded from the personal income tax base.

LO4 Explain the difference between deductions and credits.

LO5 Summarize the main deductions and credits in the calculation of tax liability.

LO6 Explain the difference between a direct expenditure and a tax expenditure.

LO7 Identify the factors affecting the effective marginal tax rates across ranges of incomes.

LO8 Explain the tradeoffs in making the unit of taxation the individual or the family.

LO9 Distinguish between real income and nominal income, and relate the distinction to bracket creep.

LO10 Contrast territorial versus global systems for treating international income.

The personal income tax is the workhorse of the Canadian tax system. In 2012, 25.5 million tax returns were filed by a Canadian population of 34.8 million. Personal income taxes generated $116 billion in revenue for the federal government and $49 billion for provincial and territorial governments in 2012. Altogether, the personal income tax accounted for 24 percent of total government revenues in 2012.[1]

Personal income tax revenues grew rapidly in the postwar period, as shown in Table 17.1. The number of returns rose from 3.2 million, 16 percent of Canada's population in 1946, to 25.5 million, 73 percent of the population in 2012. Federal plus provincial revenues increased from $671 million in 1946 to $165 billion in 2012. The personal income tax increased between 1946 and 2000, from 5.6 percent to 13.4 percent as a share of gross domestic product (GDP), and from 17.9 percent to 30.7 percent as a share of total government revenues. Table 17.2 shows that personal income taxes in Canada, relative to GDP, exceed the rates in other countries, after more than doubling from 1965 to 2000.

This chapter discusses problems associated with designing a personal income tax system, how Canada has dealt with them, and the efficiency and equity of the results. Since its inception in 1917, the income tax law has been revised many times. We devote some attention to explaining and evaluating the changes that have been made in recent years.

---

[1] Income Statistics 2014 (2012 tax year) Preliminary Table 1 and Fiscal Reference Tables (September 2015), Table 33.

TABLE 17.1

Personal Income Tax Revenues in Canada, 1933 to 2012

Year	Number of Returns (thousands)	PIT Revenues (millions $)	Per Capita 2014 $*	PERSONAL INCOME TAXES AS % OF	
				Total Revenues	GDP
1933	52	38	60	5.1	1.1
1946	3,162	671	668	17.9	5.6
1955	4,923	1,318	682	19.2	4.6
1965	7,163	3,563	1,253	20.8	6.2
1975	12,002	18,538	3,300	28.4	10.7
1985	15,864	53,262	3,815	30.5	11.0
2000	22,237	143,951	5,833	30.7	13.4
2012**	25,453	164,692	4,970	23.7	10.0

* The deflator used was the GDP price index for personal expenditure for consumer goods and services. ** The change in financial reporting from the Financial Management System (FMS) to the Government Finance Statistics (GFS) makes the 2012 figures not directly comparable to the pre-2010 figures. Under FMS, personal income tax in 2009 was $5,675 per capita (in 2014 dollars) and 30.1 and 11.6 percent of total revenues and GDP, respectively.

Sources: M. C. Urquhart and K. A. H. Buckley, *Historical Statistics of Canada,* 2nd ed. (Ottawa: Minister of Supply and Services, 1983), pp. H52–74; Statistics Canada, *Public Finance Historical Data 1965/66–1991/92,* Cat. no. 68-512 occasional (Released April 1, 1992), pp. 162–63; Statistics Canada, *Canadian Economic Observer: Historical Statistical Supplement 2010–11,* Cat. no. 11-210-XWE (July 21, 2012), Table 1.3-1 Canada Revenue Agency, *Income Statistics: Interim Statistics–Universe Data 2014 Edition (2012 Tax Year)* (Ottawa, 2014); Department of Finance, Fiscal Reference Tables (September 2015), Table 33; and Statistics Canada, CANSIM database Tables 380-0064, 051-0001, and 380-0102.

TABLE 17.2

Personal Income Taxes as a Percentage of GDP, Selected Countries, 1965 to 2008

Year	Canada	U.S.	UK	Germany	Japan
1965	5.7	7.4	9.7	8.2	3.9
1980	10.4	10.0	9.8	10.8	6.0
1990	14.4	9.7	10.0	10.6	7.9
2000	12.9	11.9	10.2	9.2	5.6
2010	10.7	7.9	9.4	8.5	5.1
2012	11.2	9.2	9.2	9.3	5.5

Source: OECD, *Revenue Statistics, 1965–2013* (Paris: OECD, 2014), Table 9.

BASIC STRUCTURE

The federal Income Tax Act requires Canadians to file an annual tax return that computes their previous year's tax liability. The individual is the taxable unit. Individuals who are resident in Canada for at least 183 days during the year are taxable on their worldwide income. The tax return is due every April 30.

FIGURE 17.1

COMPUTATION OF PERSONAL INCOME TAX LIABILITY

STEP 1:
ADD: Income from taxable sources:
- wages and other employment income
- interest
- dividends
- rent
- taxable capital gains
- alimony received
- royalties
- pension and employment insurance benefits
- net business income
- ...
  = Total income

STEP 2:
SUBTRACT: Deductions:
- union dues and certain employment expenses
- childcare expenses
- moving expenses
- interest expenses
- eligible RRSP and RPP contributions
- alimony payments
- qualifying losses
- additional deductions
  = Taxable income

STEP 3:
APPLY: Tax rate schedule to Taxable income
  = Income tax before tax credits

STEP 4:
SUBTRACT: Nonrefundable tax credits for:
- taxpayer and dependents
- medical expenses and disabilities
- age and pension income
- contributions to QPP and CPP
- premiums paid for EI
- eligible tuition and education expenses
- gifts to charities and to the Crown
- and any other tax credits
  = Federal tax payable

STEP 5:
CALCULATE: Provincial tax payable

Until 2000, provinces other than Quebec levied their income tax as a percentage of the federal tax.[2] This was known as a "tax on tax." By 2001 all provinces had shifted to a "tax on income (TONI)" system. So long as the definition of taxable income is similar to or varies from the federal definition, within limits, the federal government continues to collect the provincial as well as the federal tax in all provinces with the exception of Quebec. This permits individuals to submit payment of both the federal and provincial tax to Canada Revenue Agency. This has simplified administration and compliance. One of the strengths of the Canadian income tax system has been the integration and harmonization of federal and provincial income taxes.[3] This has been weakened by the shift to a "tax on income," which has increased complexity and differences among provinces.

The calculation of tax liability requires a series of steps summarized in Figure 17.1. The first step is to compute "total income." Total income is defined as income from all taxable sources. Taxable sources include (but are not limited to) wages, dividends, interest, realized capital gains, alimony, rents, royalties, income from pensions (including QPP and CPP), Employment Insurance (EI) and Old Age Security (OAS) benefits, and business profits, including those from farming and fishing. In the calculation of business profits, the taxpayer may deduct expenses incurred in earning income such that total income includes only net business income.

---

[2] Income taxes are not used by local governments in Canada. Income taxes are, however, a major source of revenues for local governments in countries such as Sweden and Japan. They are also an important revenue source for several major U.S. cities, including New York City and Philadelphia. Both large and small local jurisdictions in Ohio and Pennsylvania derive revenues from local income taxes.

[3] This harmonization comes at a cost, a cost that Quebec has been unwilling to pay. Therefore, Quebec (like many states in the United States) uses separate forms to collect its income taxes, permitting greater deviation from the federal tax, both its base and its rate structure. Provincial reliance on the federal tax base limits the use that provinces can make of the personal income tax for policy purposes. This has led provinces, Ontario and Alberta in particular, to consider following Quebec's example and collecting their own tax. With the provincial role growing relative to the federal role, and the cutback in federal transfers to provinces, provinces continue to press for greater freedom within the Tax Collection Agreement.

Other benefits also add to taxable income. These include gratuities, the value of room and board, the value of personal use of an employer's car, the value of below-market interest rates on loans provided by employers, benefits from share purchases at below-market rates, and benefits under deferred benefit plans.

Income in a number of forms is not taxed, including employers' contributions to employee pension plans in the year the contribution is made; nor is the income on these plans taxed in the year earned. Employer payments to group dental and medical plans, to disability insurance plans, and to supplemental unemployment benefit plans are not taxed to the employee. Nor is the value of counselling services for mental and physical health or the winnings from lotteries or other gambling taxed. Finally, several forms of income from government are excluded from taxable income: disability payments and payments from provincial Worker's Compensation Boards, and "income-tested" payments from governments, such as federal Guaranteed Income Supplements (GIS) and provincial social assistance. Several major sources of untaxed income are discussed in the following sections.

Not all of "total income" is subject to tax. The second step is to convert total income to taxable income—the amount of income subject to tax. This is done by subtracting various amounts called deductions from total income. Some deductions recognize additional expenses of earning income, and others are used by the government to encourage private savings. The former include union dues, childcare expenses, moving expenses, and some other employment expenses. The latter include contributions to retirement savings plans, such as RRSPs and RPPs. Since alimony payments to a former spouse (but not child support payments) are included in the income of the recipient, a deduction is permitted to a taxpayer required to make such payments. Deductions are discussed more fully later.

The third step is to calculate the amount of tax due before tax credits. Federal tax rates are applied to taxable income. The fourth and final step is to calculate and subtract "nonrefundable" [4] tax credits and other tax credits. These credits reduce taxes that would otherwise be due, and recognize factors that affect the taxpayer's ability to pay. However, as with deductions, credits are also used to encourage certain taxpayer behaviour. The credits recognize:

* the number of individuals supported by the taxpayer, including the taxpayer;
* age of the taxpayer, and the existence of medical expenses or disabilities;
* required contributions by the taxpayer to the Canada or Quebec Pension Plans and to Employment Insurance; and
* voluntary expenditures for education or contributions for charitable purposes.

The tax credits are subtracted to obtain the taxpayer's "federal tax." The provincial tax is calculated using a similar definition of taxable income.

For most taxpayers, some tax is withheld out of each paycheque during the year. The amount that actually has to be paid on April 30 is the difference between the tax liability and the accumulated withholding payments. If more has been withheld than is owed, the taxpayer is entitled to a refund.

It sounds fairly straightforward, but in reality, complications arise in every step of the process. We now discuss some of the major problems.

DEFINING INCOME

Clearly, the ability to identify "income" is necessary to operate an income tax. A natural way to begin this section would be to discuss and evaluate the definition of income in the Income Tax Act. However, the law provides no definition. It does indicate that income subject to tax includes that from employment in the form of wages and salaries; income from a business; income from investments, including capital gains; and income from sources such as alimony, pensions, unemployment benefits, and royalties. [5]

---

[4] The credits are nonrefundable in that if the credits exceed taxes payable, the government does not pay the difference to the taxpayer.

[5] The definition in the Income War Tax Act (1917) is as follows: "'Income' means the annual net profit or gain or gratuity, whether ascertained and capable of computation as wages, salary, or other fixed amount, or unascertained as being fees or emoluments, or as being profits from a trade or commercial or financial or other business or calling, directly or indirectly received by a person from any office or employment, or from any profession or calling, or from any trade, manufacture or business, as the case may be; and shall include interest, dividends or profits directly or indirectly received from money at interest upon any security or without security, or from stocks, or from any other investment and, whether such gains or profits are divided or distributed or not, and also the annual profit or gain from any other source; including the income from but not the value of property acquired by gift, bequest, or devise or descent; and including the income from but not the proceeds of life insurance policies paid upon the death of the person insured, or payments made or credits to the insured on life insurance endowment or annuity contracts upon the maturity of the term mentioned in the contract or upon the surrender of the contract." Statutes of Canada, 12 Parliament, 7 Session, ch. 28, p. 171.

Public finance economists have traditionally used their own standard, the **Haig-Simons (H-S) definition of income**: Income is the money value of the net increase to an individual's power to consume during a period.[6] This equals the amount actually consumed during the period plus net additions to wealth. Net additions to wealth—saving—must be included in income because they represent an increase in potential consumption. This comprehensive definition of income was behind recommendations in the 1966 Report of the Royal Commission on Taxation (Carter Commission).

Importantly, the H-S criterion requires the inclusion of all sources of potential increases in consumption, regardless of whether the actual consumption takes place, and regardless of the form in which the consumption occurs. At the same time, the H-S criterion implies that any decreases in an individual's potential to consume should be subtracted in determining income. An example is expenses that have to be incurred to earn income. If the gross revenues from an individual's business are $100,000 but business expenses are $95,000, the individual's potential consumption has only increased by $5,000.

Items Included in H-S Income

The H-S definition encompasses those items ordinarily thought of as income: wages and salaries, business profits, rents, royalties, dividends,[7] and interest. However, the criterion also includes certain unconventional items as outlined next.

Employer pension contributions and insurance purchases. Pension contributions, even though not made directly to the recipient, represent an increase in the potential to consume. In the same way, even if compensation is paid to an employee in the form of a certain commodity (such as an insurance policy) instead of cash, it is still income.

Transfer payments, including CPP/QPP retirement benefits, EI benefits, and worker's compensation payments. Any receipt, be it from the government or an employer, is income.

Capital gains. Increases in the value of an asset are referred to as **capital gains**, decreases as **capital losses**. Suppose Brutus owns some shares of Imperial Oil stock that increase in value from $10,000 to $12,500 over the course of a year. He has enjoyed a capital gain of $2,500. This $2,500 represents an increase in potential consumption and, hence, belongs in income.[8] If Brutus sells the Imperial Oil stock at the end of the year, the capital gain is said to be realized; otherwise, it is unrealized. From the H-S point of view, it is absolutely irrelevant whether it is a **realized capital gain** or an **unrealized capital gain**. It represents potential to consume and, hence, is income. If Brutus does not sell his Imperial Oil stock, in effect he chooses to save by reinvesting the capital gain in Imperial Oil. Because the H-S criterion does not distinguish between different uses of income, the fact that Brutus happens to reinvest is irrelevant. All the arguments for adding in capital gains apply to subtracting capital losses. If Casca's BlackBerry stock decreases in value by $4,200 during a given year, this $4,200 should be subtracted from other sources of income.

Income in kind. Some people receive part or all of their incomes in kind—in the form of goods and services rather than cash. Farmers provide field hands with food; corporations give employees subsidized lunches or access to company fitness centres. One important form of income in kind is the annual rental value of owner-occupied homes. A homeowner receives a stream of services from a dwelling. The net monetary value of these services—**imputed rent**—is equal to the rental payments that would have been received had the owner chosen to rent the house out, after subtracting maintenance expenses, taxes, and so on. In 2011, the average annual value of housing services in Canada was $14,008 (Brown and Dar-Brodeur, 2015).

Gifts and inheritances. Receipt of a gift or inheritance increases a taxpayer's potential to consume and based on the H-S criterion should be included in taxable income. That the donor, deceased or not, may have

---

[6] Named after Robert M. Haig and Henry C. Simons, economists who wrote in the first half of the twentieth century. See Simons (1938).

[7] While dividends are included in taxable income, Canada's "dividend tax credit" makes a provision for the fact that income from which the dividends are paid may have been subject to the corporate income tax. Detailed discussion of the dividend tax credit is deferred to Chapter 21.

[8] Only the real value of capital gains constitutes income, not gains due merely to inflation. This issue is discussed later.

previously paid tax on these funds is no more relevant than the fact that purchases of goods that contribute to the income of a shopkeeper have been made from post-tax income. Admittedly, this is not the way much of the public perceives this matter.

In all these cases, from the H-S point of view, it makes no difference whether benefits are received in monetary form or in the form of goods and services. They are all income.

Some Practical and Conceptual Problems

A number of difficulties arise in attempts to use the Haig-Simons criterion as a basis for constructing a tax system.

- Clearly, only income *net of business expenses* increases potential consumption power. But it is often hard to distinguish between consumption expenditures and costs of obtaining income. If Calpurnia buys a desk to use while working at home, but the desk is also a beautiful piece of furniture, to what extent is the desk a business expense? What portion of a "three-martini lunch" designed to woo a client is consumption, and what portion is business? (According to current law, the answer to the latter question is 50 percent is consumption. Fifty percent of business-meal expenses are deductible.)

- Capital gains and losses may be very difficult to measure, particularly when they are unrealized. For assets that are traded in active markets, the problem is fairly manageable. Even if Brutus does not sell his shares of Imperial Oil common stock, it is easy to determine their value at any time by consulting the financial section of the newspaper. It is not nearly as easy to measure the capital gain on a piece of art that has appreciated in value.

- Imputed income from durables also presents measurement difficulties. For example, it may be hard to estimate the market rent of a particular owner-occupied dwelling. Each, in some way, is unique. Similarly, measuring the imputed rental streams generated by other durables such as cars, compact disc players, and motor boats is not feasible.

- In-kind services are hard to value. One important example is the income produced by people who do housework rather than participate in the market. These services—cooking, childcare, home repairs, yard work—are clearly valuable.[9] However, even though markets exist for purchasing these services, it would be difficult to estimate whether a given home-produced service is equal to the market value.

Evaluating the H-S Criterion

Numerous additional difficulties involved in implementing the H-S criterion can be listed, but the main point is clear. No definition of income can make the administration of an income tax simple and straightforward. Arbitrary decisions about what should be included in income are inevitable. Nevertheless, the Haig-Simons criterion has often been regarded as an ideal toward which policy-makers should strive. It states that income should be defined as broadly as is feasible, and all sources of income received by a particular person should be taxed at the same rate. The Carter Commission recommendations, based on these principles, were viewed very favourably by many academics and commentators, and the tax reforms of 1971, 1981, and 1987, at least in part, drew upon these principles.[10]

Why is the H-S criterion so attractive? There are two reasons.

Fairness. Recall the traditional definition of horizontal equity from Chapter 16—people with equal incomes should pay equal taxes. For this dictum to make any sense, *all* sources of income must be included in the tax base. Otherwise, two people with identical abilities to pay could end up with different tax liabilities.

On the other hand, one can argue that as long as people's abilities to earn income differ, the H-S criterion cannot produce fair outcomes. Suppose that Popeye is endowed with a lot of brains, and Bluto with a lot of brawn. Suppose further that the work done by brawny people is less pleasant, and in far less pleasant surroundings, than that available to brainy individuals. In that case, if Bluto and Popeye have the same income, then Popeye has more utility. Is it fair to tax them as equals?

---

[9] Estimates by Statistics Canada valued housework at between 31 and 46 percent of GDP in 1992 (Chandler, 1994).

[10] See Bird (1970: 444–78), and Royal Commission on Taxation (1966).

Efficiency. Defenders of the criterion argue that it has the virtue of *neutrality*–it treats all forms of income the same and, hence, does not distort the pattern of economic activity. Following this reasoning, it is argued that the failure to tax imputed rent from owner-occupied housing leads to excessive investment in housing, other things being the same.

It is doubtless true that many departures from the Haig-Simons criterion create inefficiencies. But it does not follow that equal tax rates on all income, regardless of source, would be most efficient. Consider income from rent on unimproved land. The supply of such land is perfectly inelastic, and hence no excess burden would be created by taxing it at a very high rate.[11] An efficient tax system would tax the returns to such land at higher rates than other sources of income, and *not* tax all sources at the same rate, as dictated by the Haig-Simons criterion. More generally, the optimal tax literature discussed in Chapter 16 suggests that as long as lump-sum taxes are ruled out, efficiency is enhanced when relatively high tax rates are imposed on those activities with relatively inelastic supply. "Neutrality," in the sense of equal tax rates on all types of income, generally does *not* minimize excess burden.

Where does this leave us? McLure (2002: 118) points out that we cannot be sanguine about the possibilities for using optimal tax theory as a framework for designing the tax base, noting that optimal tax rules "generally ignore the administrative difficulty of implementation, as well as the fact that a vast amount of information is required to put them into practice." It would be unwise, therefore, to abandon the Haig-Simons criterion altogether. On the other hand, there is no reason to regard the criterion as sacred. Departures from it should be considered on their merits and should not be viewed *prima facie* as unfair and inefficient.

EXCLUDABLE FORMS OF MONEY INCOME

We have seen that some income sources that would be taxable according to the Haig-Simons criterion are omitted from the tax base for practical reasons. In addition, several forms of income that would be administratively relatively easy to tax are partially or altogether excluded from taxable income.

Capital Gains

Currently, for most taxpayers, one-half of realized capital gains are taxed as ordinary income. There is a trail of many changes over the past 25 years as we have come to this point, and further change may occur.[12]

Prior to 1971, capital gains were exempt and not included in taxable income. The Carter Commission recommended that realized capital gains be fully taxable, and the 1971 tax reform included one-half of capital gains in taxable income. The 1985 budget provided for a lifetime exemption of $500,000 in capital gains for each taxpayer (in addition to the exemption provided for principal residences). This exemption was reduced to $100,000 in the 1987 tax reform and subsequently was eliminated for real estate in 1992 and for all other assets in the 1994 budget.[13]

The 1987 reforms also changed the share of capital gains to be included in taxable income. The share of realized gains to be included in taxable income rose from one-half to two-thirds in 1988. This was further increased to three-quarters in 1990, but had been reduced to one-half by 2000. Realized capital losses–decreases in the value of an asset–can be offset only against a realized gain. Thus, if a $10,000 gain is realized on the sale of Imperial Oil common stock and a $5,000 loss on the sale of BlackBerry, the taxable gain for the year is $5,000. Moreover, capital losses in excess of capital gains in any year cannot be subtracted from ordinary income. Such losses can be carried back three years and carried forward indefinitely, but can only be used to offset capital gains.

With the taxation of one-half of capital gains and the elimination of the lifetime exemptions, movement toward the Haig-Simons criterion for capital gains has occurred. However, other aspects of the tax treatment of capital gains depart from the H-S criterion in important ways.

---

[11] This fact has long been recognized. See George (1914).

[12] Tax competition with the United States is among the factors that may contribute to further change in Canada. The maximum federal tax rate on capital gains in the U.S. is 20 percent. Currently Canadian rates, when combined with provincial rates, are higher.

[13] The capital gain exemption for qualified farms and small businesses remains and was increased from $500,000 to $800,000 in 2014. The gain arising from the sale of a principal residence is also exempted.

Only realizations taxed. Unless a capital gain is actually realized—the asset is sold—no tax is levied. In effect, the tax on a capital gain is deferred until the gain is realized. The mere ability to postpone taxes may not seem all that important, but its consequences are enormous. Consider Cassius, who purchases an asset for $100,000 that increases in value by 12 percent each year. After the first year, it is worth $100,000 × (1 + 0.12) = $112,000. After the second year, it is worth $112,000 × (1 + 0.12) = $100,000 × (1 + 0.12)^2 = $125,440. Similarly, by the end of 20 years, it is worth $100,000 × (1 + 0.12)^{20} = $964,629. If the asset is sold at the end of 20 years, Cassius realizes a capital gain of $864,629 (= $964,629 − $100,000). One-half of this, or $432,314, is taxable. Assume that the tax rate applied to the taxable gain is 50 percent. Then Cassius's tax liability is $216,157 (= $432,314 × 0.5), and his net gain (measured in dollars 20 years from now) is $648,472 (= $864,629 − $216,157).

Now assume that the 50 percent rate on the taxable share of capital gains is levied as the capital gains accrue, regardless of whether they are realized. This means that $6,000 of the $12,000 gain in the first year is subject to the 50 percent tax rate. At the end of the first year, Cassius has $109,000 [= $100,000 × (1 + 0.09)]. (Remember, $3,000 of the $12,000 gain goes to the tax collector.) Assuming that the $9,000 after-tax gain is reinvested in the asset, at the end of two years Cassius has $109,000 × (1 + .09) = $100,000 × (1.09)^2 = $118,810. Similarly, by the end of 20 years, he has $100,000 × (1 + .09)^{20} = $560,441. Cassius's after-tax capital gain is $460,441 (= $560,441 − $100,000). Comparing this with the previous $648,472 makes clear that the seemingly innocent device of letting the gain accrue without tax makes a big difference (in this case equal to $188,031). This is because the deferral allows the investment to grow geometrically at the before-tax rather than the after-tax rate of interest. In effect, the government gives the investor an interest-free loan on taxes due.

It should now be clear why a favourite slogan among tax accountants is "taxes deferred are taxes saved." Many very complicated tax-shelter plans are nothing more than devices for deferring payment of taxes.

Because only realized capital gains are subject to tax, taxpayers who are considering switching or selling capital assets must take into account that doing so will create a tax liability. As a consequence, they may be less likely to change their portfolios. This phenomenon is referred to as the **lock-in effect**, because the tax system tends to lock investors into their current portfolios. This leads to a misallocation of capital, because it no longer flows to where its return is highest. Several econometric studies have examined the tax treatment of capital gains in the United States, and a common finding is that the realization-based system for taxing capital gains does in fact produce a lock-in effect (see Ivkovich et al., 2005).

Gains realized at death. Generally speaking, Canadian law provides for the realization of gains at time of death. At death, the capital assets of an individual are deemed to be disposed of at their current market value, and half of the capital gains are taken into income in the year of death. This is particularly important in Canada since there are no death taxes.[14] However, capital property transferred from the deceased to the individual's spouse is eligible for a tax-deferred rollover of the property.

Evaluation of capital gains rules. We conclude that, in terms of the Haig-Simons criterion, the tax treatment of capital gains is mixed. The criterion requires that all capital gains be taxed, whether realized or unrealized. Whereas substantial movement has occurred toward the H-S criterion since 1971, the tax system still taxes only one-half of realized gains as ordinary income.

Further, unrealized capital gains can accrue without taxation, and significant exemptions exist for gains on principal residences, on farms, and on small businesses.

The optimal tax literature does not provide any more justification for preferential treatment of capital gains than the Haig-Simons criterion.[15] However, several rationalizations have been proposed for preferential treatment of this form of capital income. Some argue that capital gains are not regular income, but rather windfalls that occur unexpectedly. Fairness requires that such unexpected gains not create a tax liability. Moreover,

---

[14] In contrast, U.S. law permits for the transfer of assets to heirs without the capital gain being realized and taxed at death. Moreover, the cost basis for any capital gain realized by the heir is on a "stepped-up basis," equal to the market price of the asset at the time the heir receives it. In this way capital gains on assets held to the death of the owner are never taxed. However, there are estate taxes in the United States, and assets in excess of $5.43 million US in 2015 in an estate are subjected to rates up to 40 percent.

[15] However, under certain conditions, optimal tax theory suggests that no forms of capital income should be taxed. See Chapter 19 under "Personal Consumption Tax."

because investing requires the sacrifice of abstaining from consumption, it is only fair to reward this sacrifice. However, it could just as well be asserted that labour income should be treated preferentially, because it involves the unpleasantness of work, while those who receive capital gains need only relax and wait for their money to flow in. Ultimately, it is impossible to argue convincingly that production of one source of income or another requires more sacrifice and should, therefore, be treated preferentially.

Another justification for preferential taxation of capital gains is that it is needed to stimulate capital accumulation and risk taking. In the next chapter, we deal at some length with the question of how taxation affects saving and risk taking. For now, we merely note that it is not clear that special treatment for capital gains does increase saving and risk taking. If the goal is to stimulate these activities, there are probably more efficient ways to do so.

Some promote preferential treatment of capital gains because it helps counterbalance inflation's tendency to increase the effective rate at which capital gains are taxed. As we see later, under existing tax rules, inflation does produce an especially heavy burden on capital income, but arbitrarily taxing capital gains at a different rate may not be the best way to deal with this problem.

Finally, we stress that a full picture of the tax treatment of capital income requires taking into account that much of this income is generated by corporations, and corporations are subject to a separate tax system of their own. The overall tax rate on capital income thus depends on the personal and corporate rates. We discuss the effect of the corporation tax on the return to capital in Chapter 21.

Employer Contributions to Benefit Plans

Employers' contributions to their employees' retirement funds, within clearly specified limits, are not subject to tax.[16] Neither does the government tax the interest that accrues on the pension contributions over time. Only when the pension is paid out at retirement are the principal and interest subject to taxation.

As already argued, pensions represent additions to potential consumption and, hence, should be counted as income according to the Haig-Simons criterion. Similarly, the interest on pension funds should be taxable as it accrues. However, the inclusion of such items in the tax base appears to be politically infeasible.

Gifts and Inheritances

Although gifts and inheritances represent increases in the beneficiaries' potential consumption, these items are not subject to the income tax. Separate tax systems cover gifts and estates in most of the industrialized world. However, Canada is one of two countries (Australia is the other) in the industrialized world without this form of taxation. Canada's previous use of gift and estate taxes is discussed in Chapter 20.

DEDUCTIONS AND TAX CREDITS

In terms of Figure 17.1, we have now discussed issues associated with Step 1, the identification of total income. Applying existing tax rates to total income would be inappropriate for two reasons:

- expenses associated with earning this income need to be deducted to reflect "net" income available to be taxed, and
- adjustments are required to recognize costs of subsistence, and other nondiscretionary expenses. (How best to identify those expenditures that are not discretionary will always be controversial.)

In addition to these reasons, the government may choose to encourage individuals to allocate their income for specific purposes. Deductions or tax credits may be used to stimulate private saving for retirement, increased spending on education, and donations to charities.

In the case of deductions, an amount is subtracted from total income in order to reach taxable income—the deduction reduces taxable income. We then apply the tax rates to taxable income to obtain the tax payable. In the case of tax credits, the amount of the credit is subtracted from taxes that would otherwise be payable—the credit directly reduces taxes payable.

---

[16] The total allowable employer plus employee contribution was $25,370 in 2015.

Deductions

Deductibility and relative prices. Before cataloguing deductible expenditures, let us consider the relationship between deductibility of expenditures on an item and its relative price. Suppose that expenditures on commodity Z are tax deductible. The price of Z is $10 per unit. Suppose further that Cleopatra's marginal tax rate is 40 percent. Then, whenever Cleopatra purchases a unit of Z, it only costs her $6. Why? Because expenditures on Z are deductible, purchasing a unit lowers Cleopatra's taxable income by $10. Given a 40 percent marginal tax rate, $10 less of taxable income saves Cleopatra $4 in taxes. Hence, her effective price of a unit of Z is $10 minus $4, or $6.

More generally, if the price of Z is P_Z and the individual's marginal tax rate is t, allowing deduction of expenses on Z lowers Z's effective price from P_Z to $(1 - t)P_Z$. This analysis brings out two important facts:

- Because deductibility changes the relative price of the commodity involved, in general, we expect the quantity demanded to change.

- The higher the individual's value of t, the greater the value to the individual of a given dollar amount of deductions and the lower the effective price of the good.[17]

Expenses in earning income. Most deductions are for expenses incurred in order to earn taxable income. One such expense is for childcare. The need for "paid" childcare has risen as increasing numbers of women have entered the work force. A person with caregiving responsibilities would, in many cases, be unable to seek paid employment in the absence of childcare. As business expenses can be deducted in reporting business income, childcare expenses are permitted (up to $8,000 for a child under age 7 and $5,000 for a child at least 7 but not yet 17 and no more than two-thirds of the earned income of the parent with the lower income). Allowing for a deduction of childcare expenses better reflects the *net* addition to taxable income. Where there are two parents, the deduction is made by the one with the lower income.

Union dues or professional dues may also be a required expense if income is to be earned. Thus, they are deductible in calculating taxable income. Other expenses that employees may have to incur include the costs of transportation, meals, and lodging, where the employee is not reimbursed by the employer. The taxpayer must be able to prove to Canada Revenue Agency's satisfaction that the expenditures have been made. A deduction is also provided for moving expenses where the move is required to earn wages, salary, or self-employment income. Common to these deductions is that each is an expense that must be incurred to earn the taxable income. Rules apply in each of these cases in order to avoid unreasonable deductions.

Individuals may borrow money to make income-earning investments. This income may take the form of interest, dividends, capital gains, or business profits. Reasonable expenses incurred in earning this investment income, such as interest on borrowed funds and other carrying charges, are deductible. Where an interest expense exceeds the income from an investment, this expense is generally deductible against other taxable income. Taxable income is the amount after interest and other expenses, or the net income that the investment contributes.

Some interest expenses are clearly not related to earning taxable income, and are not deductible.[18] These include:

- interest paid on consumer debt, such as credit card charges or other loans for purposes of private consumption, and

- interest on mortgages for owner-occupied homes, since the imputed income from homeownership is not included in taxable income.

---

[17] Note that these observations apply more generally to expenditures on any items that are excluded from the tax base, not just deductions. For example, the value of excluding fringe benefits, such as employer-provided group life insurance or dental care, increases with the marginal tax rate, other things being the same.

[18] Interest deductibility is an area in which Canadian tax law has differed sharply from that in the United States. Mortgage interest for the purchase of up to two residences is deductible in the United States up to a limit of $1 million. Also deductible is interest on a home equity loan—a loan for which the home serves as collateral and whose proceeds can be used to finance any purchase. For example, one can obtain a home equity loan and use the money to buy a car. In effect, then, the law allows homeowners to deduct interest on consumer loans, but denies this privilege to renters. However, deductible interest on home equity loans is limited to $100,000 of debt.

Do these rules make sense in terms of the Haig-Simons criterion? For a business investment, it is clear that interest should be deductible. It is a cost of doing business and, hence, should not be subject to income tax. In the case of expenditures on consumption goods and services, it seems reasonable to argue that interest on consumer loans should be regarded merely as a higher price one pays to obtain a commodity sooner than would otherwise be possible. And where consumer durables are concerned, since imputed income from these goods is excluded (as with a house), it would be inappropriate to deduct interest.

Note that the deductibility of interest together with the exemption of certain types of capital income from taxation can lead to lucrative opportunities for smart investors. Assume that Caesar, who has a 40 percent tax rate, can borrow all the money he wants from the bank at a rate of 10 percent. Assuming that Caesar satisfies the criteria for deductibility of interest, for every dollar of interest paid, his tax bill is reduced by 40 cents. Hence, Caesar's effective borrowing rate is only about 6 percent. Suppose that the rate of return that Caesar realizes on a tax-exempt investment is 7.5 percent.[19] Then Caesar can borrow from the bank at 6 percent and make an investment at 7.5 percent. Caesar should continue to borrow as long as this opportunity exists. The process of taking advantage of such opportunities is referred to as **tax arbitrage**.

Opportunities for tax arbitrage are limited by the number of tax-free income opportunities, and because in real-world capital markets people cannot borrow arbitrarily large sums of money. Still, opportunities for gain are present. Tax authorities are vigilant on this issue, and interest on loans that are for investments in tax-deferred plans, such as RRSPs, is not deductible. Given that money can be used for many different purposes, how can it be proved that a given amount of borrowing is for one investment rather than another? This simple example illustrates some important general lessons:

- Interest deductibility in conjunction with preferential treatment of certain capital income can create major money-making opportunities.
- High-income individuals are more likely than their low-income counterparts to benefit from these opportunities. This is because they tend to face higher tax rates and to have better access to borrowing.
- The tax authorities can certainly declare various tax arbitrage schemes to be illegal, but it is hard to enforce these rules. Moreover, clever lawyers and accountants are always on the lookout for new tax arbitrage opportunities. Many inefficient investments are made, and a lot of resources are spent on tax avoidance and tax administration.

Employee savings for retirement and other purposes. (1) *Registered Pension Plans (RPPs)*: Employees may contribute to Registered Pension Plans (RPPs), matching the contributions of their employers or on some other basis. The total allowable non-taxable contribution by an employer and employee to a "money purchase plan" RPP was $25,370 per taxpayer in 2015. The larger the contribution by the employer, the smaller the tax-deductible amount that the employee is free to contribute. In 2012, RPP deductions allowed to employees totalled $17.5 billion. These funds, and the investment income earned by these funds, are not taxable until paid out as pensions. (2) *Registered Retirement Savings Plans (RRSPs)*: Under certain circumstances, individuals can engage in tax-favoured saving for their retirement or that of a spouse. Using a RRSP, an individual could, in 2015, deposit up to $24,930. (The RRSP contribution limit is equal to the total RPP contribution limit for the preceding year.) If the employee is part of a pension plan, the allowable contribution is reduced based on the pension benefits in the employer's pension plan that are accruing to the employee during the year. The objective is to encourage employee saving (RRSPs plus RPPs) toward retirement, at least to a certain level. The money contributed to an RRSP is deductible from total income. Just as in an employer-managed pension fund, the interest that accrues is untaxed. Tax is due only when the money is withdrawn or is paid out as part of a retirement plan or annuity. RRSP contributions were $32.4 billion in 2012. (3) *Tax-Free Savings Accounts (TFSAs)*: A Tax-Free Savings Account is a relatively new way to save money tax-free, in place since January 1, 2009. Canadian residents aged 18 or older can contribute up to a maximum annual amount to a TFSA. The TFSA limit in 2015 was $10,000. Unlike with RRSPs, contributions to a TFSA are not deductible in calculating taxable income, but both the investment income earned in a TFSA and withdrawals from a TFSA are tax-free. Furthermore,

---

[19] Prior to 1995, the $100,000 lifetime capital gain exemption provided a limited opportunity. In this case, if an investment paid no dividends with the total return in capital gains due to the reinvestment of earnings, the taxpayer would earn tax-exempt income, but would be able to deduct the interest on the loan.

neither income earned within a TFSA nor withdrawals from it affect eligibility for federal income-tested benefits and credits, such as Old Age Security, the Guaranteed Income Supplement, and the Canada Child Tax Benefit. Unused TFSA contribution room is carried forward into future years and withdrawals from a TFSA can be put back into the account later. The objective of TFSAs is to assist Canadians in saving for major pre-retirement purchases, such as a house, car, or vacation. The federal government estimates, however, that half of the TFSA benefits will accrue to seniors. (4) *Registered Education Savings Plans* (*RESPs*): The RESP is a tax-sheltered savings program to encourage Canadians to save for their children's education. Although contributions to RESPs are not tax deductible, the income earned on RESP accounts is not taxed as it accrues, and is taxable in the hands of the beneficiaries rather than the contributor. The benefit of an RESP is that it defers the tax on the earnings of the account, and it taxes the earnings at the (probably) lower tax rate of the student beneficiary rather than that of the contributor. There is a lifetime contribution limit of $50,000 per beneficiary.

Effect on savings. RRSPs were introduced partly to give more people the option to accumulate retirement wealth in tax-favoured funds. Part of the motivation was also to stimulate saving. However, it is not clear how aggregate saving is affected. People may merely shuffle the contents of their portfolios, reducing their holdings of some assets and depositing them into retirement accounts. Much of this does occur, and results remain unclear on the extent to which RRSPs have contributed to a higher level of private or total (public + private) saving in Canada.[20] The new TFSAs are explicitly designed to encourage saving. However, as with RRSPs, it is unclear whether total savings will increase as a result of TFSAs or whether TFSAs will displace contributions to RRSPs. In any case, it is clear that the existence of the various plans for the preferential treatment of saving represents another important departure from the H-S criterion.

Alimony. The last deduction included under Step 2 in Figure 17.1 is that for alimony payments. The deduction is permitted where the payments are made under court order or written agreement and are for the maintenance of the taxpayer's spouse or former spouse. The Income Tax Act requires that these payments be included in the income of the recipient for tax purposes.[21] Opinions will differ, but there is a certain logic in viewing the payer as a conduit for this income and including it in the income of the payee.

Tax Credits

Tax credits and relative prices. Tax credits, like deductions, alter relative prices. But their effects differ. As noted, the higher an individual's marginal tax rate, the greater the value of a deduction of a given dollar amount. In contrast, a tax credit is a subtraction from tax liability (not taxable income) and, hence, its value is independent of the *individual's* marginal tax rate. A tax credit of $100 reduces tax liability by $100 whether an individual's tax rate is 30 percent or 50 percent. In contrast, a deduction of $200 is worth $100 in tax savings to one with a 50 percent marginal tax rate and $60 to one with a 30 percent tax rate. The credit may also be set to equal x percent of the expenditure on a commodity, x being the same for all taxpayers. In such a case the price of commodity Z is reduced from P_Z to $(1 - x)P_Z$, or $0.5P_Z$ if x is set at 50 percent. If there is a 50 percent tax credit for research and development (R&D) spending, $1,000 spent on R&D costs the taxpayer only $500.

Several types of tax credits are used in Canada. One distinction is whether a tax credit is refundable or nonrefundable. *Refundable* means that if a tax credit exceeds tax that is otherwise payable, the government makes a payment to the taxpayer, creating a negative tax. In the case of *nonrefundable* credits, when a tax credit exceeds the tax otherwise owed, the government does *not* make a payment to the taxpayer. The current Goods and Services Tax (GST) credits are examples of refundable credits. The tax credit for medical expenses is nonrefundable.

Another distinction is whether the tax credit is a fixed amount or is affected by a taxpayer's circumstances or behaviour. Every taxpayer gets the same credit for the basic personal amount. It does not vary with the level of income or level of expenditure. The credit provided for medical expenses in excess of the lower of $2,208 (in 2015) or 3 percent of net income is unlimited, but since it is nonrefundable it cannot exceed taxes that would otherwise be due. The credit for charitable donations varies depending on the total amount of donations.

---

[20] From his survey of empirical studies, Milligan (1998) found evidence of some moderate net increase in savings as a result of tax-based incentive programs. Burbidge, Fretz, and Veall (1998) concluded that the savings gap between Canada and the United States cannot be reasonably explained by the timing of changes in the RRSP program.

[21] The Federal Court of Appeal ruled (in *Thibaudeau v. The Queen*, 1994) that maintenance payments *for the benefit of children* were not taxable to the recipient, a decision upheld by the Supreme Court. Such payments are not deductible to the payer.

Taxpayer and spouse. Nonrefundable tax credits recognize the need for a minimal level of income before an individual is self-supporting or able to provide a minimal level of food, housing, and other services for any dependants, including him- or herself. The credit for an individual in 2015 was $1,699.[22] Additional credits of $1,699 were provided for a spouse or a common-law partner,[23] including $1,055 if over age 65, $1,185 if disabled, and $1,005 for a dependant who is infirm. For a married or cohabiting taxpayer over 65, with a disability, the total nonrefundable credit would be $5,458. At 15 percent, taxable income would have to reach $36,387 before the nonrefundable credit is exhausted. A tax payable of $0.15 \times \$36,387 = \$5,458$ is offset by the credit of $5,458.

CPP, QPP, and EI. Nonrefundable credits are provided for nondiscretionary payments (payroll taxes) that taxpayers make for the Canada Pension Plan (CPP), Quebec Pension Plan (QPP), and Employment Insurance (EI). These required payments are set by statute and reduce funds available for taxes or other purposes. An argument could be made to treat these payments as deductions, since they could be considered an expense of earning income. Instead, the government has chosen to grant a tax credit equal to 15 percent of the contributions made, thus ensuring that equal payments for these purposes result in the same reduction in taxes whether the taxpayer is in a 30 or 50 percent tax bracket.

Medical expenses A nonrefundable tax credit is provided for medical expenses in excess of 3 percent of net income. The reason for the tax credit for medical expenses is that large medical expenses may be nondiscretionary and reduce an individual's ability to pay. It is hard to say to what extent health care expenditures are under an individual's control. A person with serious medical and dental problems may have limited choice. Nonetheless, taxpayers can and do choose among a range of medical and dental services that may not be covered by a health care system. Canadians may also claim medical expenses incurred outside of Canada; this may involve choices regarding the level of care, tests undergone, experts consulted, and elective surgery. Moreover, it may be possible for individuals to substitute preventive health care (good diet, exercise, etc.) for formal medical services.

By providing a tax credit for some medical expenses, the tax system provides a kind of social health care insurance. The terms of this "policy" are that the individual has a deductible equal to 3.0 percent of his or her net income, and after that the government pays a share equal to the federal plus provincial lowest marginal tax rate (20.05 percent in Ontario in 2015). This is in addition to the Canada Health Plan and must be considered in light of the pros and cons of providing social health insurance discussed in Chapter 9.

Charitable contributions and education. Nonrefundable credits are used to encourage private spending on charities and education. The federal credit provided for education is 15 percent of qualifying expenditures. The credit for charitable gifts totalling $200 or less is 15 percent, and for the annual amount in excess of $200 the federal credit is 29 percent regardless of the income level of the donor. Once the $200 threshold is passed, an individual receives a 29-cent federal tax credit for each $1 given to qualifying charities. This credit also reduces the provincial tax. Where the provincial tax is calculated as 10 percent of taxable income, provincial taxes are reduced by 10 cents for every $1 given, and the total tax saving is 39 cents. The net cost to the taxpayer for each dollar given is 61 cents. A supplementary federal tax credit of 25 percent is applied to money donations of up to $1,000 made after March 20, 2013, by first-time donors.

Individuals receive a tax credit for contributions made to registered religious, charitable, educational, scientific, or literary organizations. A tax credit will be given for charitable donations up to 75 percent of net income in a given year, and excess donations can be carried forward for up to five years. In 2012, individuals reported charitable deductions of $8.6 billion (CRA, 2014).

Some argue that charitable donations constitute a reduction in taxable capacity and, hence, should be excluded from taxable income. However, as long as the contributions are made voluntarily, this argument is unconvincing. If people don't receive as much satisfaction from charity as from their own consumption, why make the donations in the first place? Probably the best way to understand the presence of the credit is

---

[22] Tax would be owed when taxable income exceeded $11,327, causing the tax rate (15 percent) times taxable income to exceed the credit. Note that $0.15 \times \$11,327 = \$1,699$.

[23] In 2015, for every dollar of income earned by a spouse, the spousal credit was reduced by 15 cents. Thus, the credit for a spouse disappeared when the income of the spouse reached $11,327.

as an attempt by the government to encourage charitable giving. Setting the federal credit at 29 percent, rather than at 15 percent (as applying to qualifying education and medical expenses), indicates such encouragement.

Has the credit succeeded in doing so? The credit provision changes an individual's "price" for a dollar's worth of charity in excess of \$200 from \$1 to \$$(1 - t)$, where t is the federal tax rate of 29 percent plus the provincial rate. (If the provincial tax rate is 10 percent, t is $0.29 + 0.10 = 0.39$.) The effectiveness of the credit in encouraging giving therefore depends on the price elasticity of demand for charitable contributions. If the price elasticity is zero, charitable giving is unaffected. The credit is just a bonus for those who would give anyway. If the price elasticity exceeds zero, then giving is encouraged.

Several attempts have been made to estimate the elasticity of charitable giving with respect to its after-tax price. Estimates for Canada indicate that the price elasticity for charitable donations may be greater than unity.[24] Consider the implications of this result. Suppose a province has a combined federal plus provincial credit of 39 percent. The credit for charitable donations lowers the price of giving from \$1 to 61 cents, a reduction of 39 percent. If the elasticity is greater than one, the taxpayer increases charitable giving by more than 39 percent. Hence, charitable organizations gain more than the tax authorities lose.

Whether the government should be subsidizing gifts to private charities can be questioned. Proponents believe that in the absence of such a subsidy, many institutions now funded privately would be forced to seek more government support. Equally important, the current decentralized system is more likely to stimulate a variety of activities, encourage policy innovations, and promote a pluralistic society.

Working Income Tax Benefit. This is a refundable tax credit introduced in the federal budget of 2007 to aid working low-income individuals and families and to encourage other Canadian residents to enter the workforce. The Working Income Tax Benefit (WITB) payment is 25 percent times the amount by which earnings exceed \$3,000, up to a maximum of \$998 for single individuals without children and \$1,813 for families in 2015. As net income exceeds a threshold, which was \$11,332 for single individuals and \$15,649 for families in 2015, the WITB payment is reduced at the rate of the lowest federal marginal tax rate. Hence, when net income reached \$17,986 for a single individual or \$27,736 for a family in 2015, no WITB was paid (e.g., $\$998 = 0.15 \times [\$17,986 - \$11,332]$). There are some differences in the calculation for certain provinces as a result of agreements between the federal and provincial governments. A WITB disability supplement is also available to eligible persons.

Boutique tax credits. A recent trend in Canada is the introduction of numerous but small nonrefundable federal tax credits that target certain types of consumer purchases or behaviours deemed by the government to be meritorious. (See Chapter 2 for a discussion of merit goods.) These include the Children's Fitness Tax Credit, Public Transit Tax Credit, Textbook Tax Credit, First-Time Home Buyers' Tax Credit, Volunteer Firefighters Tax Credit, Family Caregiver Tax Credit, Children's Art Tax Credit, and the one-time Home Renovation Tax Credit (in 2009). Since 2014, the federal government added the Search and Rescue Volunteers Tax Credit and a nonrefundable tax credit called the Family Tax Cut. The estimated costs of these boutique credits in terms of forgone tax revenues are generally small. Hence, they may serve as an apparently inexpensive way for the government to draw attention to the benefits of merit goods. However, the credits also add complexity to the income tax system and to the costs of tax administration and taxpayer compliance (see Chapter 16).

Child Tax Benefits

The tax credits discussed above include a credit for the taxpayer and another for the spouse, but no credit for children who may be in the family. Although such a credit existed prior to 1993, the **Canada Child Tax Benefit** (CCTB) program, which provides non-taxable monthly payments to eligible families, has since been implemented in place of child tax credits and the taxable payments received previously under the Family Allowance program. The federal government added a **Universal Child Care Benefit** (UCCB) program to assist families with young children in 2006, but it also re-introduced a child tax credit, as well as a child fitness tax credit, on top of the Canada Child Tax Benefit program in 2007.[25] An enhanced UCCB replaced the existing child tax credit as of the 2015 taxation year.

---

[24] Hossain and Lamb (2012a, 2012b), Kitchen (1992), and Kitchen and Dalton (1990).

[25] Since its inception in 1918, various provisions of the Income Tax Act have recognized that there is a cost of providing for children. See Kesselman (1993) for a description of the many changes in methods and tax provisions for children.

The annual, basic CCTB amount in July 2015 was $1,471 per child under age 18 for the first and second child in a family, and $1,574 for the third and each additional child.[26] The benefit is taxed back (on combined net income of parents over $44,701) at 4 percent where there are two or more children and 2 percent if there is only one child. There is a supplemental child benefit for low-income families of $2,279 for the first child, $2,016 for the second, and $1,918 for the third child. These amounts are reduced by 12.2 percent (one child) to 33.3 percent (three or more children) of family income in excess of $26,021. A disability benefit paid up to $2,695 per eligible child in 2015, also subject to a tax-back when family income was more than $44,701.[27]

The newly enhanced UCCB program in 2015 paid families $160 per month for each child under the age of six and $60 per month for a child aged six to 17. The benefits are taxable as income. The child fitness tax credit is calculated as the lowest marginal tax rate times the fees paid (up to $1,000 per child) for prescribed programs of physical activity for children who are under the age of 16 at the beginning of the taxation year. An additional fitness credit is available to an individual for a child with a disability.

Kesselman (1993) points out that with the move to the Child Tax Benefit program in 1993, those with high incomes were no longer provided with any recognition of the cost of raising children. A taxpayer earning $100,000 and having three children receives no Child Tax Benefit, and pays the same income tax as a child-less taxpayer earning $100,000. It is consistent with a view that, at least for high-income households, "the presence of children is irrelevant to a household's ability to pay taxes—in effect, that the costs of raising children are simply consumer outlays like the childless family's choice to purchase a fancy boat" (Kesselman, 1993: 117). This represents a change from our past, is unusual among developed countries, and is at odds with the view that raising children involves certain nondiscretionary expenses and affects the ability to pay taxes, whatever the level of income. The introduction of the Universal Child Care Benefit in 2006 and its enhancement in 2015 is a move back in the direction of providing financial support to all families with young children. It is not clear, however, why expenses involving children should be considered nondiscretionary in the first place. Given the wide availability of contraceptive methods, many would argue that raising children is undertaken as the result of conscious choice. If one couple wishes to spend its money on European vacations whereas another chooses to raise a family, why should the tax system reward the latter?[28] On the other hand, the religions of certain people rule out effective birth-control methods, and, for them, children are not a choice as the term is conventionally defined.

Tax Credits versus Deductions

Some argue that deductions and exemptions should be converted into credits. Prior to 1988, taxpayers were permitted additional deductions to recognize some of the basic costs of providing for oneself, one's spouse, one's children, and other dependants. These deductions were referred to as the "personal exemption" and "exemptions for spouse and dependants." An additional deduction, known as the "age exemption," was provided for those who were 65 or older on December 31.

The effect of the exemptions on taxes due, like other deductions, depended on the tax rate of the taxpayer. If your marginal tax rate was 50 percent, a $5,000 personal exemption reduced taxes by $2,500; if 20 percent, by $1,000. Since the exemptions led to larger reductions for those with higher incomes, they lessened the progressivity of the tax system.

The 1987 tax reform replaced the personal, marital, age, and disability exemptions with tax credits, effective in 1988. This was a substantial change in Canadian tax policy. Deductions for the taxpayer, spouse, dependants, age, pension income, disabilities, medical expenses, charitable donations, and Canada Pension Plan and

---

[26] Benefits are paid over a 12-month period from July of one year to June of the next year. Federal legislation permits provinces to vary the payments to some extent.

[27] The National Child Benefit (NCB) is the name given to the group of programs consisting of the Canada Child Tax Benefit, the National Child Tax Benefit Supplement, and the Child Disability Benefit. The NCB is a joint initiative of the federal, provincial, and territorial governments, aimed at reducing child poverty, while minimizing the overlap and duplication of government programs. See Chapter 12 for a discussion of the work incentive effects associated with the NCB.

[28] If there are positive externalities involved in raising children, then a subsidy might be appropriate (see Chapter 5). Some would argue that because the world is overcrowded, additional children create negative externalities and, hence, should be taxed. Under China's one-child policy (which terminated in 2015), families with more than one child forfeited certain government benefits. In effect, this was a tax on children.

Employment Insurance premiums were converted to credits. The basic exemption, which would have been $4,250 with no change in tax policy, reduced taxes by $1,240 for the individual subject to a 29 percent marginal rate, and by $725 for the individual subject to a 17 percent tax rate. In contrast, the basic credit of $1,020 was independent of an individual's income level and marginal tax rate. The same is true for the other deductions that were converted to tax credits.

Proponents of credits argue that they are fairer than deductions. Under a regime of tax deductions, a poor person (with a low marginal tax rate) benefits less than a rich person (with a high marginal tax rate) even if they make identical contributions to their RRSPs. With a credit, the dollar benefit is the same.

This oversimplifies the situation. Adjustments can be made to tax rates that will offset any loss in progressivity that is due to the use of exemptions instead of credits. Moreover, the choice between deductions and credits should depend at least in part on the purpose of the exclusion. If the motivation is to correct for the fact that a given expenditure reduces ability to pay, a deduction seems appropriate. Such deductions might include the expense to feed, clothe, and house children, or for unexpected medical expenses. If the purpose is mainly to encourage certain behaviour, it is not at all clear whether credits or deductions are superior.[29]

A credit reduces the effective price of the favoured good by the same percentage for all individuals; a deduction decreases the price by different percentages for different people. If people differ with respect to their elasticities of demand, it may make sense to present them with different effective prices. For example, if the objective is to increase consumption of the good, it is ineffective to give any subsidy to someone whose elasticity of demand for the favoured good is zero.

Impact on the Tax Base and Taxes Payable

To what extent does the presence of deductions and exemptions influence the size of the tax base? To what extent do tax credits reduce the tax that would otherwise be payable? The effect of both is significant. Deductions move us from total income to taxable income. The total income on all tax returns in 2012, as shown in Table 17.3, was about $1.12 trillion. Deductions reduced this by about $120 billion, leaving about $1 trillion in taxable income. The tax expenditure estimates of the Department of Finance puts a dollar value of the revenue cost associated with these deductions at about $29 billion in 2012 for the federal government alone. Similarly, credits reduced taxes that would otherwise be payable. The total value of nonrefundable credits used to reduce taxes payable was about $68 billion in 2012. Deductions and credits play a large and important role in our income tax system.

Tax Expenditures

Failure to include a particular item in the tax base results in a loss to federal and provincial treasuries. Suppose that as a consequence of not taxing item Z, governments lose $1 billion. Compare this to a situation in which the government simply hands over $1 billion of general revenues to those who purchase item Z. In a sense, these activities are equivalent as both subsidize purchases of Z. It just so happens that one transaction occurs on the revenue side of the account and the other on the expenditure side. The former is called a *tax expenditure,* a revenue loss caused by the exclusion of some item from the tax base. Credits have a similar effect. The government can give a tax credit of $1 billion based on a certain level of charitable giving by taxpayers, or as an alternative it can give the $1 billion directly to the charities. But the credit appears on the revenue side of the account and is also a tax expenditure.

Department of Finance Canada (2015) introduces its list of tax expenditures by stating:

> The tax system can also be used directly to achieve public policy objectives through the application of special measures such as low tax rates, exemptions, deductions, deferrals, and credits.

The most prominent federal tax expenditures projected for 2014 included the CPP, QPP, and EI credit for employee contributions and the non-taxation of employer-paid premiums (totalling $12.9 billion), the partial inclusion of capital gains and the non-taxation of capital gains on principal residences (totalling $9.8 billion), the charitable donations credit ($2.3 billion), the non-taxation of business-paid health and dental benefits

---

[29] See Cloutier and Fortin (1989).

TABLE 17.3

Summary Information from Individual Income Tax Returns, 2012 ($ millions)

A. **SOURCE OF INCOME**

Employment income	$717,787
Income from OAS, CPP, QPP, and pensions	150,175
Employment Insurance benefits	16,277
Dividends, interest, rents, RSP, capital gains, and investment income	108,475
Business and professional income	40,830
Other income	87,179

Total Income Assessed = $1,120,723

B. **DEDUCTIONS (Total: $119,825)**

RPP contributions	17,453
RRSP contributions	32,402
Union and professional dues	3,916
Deduction for elected split-pension amount	11,876
Childcare and moving expenses	4,917
Capital gains deduction	4,214
Other deductions	45,047

Taxable Income Assessed = $1,000,619*

C. **NONREFUNDABLE TAX CREDITS (Total: $68,384)**

D. **TAXES PAYABLE**

Net federal tax	115,652
Net provincial tax	49,001

Total Income Tax Payable = $164,693

---

* $1,000,619 is the Canada Revenue Agency figure, although $1,120,723 − $119,825 = $1,000,898; the small difference is due to adjustments to net income for social benefits repayment.

Source: Canada Revenue Agency, *Income Statistics 2014 (2012 tax year)*, Interim Statistics–Universe Data, Table 2 at http://www.cra-arc.gc.ca. Reproduced with the permission of the Minister of Public Works and Government Services Canada, 2014.

($2.1 billion), and the non-taxation of RRSP and RPP contributions (totalling $16.7 billion, net of tax on withdrawals). The projected tax expenditures for the Canada Child Tax Benefit, Medical Expense Tax Credit, and Working Income Tax Benefit in 2014 were $10.5 billion, $1.4 billion, and $1.2 billion, respectively.

These items alone total almost $57 billion. In areas such as social services and housing, tax expenditures may be as large as direct federal expenditures. Although summing the items does not allow for interaction between the provisions or for behavioural responses to policy changes, tax expenditures are very significant relative to federal net personal income taxes collected ($116 billion in 2012). This, however, does not mean that we would be better off if the tax expenditures had been withdrawn. It is, nonetheless, apparent that tax expenditures play an important role in government policy.

The Department of Finance has published the results of its tax expenditure estimates since late 1979. These lists, and the discussion of tax expenditures in the 1981 and 1987 tax reform documents, have raised public consciousness of the symmetry between a direct subsidy for an activity via an expenditure and an implicit subsidy through the tax system. No longer are the preferences in our tax system, and the forgone revenues, as well hidden to policy-makers or the public as they once were.

The notion of a tax expenditure list and a tax expenditure budget has, however, been subject to several criticisms. First, a serious technical problem arises in the way the computations are made. It is assumed that in the absence of a deduction for a given item, all the expenditures currently made on it would flow into taxable income. Given that people are quite likely to adjust their behaviour in response to changes in the tax system, this is not a good assumption, so the tax expenditure estimates may be quite far off the mark.

Second, the tax expenditure budget is simply a list of items that either reduce the tax base by exemptions and deductions or lower taxes payable through credits. To consider these items as forgone or "lost" revenues, we must have some criterion for deciding what the tax base ought to be in the first place, and what, if any, credits are an inherent part of the tax system. As we have seen, no rigorous set of principles exists for determining what belongs in income. Nor has there been much consistency over time in protecting a minimal amount of income for a taxpayer and his or her dependants through the use of exemptions or credits. One person's loophole may be regarded by another as an appropriate adjustment of the tax base. Hence, considerable arbitrariness is inevitably involved in deciding what to include in a tax expenditure list or budget.

Finally, the concept of tax expenditures has been attacked on philosophical grounds. It is argued that the tax expenditure concept implies that the forgone revenues belong to the government. This is at odds with a view that government is "of the people" in a democracy, and property is privately held except where the polity supports the transfer of resources, through taxes or by other means, to the government.

Defenders of the tax expenditure concept have argued that the concept does not really carry these ideological implications. It is rather an attempt to force recognition of the fact that the tax system is a major method for subsidizing various activities. Moreover, even though the estimates are not exact they can still be useful for assessing the implications of tax policy. Explicit recognition of tax expenditures

* contributes to the reassessment of policies on a regular basis,
* permits a comparison of direct and indirect means of obtaining a given government objective, and
* allows, in some cases, for the use of benefit-cost analysis in the evaluation of tax expenditures, as in the evaluation of direct expenditures.[30]

The Simplicity Issue

The federal personal income tax has been railed at for its complexity and the compliance burden it has placed on taxpayers. Reference is frequently made to the growing length of the Income Tax Act and the inability of intelligent men and women to make sense of it. With some justification, it has been referred to as "the accountants and lawyers full employment act."

One of five objectives in the 1987 tax reform was that the tax system "be simpler to understand and comply with." The basic rate structure was simplified, with tax brackets reduced from 13 to 10 by the 1981 reforms and then to three in 1988.[31] The tax base was broadened (tax expenditures reduced) in order to treat income from different sources, and in the hands of different people, in a similar fashion. The general capital gains exemption was reduced from $500,000 to $100,000, and then eliminated altogether. With half of capital gains now included in taxable income, the incentive to realize income in the form of capital gains was reduced. Investments in films and in multiple unit residential buildings (MURBs) became less generously treated, and provisions that allowed income to be averaged over several years were repealed. The 1987 tax reform also replaced the personal, spousal, dependant, age, and disability exemptions with tax credits.

Nonetheless, the law is complex and will remain so. With the reduction or elimination of preferences, the conversion of exemptions and deductions to credits, and the simplification of the rate structure, taxpayers may feel the complexity of the law now contributes more to fairness and less to the special treatment of some taxpayers. However, simple rules are often inadequate when situations differ greatly in a complex world. Although it is unlikely that the Income Tax Act in Canada, or any other industrialized country, will be anything other than complex, there will always be room for improvement.

---

[30] Tax expenditures can be made through the corporate income tax, sales taxes, and property taxes, as well as through the personal income tax. It is important that provincial and local authorities, too, are aware of revenues forgone through special provisions in their laws, as well as revenues forgone due to provincial reliance on tax bases defined by the federal government. Some provincial governments, including Saskatchewan and British Columbia, have developed tax expenditure lists.

[31] The federal rate structure remains far more complex than the current basic rates of 0, 15, 22, 26, and 29 percent suggest. This is due to payroll tax rates that apply over certain ranges of earned income, and to "clawback" arrangements that reduce transfer payments as income rises. These result in marginal rates on income that substantially exceed the basic rates.

INCOME SPLITTING AND THE FAMILY TAX CUT

In the 2015 budget, the federal government of Stephen Harper implemented spousal income splitting for families with children under the age of 18. This Family Tax Cut is a refundable tax credit based on a notional transfer of income of up to $50,000 from the higher earner to the lower-earning spouse. The transfer would provide a tax savings for a family where the lesser-earning spouse is in a lower marginal tax rate bracket. For example, transferring $50,000 from a spouse facing a 29 percent federal marginal tax rate to a spouse facing a 26 percent marginal tax rate would reduce the family tax burden by $1,500. The tax savings from the measure is capped at $2,000. Proponents of the policy like its neutrality regarding a family's choice between a spouse staying at home to raise children or both spouses working and paying for day care. Opponents say it favours the rich, in particular high-income men, who, in effect, receive an unneeded tax break when their wives stay at home. And, obviously, single parents cannot get any help from income splitting at all. According to the independent Parliamentary Budget Officer, parental income splitting will benefit only 15 percent of Canadian households, about two million families, while lower income households will get virtually no benefit. Of course, well-off individuals without young children would be ineligible for the Family Tax Cut, so the estimated $2 billion in total income-splitting tax relief cannot be for only the richest 15 percent of households, despite such claims by opposition parties during the 2015 federal election campaign. A more nuanced view is provided by John Geddes in an article in *Maclean's*. He reports that, while 13 percent of the benefits of the policy will likely accrue to families with incomes above $180,000, the preponderance of benefits (52 percent) falls on middle class families with incomes between $60,000 and $120,000. However, the problem is that families with incomes below $60,000 receive only 17 percent of the tax savings. He notes that of the 1.7 million families with children and incomes falling under $60,000, only 376,000 have the income structure that allows them to gain from income-splitting: "The problem with income-splitting isn't that it is designed to benefit the best-off families; it's that it is not designed to benefit those who are really struggling to make ends meet."

Based on Lahey (2014) and "Who really benefits from income-splitting." *Mclean's*, April 24, 2015.

Complete references for this feature can be found in the References section on page 487.

RATE STRUCTURE

After calculating total income, allowed deductions, and taxable income, we have arrived at the third step in Figure 17.1—the application of tax rates to taxable income and the calculation of income tax payable *before* tax credits. A bracket system is used to define tax rates. The taxable income scale is divided into segments, and the law specifies the marginal tax rate that applies to income in that segment.

Rates and Brackets

Statutory income tax rates have changed dramatically over time. When the federal income tax was introduced in 1917, a "normal" tax rate was applied at a 4 percent rate on income over $1,500 for single individuals and over $3,000 for all others. An additional "supertax" was applied, ranging from 2 percent on income from $6,000 to $10,000 up to an additional 25 percent on income over $100,000. Thus, rates ranged from a low of zero to 29 (4 + 25) percent over eight brackets, including the first $1,500 or $3,000 subject to a zero rate.

With World War II came the need for higher rates. Rates on taxable income that had varied from 4 percent to 29 percent in 1917, ranged from 15 percent to 84 percent in 1949. Substantial compression of marginal rates has occurred since 1949, with rates on taxable income ranging from around 26 to 46 percent in 2000 (but with some differences among the provinces). The eight brackets of 1917, which had increased to 15 brackets by 1949, were reduced to 10 by the 1981 reforms and further to three by the 1987 reforms—since

TABLE 17.4

Federal and Provincial Tax Rates, and Surtaxes, 2015

1. Rates of Federal Income Tax

TAXABLE INCOME	TAX RATE	TAXABLE INCOME	TAX RATE
$44,701 or less	15%	$89,402 to $138,586	26%
$44,702 to $89,401	22%	over $138,506	29%

2. Provincial Income Tax Rates and Surtaxes

Province	Lowest Rate (%)	Highest Rate (%)	Surtax (%) (if any)	Basic Exemption ($)	Spousal Exemption ($)
Newfoundland and Labrador	7.70	14.30†		8,767	7,164
PEI	9.80	16.70	10.00	7,708	6,546
Nova Scotia	8.79	21.00		8,481	8,481
New Brunswick	9.68	25.75		9,633	8,180
Quebec	16.00	25.75		11,425	11,425
Ontario	5.05	13.16	20.0–56.0	9,863	8,375
Manitoba	10.80	17.40		9,8134	9,134
Saskatchewan	11.00	15.00		15,639	15,639
Alberta	10.00	11.25‡		18,214	18,214
British Columbia	5.06	16.8*		9,938	8,509

† 15.30 in 2016. ‡ 15.00 in 2016. * 14.70 in 2016.

Source: Canada Revenue Agency website: http://www.cra-arc.gc.ca/tx/ndvdls/fq/txrts-eng.html; and KPMG website: http://www.kpmg.com/ca/en/issuesandinsights/articlespublications/pages/taxratespersonal.aspx.

increased to four brackets. Table 17.4 shows the brackets and rates for the federal income tax in 2015, as well as information on provincial tax rates.

Frequent mention is made of top marginal rates on employment and investment income in Canada. Table 17.5 provides the maximum marginal rates that were applicable to differing forms of income in 2015,

TABLE 17.5

Maximum Federal and Provincial Combined Rates for Three Types of Income, by Province, 2015

Province	Ordinary Income (%)	Dividends (%)	Capital Gains (%)
Newfoundland and Labrador	43.30	31.57	21.65
Prince Edward Island	47.37	28.70	23.69
Nova Scotia	50.00	36.06	25.00
New Brunswick	54.75	38.27	27.38
Quebec	49.97	35.22	24.98
Ontario	49.53	33.82	24.76
Manitoba	46.40	32.26	23.20
Saskatchewan	44.00	24.81	22.00
Alberta	40.25	21.02	20.13
British Columbia	45.80	28.68	22.90

Note: These tax rates do not reflect various preferences given to certain investments in some provinces. Rather, they reflect the top marginal rates that may apply where such preferences do not exist or already have been fully realized.

Source: TaxTips website: http://www.TaxTips.ca.

by province. With the exception of New Brunswick and Quebec, the differences in top tax rates among provinces are relatively modest. As of October 1, 2015, Alberta replaced its single income tax rate of 10 percent with a schedule of progressive marginal tax rates.

Factors Affecting Marginal Rates

Unfortunately, statutory marginal tax rates seldom correspond to the actual marginal tax rates. There are three main reasons for this:

- federal and provincial surtaxes;
- payroll taxes, such as those for Employment Insurance and CPP/QPP; and
- clawbacks for the Child Tax Benefit and GST credit, EI benefits, OAS payments, and the WITB.

Surtaxes. As the federal and provincial governments more successfully addressed their deficits in the late 1990s, surtaxes were eliminated by the federal government and several provincial governments. Remaining provincial surtaxes are listed in Table 17.4. Provincial surtaxes are as high as 56 percent of the provincial tax payable in Ontario. The 56 percent surtax adds over 6 percentage points to marginal rates on higher incomes. Surtaxes raise marginal tax rates by 1 to 2 percentage points in Prince Edward Island.

Payroll taxes. Payroll taxes, discussed in Part 4, significantly raise the effective marginal rates on wages and salaries over a range of incomes. Canada Pension Plan (CPP) premiums, a form of payroll tax, are collected at a rate of 4.95 percent from employees (also 4.95 percent from the employer) and 9.9 percent from those who are self-employed. These rates apply over income ranging from $3,500 to $53,600, raising marginal tax rates on earned income by as much as 9.9 percentage points. The Quebec Pension Plan (QPP) total contribution rate in 2015 was 10.5 percent, split equally between employee and employer.

Employment Insurance (EI) premiums in 2015 were paid by each employee at a 1.88 percent rate on insurable earnings of up to $49,500. Employers contributed an additional 2.63 percent. Thus, the total tax was 4.51 percent, although the payslip taken home reflects only the 1.88 percent deducted from gross earnings. For much of earnings below $49,500, the combined effect of CPP and EI premiums raise the effective marginal tax rate on income from wages by about 14 percentage points in 2015.[32]

Clawbacks. Some benefits to taxpayers are cut back once income reaches certain levels. The loss in benefits is equivalent to a tax. This is true for the Canada Child Tax Benefit and the GST credit. The Child Tax Benefit is reduced by 4 percent (2 percent in the case of a single child) of the amount that the parents' income exceeds $44,701 in 2015. Similarly, the GST refundable tax credit, which was set at $272 each for a taxpayer and spouse and $143 per child, is reduced by 5 percent for income over $35,465. For a family with two adults and two children, the total GST credit of $830 would disappear when family income reaches $52,065. These two clawbacks raise the effective marginal tax rate above the statutory rate by nine percentage points over a range of relatively low incomes.

The clawback of EI benefits applies at higher income levels. Regular EI benefits are reduced by 30 percent of the amount that a recipient's net income exceeds $61,875 in 2015. Thus, when the income of an EI recipient exceeds this amount, marginal rates normally in the 30–35 percent range may top 60 percent until EI benefits are fully clawed back.

The OAS payments in 2015 provided about $570 per month to those over 65. Benefits are withheld when annual income is over $72,809, at a rate of 15 percent of net income over this amount. This is effectively an additional tax rate, which applies until the entire amount has been clawed back at an income level of $118,055. This creates an income range for the elderly, where marginal rates may exceed 50 percent on income between $89,402 (the start of the third federal tax bracket) and $118,055.[33]

---

[32] See the discussion of payroll tax incidence in Chapter 14. The economic incidence of payroll taxes is, over the longer run, little affected by whether the tax is collected from the employee or the employer.

[33] Since 2007, however, seniors can elect to split their pension incomes with their spouse or common-law partner. As the OAS clawback applies to the post-split income, the marginal tax rate associated with the OAS clawback is lower for many couples.

TABLE 17.6

Factors Affecting Marginal Tax Rates: An Alberta Example in 2015*

Income Level ($)	Tax Provision**	Change in Marginal Tax Rate (%)	Marginal Tax Rate (%)
0	Start of EI premiums	+ 1.88	1.88
3,500	Start of CPP premiums	+ 4.95	6.83
22,654	Start of 1st federal bracket	+15.00	21.83
35,465	Start of GST clawback	+ 5.00	26.83
36,428	Start of first Alberta bracket	+10.00	36.83
44,701	Start of CCTB clawback	+ 4.00	40.83
44,701	Start of 2nd federal bracket	+ 7.00	47.83
49,500	Maximum EI premiums	− 1.88	45.95
52,065	End of GST clawback	− 5.00	40.95
53,600	Maximum CPP premiums	− 4.95	36.00
89,402	Start of 3rd federal bracket	+ 4.00	40.00
118,251	End of CCTB clawback	− 4.00	36.00
125,000	Start of 2nd Alberta bracket	+ 0.50	36.50
138,587	Start of 4th federal bracket	+ 3.00	39.50
150,000	Start of 3rd Alberta bracket	+ 0.25	39.75
200,000	Start of 4th Alberta bracket	+ 0.25	40.00
300,000	Start of 5th Alberta bracket	+ 0.25	40.25

* This is for a one-earner married couple with two dependants between ages 7 and 17. Applicable credits include those for self, spouse, and maximum EI and CCP contributions. Only the employee share of payroll taxes are reflected in the table. The federal basic and spousal credits mean that the first $22,654 of net income is not subject to tax. Alberta provides basic and spousal exemptions each of $18,214. The rate structure is more complex for those with the National Child Benefit supplement, WITB, OAS benefits, or EI benefits as these programs have clawback provisions that add to effective marginal rates. Alberta's statutory marginal tax rates were 10%, 10.50%, 10.75%, 11%, and 11.25% in 2015, and 10%, 12%, 13%, 14% and 15% in 2016.

** EI = Employment Insurance; CPP = Canada Pension Plan; CCTB = Canada Child Tax Benefit.

The foregoing makes clear that the federal rate structure following the 1987 tax reform is anything but simple when combined with provincial rates, surtaxes, payroll tax rates, and clawbacks, all of which affect the amount a taxpayer takes home from an additional dollar of gross earnings. The rows in Table 17.6 show the federal rate structure plus the Alberta rate structure, plus CPP and EI payroll taxes, plus GST and CCTB clawbacks. Even without the further complications of clawbacks for WITB, EI benefits, the National Child Benefit supplement, and OAS payments, Table 17.6 and Figure 17.2 adequately demonstrate the complexity of existing marginal tax rates.[34] The table provides an indication of the situation in Alberta in 2015, but it illustrates the complexity that currently exists in the rate structure in all provinces.

The Alternative Minimum Tax

Under most income tax laws it is possible for some individuals with high incomes to pay little or no tax.[35] This occurs for reasons that include the form of income received and deductions allowed. Where an individual qualifies for large dividend tax credits, investment and other tax credits, and/or has large deductions due to accelerated depreciation or to contributions to deferred savings plans, taxes in a given year may appear low

---

[34] For a fuller treatment of the complexity of marginal rates due to factors discussed here, see Duclos, Fortin, and Fournier (2009). See Davies and Zhang (1996) for a discussion of marginal tax rates in Canada for the 1947 to 1991 period. They note that federal plus provincial marginal tax rates "increased very rapidly from the early 1960s to the early 1970s. There was a decline in 1975–76, and then a long fairly steady upward trend set in" (p. 974).

[35] In 2012, there were 3,750 individuals reporting total income over $100,000 and paying no personal income tax in that year (Canada Revenue Agency, 2014).

FIGURE 17.2

MARGINAL TAX RATES, 2015 (ALBERTA EXAMPLE)

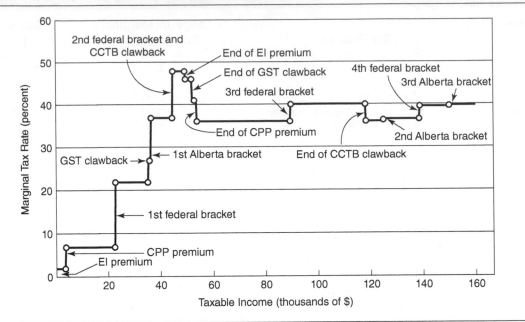

Source: Based on Table 17.6 above, but depicted only for income up to $160,000.

relative to taxes paid by those receiving income in other forms or not qualifying for similar deductions. The result may be a high income and little tax.

The Alternative Minimum Tax (AMT) took effect in 1986 and is payable if it exceeds taxes calculated in the normal way. The AMT base includes all of capital gains rather than only half, and does not allow for various tax incentives or for deductions for contributions to RPPs, RRSPs, and deferred profit sharing plans. There is provision for a $40,000 exemption, which ensures that the AMT affects only those with capital gains and dividend income, tax incentives, and deductions that are high relative to the norm. The AMT is essentially a shadow tax system with its own rules for computing the tax base. However, it applies the normal tax rates to the AMT base.

Effective versus Statutory Rates

Now is a good time to recall the distinction between statutory and effective tax rates. In this section, we have been discussing the former, the legal rates established by the law. In general, these differ from effective tax rates for at least three reasons:

- Because the tax system treats certain types of income preferentially, taxable income may be considerably lower than some more-comprehensive measures of income. The fact that tax rates rise rapidly with taxable income does not by itself tell us much about how taxes vary with comprehensive income.

- Even in the absence of loopholes, the link between statutory and effective tax rates is weak. As was emphasized in Chapter 14, taxes can be shifted, so there is no reason to believe that income taxes will really be borne by the people who pay the money to the government. The economic incidence of the income tax is determined by market responses when the tax is levied, and the true pattern of the burden is not known.

- The tax system imposes decreases in utility that exceed revenue collections. Excess burdens arise because taxes distort behaviour away from patterns that otherwise would have occurred (see Chapter 15). Similarly, the costs of compliance with the Income Tax Act, in taxpayers' own time as well as explicit payments to accountants and lawyers, must be considered.

In this connection, note that, contrary to the impression sometimes received in popular discussions, the provision of an item such as tax-free dental care paid for by an employer does not, in general, allow the taxpayer to entirely escape the burden of taxation. Consider again Caesar, whose marginal tax rate is 50 percent. The cost to the employer of providing dental care is $500. Caesar may value the service at $300, more than the after-tax $250 that he would receive if the employer increased wages by $500 instead of providing dental care. Caesar accepts the dental care, but the tax system nevertheless makes him worse off, because in its absence he would have much preferred the $500 in the form of wages rather than dental care.

Similarly, where tax incentives or preferences encourage certain types of investments, there is a general tendency for the rate of return on tax-preference items to fall by an amount that reflects the tax advantage. Because of this tendency, which results from normal market forces, the effective tax rate on capital income for those making such investments, generally high-income individuals, is higher than their tax payments would suggest.

Thus, statutory rates alone probably tell us little about the progressiveness of the current system. Conceivably, a statute with lower marginal tax rates but a broader base would lead to a system with incidence as progressive as that of the current system, and perhaps even more so. At the same time, a system with lower marginal tax rates would reduce excess burden and perhaps lower tax evasion. Such considerations have prompted a number of proposals to dramatically restructure the income tax. One plan that has received a lot of attention is the **flat tax**. A flat tax has two attributes:

- It applies the same rate of tax to everyone and to each component of the tax base.
- It allows computation of the tax base with no deductions from total income except personal exemptions and strictly defined business expenses.[36]

Assuming that a certain amount of tax revenue must be collected, under a flat tax the key tradeoff is between the size of the personal exemption and the marginal tax rate. A higher exemption may be desirable to secure relief for those at the bottom of the income schedule and to increase progressiveness (with respect to average tax rates). But a higher exemption means that a higher marginal tax rate must be applied to maintain revenues. A single tax rate of from 25 (Alberta) to 30 (Quebec) percent, with a personal and spousal exemption of $7,231 each, would have raised the same revenues in 2000 as did the existing federal and provincial personal income taxes (Emes and Clemens, 2001: 24).

Proponents of the flat tax claim that lowering marginal tax rates would reduce both the excess burden of the tax system and the incentive to cheat. Moreover, the simplicity gained would cut down on administrative costs and improve taxpayer morale. And all of this could be achieved without a serious cost in equity because, as just noted, the flat tax can be made quite progressive by suitable choice of the exemption level.

Opponents of the flat tax believe that it would redistribute the tax burden from the rich to the middle class, and there is some evidence supporting this. However, it is hard to evaluate this claim because of the usual difficulties involved in doing tax incidence analysis (Chapter 14). One way to think of the tax reforms of 1981 and 1987 is as a movement in the direction of a flat tax—the federal statutory maximum rate was lowered from 43 percent in 1981 to 34 percent in 1982, and to 29 percent in 1988, and the base was broadened by disallowing some deductions and including more investment income—interest, dividends, and capital gains—and the value of some previously untaxed fringe benefits. Whether or not there will be further movement toward a flat tax remains to be seen.

The Final Calculation

Applying the marginal tax rates to taxable income, we calculate tax that is due before credits. This brings us to Step 4 in Figure 17.1, which provides for the subtraction of tax credits from the federal income tax otherwise payable when tax rates are applied to taxable income. These include credits calculated as 15 percent of amounts provided for a taxpayer, taxpayer's spouse, disabilities, and infirm dependants, as well as 15 percent of qualifying EI, CPP/QPP, and pension contributions; $2,000 in pension income; and qualifying tuition fees and medical expenses. It allows a credit for 15 percent for the first $200 in charitable donations, and 29 percent

---

[36] In essence, then, a flat tax is just a linear income tax, as defined in Chapter 16.

for that in excess of $200. Subtracting these and a limited number of other credits from the product of the tax rates and taxable income yields **federal tax payable**. Provincial rates are then applied to taxable income and, with provincial tax credits, determine provincial tax payable (Step 5).

CHOICE OF TAX UNIT

We have discussed, at length, problems that arise in defining income for taxation purposes. Yet, even very careful definitions of income give little guidance with respect to choosing who should be taxed on the income. Should each person be taxed separately on his or her own income? Or should individuals who live together in a family unit be taxed on their joint income? We now discuss some of the difficult issues involved in the choice of taxable unit.[37]

Background

To begin, it is useful to consider the following three principles:

1. The income tax should embody increasing marginal tax rates.

2. Families with equal incomes should, other things being the same (including family size), pay equal taxes.

3. Two individuals' tax burdens should not change when they marry or live in a common-law relationship; the tax system should be **marriage neutral**.

Although a certain amount of controversy surrounds the second and third principles, it is probably fair to say they reflect a broad consensus as to desirable features of a tax system. While agreement on the first principle is weaker, increasing marginal tax rates seem to have wide political support.

Despite the appeal of these principles, a problem arises when it comes to implementing them; in general, no tax system can adhere to all three simultaneously. This point is made most easily with an arithmetic example. Consider the following simple progressive tax schedule: a taxable unit pays in tax 10 percent of all income up to $6,000, and 50 percent of all income in excess of $6,000. The first two columns of Table 17.7 show the incomes and tax liabilities of four individuals, Lucy, Ricky, Fred, and Ethel. (For example, Ricky's tax liability is $12,100 [=.10 × $6,000 + .50 × $23,000].) Now assume that romances develop—Lucy marries Ricky, and Ethel marries Fred. In the absence of joint filing, the tax liability of each individual is unchanged. However, two families with the same income ($30,000) will be paying different amounts of tax. (The Lucy–Rickys pay $12,200, while the Ethel–Freds pay only $10,200, as noted in the third column.) Suppose instead that the law views the family as the taxable unit, so that the tax schedule applies to joint income. In this case, the two families pay equal amounts of tax, but now tax burdens have been changed by marriage. Of course, the actual

TABLE 17.7					
	Tax Liabilities under a Hypothetical Tax System				
	Individual Income	Individual Tax	Family Tax with Individual Filing	Joint Income	Joint Tax
Lucy	$ 1,000	$ 100	$ 12,200	$ 30,000	$ 12,600
Ricky	29,000	12,100			
Ethel	15,000	5,100	10,200	30,000	12,600
Fred	15,000	5,100			

[37] For further details, see Mintz (2008).

[38] It may be apparent to the reader that a flat-rate tax with a single rate is marriage neutral, and will treat two couples the same regardless of the distribution of income between the two partners (assuming income in all cases is above the taxable threshold). Income-spitting problems are also minimized with a single rate since the applicable rate is more likely to be the same regardless of who reports the income.

change in the tax burden depends on the difference between the tax schedules applied to individual and joint returns. This example has assumed for simplicity that the schedule remains unchanged. But it does make the main point: given increasing marginal tax rates, we cannot have both principles 2 and 3.[38]

What choice has Canada made? The tax unit has been the individual throughout the history of the Canadian personal income tax. Nonetheless, it has been strongly argued that this is wrong-headed and that the family should be the taxable unit. An economist surveying the scene is likely to ask, "What is most efficient?" and "What is most equitable?" We discuss the choice of tax unit with these two questions in mind.

Family. The *Report* of the Royal Commission on Taxation (1966: 122–23) strongly urged that the family be the taxable unit for Canada's personal income tax:

> The family is . . . the basic economic unit in society. . . . Taxation of the individual in . . . disregard of his inevitably close financial and economic ties with the other members of the basic social unit of which he is ordinarily a member, the family, is in our view [a] striking instance of [a] lack of a comprehensive and rational pattern in . . . [a] tax system.

The commission noted that the incomes of spouses and children all contribute to the well-being of a family, and to its ability to pay taxes. With progressive tax rates based on ability to pay, it is reasonable to recognize increased ability to pay. Equity, in the eyes of the commission, is achieved only if family units with the same income pay the same tax—something that will not occur with the individual as the taxable unit.

The commission also noted that enforcement problems arise with individuals as the taxable unit. With progressive tax rates, the incentive for **income splitting** may be great. This is most likely to occur with non-labour income (dividends, interest, profits). Family members with high levels of taxable income have an incentive to shift income-generating assets to a spouse or to children with lower tax rates. Although laws may limit a taxpayer's income-splitting ability, the laws become more complex and splitting still occurs as substantial transfers are made over time. However, given the current high rates of divorce, turning property over to a spouse just for tax purposes may be a risky strategy, and there is no strong evidence that such transfers occur in massive amounts. With the family as the tax unit, there are no tax implications in the transfer of assets between spouses, or to children so long as they remain within the family unit.

The argument for the family as a unit weakens on efficiency grounds. Aggregation of the income from family members means that the additional dollar earned by a spouse or children, who individually may have little income, may be subject to high marginal tax rates if another family member has high income.[39] The effect on the labour supply may be substantial. Since married women may have more elastic labour supply schedules than their husbands (as we will note in Chapter 18), efficient taxation requires taxing wives at a relatively lower rate. This may also hold true for others in the family unit. Under a family unit, all family members face identical marginal tax rates on their last dollars of income. Hence, the family as the taxable unit is inefficient.

There is also the question of whether two partners, both of whom hold full-time jobs, such as Ethel–Fred, should pay income taxes equal to those of another couple, such as Lucy–Ricky, where one spouse working outside the home earns as much as the combined earnings of the first couple. This occurs with the family as the taxable unit, but ignores the fact that the second couple is likely to benefit more from imputed income associated with care of the home and children, more leisure, and possibly lower transportation and other work-related expenses.

Individual. Taxation of individuals avoids the inefficiency that accompanies high marginal rates on the income of secondary earners in the family unit. Adopting the family as the taxable unit would also not be a simple matter. For example, Bittker (1975: 1398) observed:

> If married couples are taxed on their consolidated income, for example, should the same principle extend to a child who supports an aged parent, two sisters who share an apartment, or a divorced parent who lives with an adolescent child? Should a relationship established by blood or marriage be demanded, to the exclusion, for example, of unmarried persons who live together, homosexual companions, and communes?

---

[39] This could not occur, so long as income is above the tax-free threshold, if there were but a single rate.

In addition to the complexities associated with adopting the family as the taxable unit, other reasons exist for choosing the individual.

There has, perhaps, never been reason to believe that full sharing of income existed within family units. A husband or wife may know relatively little of the other's income, and subjecting the earnings of one spouse to a high tax rate because the other spouse earns much more, as occurs with aggregated incomes, is seen as unfair. There has also been an increasing wish to recognize the earnings of women as theirs to use and control, recognizing that laws in the past have sometimes limited ownership rights available to women.

The earlier example of Lucy–Ricky and Ethel–Fred shows the "marriage penalty" that accompanies the use of the family as the unit of taxation. Both couples experience higher taxes on a joint basis than on an individual basis, but the difference is much greater for one couple than for the other. Continuing to tax them on an individual basis is the only way to remain neutral on the question of marriage and avoid either a marriage "penalty" or "reward" for one or the other.

With increasing numbers of two-income families, even two-city commuting families, families without children, and with high divorce rates, arguments for the individual as the tax unit have strengthened in the past several decades. The individual is expected to continue as the tax unit in Canada. This means that Canada's income tax law will continue to violate principle 2—equal taxes on families with equal incomes. Principle 3—no change in tax burdens when marriage occurs—will generally be maintained for working couples.[40] No tax system can satisfy all three criteria, and Canadian society has (for the time) made its choice. Nonetheless, the choice of taxable unit will continue to be influenced by sociological, administrative, and political as well as economic considerations.

TAXES AND INFLATION

The tax law establishes set amounts to which the 15 percent rate is applied to determine allowable tax credits. It also establishes minimum and maximum dollar amounts for each tax bracket, and thresholds at which clawbacks of tax benefits and credits, OAS payments, and EI benefits begin to apply. With inflation, the real value of these set amounts is maintained only if the amounts are adjusted upward by the rate of inflation. For example, a basic personal allowance needs to be increased from $10,000 to $10,200 in a year in which inflation is at a rate of 2 percent. Where such adjustments are automatically made as prices rise, the tax system is said to be **indexed for inflation**. The purpose is to remove automatically the influence of inflation from real tax liabilities. This section discusses motivations for tax indexing, and whether the Canadian system of indexing is an adequate response to the problems posed by inflation.

How Inflation Can Affect Taxes

Economists customarily distinguish between "anticipated" and "unanticipated" inflation. The latter is generally viewed as being worse for efficiency, because it does not allow people to adjust their behaviour optimally to price-level changes. However, with an unindexed income tax system, even perfectly anticipated inflation causes distortions.

The most popularly understood distortion is the phenomenon known as **bracket creep**. Suppose that an individual's earnings and the price level both increase at the same rate over time. Then that person's **real income** (the amount of actual purchasing power) is unchanged. However, an unindexed tax system is based on the individual's **nominal income**—the number of dollars received. As nominal income increases, the individual is pushed into tax brackets with higher marginal tax rates. Hence, the proportion of income that is taxed increases despite the fact that real income stays the same. Even individuals who are not pushed into a higher bracket find more of their income taxed at the highest rate to which they are subject. Inflation brings about an automatic increase in real tax burdens without any legislative action.

---

[40] The situation is not quite this simple. Child Tax Benefit payments and GST credits are both affected by the combined incomes of spouses. Thus, a GST credit or Child Tax Benefit that is available to a single parent is subject to clawback when the parent marries, if the couple's combined incomes exceed the threshold amount—$35,000 in 2015. Furthermore, since 2007, senior citizen couples are allowed to split pension income, and since 2015 (and retroactively to the 2014 tax year) spouses or common-law partners with a child under 18 years of age may obtain a net reduction in their combined taxes by the family tax cut.

Another effect of inflation occurs when personal and other allowances are set in nominal terms. In an unindexed system, increases in the price level decrease their real value. Again, the effective tax rate increases as a consequence of inflation.

It turns out, however, that even with a simple proportional income tax without exemptions or deductions, inflation would distort tax burdens. To be sure, under such a system, general inflation would not affect the real tax burden on wage and salary incomes. If a worker's earnings during a year doubled, so would his or her taxes, and there would be no real effects. But inflation would change the real tax burden on capital income.

Suppose Calpurnia buys an asset for $5,000. Three years later, she sells it for $10,000. Suppose further that during the three years the general price level doubled. In real terms, selling the asset nets Calpurnia zero. However, capital gains liabilities are based on the difference between the nominal selling and buying prices. Hence, Calpurnia incurs a tax liability on half of the illusory capital gain of $5,000. In short, because the inflationary component of capital gains is subject to tax, the real tax burden depends on the inflation rate.

Those who receive taxable interest income are similarly affected. Suppose that the **nominal interest rate** (the rate observed in the market) is 16 percent. Suppose further that the anticipated rate of inflation is 12 percent. Then for someone who lends at the 16 percent nominal rate, the **real interest rate** is only 4 percent, because that is the percentage by which the lender's real purchasing power is increased. However, taxes are levied on nominal, not real, interest payments. Hence, tax must be paid on receipts that represent no gain in real income.

Let us consider this argument algebraically. Call the nominal interest rate i. Then, the after-tax nominal return to lending for an individual with a marginal tax rate of t is $(1 - t)i$. To find the real after-tax rate of return, we must subtract the expected rate of inflation, π. Hence, the real after-tax rate of return r, is

$$r = (1 - t)i - \pi \tag{17.1}$$

Suppose $t = .50$, $i = 10$ percent, and $\pi = 4$ percent. Then, although the nominal interest rate is 10 percent, the real after-tax return is only 1 percent.

Now suppose that any increase in the expected rate of inflation increases the nominal interest rate by the same amount; if inflation increases by four points, the nominal interest rate increases by four points. It might be expected that the two increases would cancel out, leaving the real after-tax rate of return unchanged at 1 percent. But Equation (17.1) contradicts this prediction. If π goes from 4 percent to 8 percent and i goes from 10 percent to 14 percent, then with t equal to 0.50, r decreases to -1 percent. Inflation, even though it is perfectly anticipated, is not "neutral." This is a direct consequence of the fact that nominal rather than real interest payments are taxed.

So far, we have been considering the issue from the point of view of lenders. Things are just the opposite for borrowers. In the absence of the tax system, the real rate paid by borrowers is the nominal rate minus the anticipated inflation rate. However, assuming the taxpayer satisfies certain criteria, the tax law allows deductibility of nominal interest payments from taxable income. Thus, debtors can subtract from taxable income the payments that represent no decrease in their real incomes. The tax burden on borrowers is *decreased* by inflation.

Coping With the Tax/Inflation Problem

During the 1950s and 1960s nominal tax rates and tax brackets were unchanged. Although annual inflation during this period was generally less than 4 percent, the consumer price index (CPI) rose by 72 percent over the 22 years from 1949 to 1971, and bracket creep led to increased tax rates on individuals with unchanged levels of real income. However, real incomes also rose rapidly during this period, and Canadians paid the higher taxes that were the result of bracket creep plus higher real incomes. Personal income taxes rose from 16 percent of government revenue in 1949 to 30 percent in 1970. This rapid change was one factor that led to the overall review of the tax system by the Royal Commission on Taxation in the 1960s.[41]

---

[41] Nonetheless, at a time of modest inflation in the mid-1960s, the commission concluded, "Because it is not possible to make provision for complete recognition of declines in purchasing power brought about by inflation, we have concluded that it should not be the function of the tax system to attempt to relieve only some segments of the population from the effects of inflation. The tax system should therefore, in our opinion, continue to be based on current dollars and not on constant dollars." Royal Commission on Taxation (1966: 349).

Inflation accelerated in the early 1970s, reaching 8 percent in 1973. Lenin is alleged to have said, "The way to crush the bourgeoisie is to grind them between the millstones of taxation and inflation." Although the interaction of taxes and inflation in Canada had not created quite such drastic effects, there was growing concern over the serious distortions caused by inflation. People became acutely aware of the fact that inflation leads to unlegislated increases in the real income tax burden. A family of four with constant real income of $56,667 (2009 dollars) paid 12.7 percent of personal income in 1954 and 17.7 percent in 1970, a 30 percent increase during a period when statutory rates and brackets did not change. Increases were proportionately larger for those with lower incomes. The government, in response, partially indexed the personal income tax system. In 1974, adjustments were made to personal, marital, dependant, age, and disability exemptions; tax-free earnings of dependants were also indexed, as were tax bracket limits. These changes had a major impact on taxes otherwise payable.[42]

Indexing was neither comprehensive nor permanent. No adjustment was made to interest payments, interest receipts, capital gains, or other costs of, or returns to, capital. This is due in part to the administrative complexity such a statute would entail. For example, as suggested earlier, increases in inflation generate real gains for debtors, because the real value of the amounts they have to repay decreases. In a fully indexed system, such capital gains would have to be measured and taxed, a task that would certainly be complex. Thus, significant distortions continued to be created by taxes levied on the nominal returns on capital assets.

Full indexing of exemptions and brackets was maintained from 1974 to 1983. Adjustments in 1984 and 1985 were limited by legislation to 6 percent and 5 percent, consistent with government wage and price policies, and from 1986 to 2000 adjustments were limited to the amount by which inflation exceeded 3 percent per annum. This sharply reduced the size of adjustments from 1988 to 1992, and eliminated adjustments after 1992 when the annual rate of inflation fell below 3 percent. Full indexing of tax brackets and tax credit levels was restored in 2000.

Should indexing be maintained or diminished? Some opponents of indexing argue that a system of periodic ad hoc adjustments is a good thing because it allows legislators to examine and revise other aspects of the Income Tax Act that may need changing. Others argue that indexing of the personal income tax, as it slows growth in income tax revenues, will lead to greater reliance on less-equitable forms of taxation. Proponents of indexing argue that reducing opportunities for revising the tax act may itself be a benefit, because it is desirable to have a stable and predictable tax law. Moreover, fewer opportunities to change the law also mean fewer chances for legislative mischief. Certainly the most important argument of those who favour indexing is that it eliminates unlegislated increases in real tax rates. They believe that allowing the real tax schedule to be changed systematically by a non-legislative process is antithetical to democratic values. The amounts of money involved are substantial; one estimate is that the indexing from 1974 to 1984 resulted in federal and provincial revenues in 1984 that were $19.5 billion, or 40 percent, less than they would have been without indexing.[43]

Proponents of indexing also note that its repeal would have a disproportionately large effect on the tax liabilities of low-income families. With the value of personal allowances unadjusted, families previously free from tax move into the ranks of the taxable as nominal incomes increase while real incomes remain unchanged. The clawback on Child Tax Benefits and GST credits also occurs at lower levels of real income, unless these amounts are fully indexed.

TREATMENT OF INTERNATIONAL INCOME

We now turn to the tax treatment of individual income that is earned abroad. Such income is potentially of interest to the tax authorities of the citizen's home and host governments. Canadian law recognizes the principle that the host country has the primary right to tax income earned within its borders. Taxation in Canada

---

[42] For an explanation of the rationale behind, and the effects of, indexing when introduced in 1974, see Allen, Dodge, and Poddar (1974). See also George Vukelich, "The Effect of Inflation on Real Tax Rates," *Canadian Tax Journal* 20(4) (July–August 1972); Gregory Jarvis and Roger S. Smith, "Real Income and Average Tax Rates: An Extension for the 1970–75 Period," *Canadian Tax Journal* 25(2) (March–April 1977).

[43] This was not a surprise. See Perry (1985) and Hull and Leonard (1974).

is based on residency, and if an individual is a resident of Canada, income earned abroad is also subject to Canadian tax.[44] To avoid double taxation of foreign-source income, Canada taxes income earned abroad, but allows a credit for tax paid to foreign governments.[45] Suppose that Smith's Canadian tax liability on her income earned in Germany is $7,000, and she had paid $5,500 in German income taxes. Then Smith, a Canadian resident, can take a $5,500 credit on her Canadian tax return, so she need pay only $1,500 to Canada Revenue Agency. A Canadian resident's total tax liability, then, is based on global income.

Since the Canadian system is a residence-based system, Canadian citizens who have established residence outside of Canada are not subject to tax on income earned outside of Canada, and need not submit Canadian tax returns. This contrasts with the U.S. system; U.S. citizens, wherever they reside, are taxable on their global income, with credits permitted for taxes paid to foreign governments.

Territorial versus global systems. Most countries, like Canada, adhere to a territorial system—a citizen earning income abroad and residing outside of Canada need pay tax only to the host government. In contrast, the philosophical premise of the U.S. system is that equity in taxation is defined on a citizenship basis.[46] If you are a U.S. citizen, the total amount of tax you pay should be roughly independent of whether you earn your income at home or abroad. We refer to this as a global system. Which system is better? It is hard to build a case for the superiority of one system over the other on either equity or efficiency grounds. The following paragraphs expand on the problem.

Equity. John, a Canadian citizen, and Sam, a U.S. citizen, both live and work in Hong Kong and have identical incomes. Because Canada has a territorial system, John pays tax only to Hong Kong. Sam, on the other hand, also owes money to the United States (provided that his U.S. tax bill is higher than his Hong Kong tax payment). Thus, Sam pays more tax than John, even though they have the same income and live in the same place. Although the Canadian territorial system produces equal treatment for residents of Hong Kong regardless of their nationality, it can lead to substantially different taxes on Canadian citizens with the same income but who choose to live in different countries, whether for tax or other reasons. Should horizontal equity be defined on the basis of nationality or residence? Each principle has some merit, but in general, no system of international tax coordination can satisfy both.

Efficiency. The global system may distort international production decisions. Suppose that American firms operating abroad have to pay the U.S. income tax for their American employees. Canadian firms, which operate under the territorial system, have no analogous obligation. Other things being the same, then, the U.S. companies may end up paying more for their labour and, hence, be at a cost disadvantage.[47] Canadian firms could conceivably win more contracts than the American firms, even if they are technologically equivalent.

On the other hand, a territorial system can produce a different distortion—in people's locational decisions. Canadian citizens may find their decision to work abroad influenced by the fact that their tax liability depends on where they live. Under the U.S. global regime, you cannot escape your country's tax collector unless you change citizenship. Hence, there is less incentive to relocate just for tax purposes.

Thus, the global system may distort production decisions, and the territorial system residential decisions. It is hard to know which distortion creates a larger efficiency cost. From an enforcement perspective, it is likely that the Canadian approach is the more practical.

---

[44] Whether or not one is considered a "resident" of Canada depends on a number of factors, including length of time in Canada in a year, ownership of property, maintenance of bank accounts, membership in organizations, and the maintenance of a home. Generally, if one spends 183 days or more in Canada in a year, one is deemed a resident; however, it is possible to be deemed a resident even if in the country for less than 183 days.

[45] The credit cannot exceed what the Canadian tax on the foreign income would have been.

[46] For further details, see Ault and Bradford (1990).

[47] This assumes (a) the incidence of the U.S. tax falls on employers rather than employees, and (b) American companies cannot respond simply by hiring Canadian or other non-U.S. workers. The validity of assumption (a) depends on the elasticity of supply of U.S. workers to U.S. firms abroad. To the extent the supply curve is not horizontal, employees bear part of the tax. See Chapter 14.

SUMMARY

- Income tax systems are the primary revenue source for provinces and for the federal government. Personal income taxes account for 24 percent of total government revenues in Canada.

- Computation of individual income tax liability has four major steps: measuring total income, converting total income to taxable income, calculating tax before allowable tax credits, and deducting tax credits to obtain taxes payable.

- A traditional benchmark measure of income is the Haig-Simons definition: Income during a given period is the net change in the individual's power to consume.

- Implementation of the Haig-Simons criterion is confounded by several difficulties: (1) Income must be measured net of the expenses of earning it. (2) Unrealized capital gains are not easily gauged. (3) The imputed income from durable goods is not directly observable. (4) It is difficult to measure the value of in-kind receipts.

- Critics of the Haig-Simons criterion argue that it does not necessarily guarantee either fair or efficient outcomes.

- The Canadian income tax base excludes (1) imputed income from homeownership and other forms of imputed income; (2) employer contributions to pension, medical, and dental plans; (3) gifts and inheritances; (4) lottery winnings; and (5) half of realized capital gains.

- Deductions reduce taxable income and are allowed for expenses incurred in earning taxable income, to encourage retirement savings and to recognize alimony payments.

- Five basic marginal tax rates are applied by the federal government to taxable income—0, 15, 22, 26, and 29 percent.

- Adjustments in the form of tax credits, calculated as 15 percent of set allowances, are provided for the taxpayer and his or her dependants. These credits are subtracted from federal taxes otherwise payable.

- Tax credits are provided for charitable donations, medical expenses in excess of 3 percent of net income, certain education and tuition expenses, and required EI, CPP, and QPP premiums.

- Deductions and credits both change after-tax relative prices, and this affects economic behaviour.

- Tax expenditures are the revenues forgone due to preferential tax treatment. In some instances, a tax expenditure may be the most effective way to stimulate a particular private activity.

- Because of surtaxes, payroll taxes, and clawbacks, the effective marginal rates may be much higher, with a more complex structure, than the five basic rates of 0, 15, 22, 26, and 29 percent. Provincial rates and surtaxes further complicate applicable marginal rates.

- No system of personal income taxation can simultaneously achieve increasing marginal tax rates, marriage neutrality, and equal taxes for families with equal incomes. The Canadian tax system has generally adhered to marriage neutrality, with the individual as the taxable unit upon which the personal income tax is based.

- Bracket widths, personal and dependant tax credits, and tax-free earnings of dependants are indexed against inflation. The decision to limit indexing from 1986 to 2000 to the excess of inflation over 3 percent resulted in a substantial increase in personal income taxes on constant levels of real income.

- Canada follows a territorial, or residence-based, system with respect to the tax treatment of income earned in other countries. Canadian residents are taxed on their global incomes, but Canadian citizens who reside outside of Canada are taxed only on income earned in Canada. This contrasts with the U.S. system, which taxes global income of U.S. citizens wherever they reside. In both cases, tax credits are provided for taxes paid to the country in which income arises.

EXERCISES

1. The tax credit for charitable donations rises from 15 percent on the first $200 to 29 percent on donations over $200. Why would the heads of organizations dependent on charitable contributions think it important that the credit be at a rate of 29 percent?

2.*Jones, who has a personal income tax rate of 40 percent, holds an oil stock that appreciates in value by 10 percent each year. He bought the stock one year ago. Jones's stockbroker now wants him to switch the oil stock for a gold stock that is equally risky. Jones has decided that if he holds on to the oil stock, he will keep it only one more year and then sell it. If he sells the oil stock now, he will invest all the (after-tax) proceeds of the sale in the gold stock and then sell the gold stock one year from now. What is the minimum rate of return the gold stock must pay for Jones to make the switch? Relate your answer to the tax on capital gains and to the lock-in effect.

3. According to well-placed sources, in 1994 the Department of Finance was considering a change in the tax treatment of employer-provided dental care plans. Under the policy being considered, the value of the dental care plans would be included in workers' taxable incomes. Evaluate this proposal from the standpoint of the Haig-Simons criterion. How do you think it would alter the composition of compensation packages?

4. The purpose of this problem is to consider how effective marginal tax rates are affected by various clawbacks, payroll taxes, and surtaxes.

   a. Consider a family of four (two children, age 10 and 12, and one wage earner with a dependent spouse) whose net income places it in the range of the GST and Child Tax Benefit clawbacks—net income = $44,800—and whose taxable income places it in the 22 percent federal tax bracket. (Ignore provincial taxes.)

      i. Suppose the taxpayer's income increases by $2,500. Given a 22 percent tax rate, by how much does the tax liability increase, given the GST and Child Tax Benefit clawbacks?

      ii. The earned income of the taxpayer is subject to both CPP and EI premiums. How do these payroll taxes alter the effective marginal tax rate that applies to the additional $2,500?

      iii. Combine your answers from parts (i) and (ii) to find the effective marginal tax rate. (Divide the change in tax liability by the $2,500 change in income.)

   b. Now consider a different family (same composition with a single wage earner) with $117,000 in salary income. Suppose this taxpayer receives another $2,500 in before-tax salary income.

      i. Assuming a 26 percent federal marginal tax rate, what is the change in tax liability, given the GST and Child Tax Benefit clawbacks and the EI and CPP payroll taxes (again ignoring provincial taxes)?

      ii. Determine the effective marginal tax rate for this taxpayer.

5. Suppose that a taxpayer has a marginal personal income tax rate (including provincial taxes) of 40 percent. The nominal interest rate is 12 percent, and the expected inflation rate is 5 percent.

   a. What is the real, after-tax rate of interest?

   b. Suppose that the expected inflation rate increases by three percentage points to 8 percent, and the nominal interest rate increases by the same amount. What happens to the real after-tax rate of return?

   c.*If the inflation rate increases as in part (b), by how much would the nominal interest rate have to increase to keep the real after-tax interest rate at the same level as in part (a)? Can you generalize your answer using an algebraic formula?

---

* Difficult

6. You will need a calculator for this exercise. Sam earns $4,000, and he wants to save it for retirement, which is 10 years away. He can either pay tax on the amount and save the rest of it in a taxable account, or he can obtain a tax deduction by putting the full amount into an RRSP. When he cashes in the RRSP in 10 years he must pay tax on the principal and on the accumulated interest. Suppose that Sam can receive an annual rate of return of 8 percent, and his marginal tax rate is 25 percent today and when he retires. Determine how much net-of-tax money he will have upon retirement under each option.

7. Parents with children under 18 can split their incomes for tax purposes: one spouse may shift up to $50,000 to the other in order to lower their combined income taxes. Suppose this policy is implemented in Hibernia, where the tax structure is 20 percent of income up to $30,000, and 40 percent of all income in excess of $30,000. The table below gives the incomes of three married couples. Alyss and Will have a 6-year-old daughter, while Paulina and Halt have an 18-year-old son, and Cassandra and Horace are childless. Using the incomes in the table, compare the total tax paid by each couple before and after the tax proposal. Using your results, discuss the merits of the proposal in terms of principles 2 and 3 discussed in the chapter (where you should consider the idea of "child neutrality" in place of "marriage neutrality").

Alyss	Will	Paulina	Halt	Cassandra	Horace
$70,000	$10,000	$70,000	$10,000	$40,000	$40,000

8. Suppose the Working Income Tax Benefit (WITB) tops up a single individual's income by 25 percent of the amount that employment earnings exceed $3000, up to a maximum payment of $1000.

   a. Assume that the refundable WITB credit is reduced by 15 percent on the amount of earnings in excess of $11,500. Over what range of earnings is the credit at its maximum value? At what income is the credit reduced to zero?

   b. Now let the statutory income tax be a flat rate of 30 percent, with a basic personal exemption of $5,000. Ignoring all other taxes and program benefits in the economy, except for the income tax and the WITB, calculate and describe the effective marginal tax rate (EMTR) faced by this individual on income ranging from zero to $20,000. Discuss the incentive effects associated with this EMTR schedule, regarding the decision to join the workforce and to increase hours worked, say, from part-time to full-time.

9. The *New York Times* published an article about a man who claimed that his tax rate was 102 percent of his income (Stewart, 2012). He computed this figure by taking the ratio of his tax payments to his taxable income. Comment on whether this is a meaningful way to measure one's average tax rate. Include in your discussion a careful definition of the term *taxable income*.

CHAPTER 18

Personal Taxation and Behaviour

Neither will it be that a people overlaid with taxes should ever become valiant and martial.

—Francis Bacon (1561–1626)

AFTER READING THIS CHAPTER, THE STUDENT SHOULD BE ABLE TO:

LO1 Construct the leisure–income budget constraint and use it to analyze the effect on hours of labour supplied resulting from a proportional income tax.

LO2 Decompose the change in hours of labour supplied into a substitution effect and an income effect.

LO3 Summarize the empirical findings on labour supply elasticities.

LO4 Describe the Laffer curve and explain its relevance for tax policy.

LO5 Construct the intertemporal budget constraint and use it to analyze the effect on saving resulting from taxing interest income, both when interest payments are deductible and when interest payments are nondeductible.

LO6 Summarize the evidence on the impacts of tax-assisted savings plans on total saving.

LO7 Describe the preferential tax treatment of owner-occupied housing.

LO8 Explain why a proportional tax on the return on assets has an ambiguous effect on portfolio composition.

The theory of taxation makes clear that, ultimately, both the incidence and efficiency of a tax system depend on how it affects people's behaviour. The impact of taxes on behaviour is a matter of intense debate, both among academics and politicians. Some argue that taxes have very little effect: "Disincentives, like the weather, are much talked about, but relatively few people do anything about them" (Break, 1957: 549). Others suggest that high marginal tax rates lead to "worsening work attitudes, high absenteeism rates, reluctance to work overtime and to assume risks, and the lowest personal saving rate[s]" (Roberts, 1981: 26).

As shown in Chapter 17, the income tax affects incentives for a myriad of decisions—everything from the purchase of housing to the amount of charitable donations. We choose to focus on four particularly important topics that have been studied intensively—the effects of taxation on labour supply, saving, housing consumption, and portfolio decisions.

LABOUR SUPPLY

In 2014, about 18 million Canadians worked an average of about thirty hours per week and received total earnings of roughly $994 billion—approximately 50 percent of GDP.[1] How labour supply is determined and whether taxes affect it are the issues to which we now turn.

---

[1] Part-time workers accounted for 19 percent of employment. The data are from Statistics Canada, CANSIM database Tables 282-0087, 282-0089, 382-0006, 380-0064.

FIGURE 18.1

UTILITY MAXIMIZING CHOICE OF LEISURE AND INCOME

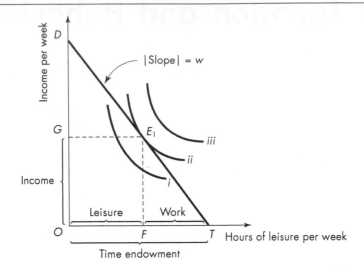

Theoretical Considerations

Hercules is deciding how much of his time to devote each week to work and how much to leisure. In Chapter 12, on welfare spending, we showed how this choice can be analyzed graphically. To review, the main points in that discussion follow:

1. The number of hours available for market work and nonmarket uses ("leisure") is referred to as the **time endowment**. In Figure 18.1, it is distance OT on the horizontal axis. Assuming that all time not spent on leisure is devoted to market work, any point on the horizontal axis simultaneously indicates hours of leisure and hours of work.

2. The budget constraint in this diagram shows the combinations of leisure and income available to an individual, given his or her wage rate. If Hercules's wage rate is $\$w$ per hour, then his budget constraint is a straight line whose slope in absolute value is w. In Figure 18.1, this is represented by line TD.

3. The particular point on the budget constraint that is chosen depends on the individual's tastes. Assume that preferences for leisure and income can be represented by normal, convex-to-the-origin indifference curves. Three such curves are labelled i, ii, and iii in Figure 18.1. Utility is maximized at point E_1, where Hercules devotes OF hours to leisure, works FT hours, and earns income OG.

We are now in a position to analyze the effects of taxation. Suppose that the government levies a tax on earnings at rate t. The tax reduces the reward for working an hour from $\$w$ to $\$(1 - t)w$. When Hercules consumes an hour of leisure, he now gives up only $\$(1 - t)w$, not $\$w$. In effect, the tax reduces the opportunity cost of an hour of leisure. This observation is represented in Figure 18.2. The budget constraint facing Hercules is no longer TD. Rather, it is the flatter line, TH, whose slope in absolute value is $(1 - t)w$. Because of the tax, the original income–leisure choice, E_1, is no longer attainable. Hercules must choose a point somewhere along the after-tax budget constraint TH. In Figure 18.2, this is E_2, where Hercules consumes OI hours of leisure, works IT hours, and has an after-tax income of OG'. The tax lowers Hercules's labour supply from FT hours to IT hours.

Can we, therefore, conclude that a "rational" individual *always* reduces labour supply in response to a proportional tax? To answer this question, consider Theseus, who faces exactly the same before- and after-tax budget constraints as Hercules, and who chooses to work the same number of hours (FT) before imposition of the tax. As indicated in Figure 18.3, when Theseus is taxed, he *increases* his hours of work from FT to JT. There is nothing "irrational" about this. Depending on a person's tastes, it is possible to want to work more, less, or the same amount after a tax is imposed.

FIGURE 18.2

PROPORTIONAL INCOME TAX DECREASING HOURS OF LABOUR SUPPLIED

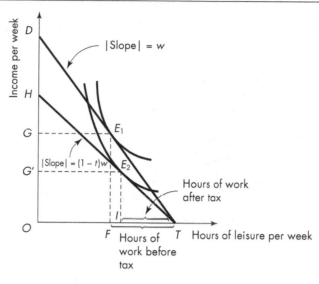

The source of the ambiguity is the conflict between two effects generated by the tax, the **substitution effect** and the **income effect**. When the tax reduces the take-home wage, the opportunity cost of leisure goes down, and there is a tendency to substitute leisure for work. This is the substitution effect, and it tends to decrease labour supply. At the same time, for any number of hours worked, the tax reduces the individual's income. Assuming that leisure is a normal good, for any number of hours worked this loss in income leads to a reduction in consumption of leisure, other things being the same. But a decrease in leisure means an increase in work. The income effect, therefore, tends to induce an individual to work more. Thus, the two effects work in opposite directions. It is simply impossible to know on the basis of theory alone whether the income effect or substitution effect dominates. For Hercules, shown in Figure 18.2, the substitution effect dominates. For Theseus, shown in Figure 18.3, the income effect is more important.

FIGURE 18.3

PROPORTIONAL INCOME TAX INCREASING HOURS OF LABOUR SUPPLIED

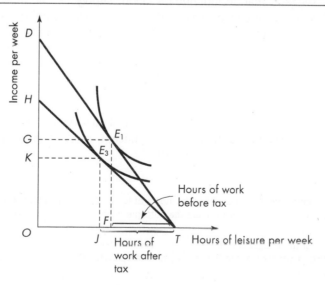

FIGURE 18.4

LEISURE–INCOME CHOICE UNDER A PROGRESSIVE INCOME TAX

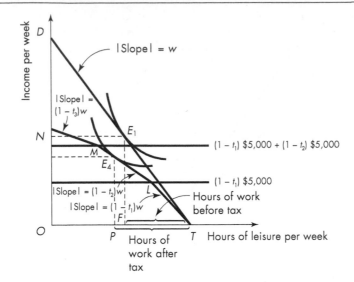

The analysis of a progressive tax system is very similar to that of a proportional tax. Suppose that Hercules is now confronted with increasing marginal tax rates: t_1 on his first $5,000 of earnings, t_2 on his second $5,000 of earnings, and t_3 on all income above $10,000. As before, prior to the tax the budget line is TD, which is depicted in Figure 18.4. After tax, the budget constraint is the kinked line $TLMN$. Up to $5,000 of before-tax income, the opportunity cost of an hour of leisure is $(1 - t_1)w$, which is the slope (in absolute value) of segment TL. At point L, Hercules's income is $(1 - t_1) \times \$5,000$. On segment ML, the absolute value of the slope is $(1 - t_2)w$. ML is flatter than TL because t_2 is greater than t_1. At point M, after-tax income is $(1 - t_1) \times \$5,000 + (1 - t_2) \times \$5,000$; this is after-tax income at point L plus the increment to income after receiving an additional $5,000 that is taxed at rate t_2. Finally, on segment MN the slope is $(1 - t_3)w$, which is even flatter. Depending on his preferences, Hercules can end up anywhere on $TLMN$. In Figure 18.4, he maximizes utility at E_4 where he works PT hours.[2]

Empirical Findings on Labour Supply

The theory just discussed suggests that an individual's labour supply decision depends on (a) variables that affect the position of the budget constraint, especially the after-tax wage,[3] and (b) variables that affect the individual's indifference curves for leisure and income, such as age, sex, and marital status. Econometricians have estimated regression equations in which they seek to explain annual hours of work as a function of such variables. Although considerable differences in estimates arise due to inevitable differences in samples, time periods, and statistical techniques, it would be fair to say that the following two important general tendencies have been observed:

1. For males between the ages of roughly 25 to 60, the effect of changes in the net wage on hours of work is small in absolute value and is often statistically insignificant. Most elasticity estimates fall in the range between −0.2 and 0.2 (Hum and Simpson, 1991: 19).

---

[2] An issue that has received substantial attention is the effect on hours of work of replacing a proportional tax with a progressive tax that yields the same tax revenue. Hemming (1980) shows that the outcome depends on the shape of the indifference curves and exactly how progressivity is defined.

[3] Another important determinant of the budget constraint is nonlabour income: dividends, interest, transfer payments, and so forth. Nonlabour income causes a parallel shift in the budget constraint; there is a constant addition to income at every level of hours worked.

2. Although estimated labour supply elasticities for women vary widely, the hours of work and labour force participation decisions of married women in Canada appear somewhat more sensitive to changes in the net wage. Estimates for elasticities of hours worked with respect to the net wage are generally between −0.2 and 0.5.[4]

The conclusion that both male and female labour supply in Canada is relatively inelastic is reinforced in a more recent study by Sand (2005), who found that the 2001 personal income tax reforms at the federal level and in British Columbia and Alberta had little impact on individual hours of work. However, there is evidence that labour force *participation* is relatively sensitive to marginal tax rates (see Meyer and Rosenbaum, 2001, and Rogerson and Wallenius, 2009).

Some Caveats

The theoretical and empirical results just described are certainly more useful than the uninformed guesses often heard in political debates. Nevertheless, we should be aware of some important qualifications.

Demand-side considerations. The preceding analyses ignore effects that changes in the supply of labour might have on the demand side of the market. Suppose that taxes on married women were lowered in such a way that their net wages increased by 10 percent. With a labour supply elasticity of 0.4, their hours of work would increase by 4 percent. If firms could absorb all of these hours at the new net wage, that would be the end of the story. More typically, as more hours of work are offered, there is a tendency to bid down the *before*-tax wage. This mitigates the original increase in the *after*-tax wage, so that the final increase in hours of work would be less than originally guessed.

The situation becomes even more complicated when we realize that major changes in work decisions could influence consumption patterns in other markets. The resulting relative price changes might feed back on labour market decisions. For example, if married women increased their hours of work, the demand for childcare would probably increase. To the extent that this raised the price of childcare, it might discourage some mothers of small children from working, at least in the short run. Clearly, tracing through these general equilibrium implications is a complicated business. Most investigators are willing to assume that the first-round effects are a reasonable approximation of the final result.

Individual versus group effects. Our focus has been on how much an individual will work under alternative tax regimes. It is difficult to use such results to predict how the total hours of work supplied by a group of workers will change. When the tax schedule changes, incentives change differently for different people. For example, in a move from a proportional to a progressive tax, low-income workers may find themselves facing lower marginal tax rates, whereas just the opposite may be true for those with high incomes. It is quite possible, then, that the labour supplies of the two groups could move in opposite directions, making the overall outcome difficult to predict. A further complication is that the labour supply elasticity might vary by income level.

Other dimensions of labour supply. The number of hours worked annually is an important and interesting indicator of labour supply. But the effective amount of labour supplied by an individual depends on more than the number of hours elapsed at the workplace. Presumably, a highly educated, healthy, well-motivated worker is more productive than a counterpart who lacks these qualities. Some have expressed fears that taxes induce people to invest too little in the acquisition of skills. Economic theory yields surprising insights into how taxes might affect the accumulation of **human capital**—investments that people make in themselves to increase their productivity.

Consider Hera, who is contemplating entering an on-the-job training program. Suppose that, over her lifetime, the program increases Hera's earnings by an amount whose present value is *B*. However, participation in the program reduces the amount of time currently available to Hera for income-producing activity, and hence costs her some amount, *C*, in forgone wages. If she is sensible, Hera enters the program only if the benefits exceed the costs:

$$B - C > 0 \qquad (18.1)$$

---

[4] See Hum and Simpson (1991: 19–23). They find that "the majority of the Canadian results . . . seem at odds with the U.S. results that female labour supply is more sensitive to wage rate variation. The results for most of the studies suggest labour supply behaviour for adult females that is not very different from that of U.S. adult males" (p. 24) (where there is little effect). Note that these estimates include both substitution and income effects. That is, they are uncompensated responses. See Hum and Simpson (1994) and Meghir and Phillips (2008) for surveys of labour supply estimation.

Now suppose that Hera's earnings are subjected to a proportional tax at rate t. The tax takes away some of the higher wages earned by virtue of participation in the training program. One might guess that the tax, therefore, lowers the likelihood that she will participate. This reasoning is misleading. To see why, assume for the moment that after the tax Hera continues to work the same number of hours as she did before.[5] The tax does indeed reduce the benefits of the training program from B to $(1 - t)B$. But at the same time, it reduces the costs. Recall that the costs of the program are the forgone wages. Because these wages would have been subject to tax, Hera gives up not C, but only $(1 - t)C$. The decision to enter the program is based on whether after-tax benefits exceed after-tax costs:

$$(1 - t)B - (1 - t)C = (1 - t)(B - C) > 0. \qquad (18.2)$$

A glance at Equation (18.2) indicates that it is exactly equivalent to Equation (18.1). Any combination of benefits and costs that was acceptable before the earnings tax is acceptable afterward. In this model, a proportional earnings tax reduces benefits and cost in the same proportion and, therefore, has no effect on human capital investment.

A key assumption here is that labour supply is constant after the tax is imposed. Suppose instead that Hera increases her supply of labour. (The income effect predominates.) In this case, the tax leads to an increase in human capital accumulation. The after-tax labour supply is, in effect, the utilization rate of the human capital investment. The more hours a person works, the greater the payoff to an increase in the wage rate from a given human capital investment. Therefore, if the tax induces more work, it makes human capital investments more attractive, other things being the same. Conversely, if the substitution effect predominates so that labour supply decreases, human capital accumulation is discouraged by the tax.

This simple model ignores the important fact that usually the returns to a human capital investment cannot be known with certainty. Moreover, some types of human capital investment involve costs other than forgone earnings. University tuition is an obvious example. Finally, when the tax system is progressive, the benefits and costs of human capital investments may be taxed at different rates. However, when such factors are considered, the basic result is confirmed—from a theoretical point of view, the effect of earnings taxation on human capital accumulation is ambiguous. Unfortunately, little empirical work on this important question is available.

The compensation package. The basic theory of labour supply assumes that the hourly wage is the only reward for working. In reality, employers often offer employees a compensation *package* that includes not only wages, but also health benefits for dental and eye care, group life insurance, pensions, and "perks," such as access to a company car and in-house sports facilities. As we noted in Chapter 17, this nonwage component of compensation may not be subject to taxation. When marginal tax rates fall, the relative attractiveness of such untaxed forms of income declines, and vice versa. Hence, changes in taxes affect the composition of the compensation package.[6]

The expenditure side. The standard analysis of labour supply and taxation ignores the disposition of the tax receipts. However, at least some of the revenues are used to purchase public goods, the availability of which can affect work decisions. If the tax money is used to provide recreational facilities, such as provincial and national parks, we expect the demand for leisure to increase, *ceteris paribus*. On the other hand, expenditure on childcare facilities for working parents might increase labour supply. Ideally, we should examine the labour supply consequences of the entire budget, not just the tax side. In practice, empirical investigators have not learned much about how public expenditures affect work decisions. This is because of the difficulties involved in determining how individuals value public good consumption, a problem that we have already discussed in several different contexts.

Labour Supply and Tax Revenues

So far, our emphasis has been on finding the amount of labour supply associated with any given tax regime. We now explore the related issue of how tax collections vary with the tax rate.

---

[5] In terms of our earlier discussion, the income and substitution effects just offset each other.

[6] In an econometric analysis of fringe benefits received by U.S. academics, Hamermesh and Woodbury (1990) found that a 1 percent increase in the value of fringe benefits resulting from higher tax rates induces an increase in fringe benefits of about 2 percent.

FIGURE 18.5

TAX RATES, HOURS OF WORK, AND TAX REVENUE

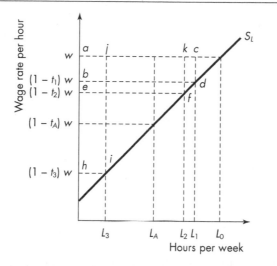

Consider the supply curve of labour, S_L, depicted in Figure 18.5. It shows the optimal amount of work for each after-tax wage, other things being the same.[7] Hours of work increase with the net wage—the substitution effect dominates. The following argument could be repeated using a labour supply curve for which the income effect is dominant.

The before-tax wage, w, is associated with L_0 hours of work. Obviously, since the tax rate is zero, no revenue is collected. Now suppose that a proportional tax at rate t_1 is imposed. The net wage is $(1 - t_1)w$, and labour supply is L_1 hours. Tax collections are equal to the tax per hour worked (ab) times the number of hours worked (ac), or rectangle $abdc$. Similar reasoning indicates that if the tax rate were raised to t_2, tax revenues would be $eakf$. Area $eakf$ exceeds $abdc$—a higher tax rate leads to greater revenue collections. Does this mean that the government can always collect more revenue by increasing the tax rate? No. For example, at tax rate t_3, revenues $haji$ are less than those at the lower rate t_2. Although the tax collected *per hour* is very high at t_3, the number of hours has decreased so much that the product of the tax rate and hours is fairly low. Indeed, as the tax rate approaches 100 percent, people stop working altogether and tax revenues fall to zero.

All of this is summarized compactly in Figure 18.6, which shows the tax rate on the horizontal axis and tax revenue on the vertical. At very low tax rates, revenue collections are low. As tax rates increase, revenues increase, reaching a maximum at rate t_A. For rates exceeding t_A, revenues begin to fall, eventually diminishing to zero. Note that it would be absurd for the government to choose any tax rate exceeding t_A, because tax rates could be reduced without the government suffering any revenue loss.

Figure 18.6 has been the centre of a major political controversy that, although centred in the United States, affected policy in Canada. This was largely due to the well-publicized assertion by economist Arthur B. Laffer that the United States has operated to the right of t_A (see Laffer, 1979). In the popular press, the tax rate–tax revenue relationship is known as the **Laffer curve.** The notion that tax rate reductions would create no revenue losses became an important tenet of the supply-side economics espoused by the Reagan administration in the United States; it continues to be a potent force in policy debates and was one of the factors contributing to reductions in marginal tax rates in the 1980s in Canada as well as in the United States.

The popular debate surrounding the Laffer curve has been confused and confusing. A few points are worth making:

- The shape of a Laffer curve is determined by the elasticity of labour with respect to the net wage. For any change in the tax rate, there is a corresponding percentage change in the net wage. Whether tax revenues rise or fall is determined by whether changes in hours worked offset the change in the tax rate. This is precisely the issue of the elasticity of labour supply investigated by public finance economists.

---

[7] The labour supply curve (or equivalently, the leisure demand curve) can be derived from the individual's indifference map.

FIGURE 18.6

TAX RATES VERSUS TAX REVENUE

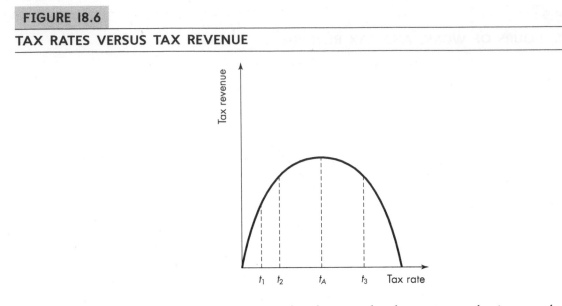

- Some critics of supply-side economics argue that the very idea that tax rate reductions can lead to increased revenue is absurd. However, the discussion surrounding Figure 18.6 suggests that, in principle, lower tax rates can indeed lead to higher revenue collections.

- It is, therefore, an empirical question whether or not the economy is actually operating to the right of t_A. As noted earlier, the consensus among economists who have studied taxes and labour supply is that the overall elasticities are modest in size. It is safe to conclude that the economy is not operating to the right of t_A.[8] Tax rate reductions are unlikely to be self-financing in the sense of unleashing so much labour supply that tax revenues do not fall.

- Changes in labour supply are not the only way in which increased tax rates can affect tax revenues. As noted earlier, people can substitute nontaxable forms of income for wages when tax rates go up, so that even with a fixed supply of labour, tax revenues can fall. In the same way, people (especially those with high incomes) can substitute nontaxable forms of capital income, such as investments in Tax-Free Savings Accounts (see Chapter 17) for taxable forms of capital income. Or individuals may cheat more when tax rates increase. Tax rates may also affect willingness to acquire new skills, assume more responsibility, work with greater intensity, move, travel, or undertake other activities that enhance productivity. Based on a survey of the literature, Feldstein (2008) concludes that tax rates have a substantial impact on taxable income. For middle- and high-income taxpayers, he estimates that the elasticity of taxable income with respect to the marginal tax rate is 0.5. This estimate implies, for example, that reducing the marginal tax rate on a typical high-income individual from 40 percent to 30 percent would increase her taxable income by more than 12 percent. Thus, the decrease in revenue would be less than if there were no behavioural response. On the other hand, the tax decrease would not be self-financing. Taxpayers with very high incomes appear to respond the most to changes in tax rates. Milligan and Smart (2014) report an elasticity of taxable income in Canada of 0.689 for the top 1 percent of earners and 1.451 for the top 0.1 percent.[9] These estimates suggest that the peak of the Laffer curve for a marginal tax rate applying to a tax bracket for the top 1 percent is about 60 percent.

- One way to substitute nontaxable for taxable income is to shift from the formal to the informal, or underground, economy. Although debate continues, there is evidence that indicates a positive linkage between tax rates in Canada (and elsewhere) and growth in the underground economy (Spiro, 1994, and Schneider and Enste, 2000). Morissette (2014) estimated the size of the underground economy in Canada to be 2.3 percent of GDP in 2011.

---

[8] Brewer and Browne (2009) estimate that t_A is about 60 percent in the United Kingdom. The figure seems plausible for Canada as well. The estimates of Dahlby and Ferede (2015: Table 2) indicate that the provincial personal income tax rates are to the left of the revenue-maximizing point.

[9] As the estimates by Milligan and Smart (2014) are based on variations in provincial tax rates, the elasticities may overestimate the impacts of changes in federal tax rates.

- Even if tax revenues fail to increase when tax rates fall, it does not mean that tax-rate reduction is necessarily undesirable. As emphasized in previous chapters, determination of the optimal tax system depends on a wide array of social and economic considerations. Those who believe that the government sector is too large should presumably be quite happy to see tax revenues reduced.

Overview

In the analysis of taxes and labour supply, economic theory tells us which variables to examine but provides no firm answers. Econometric work indicates that for prime-age males, hours of work are not much affected by taxes. For married women, on the other hand, taxes may be more likely to reduce labour force participation rates and hours of work. This, of course, may change. An important qualification is that the effect of taxes on other dimensions of labour supply, such as education and job-training decisions or the willingness to assume more on-the-job responsibility and risk, is not well understood.

Some politicians have suggested that if tax rates were cut, such large amounts of labour supply would be unleashed that Canada Revenue Agency would suffer no revenue loss. On the basis of what is known about labour supply, such an effect is unlikely. However, the notion that tax cuts might be self-financing is more plausible (although not proven) when one considers other ways in which taxpayers can substitute nontaxable forms of income for taxable ones.

SAVING

A second type of behaviour that may be affected by taxation is saving. Most modern theoretical and empirical work on saving decisions is based on the **life-cycle model**, which was introduced in Chapter 11 and says that individuals' consumption and saving decisions during a given year are the result of a planning process that considers their lifetime economic circumstances. That is, the amount you save each year depends not only on your income that year, but also on the income that you expect in the future and the income you have had in the past. This section uses a life-cycle model to explore the impact of taxes on saving decisions.

Consider Scrooge, who expects to live two periods: "now" (period 0) and the "future" (period 1). Scrooge has an income of I_0 dollars now and knows that his income will be I_1 dollars in the future. (Think of "now" as "working years," when I_0 is labour earnings, and the "future" as retirement years, when I_1 is fixed pension income.) His problem is to decide how much to consume in each period. When Scrooge decides how much to consume, he simultaneously decides how much to save or borrow. If his consumption this period exceeds his current income, he must borrow. If his consumption is less than current income, he saves.

The first step is to depict the possible combinations of present consumption (c_0) and future consumption (c_1) available to Scrooge—his **intertemporal budget constraint**. In Chapter 11, we made the following key observations about the intertemporal budget constraint:

- One option available to Scrooge is to consume all his income just as it comes in—to consume I_0 in the present and I_1 in the future. This bundle is called the endowment point. The intertemporal budget constraint must pass through the endowment point.
- Provided that the individual can borrow and lend at an interest rate of r, the constraint is a straight line whose slope in absolute value is $1 + r$.[10]

Scrooge's budget constraint is drawn as MN in Figure 18.7; note that it runs through the endowment point A. To determine which point along MN is actually chosen, we introduce Scrooge's preferences for future as opposed to present consumption, which are represented by conventionally shaped indifference curves in

---

[10] To represent the budget line algebraically, note that the fundamental constraint facing Scrooge is that the present value of his consumption equals the present value of his income. (See Chapter 3 for an explanation of present value.) The present value of his consumption is $c_0 + c_1/(1 + r)$, while the present value of his income stream is $I_0 + I_1/(1 + r)$. Thus, his selection of c_0 and c_1 must satisfy $c_0 + c_1/(1 + r) = I_0 + I_1/(1 + r)$. The reader can verify that, viewed as a function of c_0 and c_1, this is a straight line whose slope is $-(1 + r)$ and that passes through the point (I_0, I_1).

FIGURE 18.7

UTILITY MAXIMIZING CHOICE OF PRESENT AND FUTURE CONSUMPTION

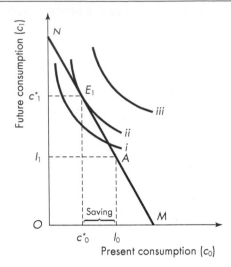

Figure 18.7. Under the reasonable assumption that more consumption is preferred over less consumption, curves farther to the northeast represent higher levels of utility.

Subject to budget constraint MN, the point at which Scrooge maximizes utility is E_1. At this point, Scrooge consumes c_0^* in the present and c_0^* in the future. With this information, it is easy to find how much Scrooge saves. Because present income, I_0, exceeds present consumption, c_0^*, then by definition the difference, $I_0 - c_0^*$, is saving.

IN THE NEWS

MARGINAL TAX RATES IN THE 2015 FEDERAL ELECTION

The platform of the Liberal party in the 2015 federal election included a change in marginal tax rates on personal income. Those earning between $44,700 and $89,401 would see their federal marginal tax rate drop from 22 percent to 20.5 percent, while the rate on incomes above $200,000 would increase from 29 to 33 percent. The rate changes were intended as a revenue-neutral swap: up $3 billion at the top and down $3 billion in the middle. Reaction to the party's proposal to raise the top income tax rate illustrates the perennial debate about the incentives created by income taxes. The reform would push the combined federal-provincial top marginal tax rate above 50 percent in some provinces (53.53% in Ontario and 53.3% in Quebec), "a psychological threshold that economists have long warned will encourage tax avoidance and disappoint government expectations for extra cash," wrote one columnist. A former chief economic analyst at Statistics Canada elaborated with, "The tax base shrinks as taxes go up because high earners resort more to tax avoidance—by changing their residency, sheltering income, getting paid in stock options, or hiring even better accountants." Not everyone agrees that the rich would flee from the tax hike. An editorial noted that in New York City the combined federal, state, and city marginal tax rate is 50.7 percent on incomes above $411,000, while it is 50.9 percent in California. The Canadian political debate over increasing income taxes on the "top 1 percent," which is echoed in the United States and in European countries, clearly pits concerns about rising income inequality with the efficiency costs of tax avoidance behaviour.

Based on Den Tandt (2015), Clark and DeVries (2015), and "Trudeau's new high-income bracket may encourage tax avoidance, economists warn." *The Globe and Mail*, May 5, 2015.

Complete references for this feature can be found in the References section on page 488.

FIGURE 18.8

INTEREST TAXED AND INTEREST PAYMENTS DEDUCTIBLE: SAVING DECREASES

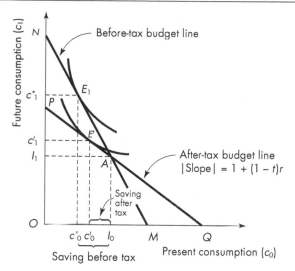

Of course, this does not prove that it is always rational to save. If the highest feasible indifference curve had been tangent to the budget line below point A, present consumption would have exceeded I_0, and Scrooge would have borrowed. Although the following analysis of taxation assumes Scrooge is a saver, the same techniques can be applied if he is a borrower.

We now consider how the amount of saving changes when a proportional tax on interest income is introduced.[11] In this context, it is important to specify whether payments of interest by borrowers are deductible from taxable income. While interest payments for consumption expenditures are generally not deductible, it may, in some cases, be possible to structure a transaction so that interest is effectively deductible. We therefore analyze the effect on saving both with and without deductibility.

Case I: Deductible interest payments. How does the budget line in Figure 18.7 change when interest is subject to a proportional tax at rate t, and interest payments by borrowers are deductible? Figure 18.8 reproduces the before-tax constraint MN from Figure 18.7. The first thing to note is that the after-tax budget constraint must also pass through the endowment point (I_0, I_1), because, interest tax or no interest tax, Scrooge always has the option of neither borrowing nor lending.

The next relevant observation is that the tax reduces the rate of interest received by savers from r to $(1 - t)r$. Therefore, the opportunity cost of consuming a dollar in the present is only $[1 + (1 - t)r]$ dollars in the future. At the same time, for each dollar of interest Scrooge pays, he can deduct \$1 from taxable income. This is worth \$$t$ to him in lower taxes. Hence, the effective rate that has to be paid for borrowing is $(1 - t)r$. Therefore, the cost of increasing current consumption by one dollar, in terms of future consumption, is only $[1 + (1 - t)r]$ dollars. Together, these facts imply that the after-tax budget line has a slope (in absolute value) of $[1 + (1 - t)r]$.

The budget line that passes through (I_0, I_1) and has a slope of $[1 + (1 - t)r]$ is drawn as PQ in Figure 18.8. As long as the tax rate is positive, it is necessarily flatter than the pretax budget line MN.

To complete the analysis, we draw in indifference curves. The new optimum is at E_t, where present consumption is c_0^t, and future consumption is c_1^t. As before, saving is the difference between present consumption and present income, distance $c_0^t I_0$. Note that $c_1^t I_0$ is less than $c_0^t I_0$, the amount that was saved before the tax was imposed. Imposition of the interest tax thus lowers saving by distance $c_0^* c_0^t$.

---

[11] We could consider an income tax with a base of both labour and capital income, but this would complicate matters without adding any important insights.

FIGURE 18.9

INTEREST TAXED AND INTEREST PAYMENTS DEDUCTIBLE: SAVING INCREASES

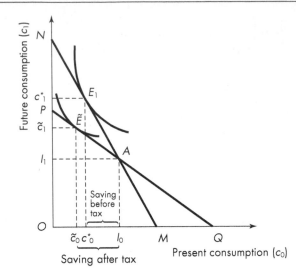

However, saving does not always fall. For a counter example, consider Figure 18.9. The before- and after-tax budget lines are identical to their counterparts in Figure 18.8, as is the before-tax equilibrium at point E_1. But the tangency of an indifference curve to the after-tax budget line occurs at point $\tilde{E}$, to the left of E_1. Consumption in the present is $\tilde{c}_0$, and in the future, $\tilde{c}_1$. In this case, a tax on interest actually increases saving, from $c_0^* I_0$ to $\tilde{c}_0 I_0$. Thus, depending on the individual's preferences, taxing interest can either increase or decrease saving.

The source of this ambiguity is the conflict between two different effects. On the one hand, taxing interest reduces the opportunity cost of present consumption, which tends to increase c_0 and lower saving. This is the substitution effect, which comes about because the tax changes the price of c_0 in terms of c_1. On the other hand, the fact that interest is being taxed makes it harder to achieve any future consumption goal. This is the income effect, which arises because the tax lowers real income. If present consumption and present saving are normal goods, a decrease in income lowers both. Just as in the case of labour supply, whether the substitution or income effect dominates cannot be known on the basis of theory alone.

If the notion that a rational person might actually increase saving in response to an increased tax on interest seems bizarre, consider the extreme case of a "target saver," whose only goal is to have a given amount of consumption in the future—no more and no less. (Perhaps the person wants to save just enough to pay his or her children's future college tuition.) If the tax rate goes up, then the only way for this person to reach his or her target is to increase saving, and vice versa. Thus, for the target saver, saving and the after-tax interest rate move in opposite directions.

Case II: Nondeductible interest payments. We now consider how the budget constraint changes when interest is taxed at rate t, but borrowers cannot deduct interest payments from taxable income. Figure 18.10 reproduces again the before-tax budget constraint NM from Figure 18.7. As was true for Case I, the after-tax budget constraint must include the endowment point (I_0, I_1). Now, starting at the endowment point, suppose Scrooge decides to save $1; that is, move $1 to the left of point A. Because interest is taxed, this allows him to increase his consumption next period by $[1 + (1 - t)r]$ dollars. To the left of point A, then, the opportunity cost of increasing present consumption by $1 is $[1 + (1 - t)r]$ dollars of future consumption. Therefore, the absolute value of the slope of the budget constraint to the left of point A is $[1 + (1 - t)r]$. This coincides with segment PA of the after-tax budget constraint in Figure 18.9.

Now suppose that, starting at the endowment point, Scrooge decides to borrow $1; that is, move $1 to the right of point A. Because interest is nondeductible, the tax system does not affect the cost of borrowing. Thus, the cost to Scrooge of borrowing the $1 now is $(1 + r)$ dollars of future consumption, just as it was before the interest tax. Hence, *to the right of point A*, the opportunity cost of increasing present consumption by a dollar is $(1 + r)$ dollars. This coincides with segment AM of the before-tax budget constraint NM.

FIGURE 18.10

INTEREST TAXED AND INTEREST PAYMENTS NONDEDUCTIBLE

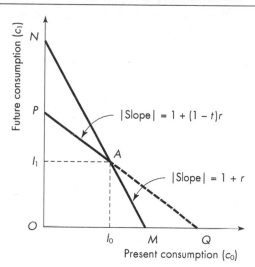

Putting all this together, we see that when interest receipts are taxable but interest payments are nondeductible, the intertemporal budget constraint has a kink at the endowment point. To the left of the endowment point, the absolute value of the slope is $[1 + (1 - t)r]$; to the right, it is $(1 + r)$. What is the impact on saving? If Scrooge was a borrower before the tax was imposed, the system has no effect on him. That is, if Scrooge maximized utility along segment AM before the tax was imposed, he continues to do so after. On the other hand, if Scrooge was a saver before the tax, his choice between present and future consumption must change, because points on segment NA are no longer available to him. However, just as in the discussion surrounding Figures 18.8 and 18.9, we cannot predict *a priori* whether Scrooge will save more or less. It depends on the relative strengths of the income and substitution effects.

Some additional considerations. This simple two-period model ignores some important real-world complications:

- The analysis, as usual, is couched in *real* terms—it is the real net rate of return that governs behaviour. As was emphasized in Chapter 17, care must be taken to correct the *nominal* rates of return observed in the market for inflation.

- In the model, there is one vehicle for saving, and the returns to saving are taxed at a single rate. In reality, there are numerous assets, each with its own before-tax rate of return. Moreover, as observed in the last chapter, the returns to different assets are taxed at different rates. It is, therefore, an oversimplification to speak of how changes in "the" after-tax rate of return influence saving.

- The model focuses only on private saving. For many purposes, the important variable is *social saving*, defined as the sum of government and private saving. For example, if the government were to save a sufficiently high proportion of tax receipts from an interest tax, social saving could go up even if private saving decreased.

- Some investigators have questioned the validity of the life-cycle model itself. The life-cycle hypothesis posits that people are forward looking; critics argue that a more realistic assumption is that people are myopic. The life-cycle model also assumes that people can borrow and lend freely at the going rate of interest; critics point out that many people are not able to borrow. Of course, neither the proponents of the life-cycle view nor its detractors need be 100 percent correct. At any given time, some families' saving behaviour may be explained by the model, while others' saving behaviour may be myopic or constrained.

Despite the controversies surrounding the life-cycle hypothesis, most economists are willing to accept it as a pretty good approximation to reality.

Empirical Findings on Saving

Several econometric studies have estimated the effect of taxation on saving. In a typical study, the quantity of saving is the left-hand variable and the explanatory variables are the rate of return to saving, disposable income, and other variables that might plausibly affect saving. If the coefficient on the rate of return is positive, the conclusion is that increases in taxes (which decrease the rate of return) depress saving, and vice versa.

Beach, Boadway, and Bruce (1988) found that the impact on saving of changes in the real, after-tax rate of return is small in Canada. Although they found an average interest elasticity of savings over all ages of about 0.5 in Canada, they also found that the interest elasticities of savings varied significantly by age cohort (positive for younger cohorts and negative for older cohorts), and depend on the after-tax, real interest rate itself. Thus, the issue is a complex one, with interest elasticity changing with demography, the real interest rate, and other factors.

In sum, as McLure (1980: 318) noted some years ago, "Determining the effect interest rates have on saving is no mean trick. It involves considerable conceptual and econometric difficulties that still defy the best efforts of bright and dedicated economists." For Canada as well as for the United States, the conclusion by the Joint Committee on Taxation (2005) that the long-run savings elasticity is about 0.29 seems reasonable.

RRSPs, RPPs, TFSAs, and Saving

As noted in the previous chapter, taxpayers are allowed each year to save (up to $25,370 in 2016) in tax-deductible retirement savings plans (RRSPs) and pension plans (RPPs). Because the amounts contributed to these plans are tax deductible, and the interest earnings are not taxed until paid out, these are an attractive form of saving for qualified taxpayers. RRSPs and RPPs have been popular; $52 billion was claimed in contributions to RRSPs and RPPs in 2012 (Canada Revenue Agency, *Income Statistics 2014, 2012 tax year*).

In addition, individuals can save up to $10,000 per year in Tax-Free Savings Accounts (TFSAs) in 2016. Unlike RRSPs, contributions to TFSAs are not tax deductible, but the investment income earned in the account is tax-free, even when it is withdrawn (see Chapter 17).

There have been frequent proposals to increase annual limits on RRSP contributions as a way to increase private saving. The central question in debates over proposals to raise the limits is whether RRSPs stimulate new saving. To think about this issue, note the three sources from which RRSPs could be funded. First, households could cut back on their consumption, putting the new saving into an RRSP. Second, they could put money into RRSPs that would otherwise have been saved in some other form; such asset transfers are clearly not new saving. Third, part of the money used to fund an RRSP could come from the tax savings generated by the RRSP itself.[12]

In earlier work on the effect of a $1,000 investment income exclusion as well as RRSPs, Jump (1982) concluded that the effect of these incentives was not at the margin for most people, and that the RRSP deduction would *not* affect taxpayers who were already saving an amount in excess of the contribution limit. They would simply reallocate their saving. This would result in a fall in government revenues, and possibly a fall in total (private plus government) saving. In contrast, Carroll and Summers (1987) concluded that sheltered savings plans such as RRSPs contributed significantly to higher private saving rates in Canada in the 1970s. Beach, Boadway, and Bruce (1988) also found that tax sheltering of savings by RRSPs and other means, by keeping the after-tax real interest rate on savings in Canada at a higher level, may have kept Canada's private savings rate from falling in the 1970s, as had occurred in the United States.[13] And a study by Engelhardt (1996) found that saving increased due to Canada's Registered Home-Ownership Savings Program (RHOSP). This program (from 1974 to 1985), with tax features similar to RRSPs, allowed renters to deduct savings (up to $1,000 annually)

---

[12] Note that if the government borrowed to make up for the decrease in tax revenue, then, even if households saved the entire tax cut, there would be no net increase in the level of social saving.

[13] Individual Retirement Accounts (IRAs) are the U.S. policy tool that is similar to Canada's RRSPs. The controversy over the effects of IRAs in the U.S. and RRSPs in Canada continues. Hubbard and Skinner (1996) concluded that such "saving incentives generate substantial net capital accumulation," and Poterba, Venti, and Wise (1996) conclude that IRA and 401(k) programs, like RRSPs in Canada, are likely to increase saving. In contrast, Engen, Gale, and Scholz (1996) find little effect of such programs on the level of saving. Morissette and Drolet (2001) conclude that it is "unclear" whether RRSPs lead to increased saving, and Milligan (2002) finds that marginal tax rates had only a small effect on participation in RRSPs in the period from 1982 to 1996. A study by Benjamin (2003) suggests that tax-favoured saving options stimulate at least some new saving.

to accumulate funds (up to $10,000) for a home purchase. Engelhardt found that the program had "a substantial impact on saving: each dollar contributed to the program represented 56–93 and 20–57 cents of new household and national saving, respectively" (p. 1237).

Taxes and the Capital Shortage

As a political issue, the taxation of capital income receives at least as much public discussion as the taxation of wages. Much of the debate has centred on the proposition that, by discouraging saving, the tax system contributed to a decline in investment, and in the capital stock of the country. This, in turn, contributes to slower productivity growth than otherwise. This leads to a claim that a reduction of taxes on capital is needed to end the so-called productivity crisis.

A major problem with this line of reasoning is that, as we have just shown, it is not at all obvious that taxation has reduced the supply of saving. Let us assume, for the sake of argument, that saving has indeed declined as a consequence of taxes. Nevertheless, as long as the capital market is competitive, a decrease in saving does not create a gap between the demand for investment funds and their supply. Indeed, in a small, open economy, we can expect investment opportunities to attract savings from other countries. Where the gap is less than completely filled by foreign saving, the interest rate adjusts to bring quantities supplied and demanded into equality. The new equilibrium may or may not involve a lower rate of investment and a lower level of productivity growth, depending on the inflow of savings from other countries.

But to look only at these issues is unfair. Taxation of *any* factor may reduce the equilibrium quantity. Just as in any other case, the important efficiency question is whether taxation of capital income has led to large excess burdens compared to other ways of raising tax revenues. We defer to Chapter 20 a discussion of whether economic efficiency would be enhanced if taxes on capital were eliminated. In the meantime, we note that there is no reason a high rate of investment alone is a desirable objective. In a utilitarian framework, at least, capital accumulation is a means of enhancing individual welfare, not an end in itself.

Finally, we emphasize that the entire argument that saving incentives can help increase the capital stock rests on the premise that investment in the economy depends on its own rate of saving: all national saving is channelled into national investment. This is true in an economy that is closed to international trade. In an open economy, however, domestic saving can be invested abroad. This means that tax policy designed to stimulate saving may not lead to more domestic investment. To the extent that saving flows freely across national boundaries to whatever investment opportunities seem most attractive, the ability of tax policy to stimulate investment through saving is greatly diminished.

How open is the Canadian economy? Empirical studies indicate that countries with high domestic saving tend to have high domestic investment, and vice versa.[14] Although the data are open to other interpretations, this suggests that saving may not flow into and out of the economy as freely as one would expect in a completely integrated world capital market (Kho, Stulz, and Warnock, 2009).[15] As long as saving and investment are correlated, tax policy that affects saving can generally be expected to affect investment. The size of the effect, however, is considerably smaller than one would find in a completely closed economy.

HOUSING DECISIONS

When people talk of a capital shortage, they are usually concerned with the amount of capital available to businesses for producing goods. Such capital is only part of the nation's stock. Some capital, such as schools, hospitals, and roads, is government-owned infrastructure. Some capital, such as pollution abatement equipment, is used by business, but not for increasing output as conventionally measured. Other capital is in the hands of households, with owner-occupied housing being the prime example. Even a tax act that has little impact on the overall level of saving can have significant effects on the allocation of saving across these different types of investment. As we see in this section, the Canadian income tax system favours investment in housing.

---

[14] This is disputed by Kim and Oh (2008), who conclude that "capital has long been perfectly mobile in Canada."

[15] Interestingly, Helliwell and McKitrick (1999) find that, while there is a high correlation between national savings and investment, the effect is absent between provinces.

Income for owner-occupied housing is not subjected to taxes that apply to income from other investments. Neither imputed rent nor capital gains from a primary residence are taxed in Canada. Consider Macbeth, who has an amount, K, in assets. He is choosing between (a) buying a home for an amount equal to K, or (b) continuing to rent and investing K in alternative income-earning assets.

If he buys his own house, Macbeth and his wife derive services from it that have a market value equal to its rental value, R. (In order to keep things simple, we assume that R is net of property taxes and maintenance expenses.) Of course, they do not receive this income in dollars—the income is in kind. However, under a comprehensive income tax system, the form in which the income is received is irrelevant, and the imputed rent from owner-occupied housing is part of taxable income. Moreover, any increase in the market value of the house, C, is income, and should be taxed as a capital gain as with any other asset. (Decreases in house value lower income.) The return that Macbeth receives on his owner-occupied home is $(R + C)/K$, and this return is not reduced by the income tax.

If Macbeth invests in an alternative asset that yields taxable income, the return will be $[(1 - t)(R' + C')/K]$. R' and C' represent the flow of money income from the asset and capital gain (or loss), respectively. The before-tax return on other investments must be $1/(1 - t)$ times that on housing in order to yield the same after-tax return. If Macbeth's tax rate is 40 percent, the return on the alternative investment must be 16.67 percent if the return on his housing investment is 10 percent.

An investment in owner-occupied housing is attractive, due to the exemption of imputed rent and capital gains, even though the before-tax return on housing is substantially below that on other forms of capital.[16] In this way, investment is diverted into housing when it could be more productively used in other areas. The precise size of the increase in demand for owner-occupied housing is difficult to determine, because the demand for housing is influenced by many factors. Owner-occupied housing in the United States, where mortgage interest payments and property taxes can be deducted in calculating taxable income, has received even more favourable treatment than in Canada. Yet, owner-occupancy rates and the ratio of owner-occupied capital to total capital stock may be about the same in the United States as in Canada.[17]

Exemption of imputed income and nontaxation of capital gains on principal residences have been sizable benefits to homeowners. Federal personal income tax revenues forgone due to the capital gain exemption were estimated to be $4.8 billion in 2014. Revenue forgone due to exemption of imputed rent, although not estimated, is likely much larger. This compares with federal personal income taxes of $131 billion in 2014.[18] Provinces, through their provincial income taxes, forgo half again as much. The implicit subsidy affects not only how much housing people purchase, but also whether they become owners or renters in the first place. In fact, the owner-occupancy rate in 1951 was about the same as it is today—65 percent.[19]

Another benefit to homeowners is an interest-free loan to which first-time buyers have access from their RRSP accounts. A provision introduced in 1992 allows a taxpayer to withdraw up to $25,000 (in 2016) tax-free from his or her RRSP for the purchase of a home. Although the funds must be paid back to the RRSP account over a 15-year period, no interest is to be paid on them. The availability of these funds to purchase a house, but not for other purposes, further contributes to the use of capital to purchase housing rather than other consumption goods or capital assets.

[16] See Ibbotson and Siegel (1984) and Webb and Rubens (1987).

[17] The owner-occupancy rate in 2006 was 68 percent in Canada (Statistics Canada, 2008: 6) and principal residences accounted for $1.1 trillion, or 38 percent, of household assets in 1999 (Statistics Canada, 2001: 22). A study by Poterba (1992: 283) found that owner-occupied capital in the United States accounted for 27 percent of total capital in 1989 compared to 27.4 percent in Canada.

[18] See *Tax Expenditures and Evaluations 2014* (Department of Finance Canada, 2015) and *Public Accounts of Canada 2014* (Ottawa: Public Works and Government Services Canada, 2015).

[19] Evidence concerning the effect of housing incentives is stronger in the United States than in Canada. The share of owner-occupiers in the United States rose from 43.6 percent in 1940 to 63.7 percent by 1986. Smith, Rosen, and Fallis (1988), in a review of the literature, found that "although the research on income tax incentives has taken numerous approaches, these studies have reached remarkably similar conclusions. They have concluded that tax preferences have strongly favoured and encouraged homeownership, have transferred resources to more heavily subsidized owner-occupiers from generally less-subsidized renters, have raised the gross price of home ownership housing services but lowered the net after-tax price, and have directed resources in favour of housing and away from other capital uses. Empirical estimates (for the United States) suggest that personal income tax benefits for homeownership increased the proportion of homeowners by approximately 4 percentage points (or 7 percent), and that approximately one-quarter of the increase in home ownership since World War II can be attributed to these tax factors (p. 55).

So far we have discussed only tax policies affecting owner-occupied housing and ignored rental housing. Historically, however, the Canadian system has provided generous subsidies to the owners of rental housing. (These included accelerated depreciation and the right to create losses that could be offset against other income, discussed in Chapter 21.) These provisions reduced the cost of renting to individuals, although one cannot know by how much without information on the relevant supply and demand elasticities.[20]

Proposals for Change

A number of proposals have been made to reform the tax treatment of housing. Probably the most radical change would be to include net imputed rent in taxable income. Such a move would create an administrative challenge since authorities would have to determine the potential market rental value of each house, allowing for appropriate costs, to arrive at "net" rent. Nevertheless, a portion of imputed rental income is taxed in European countries such as the Netherlands and Belgium. It is, however, highly unlikely that taxing imputed rent would be politically feasible. Homeowners are more likely to perceive their houses as endless drains on their financial resources than as revenue producers. It would not be easy to convince homeowners—who comprise more than half the electorate—that taxation of imputed rental income is a good idea.

Finally, we note that much of the debate over the tax treatment of housing implicitly assumes that full taxation of imputed rent would be the most efficient solution. Recall from the theory of optimal taxation (Chapter 16) that if lump-sum taxes are excluded, the efficiency maximizing set of tax rates is generally a function of the elasticities of demand and supply for all commodities. Only in very special cases do we expect efficiency to require equal rates for all sources of income. We must also recognize the favourable treatment of investment in other sectors and regions under the income tax. On the other hand, it is highly improbable that the efficient tax rate on imputed rental income is zero. Determining the appropriate rate is an important topic for further research.

PORTFOLIO COMPOSITION

Taxes may affect not only the total amount of wealth that people accumulate, but the assets in which that wealth is held as well.[21] Some argue that lowering taxes would encourage people to hold riskier assets. Superficially, this proposition seems plausible. Why take a chance on a risky investment if your gains are going to be grabbed by the tax collector? However, the problem is considerably more complicated than this line of argument suggests.

Most modern theoretical work on the relationship between taxes and portfolio composition is based on the path-breaking analysis of Tobin (1958). In Tobin's model, individuals make their decisions about whether to invest in an asset on the basis of two characteristics—the expected return on the asset, and how risky that return is. Other things being the same, investors prefer assets that are expected to yield high returns. At the same time, investors are assumed to dislike risk; other things being the same, investors prefer safer assets.

Suppose there are two assets. The first is perfectly safe, but it yields a zero rate of return. (Imagine holding money in a world with no inflation.) The second is a bond that *on average* yields a positive rate of return, but it is risky—there is some chance that the price will go down, so the investor incurs a loss.

Note that the investor can adjust the return and risk on the entire portfolio by holding different combinations of the two assets. In one extreme case he or she could hold only the safe asset—there is no return, but also no risk. On the other hand, the investor could hold only the risky asset—his or her expected return rises, but so does the risk involved. The typical investor holds a combination of both the risky and safe assets to suit tastes concerning risk and return.

---

[20] Some provisions favourable to real estate in Canada were eliminated in the 1980s. Prior to 1985, Registered Home-Ownership Savings Plans (RHOSPs) permitted first-time home-buyers to make a tax-deductible contribution of $1,000 a year, to a limit of $10,000, with the interest earned in the account tax exempt. The proceeds could be withdrawn, tax free, from the RHOSP account when applied to the purchase of a first home. Poterba (1992) estimated that "for a household participating in this program and purchasing a median-priced house in 1980, the subsidy would have amounted to 7–9 percent of the house value" (p. 277). Reforms in 1981 and 1987 limited the extent to which losses on rental property that were due to capital cost allowances could be deducted against other sources of income. This made investment in rental properties by high-income individuals less attractive.

[21] This should be apparent from the previous section. Housing is the most important single element in the portfolios of most Canadians.

Now assume that a proportional tax is levied on the return to capital assets. Assume also that the tax allows for **full loss offset**—individuals can deduct all losses from taxable income. Because the safe asset has a yield of zero, the tax has no effect on its rate of return—the return is still zero. In contrast, the risky asset has a positive expected rate of return, which is lowered by the presence of the tax. It seems that the tax reduces the attractiveness of the risky asset compared to the safe asset.

However, at the same time that the tax lowers the return to the risky asset, *it lowers its riskiness as well.* Why? In effect, introducing the tax turns the government into the investor's silent partner. If the investor wins (in the sense of receiving a positive return), the government shares in the gain. But because of the loss-offset provision, if the individual loses, the government also shares in the loss. Suppose, for example, that an individual loses $100 on an investment. If the tax rate is 40 percent, the ability to subtract the $100 from taxable income lowers the tax bill by $40. Even though the investment lost $100, the investor loses only $60. In short, introduction of the tax tightens the dispersion of returns—the highs are less high and the lows are less low—and, hence, reduces the risk. Thus, although the tax makes the risky asset *less* attractive by reducing its expected return, it simultaneously makes it *more* attractive by decreasing its risk. If the second effect dominates, taxation can, on balance, make the risky asset more desirable.

An important assumption behind this discussion is the existence of a perfectly riskless asset. This is not a very realistic assumption. In a world where no one is sure exactly what the inflation rate will be, even the return on money is risky. But the basic reasoning still holds. *Because taxes decrease risk as well as returns, the effect of taxes on portfolio choice is ambiguous.*

Resolving this ambiguity econometrically is very difficult. A major problem is that it is hard to obtain reliable information on just which assets people hold. Individuals may not accurately report their holdings to survey takers because they are not exactly sure of the true values at any point in time. Alternatively, people might purposely misrepresent their asset positions because of fears that the information will be reported to the tax authorities. In one study using a fairly reliable data set, Poterba and Samwick (2003) found that, other things being the same, people in higher tax brackets hold a higher proportion of their portfolios in common stock, which is quite risky. This finding lends at least tentative support to the notion that taxation *increases* risk taking. But the issue is far from being resolved.

A NOTE ON POLITICS AND ELASTICITIES

Despite much investigation, the effect of income taxation on several important kinds of behaviour is not known for sure. Different "experts" are, therefore, likely to give policy makers different pieces of advice. In this situation, it is almost inevitable that policy makers will adopt behavioural assumptions that enhance the perceived feasibility of their goals. Although it is dangerous to generalize, liberals tend to believe that behaviour is not very responsive to the tax system, while conservatives take the opposite view. Liberals prefer low elasticities because they can raise large amounts of money for public sector activity without having to worry too much about charges that they are "killing the goose that laid the golden egg." In contrast, conservatives like to assume high elasticities because this limits the volume of taxes that can be collected before serious efficiency costs are imposed on the economy. Thus, when journalists, politicians, and economists make assertions about how taxes affect incentives, it is prudent to evaluate their claims in light of what their hidden agendas might be.

SUMMARY

- The Canadian personal income tax affects many economic decisions, including labour supply, saving, residential housing consumption, and portfolio choice.
- For labour supply, saving, and choice of portfolio, the direction of the effect of taxation is theoretically ambiguous. Further, in each area, the size of tax-induced behavioural changes may be determined only by empirical investigation. For these reasons, the effect of taxation is among the most contentious of all areas of public policy.

- Empirical studies of labour supply indicate prime-age males vary their hours only slightly in response to tax changes, while the hours of married women are more sensitive to variations in the after-tax wage rate.

- Earnings taxes can increase, decrease, or leave unchanged the amount of human capital investments. The outcome depends in part on how taxes affect hours of work.

- The effect of tax rates on tax revenues depends on the responsiveness of labour supply to changes in tax rates and on the extent of substitution between taxable and nontaxable forms of compensation.

- The effect of taxes on saving may be analyzed using the life-cycle model, which assumes that people's annual consumption and saving decisions are influenced by their lifetime resources. Taxing interest income lowers the opportunity cost of present consumption and thereby creates incentives to lower saving. However, this substitution effect may be offset by the fact that the tax reduces total lifetime resources, which tends to reduce present consumption; that is, increase saving. The net effect on saving is an empirical question.

- Empirical studies of saving behaviour have foundered on both conceptual and practical difficulties. As a result, there is no firm consensus of opinion on the effects of taxation on saving.

- The personal income tax excludes the imputed rent (and capital gains) from owner-occupied housing from taxation. *Ceteris paribus,* this increases both the percentage of those choosing to own their homes and the quantity of owner-occupied housing. Proposals to modify the tax treatment of housing include making imputed rent part of taxable income.

- The theoretical effects of taxation on portfolio composition are ambiguous. Taxes reduce the expected return on a risky asset, but also lessen its riskiness. The net effect of these conflicting tendencies has not been empirically resolved.

EXERCISES

1. In January 2000, delegates at the founding convention of the Canadian Alliance (a predecessor to the current Conservative Party) voted to make a 17 percent "flat-rate" tax the cornerstone of the new party's election platform. The shift would reduce the top marginal rate applied to high-income individuals. Part of the rationale was to give highly productive Canadians renewed incentives for work. Use the graphical model of leisure-income decisions to analyze the effect of a lower marginal tax rate on a high-income individual.

2. Suppose that individuals view their loss of income from income taxes as offset by the benefits of public services purchased with the revenues. How are their labour supply decisions affected? (*Hint:* Break down the change in hours worked into income and substitution effects.)

3. Brian Mulroney's 1987 tax reform included a substantial gradual increase in the limit, from $7,500 to $15,500, for contributions to registered retirement savings plans (RRSPs). The interest earned on RRSPs is not subject to income tax until it is withdrawn. Sketch the intertemporal budget constraint associated with an RRSP. Will RRSPs increase private saving? What about social saving (the sum of private and public saving)?

4. In the mid-1990s, the Japanese government implemented a set of very large, temporary tax cuts. These cuts had very little impact on personal consumption (Watanabe et al., 2001). Is this finding consistent with the life-cycle model of consumer behaviour? If the life-cycle model is correct, and the Japanese government wishes to use tax policy to stimulate consumption, what advice would you give?

5. Use the life-cycle model to evaluate whether a rational saver would follow this piece of advice: "To compensate for falling interest rates, aim to save more every month."

6. Apollo has T hours to allocate between work and leisure. His wage rate is w and he also has nonlabour income equal to a fixed amount, A. The income tax rate is t. Write an algebraic expression for Apollo's after-tax budget constraint. Illustrate his before-tax and after-tax budget constraints with a diagram.

7. According to Nobel Laureate Ed Prescott, "Increasing tax rates [in Europe] will not increase revenue" (Prescott, 2004: 2). What assumptions must hold in order for this statement to be correct?

8. The U.S. Immigration Act of 1965 imposed severe restrictions on the emigration of Canadians to the United States until the Free Trade Agreement of 1988 (Davies and Winer, 2011). What impact might you expect the restrictions, and their subsequent removal, to have on the elasticity of *total* labour supply in Canada? What would be the policy implications for personal income taxation in Canada?

9. In an economy, the supply curve of labour, S, is given by

$$S = -100 + 200w_n$$

where w_n is the after-tax wage rate. Assume that the before-tax wage rate is fixed at 10.

a. Write a formula for tax revenues as a function of the tax rate, and sketch the function in a diagram with the tax rate on the horizontal axis and tax revenues on the vertical axis. (*Hint*: Note that $w_n = (1 - t)10$, where t is the tax rate, and that tax revenues are the product of hours worked, the gross wage, and the tax rate.) Suppose that the government currently imposes a tax rate of 70 percent. What advice would you give?

b. Try this problem if you know some calculus: at what tax rate are tax revenues maximized in this economy?

10. An editorial in the *Wall Street Journal* (2001) argued, "high marginal tax rates . . . discourage incentives . . . to take risks," The proposition seems plausible. Why take a chance on a risky investment if your gains are going to be grabbed by the tax collector? Use the theory of portfolio composition to explain why the problem is more complicated than this line of argument suggests.

11. Define the "after-tax share" as one minus the marginal tax rate. Heim (2009) recently estimated the elasticity of taxable income with respect to the after-tax share is 1.2 for people with incomes above $500,000. If this estimate is correct, what would be the revenue consequences of raising the marginal tax rate on very high-income people from 40 percent to 45 percent?

CHAPTER 19

Consumption Taxation

But when the impositions are laid upon those things which men consume, every man payeth equally for what he useth: nor is the common wealth defrauded by the luxurious waste of private men.

–Thomas Hobbes

AFTER READING THIS CHAPTER, THE STUDENT SHOULD BE ABLE TO:

LO1 Explain how a consumption tax and an income tax differ in their treatment of saving.

LO2 Discuss the distributional effects of a consumption tax.

LO3 Distinguish between a retail sales tax and a value-added tax.

LO4 Explain the role of input tax credits in calculating the net amount of Goods and Services Tax (GST) owed by a firm.

LO5 Distinguish between zero-rated and tax-exempt items.

LO6 Summarize the use of excise taxes by the federal and provincial governments.

LO7 Explain how tax liability is calculated for a personal consumption tax.

LO8 Discuss the advantages of a personal consumption tax over an income tax.

Most of our attention in this part of the book has been devoted to various kinds of income taxes. As noted in Chapter 17, the base of an income tax is *potential* consumption. This chapter discusses taxes that are imposed on *actual* consumption. There is no reason to believe that actual or potential consumption is inherently the fairer tax base. The following chapter will consider taxes on wealth whose base is accumulated saving; that is, the accumulated difference between potential and actual consumption.

OVERVIEW

In Canada today, the most important consumption taxes are those levied on the purchases of a wide variety of goods and services. Referred to as **general sales taxes**, or **broad-based sales taxes**, these are generally in a form that imposes the same tax rate on most final purchases. The two distinct forms of such taxes in Canada, one used by the federal government and the other by some provincial governments, are the federal Goods and Services Tax (GST) and the various provincial retail sales taxes (RSTs). Although both of these taxes exempt a variety of goods and services, the GST has the broader base because it taxes some goods and many services that are exempt under provincial retail sales taxes. All the provinces have had an RST at one time or another, but several provinces have now blended their sales tax with the GST tax base to form a Harmonized Sales Tax (HST). The HST tax rate in a participating province is the sum of the GST rate and the provincial sales tax rate. The GST and HST are examples of a **value-added tax (VAT)**, used today by over 130 countries. In the industrialized world, only the United States has not implemented such a tax.

Selective sales taxes, also referred to as **excise taxes**, or **differential commodity taxes**, are levied at different rates on the purchase of different commodities by both the federal government and the provinces. **Customs duties** are a form of selective sales tax levied on different commodities at different rates at the time the goods are imported into the country, and can be used only by the federal government.

Sales taxes generally take one of two forms. A **unit tax** is a given amount for each unit purchased. For example, most provinces levy a tax on motor fuel that is a certain number of cents per litre; a typical rate is around 15 cents. In contrast, an **ad valorem tax** is computed as a percentage of the value of the purchase. For example, the federal excise tax rate on insurance premiums is 10 percent.

A distinguishing feature of sales taxes is that the legal incidence falls upon businesses. Consumers make no explicit payments to the government (although they bear a share of the economic incidence). Some recent proposals for tax reform have centred on *personal* consumption taxes, which require individuals to file returns and write cheques to the government. Unlike sales taxes, these systems allow individuals' tax liabilities to depend on their personal circumstances. The best known of these proposals is the *flat tax* put forward by Hall and Rabushka (H&R) (2007), which we describe later in the chapter. However, except for the possibility of building some progressivity into the system, the H&R flat tax is essentially equivalent to a general sales tax, since both approaches amount to a proportional tax on consumption. Thus, to all intents and purposes, any results pertaining to the economic effects of a general sales tax apply to the H&R flat tax.

Consolidated revenues. Consumption taxes raised $150 billion for the federal and provincial governments in the 2014–15 fiscal year.[1] Consumption taxes declined from about 35 percent of consolidated government revenues in 1965–66 to 20 percent in 2014–15. This decline was largely due to rapid growth in income tax revenues rather than to any decrease in consumption taxes. Figure 19.1 shows the revenue shares of the main consumption taxes.[2] *General* sales taxes have become more important over the past five decades,

---

FIGURE 19.1

COMPOSITION OF CONSUMPTION TAX REVENUE BY TAX CATEGORY, 1965–66 AND 2008–09 (CONSOLIDATED FEDERAL, PROVINCIAL, AND LOCAL GOVERNMENT REVENUE)

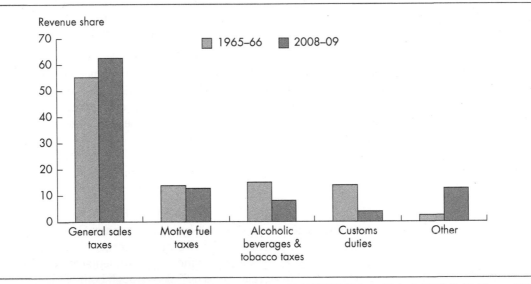

Sources: Adapted from the Statistics Canada, *Public Sector Statistics,* Cat. no. 68-213-XWE (Released July 8, 2008); *Public Finance Historical Statistical Data 1965/66–1991/92,* Cat. no. 68-512 (released April 1, 1992) and CANSIM II database http://cansim2.statcan.ca/ Table 385-0001.

---

[1] Consumption taxes are calculated as the sum of taxes on goods and services and taxes on international trade and transactions using Statistics Canada's CANSIM database, Table 385-0032.

[2] As a result of the change in the government accounting framework from FMS to GFS, the decomposition of consumption taxes into categories is unavailable after 2008–09 for either the aggregate of provincial governments or the consolidated government sector.

up from 55 to 63 percent of revenues, whereas selective sales taxes, especially customs duties, declined in importance. Lottery profits, another form of consumption taxation, are the main reason for the increase in the category labelled "Other." The growth in general sales tax revenues is due to a need for greater revenue and to equity, efficiency, and administrative concerns related to heavier use of selective sales taxes.

Federal revenues. Consumption taxes—in the form of customs duties and excise taxes—accounted for *all* federal tax revenues from the time of Confederation until World War I. The income tax was enacted in 1917. Although consumption taxes still accounted for about 18 percent of federal revenues in 2014-15, income taxes are now by far the most important source of federal revenues.

The mix of federal consumption tax revenues has also changed over time. Customs and excise duties play a smaller role than initially, whereas the federal general sales tax and taxes on motor fuels have grown in importance. Federal taxes on motor fuels, introduced at the time of the energy crisis in the 1970s, accounted for 12 percent of federal consumption taxes in 2013-14. The general sales tax accounted for 67 percent of federal consumption tax revenues in 2013-14 and other consumption taxes (especially taxes on tobacco products and alcoholic beverages) for 12 percent.[3] Customs duties make up the rest.

REASONS FOR CONSUMPTION TAXES

The need for revenues continues to be the primary reason for using consumption taxes. This was true prior to Confederation, when public revenues were needed to support the construction of canals, bridges, roads, and other public activity, and it continues to be true. But why consumption taxes rather than other forms of taxation?

Administrative Considerations

A main attraction of consumption taxes in the form of general sales taxes, customs duties, and excise taxes has always been ease of administration. Early in Canada's history, customs duties could be collected at the time goods were imported into the country, and excise duties could be collected at the time of import or from the few producers of the commodities subjected to these duties. As consumption taxes were expanded to include taxes on motor fuels and broad-based federal and provincial sales taxes, administrative ease continued to be an important factor.

The federal broad-based sales tax, introduced in 1924 and levied on manufactured goods, was collected from relatively few taxpayers. Provincial retail sales taxes, generally collected from sellers at the retail level, require tax authorities to deal with a much larger number of taxpayers, but far fewer than for a personal income tax. Relative to an income tax, there are fewer individuals whose behaviour has to be monitored by the tax authorities. This is not to say that administering a sales tax is without complications. Many difficulties arise because it is unclear whether a given transaction creates a tax liability. Whether at the federal or provincial level, lines have been drawn between taxable and exempt goods. For provincial sales taxes this may involve a distinction between children's clothing and other clothing, prescription drugs and other medications, or restaurant meals above or below a specified threshold. The federal Goods and Services Tax (GST), which replaced the federal sales tax on manufactured products in 1991, has confronted similar problems, with a parliamentary committee noting that "under the current legislation, a single plain croissant is not taxed; a single chocolate filled croissant is taxed; however, a package containing six or more chocolate croissants is not taxed."[4]

The point is that defining the base for a sales tax involves arbitrary distinctions, as is true in the case of the personal and corporate income taxes. Moreover, just as is true for other taxes, tax evasion can be a real problem. As noted in Chapter 16, by early 1994 federal and provincial taxes on cigarettes had reached a level that resulted in cigarette smuggling across the U.S. border that was costing millions of dollars in lost tax revenues each month. And there is evidence that the federal GST caused many workers, particularly in the service sector, to shift to the underground economy in order to evade taxes.[5]

---

[3] Calculations based on Government of Canada (2014).

[4] House of Commons (1994: 16).

[5] See Spiro (1993 and 1994).

Nevertheless, sales taxes are probably easier to administer than income taxes. Taxes on consumption are, therefore, an attractive option in less-developed countries, where individual record keeping is not widespread, and where the resources available for tax administration are quite limited. In countries with high literacy and good record keeping, these administrative arguments are less compelling. Are there any other justifications?

Efficiency Issues

An important difference between taxing consumption versus income is that consumption taxes do not distort decisions related to saving and investment. The efficiency implications of this observation can be examined with the life-cycle model of consumption and saving used in Chapters 11 and 18. In that model, the individual's labour supply in each period is fixed. The two commodities she purchases are present consumption, c_0, and future consumption, c_1. If r is the interest rate, every additional dollar of consumption today means that the individual's future consumption is reduced by $(1 + r)$. Hence, the relative price of c_0–its opportunity cost–is $(1 + r)$.

Consider now the case of Juliet, on whom a 30 percent income tax is levied. Assuming that the tax allows for the deductibility of interest payments, how does this affect the relative price of c_0? If Juliet saves a dollar and it earns a return of r, the government taxes away 30 percent of the return, leaving her only $.70 \times r$. If she borrows a dollar, the interest payments are deductible, so the cost of borrowing is reduced to $.70 \times r$. In short, as a consequence of the income tax, the relative price of present consumption falls from $(1 + r)$ to $(1 + .70r)$. A wedge is inserted between the amounts a borrower pays and a lender receives. As we showed in Chapter 15, the presence of such a tax wedge creates an excess burden. We conclude that an income tax generates an excess burden.

Now consider a general sales tax that raises the same amount of revenue as the income tax. The key thing to note in this context is that the sales tax leaves unchanged the market rate of return available to Juliet. This is because the receipt of interest income by itself does not create a tax liability–only consuming it does. Hence, after the sales tax, the relative price of c_0 is still $(1 + r)$. Unlike the income tax, there seems to be no tax wedge, and, hence, no excess burden. This neutral treatment of saving is frequently cited as the key advantage of a consumption tax. As Lazear and Poterba (2006: 4) write, "By eliminating the favored treatment of present consumption over future consumption that results from the taxation of saving in an income tax, a consumption tax removes the disincentive to save." Apparently, consumption taxation is superior to income taxation on efficiency grounds.

Although the sales tax, unlike the income tax, leaves unchanged the rate at which Juliet can trade off consumption between the two periods, in general, it *does* distort the rate at which she can trade off leisure against consumption. Recall from Chapter 15 that even a tax at the same rate on every commodity distorts the choice between leisure and each of the taxed commodities, so it is not clear that taxing all commodities at the same rate is efficient. The key insight is that a consumption tax distorts the choice between consumption and leisure. To see why, suppose that Juliet has a wage of $5 per hour. Suppose further that the price of the good she consumes is $1 per unit. Then, for each hour of leisure she gives up, Juliet can get 5 units of consumption goods. Now suppose that a sales tax of 25 percent is levied, so the price of the consumption good increases to $1.25. Now Juliet can only get 4 units of the consumption good for each hour of leisure she gives up (because $5/1.25 = 4$). Hence, the sales tax distorts the decision between leisure and consumption. The argument in the preceding paragraphs was built on the *assumption* that the supply of labour is fixed.

Once the possibility is raised that labour–supply decisions are choices, it is no longer true that a consumption tax is *necessarily* more efficient than an income tax. Although an income tax distorts the saving decision and a consumption tax does not, both taxes distort the labour supply decision. One cannot simply conclude that a consumption tax is preferable because it only distorts one market instead of two. Rather, both systems induce an efficiency cost, and only empirical work can determine which tax's cost is smaller. Nonetheless, most studies indicate that given what is known about labour supply and saving behaviour, a consumption tax creates a smaller excess burden than an income tax, even when labour supply distortions created by both taxes are taken into account. (See, for example, Feldstein, 2006). The Economic Council of Canada (1987) analyzed the impact of replacing the personal income tax system in Canada with a comprehensive proportional consumption tax, like a VAT, and found that in the long run it would increase income by about 7 percent. Altig et al. (2001) estimated that replacing the existing U.S. tax system with a proportional consumption tax would increase income by about 9 percent. Dahlby and Ferede (2015) estimated the marginal cost of public funds (see Chapter 4) for the major taxes and found that consumption is the least distortionary of the tax bases used by the provincial governments in Canada. For example, their estimates for Saskatchewan suggest that replacing $10 million of personal income tax revenues with $10 million more in sales tax revenues would generate a welfare gain of $9.98 million.

Equity Issues

Progressiveness. The conventional view of the distributional effects of sales taxes is that they are regressive. This is because higher-income people spend a smaller proportion of their annual income. Where consumption equals 70 percent of the income of a high-income individual, a 10 percent consumption tax equals 7 percent of income. A person with low income who draws down saving to consume 110 percent of annual income pays a consumption tax equal to 11 percent of income. One study estimates that the consumption taxes consistently fell from 14.0 percent of income for the lowest decile of taxpayers to 5.9 percent for the highest decile.[6]

There are three problems with this line of reasoning. First, it looks at the tax as a proportion of *annual* income. In the absence of severe credit market restrictions, *lifetime* income is more relevant, and there is reasonably strong evidence that the proportion of lifetime income devoted to consumption is about the same at all levels.[7] Indeed, computations by Davies, St-Hilaire, and Whalley (1984) suggest that general sales taxes may be roughly proportional when measured with respect to lifetime (rather than annual) income. Second, and perhaps more fundamentally, the conventional view totally ignores the theory of tax incidence. Implicitly (or explicitly), it is assumed that the taxes on a good are borne entirely by the consumers of that good. As emphasized in Chapter 14, however, a commodity tax is generally shifted in a complicated fashion that depends on the supply and demand responses when the tax is imposed. Finally, the incidence of sales taxes, whether selective or general, depends crucially on which goods are taxed at low rates or exempted altogether, and on refundable sales tax credits provided through the income tax system or by some other means. By exempting goods consumed by the poor, for example, the after-tax income distribution can be made more equal, other things being the same. The overall effect of sales taxes on the distribution of income remains an open question.

Ability to pay. Those who favour the income base argue that *actual* consumption is merely one component of *potential* consumption. It is the power to consume, not necessarily its exercise, that is relevant. They point out that under a consumption tax it would be possible for a miserly millionaire to have a smaller tax liability than a much poorer person. A possible response is that it is fairer to tax an individual according to what he or she "takes out" of the economic system, in the form of consumption, than what he or she "contributes" to society, as measured by income. As Thomas Hobbes said in the seventeenth century:

> For what reason is there, that he which laboureth much, and sparing the fruit of his labour, consumeth little, should be more charged, than he that liveth idly, getteth little, and spendeth all he gets; seeing the one hath no more protection from the commonwealth than the other. (1651/1963: 303)

From this point of view, if the miserly millionaire chooses not to consume very much, that is all to the good, because the resources he or she saves become available to society for capital accumulation.

A related question is whether or not an income tax results in double taxation of interest income. Some argue that an income tax is unfair because it taxes capital income twice: once when the original income is earned, and again when the investment produces a return. However, the logic of income taxation impels the return to saving to be taxed. Whether or not this is fair depends, as usual, on value judgments.

Annual versus lifetime equity. Events that influence a person's economic position for only a very short time do not provide an adequate basis for determining ability to pay. Indeed, some have argued that, ideally, tax liabilities should be related to lifetime income. Proponents of consumption taxation point out that an annual income tax leads to tax burdens that can differ quite substantially even for people who have the same lifetime wealth.

To see why, consider Mr. Grasshopper and Ms. Ant, both of whom live for two periods. In the present, they have identical fixed labour incomes of I_0, and in the future they both have labour incomes of zero. (The assumption of zero second-period income is made solely for convenience.) Grasshopper chooses to consume heavily

---

[6] The assumption which this result is based on is that "commodity taxes are borne by consumers except for the share of such taxes on government purchases which is borne by personal income taxpayers and the share on purchases of capital goods and exports, the common portion of which is borne by consumers and the differential portion of which is borne by labour" (Vermaeten, Gillespie, and Vermaeten, 1995: 323) A study by Dynan, Skinner, and Zeldes (2004) confirms that the rich do save proportionately more.

[7] See Friedman (1957).

early in life because he is not very concerned about his retirement years. Ant chooses to consume most of her wealth later in life, because she wants a lavish retirement.[8]

Define Ant's present consumption in the presence of a proportional income tax as c_0^A, and Grasshopper's as c_0^G. By assumption, $c_0^G > c_0^A$. Ant's future income before tax is the interest she earns on her savings: $r(I_0 - c_0^A)$. Similarly, Grasshopper's future income before tax is $r(I_0 - c_0^G)$. Now, if the proportional income tax rate is t, in the present Ant and Grasshopper have identical tax liabilities of tI_0. However, in the future Ant's tax liability is $tr(I_0 - c_0^A)$, while Grasshopper's is $tr(I_0 - c_0^G)$. Because $c_0^G > c_0^A$, Ant's future tax liability is higher. Solely because Ant has a greater taste for saving than Grasshopper, her lifetime tax burden (the discounted sum of her tax burdens in the two periods) is greater than Grasshopper's.

In contrast, under a proportional consumption tax, lifetime tax burdens are independent of tastes for saving, other things being the same. To prove this, all we need to do is write down the equation for each taxpayer's budget constraint. Because all of Ant's noncapital income (I_0) comes in the present, its present value is simply I_0. Now, the present value of lifetime consumption must equal the present value of lifetime income. Hence, Ant's consumption pattern must satisfy the relation

$$I_0 = c_0^A + \frac{c_1^A}{1 + r} \qquad (19.1)$$

Similarly, Grasshopper is constrained by

$$I_0 = c_0^G + \frac{c_1^G}{1 + r} \qquad (19.2)$$

Equations (19.1) and (19.2) say simply that the lifetime value of income must equal the lifetime value of consumption.

If the proportional consumption tax rate is t_c, Ant's tax liability in the first period is $t_c c_0^A$; her tax liability in the second period is $t_c c_1^A$; and the present value of her lifetime consumption tax liability, R_c^A, is

$$R_c^A = t_c c_0^A + \frac{t_c c_1^A}{1 + r} \qquad (19.3)$$

Similarly, Grasshopper's lifetime tax liability is

$$R_c^G = t_c c_0^G + \frac{t_c c_1^G}{1 + r} \qquad (19.4)$$

By comparing Equations (19.3) and (19.1), we see that Ant's lifetime tax liability is equal to $t_c I_0$. (Just multiply Equation (19.1) through by t_c.) Similar comparison of Equations (19.2) and (19.4) indicates that Grasshopper's lifetime tax liability is also $t_c I_0$. We conclude that, under a proportional consumption tax, two people with identical lifetime incomes always pay identical lifetime taxes (where lifetime is interpreted in the present value sense). This stands in stark contrast to a proportional income tax, where the pattern of lifetime consumption influences lifetime tax burdens.

A related argument in favour of the consumption tax centres on the fact that income tends to fluctuate more than consumption. In years when income is unusually low, individuals may draw on their savings or borrow to smooth out fluctuations in their consumption levels. Annual consumption is likely to be a better reflection of lifetime circumstances than annual income.[9]

Opponents of consumption taxation would question whether a lifetime point of view is really appropriate. There is too much uncertainty in both the political and economic environments for a lifetime perspective to be very realistic. Moreover, the consumption smoothing described in the lifetime arguments requires that

---

[8] Venti and Wise (2001) found that "the bulk of dispersion in wealth at retirement results from the choice of some families to save while other similarly situated families choose to spend" (p. 4). Differences in saving among families with similar lifetime incomes leads to tremendous variation in accumulated wealth.

[9] A tax on consumption is a tax on lifetime income if the tax return in the year of death includes all bequests as part of consumption in the final year. In this case, all income over a lifetime is consumed.

individuals be able to save and borrow freely at the going rate of interest. Given that individuals often face constraints on the amounts they can borrow, it is not clear how relevant the lifetime arguments are. Although a considerable body of empirical work suggests the life-cycle model is a good representation for most households (see Browning and Crossley, 2001), this argument still deserves some consideration.

Having investigated the efficiency and equity implications of taxing consumption, we now discuss, in turn, each of the main consumption taxes used in Canada: the federal Goods and Services Tax and the joint federal/provincial Harmonized Sales Tax, provincial retail sales taxes, and the excise taxes and duties used by provincial and federal levels of government.

CANADA'S VALUE-ADDED TAX: THE GST AND HST

The Goods and Services Tax (GST) replaced the federal sales tax (FST) in 1991.[10] The FST was regarded as a "notoriously defective levy" (McLure, 1992: 295). One problem with the FST was that it was imposed on a narrow tax base—manufactured goods, which included only a third of total consumption. The narrow base required a higher tax rate to raise needed revenues, and the higher rate has a larger effect on the price of manufactured goods relative to untaxed goods and services. A broader base and lower rates would result in fewer distortions in the individual's consumption decisions.

The taxation of manufactured goods under the FST also resulted in a large share of FST revenues being collected on the *inputs* to production processes, rather than only at the time of final consumption. Taxed inputs were often used in the production of manufactured goods, resulting in a tax being imposed on a tax. This is referred to as *tax cascading*, and one result was that the tax component in the final price of different manufactured goods varied. Tax cascading also meant that the FST added to the cost of goods produced for export, reducing Canada's competitiveness. Although exports could be exempted from the FST at point of export, it was not possible to adjust export prices to eliminate the effect of the higher price caused by the FST charged on the inputs.

Effective tax rates on goods also differed because the FST excluded costs incurred beyond the manufacturing stage. Mark-ups subsequent to manufacturing varied from good to good, and led to different effective rates on manufactured goods. This contrasts with the result of a broad-based sales tax applied at a uniform rate on the pretax price of a good at the final point of sale.

Finally, the FST was complex to administer, even though it was applied to relatively few taxpayers compared with the GST. A line had to be drawn between the manufacturing stage and later stages, which included, *inter alia*, advertising, marketing, transportation, retail, and wholesale activities. Lines between the activities are particularly difficult to draw in vertically integrated organizations, and the division of activity sometimes differed for domestic and imported goods, to the disadvantage of domestic producers. This resulted in complex regulations and arbitrary decisions.

The GST was designed to address many of the problems of the FST. The tax base was broadened to include services, and it was extended to include marketing and distribution activities through the wholesale and retail levels. The GST nearly doubled the tax base of the FST, even with food excluded from the tax, and allowed the rate of the federal government's broad-based sales tax to be lowered from 13.5 percent in 1990 (under the FST) to 7.0 percent in 1991 (under the GST) while maintaining revenues. Increased uniformity of effective tax rates and lower rates on final goods and services reduced distortions and lowered excess burdens.[11] As we shall see, the invoice–credit system allowed taxpayers to claim a credit for taxes paid at earlier stages in the production process, and to pay a tax only on the value they added. This avoided the problem of tax cascading, permitted a refund of taxes at point of export, and improved Canada's competitiveness. Nonetheless, the GST has been subjected to intense criticism. The rate was lowered to 6 percent by the Conservative Party led by Prime Minister Stephen Harper on July 1, 2006, and again by the same government to 5 percent on January 1, 2008. The attractive features of the GST led six provinces to replace their retail sales taxes with provincial sales taxes that were harmonized

---

[10] The FST was generally referred to as the Manufacturers' Sales Tax (MST) prior to the 1987 tax reform. The FST and MST are one and the same; students who examine earlier literature will find frequent reference to the MST.

[11] Estimates of the expected efficiency gain differed greatly. The Department of Finance estimated that replacing the FST with the GST would cause GDP to be $9 billion, or 1.5 percent, higher. Hamilton and Whalley estimated the efficiency gain from this change to be 0.31 percent of GDP, or one-fifth as large. See Department of Finance (1989), and Hamilton and Whalley (1989).

TABLE 19.1				
Implementation of a Value-Added Tax (VAT)				
Producer	Purchases	Sales	Value Added	VAT at 10 Percent Rate
Farmer	$ 0	$ 400	$ 400	$ 40
Miller	400	700	300	30
Baker	700	950	250	25
Grocer	950	1,000	50	5
Total	$2,050	$3,050	$1,000	$100

with the GST. However, controversy over these reforms is evident in the fact that British Columbia voters decided in a mail-in referendum (held in summer 2011) to rescind the HST and reinstate a retail sales tax.

How a Value-Added Tax Works

Typically, goods are produced in several stages. Consider a simple model of bread production. The farmer grows wheat and sells it to a miller who turns it into flour. The miller sells the flour to a baker who transforms it into bread. The bread is purchased by a grocer who sells it to consumers. A hypothetical numerical example is provided in Table 19.1. Column 1 shows the purchases made by the producer at each stage of production, and column 2 shows the sales value at each stage. For example, the miller pays $400 to the farmer for wheat, and sells the processed wheat to the baker for $700. The *value added* at each stage of production is the difference between the firm's sales and the purchased material inputs used in production. The baker paid $700 for the wheat and sold the bread for $950, so the baker's value added is $250. The value added at each stage of production is computed by subtracting purchases from sales, shown in column 3.[12]

A **value-added tax (VAT)** is a percentage tax on value added applied at each stage of production. For example, if the rate of the VAT is 10 percent, the grocer would pay $5, which is 10 percent of $50. Column 4 shows the amount of VAT liability at each stage of production. The total revenue created by the VAT is found by summing the amounts paid at each stage, and equals $100.

The identical result could have been generated by levying a 10 percent tax at the retail level; that is, by a tax of 10 percent on the value of sales made to consumers by the grocer. In essence, then, a VAT is just an alternative method for collecting a sales tax,[13] and this is the method chosen by the federal government when it introduced the GST. In contrast to "single-stage" sales taxes, the GST is a "multi-stage" sales tax. Retail sales taxes, which are still used in Manitoba, Saskatchewan, and British Columbia, are collected only at the retail level. Value-added taxes are collected at each stage, including the retail stage, as value is added. Ontario, Quebec, and the Atlantic provinces have replaced their retail sales taxes with provincial sales taxes that are integrated with the GST. One advantage of the multi-stage tax is that with a portion of the tax collected at each stage, the incentive to evade the tax on the final sale is much reduced in many cases.

Implementation Issues

Certain administrative decisions have a major impact on a VAT's ultimate economic effects. We discuss three key implementation decisions.

First, it must be decided how purchases of investment assets by firms will be treated in the computation of value added. There are three possibilities:

1. The purchase of an investment good is treated like any other material input. Its full value is subtracted from sales in the computation, despite the fact that it is durable. This is referred to as a **consumption-type VAT** because the tax base excludes investment and involves only consumption.

---

[12] By definition, value added must equal the sum of factor payments made by the producer: wages, interest, rent, and economic profits.

[13] In this example, net income is $1,000, the same as value added. Hence, the VAT is equivalent to a proportional income tax. As we will see later, this is not always true.

2. Each period, firms may deduct only the amount by which investment goods depreciate. The tax base is thus total income net of depreciation, which is why this is characterized as a **net income–type VAT**.

3. Firms are allowed no deductions for investment and depreciation. This is called a **gross income–type VAT**.

Thus, by making different provisions with respect to the treatment of investment goods, a VAT can be transformed into three distinct taxes, each of which has different efficiency and distributional effects. A VAT does not necessarily have to be a tax on consumption, but in Canada, as in most of Europe, VATs are of the consumption type.

Second, a procedure for collection must be devised. The Canadian GST adopted the method long used in Europe–the **invoice-credit method**, which can be illustrated in the hypothetical example in Table 19.1. Each firm is liable for tax on the basis of its total sales, but it can claim the taxes already paid by its suppliers as a credit against this liability. For example, the baker is liable for taxes on his $950 in sales, giving him a tax obligation of $95 (=.10 × $950). However, he can claim a credit of $70 for the GST he paid to the miller when buying the processed wheat (which is the sum of the GST remitted to the government by the farmer and the miller), leaving him a net obligation of $25. The catch is that the credit is allowed only if supported by invoices provided by the baker and the miller. This system provides an incentive for the producers to police themselves against tax evasion. Whatever taxes the farmer and miller evade must be paid by the baker, so the baker will only do business with firms that provide proper invoices. The invoice-credit method cannot eliminate evasion completely. For example, producers can collude to falsify invoices. Nevertheless, there appears to be some evidence that multi-stage collection has cut down on fraud.[14]

Finally, a rate structure must be established. In our simple example in Table 19.1, all commodities are taxed at the same rate. Under the GST, commodities are taxed differentially. Basic food, prescription drugs, and medical devices are not taxed at all; and some services, such as childcare and dental care, receive preferential treatment, presumably because of equity considerations. For reasons of administrative feasibility, firms with gross annual sales below $30,000 are exempted from the GST. Similarly, banking and finance institutions escape taxation because they tend to provide services in kind; therefore, it is difficult to compute value added. The consumption of services generated by owner-occupied housing is exempt from tax for the same reasons that it is usually exempted from income taxation (see Chapter 17).

Non-uniform taxation increases administrative complexity, especially when firms produce multiple outputs, some of which are taxed and some of which are not. But can non-uniform GST rates be justified by the theory of optimal taxation?

Efficiency and Distributional Implications of the Rate Structure

In an optimal tax framework, the key question is what role differential commodity taxation can play given that an income tax is already in place? Atkinson and Stiglitz (1980) showed that if the income tax schedule is chosen optimally, then, under fairly reasonable conditions, social welfare cannot be improved by levying differential commodity taxes.[15] However, if for some reason the income tax is not optimal, differential commodity taxes can improve welfare. For example, if society has egalitarian goals but income taxes are not set optimally, social welfare can be improved by taxing luxury goods at relatively high rates and taxing the commodities that make up a high proportion of the budgets of the poor at relatively low rates. This may explain why the federal government omits food from the GST base.[16]

---

[14] For a discussion of the various problems confronted in the administration of value-added taxes, see Tait (1988: ch. 14). According to Tait: "All commentators describe the theoretical self-checking mechanism of VAT and all go on to elaborate on how this does not work" (p. 304). Tax authorities do not have the resources required to cross-match sales with invoices, and computers have not provided the solution. False invoices are also a potentially serious problem.

[15] Suppose the utility function of each individual is a function of his or her consumption of leisure and a set of other commodities. Then as long as the marginal rate of substitution between any two commodities is independent of the amount of leisure, differential commodity taxation cannot improve social welfare in the presence of an optimal earnings tax.

[16] Also recall from Chapter 16 that uniform commodity taxation is not optimal if some goods are more substitutable or complementary with leisure than other goods. (This is the case if the condition on the utility function described in the previous footnote does not hold.) Nevertheless, given that the information required to determine fully efficient commodity taxes in the general case is not currently available, uniform tax rates may not be a bad approach. Recent advances in optimal tax theory suggest that the information required to implement efficient commodity taxes may be easier to obtain than previously believed. See the study by Sørensen (2007).

But problems can arise with attempts to achieve equality in this way. Even if it is true that food expenditures, on average, play an especially important role in the budgets of the poor, there are still many upper-income families whose food consumption is proportionally very high. Furthermore, while there may be obstacles to setting income taxes optimally in less-developed countries (see Bird and Zolt, 2005), it can be argued that tax policy in Canada should address concerns about equity by adjusting the income tax schedule rather than by setting differential commodity tax rates (see Kaplow, 2006). As Michael Wilson, then Minister of Finance, argued when the GST was proposed in 1987:

> A better way to make the sales tax fair [than by exempting items from the GST] is to offset the effects of the total tax paid by lower-income families with a refundable sales tax credit. By making the credit refundable, all low-income Canadians receive the credit, even if they do not pay income tax. What is required to qualify is to file a tax return, as most Canadians already do. By phasing the credit out for households with income above a threshold level, the benefits are appropriately targeted to lower-income families. By prepayment of this credit, those in need will receive a payment before they have to purchase goods and services and pay the sales tax.[17]

The refundable credit that accompanied the GST has, even if unnoticed, been sufficient to compensate for any additional regressivity contributed by the GST.[18] Nevertheless, the GST excludes certain items from the consumption tax base. There are two ways to implement the non-taxation of consumption items under the GST: zero-rated (tax free) and tax-exempt items. There is an important difference between zero-rated and tax-exempt items, which we now explain.

Zero-rated (tax-free) and tax-exempt items. Zero-rated items include basic groceries, prescription drugs, medical devices, and exports. For these items, the seller does not pay the GST on the value added at

---

TABLE 19.2

Value-Added Tax with Zero-Rated and Tax-Exempt Items

A. Value-Added Tax with Groceries Zero-Rated

Producer	Purchases	Sales	Tax on Sales	Credit Allowed	Tax Due
Farmer	$ 0	$ 400	$ 40	$ 0	$ 40
Millert	400	700	70	40	30
Baker	700	950	95	70	25
Grocer	950	1,000	0	95	−95
Total					$ 0

B. Value-Added Tax with Groceries Tax-Exempt

Producer	Purchases	Sales	Tax on Sales	Credit Allowed	Tax Due
Farmer	$ 0	$ 400	$ 40	$ 0	$ 40
Miller	400	700	70	40	30
Baker	700	950	95	70	25
Grocer	950	1,000	0	0	0
Total					$ 95

C. Value-Added Tax with Milled Flour Tax-Exempt

Producer	Purchases	Sales	Tax on Sales	Credit Allowed	Tax Due
Farmer	$ 0	$ 400	$ 40	$ 0	$ 40
Miller	400	700	0	0	0
Baker	700	950	95	0	95
Grocer	950	1,000	100	95	5
Total					$140

---

[17] Department of Finance (1987: 64).

[18] See Bird (1994: 2). For a discussion of the distributional effects of zero-rating certain items and providing refundable credits as part of a value-added tax system, see Metcalf (1994).

this stage of production and can claim a tax credit for taxes paid at earlier stages. In Table 19.2 part A we consider how groceries, a zero-rated item, are treated under the GST. (A 10 percent tax rate is assumed in Table 19.2.) The tax is collected from the farmer, miller, and baker—a total of $95 to that point. Since food from the grocer is a tax-free item, the grocer pays no GST on the $50 of value added, *and* in addition is able to claim a credit for the $95 of GST paid on its purchases. The result is that the final price of the food is free of GST. (See the last column in the table.)

Tax-exempt items include residential rents, most health and dental services, daycare services, municipal transit, most educational services, and many financial services.[19] If food were a tax-exempt item instead, as in Table 19.2 part B, the grocer would not pay the $5 tax on the $50 of value added at this stage, and would *not* be able to claim a tax credit for the $95 in GST paid on its purchases. Thus, the final price of the groceries would include the $95 in GST previously paid. If all of the value added were in the final stage of production (i.e., the grocer produces the wheat, mills the flour, and bakes and sells the bread), zero-rated and tax-exempt treatment would be the same. Thus, the importance of tax-exempt treatment depends on where value is added. Moreover, the exemption of goods at an intermediate stage of production may have the perverse effect of increasing the tax component in the price of the final good. This is because the credit given for value added at earlier stages is lost. Table 19.2 part C provides such an example. In this case, the flour sold by the miller is exempt. The miller does *not* owe the GST, nor is he able to take a tax credit for the $40 in GST paid on his purchases from the farmer. Thus, under the credit–invoice system the baker owes 10 percent of the total value added, or $95, and is unable to take a credit against this since the invoice from the miller, due to his exemption, does not include any GST information. The GST in this case totals $140 by the time the groceries are sold; since the chain of credits was interrupted, the credit of $40 paid by the farmer is lost.

Improving the GST

The Liberal government was elected in 1994 on a platform that included a commitment to repeal the GST. The government was unable to honour this commitment, even though the GST was "broadly and deeply resented by Canadians," because none of the alternative taxes is particularly attractive. We discussed, previously, the reasons for Canada's adoption of a VAT (the GST). We turn now to some of the problems with the GST, and changes that will improve the GST.

Harmonization efforts. The Standing Committee on Finance recognized that "in designing a replacement for the GST it is necessary to try to preserve some of the most beneficial aspects of an invoice credit VAT," and recommended "replacing the GST with a federal–provincial, integrated, value-added tax."[20] With integration, the sales tax base would be uniform across Canada and the combined federal and provincial rate would vary from province to province depending on the rates chosen by provinces.

Although Quebec integrated its provincial sales tax with the GST, and Newfoundland, Nova Scotia, and New Brunswick reached an agreement in early 1996 to do so, other provinces have been reluctant to give up their autonomy. It was not until July 1, 2010, that Ontario and British Columbia integrated their sales taxes with the GST. Then in August 2011, British Columbia decided to return to a provincial retail sales tax, effective April 1, 2013. Prince Edward Island implemented an integrated sales tax in 2013.

The challenge for tax harmonization is to find solutions that respond to the need for provincial and federal autonomy while achieving efficiencies by broadening the consumption tax base and reducing compliance and administration costs. The federal government also needs to work with provinces to eliminate the complex system of rebates, which ensures that the municipalities, universities, schools, and hospitals (the MUSH sector) pay no more in federal sales taxes than before the GST.

The integrated sales tax in Newfoundland, Prince Edward Island, Nova Scotia, New Brunswick, and Ontario, is called the Harmonized Sales Tax (HST). The tax base for the HST is essentially the same as the GST and the HST rate is the sum of the 5 percent GST and the provincial sales tax rate. The federal government collects HST revenues and remits the appropriate amounts to the participating provinces. The integrated provincial

---

[19] The resale of homes is not subject to the GST. New homes receive special treatment. Those that cost more than $450,000 pay the full 5 percent. Those below $350,000 receive a 1.8 percentage point rebate, resulting in a 3.2 percent tax rate. For new homes between $350,000 and $450,000, the rebate is gradually phased out.

[20] House of Commons (1994: 39–40).

sales tax in Quebec, called the Quebec Sales Tax (QST), contains certain exemptions not available under the GST, and, unlike in the HST provinces, the tax is administered by the provincial government.[21]

Compliance and administration costs. The introduction of the GST added a significant new tax burden plus tax compliance costs on small businesses in the service sector. Services are an area of activity where (a) home production can often be readily substituted for market production, and (b) much of the value is contributed in the form of labour in the final stage of production. These characteristics make tax avoidance and evasion activity more prevalent in the service industries, even in the best of circumstances.

Small businesses are less likely to have record-keeping systems, or in-house expertise, that facilitate ready response to new demands by tax authorities. Compliance costs expressed as a percentage of taxable sales, or as a percentage of revenues collected, are much higher than for large businesses.[22]

Zero-rated and tax-exempt items complicate the administration of the GST, and also make the tax more difficult to understand. From the foregoing, it may be apparent that asking small retailers to differentiate between zero-rated and taxable goods and services complicates compliance by taxpayers, and that exemptions add further complications.

Another problem for the GST is that the United States has no national sales tax. Some U.S. border states (New Hampshire and Montana) have no sales tax, and others (New York at 4 percent and Michigan at 6 percent) have sales taxes that are quite low. Combined federal and provincial sales tax rates were 12 percent in British Columbia, 14.975 percent in Quebec, and 13 percent in Ontario, in 2015. In addition to problems inherent in assessing the GST on goods brought in by shoppers, services purchased abroad by Canadians—such as car repairs, cosmetic surgery, and legal and financial services—are unlikely to be visible to Canadian tax authorities. A related and growing problem with the GST is the challenge posed by the sales of digitized products that take place across international borders. Unless consumers self-assess the GST owed on the imported digitized product (which they have no incentive to do), the situation results in a leakage of tax revenues and can put domestic suppliers at a competitive disadvantage. OECD (2006) recommends lowering the threshold requirements for GST registration of non-resident e-commerce businesses. Canada Revenue Agency has tried to oblige certain non-resident businesses to register for the GST by asserting that they are carrying on business in Canada.

The GST could be improved by simplifying tax compliance for the many small businesses. Raising the sales threshold at which small businesses are required to file GST returns only once a year would increase acceptability.[23]

Other improvements. Another improvement in the GST would be to include basic groceries. This would broaden the tax base and reduce compliance costs. New Zealand and Singapore are examples of countries where basic groceries are taxed under the VAT. A more controversial change may be the move to hide the tax. Surveys indicate that consumers prefer *tax-inclusive pricing*, where advertised and publicized prices include the GST. The GST requires that the tax be made visible either by adding the tax at the cash register and/or by clearly identifying the tax on cash register receipts.[24] Economists commonly argue for the visibility of taxes, ensuring that taxpayers within a democracy are aware of taxes they are paying. Indeed, the move from a hidden FST to a visible GST in 1991 was, among other things, a conscious effort to make the federal sales tax more visible. The extent to which the GST should be hidden will continue to be debated.[25]

---

[21] Prior to 2013, the QST was charged on the selling price *including* GST. Quebec moved toward nearly full harmonization with the GST in 2013.

[22] Compliance costs for businesses with annual sales of $100,000 or less were estimated at 16.97 percent of taxes collected, and for businesses with sales over $1 million at 2.65 percent of taxes collected (House of Commons, 1994: 17). Sandford et al. (1989: 116) have estimated compliance costs for the VAT in the United Kingdom in 1986–87, finding that these costs, expressed as a percentage of taxable sales, varied from a high of 1.94 percent for taxpayers with sales of less than £20,500 per annum to 0.003 percent for those with sales in excess of £10 million per annum.

[23] Requiring small businesses to pay their GST only once a year will increase funds available to them during the year by the amount of GST collected. For example, if an average of $10,000 in GST is held by a business during a year, at an interest rate of 8 percent this is worth $800 to the business and helps to reduce the net cost of complying with the GST. See Sandford et al. (1989: ch. 8).

[24] The visibility of the GST to consumers contributed to its unpopularity when it replaced the FST, which had been invisible. This made the GST look like a new tax rather than a replacement tax.

[25] See Bird (2010) for a detailed discussion about the pros and cons of including the GST in prices.

AN OPTIMAL GAS TAX FOR TORONTO

Federal and provincial gasoline taxes are used in part to pay for investments in municipal infrastructure; for example, public transit, highways, hospitals, and schools. The federal Gas Tax Fund (GTF) distributes $2 billion annually to municipalities across the country. Toronto has used its funding in the past to invest in the city's transit system. *Ontario Budget 2015* promised to dedicate 7.5¢ per litre of the existing provincial gas tax to new infrastructure. (The provincial tax rate in Ontario is 14.7¢ per litre of unleaded gasoline.) Recently, there have been calls for raising the gasoline tax to pay for new transit in the Greater Toronto and Hamilton Area (GTHA). One report proposed a rise in gasoline taxes of 3¢ per litre starting in 2015–16, followed by 1¢ annual increases. A case for a higher gas tax has also been made on environmental grounds. As another report explained, "The higher cost of driving would nudge motorists to more efficient cars, reduce the distance they travel and cut greenhouse gas emissions." Most recently, an academic study by Joel Wood from Thompson Rivers University surveyed estimates of how consumers respond to gasoline taxes, the costs of traffic congestion, the costs of air pollution, and many other parameters. He then used these estimates in an economic model to calculate the optimal gasoline taxes for the GTHA (taking into account pre-existing distortionary income taxes). The results suggest that the optimal gasoline tax for the GTHA is about 15 cents per litre higher than the existing federal-Ontario gas taxes (for a total gasoline tax bill of 40.57 cents per litre) in 2006 prices, which is more than the recently proposed increases. However, proposals for a higher gas tax are opposed by some MPPs: "It's a sin tax for drivers," said one. "It's a direct hit on average families," commented another.

Based on Kalinowsky (2015), Wood (2015), and "Up to 10¢/L gas tax hike to fund Ontario transit, panel recommends." *Toronto Sun*, December 12, 2013.

Complete references for this feature can be found in the References section on page 489.

There is an additional argument that the introduction of the GST will contribute to further expansion of the public sector at the expense of the private sector. Indeed, in virtually all countries with a VAT, the rate has increased over time, as has the share of gross domestic product devoted to taxes.[26] In a world where political institutions accurately reflect the wishes of the citizenry, this observation may not be troubling.

PROVINCIAL BROAD-BASED SALES TAXES

Retail sales taxes (RSTs) are the second form of general, or broad-based, sales tax widely used in Canada. The RST is a single-stage tax that is collected by retailers at the point of sale. Provincial revenue needs created by the Great Depression led to the introduction of provincial retail sales taxes, first in Alberta in 1936 and then in Saskatchewan in 1937. Alberta, although first in, was first out, repealing its tax in 1937. It remains the only province without a broad-based sales tax. By 1950, Quebec, Newfoundland, Nova Scotia, and British Columbia had enacted retail sales taxes, and by 1967, the four remaining provinces all had RSTs. The conversion from RSTs to HSTs in six provinces was discussed above. Nine of Canada's 10 provinces have an RST or an HST.

A consumption type of VAT, such as the GST or an HST, and a retail sales tax can be designed to be equivalent. For example, a 10 percent RST on the $1,000 sale by the grocer in Table 19.1 has the same effect and raises the same revenue as the 10 percent VAT. A main difference is that the VAT is collected in smaller amounts for several taxpayers, while the RST results in a larger amount collected from a single taxpayer. This difference has several implications. One is that the paper trail left by the VAT's invoice-credit system, and the assistance it provides to

---

[26] For example, when Denmark introduced a VAT of 10 percent in 1967, total tax revenues as a percent of gross domestic product were 36.1 percent. By 1978, the VAT rate was 22 percent, and the ratio of taxes to gross domestic product was 43.6 percent (Aaron, 1981: 14). Of course, this does not prove that the VAT was responsible for a larger government sector (see Stockfisch, 1985, Becker and Mulligan, 2003, and Keen, 2007).

TABLE 19.3

	Provincial Consumption Tax Rates (2015) and Revenues from Provincial Consumption Taxes (2013-14)					
Provincial	RST Rate or Provincial Portion of HST (%)	RST/HST Per Capita Revenue* ($)	Tax Rate on Cigarettes (¢/cig.)	Tax Rate on Gasoline (¢/litre)	Consumption Tax Revenue** ($ millions)	Consumption Tax Share of Own-Source Revenue (%)
Newfoundland and Labrador	8	$1,717	23.50	16.5	$1,093	17.9
Prince Edward Island	9	1,678	22.50	13.1	310	29.8
Nova Scotia	10	1,761	25.52	15.5	2,085	31.3
New Brunswick	8	1,370	19.00	13.6	1,455	30.0
Quebec	9.975	1,626	14.90	19.2	16,581	22.2
Ontario	8	1,511	13.97	14.7	24,672	26.3
Manitoba	8	1,603	29.50	14.0	2,381	23.0
Saskatchewan	5	1,199	25.00	15.0	2,112	17.0
Alberta	–	–	22.52	13.0	1,847	4.4
British Columbia	7	1,156	23.90	21.17	6,938	19.1
Northwest Territories	–	–	28,60	10.7	34	9.2
Nunavut	–	–	25.00	10.7	21	5.2
Yukon	–	–	21.00	6.2	19	1.6

* Based on 2013 population figures from CANSIM II database http://cansim2.statcan.ca/ Table 051-0001.
** Only includes HST/RST, taxes on cigarettes, and taxes on gasoline.
Sources: Provincial *Public Accounts 2014* and provincial budgets.

tax authorities, does not exist with the RST. A second is that the exemption of smaller retailers (and hence their value added) under a VAT leads to the loss of much less revenue than if small retailers are exempt from the RST, since under the RST the tax applying to the value added at previous stages of production is also lost. A third is that a VAT, since it is collected at each stage of production, must be collected from many more taxpayers.

The primary advantages of an RST over a VAT are that it is easier to understand and has fewer points of collection. A VAT, on the other hand, is better able to avoid tax cascading and the taxation of goods used as inputs in the production of other goods. Bird and Smart (2009) estimate that 43 percent of RST revenues in Canada come from taxing business inputs. The authors show that when Quebec, Newfoundland, Nova Scotia, and New Brunswick switched from RSTs to provincial value-added taxes (QST and HSTs), investment in these provinces increased, compared with investments in the provinces that retained their RSTs.

Rates and revenues. Provincial sales tax rates have steadily risen since the first RSTs were introduced at a 2 percent rate. Rates and revenues differ substantially from province to province. As Table 19.3 shows, aside from Alberta, which has no general sales tax, 2015 rates ranged from 10 percent in Prince Edward Island to 5 in Saskatchewan. Per capita revenues in 2013-14 were $1,761 in Nova Scotia and $1,156 in British Columbia. RSTs and HSTs account for about 59 percent of provincial consumption taxes.[27] Broad-based sales taxes have been a very important tax policy tool for provinces.

Tax base. Tax bases also differ from province to province. All provinces exempt most food from the tax base, but there is substantial variation in the treatment of prepared meals. Children's clothing is also exempt, but the treatment of other clothing varies among provinces. Although there is no basis in economic theory for the exemption of services that account for a large and growing share of consumption, most services are exempted from provincial RSTs. One result is that the tax base for the federal GST and the HST or QST is broader than

---

[27] Based on data for 2008-09 (see footnote 2).

the remaining provincial RSTs. Services that are usually in the RST base include telephones, cable television, temporary accommodations, and dry cleaning; there is substantial variation in the treatment of maintenance, repair, and other services. Whereas the exemption of services undoubtedly reduces administration and compliance costs, the narrowness of the RST tax bases leads to significant distortions that favour the choice of exempt services over taxed goods. RSTs, like the former FST, continue to fall on many goods that are used as inputs in the production of other goods, resulting in tax cascading and higher effective tax rates on the final goods.

EXCISE TAXES AND CUSTOMS DUTIES

Customs duties, those taxes levied on goods at the time of import or export, are the sole purview of the federal government. As noted in Chapter 1, the Constitution Act of 1867 prohibited provinces from taxing international or interprovincial trade. At the time of Confederation, customs duties raised $9 million and accounted for 75 percent of federal government revenues. In 2013–14 they generated $4.2 billion, 1.5 percent of federal revenue, on $524 billion of imported goods and services. These revenues have decreased steadily as international negotiations through the General Agreement on Tariffs and Trade (GATT) (now the World Trade Organization (WTO)) and bilateral agreements such as the North American Free Trade Agreement (NAFTA) have lowered tariff barriers. Although most raw materials are free of tax, import duties on manufactured goods depend in part on whether similar goods are produced in Canada, with higher taxes applied to imported goods that compete with Canadian goods. Choice is intentionally distorted, with these distortions decreasing as tariff rates are lowered.

Excise taxes continue as an important revenue source. The major excise taxes imposed by the provincial and federal governments in 2015 are listed in Table 19.3 and Table 19.4.[28] Excise taxes on motor fuels, at about

TABLE 19.4

Rates for Federal Excise Taxes and Duties, 2015	
A. Federal Excise Taxes	
Gasoline	10.0¢/litre
Diesel and aviation fuel	4.0¢/litre
Cigarettes	52.58¢/5 cigarettes
Manufactured tobacco	$131.44/kg
Cigars	$22.89/1,000 plus 82%
Tobacco sticks	10.52¢/stick
Wines	
Alcohol, 1.2% or less	2.05¢/litre
Alcohol, 1.2% to 7%	29.50¢/litre
Alcohol, over 7%	62.0¢/litre
Automobile air conditioners	$100/unit
B. Federal Excise Duties (in addition to the federal excise taxes)	
Distilled spirits	$11.696/litre of alcohol
Mixed beverages up to 7% alcohol	29.50¢/litre
Beer	
Up to 1.2% alcohol	$2.59/hectolitre
1.2% to 2.5% alcohol	$15.61/hectolitre
Over 2.5% alcohol	$31.22/hectolitre

Source: Canada Revenue Agency, *Excise Tax Act, 2001-Technical Information, Excise Duty Rates*, http://www.cra arc.gc.ca/E/pub/em/edm1-5-1/edm1-5-1-e.html; accessed September 9, 2015.

---

[28] In Table 19.4, federal excise taxes apply to domestic and foreign goods sold in Canada. Excise duties apply only to domestically produced goods. However, customs duties on imports exceed the excise duty exemption on imports.

25 to 30 cents per litre, raised $14.3 billion in 2013–14, while cigarette taxes generated $4.5 billion for the provinces, and non-energy federal excise taxes and customs import duties raised $8.7 billion for the federal government. Tax authorities are able to collect the bulk of these tax revenues from the relatively few producers of motor fuels, alcoholic beverages, and tobacco products, or at the time of import. Although excise taxes are generally among the easiest and most cost-effective to administer, the explosion in cigarette smuggling in 1993 and 1994 after tobacco taxes increased 48 percent in four years made clear that there are limits on the use of excise taxes as a source of revenue.

Within the conventional welfare economics framework, another justification for a selective sales tax is the presence of externalities. If consumption of a commodity generates costs not included in its price, then, in general, efficiency requires a tax on the use of that good (see Chapter 5). The high tax rates on tobacco—provincial plus federal rates in 2015 ranged from a low of $48.97 in Ontario to a high of $80.03 in Manitoba per carton of 200 cigarettes (from $6.12 to $10.00 per pack of 25)—are sometimes rationalized in this way. Smokers impose higher costs on our public health care system, so a tax on tobacco may enhance efficiency by equalizing the private and the total social cost of smoking.[29] Excise taxes on luxury goods are sometimes used to raise revenues while addressing distributional concerns. A 10 percent federal excise tax on jewellery, watches, and clocks was repealed in 2006.

In some cases, selective sales taxes can be viewed as substitutes for user fees. With current technology, it is not feasible to charge motorists a fee for every kilometre driven, even though the process of driving creates costs in terms of road damage, congestion, and so on. Because the amount of road use is related to gasoline consumption, road use can be taxed indirectly by putting a tax on gasoline. Of course, the correspondence is far from perfect: some cars are more fuel efficient than others, and some do more damage than others. Still, some positive user fee may be more efficient than none at all.

Other rationalizations for differential commodity taxation lie outside the framework of conventional economics. Certain excises can be regarded as taxes on "sin." A particular commodity, such as tobacco or alcohol, is deemed to be bad per se, and its consumption is, therefore, discouraged by the state. Such commodities are just the opposite of "merit goods" (see Chapter 2), which are viewed as being good per se. In both cases, the government is essentially imposing its preferences on those of the citizenry.

PERSONAL CONSUMPTION TAX

A major objection to both retail sales taxes and value-added taxes, such as the GST, and to many excise taxes is that they do not allow personal circumstances to be considered when determining tax liabilities. In particular, differentiating among people on the basis of ability to pay is difficult.

In contrast, a personal tax based on total consumption expenditures during a given period allows the tax authorities to take individual characteristics into account in determining tax liability. Under a **personal consumption tax** (also referred to as a **personal expenditure tax**), each household files a return reporting its consumption expenditures during the year. Table 19.5 outlines how this might be done. Unlike an income tax, the base of a consumption tax excludes unconsumed additions to wealth: saving. Whereas, under a personal income tax the tax base is defined as

$$income = consumption + change\ in\ net\ wealth,$$

under a personal consumption tax the tax base is

$$consumption = income - change\ in\ net\ wealth.$$

Moreover, just as under the personal income tax, under a consumption tax, various exemptions and deductions can be taken to allow for special circumstances, such as extraordinary medical expenses. Each individual's tax bill is then determined by applying a rate schedule to the adjusted amount of consumption. The rate schedule can be as progressive as policy-makers desire.

---

[29] An offsetting effect of smoking is the reduction in expenditures for health and other care in old age for smokers who die younger than nonsmokers. Smokers also create a second-hand smoke problem, but this externality is best handled through zoning—creating nonsmoking areas in restaurants and office buildings—because a tax on tobacco does not affect the location of cigarette consumption.

TABLE 19.5

Calculating a Personal Consumption Tax

Include:
- wages, salaries, interest, dividends, rent, profits, royalties, transfer payments, and other income (excluding capital gains)
- proceeds from the sale of real and financial assets
- proceeds from borrowing
- gifts and bequests
- withdrawals from savings accounts and other investments

Deduct:
- cost of real and financial assets purchased
- capital contributed to partnerships or proprietorships
- repayment of interest and principal on borrowed funds
- deposits into savings accounts and other investments
- other permitted deductions, such as extraordinary medical expenses, as might also be provided under an income tax

Equals:
- tax base

Tax base × applicable tax rates = tax liability

Some argue that if the income tax were replaced by a consumption tax, efficiency, equity, and administrative simplicity would be enhanced. Indeed, it is argued that we are well on our way to a personal consumption tax in Canada, since "a consumption tax can essentially be achieved by extending the Registered Pension Plans (RPP) and Registered Retirement Savings Plan (RRSP) provisions which currently exist in the present system."[30] One well-known proposal for a personal consumption tax is that put forward by Hall and Rabushka (H&R) (2007), which they call a *flat tax*.

Hall-Rabushka Flat Tax

The H&R proposal has two tax-collecting vehicles: a business tax and an individual compensation tax. The coordinated use of these two instruments allows the government to levy a progressive tax.

The calculation of the business tax base begins with a computation like that of a consumption-type VAT—sales less purchases from other firms. The key difference is that *the firm also deducts payments to its workers*. Firms then pay a flat rate of tax on the final amount.

The base for the individual tax is the payments received by individuals for their labour services. No capital income is taxed at the individual level. In principle, any tax schedule could be applied to this base; the tax rate could be flat to increasing, and an exemption might or might not be allowed. The same or differing rates could be applied at the business and individual levels. Progressivity can be built into the system by providing an exemption of $X for a family. No other deductions would be allowed, and this allows for a lower rate.

At this point you might be wondering why the H&R tax is a consumption tax. To see why, consider a VAT that taxes all goods and services at the same rate, say 20 percent. It has already been shown that this is equivalent to a 20 percent retail sales tax. Now consider an H&R-type flat tax that taxes both individuals and firms at 20 percent and that has no exemptions or deductions at the personal level. Recall that under the VAT, the firm's tax base is sales minus purchases from other firms. Wage payments are not deductible. In effect, then, wage payments are subject to a 20 percent tax. Under the H&R tax, wage payments are deductible at the firm level, but they are taxed at the individual level. The amount of tax is exactly the same as under a VAT; all that changes is the point of collection for part of the tax. The personal exemption simply builds some

---

[30] Beach, Boadway, and Bruce (1988: 106).

progressivity into the system. In short, except for the exemption, the H&R flat tax is essentially equivalent to a VAT or retail sales tax.

The defenders of the income tax have argued that the case for personal expenditure taxation, whether of the H&R type or that outlined in Table 19.5, is seriously flawed. We now discuss the controversy.

Administrative Issues

In discussions of personal consumption taxation, administrative issues are of more than usual interest. This is because such a tax system has never been implemented successfully.[31] Indeed, for many years, a consumption tax has been viewed mostly as an intellectual curiosity rather than a realistic policy option. But, recently, growing numbers of economists and lawyers have suggested that a consumption tax is feasible and not as different from the current income tax system as one might think.[32]

If the only way to compute annual consumption were to add up all expenditures made over the course of a year, taxpayers would have to keep records and receipts for every purchase. This would be administratively infeasible. All taxpayers cannot be expected to maintain complete balance sheets.

An alternative is to measure consumption on a cash flow basis, meaning that it would be calculated simply as the difference between all cash receipts and saving. To keep track of saving, qualified accounts would be established at savings banks, security brokerage houses, and other types of financial institutions. Funds that were certified by these institutions as having been deposited in qualified accounts would be exempt from tax. Most of the record-keeping responsibility would be met by these institutions and would not involve more paperwork than exists already. As long as capital gains and interest from such accounts were retained, they would not be taxed. For some taxpayers, such qualified accounts already exist in the forms of RRSPs, RPPs, and Tax-Free Savings Accounts (TFSAs) (see Chapter 17). One way to look at a consumption tax is simply as an expansion of the opportunities to invest in such accounts.

A potentially important administrative problem concerns the valuation of the consumption benefits produced by durable goods. The purchase of a durable is an act of saving and, hence, would be deductible under a consumption tax. Over time, the durable generates consumption benefits subject to tax. But here the usual problems of imputing consumption streams arise. How do we measure the annual flow of benefits produced by a house or a car?

Proponents of a personal consumption tax argue that this problem is avoidable if a **tax prepayment approach** for durables is used. When the original durable investment is made, it is taxed as if it were consumption. There is no attempt later to tax the returns generated by the investment. Thus, imputation problems are avoided. But does prepayment yield the appropriate amount of tax? In present value terms, tax prepayment does, indeed, yield the right amount as long as the tax rate is fixed. To see why, suppose that the durable lasts for T years and produces expected consumption benefits of c_1 in year 1, c_2 in year 2, and so forth. In equilibrium, the price of the durable, V, just equals the present value of the stream of consumption the durable generates:

$$V = \frac{c_1}{(1+r)} + \frac{c_2}{(1+r)^2} + \cdots + \frac{c_T}{(1+r)^T} \tag{19.5}$$

where r is the interest rate. Now, if consumption is taxed at rate t_c, revenue collections under the tax prepayment approach are $t_c V$. On the other hand, if consumption is taxed when it occurs, the present value of the tax proceeds (R_c) is

$$R_c = \frac{t_c c_1}{(1+r)} + \frac{t_c c_2}{(1+r)^2} + \cdots + \frac{t_c c_T}{(1+r)^T} \tag{19.6}$$

Examining Equations (19.5) and (19.6) together, we note that R_c is exactly equal to $t_c V$. Hence, the same amount of tax is collected in present value terms.

---

[31] India and Sri Lanka were the only two countries to adopt a personal consumption tax, and both nations soon abandoned it.

[32] A version of the H&R proposal was the centrepiece of 2000 U.S. presidential candidate Steve Forbes's campaign.

Advantages of a personal consumption tax. Although many people believe that personal consumption taxation would be an administrative nightmare and that switching to it would be accompanied by enormous transitional problems, many others have become convinced that personal consumption taxation is practical. We now catalogue some *advantages* of personal consumption taxation relative to income taxation.

• *No need to measure capital gains and depreciation.* Some of the most vexing problems in administering an income tax arise from difficulties in measuring additions to wealth. For example, it requires calculation of capital gains and losses even on those assets not sold during the year, a task so difficult that it is not even attempted under the current system. Similarly, for those who have income produced by capital equipment, additions to wealth must be lowered by the amount the equipment depreciates during the year. As we note in Chapter 21, very little is known about actual depreciation patterns. One result of our inability to accurately measure depreciation is the variation in effective tax rates on income arising from different investments. Although the total level of investment may be little affected by our choice between an income or consumption tax, the income tax may lead to a very inefficient allocation of capital. Andrews (1983: 282) views the inability of real-world income tax systems to measure and tax additions to wealth as their fatal flaw: "A comprehensive income tax ideal with an immediate concession that taxation is not to be based on actual value is like a blueprint for constructing a building in which part of the foundation is required to be located in quicksand. If the terrain cannot be changed, the blueprint had better be amended." Under a consumption tax, all such problems disappear because additions to wealth, per se, are no longer part of the tax base.

• *Fewer problems with inflation.* In the presence of a non-indexed income tax, inflation creates important distortions. Some of these are a consequence of a progressive rate structure, but some would occur even if the tax were proportional. These distortions occur because computing capital income requires the use of figures from years that have different price levels. For example, if an asset is sold, calculation of the capital gain or loss requires subtracting the value in the year of purchase from its value in the current year. In general, part of the change in value is due to inflation, so individuals are taxed on gains that do not reflect increases in real income, and the lock-in effect may be significant.[33] With a consumption tax, the sale of an asset results in no change in the tax base if the proceeds of the sale are reinvested in the same year.

As noted in Chapter 17, setting up an appropriate scheme for fully indexing income generated by investments is very complicated and has not been attempted in Canada. In contrast, under a consumption tax, calculation of the tax base involves only current-year transactions. Therefore, any distortions associated with inflation are likely to be much less of a problem.

• *No need for separate corporation tax.* Some argue that implementation of a personal consumption tax would allow removal of the corporation income tax, at least in theory. We will see in Chapter 21 that one of the main justifications of the corporation tax is to get at income that people accumulate in corporations. If accumulation, per se, were no longer part of the personal income tax base, this would not be necessary. Elimination of the corporation tax would probably enhance efficiency. However, to receive part of the profit generated by foreign-owned companies operating in Canada, withholding on income arising in Canada would continue to be necessary.

Assessment. Advocates of a consumption tax often point out that adoption would not be as radical a move as first appearances might suggest. In some respects, the present income tax system in Canada *already* looks very much like a consumption tax:

1. For some taxpayers, income is exempt from taxation when it is saved in certain forms such as RRSPs, RPPs, and TFSAs.
2. Unrealized capital gains on financial assets are untaxed, as are virtually all capital gains on housing.
3. Accelerated depreciation reduces the amount of investment purchases included in the tax base.

In light of these considerations, characterizing the status quo as an income tax is a serious misnomer; it is more a hybrid between income and consumption taxation. Moreover, the importance of the GST/HST as a source of revenues means that consumption as a tax base is well-established in Canada (unlike in the United

---

[33] Suppose, for example, that Smith buys an asset for $100. After a year, the asset is worth $200, but the price level has also doubled. In real terms, there has been no increase in income, yet Smith nevertheless has incurred a tax liability.

States, which does not have a federal sales tax). For these reasons, the benefits of moving from income taxation to a personal consumption tax are limited. However, see Kesselman (1994) for a favourable assessment of replacing the GST with a personal consumption tax.

SUMMARY

- Sales taxes may be levied per unit or as a percentage of purchase value (ad valorem), on all (general sales tax) or specific (excise tax) purchases. General sales and excise taxes are important revenue sources for both the federal and the provincial governments.

- A major attraction of general sales taxes and selective sales taxes is that they are relatively easy to administer. Some sales taxes, such as the excise taxes on tobacco products, alcoholic beverages, and motor fuels, can be justified as correctives for externalities or as substitutes for user fees.

- Unlike income taxes, taxes on consumption do not distort an individual's decisions about saving and investment. However, both forms of taxation distort the choice between leisure and work.

- Taxes on consumption, both general sales taxes and selective taxes, are typically viewed as regressive. However, this view is based on calculations involving annual rather than lifetime income, and assumes that the incidence of the tax lies with the purchaser.

- The Goods and Services Tax (GST) is a value-added tax (VAT). This multi-stage tax, although levied on a similar tax base, differs from a single-stage retail sales tax (RST), which is collected only upon the sale of the final good. A VAT is levied on the difference between sales revenue and cost of purchased commodity inputs at all stages of production. Depending on the treatment of capital inputs, a VAT may be equivalent to a tax on consumption, net income, or gross income. The GST treats investment goods like any other material goods, permitting their full value to be subtracted from sales in the tax computation, and is therefore a consumption-type VAT. A frequent problem with a RST is that some intermediate goods, those used in the production of other goods, may be taxed. This results in tax cascading.

- Most provinces have integrated their provincial sales tax with the GST to form the Harmonized Sales Tax (HST).

- The base of a personal consumption tax is found by subtracting additions to wealth from income: consumption = income − change in net wealth.

- Proponents of the personal consumption tax argue that it eliminates double taxation of interest income, promotes lifetime equity, taxes individuals on the basis of the amount of economic resources they use, may be adjusted to achieve any desired level of progressiveness, and is administratively superior to an income tax.

- Canada's income tax system includes preferential treatment of some forms of savings—for example, RRSP and RPP contributions. Thus, the current income tax system is a hybrid system that includes characteristics of both a personal income tax and a personal consumption tax.

EXERCISES

1. Zach lives two periods, earning $31,500 in the first and nothing in the second. The rate of return on savings is 8 percent. Zach faces a sales tax rate of 5 percent and a tax rate on interest income of 20 percent. His after-tax consumption level in the first period is $16,000. The rest of his earnings are used to pay the sales tax and to save for the second period. Determine how much Zach saves and how much he consumes in the second period. Determine how much Zach pays in sales taxes in each period and how much he pays in interest income tax.

2. Amy and Shirley both live two periods. Both have earnings of $1,000 in the present and zero in the future. The interest rate is 8 percent. Suppose that they are each subject to an income tax, and Amy's first period consumption is $200 while Shirley's is $300. Who has the higher lifetime tax burden? Under a proportional consumption tax, how would their lifetime tax burdens compare?

3. On July 1, 2006, the federal government reduced the GST rate but raised the income tax rate in the lowest tax bracket to help make up for the lost revenues. Discuss the possible effects of this reform on the incentives to save and to work.

4. Rich lives two periods. His earnings in the present are $100; in the future they are $75.6. The interest rate is 8 percent.

   a. Suppose Rich's earnings are subject to a 25 percent tax. Suppose also that interest earnings are taxed at the same rate and interest paid is tax deductible. Using our life-cycle model, show that this tax generates an excess burden. (*Hint:* How does the tax change the intertemporal budget constraint?)

   b. Suppose now that interest payments are not tax deductible. Does this tax generate an excess burden if Rich is a borrower?

   c. Now assume the tax is scrapped in favour of a consumption tax. What consumption tax rate would yield the same tax revenue? Does this tax distort the choice between present and future consumption?

   d. Now assume the consumption tax in part (c) is instituted, but the deduction of interest payments remains. Does this tax distort the choice between present and future consumption?

5. In the table below, with a GST rate of 5 percent, how much does each producer (a) collect in GST; (b) receive as a GST credit; and (c) remit to the government?

	Sale by producer X to producer Y	Sale by producer Y to producer Z	Sale by producer Z to consumer
Sale value	$200.00	$600.00	$1,600.00
GST collected			
GST credit			
GST remitted			

6. Use the same table as in Exercise 5 above but assume now that the retail item (the sale by Z to the consumer) is *exempt* from GST. How much does each producer (a) collect in GST, (b) receive as a GST credit, and (c) remit to the government?

7. Measuring income on an accrual basis creates serious problems for an income tax system. Explain the nature of these problems and how a shift to a personal consumption tax would help to eliminate the problems.

8. Evaluate the following critique of the Hall-Rabushka flat tax: "The flat tax does not treat all income the same. It taxes only salaries and wages and leaves investment income untouched" (Chait, 1996: A17).

9. The table below shows the value added at each stage in the production and sale of furniture.

   a. Fill the blanks in the table, assuming a GST rate of 5 percent.

   b. Repeat the calculations in part (a), but now suppose that the *retail sector is tax exempt*.

	Value Added	GST	Input Tax Credit	Net Tax Due
Producer				
Lumberjack	$100			
Furniture Maker	400			
Wholesaler	200			
Retailer	100			
Total	$800			

CHAPTER 20

Taxes on Wealth and Property

What I, therefore, propose, as the simple yet sovereign remedy, which will raise wages, increase the earnings of capital, extirpate pauperism, abolish poverty, give remunerative employment to whoever wishes it, afford free scope to human powers, lessen crime, elevate morals, and taste, and intelligence, purify government and carry civilization to yet nobler heights, is–to expropriate rent by taxation.

–Henry George[1]

AFTER READING THIS CHAPTER, THE STUDENT SHOULD BE ABLE TO:

LO1 Describe different forms of wealth taxes.

LO2 Explain how a taxpayer's property taxes are determined.

LO3 Summarize the view that the property tax is an excise tax.

LO4 Summarize the view that the property tax is a capital tax.

LO5 Summarize the view that the property tax is a user fee.

LO6 Understand why each view of the incidence of the property tax is valid in different contexts.

The taxes we have discussed so far are levied on items such as income, consumption, and sales. In the jargon of economics, these are known as **flow variables** because they are associated with a time dimension. For instance, income is a flow, because the concept is meaningful only when put in the context of some time interval. If you say, "My income is $10,000," it means nothing unless one knows whether it is over a week, month, or year. A **stock variable**, on the other hand, has no time dimension. It is a quantity at a point in time, not a rate per unit of time. Wealth is a stock, because it refers to the value of the assets an individual has accumulated as of a given time. This section discusses some taxes that are levied on some form of wealth.

WEALTH TAXES

There are many types of wealth taxes. The tax in Canada that most closely resembles a tax on personal wealth is the tax on owner-occupied homes, which is a major tax revenue source for local governments. Other forms of taxation on wealth in Canada are the taxes levied on business properties by provincial and local governments

---

[1] Henry George, *Progress and Poverty* (New York: The Modern Library, originally published in 1879), pp. 405–6.

and the taxes on "paid-up" capital[2] of financial institutions, now used by the federal government and all provincial governments except Alberta. With none of these taxes, however, is the amount of revenue collected closely related to the personal circumstances of individual taxpayers. In the case of property taxes on home-owners, the tax does not reflect the equity of the homeowner—that is, the value of the house net of the mortgage. Instead, it is based on the gross value of the real estate. The net wealth of a taxpayer with a $100,000 home and $75,000 mortgage may be $25,000, but the tax due is still based on the $100,000 value. Similarly, taxes on paid-up capital of corporations and on business property do not reflect individual circumstances, and the incidence of such taxes is far from certain.

Some forms of wealth taxation used in other countries are more closely related to personal circumstances, and allow for an adjustment for liabilities. An example is an *annual tax on the net wealth* of the individual taxpayer. "Net wealth" for such a tax is normally the market value of the nonhuman capital owned by the taxpayer net of his or her liabilities. An *inheritance tax* and *gift tax* can also be adjusted to reflect individual circumstances—the wealth or income of the recipient, or the total amounts received as bequests or gifts. An *estate tax* based on the net value of an estate at the time of death reflects individual wealth at a point in time, although it may be a poor reflection of the taxpaying ability of heirs. Net wealth taxes (NWTs) and death (inheritance and estate) taxes are to some degree adjusted to personal circumstances.

Some wealth taxes, such as the estate tax levied at time of death, are applied once in a generation. Other taxes are applied annually; these include taxes on immovable property in Canada, and annual net wealth taxes in several European countries. Still others are applied periodically, such as gift taxes, which are levied whenever gifts occur. A once-a-generation tax, such as an estate tax, may be levied at relatively high rates (often over 50 percent), while annual net wealth taxes and taxes on immovable properties are generally applied at rates ranging from well below 1 percent to less than 3 percent.

With increased movement of capital and labour across national borders there has been growing reluctance to tax factors of production that are particularly mobile. Policy-makers have become less willing to rely on taxes that fall on capital, such as those on corporate income, capital gains, business properties, personal net wealth, or the transfer of wealth. Evidence of rapid growth in countries with a high rate of private saving—Japan, South Korea, Botswana in the 1980s and 1990s—has also led to a desire for policies that are believed to encourage saving and the accumulation of capital. Although the evidence is mixed on how the after-tax rate of return affects private saving, in the absence of conclusive evidence countries attempt to encourage saving by reducing taxes on the return to some forms of saving. Thus, a wish to increase private saving as well as the concern over factor mobility has decreased the emphasis placed on taxes that fall on wealth, relative to other taxes, over the past 30 years. Establishing and maintaining records of property ownership (e.g., art, coin, and stamp collections), and valuing such property, is accompanied by a substantial set of administrative problems.

Even with the difficulties associated with implementation of such taxes, proponents continue to argue for increased taxation of personal wealth. Why? We saw in Chapter 6 that the distribution of (annual) income in Canada is quite unequal. Evidence suggests that the distribution of wealth may be even more unequal.[3] Statistics Canada estimated that the top 10 percent of wealth holders owned 48 percent of wealth in Canada in 2012 (see Table 20.1). Wealth concentration increased since the 1980s due to the rise in value of North American common stocks (see Wolf, 1998, 2010) and the growth in home equity.[4] Hence, proponents argue that taxes on personal net wealth and wealth transfer taxes are needed to

---

[2] The definition of paid-up capital varies somewhat in federal and provincial statutes. Paid-up capital generally includes the amount received by corporations on stock that has been issued after deducting discounts given and including premiums received. It also includes items such as government grants, retained earnings, all long- and short-term loans from banks and other financial institutions, and all loans from other corporations or shareholders. The federal capital tax on non-financial, large corporations was eliminated in 2006. Similarly, all provincial general capital taxes were eliminated by 2012.

[3] Brzozowski et al. (2010) report Gini indices of 0.34 for disposable income and 0.66 for net total wealth in Canada in 2005.

[4] When wealth is more broadly defined to include the value of employee pensions and public pensions (social insurance), it is more equally distributed than Table 20.1 may suggest. For example, in Canada in 2005 the share of wealth held by the top 10 percent fell from 58 to 51 percent with the inclusion of employer pension plan wealth (Van Rompaey et al. 2006: 18). If we include the value of human capital—the discounted stream of future employment earnings—wealth is even more evenly distributed.

TABLE 20.1

Distribution of Wealth* in Canada in 2012 by Wealth Decile (Families and Unattached Individuals)

	WEALTH DISTRIBUTION BASED ON	
Net Worth Decile	Share of Total Net Wealth (%)	Median Net Worth ($)
1 (lowest)	0	−5,100
2	0	5,000
3	1	30,000
4	2	92,400
5	3	183,300
6	6	312,600
7	9	479,100
8	13	705,000
9	19	1,060,300
10 (highest)	48	2,103,200
Total and overall median	100**	84,800

* Wealth in the survey included bonds, stocks and shares, deposits, owner-occupied homes, cars, and net investments in personal businesses. It excluded equity in private pension funds and insurance policies. It also excluded the value of public pensions, human capital, and other public services and goods such as medical care. ** Subject to rounding error.

Sources: Broadbent Institute, "Haves and Have-Nots: Deep and Persistent Wealth Inequality in Canada," (September 2014) and personal correspondence; Statistics Canada, *Survey of Financial Security, 2012*; and René Morissette and Xuelin Zhang, "Revisiting Wealth Inequality," *Perspectives on Labour and Income* 7(2), Statistics Canada Cat. No. 75–001 (December 13, 2006).

improve wealth distribution (see Davies, 1982, 1991). They also argue that such taxes relate closely to "ability to pay," increase the progressivity of the tax system, fill holes in the income tax system, and generally make the tax system more efficient. Each of these arguments is explored in some depth in Canadian fiscal literature.[5]

The role of several different forms of taxes on wealth and property in the tax systems of various industrialized countries is illustrated in Table 20.2. Countries that rely more heavily on taxes on wealth and property are those that draw substantial revenues from taxes on immovable property owned by individuals and businesses.[6] The United States, the United Kingdom, and Canada stand out in this regard, although Japan, France, and Australia also have quite significant taxes on immovable property. Thus, although the immovable property tax base in Canada does not, in most cases, accurately reflect personal net wealth, Canadians may feel that wealth in Canada is taxed relatively heavily. Other taxes on wealth raise substantially less revenue than do property taxes, although Switzerland appears to draw significant revenues from net wealth taxes, and Japan, Belgium, and France rely relatively heavily on wealth transfer taxes.[7]

Taxes on net wealth have not been used in Canada, whereas wealth transfer taxes, which were used in Canada from 1894 to 1985, are no longer used. Canada and Australia were the only industrialized countries without wealth transfer taxes in 2012. The remainder of this chapter focuses on the use and the effects of taxes on real property.

---

[5] For a detailed discussion of the literature on net wealth taxes and wealth transfer taxes, and the history of wealth transfer taxes in Canada, see Smith (1993 and 2001).

[6] Immovable property is also called real property or real estate.

[7] Although Canada has no estate or inheritance tax, it includes unrealized capital gains in taxable income in the final personal income tax return. In contrast, the United States permits a step-up at time of death, thus allowing unrealized capital gains accruing over the life of the deceased to permanently escape the personal income tax. With a top tax rate of 40 percent on U.S. estates, and maximum rates on capital gains in Canada from 20–25 percent, wealthy Canadians may have an advantage over wealthy Americans. However, given the estate tax exemption in the U.S., at US$5.43 million in 2015, those with modest estates and substantial unrealized capital gains (or their beneficiaries) may be better off in the U.S. than in Canada.

TABLE 20.2

Revenues from Net Wealth Taxes, Wealth Transfer Taxes, Taxes on Immovable Property, and Total Taxes on Property as a Percent of Total Taxes; Selected Countries, 2012

Country	Recurrent Taxes on Immovable Property	Recurrent Net Wealth Taxes*	Estate, Inheritance & Gift Taxes	Total Taxes on Property***
		(Percent of Total Tax Revenues)		
CANADA	9.08	0.12	–**	10.6
Australia	5.23	–	–	8.6
Austria	0.51	–	0.00	1.3
Belgium	2.95	0.34	1.87	7.5
Denmark	2.86	–	0.42	3.8
Finland	1.58	–	0.68	2.8
France	5.65	0.45	1.09	8.5
Germany	1.20	0.00	0.45	2.4
Ireland	3.85	1.01	0.61	7.0
Italy	2.93	0.38	0.09	6.3
Japan	7.03	–	1.08	9.1
Netherlands	1.94	0.00	0.59	3.0
Norway	0.86	1.38	0.18	2.9
Sweden	1.90	–	0.00	2.4
Switzerland	0.58	4.13	0.52	6.6
U.K.	9.69	–	0.60	11.9
U.S.	10.56	–	0.58	11.8
Unweighted avg.				5.5

* These refer only to taxes on "individual" net wealth.
** This indicates that no revenues are reported for such a tax.
*** Taxes included are those on immovable property, net wealth taxes on individuals and corporations, estate taxes, gift taxes, inheritance taxes, taxes on financial and capital transactions, non-recurrent taxes on property such as betterment levies, and recurrent taxes on properties such as jewellery or cattle.

Source: Organisation for Economic Co-operation and Development, *Revenue Statistics, 1965–2013* (Paris: OECD, 2014), Tables 37, 41, 58, and 62.

PROPERTY TAXES

A tax on real property is the major form of wealth taxation in Canada. The property tax in Canada is predominantly a local tax, with provincial governments accounting for less than 16 percent of taxes on real property.[8] There is no federal property tax. In 2013, property and related taxes raised about $49 billion for the local governments in Canada, or 48 percent of local government revenues (including grants from other levels of government). Although it is not as important as many other taxes when viewed from a national perspective, the property tax plays a key role in local public finances. This is most evident in Nova Scotia, where property taxes accounted for 68 percent of total local government revenue in 2013 (see Table 20.3).

In 1933, the property tax accounted for 32 percent of tax revenues raised by all levels of government (see Table 20.4). By the mid-1980s, property taxes had fallen to under 9 percent of total tax revenues. The rapid growth of federal and provincial income tax and sales tax revenues since the 1930s sharply reduced the *relative* importance of property taxes as a revenue source. In 2012, property taxes were 8.7 percent of total government revenues. Nonetheless, property taxes constantly increased in real per capita terms over this period. Real per capita revenue stood at $1,789 in 2012.

---

[8] In British Columbia, Prince Edward Island, and New Brunswick, however, the provincial share of property taxes exceeds 40 percent.

TABLE 20.3

Local Government Property and Related Tax Revenue, 2013

Province	Local Government Revenue from Property and Related Taxes* (in $ thousands)	Percentage of Total Local Government Revenue
Newfoundland	$365,000	44.6%
PEI	47,000	37.3
Nova Scotia	1,218,000	68.2
New Brunswick	645,000	53.9
Quebec	11,322,000	60.4
Ontario	18,571,000	45.6
Manitoba	990,000	39.7
Saskatchewan	705,000	26.7
Alberta	5,945,000	42.2
British Columbia	4,949,000	48.4
NWT	39,000	18.0
Nunavut	14,000	6.1
Yukon	39,000	45.3
All Canada	44,849,000	48.0

* Includes recurrent taxes on immovable property; recurrent taxes on net wealth, estate, inheritance, and gift taxes; recurrent and non-recurrent other taxes on property.

Source: CANSIM II database http:/ /cansim2.statcan.ca/ Table 385-0037.

TABLE 20.4

Real Property Taxes in Canada, 1933–2012

	PROPERTY TAXES* AS A SHARE OF			
Year	Government** Revenue	GDP***	Personal Income	Per Capita (2014 $)****
1933	31.7%	6.5%	8.3%	$390
1945	7.8	2.4	3.1	321
1955	11.2	2.7	3.6	436
1965	11.6	3.2	4.4	680
1975	8.9	3.3	4.1	1,041
1985	8.7	3.4	3.9	1,201
2005	8.7	3.8	4.7	1,784
2012	8.7	3.5	–	1,789

* Property and related taxes. ** Consolidated federal, provincial, and local government revenues. *** GDP at basic prices. **** Inflation adjustment using CPI.

Sources: Adapted from M. C. Urquhart and K. A. H. Buckley, *Historical Statistics of Canada*, 2nd ed. (Ottawa: 1983); Statistics Canada, *Public Finance Historical Statistical Data, 1965/66-1991/92*, Catalogue 68-512 (Ottawa: April 1, 1992) and *Canadian Economic Observer: Historical Statistical Supplement*, Catalogue 11-210-X (Ottawa: August 12, 2010); and CANSIM II database http://cansim2.statcan.ca/ Tables 326-0021, 379-0024, 379-0029, 384-0012, 051-0001, 385-0003, 385-0032.

Property Tax Assessments

How is the tax liability on a given piece of property determined? An individual's property tax liability is the product of the tax rate and the property's **assessed value**–the value the jurisdiction assigns to the property. In most cases, jurisdictions attempt to make assessed values correspond to market values. However, if a piece of property has not been sold recently, the tax collector does not know its market value and must therefore make an estimate, perhaps based on the market values of comparable properties that have been sold recently.

TABLE 20.5

Residential and Commercial Property Tax Rates Effective Tax Rates (Selected Cities, 2015)		
City	Residential Property	Commercial Property
Vancouver	0.37%	1.59%
Calgary	0.61	1.41
Edmonton	0.80	1.80
Halifax	1.21	3.40
Toronto	0.72	2.90
Saskatoon	1.26	1.76
Montreal	0.83	3.71
Ottawa	1.13	3.04
Regina	1.37	2.14
Winnipeg	1.21	2.50

Source: Altus Group, prepared for Real Property Association of Canada, "2015 Property Tax Rate Analysis" (September 2015).

Market and assessed values diverge to an extent that depends on the accuracy of the jurisdiction's estimating procedure. The ratio of the assessed value to market value is called the **assessment ratio**. If all properties have the same statutory rate and the same assessment ratio, their effective tax rates are the same. Suppose, however, that assessment ratios differ across properties. Ophelia and Hamlet both own properties worth $100,000. Ophelia's property is assessed at $100,000 and Hamlet's at $80,000. Clearly, even if they face the same statutory rate (say 2 percent), Ophelia's effective rate of 2 percent (= $2,000/$100,000) is higher than Hamlet's 1.6 percent (= $1,600/$100,000). In fact, in many communities, due to assessment errors, properties with the same statutory rate differ drastically with respect to effective rates.

It is not unusual for assessment ratios to differ systematically for different types of property. Business properties are often assessed at higher ratios than are single and double family dwellings, and the assessment ratio for manufacturing and industrial property may differ from that for professional and commercial property.

To analyze the property tax, one must realize at the outset that property tax systems in Canada differ from province to province, and even within provinces there may be significant differences. No jurisdiction includes a comprehensive measure of wealth in its tax base, but there are major differences with respect to just what types of property are excludable and what rates are applied. Churches, educational properties, hospitals, and cemeteries are generally among properties that are exempt, but there are some differences among provinces. Charitable organizations are also often exempt. The tax rate on commercial properties is higher than on residential properties, although some communities tax new business plants preferentially, presumably to attract more commercial activity.[9] Few areas tax personal wealth other than homes, so items such as cars, jewels, and stocks and bonds are exempt. Typically, structures and the land on which they are built are subject to tax. But, as Table 20.5 demonstrates, the effective rates differ substantially across cities and type of properties.

Thus, although we continue to describe the subject matter of this section as "the" property tax, it should now be clear that there is no such thing. The fact that there are many different property taxes is crucial to assessing the economic effects of the system as a whole. There is considerable controversy as to who ultimately bears the burden of the property tax. We discuss three different views and then try to reconcile them.

Incidence and Efficiency Effects: Traditional View—Property Tax as an Excise Tax

The traditional view is that the property tax is an excise tax that falls on land and structures. Incidence of the tax is determined by the shapes of the relevant supply and demand schedules in the manner explained in Chapter 14. The shapes of the schedules are different for land and structures.

---

[9] From an efficiency standpoint, it can be argued that commercial and industrial properties should be taxed more lightly than residential properties, because businesses tend to be more mobile than homeowners (see Chapter 15).

IN THE NEWS

IS TAXPAYER SATISFACTION AN OXYMORON?

If citizens perceive a clear connection between their residential property taxes and the financing of local services, then the link encourages local politicians to make efficient fiscal decisions, and taxpayers will be more inclined to view their property taxes as a form of user charge for good schools, public parks, access to roads and transit, snow removal, and so on. However, the visibility of property taxes—they appear as a bill, rather than being withheld at source—can also make them unpopular. Several municipalities in Canada use surveys to gauge the satisfaction of their citizens with their property taxes and service levels. Calgary's 2015 Citizen Satisfaction Survey is an example. One of the questions asked about "the value you feel you receive from your municipal property tax dollars using a scale of 1 to 10 where '1' represents 'very poor value' and '10' represents 'very good value'." Sixty-four percent of respondents said they received "good value" (interpreted by the survey as numerical responses from 7 to 10). Another question stated, "Due to the increased cost of maintaining current service levels and infrastructure, the City must balance taxation and service delivery levels. To deal with this situation, which of the following four options would you most like the City to pursue?" A perhaps surprising 59 percent opted for "increase taxes" while 36 percent opted for "cut services." Sixty-five percent of people agreed with the statement, "the City does a good job of providing citizens with information about how their property tax dollars are invested in various City services." Mayor Naheed Nenshi said, "Research like this helps guide Council as we make decisions about capital investments and how the City can support the quality of life we all enjoy."

Based on Kaufman (2015), Ipsos Public Affairs (2015), Slack (2011), and "Results are in from 2015 Citizen Satisfaction Survey & Research on Calgary's Economy." 660 News, November 23, 2015.

Complete references for this feature can be found in the References section on page 490.

Land. As long as the amount of land cannot be varied, its supply curve is, by definition, perfectly vertical. A factor with such a supply curve bears the entire burden of a tax levied on it. Intuitively, because its quantity is fixed, land cannot "escape" the tax. This is illustrated in Figure 20.1. S_L is the supply of land. Before the tax, the demand curve is D_L, and the equilibrium rental value of land is P_0^L. The imposition of an ad valorem tax on land pivots the demand curve. The after-tax demand curve is D_L'. The rent received by suppliers of land (landowners) is found at the intersection of the supply curve with D_L' and is given by P_n^L. The rent paid by the users of land is found by adding the tax per acre of land to P_n^L, giving P_g^L. As expected, the rent paid by the users of the land is unchanged $(P_0^L = P_g^L)$; the rent received by landowners falls by the full amount of the tax. Landowners bear the entire burden of the tax.

As discussed in Chapter 14, under certain circumstances the tax is *capitalized* into the value of the land. Prospective purchasers of the land take into account the fact that if they buy the land, they also buy a future stream of tax liabilities. This lowers the amount they are willing to pay for the land. Therefore, the person who bears the full burden of the tax is the landlord at the time the tax is levied. To be sure, future landlords make payments to the tax authorities, but such payments are not really a burden because they just balance the lower price paid at purchase. Capitalization complicates attempts to assess the incidence of the land tax. Knowing the identities of current owners is not sufficient; we must know who the landlords *were* at the time the tax was imposed.[10]

To the extent that land is *not* fixed in supply, the preceding analysis requires modification. For example, the supply of urban land can be extended at the fringes of urban areas that are adjacent to farmland. Similarly, the amount of land can be increased if landfills or reclamation of wasteland is feasible. In such cases, the tax on land is borne both by landlords and the users of land, in proportions that depend on the elasticities of demand and supply. But it is usually assumed that a vertical supply curve for land is a good approximation of reality.

---

[10] A study by Dachis, Duranton, and Turner (2012) finds the land transfer tax imposed by Toronto in 2008 on purchases of real estate was fully capitalized into lower purchase prices.

FIGURE 20.I

INCIDENCE OF A TAX ON LAND

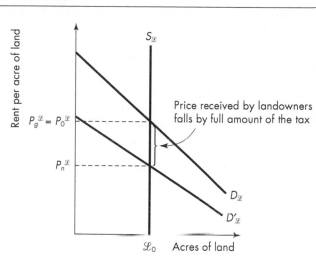

Structures. To understand the traditional view of the tax on structures, we begin by considering the national market for capital. Capital can be used for many purposes: construction of structures; equipment for manufacturing; public sector projects, like dams; and so forth. At any given time, capital has some price that rations the capital among alternative uses. According to the traditional view, in the long run, the construction industry can obtain all the capital it demands at the market price. Thus, the supply curve of structures is perfectly horizontal—a higher price is not required to obtain more of them.

The market for structures under these conditions is depicted in Figure 20.2. Before the tax, the demand for structures by tenants is D_B, and the supply curve, S_B, is horizontal at the going price, P_0^B. At price P_0^B the quantity exchanged is B_0. On imposition of the tax, the demand curve pivots to D_B', just as the demand for land pivoted in Figure 20.1. But the outcome is totally different. The price received by the suppliers of structures, P_n^B, is the same as the price before the tax was imposed ($P_n^B = P_0^B$). Demanders of structures pay a price, P_g^B, which exceeds the original price, P_0^B, by precisely the amount of the tax. Hence, the burden is shifted entirely to tenants. This result, of course, is a consequence of the assumption that the supply curve is horizontal.

FIGURE 20.2

INCIDENCE OF A TAX ON STRUCTURES

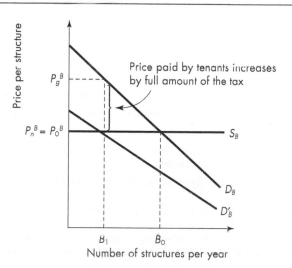

Intuitively, the horizontal supply curve means capital will not stay in the housing sector if it does not receive a return of at least P_0^B. But if the price received by the suppliers of capital cannot be lowered, the tax must be borne entirely by tenants.

The traditional view is based on the assumption that imposing a property tax on structures does not affect the position of the demand curve for land. In other words, the traditional view of the property tax ignores the interaction between the demand for land and rate of return on capital (structures). If the demand for land increases because builders substitute land for structures when the price of structures increases, then the rental price of land will increase, and landowners will bear less than the full burden of the property tax on land. On the other hand, if the demand curve for land shifts to the left because of the reduced demand for housing and other services in the community that has imposed the higher property tax, then the rental price of land will go down, the owners of land will bear more than the burden of the property tax on land, and tenants will bear less than the burden on structures.

Summary of the traditional view. The part of the property tax that is on land is borne by landowners (or at least the landowners at the time the tax is levied); the tax on structures is passed on to tenants. Therefore, the land part of the property tax is borne by people in proportion to the amount of rental income they receive, and the structures part of the tax is borne by people in proportion to the amount of housing they consume.

Implications for progressiveness. With these observations in mind, we can assess the distributional implications of the traditional view of the property tax. The effect of the land part of the tax on progressiveness hinges on whether or not the share of income from land ownership tends to rise with income. There is fairly widespread agreement that it does, so this part of the tax is progressive.

Similarly, the progressiveness of the tax on structures depends critically on whether the proportion of income devoted to housing rises or falls as income increases. If it falls, then the structures part of the tax tends to be regressive, and vice versa.

An enormous amount of econometric work has been done to estimate how housing expenditures actually do respond to changes in income. The ability to reach a consensus has been impeded by disagreement over which concept of income to use. Some investigators use *yearly* income. They tend to find that the proportion of income devoted to housing falls as income increases, suggesting that the tax is regressive. Other investigators believe that some measure of *normal* or *permanent* income is more relevant to understanding housing decisions. According to this view, the fact that a family's annual income in a given year happens to be higher or lower than its normal income should not have much of an impact on that year's housing consumption. Housing decisions are made in the context of the family's long-run prospects, not yearly variations.

Of course, those who believe that permanent income is the appropriate variable must find some way to estimate it. One approach is to define permanent income as the average of several years' annual incomes. Housing expenditures turn out to be more responsive to changes in permanent income than to changes in annual income. Indeed, although the evidence is mixed, it appears reasonable to say that housing consumption is roughly proportional to permanent income. Hence, the structures part of the tax is probably neither regressive nor progressive. Unfortunately, analyses based on annual income, which suggest the tax is regressive, have tended to have the greater influence on public discussion of the tax.

Implications for efficiency. Since the supply of land is more or less fixed, the portion of the property tax falling on land is equivalent to a lump-sum tax.[11] The property tax on structures, on the other hand, creates inefficiency by discouraging new construction and repairs to the existing stock of buildings.[12] These considerations have led some jurisdictions to levy property taxes on land values rather than on real estate.[13]

---

[11] When the effective tax rate varies according to *how* the land is used, the property tax distorts the allocation of land between residential and non-residential usages, resulting in an excess burden.

[12] The tax on structures may also encourage urban sprawl by reducing the capital intensity of land usage (i.e., less floor space per building); see Brueckner and Kim (2003).

[13] Several cities in Australia use land value taxation and, following the reforms in Pittsburgh in 1979, nearly 20 Pennsylvanian cities currently levy a much higher tax rate on land than on structures. See Oates and Schwab (1997) for an empirical assessment of Pittsburgh's split-rate policy. Local governments in western Canadian provinces taxed mainly land values by exempting improvements from property taxes in the 1910s, which may have stimulated building construction and the rapid settlement of the region (Newcomer and Hutchinson, 1932).

Incidence and Efficiency Effects: New View—Property Tax as a Capital Tax

The traditional view uses a standard partial equilibrium framework. As we noted in Chapter 14, although partial equilibrium analysis is often useful, it may produce misleading results for taxes that are large relative to the economy. The new view of the property tax proposed by Mieszkowski (1972) takes a general equilibrium perspective and leads to some surprising conclusions.

According to the new view, it is best to think of the property tax as a general wealth tax with some assets taxed below the average rate and some taxed above. Both the average level of the tax and the deviations from that average have to be analyzed.

General tax effect. Assume for the moment that the property tax can be approximated as a uniform tax on all capital. Then the property tax is just a general factor tax on capital. Now assume further that the supply of capital to the economy is fixed. As shown in Chapter 14, when a factor is fixed in supply, it bears the full burden of a general tax levied on it. Hence, the property tax falls entirely on owners of capital. And since the proportion of income from capital tends to rise with income, a tax on capital tends to be progressive. Thus, the property tax is progressive, a conclusion that turns the traditional view exactly on its head!

Table 20.6 illustrates the difference in results when incidence estimates are based on the traditional view (columns (c) and (d) showing different years), and when incidence is based on the "general tax effect" of the new view (column (a)), and on lifetime income combined with the new view (column (b)). Where the property tax on land is borne by owners of land and that on residential structures by homeowners and renters, the incidence is consistently regressive, as in columns (c) and (d). In contrast, where property taxes are borne by recipients of investment income, the property tax becomes significantly progressive at higher income levels (column (a)). And when the new view is combined with "lifetime" as opposed to "annual" incidence, the incidence of the property tax appears moderately progressive.

TABLE 20.6

Estimates of Property Tax Incidence: Annual Incidence versus Lifetime Incidence

Income Decile	New View (1971-Davies et al.)		Traditional View** (1969-Vermaeten et al.)	(1988-Vermaeten et al.)
	Annual	Lifetime*		
	(A)	(B)	(C)	(D)
1 (low)	1.1	2.4	8.5	8.0
2	1.5	3.1	5.8	6.5
3	1.8	2.8	5.7	5.7
4	1.7	3.3	5.3	5.1
5	1.3	3.2	4.5	4.8
6	1.5	3.6	4.4	4.2
7	1.3	3.6	4.1	3.8
8	1.9	4.5	4.1	3.6
9	2.9	3.7	3.7	3.3
10 (high)	10.6	5.6	3.6	3.0
All	4.5	3.9	4.1	3.8

* Deciles for lifetime incidence are ranked by lifetime resources, and the property tax is calculated as a share of resources available over lifetimes. Here it is assumed that property taxes are borne by recipients of investment income.
** Property taxes are expressed as a share of "broad income," which includes employment and investment income; non-taxed income, such as capital gains on residences, retirement savings earnings, and inheritances; and government transfer payments. The share of property taxes on land is assumed to be borne by owners and the share on residential structures by homeowners and renters. The tax on business structures is borne by consumers.

Sources: J. Davies, France St-Hilaire, and J. Whalley, "Some Calculations of Lifetime Tax Incidence," *American Economic Review* 74(4) (September 1984): 633–49; A. Vermaeten, W.I. Gillespie, and F. Vermaeten, "Who Paid the Taxes in Canada, 1951–1988?" *Canadian Public Policy* 21(3) (September 1995).

Excise tax effects. As noted earlier, the property tax is emphatically not a uniform tax. Rates vary according to the type of property and the jurisdiction in which it is located. Some rates are higher than average, and some are lower. Hence, the property tax is a set of excise taxes on capital. According to the new view, capital tends to migrate from areas where it faces a high tax rate to those where the rate is low. In a process reminiscent of the Harberger model presented in Chapter 14, as capital migrates into low-tax-rate areas, its before-tax rate of return there is bid down. At the same time, the before-tax rate of return in high-tax areas increases as capital leaves. The process continues until after-tax rates of return are equal throughout the economy. In general, as capital moves, returns to other factors of production also change. The impact on the other factors depends in part on their mobility. Land, which is perfectly immobile, cannot shift the tax. (In this conclusion, at least, the new and old views agree.) Similarly, the least-mobile types of capital are most likely to bear the tax.

As is usually the case in general equilibrium models, the ultimate incidence depends on how production is organized, the structure of consumer demand, and the extent to which various factors are mobile.

Long-run effects. In our discussion of the general tax effect of the property tax, we assumed that the amount of capital available to the economy is fixed. However, in the long run, the supply of capital may depend on the tax rate. If the property tax decreases the supply of capital, the productivity of labour, and hence the real wage, falls. Moreover, the decrease in capital accumulation as a result of property taxation will generate an excess burden (see Chapter 15). Jorgenson and Yun (1993) estimated a marginal excess burden of about 18 cents per dollar of additional property tax revenues in the United States, which was smaller than their estimate of the marginal excess burden associated with income taxation.

Summary of the new view. The property tax is a general tax on capital with some types of capital taxed at rates above the average, others below. The general effect of the tax is to lower the return to capital, which tends to be progressive in its impact on the income distribution. The differentials in tax rates create excise effects, which tend to hurt immobile factors in highly taxed jurisdictions. The adjustment process set in motion by these excise effects is very complicated, and not much is known about their effects on progressiveness. Neither can much be said concerning the importance of long-term effects created by changes in the size of the capital stock. If the excise and long-run effects do not counter the general effect too strongly, the overall impact of the property tax is progressive.

Incidence and Efficiency Effects: Property Tax as a User Fee

The discussion so far has ignored the fact that property taxes are often used by communities to purchase public services, such as education and police protection. In light of this reality, it may be appropriate to view the property tax as just the cost of purchasing public services. Each individual buys the amount he or she desires by selecting the community in which to live based on the package of local public services (quantity) and the property taxes (price) (see the discussion of the Tiebout model in Chapter 8). Thus, the property tax is really not a tax at all; it is more like a user fee for public services.[14] This view has two important implications:

1. The notion of the *incidence of the property tax* is meaningless because the levy is not a tax in the normal sense of the word.
2. The property tax creates no excess burden. As Hamilton (1975: 13) points out, "If consumers treat the local property tax as a price for public services, then this price should not distort the housing market any more than the price of eggs should distort the housing market."

As noted earlier, the link between property taxes and services received is often tenuous, so we should not take the notion of the property tax as a user fee too literally. Nevertheless, this line of reasoning has interesting implications. For example, if people care about the public services they receive, we expect that the depressing effects of high property taxes on housing values may be counteracted by the public services financed by these taxes. In a classic paper, Oates (1969) constructed an econometric model of property value determination.

---

[14] This view appears to exist in New Zealand where the central government's sales tax (GST) is levied on the property tax bills paid by New Zealanders to their local governments. Where property taxes are, in effect, a fee for local services, this is necessary to ensure that services provided by the public sector are not favoured relative to goods and services provided by the private sector. The fees paid for public services must also be taxed if relative prices are to remain unchanged. It is difficult to imagine Canadians accepting that the GST should be levied on the property taxes paid to local and provincial governments.

In his model, the value of homes in a community depends positively on the quality of public services in the community and negatively on the tax rate, other things being the same. Of course, across communities, factors that influence house prices do differ. These include physical characteristics of the houses, such as number of rooms, and characteristics of the communities themselves, such as distance from an urban centre. These factors must be considered when trying to sort out the effects of property taxes and local public goods on property values. Oates used multiple regression analysis to do so.

Oates's regression results suggest that increases in the property tax rate decrease housing values, while increases in per pupil schooling expenditures increase housing values. Moreover, the parameter values implied that the increase in property values created by expanding school expenditures approximately offset the decrease generated by the property taxes raised to finance them. These results need to be interpreted with caution. For one thing, expenditure per pupil may not be an adequate measure of local public services. Localities provide many public services other than education, such as police protection, parks, and libraries. Furthermore, even if education were the only local public good, expenditure per pupil might not be a good measure of educational quality. It is possible, for example, that expenditures in a given community are high because the community has to pay a lot for its teachers, its schools are not administered efficiently, or its students are particularly difficult to educate.

Subsequent to Oates's study, a number of other investigators have examined the relationships among property values, property taxes, and local public goods using data from different geographical areas and employing different sets of explanatory variables. Although the results are a bit mixed, Oates's general conclusion seems to be valid—property taxes and the value of local public services are capitalized into housing prices. See, for example, Nguyen-Hoang and Yinger. (2011).[15] Thus, if two communities have the same level of public services but the first has higher taxes than the second (perhaps because its cost of providing the services is greater), we expect the first to have lower property values, other things being the same. More generally, these results imply that to understand how well off members of a community are we cannot look at property tax rates in isolation. Government services and property values must also be considered.

Reconciling the Three Views

It is a mistake to regard the three views of the property tax as mutually exclusive alternatives. Each may be valid in different contexts. If, for example, we want to find the consequences of eliminating all property taxes and replacing them with an increase in the federal GST rate, the "new view" is appropriate because a change that affects all communities requires a general equilibrium framework. On the other hand, if a given community is considering lowering its property tax rate and making up the revenue loss from a local sales tax, the "traditional view" offers the most insight. This is because a single community is so small relative to the economy that its supply of capital is essentially perfectly horizontal, and Figure 20.2 applies. Finally, when taxes and benefits are jointly changed and there is sufficient mobility for people to pick and choose communities, the "user fee view" is useful.

The Future of the Property Tax

In the past 35 years, governments in the United States and the United Kingdom have acted to sharply reduce reliance on property taxes for the financing of local governments. In 1978, California voters put a 1 percent ceiling on the property tax rate that any locality could impose, limited the assessed value of property to its 1975 value,[16] and forbade state and local governments from imposing any additional property taxes without approval by a two-thirds' majority local vote. Property taxes were reduced in 37 U.S. states in 1978 and 1979 alone, and the move against property taxes continued. Although subsequently repealed in the U.K., Prime Minister Margaret Thatcher replaced taxes on residential properties with a poll, or head, tax as the primary way to finance local services.

In Canada, provincial action to improve property tax administration and limited growth in property tax revenues in the 1970s and 1980s may have resulted in more modest opposition to this form of taxation.[17]

---

[15] For a critical discussion of empirical findings on tax and benefit capitalization, see Mieszkowski and Zodrow (1989).

[16] For property transferred after 1975, the assessed value was defined as the market value at which the transaction took place.

[17] See Smith (1990).

Nonetheless, with increased reliance on property taxes in the 1990s to offset reduced grants from higher levels of government, resistance to property taxes is growing in Canada. This resistance is seen in the public pressure to implement limits on property tax increases in Ontario (Slack, 2010).

There are several reasons why property taxes will continue to be an appropriate target for criticism by those who seek fair and efficient taxes:

1. As noted earlier, because housing market transactions typically occur infrequently, the property tax must be levied on an estimated value. To the extent that this valuation is done incompetently, or political forces prevent valuations based on current market values, the tax is perceived as unfair.

2. The property tax is highly visible. Under the federal and provincial income and payroll taxes, payments are withheld from workers' paycheques, and the employer sends the proceeds to the government. In contrast, the property tax is often paid directly by the taxpayer. Moreover, the payments are often made on a quarterly or an annual basis, so each payment comes as a large shock.

3. The property tax is perceived as being regressive. This perception is partly a consequence of the fact that the "traditional view" of the property tax continues to dominate public debate. It is reinforced by the fact that some property owners, particularly the elderly, do not have enough cash to make property tax payments and may therefore be forced into selling their homes. All provinces have responded to this phenomenon with one or more programs. Five provinces allow some portion of property taxes to be credited against personal income taxes payable, with the value of the credit declining as taxable income increases. Other relief includes a partial exemption from property taxes for those with incomes below a certain level, grants that fully or partially offset property taxes, and the deferral of property taxes (with a lien against a property) until the time when the property is transferred.

4. Taxpayers may dislike other taxes as much as the property tax, but they feel powerless to do anything about the others. It is relatively easy to take aim at the property tax, where it is levied locally. In contrast, mounting a drive against, say, the federal income tax is more difficult, if for no other reason than a national campaign would be necessary and, hence, involve large coordination costs.

In light of objections to the property tax, it is natural to ask whether there are any ways to improve it. A modest proposal is to improve assessment procedures. The use of computers and modern valuation techniques can make assessments more frequent and uniform.[18] Where effective tax rates differ within a jurisdiction, uniform tax rates would probably enhance efficiency. The equity issues are more complicated. On one hand, it seems a violation of horizontal equity for two people with identical properties to pay different taxes on them. However, the phenomenon of capitalization requires that we distinguish carefully between the owners at the time the tax is levied and the current owners. A property with an unduly high tax rate can be expected to sell for a lower price, other things being the same. Thus, a high tax rate does not necessarily make an individual who buys the property after the tax is imposed worse off. Indeed, equalizing assessment ratios could generate a whole new set of horizontal inequities.

A more ambitious reform of the property tax would be to convert it into a tax on personal net wealth. An advantage of such a system over a property tax is that by allowing for deduction of liabilities, it provides a better index of ability to pay. Moreover, because it is a personal tax, exemptions can be built into the system and the rates can be varied to attain the desired degree of progressivity. However, administrative problems associated with a net wealth tax are formidable. Difficulties that arise in valuing housing for property tax purposes are likely to pale in comparison to valuing assets such as paintings, antiques, or Persian rugs. Moreover, while a house is difficult to conceal, other types of assets are relatively easy to hide from the tax collector. Note also that because individuals can have assets and liabilities in different jurisdictions, a net wealth tax would undoubtedly have to be administered by the federal government.

In the face of strong criticism, two lines of argument appear foremost in justifying continued reliance on the current system of property taxation as the way to finance local services. The first argument is the local autonomy that is provided by taxes on real property. The second is based on the extent to which the property tax serves as a user fee for locally provided services.

---

[18] For example, properties in Alberta were appraised for market value once every eight years prior to 1995, whereas now they are assessed annually.

Whatever its flaws, the property tax can be administered locally. Hence, it provides local government with considerable fiscal autonomy. As one observer put it, "Property taxation offers people in different localities an instrument by which they can make local choices significant" (Harris, 1978: 38). According to this view, elimination of the property tax would ultimately destroy the economic independence of local units of government.

Over the past two decades, several provincial governments–Ontario, Manitoba, Alberta, and British Columbia– have increased their involvement in the property tax field. This has, in some cases, reduced local autonomy as provinces seek to achieve "provincial standards" in areas such as education. This is likely to raise concern over increased concentration of power to set policies and priorities at provincial rather than local levels. Just as provinces have been concerned about undue federal influence through excessive control of revenue sources, local citizens may have similar concern regarding control at the provincial level. Even though municipalities may have access to other tax bases, the political role of the property tax needs to be taken seriously in any discussion of its reform.

SOME FINAL COMMENTS

Canadians rely heavily on "personal consumption" and "personal income" as tax bases from which to raise substantial government revenue. This is not so for "personal wealth." The property tax applies only to a small share of the wealth of many Canadians. Moreover, to the extent that the property tax is a user fee for local services, it is a payment for services rendered rather than a tax, and in this regard differs from the broad-based personal income and consumption taxes.

We should not expect Canadian policy-makers to turn to a personal net wealth tax or wealth transfer taxes as a new or significant revenue source. Interprovincial and international tax competition contributed to the demise of wealth transfer taxes in Canada from 1967 through 1985. Ontario's Fair Tax Commission, reporting in 1993, was unable to recommend the reintroduction of estate or inheritance taxes. There is general agreement that any such tax would need to be nationwide, even if the revenues went to the provinces, in order to avoid interprovincial tax competition. In addition, tax competition with the United States makes it difficult for Canada to employ a significant estate tax while continuing to deem capital gains to be realized at time of death for income tax purposes. Although the United States has an estate tax, it exempts accrued, but unrealized, gains at time of death from its income tax. Nonetheless, estate and inheritance taxes may continue to strike a sympathetic note with many Canadians who seek a "more equal start" for all Canadians, as long as wealth remains concentrated in the hands of a relatively small minority.

SUMMARY

- Wealth taxes are assessed on a tax base that is a stock of assets instead of a flow, such as income or sales.

- Proponents of wealth taxes believe that they help to correct the income tax for unrealized capital gains, reduce the concentration of wealth, and compensate for benefits received by wealth holders. Some also argue that wealth by itself is a good index of ability to pay and should, therefore, be subject to tax.

- Property taxes are an important revenue source for provincial and local governments. There are three, not mutually exclusive, views on the incidence and efficiency effects of the property tax. The "traditional view" is that the property tax is an excise tax on land and structures. The "new view" is that the property tax is a general tax on all capital with rates that vary across jurisdictions and different types of capital. The "user fee view" regards property taxes as payment for local public services.

- The property tax is a very imperfect tax on personal wealth. It is unlikely that it can be extended to become part of an effective tax on personal net wealth, allowing for the full recognition of liabilities as well as assets. Such a change would be administratively complex and may undermine the most appealing aspect of the property tax in the context of a federal system—local administration.

EXERCISES

1. As a result of Brian's will, $100,000 is paid to his son John at the time of Brian's death in 2012. The $100,000 is not to be included in the income of John. However, this is not a flaw in the income tax system since the $100,000 was never allowed as a deduction for Brian for income tax purposes while he was alive. Comment.

2. David and Jonathan own identical homes. David has owned his home for many years and paid $100,000 for it. Jonathan purchased his home after a recent property tax increase and paid $80,000. Should the local assessor change the assessed value of Jonathan's home to maintain horizontal equity? (Assume there has been no inflation in housing prices since David purchased his home and that David and Jonathan value equally all public services provided in the local community.) In your answer, carefully define all key concepts.

3. Residential properties typically face a lower tax rate than commercial and industrial properties. Explain how the allocation of resources might change in a city if it were to raise the tax rate on homes and decrease the tax rate on business properties. What are the efficiency and equity implications of your analysis of this policy reform?

4. Opponents argue that taxes on the transfer of wealth will reduce work effort, reduce saving, and reduce the willingness to make risky investments. Whether or not you agree with this assessment, explain why many people, supported by economic theory, think it may not be true.

5. The City of Ottawa charges the developers of residential housing for the cost of constructing storm sewers, roads, street lights, libraries, police stations, parks, and community recreation facilities. Discuss the efficiency and equity aspects of this policy from the perspective of the property tax as a user fee.

6. Suppose Toronto adopted a tax on land value instead of a property tax (while collecting the same revenue). Would downtown parking become scarcer? Would the reform in Toronto have an effect on the value of land in nearby Hamilton? Explain.

7. The City of Calgary opened a new airport runway in 2014. To avoid having to close direct road access to the airport from the city's northeast, the city plans to build a tunnel under the new runway. The cost of the tunnel is about $300 million and is to be financed mainly by an increase in property tax rates in Calgary. Discuss the incidence and efficiency effects of the tunnel project from a capital tax view and a user fee view of the property tax. Which view of the property tax do you think is more appropriate for the tunnel project? Explain your reasoning.

8. Heal (2001, p. 1) notes that when Frederick Law Olmsted, the developer of New York City's Central Park, was asked how the city would pay for the park, "he responded that its presence would raise property values and the extra tax revenues would easily repay the construction costs. History shows that he was correct." This episode illustrates best which of the three views of the nature of the local property tax?

9. A predecessor of the modern property tax was a tax levied on dwellings based on the number of windows they had. (The window tax was introduced in England in 1696 by King William III.) Oates and Schwab (2015) estimated that raising an additional $1 of tax revenue through the window tax generated an additional $0.23 of excess burden, as a result of residents reducing the number of windows. The authors noted that, despite its evident inefficiency, the window tax persisted over a long period, perhaps because "these were years of intense fiscal pressures, involving at various junctures massive military expenditures." Based on these observations, discuss the relevance of each of the three views of the property tax for assessing the equity and efficiency consequences of the window tax.

CHAPTER 21

The Corporation Tax

To excel in the global economy, Canada needs a competitive business tax system. We need to create a climate that encourages capital investment and innovation.

—James M. Flaherty, Minister of Finance (May 2006)

AFTER READING THIS CHAPTER, THE STUDENT SHOULD BE ABLE TO:

LO1 Discuss five potential justifications for taxing corporations.

LO2 Describe the allowable deductions for calculating taxable corporate income.

LO3 Contrast the tax treatment of interest payments, dividends, and retained earnings.

LO4 Understand the purpose and the application of the dividend tax credit.

LO5 Compare a tax on corporate capital with a tax on economic profits.

LO6 Derive expressions for the user cost of capital and the marginal effective tax rate.

LO7 Summarize the empirical results of the effects of the corporate income tax on investment behaviour.

LO8 Assess the tax incidence and excess burden aspects of the corporate income tax.

LO9 Discuss the possible effects of the corporate income tax on corporate finance.

LO10 Contrast a credit versus a deduction for foreign taxes in calculating the tax liability.

LO11 Discuss methods of fully integrating corporate and personal income taxes.

INTRODUCTION

In 2014, corporations in Canada had $3.7 trillion in operating revenues, and generated $307 billion in before-tax profits.[1] Federal and provincial corporate income tax revenues were $64.2 billion. Clearly, corporations play a major role in the Canadian economy.

A corporation is a form of business organization. It is owned by its shareholders, with ownership usually represented by transferable stock certificates. The shareholders have limited liability for the acts of the corporation. This means that their liability to the creditors of the corporation is limited to the amount they have invested in the corporation.

Corporations are independent legal entities and as such are often referred to as artificial legal persons. A corporation may make contracts, hold property, incur debt, sue, and be sued. And, just like any other person,

---

[1] Statistics Canada, *Quarterly Financial Statistics for Enterprises, Second Quarter, 2015*, Cat. No. 61-008-X (Ottawa: September 2015), and CANSIM II database http://cansim2.statcan.ca/ Table 187-0001.

TABLE 21.1

Corporate Income Taxes in Canada, 1945 to 2014

Year	Federal Revenue (millions)	Provincial Revenue (millions)	Federal + Provincial (millions)	As a Percent of Government Revenue (%)	Per Capita ($2014)
1945	$ 645	$ —	$ 645	17.8	$ —
1955	1,081	54	1,135	16.5	642
1965	1,759	523	2,282	13.7	866
1975	5,748	2,091	7,921	12.6	1,477
1985	9,210	4,033	13,243	7.3	1,019
1995	12,432	7,093	19,525	6.1	952
2005	30,528	16,400	46,928	8.7	1,592
2009	31,273	19,005	50,277	7.9	1,632
2014*	36,587	27,629	64,216	8.8	1,807

* Authors' calculations for 2014 from the federal and provincial *Public Accounts* for 2013/14 and consolidated government revenues for Canada from CANSIM II Table 385-0032.

Sources: Adapted from the Statistics Canada publications "Historical Statistics of Canada," 1983, Catalogue 11-516, released July 29, 1999; "Public Finance Historical Statistical Data," 1965/66-1991/92, Catalogue 68-512, released April 1, 1992; "Public Sector Statistics," 2007/08, Catalogue 68-213-X, released July 14, 2008 (Tables 2-3, 2-4, 2-6); and CANSIM II database http://cansim2.statcan.ca/ Tables 385-0001, 385-0032, 326-0021, 109-5325.

a corporation must pay tax on its income. This chapter explains the structure of the federal and provincial corporation income taxes and analyzes their effect on the allocation of resources.

Table 21.1 shows that the relative importance of corporation income taxes had fallen from 17.8 percent of government revenues at the end of World War II to 6.1 percent in 1995. This share had risen to 8.7 percent by 2005 due to increased profits from economic growth and the 1987 tax reforms that broadened the tax base and reduced investment tax credits. Real per capita corporation tax revenues fell from 1975 through the mid-1990s, but nearly doubled from 1995 to 2005, despite reductions in the corporate tax rate after 2000.

Corporation income taxes remain important in the formulation of tax policy. The theory of excess burden suggests that a tax may create efficiency costs far out of proportion to the revenues yielded. There is some evidence that the corporation income tax is an example of this important phenomenon.

At the end of 1997, the Technical Committee on Business Taxation[2] reported a variety of deficiencies in Canada's corporate income taxes to the finance minister. These included the following:

- Higher corporate income tax rates on non-manufacturing activities in Canada compared with the United States and other countries.
- An erosion of Canada's corporate income tax base—higher tax rates in Canada encourage multinational companies to do their debt financing with debt expense deduction in Canada.
- Distortions that favour debt over equity financing.
- Distortions among industrial sectors with differing tax rates across industries.
- Distortions among kinds of assets due to preferential tax treatment of some assets relative to others.
- Distortions that favour small corporations over large corporations.

These problems adversely affect economic efficiency, fairness, and administrative and compliance costs. Important reforms to business taxation in Canada during the past decade have alleviated many, but not all, of these problems. Sections of this chapter will explain in more detail the nature of the problems arising from taxing corporate income.

[2] Department of Finance, *Report of the Technical Committee on Business Taxation* (Ottawa: December 1997).

WHY TAX CORPORATIONS?

Before undertaking a description and analysis of the tax, we should ask whether it makes sense to have a special tax system for corporations in the first place. To be sure, from a legal point of view, corporations are people. But from an economic standpoint, this notion makes little sense. As we stressed in Chapter 14, only real people can pay a tax. If so, why should corporate activity be subject to a special tax? Is it not sufficient to tax the incomes of the corporation owners via the personal income tax?

A number of justifications for a separate corporation tax have been proposed. First, contrary to the view just stated, corporations—especially very big ones—really are distinct entities. Large corporations have thousands of shareholders, and the managers of such corporations are controlled only very loosely, if at all, by the shareholder/owners. Most economists would certainly agree that there is separation of ownership and control in large corporations, and that this creates important problems for understanding just how corporations function. Nevertheless, it does not follow that the corporation should be taxed as a separate entity.

A second justification for corporate taxation is that the corporation receives a number of special privileges from society, the most important of which is limited liability of the shareholders. The corporation tax can be viewed as a user fee for this benefit. However, the tax is so structured that there is no reason to believe that the revenues paid approximate the benefits received.

Third, the corporate tax serves as a withholding tax. With substantial foreign ownership of corporations operating in Canada, if a tax were not levied at the corporate level much income arising in the corporate sector could flow to foreign owners without taxes being paid to Canadian governments. Direct investment in Canada by foreign corporations amounted to $686 billion in 2013.[3]

Fourth, the corporate income tax serves as a rent-gathering device. Canadian corporations operating in the resource sector, and other corporations given privileges by the state, realize economic rent from their activities. Royalties on resource production and the sale of Crown leases for the exploration and development of resources capture only a portion of the economic rent. The corporate income tax permits the provincial and federal governments to share in remaining rents.[4]

A final justification is that the corporation tax protects the integrity of the personal income tax. Suppose that Karl's share of the earnings of a corporation during a given year is $10,000. According to the standard convention for defining income, this $10,000 is income whether the money happens to be retained by the corporation or paid out to Karl. If the $10,000 is paid out, it is taxed in an amount that depends on his personal income tax rate. In the absence of a corporation tax, the $10,000 creates no tax liability if it is retained by the corporation since the personal income tax does not tax capital gains on an accrual basis. Hence, unless corporation income is taxed, Karl can reduce his tax liability by accumulating income within the corporation. Of course, the money will be taxed when it is eventually paid out, but in the meantime the full $10,000 grows at the before-tax rate of interest. Remember from Chapter 17, taxes deferred are taxes saved.

It is certainly true that if corporate income goes untaxed, opportunities for personal tax avoidance are created. But a special tax on corporations is not the only way to include earnings accumulated in corporations. We discuss an alternative method, one partially adopted in Canada and viewed by many economists as superior, in later sections of this chapter.

STRUCTURE

Corporate Income Tax Statutory Rates

In addition to the federal tax, all 10 provinces, as well as Yukon, Nunavut, and the Northwest Territories, levy a tax on corporate income. Provincial corporate income taxes generated $28 billion in 2014, compared to the $37 billion from the federal tax. The total equalled 8.8 percent of the federal and provincial revenues. Provinces raised four times as much through their taxes on personal income, and the federal government raised three and one-half times as much.

---

[3] Statistics Canada, CANSIM II database Table 376-0051.

[4] For a general discussion of federal and provincial natural resource revenues, see Trett and Perry (2007: ch. 7), and *Report of the Technical Committee on Business Taxation* (1997): 5.23–5.31.

TABLE 21.2

Combined Federal and Provincial Corporate Income Tax Rates, 2015

	Small Business	Manufacturing and Processing	General
Federal	11.0%*	15.0%	15.0%
Province (federal plus provincial)			
Newfoundland and Labrador	14.0	20.0	29.0
Prince Edward Island	15.5	31.0	31.0
Nova Scotia	14.0	31.0	31.0
New Brunswick	15.0	27.0	27.0
Quebec	19.0	26.9	26.9
Ontario	15.5	25.0	26.5
Manitoba	11.0	27.0	27.0
Saskatchewan	13.0	25.0	27.0
Alberta	14.0	26.0**	26.0**
British Columbia	13.5	26.0	26.0
Northwest Territories	11.0	26.5	26.5
Nunavut	11.0	27.0	27.0
Yukon	11.0	17.5	30.0
Unweighted Average	13.7	25.8	27.7

* 10.5% in 2016 and announced rates of 10.0% in 2017, 9.5% in 2018, and 9.0% in 2019. ** Average for the year, as Alberta's rate was raised from 25% to 27% on July 1, 2015.

Sources: Canada Revenue Agency website (http://www.cra-arc.gc.ca/menu-eng.html) and KMPG website (http://www.kpmg.com/ca/en/Pages/default.aspx).

Room has been made for provincial taxes on corporate income through a federal–provincial agreement that provides a credit of up to 10 percent of corporate income earned in a province against federal tax that would otherwise be payable. For example, a federal tax that would be at a 25 percent rate is 15 percent if the provincial tax is imposed at a rate of at least 10 percent. General corporate income tax rates of all provinces equalled or exceeded 10 percent in 2015.

The federal government collects the provincial corporate income tax on behalf of eight provinces on the understanding that the provincial tax base differs only to a limited degree from the federal tax base. Quebec and Alberta administer their own corporate income taxes; these provinces, as a result, have greater freedom to alter their tax base from the federal base, and increased freedom to use the corporate income tax as an economic policy instrument. Such freedom is purchased at the cost of somewhat higher administrative and compliance costs.

Table 21.2 provides the combined federal and provincial corporate income tax rates for 2015. The federal government's general rate was 15 percent and its rate on small business income was 11.0 percent.[5] The provincial income tax rates can be calculated by subtracting the federal rate from the total tax rates in Table 21.2. Newfoundland, Ontario, Saskatchewan, and Yukon apply reduced rates for manufacturing and processing. Prior to 2001, the federal general tax rate was 28 percent but the federal rate on manufacturing and processing was 21 percent. This cross-industry difference in federal tax rates was removed by 2004, thereby addressing one of the deficiencies identified by the Technical Committee on Business Taxation (1997).

Since 2000 the federal and provincial governments have reduced taxes on corporate income, and further reductions for small businesses have been announced until 2019. The general federal rate decreased from 18 to 16.5 percent in 2011 and to 15 percent in 2012. A federal capital tax and corporate surtax were eliminated in 2006 and 2008, respectively. Nevertheless, Canada's corporate tax rates remain higher than in several other OECD countries, as indicated in Table 21.3.

---

[5] The federal and provincial small business tax rate reduction applies to the first $500,000 of income of Canadian-controlled private corporations, and is reduced when taxable capital of a corporation is over $10 million and eliminated if taxable capital exceeds $15 million.

TABLE 21.3

Corporate Tax Rates for Selected OECD Countries (%)		
	2000	**2015**
Australia	36.0	30.0
Canada	44.6	26.5
France	36.7	33.3
Germany	51.6	29.7
Ireland	24.0	12.5
Italy	41.3	31.4
Japan	42.0	33.1
Poland	30.0	19.0
Sweden	28.0	22.0
U.K.	30.0	20.0
U.S.	40.0	40.0

Source: KPMG International's *Corporate and Indirect Tax Survey 2007* (June 2007) and *2015 KPMG Global Tax Survey* (October 2015).

As in the case of the personal income tax, knowledge of the rate applied to taxable income by itself gives relatively little information about the effective burden. To compute taxable income, we must know exactly which deductions from before-tax corporate income are allowed. Accordingly, we now discuss the rules for defining taxable corporate income.[6]

Wage Payments Deducted

As we saw in Chapter 17, a fundamental principle in defining personal income is that income should be measured net of the expenses incurred in earning it. The same logic applies to the measurement of corporate income. One important business expense is labour, and wages paid to workers are excluded from taxable income.

Depreciation Deducted

Suppose that during a given year the XYZ Corporation makes two purchases: (1) $1,000 worth of stationery, which is used up within the year; and (2) a $1,000 drill press, which will last for 10 years.[7] Should there be any difference in the tax treatment of these expenditures?

From the accounting view, these are very different items. Because the stationery is entirely consumed within the year of purchase, its entire value is deductible from that year's corporate income. But the drill press is a durable good. When the drill press is purchased, the transaction is merely an exchange of assets—cash is given up in exchange for the drill press. Thus, unlike stationery, a drill press is not entirely consumed during the year. To be sure, during its first year of use some of the machine is used up by wear and tear, which decreases its value. This process is called **economic depreciation**. But at the end of the year the drill press is still worth something to the firm, and, in principle, could be sold to some other firm at that price.

We conclude that during the first year of the life of the drill press a consistent definition of income requires that only the economic depreciation experienced that year be subtracted from the firm's before-tax income. Similarly, the economic depreciation of the machine during its second year of use should be deductible from that year's gross income, and so on for as long as the machine is in service.

It is a lot easier to state this principle than to apply it. In practice, the tax authorities do not know exactly how much a given investment asset depreciates each year, or even what the useful life of the machine is. The tax law has rules that indicate for each type of asset what proportion of its acquisition value can be depreciated each year (referred to as the **capital cost allowance**, or **CCA**), and over how many years depreciation can be taken—the **tax life** of the asset. Next, we discuss these rules, which often fail to reflect true economic depreciation.

---

[6] Note also that many of these rules apply to noncorporate businesses. As in the case for the personal income tax, there is a corporate alternative minimum tax.

[7] Understanding the impact of depreciation allowances requires the concept of present value (see Chapter 3).

Calculating the value of depreciation allowances. Assume that the tax life of the $1,000 drill press is 10 years, and a firm is allowed to depreciate 1/10th the machine's value each year. How much is this stream of depreciation allowances worth to the XYZ Corporation?

At the end of the first year, XYZ is permitted to subtract 1/10th the acquisition value, or $100, from its taxable income. With a corporation income tax rate of 35 percent, this $100 deduction saves the firm $35. Note, however, that XYZ receives this benefit a year after the machine is purchased. The present value of the $35 is found by dividing it by $(1 + r)$, where r is the opportunity cost of funds to the firm.

At the end of the second year, XYZ is again entitled to subtract $100 from taxable income, which generates a saving of $35 that year. Because this saving comes two years in the future, its present value is $35/(1 + r)^2$. Similarly, the present value of depreciation taken during the third year is $35/(1 + r)^3$, during the fourth year, $35/(1 + r)^4$, and so on. The present value of the entire stream of depreciation allowances is

$$\frac{\$35}{1 + r} + \frac{\$35}{(1 + r)^2} + \frac{\$35}{(1 + r)^3} + \cdots + \frac{\$35}{(1 + r)^{10}}$$

For example, if $r = 10$ percent, this expression is equal to $215.10. In effect, then, the depreciation allowances lower the price of the drill press from $1,000 to $784.90 (= $1,000 − $215.10). Intuitively, the effective price is below the acquisition price because the purchase leads to a stream of tax savings in the future.

More generally, suppose that the tax law allows a firm to depreciate a given asset over T years, and the proportion of the asset that can be written off against taxable income in the nth year is $D(n)$. The $D(n)$ terms sum to one, meaning that the tax law eventually allows the entire purchase price of the asset to be written off. (In the preceding example, T was 10, and $D(n)$ was equal to 1/10th every year. There are, however, several depreciation schemes for which $D(n)$ varies across years.) Consider the purchase of an investment asset that costs $1. The amount that can be depreciated at the end of the first year is $D(1)$ dollars, the value of which to the firm is $\theta \times D(1)$ dollars, where θ is the corporation tax rate. (Because the asset costs $1, $D(1)$ is a fraction.) Similarly, the value to the firm of the allowances in the second year is $\theta \times D(2)$. The present value of all the tax savings generated by the depreciation allowances from a $1 purchase, which we denote ψ, is

$$\psi = \frac{\theta \times D(1)}{1 + r} + \frac{\theta \times D(2)}{(1 + r)^2} + \cdots + \frac{\theta \times D(T)}{(1 + r)^T} \qquad (21.1)$$

Because ψ is the tax saving for one dollar of expenditure, it follows that if the acquisition price of an asset is $q, the presence of depreciation allowances lowers the effective price to $(1 − \psi)q$. For example, a value of $\psi = 0.25$ indicates that for each dollar spent on an asset, 25 cents worth of tax savings are produced. Hence, if the machine cost $1,000 ($q = $1,000), the effective price is only 75 percent of the purchase price, or $750.

Equation (21.1) suggests that the tax savings from depreciation depend critically on the value of T and the function $D(n)$. In particular, the tax benefits are greater (1) the shorter the time period over which the machine is written off—the lower is T; and (2) the greater the proportion of the machine's value that is written off at the beginning of its life—the larger the value of $D(n)$ when n is small. Schemes that allow firms to write off assets faster than true economic depreciation are referred to as **accelerated depreciation**. An extreme possibility is to allow the firm to deduct from taxable income the asset's full cost at the time of acquisition. This is referred to as **expensing**, and, in this case, $\psi = \theta$ in Equation (21.1).

Under current law, every depreciable asset is assigned to one of more than forty classes, with special rules applying in some cases. The rate at which an asset can be written off differs among the classes, but, generally, the permitted write-off is faster than economic depreciation. This has potential consequences for corporate investment behaviour, which we discuss later. With respect to the rate at which assets can be depreciated, two methods are currently relevant.

Declining-balance method. The declining-balance method applies in most cases under existing Canadian law. Existing rates are generally between 4 percent and 55 percent when expensing is not permitted. These rates apply to the full cost of the asset in the first year and to the remaining undepreciated cost in subsequent years. For example, if the applicable rate is 20 percent and the cost of the depreciable asset is $1,000, the deduction permitted is $200 (0.2 × 1,000) in the first year, $160 (0.2 × 800) in the second year, and $128 (0.2 × 640) in the third year, and so on. It should be apparent that this provides for a slower write-off than if a 20 percent rate were applied to the original cost and the asset were fully written off over five years.[8]

Straight-line method. The straight-line method applies in a few special cases in Canada and is widely used elsewhere in the world. This is the method we have been using for our examples so far. If the tax life of the asset is T years, the firm can write off $1/T$th of the cost each year. Thus, for a $1,000 asset that may be depreciated over five years, $200 is deducted each year.[9]

Investment Tax Credits

Over the years, the Income Tax Act has included sizable **investment tax credits (ITCs)** to encourage new investment and to achieve development objectives in depressed areas of the country. The ITCs permit a firm to subtract some portion of the purchase price of an asset from its tax liability at the time the asset is acquired. If a drill press costs $1,000, and if the XYZ firm is allowed an investment tax credit of 10 percent, the purchase of a drill press lowers XYZ's tax bill by $100. The effective price of the drill press (before depreciation allowances) is thus $900. More generally, if the investment tax credit is k and the acquisition price is q, the effective price of the asset is $(1 - k)q$. In contrast to depreciation allowances, the value to the firm of an ITC does not depend on the corporate income tax rate. This is because the credit is subtracted from tax liability rather than taxable income.

The general ITC was 7 percent in 1987; investment for manufacturing and processing in certain slow-growth areas qualified for a 40 percent ITC, and ITCs were at 20 percent for the Atlantic region as a whole and at 60 percent for Cape Breton. The general ITC was eliminated by 1989; what remains after the 1994 federal budget is a 10 percent federal ITC for certain investments in the Atlantic provinces and the Gaspé region, and the continuation of a 20 to 35 percent ITC for qualifying expenditures on research and development.[10] As with gophers that keep popping out of holes as part of a carnival game, ITCs are likely to re-emerge as they are a readily understood investment incentive and likely to remain popular among policy-makers.

Treatment of Interest

When corporations borrow, interest payments to lenders are excluded from taxable income. Again, the justification is that business costs should be deductible. However, when firms finance their activities by issuing stock, the dividends paid to the shareholders are not deductible from corporate earnings. We discuss the consequences of this asymmetry in the treatment of interest and dividends later. Now we briefly look at the effect of deducting interest on the cost of an investment.

Calculating the value of interest deductions. Assume that a firm borrows $1,000 to invest in a machine that has a 10-year life. The firm pays annual interest of 7.5 percent, or $75, for the duration of the loan, and repays the full $1,000 after 10 years. With interest deductible, taxable income is reduced by $75 each year, and if the corporate tax rate is 35 percent this saves $26.25 each year. The present value of this stream of tax savings is:

$$\frac{\$26.25}{1 + r} + \frac{\$26.25}{(1 + r)^2} + \cdots + \frac{\$26.25}{(1 + r)^{10}}$$

---

[8] Since 1981 the government has limited the capital cost allowance (CCA) to one-half of the normal CCA rate in the year of acquisition. Although this rule applies for most classes of assets, there are some exceptions.

[9] A variety of other methods have been used to permit faster write-offs in Canada or other countries. The double declining balance method allows twice the percentage applied under the declining balance method. Other possible methods may permit a company to deduct a substantial portion of the investment in the first year, and this may or may not reduce deductions in subsequent years. Thus, the total write-off over the life of the asset could, in some cases, exceed 100 percent of the original investment.

[10] Several provinces also provide investment tax credits for certain types of investments, including those for research and development purposes. For more detail, see Treff and Ort (2011: 4–5).

If r is equal to 10 percent, this expression is worth $161.33, and the cost of the machine is reduced from $1,000 to $838.67. More generally, the present value of the tax saving resulting from the deductibility of interest for each dollar of capital is:

$$\lambda = \frac{[\theta \times R]}{[1 + r]} + \frac{[\theta \times R]}{[1 + r]^2} + \cdots + \frac{[\theta \times R]}{[1 + r]^T} \qquad (21.2)$$

where T is the life of the loan, θ is the tax rate, R is the interest deduction resulting from $1 of capital, and r is the discount rate. Effectively, the price of the asset is reduced by λ. If the cost of acquiring an asset was q prior to allowing for deduction of interest, and q were borrowed to make the purchase, it becomes $(1 - \lambda)\$q$ with the deduction. We will use this result later. If equity financing were used, with dividends not deductible, the cost remains at q.

Treatment of Dividends

So far we have been focusing on taxes directly payable by the corporation. For many purposes, however, the important issue is not the corporation's tax liability per se, but rather the total tax rate on income generated in the corporate sector. As noted in Chapter 17, corporate dividends received by individuals are subject to the personal income tax. Understanding how the corporate and personal tax structures interact is important.

Corporate profits may either be retained by the firm or paid to shareholders in the form of dividends. Dividends paid are *not* deductible from corporation income and, hence, are subject to the corporation income tax. At the same time, shareholders who receive dividends must pay personal income tax in an amount that depends on their marginal tax rates. This gives rise to the possibility that corporate earnings are taxed twice—once at the corporate level and once again when distributed to the shareholder. The **double taxation** of dividends increases the relative cost of using equity to finance investments in the corporate sector. Eliminating double taxation is a prime objective of many reformers, and was foremost in the minds of Canada's Royal Commission on Taxation in the 1960s and more recently the Technical Committee on Business Taxation. The dividend tax credit system is used in Canada as a way to integrate the personal and corporate tax systems.

Canada's dividend tax credit. Shareholders are given a dividend tax credit to offset some of the tax paid at the corporate level. The example below illustrates the method for an assumed corporate income tax rate of 20 percent. Dividends ($100) are grossed up by an amount that approximates the taxes paid at the corporate level ($25). The grossed-up amount ($125) is then included in the taxable income of an individual, the appropriate personal income tax rate (say 40 percent) is applied to determine the individual's tax liability (0.4 × $125 = $50), and a tax credit ($25) is allowed for the grossed-up amount. The result is that the individual pays an additional $25 (or $50 − $25), and the combined corporate and personal income tax collected on the $125 originating in the corporate sector is $50, or 40 percent. This is the applicable marginal tax rate for this individual. The corporate tax served to withhold the first $25, and credit is later given through the personal income tax system for this withholding. The situation is summarized as follows:

a)	Taxable corporate income	$125
b)	− Corporate tax collected at a 20% tax rate	25
c)	= Corporate income for distribution [(a) − (b)]	100
d)	Paid as dividends to individual =	100
e)	Gross-up of dividends by 25 percent [0.25 × (d)]	25
f)	Taxable individual income [(d) + (e)]	125
g)	Individual tax liability at a 40% tax rate [0.4 × (f)]	50
h)	− Dividend tax credit [20% of (f)]	25
i)	Individual tax payable after credit [(g) − (h)]	25
j)	Total tax on $125 originating in a corporation = (b) + (i)	50

The preceding hypothetical example reflects a situation of full integration, whereby the total tax on corporate income ($50) is identical to the amount of personal income tax that would be paid by the owner of an unincorporated business earning the same income (40 percent times $125 = $50). The total marginal tax rate on the corporate taxable income is 40 percent ($50/$125), which is the same as the assumed personal marginal tax rate.[11]

One of the purposes of the dividend tax credit mechanism is to avoid distorting the decisions of small businesses about whether to be incorporated or unincorporated. However, most dividends are paid by corporations that do not qualify for the small business tax rate. To offset the higher general tax rate faced by medium and large corporations, an *enhanced* dividend tax credit is provided to their shareholders. Before the May 2006 federal budget, this was not the case. At that time, the dividend gross-up rate and tax credit rate, which provided approximate tax neutrality on dividends from small corporations, were the same for all domestic corporations.[12] Consequently, there was a substantial degree of double taxation on dividends paid by corporations subject to tax rates in excess of the small business tax rate.[13]

At the time of writing in 2016, the federal gross-up rate was 17 percent for dividends received from small Canadian corporations, while the gross-up rate for the enhanced dividend tax credit was 38 percent. The corresponding federal dividend tax credit rates were 10.5 percent and 15.02 percent. Although most of the provinces apply the federal gross-up rates, their dividend tax credit rates vary by province.[14]

The move from partial to fuller integration in 2006 reduced the tax discrimination against the corporate sector. But even so, integration may be excessive or inadequate. The dividend tax credit is allowed for dividends paid even when the corporation has paid no tax. In that case, the result is a total tax below that paid on income from other sources, and "overintegration" occurs. Where dividends are paid from past profits, and the permitted credit does not reflect the time value of corporate taxes paid in the past, "underintegration" may occur. Furthermore, the enhanced dividend tax credit does not precisely offset the existing general corporate tax rates. Thus, through its dividend tax credit system, Canada has achieved a *partial* integration of the personal and corporate income tax systems. The last section of this chapter discusses further reforms that would eliminate the remaining deficiencies in the integration of personal and corporate income taxes.

Treatment of Retained Earnings

To assess the tax consequences to the shareholder of retained earnings is a bit more complicated. Suppose that XYZ retains $1 of earnings. To the extent that the stock market accurately values firms, the fact that the firm now has one more dollar causes the value of XYZ stock to increase by $1. But as we saw in Chapter 17, income generated by increases in the value of stock—capital gain—is treated preferentially for tax purposes. This is because the gain received by a typical XYZ shareholder is not taxed until it is realized, and even then only half of the gain is taxable. The tax system thus creates incentives for firms to retain earnings rather than pay them out as dividends.

Tax Expenditures under the Corporate Income Tax

As with the personal income tax, "special" provisions that exclude an item from the tax base permit a deduction in calculating the tax base or tax liability, and create preferential rates that result in losses to federal and provincial treasuries. Governments may, and do, use the corporate income tax structure to channel assistance to particular industries. Where the tax structure, rather than direct expenditure, encourages industrial development in a particular region, expenditures on research, or renewal of the manufacturing sector, a tax expenditure occurs and the structure of the corporate income tax is changed. Federal tax expenditures made through the corporate income tax in 2014 included the deductibility of charitable donations ($340 million), the Canadian

---

[11] The total marginal tax rate on before-tax corporate income will coincide with the personal marginal income tax rate on unincorporated business income if the gross-up rate equals the corporate tax rate divided by one minus the corporate tax rate, and the dividend tax credit rate is the same as the corporate tax rate.

[12] Dividends paid by foreign corporations are not eligible for the dividend tax credit.

[13] To see this, recalculate the example above with the tax rate faced by large corporations in 2006 (about 40 percent) in line (b), but keep the gross-up of dividends at 25 percent (the rate applicable to small corporations until 2014) and the value of the dividend tax credit at 20 percent of taxable individual income in line (h). The resulting total tax is about $68.75, or 55 percent of the $125 originating in the corporation. This rate exceeds the personal marginal income tax rate of 40 percent because of double taxation.

[14] In Ontario, for example, the 2016 tax credit for small business dividends is 4.29 percent and it is 10 percent for dividends eligible for the enhanced tax credit.

film or video production tax credit ($280 million), the Atlantic investment tax credit ($186 million), the Scientific Research and Experimental Development investment tax credit ($3,135 million), and the low tax rate for small businesses ($3,170 million).[15]

Effective Tax Rate on Corporate Capital

We began this section by noting that the statutory tax rate on capital income in the corporate sector is currently about 28 percent when provincial and federal rates are combined. Clearly, it would be most surprising if this were the effective rate as well. At the corporate level, computing the effective rate requires considering the effects of interest deductibility, depreciation allowances, and inflation. Moreover, as just noted, corporate income in the form of dividends and realized capital gains is also taxed at the personal level. Finally, some corporate income is affected by provincial and local property taxes. Allowing for all these considerations, the estimated effective tax rate on marginal investments for non-financial industries was (on average) 19.0 percent in 2014 (Chen and Mintz, 2015). This varied from a high of 25.8 percent for large firms in the other services industry and 24.8 in construction to lows of 3.2 percent for large firms in forestry and 8.2 percent for large firms in manufacturing.[16] The low marginal effective tax rates in forestry and manufacturing are attributable to accelerated depreciation allowances in these industries, which have the effect of increasing the value of Ψ in Equation (21.1) above.

Of course, any such calculation requires assumptions on items such as the appropriate choice of discount rate [r of Equation (21.1)], the expected rate of inflation, the extent of true economic depreciation, and so forth. Moreover, as we will see below, the effective burden of the corporate tax depends in part on how investments are financed—by borrowing, issuing stock, or using internal funds. It is, therefore, likely that investigators using other assumptions would generate a somewhat different effective tax rate. It is unlikely, however, that alternative methods would modify the difference between statutory and effective marginal tax rates very much.

Some effects of inflation. Studies during the 1970s highlighted the impact that inflation has on effective corporate tax rates. Inflation affects taxable income in three important ways, two of which cause an overstatement of taxable income and one of which results in an understatement. The first is the failure to recognize the cost of replacing goods sold from inventories that were acquired at a lower cost. Canadian law requires that accounts be kept on a first-in, first-out (FIFO) basis. A good acquired for $100 a year ago is deducted at that cost, even though increases in the general price level have raised its replacement cost to $110. If this good is sold for $150 and inventory is replaced for $110, the taxable profit based on FIFO accounting is $50, whereas the firm has realized real income of only $40. Taxable income is overstated by $10.

Second, depreciation allowances for capital assets are based on historical cost, and not on replacement cost. In a time of inflation, depreciation based on historical cost results in an overstatement of taxable income. Capital equipment with a five-year life and costing $500 would, on a straight-line basis, be depreciated at $100 a year. If, due to a 10 percent rise in the general price level, the replacement cost increases to $550, annual depreciation should be $110. Failure to make this adjustment overstates profits by $10.

Finally, the current system leads to an understatement of taxable income to the extent that deductible interest payments include an element that compensates the lender for the decline in the real value of the debt that occurs as prices rise. Where this occurs, the borrower is in effect deducting part of the repayment of the loan in calculating taxable income. In general, repayment of principle is not deductible.

With inflation at low rates, these factors may have little impact on corporate taxes. However, if price increases are significant and unpredictable, the effects can be great. From 1973 through 1982 the annual change in the consumer price index (CPI) reached a high of 12.4 percent and was never below 7.8 percent. Bossons (1977: 95) found that pretax income for 279 large Canadian companies was reduced by 43 percent in 1975 when adjustments were made for the above three factors. Corporate income taxes, although 44 percent of "reported" pretax income, were 77 percent of "real" pretax income.[17]

The corporate income tax's lack of adjustment for inflation affects some industries much more severely than others. The effect depends on the importance of inventories, capital equipment, and debt finance. Inflation-induced distortions in the early 1970s were particularly severe in capital-intensive sectors, such as forest

---

[15] Projections of the Department of Finance Canada (2015).

[16] A further discussion of marginal effective tax rates is provided later in the chapter.

[17] See Bossons (1977). For further discussion of these issues, also see Jenkins (1977).

WORLD'S BEST TAX HAVENS

Tax havens are countries with very low or nonexistent tax rates. They also tend to be secretive about financial information. Multinational corporations shift their profits to subsidiaries in offshore tax havens so that they can avoid paying Canadian taxes. According to an estimate by Canadians for Tax Fairness, a not-for-profit, non-partisan organization, Canadian corporations held nearly $200 billion in assets in the world's top 10 tax havens in 2014, including $71 billion in Barbados and $36 billion in the Cayman Islands. It was estimated that the sheltered money cost Canadian governments $7.8 billion in lost revenues in 2014. These figures don't include money held in tax havens by individual Canadians. The tax avoidance problem confronts almost all governments of industrialized countries. In the United States, Apple alone hides $181 billion offshore so it can avoid $59 billion in taxes it would owe if the money were brought back to the U.S., according to another study. Not surprisingly, critics of perceived government inaction have said, "Tax havens undermine democracy." Yet, tax havens may also have a useful function. A study by Smart and Hong (2007) shows how tax havens can facilitate real investments (e.g., plant and equipment) in the industrialized countries by reducing the tax burdens on mobile capital, through the financial manipulations that corporations use to shift profits for tax reporting purposes, while at the same time exposing non-mobile capital to larger tax rates. In this way, corporate tax revenues can be collected without unduly sacrificing industrial investments by footloose multinational firms.

Based on Bowles (2015), Smart and Hong (2010), Thompson Reuters (2015), and "Canadian Corporations had $200 Billion in World's Top Tax Havens Last Year: Report," The Huffington Post Canada, June 16, 2015.

Complete references for this feature can be found in the References section on page 491.

products and chemicals, and much less severe for merchandising businesses. Inflation resulted in a tax on real profits that was well in excess of 100 percent for some companies. Thus, the effect of inflation on tax rates may have a major influence on investment decisions in a time of rapid price changes.

INCIDENCE AND EXCESS BURDEN

Understanding tax rules and computing effective tax rates is only the first step in analyzing the corporation tax. We still must determine who ultimately bears the burden of the tax and measure the costs of any inefficiencies it induces. The economic consequences of the corporation tax are among the most controversial subjects in public finance. An important reason for the controversy is disagreement with respect to just what kind of tax it is. We can identify several views.

A Tax on Corporate Capital

Recall from our discussion of the structure of the corporation tax that the firm is not allowed to deduct from taxable income the opportunity cost of capital supplied by shareholders. Since the opportunity cost of capital is included in the tax base, it appears reasonable to view the corporation tax as a tax on capital used in the corporate sector. In the classification scheme developed in Chapter 14 under "General Equilibrium Models," the corporation tax is a partial factor tax. This is the view that predominates in most writing on the subject.

In a general equilibrium model, the tax on corporate capital leads to a migration of capital from the corporate sector until after-tax rates of return are equal throughout the economy. Evidence that the corporation tax does, indeed, lead to less economic activity being undertaken by corporations is provided by Goolsbee (2004), who notes that in U.S. states with relatively high corporation income tax rates the number of firms doing business as corporations is relatively low, other things being the same. As capital moves to the noncorporate sector, the rate of return to capital is depressed so that ultimately *all* owners of capital, not just those in the corporate sector, are affected. The reallocation of capital between the two sectors also affects the return to labour. The extent to which capital and labour bear the ultimate burden of the tax depends on the technologies used in production in each of the sectors, as well as the structure of consumers' demands for corporate and noncorporate goods. In their survey of public finance economists, Fuchs et al. (1998) found that virtually all of them believe that the burden of the corporate income tax is shared by both capital and labour, "but there is significant disagreement about the precise division."

Turning now to efficiency aspects of the problem, we discussed computation of the excess burden of a partial factor tax in Chapter 15. By inducing less capital accumulation in the corporate sector than otherwise would have been the case, the corporation tax diverts capital from its most productive uses and creates an excess burden. A further distortion occurs if the corporate tax influences how a business is organized. For example, sole proprietorships and partnerships forgo some benefits of incorporation, such as limited liability, centralized management, and better access to financing. Similarly, prior to the October 2006 decision of the federal government to tax income trusts at the corporate rate, businesses had an incentive to organize themselves as income trusts to avoid paying corporation income tax, even if this noncorporate form increased "governance costs."[18] The increase in excess burden when one more dollar is raised via the corporation tax—the marginal excess burden—may well be in excess of $1.50.[19]

The Harberger model assumes perfect competition and profit-maximizing behaviour (see Chapter 14). Without these conditions, a tax on corporate capital may have quite different incidence and efficiency implications. Moreover, the model is static—the total amount of capital to be allocated between the corporate and noncorporate sectors is fixed. Suppose that, over time, the tax on corporate capital changes the total amount of capital available to the economy. If the tax lowers the total amount of capital, the marginal product of labour, and hence the wage rate, falls. Thus, labour bears a greater share of the burden than otherwise would have been the case. If the tax increases the amount of capital, the result is just the opposite. Hence, even if we accept the view of the corporation tax as a partial factor tax, its efficiency and incidence effects are not at all clear.

A Tax on Economic Profits

An alternative view is that the corporation tax is a tax on economic profits. This view is based on the observation that the tax base is determined by subtracting costs of production from gross corporate income, leaving only "profits." As we explained in Chapter 14, analyzing the incidence of a tax on economic profits is straightforward. As long as a firm maximizes economic profits, a tax on them induces no adjustments in firm behaviour—all decisions regarding prices and production are unchanged. Hence, there is no way to shift the tax, and it is borne by the owners of the firm at the time the tax is levied. Moreover, by virtue of the fact that the tax leaves behaviour unchanged, it generates no misallocation of resources. Hence, the excess burden is zero.

Modelling the corporation tax as a simple tax on economic profits is almost certainly wrong. Recall that the base of a pure profits tax is computed by subtracting from gross earnings the value of *all inputs, including* the opportunity cost of the inputs supplied by the owners. As noted earlier, no such deduction for the capital supplied by shareholders is allowed, so the base of the tax includes elements other than economic profits.

Nevertheless, there are circumstances under which the corporation tax is *equivalent* to an economic profits tax. Stiglitz (1973) showed that under certain conditions, as long as the corporation is allowed to deduct interest payments made to its creditors, the corporation tax amounts to a tax on economic profits.

To understand the reasoning behind Stiglitz's result, consider a firm that is contemplating the purchase of a machine costing $1. Suppose the before-tax value of the output produced by the machine is known with certainty to be G dollars. To finance the purchase, the firm borrows $1 and must pay an interest charge of r dollars. In the absence of any taxes, the firm buys the machine if the net return (total revenue, minus depreciation, minus interest) is positive. Algebraically, the firm purchases the machine if

$$G - r > 0 \tag{21.3}$$

Now assume that a corporation tax with the following features is levied: (1) net income is taxed at rate θ, and (2) net income is computed by subtracting interest costs from total revenue. How does such a tax influence the firm's decision about whether to undertake the project? Clearly, the firm must make its decision on

---

[18] Prior to the 2007 tax year, the earnings of income trusts were not subject to corporate tax but flowed directly to investors and were taxed only at the personal level. See McKenzie (2006) for an appraisal of the effect of taxing income trusts.

[19] Dahlby and Ferede (2011) estimated the excess burden of one more dollar raised by the federal corporate income tax in Canada to equal $1.61 in 2006. They estimated the marginal excess burden of provincial corporate taxes to be even higher.

the basis of the *after-tax* profitability of the project. In light of feature 2, the firm's taxable income is $G - r$. Given feature 1, the project therefore creates a tax liability of $\theta (G - r)$, so the after-tax profit on the project is $(1 - \theta)(G - r)$. The firm does the project only if the after-tax profit is positive; that is, if

$$(1 - \theta)(G - r) > 0 \qquad (21.4)$$

Now note that any project that passes the after-tax criterion, Equation (21.4), also satisfies the before-tax criterion, Equation (21.3). (Just divide Equation (21.4) through by $(1 - \theta)$ to get Equation (21.3).) Hence, imposition of the tax leaves the firm's investment decision unchanged—anything it would have done before the tax, it will do after. The owners of the firm continue to behave exactly as they did before the tax; they simply lose some of their profit on the investment to the government. In this sense, the tax is equivalent to an economic profits tax. And like an economic profits tax, its incidence is on the owners of the firm, and it creates no excess burden.

This conclusion depends critically on the underlying assumptions, and these can easily be called into question. In particular, the argument assumes that firms finance their additional projects by borrowing. There are several reasons why they might instead raise money by selling shares or using retained earnings. For example, firms may face constraints in the capital market and be unable to borrow all they want. Alternatively, if a firm is uncertain about what the project's return will be, it might be reluctant to finance the project by borrowing. If things go wrong, the greater a firm's debt is, the higher the probability of bankruptcy, other things being the same.

Hence, the main contribution of Stiglitz's analysis is not the conclusion that the corporate tax has no excess burden. Rather, the key insight is that the way in which corporations finance their investments has a major influence on how the corporation tax affects the economy.

EFFECTS ON BEHAVIOUR

The corporation tax influences a wide range of corporate decisions. In this section we discuss three important types: (1) the total amount of physical investment (equipment and structures) to make, (2) the types of physical assets to purchase, and (3) the way to finance these investments. For expositional ease, we discuss these decisions separately, even though the firm makes them simultaneously.

Total Physical Investment

A firm's net investment during a given period is the increase in physical assets during that time. The main policy question is whether features such as accelerated depreciation and the investment tax credit stimulate investment demand. The question is important. For example, when the minister of finance, Paul Martin, reduced regionally based investment tax credits in 1994, he argued that the credits had not been cost effective in encouraging new investment. Yet, when these and other investment tax credits were enacted, ministers of finance argued that the ITCs increase investment substantially. Who was right?

The answer depends in part on your view of how corporations make their investment decisions. Many different models have been proposed, and there is no agreement on which is the best.[20] We discuss three investment models that have received a lot of attention.

Accelerator model. Suppose the ratio of capital to output in production is fixed. For example, production of every unit of output requires three units of capital. Then, for each unit increase in output, the firm must increase its capital stock—invest—three units of capital. Thus, the main determinant of the amount of investment is changes in the level of output.

This theory, sometimes referred to as the accelerator model, implies that depreciation allowances and ITCs are basically irrelevant when it comes to influencing physical investment. It is only the quantity of output that influences the amount of investment, because technology dictates the ratio in which capital and output must be used. In other words, tax benefits for capital (such as ITCs) may make capital cheaper, but in the accelerator model this does not matter, because the demand for capital does not depend on its price.

---

[20] See Chirinko (1993) for a survey of various models.

Neoclassical model. A less extreme view of the investment process is that the ratio of capital to output is not technologically fixed. Rather, the firm can choose among alternative technologies. But how does it choose? According to Jorgenson's (1963) neoclassical model, a key variable is the firm's **user cost of capital**–the cost the firm incurs as a consequence of owning an asset. As we show later, the user cost of capital includes both the opportunity cost of forgoing other investments and direct costs, such as depreciation and taxes. The user cost of capital indicates how high a project's rate of return has to be to be profitable. For example, if the user cost of capital on a project is 15 percent, a firm undertakes the project only if its rate of return exceeds 15 percent. The higher the user cost of capital, the lower the number of profitable projects and the lower the firm's desired stock of capital. In the neoclassical model, when the cost of capital increases, firms choose less–capital-intensive technologies, and vice versa. To the extent that tax policy reduces the cost of capital, it can increase the amount of capital that firms desire and, hence, increase investment.

All of this leaves open two important questions: (1) how do changes in the tax system change the user cost of capital, and (2) just how sensitive is investment to changes in the user cost of capital? To examine these points, we must first calculate the user cost of capital.

The user cost of capital. Consider the Leona Corporation, a company that operates a chain of hotels. The corporation can lend its money and receive an after-tax rate of return of 10 percent. Because it can always earn 10 percent simply by lending in the capital market, the Leona Corporation will not make any investment in the hotel that yields less than that amount.[21] Assume that the corporation is considering the acquisition of a vacuum cleaner that would experience economic depreciation of 2 percent annually. Ignoring taxes for the moment, the user cost of capital for the vacuum cleaner would be 12 percent, because the vacuum cleaner would have to earn a 12 percent return to earn the Leona Corporation the 10 percent return that it could receive simply by lending its money. Algebraically, if r_t is the after-tax rate of return and δ is the economic rate of depreciation, the user cost of capital is $(r_t + \delta)$. If the vacuum cleaner cannot earn $(r_t + \delta)$ (or 12 percent) after taxes, there is no reason for the firm to purchase it.

Now assume that the corporate tax rate is 45 percent. Then if the corporation earns \$1, a corporation tax of \$0.45 (= 0.45 × \$1) is due, leaving \$0.55 available to distribute or reinvest. If θ is the corporate tax rate, the after-tax return from \$1 of corporate profits is $(1 - \theta) \times \$1$.

How does the corporate tax affect the cost of capital? We have to find a before-tax return such that, after the corporate tax, the Leona Corporation receives 12 percent. Calling the user cost of capital C, then C must be the solution to the equation $(1 - .45) \times C = 12$ percent, or C = 21.8 percent. Thus, the corporation is unwilling to purchase the vacuum cleaner unless its before-tax return is 21.8 percent or greater. Using our algebraic notation, the user cost of capital is the value of C that solves the equation $(1 - \theta) \times C = (r_t + \delta)$, or

$$C = \frac{r_t + \delta}{(1 - \theta)} \qquad (21.5)$$

So far, we have shown how the corporate tax rate increases the user cost of capital. However, certain provisions in the Income Tax Act, such as accelerated depreciation and interest deductibility, tend to lower the cost of capital. In Equations (21.1) and (21.2), we defined ψ and λ as the present value of depreciation allowances and the interest deductions that flow from a \$1 investment.[22] First, consider depreciation. Suppose that ψ for the vacuum cleaner is 0.25. In effect, then, depreciation allowances reduce the cost of acquiring the vacuum cleaner by one-fourth and, hence, lower by one-fourth the before-tax return that the firm has to earn to attain any given after-tax return. In our example, instead of having to earn 21.8 percent, the Leona Corporation now only has to earn 16.4 percent [= 21.8 × (1 − 0.25)]. Algebraically, depreciation allowances lower the cost of capital by a factor of $(1 - \psi)$, and $C = [(r_t - \delta) \times (1 - \psi)]/(1 - \theta)$.

Referring back to Equation (21.1), recall that if the Leona Corporation were able to immediately write off, or expense, the investment, then $\psi = \theta$, and the cost of the asset is reduced by θ. In this case, $C = [(r_t + \delta) \times (1 - \theta)]/(1 - \theta)$, which collapses to $r_t + \delta$. The result is that the corporate tax has no effect on the user cost

---

[21] The example assumes that Canada is a small, open economy, so that the after-corporate-tax rate of return is determined by arbitrage in the international capital market and is taken as a given by Leona Corporation.

[22] Note from Equation (21.1) that ψ depends on the statutory rate θ, and increases as θ increases.

of capital, and is neutral with respect to the investment decision. Where the asset is written off over a longer period, $\psi < \theta$, the user cost of capital is higher, and investment is lower.

Similarly, we showed that an investment tax credit at rate k reduces the cost of a $1 acquisition to $(1 - k)$ dollars. In the presence of both depreciation allowances and an investment tax credit, the cost of capital is reduced by a factor of $(1 - \psi - k)$.[23] Thus, the expression for C in Equation (21.5) must be multiplied by $(1 - \psi - k)$ to adjust for the presence of accelerated depreciation and investment tax credits:

$$C = \frac{(r_t + \delta) \times (1 - \psi - k)}{(1 - \theta)} \tag{21.6}$$

Equation (21.6) summarizes how the corporate tax system influences the firm's user cost of capital for investments that are financed from retained earnings or by other equity financing. By taxing corporate income, the tax makes the user cost of capital more expensive, other things being the same. However, depreciation allowances and ITCs tend to lower the user cost of capital.

We now refer back to Equation (21.2). Where debt is used to finance an investment, the deductibility of interest payments reduces the user cost of capital. If λ represents the present value of deductible interest for $1 of capital, then the user cost of capital, C, equals $[(r_t + \delta) \times (1 - \lambda - \psi - k)]/(1 - \theta)$, where depreciation and interest are deductible, and where there is also an ITC.[24] The user cost of capital is lower by λ than for equity-financed investments.

The corporate tax, by itself, increases the user cost of capital. Where an equity-financed investment is expensed rather than written off over time, the user cost of capital is unchanged and investment decisions are unaffected. The result is similar for expensing of a debt-financed investment so long as interest is not deductible. Depreciation allowances, ITCs, and interest deductibility all lower the user cost of capital. Such provisions may more than offset the increase in the user cost of capital caused by the corporate tax. Where this occurs, the overall effect is the subsidization of investment by the government, or negative tax rates. In sum, changes in tax rates, depreciation allowances, ITCs, and interest deductibility influence θ, ψ, k, and λ, and affect investment decisions through the user cost of capital.[25]

Effect of user cost on investment. After determining how the tax system affects the user cost of capital, the next step is to ascertain how changes in the user cost influence investment. If the accelerator model is correct, even drastic reductions in the user cost have no impact on investment. On the other hand, if investment is responsive to the user cost of capital, tax rate reductions, depreciation allowances, and ITCs can be powerful tools for influencing investment.

Empirical evidence supports the conclusion that depreciation and tax credits affecting the cost of capital influence investment, although the effect may be more modest than originally thought. Chirinko, Fazzari, and Meyer (1999) found an elasticity of the user cost of capital of 0.25 for the United States. Using Canadian data, Schaller (2006) estimated elasticities of the user cost of capital of 1.6 for equipment and zero for non-residential construction. And McKenzie and Sershun (2010) found that lowering the user cost of capital for R&D through tax subsidies increases the amount spent on R&D—with elasticity of 0.83. Investment does respond to changes in the tax system. While there are differences in the literature, an elasticity of investment with respect to the user cost of 0.4 is plausible (Chirinko, 2002).

An important implicit assumption in this discussion is that the before-tax price of capital goods is not affected by tax-induced changes in the user cost of capital. If, for example, firms start purchasing more capital goods in response to the introduction of the investment tax credit, this does not increase the price of capital goods. In more technical terms, the supply curve of capital goods is perfectly horizontal. However, Goolsbee

---

[23] This assumes the basis used to compute depreciation allowances is not reduced when the firm takes the ITC. Generally, an ITC reduces the cost of an asset for depreciation purposes by the amount of the tax credit, k. Where this is true, the cost of capital is reduced by a factor of $(1 - k) \times (1 - \psi)$.

[24] In the case of debt-financed investments, the cost of finance, r_t in Equation (12.6), refers to the interest rate for borrowing in the international capital market.

[25] For a more comprehensive, and somewhat more technical, study of the neoclassical theory of investment, see Boadway (1979: 265–76).

(2003) found that the introduction of an investment tax credit increases the relative wages of workers who produce capital goods. Hence, some of the increase in investment induced by the credit is dampened by an increase in the before-tax price of capital goods.

Finally, we must remember that Canada is, to a large extent, an open economy. If the tax law makes investment in Canada more attractive to foreigners, saving from abroad can finance investment in this country. The consequence for tax policy toward investment is the flip side of the relationship we saw in Chapter 18 between tax policy and saving; the possibility of domestic saving flowing out of the country makes it harder to stimulate domestic investment indirectly by manipulating saving, but the possibility of attracting foreign capital makes it easier to stimulate investment through direct manipulation of the user cost of capital. Investment in Canada is not determined, alone, by the amount Canadians save.

Cash flow model. If you ask people in business what determines the amount of investment they make, they likely will mention **cash flow**—the difference between revenues and expenditures for inputs. The more money there is on hand, the greater the capacity for investment. In contrast, cash flow is irrelevant in the neoclassical investment model. In that model, if the return on manufacturing a new kind of computer chip exceeds the opportunity cost, the firm will make the chip, whether it has to borrow the money or use internal sources. But if the return on the project is below the opportunity cost, the firm will not make the chip because the borrowing cost will be higher than the return. Further, even if the firm has internal funds on hand, it will not make the chip, because the firm can make more money by lending the funds to someone else than by investing in a substandard project.

A critical assumption behind the neoclassical story is that the cost to the firm of internal and external funds is the same. Many economists believe that this is a bad assumption. To see why, suppose that the managers of the firm have better information about the prospects for the computer chip than the potential lenders do. In particular, the lenders may view the project as being more uncertain than management and, thus, charge a very high interest rate on the loan. Or they might not be willing to lend any money at all. Thus, the cost of internal funds is lower than the cost of external funds, so the amount of investment depends on the flow of these internal funds, the cash flow.

There does indeed seem to be a statistical relationship between cash flow and investment (Stein, 2003). However, the interpretation of this finding is not quite clear. Do firms invest because their cash flow is high, or do successful firms have both high cash flow and investment? In any case, if the cash flow theory is correct, it has major implications for the impact of taxes on investment behaviour. For example, in the neoclassical model, a lump-sum tax on the corporation would have no effect on investment. In contrast, in a cash flow model, investment would fall. Currently, cash flow models are an active subject of research.[26]

Types of Asset

So far, our focus has been the total volume of investment spending without much attention to its composition. It is likely, though, that the tax system affects the types of assets purchased by firms, and investment by industry sector. Purchases of assets that receive relatively generous depreciation allowances tend to be encouraged, other things being the same, and investment is likely to flow to those industries that are more lightly taxed. Several studies have examined the effect of taxes on the user cost of capital, calculating the marginal effective tax rate (METR) for different investments. The METR is the tax paid as a proportion of the income generated by the last, or marginal, dollar of capital invested.[27]

Table 21.4 shows the METR values across industries and types of assets in Canada for 1997 and 2014. The table indicates that a marginal investment in inventories is taxed more heavily than investments in other assets in 2014. This is, in part, due to FIFO (first in, first out) accounting, as previously discussed, and to faster write-offs of capital equipment than warranted by rates of economic depreciation. Because the mix of assets differs among industries,

---

[26] A Statistics Canada survey of 186 large corporations in 1992 examined the sources of financing capital expenditures in the corporate sector. Although 1992 was at the bottom of an economic cycle and retained earnings were relatively scarce, operating funds were the most important source, accounting for 27 percent of capital expenditures. Funds from the sale of other assets accounted for another 20 percent, with bond and equity issues accounting for 16 and 13 percent, respectively. Other sources included cash (3%), commercial paper (6%), bank loans (3%), mortgage loans (6%), and loans from affiliates (6%). Statistics Canada, *Quarterly Financial Statistics for Enterprises*, Second Quarter 1994, Cat. no. 61-008 (Ottawa: October 1994).

[27] The METR can be derived from the user cost of capital, C in Equation (21.6), as METR $= [C - \delta - r_i]/[C - \delta]$.

TABLE 21.4

Marginal Effective Corporation Tax Rates in Canada, 1997 and 2014: (a) by Industry, and (b) by Asset Type (Medium and Large Firms)

	Percent	
Industry	**1997**	**2014**
Forestry	31.6%	3.2%
Manufacturing	37.5	8.2
Construction	48.8	24.8
Transportation	41.3	19.8
Communication	54.2	23.9
Public Utilities	44.6	19.3
Wholesale Trade	47.4	23.1
Retail Trade	48.0	23.5
Other Service Industries	50.0	25.4
Asset		
Buildings	47.8	22.3
Machinery	43.6	16.2
Land	23.9	10.7
Inventory	42.4	24.4
TOTAL	44.3	19.0

Sources: Duanjie Chen and Jack Mintz, *Federal/Provincial Combined Marginal Effective Tax Rates on Capital 1997–2006, 2010* (C. D. Howe Institute e-brief, June 20, 2006); Duanjie Chen and Jack Mintz, "The 2014 Global Tax Competitiveness Report: A Proposed Business Tax Reform Agenda," University of Calgary, SPP Research Papers vol. 8(4) (February 2015), table 2a; and authors' correspondence with Duanjie Chen.

we can expect marginal effective tax rates to differ among industries. Table 21.4 shows that marginal investments in construction and "other service industries" are taxed more than investments in manufacturing and forestry. These differences result in distortions in investment decisions and the accompanying excess burdens. Nonetheless, the effective tax rates on the physical investments of corporations are considerably lower than in 1997. These reductions are due to lower statutory tax rates, as well as to adjustments in capital cost allowances to better match economic depreciation rates, and to the harmonization of Ontario's retail sales taxes with the GST in 2010.

As emphasized earlier, computations like those in Table 21.4 require making a number of assumptions. For example, the value of depreciation allowances depends on the discount rate used by firms [see Equation (21.1)], and different values lead to different answers. Hence, it is possible that different investigators might find results somewhat different from those in the table. There is little doubt, however, that the qualitative picture suggested in the table is correct.

Corporate Finance

In addition to "real" decisions concerning physical investment, the owners of a firm must determine how to finance the firm's operations and whether to distribute profits or retain them. We discuss the effects of taxes on these financial decisions in this section.

Why do firms pay dividends? Profits earned by a corporation may be either distributed to shareholders in the form of dividends or retained by the company. If it is assumed that (1) outcomes of all investments are known in advance with certainty, and (2) there are no taxes, then the owners of a firm are indifferent in choosing between a dollar of dividends and a dollar of retained earnings. Provided that the stock market accurately reflects the firm's value, $1 of retained earnings increases the value of the firm's stock by $1. This $1 capital gain is as much income as a $1 dividend receipt. Under the previous assumptions, then, shareholders do not care whether profits are distributed.[28]

---

[28] For a rigorous discussion of this argument, see Fama and Miller (1972: 80–81).

Of course, in reality, considerable uncertainty surrounds the outcomes of economic decisions, and corporate income is subject to a variety of taxes. As already noted, when dividends are paid out, the shareholder will often incur a tax liability even with the dividend tax credit; retained earnings generate no concurrent tax liability. True, retention creates a capital gain for the shareholder, but no tax is due until the gain is realized.

On the basis of these observations, it appears that paying dividends is often equivalent to giving away money to the tax collector, and we would expect large firms to retain virtually all of their earnings. Surprise! From 2001 through 2011, about 34 percent of after-tax corporate profits in Canada were paid out as dividends.[29] This phenomenon continues to baffle many students of corporate finance.

One possible explanation is that dividend payments signal the firm's financial strength. If investors perceive firms that regularly pay dividends as "solid," then paying dividends enhances the value of the firms' shares. In the same way, a firm that reduces its dividend payments may be perceived as being in financial straits. However, although it is conceivable that the owners of a firm would be willing to pay some extra taxes to provide a positive signal to potential shareholders, it is hard to imagine that the benefits gained are worth the huge sums sacrificed. After all, there are certainly ways other than dividend policy for potential investors to obtain information about a firm's status.

Another explanation centres on the fact that not all investors have the same marginal tax rate. High-income individuals currently face rates as high as 46 percent, while untaxed institutions (such as pension funds and universities) face a rate of zero. Those with low marginal tax rates would tend to put a relatively high valuation on dividends, and it may be that some firms "specialize" in attracting these investors by paying out dividends. This is referred to as a **clientele effect**, because firms set their financial policies to cater to different clienteles.

Econometric studies of the clientele effect are hindered by the lack of data on just who owns shares in what firms. However, there is some evidence that mutual funds, whose shareholders are taxable, tend to hold stocks with low dividend yields, while untaxed institutions show no preference between low- and high-dividend stocks (Graham, 2003).

Effect of taxes on dividend policy. Because the tax system appears to bias firms against paying dividends (although it by no means discourages them completely), the natural question is how corporate financial policy would change if the tax treatment of dividends vis-à-vis retained earnings were modified. Suppose that, for whatever reasons, firms want to pay some dividends as well as retain earnings. One factor that determines the desired amount of retained earnings is the opportunity cost in terms of after-tax dividends paid to shareholders. For example, if there were no taxes, the opportunity cost of $1 of retained earnings would be $1 of dividends. On the other hand, if the shareholder faces a 25 percent marginal income tax rate (even after the dividend tax credit), the opportunity cost of retaining a dollar in the firm is only 75 cents of dividends.[30] In effect, then, the current tax system lowers the opportunity cost of retained earnings.

Several studies have found that when the opportunity cost of retained earnings decreases, dividend payments go down, and vice versa. Chetty and Saez (2005) estimated that the elasticity of dividend payments with respect to the marginal tax rate on dividend income is about −0.5. It appears, then, that the tax system does indeed affect corporate retained earnings. Some argue that this is desirable because increasing retained earnings makes more money available for investment. Now, it is true that retained earnings represent saving. However, it may be that shareholders take corporate saving into consideration when making their personal financial decisions. Specifically, if owners of the firm perceive that the corporation is saving a dollar on their behalf, they may simply reduce their personal saving by that amount. Thus, although the composition of overall saving has changed, its total amount is just the same as before the retention. There is indeed some econometric evidence that personal and corporate saving are somewhat offsetting (Poterba, 1991). This analysis illustrates once again the pitfalls of viewing the corporation as a separate person with an existence apart from the shareholders.

Debt versus equity finance. Another important financial decision for a corporation is how to raise money. The firm has basically two options. It can borrow money (issue debt); however, the firm must pay interest on

---

[29] Statistics Canada, CANSIM II database Table 380-0014.

[30] A more careful calculation would take into account the effective capital gains tax liability that is eventually generated by the retention. This is ignored for purposes of illustration.

its debt, and inability to meet the interest payments or repay the principal may have serious consequences. A firm can also issue shares of stock (equity), and shareholders may receive dividends on their shares.

Recall that under the Canadian tax system, corporations are permitted to deduct payments of interest from taxable income, but are not allowed to deduct dividends. Interest deductibility can therefore build in a bias toward debt financing. This bias is reduced by Canada's dividend tax credit, which does not exist in the United States. It is difficult to precisely estimate the impact that this bias has had on the debt–equity choice, but there is evidence that the effective tax rates of debt-financed investments may be significantly lower than on equity-financed investments (see Daly et al., 1993: 117). In one U.S. econometric study, Gordon and Lee (2001) found that taxes have a strong effect on debt levels–lowering the corporate tax rate by 10 percentage points (say from 40 to 30 percent) would lower the percentage of a firm's assets financed by debt by 4 percent.

Indeed, we might wonder why firms do not use debt financing exclusively. Part of the answer lies in the fact that the outcomes of a firm's decisions are uncertain. There is always some possibility of a very bad outcome and therefore a fear of bankruptcy. Indeed, heavy reliance on debt finance has led some major corporations in Canada to declare bankruptcy, including Campeau Corporation (the parent company of several major department stores), and Olympia and York (a major real estate development company). It has been argued that by encouraging the use of debt, the tax system has had the undesirable effect of increasing probabilities of bankruptcy above levels that otherwise would have prevailed.

TAXATION OF MULTINATIONAL CORPORATIONS

Canadian firms do a substantial amount of business abroad. Canadian-held assets due to direct investment in foreign subsidiaries and branches totalled $779 billion in 2013. The income flowing back to Canada from these direct investments was $91 billion in 2013. Canadians held an additional $610 billion in portfolio investments in foreign stocks and bonds, plus another $483 billion in foreign assets.[31] The tax treatment of foreign-source income is of some importance.

"Active business income" versus "passive investment income." The Canadian approach to the taxation of foreign-source income attempts to be neutral with respect to the place of investment while maintaining the integrity of the Canadian tax system. The government wishes to minimize personal or corporate tax avoidance through financial manipulations. However, it does not wish to discourage foreign investment by Canadians and Canadian corporations, and attempts to ensure that investments abroad are not subject to higher taxes than similar investments made at home. Although it is difficult to achieve these objectives, the following policies are designed with them in mind.

- First, the Income Tax Act attempts to prevent Canadian corporations from easily avoiding or postponing Canadian taxes on "passive"[32] investment income by diverting this income (FAPI, or Foreign Accrual Property Income) to foreign corporations and trusts. Income from such "passive" investment in foreign assets must be included in the taxable income in the year in which it is earned. Credit, within limits, is given for foreign taxes paid.

- Second, "active" business income of foreign affiliates is generally subject to tax only in the source country. Foreign affiliates, as **incorporated subsidiaries** and separate legal entities, are subject to the laws of the source country. Where there is a tax treaty between Canada and the source country, the active business income of foreign affiliates goes into an "exempt surplus" account. This income is not subject to Canadian tax when earned, and is *not* subject to Canadian tax when paid as dividends to Canadian owners. Most dividends now come from countries with which Canada has a tax treaty.

  Where dividends received come from a foreign affiliate in a country with which Canada does not have a tax treaty, the dividends must be included in the taxable income of the Canadian owner. In this case, the Canadian company may credit foreign tax paid on the dividend income against Canadian taxes, up to

---

[31] Statistics Canada, CANSIM II database Tables 376-1041 and 376-0012.

[32] "Passive" income is income from sources other than an active business and includes portfolio income in the form of interest, property income, some capital gains, and income that results from non–arm's length transactions.

the amount of the Canadian tax that would otherwise be due. Where tax rates in the source country are as high or higher than in Canada, no additional tax is due. In sum, dividends from foreign-source, active business income are seldom subject to further tax in Canada.

- Third, income from **branch operations** of Canadian corporations in foreign countries must be included in the taxable income of the Canadian corporations in the year it is earned. Unincorporated branches are used primarily by financial institutions, where incorporated subsidiaries would deprive foreign depositors of the security provided by the Canadian institution. Credit is given for taxes paid to the source country, and the credit cannot exceed the Canadian tax on the foreign income.[33]

This brief discussion does not reflect the difficulties that may exist in distinguishing between the active business income and passive investment income of controlled affiliates, or the continuing opportunities to avoid Canadian taxation through the use of holding companies located in other countries.[34]

Income allocation. It is often difficult to know how much of a multinational firm's total income to allocate to its operations in a given country. The procedure now used for allocating income between domestic and foreign operations is the **arm's length system**. This means that the domestic and foreign operations are treated as separate enterprises doing business independently ("at arm's length"). The taxable profits of each entity are computed as its own sales minus its own costs. The problem is that it is not always clear how to allocate costs to various locations, and this can lead to major opportunities for tax avoidance. To see why, consider a multinational firm that owns a patent for a gene-splicing process. One of the subsidiaries owns the patent, and the other subsidiaries pay royalties to it for the privilege of using the process. The company has an incentive to assign the patent to one of its subsidiaries in a low-tax country, so that the royalties received from the other subsidiaries will be taxed at a relatively low rate. At the same time, it wants the subsidiaries that use the patent to be in relatively high-tax countries—high tax rates mean that the value of the deductions associated with the royalty payments is maximized. Indeed, since the transaction is entirely internal to the company, it will set the royalty payment as high as possible in order to maximize the tax benefits of this arrangement. And if there is no active market for the rights to the patent outside the company, then the tax authorities have little basis for deciding whether or not the royalty payment is excessive.

This relates to the **transfer price** and is called the transfer-pricing problem, because it refers to the price that one part of the company uses for transferring resources to another. Given that it is essentially arbitrary how costs for many items are assigned to various subsidiaries, multinational corporations and the tax authorities are constantly at odds over whether the companies have done their transfer pricing appropriately. This has become one of the most complicated areas of tax law.

Evaluation

An evaluation of the Canadian tax treatment of multinational firms requires a careful statement of the policy goal. One possible objective is to maximize worldwide income; another is to maximize national income. A system that is optimal given one goal may not be optimal given another.

Maximization of world income. The maximization of world income requires that the before-tax rate of return on the last dollar invested in each country—the marginal rate of return—be the same.[35] To see why, imagine a situation in which marginal returns are not equal. Then it would be possible to increase world income simply by taking capital from a country where its marginal return was low and moving it to one where the marginal return was high. Algebraically, if r_c is the marginal rate of return in Canada and r_f is the marginal rate of return in a given foreign country, then worldwide efficiency requires

$$r_f = r_c \qquad (21.7)$$

What kind of tax system induces profit-maximizing firms to allocate their capital so that the outcome is consistent with Equation (21.7)? The answer hinges on the fact that investors make their decisions on the basis of

---

[33] Where foreign tax exceeds the Canadian tax due, the excess can be carried forward for crediting purposes for seven years.

[34] See Arnold and Harris (1994) for a very useful summary of Canadian taxation of foreign-source income, particularly as it relates to NAFTA.

[35] As usual, we refer here to rates of return after differences in risk are taken into account.

after-tax returns. They, therefore, allocate their capital across countries so that the after-tax marginal return in each country is equal. If t_C is the Canadian tax rate and t_f is the foreign tax rate, a firm allocates its capital so that

$$(1 - t_f)r_f = (1 - t_C)r_C \qquad (21.8)$$

Clearly, the equilibrium condition (21.8) is satisfied if and only if t_f equals t_C. Intuitively, if we want capital allocated efficiently from a global point of view, capital must be taxed at the same rate wherever it is located.

The policy implication seems to be that if Canada cares about maximizing world income, it should devise a system that makes its firms' tax liabilities independent of their location. A *full* credit against foreign taxes paid would do the trick. However, as already noted, the Canadian system allows a tax credit *only* up to the amount that Canadian tax on the foreign earnings would have been.

Why is the credit limit present? Our model implicitly assumes the behaviour of foreign governments is independent of Canadian government actions. Suppose Canada announces it will pursue a policy of allowing a full foreign tax credit to its multinational firms. Then foreign governments have an incentive to raise their own tax rates on Canadian corporations virtually without limit. Doing so will not drive out the foreign countries' Canadian firms, because the tax liability for their domestic operations is reduced by a dollar for every dollar foreign taxes are increased.[36] Essentially, the program turns into a transfer from Canada to foreign treasuries. Limiting the credit is an obvious way to prevent this from happening.

Maximization of national income. At the outset, we noted the importance of defining the objectives of tax policy on foreign-source corporate income. Some have argued that tax policy should maximize not world income, but national income. Some care must be taken in defining national income here. It is the sum of *before*-tax, domestically produced income and foreign-source income *after* foreign taxes are paid. This is because taxes paid by Canadian firms to the Canadian government, although not available to the firms themselves, are still part of Canadian income. Thus, domestic income is counted before tax. However, taxes paid to foreign governments are not available to Canadian citizens, so foreign income is counted after tax.

National income maximization requires a different condition than that in Equation (21.7). The difference arises because marginal rates of return must now be measured from the Canadian point of view. According to the Canadian perspective, the marginal rate of return abroad is $(1 - t_f)r_f$; foreign taxes represent a cost from the Canadian point of view and, hence, are excluded in valuing the rate of return. The marginal return on investments in Canada is measured at the before-tax rate, r_C. Hence, maximization of national income requires

$$(1 - t_f)r_f = r_C \qquad (21.9)$$

A comparison with Equation (21.7) suggests that under a regime of world income maximization, investments are made abroad until $r_f = r_C$, while if national income maximization is the goal, foreign investment is carried to the point where $r_f = r_C/(1 - t_f)$. In other words, if national income maximization is the goal, the before-tax marginal rate of return on foreign investment is higher than it would be if global income maximization were the goal. (As long as t_f is less than one, $r_C < r_C/(1 - t_f)$.) But under the reasonable assumption that the marginal return to investment decreases with the amount of investment, a higher before-tax rate of return means less investment. In short, from a national point of view, world income maximization results in "too much" investment abroad.

What kind of tax system induces Canadian firms to allocate their capital so that Equation (21.9) is satisfied? Suppose that multinational firms are allowed to deduct foreign tax payments from their Canadian taxable income. (For example, a firm with domestic income of $1,000 and foreign taxes of $200 would have a Canadian taxable income of $800.) Given that foreign tax payments are deductible, a firm's overseas return of r_f increases its taxable Canadian income by $r_f(1 - t_f)$. Therefore, after Canadian taxes, the return on the foreign investment is $r_f(1 - t_f)(1 - t_C)$. At the same time, the after-tax return on investments in Canada is $r_C(1 - t_C)$. Assuming that the investors equalize after-tax marginal returns at home and abroad,

$$r_f(1 - t_f)(1 - t_C) = r_C(1 - t_C) \qquad (21.10)$$

---

[36] The amount the foreign government can extract in this way is limited to the firm's tax liability to Canada on its domestic operations. Suppose the firm's tax liability on its Canadian operations is $1,000. If the foreign government levies a tax of $1,000, under a full credit, the firm's Canadian tax liability is zero. If the foreign government raises the tax to $1,001, the firm's domestic tax liability cannot be reduced any further (assuming there is no negative income tax for corporations).

Clearly, Equations (21.9) and (21.10) are equivalent. Just divide both sides of Equation (21.10) by $(1 - t_c)$. Because Equation (21.9) is the condition for national income maximization, this implies that deduction of foreign tax payments leads to a pattern of investment that maximizes Canadian income.

Such reasoning may lead to arguments to replace credits for foreign taxes paid with deductions. One important problem with the case for deductions is that the analysis assumes the capital-exporting country can impose the tax rate that maximizes its income, while the capital-importing foreign countries passively keep their own tax rates constant. Suppose, to the contrary, that the capital-exporting country takes into account the possibility that changes in its tax rate may induce changes in the host countries' tax rates. If Canada lowers its tax rate on capital invested abroad, host governments do the same. In this case, it may be worthwhile for Canada, as a capital-importing country, to preferentially tax income earned abroad. Of course, it is also possible that host governments could choose to raise their tax rates when the Canadian rate goes down. The point is that when interdependent behaviour is allowed, the national income-maximizing tax system generally does not consist of a simple deduction for foreign taxes paid. The effective tax rate on foreign-source income can be either larger or smaller than that associated with deductibility. Just as in the strictly domestic context, optimal tax theory shows that simple rules of thumb for tax policy do not necessarily achieve a given goal.

In general, the Canadian tax system treats foreign-source income of Canadian corporations, and hence foreign investment, quite favourably. Where foreign tax rates approximate rates in Canada, Canada's policy of exempting foreign-source income from further tax is comparable to giving a credit for the foreign tax. And where taxes are imposed when profits are repatriated, tax credits rather than deductions are permitted. Thus, existing Canadian policy is more in line with maximizing world income rather than national income. Such a policy encourages foreign investment, and better enables Canada to advocate similar policies globally.[37] As a net importer of capital, Canada is likely to be well served by policies that reduce barriers to the international movement of capital.

CORPORATION TAX REFORM

Toward the beginning of this chapter, we observed that if corporation income were untaxed, individuals would be able to avoid personal income taxation by accumulating income within corporations. Evidently, this would lead to serious equity and efficiency problems. The government's response has been to construct a system that taxes some of corporate income twice: first at the corporate level, where the combined federal and provincial tax rate for large corporations is around 28 percent, and again when dividends are received by individuals and included in their taxable personal income. The introduction of the enhanced dividend tax credit in 2006 has considerably alleviated this double taxation. However, Canada's dividend tax credit is a **partial imputation** system, similar to those used by several countries in the industrialized world. It is "partial" in the sense that only a portion of corporate income, dividends, is attributed or imputed at the personal level. Retained earnings are taxed only at the corporate level. Such a system includes in taxable personal income the dividend, "grossed-up" for the corporate tax that has been paid. The personal tax is calculated on the grossed-up amount, and a credit is permitted for the tax paid at the corporate level. In this way, double taxation of corporate income that is paid out as dividends is reduced or eliminated.

As noted earlier, the dividend tax credit system has serious shortcomings. One that astounds many observers is the granting of credits even when no tax has been paid at the corporate level. A second is the partial nature of the relief provided. Third is the unevenness in relief given to different taxpayers (end-of-chapter Exercise 7 makes this clear). A number of other proposals have been made to integrate personal and corporate income taxes into a single system.

The Partnership Method

The most radical approach is the **partnership method**, sometimes also referred to as **full integration**. Under this approach, all earnings of the corporation during a given year, whether they are distributed or not, are attributed to shareholders just as if the corporation were a partnership. Each shareholder is then liable for personal income tax on his or her share of the earnings. Thus, if Karl owns 2 percent of the shares of Stelco,

---

[37] Note that lower tax rates in other countries also may encourage Canadians to invest abroad.

each year his taxable income includes 2 percent of Stelco's taxable earnings. The corporation tax as a separate entity is eliminated. This was the approach followed in the report of the Royal Commission on Taxation, although it was never enacted.

Other Methods

There are a number of other ways to reduce the degree of double taxation. These include the **dividend exclusion method**, which exempts dividends from taxation at the level of the individual. Corporate income is taxed but once, at the corporate rate. Hence, the tax paid does not reflect individual circumstances, and a low-income corporate shareholder pays the same tax on dividend income as a high-income shareholder. This is perceived by many to be unfair and, as a result, is seldom used. Alternatively, the **dividend deduction method** allows corporations to deduct dividends in calculating taxable income, just as interest is deductible. The dividends would be taxable to the recipients. In such a case, withholding taxes would have to be used if tax revenues were not to be lost when untaxed corporate profits were paid to foreign shareholders. A few countries use this method. As a modification of the dividend deduction method, the **split-rate method** may be used to apply a lower corporate rate (rather than a zero rate) to that part of corporate income distributed as dividends, or a preferential rate may be applied to dividend income under the personal income tax. A number of countries currently apply lower rates to dividend income as a form of relief. Finally, several Nordic countries use a **dual income tax**—income is separated as either capital income or labour income. All capital income is taxed at a proportional rate, and labour income may be subjected to progressive rates. Double taxation of capital income is avoided by a system of imputation at the shareholder level, or by exempting dividend income at the shareholder level. Each of these methods eliminates or lessens the double taxation of corporate dividends, but each maintains the corporation tax as a separate entity.[38]

High effective marginal tax rates on income in the corporate sector ensure that the debate will continue on whether a more complete shift to the "partnership method," or to some other means of lessening distortions created by taxes on capital income, should be adopted. The debate has focused on the following issues.

Nature of the Corporation

Those who favour full integration emphasize that a corporation is, in effect, merely a conduit for transmitting earnings to shareholders. It makes more sense to tax the people who receive the income than the institution that happens to pass it along. Those who oppose full integration argue that, in large modern corporations, it is ridiculous to think of the shareholders as partners, and that the corporation is best regarded as a separate entity.

Administrative Feasibility

Opponents of full integration stress the administrative difficulties that it would create.[39] How are corporate earnings imputed to individuals who hold stock for less than a year? Would shareholders be allowed to deduct the firm's operating losses from their personal taxable income? Proponents of full integration argue that a certain number of fairly arbitrary decisions must be made to administer any complicated tax system. The administrative problems here are no worse than those that have arisen in other parts of the tax laws and can probably be dealt with satisfactorily.

Effects on Efficiency

Those who favour integration point out that the current corporate tax system results in the economy carrying excess burdens, many of which would be eliminated or at least lessened under full integration. The economy would benefit from four types of efficiency gains:

- Elimination of the misallocation of resources between the corporate and noncorporate sectors.
- To the extent that integration lowered the rate of taxation on the return to capital, tax-induced distortions in savings decisions would be reduced.

---

[38] A useful survey of methods used by different countries to reduce double taxation of dividends is found in Cnossen (1993). For a discussion of dual income taxes see Cnossen (2000).

[39] Administrative issues are discussed carefully by the U.S. Department of the Treasury (1992).

- Removal of the incentives for "excessive" retained earnings that characterize the current system. Firms with substantial amounts of retained earnings do not have to enter capital markets to finance new projects. Without the discipline that comes from having to convince investors that projects are worthwhile, such firms may invest inefficiently.
- Removal of the bias toward debt financing that occurs in the present system because there would be no separate corporate tax base from which to deduct payments of interest. High ratios of debt to equity increase the probability of bankruptcy. This increased risk and the actual bankruptcies that do occur lower welfare without any concomitant gain to society.

Although it is difficult to determine the value of all these efficiency gains, some estimates suggest that they may be quite high.[40]

Opponents of full integration point out that given all the uncertainties concerning the operation of the corporation tax, the supposed efficiency gains may not exist at all. For example, as discussed earlier, to the extent that Stiglitz's view of the tax as equivalent to a levy on pure profits is correct, the tax induces no distortion between the corporate and noncorporate sectors. Similarly, there is no solid evidence that corporations invest internal funds less efficiently than those raised externally.

Effects on Saving

Some argue that full integration would lower the effective tax rate on capital and, therefore, lead to more saving. As we saw in Chapter 18, this is a non sequitur. From a theoretical point of view, the volume of saving may increase, decrease, or stay the same when the tax rate on capital income decreases. Econometric work has not yet provided a definitive answer.

Effects on the Distribution of Income

If the efficiency arguments in favour of full integration are correct, then, in principle, all taxpayers could benefit if it were instituted. Still, people in different groups would be affected differently. For example, shareholders with relatively high personal income tax rates would tend to gain less from integration than those with low personal income tax rates (see the end-of-chapter Exercise 10). At the same time, integration would tend to benefit those individuals who receive a relatively large share of their incomes from capital. Taking these effects together, there may be a roughly U-shaped pattern to the distribution of benefits of full integration—people at the high and low ends of the income distribution gain somewhat more than those in the middle.

Overview

Clearly, there is considerable uncertainty surrounding the likely impact of full integration. This simply reflects our imperfect knowledge of the workings of the current system of corporate taxation. There is by no means unanimous agreement that introducing the partnership method would be a good thing. However, on the basis of the existing and admittedly imperfect evidence, many economists have concluded that both efficiency and equity would be enhanced if the personal and corporate taxes were fully integrated.

SUMMARY

- Corporations are subject to separate federal and provincial income taxes. These taxes account for about 9 percent of all government revenues.
- All provinces and the three territories have their own corporate income taxes. In all but two provinces (Quebec and Alberta) these taxes are collected for the provinces by the federal government. The possibilities for tax exporting and interprovincial mobility of factors of production complicate analysis of these taxes.

---

[40] For the United States, where no integration currently exists, Jorgenson and Yun (2001) found that the present value of the lifetime efficiency gain from full integration would be more than $250 billion.

- Before applying the corporate income tax rate, often around 28 percent, firms may deduct wage payments, interest payments, and depreciation allowances. These are meant to measure the cost of producing revenue. Dividends, the cost of acquiring equity funds, are not deductible.

- Investment tax credits (ITCs) are deducted from the firm's tax bill when particular physical capital assets are purchased. Tax reforms since 1986 have repealed many ITCs. Remaining federal ITCs encourage investment in the Atlantic and Gaspé regions, and investment in Scientific Research and Experimental Development (SR&ED). Several provinces use ITCs to encourage specific investments.

- Canada partially integrates its corporate and personal income taxes through a system of dividend tax credits. A gross-up factor is applied to the dividends received by shareholders of Canadian corporations and the grossed-up dividends are taxed at the shareholder's personal marginal tax rate. A dividend tax credit allows shareholders to reduce their tax liabilities on dividends at the individual level. Integration through the dividend tax credit in Canada is incomplete because various circumstances cause differences between the marginal tax rates on incorporated versus unincorporated business income.

- The corporate tax has been viewed either as an economic profits tax or as a partial factor tax. In the former case, the tax is borne entirely by owners of firms, while in the latter the incidence depends on capital mobility between sectors, substitution of factors of production, the structure of consumer demand, and the sensitivity of capital accumulation to the net rate of return.

- The effect of the corporate tax system on physical investment depends on (1) its effect on the user cost of holding capital goods, and (2) the sensitivity of investment to changes in the user cost. In the accelerator model, investment depends only on output, making the user cost irrelevant. The neoclassical model incorporates both effects.

- In the neoclassical investment model, the user cost of capital is:

$$C = \frac{(r_1 + \delta) \times (1 - \psi - k)}{(1 - \theta)}$$

where C is the user cost, r_t the after-tax interest rate, δ the economic depreciation rate, θ the corporation tax rate, k the ITC, ψ the present value of depreciation allowances per dollar, and λ the present value of deductible interest payments per dollar. Thus, corporate taxation raises the user cost, while ITCs, depreciation allowances, and interest deductibility reduce it.

- Estimates of the effect of the user cost on investment vary greatly. One reason is the critical role played by unobservable changes in expectations.

- Effective tax rates vary between machinery, buildings, land, and inventory, creating efficiency losses. Reductions in corporate tax rates from 2001 to 2012 substantially lowered the overall effective tax rate in Canada.

- Due to combined corporate and personal income taxation of dividends, it is somewhat surprising that firms continue to pay out so much in dividends. Dividends may serve as a signal of the firm's financial strength, or be used to cater to particular clienteles.

- Interest deductibility provides a strong incentive for debt finance. However, increasing the proportion of debt may lead to larger bankruptcy costs.

- Most foreign-source income of Canadian subsidiaries is subject to tax only in the source country. Where the Canadian corporate income tax applies, Canadian corporations are allowed tax credits for taxes paid to foreign governments. Complications may arise due to the need to distinguish between passive and active business income, due to the use of holding companies, and due to the need to allocate net income to countries in which a multinational operates.

- One possible corporate tax reform is full integration of the corporate and personal income taxes. Owners of stock would be taxed on their share of corporate income as if they were partners. The corporation tax as a separate entity would cease to exist. Canada's dividend tax credit is a step in this direction, but achieves less than full integration for most income arising in the corporate sector.

EXERCISES

1. Some Canadian political leaders have referred to "those corporate welfare bums" when average tax rates on corporate-source income have been low. What view of the corporation is implicit in this statement? Contrast this view with the view of conventional economics.

2. Under Canadian law, depreciation allowances are based on the original cost of acquiring the asset. No account is taken for the effects of inflation on the price level over time.

   a. How does inflation affect the real value of depreciation allowances? Organize your answer around Equation (21.1).

   b. When inflation increases, what is the impact on the user cost of capital? Organize your answer around Equation (21.6).

   c. Suggest a policy that could undo the effects on inflation from part (b).

3. Finance Minister Michael Wilson's 1987 tax reform contained several provisions that increased corporate taxes. The White Paper that accompanied the tax reform did not include an analysis of the distributional implications of corporate income tax changes, although it did include analysis regarding the distributional effects of other changes. How would you have distributed an increase in corporate taxes across households? How did the failure to distribute the corporate provisions bias the analysis of the distributional implications, across income classes, of the tax reform as a whole?

4. Canada, through its dividend tax credit, has achieved partial integration of its corporate income tax with its personal income tax. Would a move to more complete integration, or some other means of eliminating "double" taxation of corporate sector income, make sense from the standpoint of the Haig-Simons definition of income? How would you expect a move to full integration to affect the following in Canada: the allocation of capital between the corporate and noncorporate sectors, the share of corporate earnings that is distributed, and the ratio of debt to equity?

5. "Small corporations should face lower tax rates than large businesses, just as individuals with low incomes should face lower income tax rates than those with high incomes." What view of the corporation is implicit in this statement? Contrast this view with the view of conventional economics.

6. The ABC Corporation is contemplating purchasing a new computer system that would yield a before-tax return of 30 percent. The system depreciates at 10 percent a year. The after-tax interest rate is 8 percent, the corporation tax rate is 35 percent, and depreciation allowances follow the straight-line method over five years. There is no investment tax credit. Do you expect ABC to buy the new computer system? Explain your answer. (*Hint:* Use Equation (21.6).)

7. Ahmed's personal marginal income tax rate is 15 percent at the federal level and 5 percent at the provincial level. Bindi's federal and provincial personal marginal income tax rates are 29 percent and 13 percent, respectively. Both individuals receive dividends that are eligible for the enhanced dividend tax credit. Suppose that the combined federal and provincial corporate tax rate is 26.5 percent and the dividend gross-up rate is 38 percent, while the federal and provincial the dividend tax credit rates are 15 percent and 10 percent of the grossed-up dividends, respectively. (These were the approximate rates for Ontario taxpayers in 2015.) Assume that the corporation earns $200 in before-tax profits for each individual, all of which is distributed as dividends, after paying corporate taxes.

   a. Calculate the amount of corporate income tax paid on $200 of before-tax corporate income.

   b. Calculate the federal personal income tax liabilities of Ahmed and Bindi net of the federal dividend tax credit.

   c. Calculate the provincial personal income tax liabilities of Ahmed and Bindi net of the provincial dividend tax credit.

    d. What is the total tax rate (the combined corporate and personal income taxes) on the $200 in before-tax corporate income earned on behalf of Ahmed and Bindi?

    e. How does the total tax rate faced by each person compare with their individual personal marginal income tax rate?

    f. Comment on the extent to which the dividend tax credit integrates personal and corporate income taxes in the cases of Ahmed and Bindi.

8. The Quebec government provides a tax holiday—a temporary reduction in the corporate tax rate for several years—for small- and medium-sized manufacturing companies investing in remote regions. Discuss how this policy might distort the allocation of resources between long-lived and short-lived capital investments if depreciation allowances cannot be deferred to the period after the holiday ends. (*Hint:* Observe that the tax holiday changes the tax saving generated by the depreciation allowances.)

9. Assume Canada is a small, open economy such that the supply of capital is perfectly elastic at a net rate of return equal to 10 percent. Suppose the demand for capital in Canada is a downward sloping function of the net-of-tax rate of return r_t. Depict the equilibrium quantity of capital in Canada and the user cost of capital net of economic depreciation ($C - \delta$) in the case where

    a. There is no corporate taxation in Canada.

    b. There is a corporate tax in Canada and the marginal investment is financed by the equity.

    c. There is a corporate tax in Canada and the marginal investment is financed by debt.

10. Jimbo Corporation distributes its after-tax earnings to shareholders as dividends. Jimbo's before-tax earnings per share are $200 and the corporate tax rate is 50 percent. Roodly and Drey each own one share in Jimbo and they face marginal personal income tax rates of 20 percent and 40 percent, respectively. Give the total tax rates (corporate plus personal) faced by Roodly and Drey on the $200 per share of corporate earnings, if

    a. The corporate and personal income tax systems are not integrated.

    b. The corporate and personal income tax systems are fully integrated via the partnership method.

    c. Show that full integration reduces the total tax rate faced by Roodly by more than it reduces it for Drey.

11. Suppose that corporation XYZ has a domestic income of $1,000,000 and paid foreign taxes of $200,000. If the domestic corporate tax rate is 25 percent, how much will XYZ pay in domestic taxes if multinational firms are allowed to deduct foreign tax payments from their domestic taxable income? How much would XYZ pay in domestic taxes if the domestic government provides a tax credit for the foreign taxes paid? How would these alternative methods of treating foreign taxes affect XYZ's decision between making a domestic versus a foreign investment, when the before-tax incomes are identical across the two countries?

Glossary

Abatement Activities Emission-reducing activities that include changing production technology, switching to cleaner inputs, or reducing output.

Ability to Pay Principle A principle for equitable taxation that maintains that the tax burden should be distributed in relation to individuals' ability to pay taxes.

Absolute Tax Incidence The effect of a tax on the distribution of income when there is no change in either other taxes or government spending.

Accelerated Depreciation Allowing firms to take depreciation allowances faster than true economic depreciation.

Active Business Income Business income of a corporation other than from a specified investment business or a personal services business that includes an adventure or concern in the nature of trade.

Actuarially Fair Insurance Premium An insurance premium for a given time period set equal to the expected payout for the same time period.

Additive Social Welfare Function An equation defining social welfare as the sum of individuals' utilities.

Ad Valorem Tax A tax computed as a percentage of the purchase value.

Adverse Selection The situation that occurs when the people who are most likely to receive benefits from a certain type of insurance are the ones who are most likely to purchase it.

Agenda Manipulation The process of organizing the order in which votes are taken to ensure a favourable outcome.

Allowance An income-tested benefit that is paid to the spouse or partner of an OAS pension recipient.

Alternative Minimum Tax The tax liability calculated by an alternative set of rules, designed to force individuals with high levels of preference income to incur at least some tax liability.

Altruistic An individual who feels that he or she is better off when other individuals are better off.

Annuity Insurance plan that charges a premium and then pays a sum of money at some regular interval for as long as the policy holder lives.

Arm's-Length System A method of calculating taxes for multinational corporations by treating transactions between domestic and foreign operations as if they were separate enterprises.

Arrow's Impossibility Theorem It is impossible to translate individual preferences into collective preferences without violating at least one of a specified list of ethically reasonable conditions.

Assessed Value The value a jurisdiction assigns to a property for tax purposes.

Assessment Ratio The ratio of a property's assessed value to its market value.

Asymmetric Information A situation in which one party engaged in an economic transaction has better information about the good or service traded than the other party.

Automatic Stabilizers Taxes (expenditures) that rise (decline) when the economy is strong and decline (rise) when the economy is weak.

Average Tax Rate The ratio of the total tax paid to the total tax base.

Balanced-Budget Incidence The combined distributional effect of levying taxes and the government spending financed by those taxes.

Benefit–Cost Ratio The ratio of the present value of a stream of benefits to the present value of a stream of costs for a project.

Benefits-Received Principle Consumers of a publicly provided service should be the ones who pay for it.

Bequest Effect Individuals save more to counteract the redistribution of income from children to parents implicit in the public pension system. The increased saving is used to finance a larger bequest to children.

Bracket Creep When an increase in an individual's nominal income pushes him or her into a higher tax bracket despite the fact that the individual's real income is unchanged. *See also* **Tax Indexing**.

Branch Operations Parts of a Canadian corporation that operate in a foreign country and are not established as separate legal entities through incorporation in the foreign country.

Broad-Based Sales Taxes Levied on the purchases of a wide variety of goods and services; referred to as general sales taxes.

Budget Constraint The representation of the bundles among which consumers may choose, given their income and the prices they face.

Budget Line *See* **Budget Constraint**.

Canada Child Tax Benefit Non-taxable monthly payments to eligible families.

Canada Health and Social Transfer (CHST) A federal block grant to the provinces that funds spending on welfare, health care, and post-secondary education.

Canada Pension Plan (CPP) A contributory pension plan administered by the federal government. Contributions are collected from the employers and employees. The Quebec Pension Plan (QPP) operates in Quebec.

Cap and Trade A policy of granting permits to pollute. The number of permits is set at the desired pollution level and polluters may trade permits.

Capital Cost Allowance (CCA) The term in the Income Tax Act that refers to the depreciation of capital assets allowed for income tax purposes.

Capital Gains An increase in the value of an asset.

Capital Losses A decrease in the value of an asset.

Capital Intensive An industry in which the ratio of capital to labour inputs is relatively high.

Capitalization The process by which a stream of tax liabilities becomes incorporated into the price of an asset.

Cartel   Arrangement under which suppliers band together to restrict output and raise prices.

Cash Flow   The difference between the revenues obtained from the sale of output and assets and the expenditures on the purchase of inputs.

Categorical Grants   Grants for which the donor specifies how the funds can be used.

Certainty Equivalents   The value of an uncertain project measured in terms of how much certain income an individual would be willing to give up for the set of uncertain outcomes generated by the project.

Ceteris Paribus   Other things being the same.

Child Tax Benefit   An annual amount paid by the government to parents for each child under the age of 18. The benefit is reduced when the income of parents reaches a certain level and eventually disappears as income rises.

Clawbacks   Provisions in the law that reduce benefits once incomes reach a certain level. The child tax benefit, GST credits, and Employment Insurance benefits are all subject to clawbacks.

Clientele Effect   Firms structure their financial policies to meet different clientele needs. Those with low dividend payments attract shareholders with high marginal tax rates, and vice versa.

Coase Theorem   Provided that transaction costs are negligible, an efficient solution to an externality problem is achieved as long as someone is assigned property rights, independent of who is assigned those rights.

Coinsurance Rate   The proportion of costs above the deductible for which an insured individual is liable.

Command and Control Regulation   Policies that require a certain amount of pollution reduction with limited or no flexibility in how it may be achieved

Commodity Egalitarianism   The idea that some commodities ought to be made available to everybody.

Compensated Demand Curve   A demand curve that shows how quantity demanded varies with price, holding utility constant.

Compensated Response   How a price change affects quantity demanded when income is simultaneously altered so that the level of utility is unchanged.

Complements   Two goods are complements if an increase in the price of one good leads to decreased consumption of the other good.

Conditional Grants   *See* **Categorical Grants**.

Consumer Surplus   The amount by which consumers' willingness to pay for a commodity exceeds the sum they actually have to pay.

Consumption Smoothing   Reducing consumption in high-earning years in order to increase consumption in low-earning years.

Consumption-Type VAT   Capital investments are subtracted from sales in the computation of the value added.

Contract Curve   The locus of all Pareto-efficient points.

Corlett–Hague Rule   Efficient taxation requires taxing commodities that are complementary to leisure at relatively high rates.

Corporation   A state-chartered form of business organization, usually with limited liability for shareholders (owners) and an independent legal status.

Cost–Benefit Analysis   A set of procedures based on welfare economics for guiding public expenditure decisions.

Cost-Effective   When an outcome is achieved at the lowest possible cost.

Cost-Effectiveness Analysis   Comparing the cost of the various alternatives that attain similar benefits to determine which one is the cheapest.

Credit Budget   An annual statement that estimates the volume of new direct loans and loan guarantees made by the federal government for the fiscal year.

Crowding Out Hypothesis   Government borrowing decreases private investment by raising the market interest rate.

Customs Duties   Taxes imposed on imported and exported goods and services that may be in addition to all other taxes.

Cycling   When paired majority voting on more than two possibilities goes on indefinitely without a conclusion ever being reached.

Deadweight Loss   A pure waste with no accompanying gain; the inefficiency.

Debt   The total amount owed at a given point in time; the sum of all past deficits.

Deductible   The expenses an individual must pay out of pocket before an insurance policy makes any contribution.

Deductions   Certain expenses that may be subtracted from adjusted gross income in the computation of taxable income.

Deficit   The excess of expenditures over revenues during a period of time.

Demand Curve   A graph of the demand schedule.

Demand Schedule   The relation between the price of a good and the quantity demanded, ceteris paribus.

Differential Commodity Taxes   *See* **Excise Taxes**.

Differential Tax Incidence   The effect on income distribution of a change in taxes, with government expenditures held constant.

Diminishing Marginal Rate of Substitution   The marginal rate of substitution falls as we move down along an indifference curve.

Discount Factor   The number by which an amount of future income must be divided to compute its present value. If the interest rate is r and the income is receivable T periods in the future, the discount factor is $(1 + r)^T$.

Discount Rate   The rate of interest used to compute present value.

Discouraged Workers   Individuals who have stopped looking for a job because they think that the probability of finding a job is very low.

Dividend Deduction Method   When corporate income distributed as dividends is exempted from taxation at the corporate level in recognition that it is taxed at the individual level. It is a means of reducing "double taxation."

Dividend Exclusion Method When dividends are exempted from taxation at the individual level in recognition that corporate taxes are applied prior to distribution. It is a means of reducing "double taxation."

Dividend Relief Approach A method for relieving double taxation under which the corporation deducts dividends paid to the stockholders.

Dividend Tax Credit The credit allowed to taxpayers receiving taxable dividends in recognition of taxes that may have been paid on income at the corporate level prior to distribution.

Double-Peaked Preferences If, as a voter moves away from his or her most preferred outcome, utility goes down but then goes back up again.

Double Taxation Taxing corporate income first at the corporate level and again when it is distributed to shareholders.

Dual Income Tax An income tax system, as in several Nordic countries, where labour income and capital income are separated and taxed at different rates.

Earnings Test An individual whose earnings exceed a certain ceiling faces a reduction in concurrent social security benefits.

Econometrics The statistical tools for analyzing economic data.

Economic Depreciation The extent to which an asset decreases in value during a period of time.

Economic Incidence The change in the distribution of real income induced by a tax.

Economic Profits The return to owners of a firm above the opportunity costs of all the factors used in production. Also called supranormal or excess profit.

Edgeworth Box A device used to depict the distribution of goods in a two good–two person world.

Efficient *See* **Pareto Efficient**.

Elasticity of Substitution A measure of the ease with which one factor of production can be substituted for another.

Emissions Fee A tax on each unit of pollutant instead of each unit of output.

Empirical Work Analysis based on observation and experience as opposed to theory.

Employment Rate The ratio of the total number of employed individuals to the total working-age population.

Endowment Point The consumption bundle that is available if there are no exchanges with the market.

Equilibrium A situation that tends to be maintained unless there is an underlying change in the system.

Equivalent Variation A change in income that has the same effect on utility as a change in the price of a commodity.

Excess Burden A loss of welfare above and beyond taxes collected. Also called welfare cost or deadweight loss.

Excise Taxes Tax levied on the purchase of a particular commodity.

Exclusionary Zoning Laws Statutes that prohibit certain uses of land.

Exemption When calculating taxable income, the amount per family member that can be subtracted from adjusted gross income.

Expected Loss The probability of a loss times the magnitude of the loss.

Expected Utility The average utility over all possible uncertain outcomes, calculated by weighting the utility for each outcome by its probability of occurring.

Expected Value The average value over all possible uncertain outcomes, with each outcome weighted by the probability of it occurring.

Expenditure Decentralization Ratio The share of total government expenditures made by subnational governments, exclusive of grants received from the central government.

Expenditure Incidence The impact of government expenditures on the distribution of real income.

Expenditure Tax *See* **Personal Consumption Tax**.

Expensing Deducting the entire value of an asset in the computation of taxable income.

Experience Rating A method of determining what employment

insurance tax rate a firm should pay based on the firm's past layoff experience.

External Debt The amount a government owes to foreigners.

Externality An activity of one entity affects the welfare of another entity in a way that is outside the market.

Factors of Production *See* **Inputs**.

Federal Sales Tax (FST) The federal sales tax imposed on manufactured goods, known also as the Manufacturers' Sales Tax (MST), prior to the enactment of the GST.

Federal Tax Payable The amount of income tax levied by the federal government on a taxpayer.

Fiscal Federalism The study of the public finances of a federation.

Flat Tax A tax schedule for which the marginal tax rate is constant throughout the entire range of incomes.

Flow Variables Variables that are measured over a period of time. *See also* **Stock Variable**.

Flypaper Effect A dollar received by the community in the form of a grant to its government results in greater public spending than a dollar increase in community income.

Foreign Subsidiary A company incorporated abroad, but owned by a Canadian corporation.

Free-Rider Problem The incentive to let other people pay for a public good while you enjoy the benefits.

Full Integration *See* **Partnership Method**.

Full Loss Offset Allowing individuals to deduct from taxable income all losses on capital assets.

Functional Distribution of Income The way income is distributed among people when they are classified according to the inputs they supply to the production process (for example, landlords, capitalists, labourers).

Functional Finance Using fiscal policy to keep aggregate demand at the desired level, regardless of the impact on deficits.

General Agreement on Tariffs and Trade (GATT) A multinational pact that regulated international trade practices. GATT has been superseded by the World Trade Organization (WTO).

General Equilibrium Analysis The study of how various markets are interrelated.

General Sales Tax A tax levied at the same rate on the purchase of all commodities. Also referred to as broad-based sales tax.

Generation Skipping Arranging an estate in such a way that one or more generations avoid paying taxes on it.

Gini Coefficient A common measure of inequality.

Global System A system under which an individual is taxed on income whether it is earned in the home country or abroad.

Goods and Services Tax (GST) Canada's value-added tax. *See* **Value-Added Tax**.

Gross Income-Type VAT No deductions are allowed for capital investments when calculating value added.

Gross Replacement Rate The proportion of pretax earnings replaced by employment insurance.

Guaranteed Income Supplement (GIS) A negative income tax program for the elderly. Benefits are reduced as income increases.

Haig-Simons (H-S) Definition of Income Money value of the net increase to an individual's power to consume during a period.

Herd Immunity Situation where enough individuals in the community have been vaccinated so that the risk of infection to anyone else is negligible.

Hicks–Kaldor Criterion A project should be undertaken if it has a positive net present value, regardless of the distributional consequences.

Horizontal Equity People in equal positions should be treated equally.

Horizontal Summation The process of creating a market demand curve by summing the quantities demanded by each individual at every price.

Human Capital The investments that individuals make in education, training, and health care that raise their productivity.

Impure Public Good A good that is rival to some extent. *See* **Public Good**.

Imputed Rent The net monetary value of the services a home owner receives from a dwelling.

Incentive Contract A contract specifying that the contracting firm receives a fixed fee plus some fraction of the cost of the project.

Income After Taxes and Transfers Total income minus taxes.

Income Allocation Formula A formula that allocates a firm's income (based on sales and wages) among the provinces in order to determine how much income tax should be paid in each province.

Income Effect The effect of a price change on the quantity demanded due exclusively to the fact that the consumer's real income has changed.

Income Splitting Lowering total family income tax payments by assigning ownership of income-producing assets to the members of the family with the lowest incomes.

Incorporated Subsidiaries Foreign corporations owned by a Canadian corporation, but established as separate legal entities in the country in which each is located.

Independence of Irrelevant Alternatives Society's ranking of two different projects dependent only on individuals' rankings of the two projects, not on how individuals rank the two projects relative to other alternatives.

Indexed for Inflation Tax credits and tax brackets adjusted by the increase in the price level to prevent an increase in the real tax burden.

Indifference Curve The locus of consumption bundles that yield the same total utility.

Indifference Map The collection of all indifference curves.

Inferior Good A good whose demand decreases as income increases.

Inheritance Tax Tax levied on an individual receiving an inheritance.

In-Kind Transfers Payments from the government to individuals in the form of commodities or services rather than cash.

Inputs Factors that are used in the production process.

Insurance Premium Money paid to an insurance company in exchange for compensation if a specified adverse event occurs.

Internal Debt The amount that a government owes to its own citizens.

Internal Rate of Return The discount rate that would make a project's net present value zero.

Intertemporal Budget Constraint The schedule showing all feasible consumption levels across time.

Inverse Elasticity Rule For goods that are unrelated in consumption, efficiency requires that tax rates be inversely proportional to elasticities.

Investment Tax Credit (ITC) A reduction in tax liability equal to some portion of the purchase price of an asset.

Invoice-Credit Method Each firm is liable for taxes on total sales, but can claim the taxes already paid by suppliers as a credit against this liability, provided this tax payment is verified by invoices from suppliers.

Job-finding Rate The probability that an unemployed workers finds an acceptable job over a given week.

Labour Force The total number of individuals who are employed or unemployed and willing to work.

Labour Force Participation Rate The labour force as a percentage of the working-age population.

Labour Intensive An industry in which the ratio of capital to labour inputs is relatively low.

Laffer Curve A graph of the tax rate–tax revenue relationship.

Learning by Doing The process of generating knowledge and technological know-how that can benefit other firms that occurs when a firm undertakes an investment.

Life-Cycle Model Individuals' consumption and saving behaviour during a given year is the result of a planning process that considers their lifetime economic circumstances.

Lindahl Prices The tax share an individual must pay per unit of public good.

Linear Income Tax Schedule *See* Flat Tax.

Loading Fee The difference between the premium an insurance company charges and the actuarially fair premium level.

Loan Guarantees Promises to repay principal and interest on a loan in case the borrower defaults.

Local Public Good A public good that benefits only the members of a particular community.

Lock-In Effect The disincentive to change portfolios that arises because an individual incurs a tax on realized capital gains.

Logrolling The trading of votes to obtain passage of a package of legislative proposals.

Lorenz Curve Used to illustrate the distribution of income. It shows the share of income going to the poorest x percent of individuals.

Low Income Gap Ratio A measure that attempts to capture the depth of poverty.

Low Income Rate The percentage of a given population with low income.

Lump-Sum Tax A tax whose value is independent of the individual's behaviour.

Majority Voting Rule One more than half of the voters must favour a measure for it to be approved.

Marginal Incremental, additional.

Marginal Abatement Cost The additional cost associated with a one-unit reduction in emissions.

Marginal Congestion Cost Measure of the dollar cost of the incremental congestion created by each new member.

Marginal Cost The incremental cost of producing one more unit of output.

Marginal Cost of Public Funds (MCF) The cost to the economy of raising an additional dollar of tax revenue.

Marginal Effective Tax Rate Tax paid as a proportion of the income generated by the last, or marginal, dollar of capital invested.

Marginal Rate of Substitution The rate at which an individual is willing to trade one good for another; it is the slope of an indifference curve.

Marginal Rate of Transformation The rate at which the economy can transform one good into another good; it is the slope of the production possibilities frontier.

Marginal Tax Rate The proportion of the last dollar of income taxed by the government.

Market Income Receipts from employment, investment, retirement pensions, and other non-government sources.

Marriage Neutral Individuals' tax liabilities are independent of their marital status.

Maximin Criterion Social welfare depends on the utility of the individual who has the minimum utility in the society.

Means-Tested A spending program whose benefits flow only to those whose financial resources fall below a certain level.

Mechanistic View of Government Government is a creation of individuals to better achieve their individual goals.

Median Voter The voter whose preferences lie in the middle of the set of all voters' preferences; half the voters want more of the item selected, and half want less.

Median Voter Theorem As long as all preferences are single-peaked and several other conditions are satisfied, the outcome of majority voting reflects the preferences of the median voter.

Merit Goods Commodities that ought to be provided even if people do not demand it.

Monopoly A market with only one seller of a good.

Moral Hazard Arises in an insurance market when an individual can influence the probability, or the magnitude, of a loss by undertaking an action that the insurance company cannot observe.

Multiple Regression Analysis An econometric technique for estimating the parameters of an equation involving a dependent variable and more than one explanatory variable.

Natural Monopoly A situation in which factors inherent to the production process lead to a single firm supplying the entire industry's output.

Negative Income Tax An income support program that provides a basic level of support and that allows recipients to keep a fraction of their earnings.

Neoclassical Model A model in which the cost of capital is the primary determinant of the amount of capital investment.

Net Fiscal Benefits The value of publicly provided services minus their cost to the recipient.

Net Income-Type VAT The tax base for the VAT is based on net income so that depreciation is excluded from the base.

Net Wage The wage after taxes.

Net Wealth Tax A tax based on the difference between the market value of all the taxpayer's assets and liabilities.

Neutral Taxation Taxing each good at the same rate.

Nominal Amounts Amounts of money that are valued according to the price levels that exist in the year that the amount is received.

Nominal Income Income measured in terms of current prices.

Nominal Interest Rate The interest rate observed in the market.

Nonexcludable Good When an individual or firm cannot charge others for the goods that they produce because they cannot prevent them from benefiting from the goods.

Nonrival Good When the consumption of a good by one individual does not reduce the benefit that another individual receives from that good.

Normal Good A good whose demand increases as income increases.

Normative Analysis The method of evaluating policies according to certain ethical criteria.

Normative Economics The study of whether or not the economy produced socially desirable results.

Not in the Labour Force Individuals who do not have a job and are not looking for a job.

Old Age Security Pension (OAS) A federal pension for those 65 years and older. There is a clawback of benefits for high-income recipients.

Oligopoly A market structure where there are very few sellers of a good.

Organic View of Government The political philosophy that views society as a natural organism with the government as its heart.

Original Position An imaginary situation in which people have no knowledge of what their economic status in society will be.

Overlapping Generations Model A model that takes into account the fact that several different generations may exist simultaneously.

Parameters In econometrics, the coefficients of the explanatory variables that define the relationship between a change in an explanatory variable and a change in the dependent variable.

Pareto Efficient An allocation of resources such that no person can be made better off without making another person worse off.

Pareto Improvement A reallocation of resources that makes at least one person better off without making anyone else worse off.

Partial Equilibrium Models Models that study only one market and ignore possible spillover effects in other markets.

Partial Factor Tax Tax levied on an input in only some of its uses.

Partial Imputation An income tax measure in which "part" of the income at the corporate level is attributed to the individual shareholder and taxed at the individual's tax rate. Canada's dividend tax credit is such a measure.

Partnership Method When all earnings of a corporation, whether distributed or not, are attributed to shareholders as would be done in a partnership, and are taxed at the personal income-tax rate of the individual shareholders.

Passive Investment Income Income of a corporation that includes property income—such as interest, dividends, and rents—that is generally seen as income requiring limited effort on the part of the recipient, and where such investments may be viewed primarily as tax shelters. *See* **Active Business Income**.

Pay-As-You-Go A public pension system under which benefits paid to current retirees come from payments made by current workers.

Peak A point on the graph of an individual's preferences at which all the neighbouring points have lower utility.

Pecuniary Externalities Effects on welfare that are transmitted via the price system.

Perfect Price Discrimination When a producer charges each person the maximum he or she is willing to pay for the good.

Performance Standard A type of command and control regulation that sets an emissions goal for each polluter and allows for some flexibility in meeting that goal.

Personal Consumption Tax A system under which each household's tax base is its consumption expenditures.

Personal Expenditure Tax *See* **Personal Consumption Tax**.

Pigouvian Tax A tax levied on each unit of a polluter's output in an amount equal to the marginal damage that it inflicts at the efficient level of pollution.

Positive Analysis The method of predicting the consequences of policies.

Positive Economics The study of how the economy actually functions (as opposed to how it ought to function).

Potential Pareto Improvement A reallocation of resources where the gains achieved by those who are made better off exceed the losses sustained by those who are made worse off.

Poverty Lacking sufficient resources to meet current needs.

Poverty Gap The amount of money that would be required to raise the incomes of all poor households to the poverty line, calculated as a percentage of the poverty line income.

Poverty Line A fixed level of real income considered enough to provide a minimally adequate standard of living.

Present Value The value today of a certain amount of money to be paid or received in the future.

Present Value Criteria Rules for evaluating projects stating that (1) only projects with positive net present value should be carried out; and (2) of two mutually exclusive projects, the preferred project is the one with the higher net present value.

Price Elasticity of Demand The absolute value of the percentage change in quantity demanded divided by the percentage change in price.

Price Elasticity of Supply The absolute value of the percentage change in quantity supplied divided by the percentage change in price.

Price Taker An agent unable to affect the price of a good.

Principal–Agent Problem When one person (the principal) wants another person (the agent) to perform a task, the principal has to design the agent's incentives so that the principal's expected gain is maximized.

Private Good A good that is rival and excludable.

Privatization The process of changing ownership or control of an enterprise from the public to the private sector.

Production Possibilities Curve A graph that shows the maximum quantity of one output that can be produced, given the amount of the other output.

Production Possibilities Frontier The set of all the feasible combinations of goods that can be produced with a given quantity of efficiently employed inputs.

Progressive A tax system under which an individual's average tax rate increases with income.

Proportional A tax system under which an individual's average tax rate is the same at each level of income.

Public Choice The field of applying economic principles to the understanding of political decision making.

Public Economics *See* **Public Finance**.

Public Finance The field of economics that analyzes government taxation and spending policies.

Public Good A good that is nonrival and nonexcludable. *See* **Nonrival Good; Nonexcludable Good**.

Public Pension Wealth The present value of future public pension benefits.

Public Sector Economics *See* **Public Finance**.

Publicly Provided Private Goods Rival and excludable commodities that are provided by governments.

Pure Public Good A commodity that is nonrival and nonexcludable in consumption.

Quebec Pension Plan (QPP) The Quebec equivalent of the Canada Pension Plan.

Ramsey Rule To minimize total excess burden, tax rates should be set so that the tax-induced percentage reduction in the quantity demanded of each commodity is the same.

Random Error The term of a regression equation representing the unexplained difference between the dependent variable and its value as predicted by the model.

Rate Schedule A list of the tax liabilities associated with each level of taxable income.

Real Amounts Amounts of money adjusted for changes in the general price level.

Real Income A measure of income taking into account changes in the general price level.

Real Interest Rate The nominal interest rate corrected for changes in the level of prices by subtracting the expected inflation rate.

Realized Capital Gain A capital gain resulting from the sale of an asset.

Regional Extended Benefits A feature of the Employment Insurance program whereby unemployed workers in high-unemployment regions receive benefits for a longer period of time.

Registered Education Savings Plan (RESP) A plan to encourage saving for education. Contributions are not deductible, but interest on the plan would be taxable to the beneficiary (i.e., student) of the plan at the time of withdrawal. The beneficiary may have a much lower tax rate than the contributor (i.e., parent). Income earned on RESP accounts is not taxed as it accrues.

Registered Homeownership Savings Plan (RHOSP) A savings plan (terminated in 1985) that permitted specified amounts (to a maximum of $10,000) if placed in an RHOSP to be deducted in calculating taxable income. Funds, accumulated contributions plus earned interest, could be withdrawn, tax free, from the RHOSP for "first home" purchases.

Registered Pension Plan (RPP) Pension plans operated by public and private organizations, funded by employers and employee contributions, and benefiting from the deferral of taxes on contributions and the income earned by the plans.

Registered Retirement Savings Plan (RRSP) Savings plans for employees and the self-employed that permit a specified annual contribution, if placed in an RRSP, to be deducted in calculating taxable income. The tax on the contribution and the interest earned in the RRSP is deferred.

Regression Coefficient *See* **Parameters**.

Regression Line The line that provides the best fit through a scatter of points.

Regressive A tax system under which an individual's average tax rate decreases with income.

Regulatory Budget An annual statement of the costs imposed on the economy by government regulations. (Currently, there is no such budget.)

Rent Seeking Using the government to obtain higher than normal returns ("rents").

Repatriate To return the earnings of a foreign subsidiary to its parent company.

Retirement Effect Public pensions may induce an individual to retire earlier, which means that, ceteris paribus, he or she has to save more to finance a longer retirement period.

Risk Aversion A preference for paying a more than the actuarially fair premium in order to guarantee compensation if an adverse event occurs.

Risk Pooling The mechanism whereby risk is reduced when a number of risky projects or risky assets are combined.

Risk Premium The amount above the actuarially fair premium that a risk-averse person is willing to pay to guarantee compensation if the adverse event occurs.

Risk Smoothing Paying money in order to guarantee a certain level of consumption should an adverse event occur.

Risk Spreading The mechanism whereby risk is reduced when a number of individuals share the gains and losses from a risky project.

Rule definition of horizontal equity The rules that govern the selection of taxes are more important for judging fairness than the outcomes themselves.

Selective Sales Taxes *See* **Excise Taxes**.

Separation Rate The rate at which individuals are laid off or quit their jobs.

Shadow Price The underlying social cost of an input.

Single-Peaked Preferences Utility consistently falls as a voter moves away from his or her most preferred outcome.

Size Distribution of Income The way that total income is distributed across income classes.

Slope The change in the variable measured on the vertical axis divided by the change in the variable measured on the horizontal axis.

Social Insurance Government programs that replace income losses that are, at least in part, outside personal control.

Social Marginal Benefit The sum of marginal benefits to all of the individuals in the society.

Social Rate of Discount The rate at which society is willing to trade off present consumption for future consumption.

Social Security Wealth The present value of expected future social security benefits.

Social Welfare Function A function reflecting society's views on how the utilities of its members affect the well-being of society as a whole.

Split-Rate Method When a lower corporate income tax rate is applied to the share of corporate income distributed as dividends than to corporate income that is retained. It is a modification of the "dividend deduction method."

Standard Error A statistical measure of how much an estimated parameter might vary from its true value.

Statistically Significant When the standard error of a regression coefficient is low in relation to the size of the estimated parameter.

Statutory Incidence Indicates who is legally responsible for a tax.

Stock Variable Variable that is measured as of a given point in time. *See also* **Flow Variables**.

Subsidiary A company owned by one corporation, but chartered separately from the parent corporation.

Substitutes Two goods are substitutes if an increase in the price of one good leads to increased consumption of the other good.

Substitution Effect The tendency of an individual to consume more of one good and less of another because of a change in the two goods' relative prices.

Supply Schedule The relation between market price of a good and the quantity that producers are willing to supply, ceteris paribus.

Taxable Income The amount of income subject to tax.

Tax Amnesty Allowing delinquent taxes to be paid without prosecution.

Tax Arbitrage Producing a risk-free profit by exploiting inconsistencies in the tax act.

Tax Avoidance Altering behaviour in such a way to reduce your legal tax liability.

Tax Credit A subtraction from tax liability (as opposed to a subtraction from taxable income).

Tax Effort The ratio of tax collections to tax capacity.

Tax Evasion Not paying taxes legally due.

Tax Expenditures Loss of tax revenue because some item is excluded from the tax base or given preferential tax treatment in some way.

Tax Indexing Automatically adjusting the tax schedule to compensate for inflation so that an individual's real tax burden is independent of inflation.

Tax Life The number of years an asset can be depreciated.

Tax Prepayment Approach Under a personal consumption tax, durables are taxed when they are purchased, and future consumption benefits generated by the durable are not taxed.

Tax Shifting The difference between statutory incidence and economic incidence.

Tax Wedge The tax-induced difference between the price paid by consumers and the price received by producers.

Technology Standard Requires polluters to install a certain technology; for example, "scrubbers" in power plants to clean up or reduce emissions.

Territorial System A system under which an individual earning income in a foreign country owes taxes only to the host government. Also known as the exemption system.

Theory of the Second Best In the presence of existing distortions, policies that in isolation would increase efficiency can decrease it, and vice versa.

Third-Party Payment Payment for services by someone other than the provider or the consumer.

Time Endowment The maximum number of hours per year an individual can work.

Time Inconsistency of Optimal Policy The best fiscal policy, after individuals and firms have made investment decisions and other commitments, may be different from the best policy before those decisions and commitments were made.

Total Income Includes receipts from non-government sources as well as cash transfers from the government.

Transfer Price The price that one subsidiary charges another for some input.

Transitional Equity Fairness in changing tax regimes.

Turnover Tax A tax whose base is the total value of sales at each level of production.

Two-Part Tariff A system under which a consumer first pays a lump sum for the right to purchase a good and then pays a price for each unit of the good actually purchased.

Uncompensated Response The total change in quantity in response to a price change, incorporating both the substitution and the income effects.

Underground Economy Those economic activities that are either illegal, or legal but hidden from tax authorities.

Unearned Income Income, such as dividends and interest, that is not directly gained through supplying labour.

Unemployed Individuals who do not have a job but are available for work and have made an effort to find a job.

Unemployment Rate The percentage of the labour force that is unemployed.

Universal Child Care Benefit A program to assist families with young children, introduced in 2006.

Unit Tax A tax levied as a fixed amount per unit of commodity purchased.

Unrealized Capital Gain A capital gain on an asset not yet sold.

User Cost of Capital The opportunity cost to a firm of owning a piece of capital.

User Fee A price paid by users of a government-provided good or service.

Utilitarian Social Welfare Function An equation stating that social welfare is the sum of individuals' utilities.

Utility The amount of satisfaction a person derives from consuming a particular bundle of commodities.

Utility Definition of Horizontal Equity A method of classifying people of "equal positions" in terms of their utility levels.

Utility Possibilities Curve A graph showing the maximum amount of one person's utility given each level of utility attained by the other person.

Value Added The difference between sales and the cost of purchased material inputs.

Value-Added Tax (VAT) A percentage tax on value added at each stage of production.

Value of the Marginal Product (VMP) The value of the additional output obtained by using an additional unit of an input.

Vertical Equity Distributing tax burdens fairly across people with different abilities to pay.

Vertical Summation The process of creating an aggregate demand curve for a public good by adding the prices each individual is willing to pay for a given quantity of the good.

Voting Paradox With majority voting, community preferences can be inconsistent even though each individual's preferences are consistent.

Wagner's Law Government expenditures rise faster than incomes.

Wealth Neutrality Expenditure on a public good or service in a jurisdiction is not dependent on its level of wealth.

Wealth Substitution Effect Individuals save less in anticipation of the fact that they will receive public pension benefits after retirement, ceteris paribus.

Welfare Economics The branch of economic theory concerned with the social desirability of alternative economic policies.

Working-Age Population Individuals between the ages of 15 and 64.

Yearly Maximum Pensionable Earnings (YMPE) The maximum earnings that are used to compute an individual's CPP contribution and benefit.

Year's Basic Exemption (YBE) An individual's CPP contributions are based on his or her annual earnings in excess of the YBE.

References

CHAPTER 1

Adams, Charles. *For Good and Evil: The Impact of Taxes on the Course of Civilization.* Maryland: Madison Books, 1993.

Arrow, Kenneth J. *The Limits of Organization.* New York: W.W. Norton, 1974.

Canada. The Royal Commission on Dominion–Provincial Relations. Ottawa: King's Printer, 1940.

Canada. Public Accounts of Canada, 2014. Volume 1. http://www.tpsgc-pwgsc.gc.ca/recgen/cpc-pac/2014/vol1/intro-eng.html (Accessed June 3, 2015)

Creighton, Donald G. *British North America at Confederation: A Study Prepared for the Royal Commission on Dominion–Provincial Relations.* Ottawa, 1939.

Cross, Philip. *Estimating the True Size of Government: Adjusting for Regulation.* Macdonald-Laurier Institute, 2014. http://www.macdonaldlaurier.ca/mli-report-government-controls-nearly-two-thirds-of-the-canadian-economy/ (Accessed June 1, 2015)

Department of Finance. *Tax Expenditures and Evaluations, 2014.* Ottawa: Department of Finance, 2014.

Di Matteo, Livio, and Michael Shannon. "Payroll Taxation in Canada: An Overview." *Canadian Business Economics* 3(4) (1995): 5–22.

Eggleston, Wilfred, and C.T. Kraft. *Dominion–Provincial Subsidies and Grants: A Study Prepared for the Royal Commission on Dominion–Provincial Relations.* Ottawa, 1939.

Ferris, J. Stephen, and Stanley L. Winer. "Just How Much Bigger Is Government in Canada? A Comparative Analysis of the Size and Structure of the Public Sectors in Canada and the United States, 1929–2004." *Canadian Public Policy* 33(2) (June 2007): 173–206.

Lin, Zhengxi. *Payroll Taxes in Canada Revisited: Structure, Statutory Parameters, and Recent Trends.* Analytical Studies Branch Research Paper No. 149. Ottawa: Statistics Canada, September 2001.

Lowi, Theodore J. *The End of Liberalism.* New York: W.W. Norton, 1979.

North, Douglas. *Institutions, Institutional Change and Economic Performance.* New York: Cambridge University Press, 1990.

Perry, J. Harvey. *Taxation in Canada,* 5th ed. Toronto: Canadian Tax Foundation, 1990.

Sheikh, Munir A. *Estimating the True Size of Government: Adjusting for Tax Expenditures.* Macdonald-Laurier Institute, 2014. http://www.macdonaldlaurier.ca/mli-report-munir-sheikh-finds-tax-expenditures-dramatically-increase-size-of-government/ (Accessed June 2, 2015)

Stone, Lawrence. *The Family, Sex, and Marriage in England, 1500–1800.* New York: Harper and Row, 1977. 18, 1987.

IN THE NEWS

Robinson, Bill. *Canadian Military Spending 2010–11.* Foreign Policy Series, Canadian Centre for Policy Alternatives, March 2011. https://www.policyalternatives.ca/sites/default/files/uploads/publications/National%20Office/2011/03/Canadian%20Military%20Spending%202010.pdf

Starr, Katharine. "'Jason Kenney says $12B military budget boost a 'huge improvement'." CBC News Posted: Apr 22, 2015. http://www.cbc.ca/news/politics/jason-kenney-says-12b-military-budget-boost-a-huge-improvement-1.3044771

"What Canada did—and did not—achieve in Afghanistan." Editorial. *The Globe and Mail,* Mar. 14, 2014. http://www.theglobeandmail.com/globe-debate/editorials/now-that-our-war-in-afghanistan-is-over/article17501889/

CHAPTER 2

Baumol, William J., and Hilda Baumol. "Book Review." *Journal of Political Economy* 89(2) (April 1981): 425–28.

Harford, Tim. *The Undercover Economist.* Oxford: Oxford University Press, 2006.

Musgrave, Richard A. *The Theory of Public Finance.* New York: McGraw-Hill, 1959.

Tucker, Robert C., ed. *The Marx-Engels Reader,* 2nd ed. New York: W.W. Norton, 1978.

Willig, Robert. "Consumer's Surplus without Apology." *American Economic Review* (September 1976): 589–97.

IN THE NEWS

CBC News. October 17, 2014. "Uber warning issued by Canada's insurance industry." http://www.cbc.ca/news/canada/calgary/uber-warning-issued-by-canada-s-insurance-industry-1.2804413

Hui, Ann. "Court case between Toronto, Uber pushed back until June." *The Globe and Mail,* May 11, 2015. http://www.theglobeandmail.com/news/toronto/court-case-between-toronto-uber-pushed-back-until-june/article24379546/

Kerr, Dara. "Sharing economy's apps to boom with their lure of cheap and easy." CNET, April 14, 2015. http://www.cnet.com/news/sharing-economy-expected-to-boom-customers-say-it-makes-life-cheap-and-easy/

CHAPTER 3

Ackerman, Frank, and Lisa Heinzerling. *Priceless: On Knowing the Price of Everything and the Value of Nothing.* New York: New Press, 2005.

Arrow, Kenneth J. "The Economic Implications of Learning by Doing." *Review of Economic Studies* 29 (1962): 155–73.

Bellavance, François, Georges Dionne, and Martin Lebeau. "The Value of a Statistical Life: A Meta-Analysis with a Mixed Effects Regression Model." *Journal of Health Economics* 28(2) (March 2009).

Boardman, Anthony E., and Diane Forbes. "A Benefit–Cost Analysis of Private and Semi-Private Hospital Rooms." *Journal of Benefit-Cost Analysis* 2(1) art. 3 (2011): 1–25.

Boardman, Anthony, David Greenberg, Aidan Vining, and David Weimer. *Cost–Benefit Analysis: Concepts and Practice,* 4th ed. New York: Prentice Hall, 2011.

Boardman, Anthony E., Mark A. Moore, and Aidan R. Vining. "The Social Discount Rate in Canada Based on Future Growth in Consumption." *Canadian Public Policy* 36(3) (September 2010): 325–343.

Boardman, Anthony E., Wendy L. Mallery, and Aidan R. Vining. "Learning from Ex Ante/Ex Post Cost-Benefit Comparisons: The Coquihalla Highway Example." *Socio-Economic Planning Sciences* 28(2) (June 1994): 69–84.

Broome, J. "Trying to Value a Life." *Journal of Public Economics* (February 1978): 91–100.

Brookes, Peter, and J.D. Foster. "Better Green Jobs: The One-Word Solution." The Heritage Foundation (March 20, 2009).

The Economist. 2007. "Vote for Me, Dimwit" (June 16, 2007): p. 42.

Garen, J. "Compensating Wage Differentials and the Endogeneity of Job Riskiness." *Review of Economics and Statistics* 70(1) (February 1988).

Goldsmith, Charles. "Is There a Doctor in the Plane? Yes, If He Can Bill His Bill Pad." *The Wall Street Journal,* October 8, 1998, p. B1.

References

Harberger, Arnold. "The Incidence of the Corporation Income Tax," in *Taxation and Welfare*, ed. Arnold C. Harberger. Boston: Little, Brown, 1974.

Marv Anderson and Associates Ltd. *Oldman River Basin Study. Phase II, Economic Analysis of Water Supply Alternatives*, 1978.

McHugh, Darren. "A Cost–Benefit Analysis of an Olympic Games." Queen's Economics Department Working Paper No. 1097 (August 2006).

Pigou, A.C. *The Economics of Welfare*. New York: Macmillan, 1932.

Treasury Board of Canada Secretariat. *Canadian Cost Benefit Analysis Guide: Regulatory Proposals*. Ottawa (2007).

Tresch, Richard W. *Public Finance: A Normative Theory*, 2nd ed. New York: Academic Press, 2002.

Viscusi, W. Kip, and Joseph E. Aldy. "The Value of a Statistical Life: A Critical Review of Market Estimates throughout the World." *Journal of Risk and Uncertainty* 27(1) (2003): 5–76.

Von Wartburg, Markus, and William G. Waters II. "Congestion Externalities and the Value of Travel Time Savings," in *Towards Estimating the Social and Environmental Costs of Transport in Canada: A Report for Transport Canada*, eds. Anming Zhang, Anthony E. Boardman, David Gillen, and William G. Waters II. Vancouver, Canada: Centre for Transportation Studies, University of British Columbia (2004).

Will, George F. "You Ain't Seen Nothing Yet!" *Newsweek*, December 23, 1985, p. 84.

Zhang, Anming Anthony E. Boardman, David Gillen, and William G. Waters II (eds.). Vancouver, Canada: Centre for Transportation Studies, University of British Columbia (2004).

IN THE NEWS

Allan, Robyn. "An Economic Assessment of Northern Gateway." http://www.robynallan.com/wp-content/uploads/2012/02/Economic-Assessment-of-Northern-Gateway-January-31-2012.pdf

CBC News. "Northern Gateway Pipeline approved: B.C. reacts: B.C. reaction is rolling in to the federal government's decision to approve the Enbridge pipeline." June 11, 2014. http://www.cbc.ca/news/canada/british-columbia/northern-gateway-pipeline-approved-b-c-reacts-1.2672279

Hunter, Justine, and Wendy Stueck. "B.C. government to Northern Gateway pipeline proposal: 'No'." June 17, 2014. http://www.theglobeandmail.com/news/british-columbia/bc-to-northern-gateway-no/article19213866/

Wright Mansell Research Ltd. "Public Interest Benefit Evaluation of the Enbridge Northern Gateway Pipeline Project: Update and Reply Evidence." https://docs.neb-one.gc.ca/ll-eng/llisapi.dll/fetch/2000/90464/90552/384192/620327/624798/833081/B83-4_-_Attachment_2_-_Public_Interest_Benefit_Evaluation_-_Update_and_Reply_Evidence_-_A2V1R8.pdf?nodeid=832978&vernum=0

CHAPTER 4

Atkinson, Anthony B., and Nicholas H. Stern. "Pigou, Taxation and Public Goods." *Review of Economic Studies* 41 (1974): 119–28.

Caves, Douglas W., and Laurits R. Christensen. "The Relative Efficiency of Public and Private Firms in a Competitive Environment: The Case of Canadian Railroads." *Journal of Political Economy* 88(5) (October 1980): 958–76.

Chan, Kenneth S., Stuart Mestelman, Rob Moir, and R. Andrew Muller. "The Voluntary Provision of Public Goods Under Varying Income Distributions." *Canadian Journal of Economics* 29(1) (February 1996): 54–69.

Cinyabuguma, Matthias, Talbot Page, and Louis Putterman. "Cooperation Under the Threat of Expulsion in a Public Goods Experiment." *Journal of Public Economics* 89 (2005): 1421–1435.

Coase, Ronald H. "The Lighthouse in Economics." *Journal of Law and Economics* (October 1974): 357–76.

Ehrlich, Isaac, Georges Gallais-Mamonno, Zhiqiang Liu, and Randall Lutter. "Productivity Growth and Firm Ownership: An Empirical Investigation." *Journal of Political Economy* 1002(4) (August 1994): 1006–38.

Groves, Theodore, and Martin Loeb. "Incentives and Public Inputs." *Journal of Public Economics* 4(3) (1975): 211–226.

Hart, Oliver, Andrei Shleifer, and Robert W. Vishny. "The Proper Scope of Government: Theory and an Application to Prisons." *Quarterly Journal of Economics* 112(4) (1997): 1127–1161.

Johansen, Leif. "The Theory of Public Goods: Misplaced Emphasis?" *Journal of Public Economics* 7(1) (February 1977): 147–52.

Megginson, William L., and Jeffry M. Netter. "From State to Market: A Survey of Empirical Studies on Privatization." *Journal of Economic Literature* 39 (June 2001): 321–89.

Samuelson, Paul A. "Diagrammatic Exposition of a Theory of Public

Expenditure." *Review of Economics and Statistics* 37 (1955): 350–56.

Sheshinski, Eytan, and Luis Felipe Lopez-Calva. "Privatization and Its Benefits: Theory and Evidence." Working Paper. Harvard Institute for International Developement, January 1999.

Shleifer, Andrei. "State versus Private Ownership." *Journal of Economic Perspectives* 12(4) (1998): 133–150.

Thurow, Lester C. "The Income Distribution as a Pure Public Good." *Quarterly Journal of Economics* (May 1971): 327–36.

Tobin, James. "On Limiting the Domain of Inequality." *Journal of Law and Economics* 13 (1970): 263–77.

Vickers, John, and George Yarrow. "Economic Perspectives on Privatization." *Journal of Economic Perspectives* 5 (Spring 1991): 111–32.

West, Douglas S. "The Privatization of Liquor Retailing in Alberta." Public Policy Sources #5. Vancouver: The Fraser Institute, 1997.

IN THE NEWS

CTVNews.ca Staff. "Ottawa to invest $75M in anti-terrorism drone technology." March 23, 2015. http://www.bnn.ca/News/2015/3/23/Ottawa-to-invest-in-anti-terrorism-drone-technology.aspx

Mackin, Bob. "BC Quietly Scopes Out Drones." *The Tyee*, November 15, 2013. http://thetyee.ca/News/2013/11/15/BC-Drone-Industry/

Quan, Douglas. "RCMP drone expansion comes with hefty price tag, prompts concerns of 'mission creep'." *National Post*, December 31, 2014. http://news.nationalpost.com/news/canada/rcmp-drone-expansion-comes-with-hefty-price-tag-prompts-concerns-of-mission-creep

CHAPTER 5

Chay, Kenneth Y., and Michael Greenstone. "The Impact of Air Pollution on Infant Mortality: Evidence from Geographic Variation in Pollution Shocks Induced by a Recession." *Quarterly Journal of Economics* 118(3) (2003): 1121–1167.

Coase, Ronald H. "The Problem of Social Cost." *Journal of Law and Economics* (October 1960): 1–44.

Conda, Cesar V. "An Environment for Reform." *The Wall Street Journal*, January 23, 1995, p. A18.

Congressional Budget Office (CBO). "Fuel Economy Standards Versus a Gasoline Tax." *Economic and Budget Issue Brief*, March 9, 2004.

Currie, Janet, and Matthew Neidell. "Air Pollution and Infant Health: What Can We Learn from California's Recent Experience?" *Quarterly Journal of Economics* 120(3) (2005): 1003–1030.

Cushon, Jennifer A., Cory O. Neudorf, Tanis M. Kershaw, Terry G. Dunlop, and Nazeem Muhajarine. "Coverage for the Entire Population: Tackling immunization rates and disparities in Saskatoon Health Region." *Canadian Journal of Public Health* 103(Suppl. 1) (2012): S37–S41.

Executive Office of the President Council of Economic Advisers. *Economic Report of the President, 2003.* Washington, D.C.: U.S. Government Printing Office, 2003.

Environment Canada. "Canada Lists Emissions Target under the Copenhagen Accord." News Release, February 1, 2010. http://www.ec.gc.ca.

Environment Canada. *An Introduction to Climate Change: A Canadian Perspective.* Ottawa: Minister of Public Works and Government Services Canada, 2005.

Gayer, Ted. "Neighbourhood Demographics and the Distribution of Hazardous Waste Risks: An Instrumental Variable Estimation." *Journal of Regulatory Economics* 17(2) (2000): 131–155.

Gardam, Michael, and Camille Lemieux. "Mandatory influenza vaccination? First we need a better vaccine." *Canadian Medical Association Journal* 185(8) (May 14, 2013): 639–640.

Grainger, Corbett A., and Charles D. Kolstad. "Who Pays a Price on Carbon." *NBER Working Paper No. 15239.* Cambridge, MA: National Bureau of Economic Research, 2009.

Heal, Geoffrey. "Bundling Biodiversity." *European Economic Association* 1(2–3) (2003): 553–560.

Kennedy, Mark. "Stephen Harper and Australia's Tony Abbott won't let climate policies kill jobs." *Ottawa Citizen.* June 9, 2014. http://ottawacitizen.com/news/national/stephen-harper-and-australias-tony-abbott-wont-let-climate-policies-kill-jobs (accessed August 1, 2014)

Komarnicki, Jamie. "Province eyes manadatory flu shots for health workers." *Calgary Herald,* June 11, 2014. http://www.calgaryherald.com/news/alberta/Province+eyes+mandatory+shots+health+workers/9930118/story.html (accessed August 8, 2014)

M. K. Jaccard and Associates Inc. *Exploration of Two Canadian Greenhouse Gas Emissions Targets: 25% Below 1990 and 20% below 2006 levels by 2020.* Final report prepared for the Pembina Institute and the David Suzuki Foundation (M. K. Jaccard and Associates Inc.) 2009.

Mishan, E.J. "The Postwar Literature on Externalities: An Interpretative Essay." *Journal of Economic Literature* 9(1) (March 1971): 1–28.

Parry, Ian W. H. *How Much Should Highway Fuels be Taxed?* Resources for the Future Discussion Paper 09–52, December 2009.

Parons, Mark, and Nicholas Phillips. *An Evaluation of the Federal Tax Credit for Scientific Research and Experimental Development.* Department of Finance Working Paper 2007-08, 2007.

Rucker, Randal R., Walter N. Thurman, and Michael Burgett. "Honey Bee Pollination Markets and the Internalization of Reciprocal Benefits." *American Journal of Agricultural Economics* 94(4) (2012): 956–977.

Snoddon, T., and R. Wigle. "Regional Incidence of the Costs of Greenhouse Policy." *Canadian Journal of Regional Science* 30(2) (2007): 313–336.

Stavins, Robert N. "Experience with Market-based Environmental Policy Instruments," in *Handbook of Environmental Economics*, Volume 1, eds. Karl-Goran Maler and Jeffrey R. Vincent. Amsterdam: North Holland, 2003.

Sugg, Ike C. "Selling Hunting Rights Saves Animals." *The Wall Street Journal,* July 23, 1996, p. A22.

Walkinshaw, Erin. "News: Mandatory vaccinations: The international landscape." *Canadian Medical Association Journal* 183(16) (Nov. 8, 2011): E1165–E1166.

IN THE NEWS

Beaty, R. R. Lipsey, and S. Elgie. "The shocking truth about B.C.'s carbon tax: It works." *The Globe and Mail,* July 9, 2014.

British Columbia Ministry of Finance. *Budget and Fiscal Plan 2014/15 to 2016/17.* February 14, 2014. http://www.bcbudget.gov.bc.ca/2014/bfp/2014_Budget_Fiscal_Plan.pdf (accessed July 16, 2014)

Corcoran, Terence. "Time to bury B.C.'s carbon tax myth," *National Post.* June 18, 2015.

Elgie, Stewart, and Jessica McClay. "BC's Carbon Tax Shift Is Working Well after Four Years (Attention Ottawa)." *Canadian Public Policy,* Vol. 39, Supplement, (August 2013): S1-S10.

Reguly, Eric. "A revenue neutral, comprehensive carbon tax is the least bad option." *The Globe and Mail,* November 29, 2013. http://www.theglobeandmail.com/report-on business/industry-news/energy-and-resources/politically-unpopular-carbon-tax-wont-work/article15691281/ (accessed July 16, 2014)

CHAPTER 6

Blackorby, C., and D. Donaldson. "Cash Versus Kind, Self-Selection, and Efficient Transfers." *American Economic Review* 78 (1988): 691–700.

Blanchard, Lois, J.S. Butler, T. Doyle, R. Jackson, J. Ohis, and Barbara Posner. *Final Report, Food Stamp SSI/Elderly Cash-out Demonstration Evaluation.* Princeton, NJ: Mathematica Policy Research, 1982.

Browning, Edgar. "The Case Against Income Redistribution." *Public Finance Review,* 30(6) (2002): 509–530.

Burbridge, J., L. Magee, and A. Robb. "The Education Premium in Canada and the United States." *Canadian Public Policy* 28(2) (2002): 203–217.

Chen, Wen-Hao. "Cross-National Differences in Income Mobility: Evidence from Canada, the United States, Great Britain, and Germany." *Review of Income and Wealth,* 55(1) (2009): 75–100.

Crutsinger, Martin. "Greenspan Talk Doesn't Roil Markets," *The Washington Post, Tuesday,* March 13, 2007. http://www.washingtonpost.com/wp-dyn/content/article/2007/03/13/AR2007031300744.html (accessed January 9, 2015)

Cushing, Matthew J., and Mary G. McGarvey. "The Efficiency of Race- and Gender-Targeted Income Transfers." *Public Finance Review* 31(5) (2003): 455–486.

Dahlby, Bev G. *The Marginal Cost of Public Funds: Theory and Applications.* Boston: The MIT Press, 2008.

Dahlby, Bev G., and Guiseppe C. Ruggeri. "The Marginal Cost of Redistribution: Comment." *Public Finance Quarterly* 24 (1996): 44–62.

Fair, Ray C. "The Optimal Distribution of Income." *Quarterly Journal of Economics* 85 (1971): 551–79.

Feldstein, Martin S. "On the Theory of Tax Reform." *Journal of Public Economics* 6 (1976): 77–104.

Frenette, Marc., David Green, and Kevin Milligan. "Revisiting Recent Trends in Canadian After-Tax Income Inequality Using Census Data." Analytical Studies Branch Research Paper Series 2006274e. Statistics Canada, Analytical Studies Branch, 2006.

Hobbes, Thomas. *Leviathan.* New York: Meridian Books, 1963 (1651).

Jenkins, Holman, Jr. "The 'Poverty' Lobby's Inflated Numbers." *The Wall Street Journal*, December 14, 1992, p. A10.

Nozick, Robert. *Anarchy, State, and Utopia*. Oxford: Basil Blackwell, 1974.

OECD. "Focus on Top Incomes and Taxation in OECD Countries: Was the crisis a game changer?" Paris: OECD, 2014. www.oecd.org/social/inequality.htm

Osberg, Lars. *A Quarter Century of Economic Inequality in Canada: 1981-2006* (Toronto: Canadian Centre for Policy Alternatives, 2008).

Rawls, John. *A Theory of Justice*. Cambridge, MA: Harvard University Press, 1971.

Saez, Emmanuel, and Michael Veall. "The Evolution of High Incomes in Northern America: Lessons from Canadian Evidence," *American Economic Review* 95(3) (2005): 831-849.

Statistics Canada. *Low Income Cut-offs for 2008 and Low Income Measures for 2007*. Ottawa: Ministry of Industry, 2009.

Statistics Canada. *Low Income Lines, 2010-2011*, no. 2. Ottawa: Ministry of Industry, 2012. http://www.statcan. gc.ca/pub/75f0002m/75f0002m2012002-eng.htm

Stein, Herbert. "The Income Inequality Debate." *The Wall Street Journal*, May 1, 1996, p. A14.

Thurow, Lester C. "The Income Distribution as a Pure Public Good." *Quarterly Journal of Economics* (May 1971): 327-36.

Tobin, James. "On Limiting the Domain of Inequality." *Journal of Law and Economics* 13 (1970): 263-77.

Whitmore, Diane. "What are Food Stamps Worth?" Industrial Relations Section Working Paper No. 468. Princton, NJ: Princton University, 2002.

IN THE NEWS

Beltrame, Julian. "Canadian income disparity growing: Income Disparity in Canada among fastest growing in the OECD." *Maclean's*, April 30, 2014. http://www.macleans.ca/economy/business/canadian-income-disparity-growing (accessed November 24, 2014)

Davies, James B. *Redistribution of Income: Policy Directions*. School of Public Policy Research Paper, Vol. 6(23) (Calgary: the School of Public Policy, 2013).

Jackson, Andrew. "Economy Lab: Government policies have widened Canada's income gap." *The Globe and Mail*, March 17, 2014. http://www. theglobeandmail.com/report-on-business/economy/economy-lab/government-policies-have-widened-canadas-income-gap/article17517631 (accessed November 6, 2014)

Milligan, Kevin. *Income Inequality and Income Taxation in Canada: Trends in the Census 1980-2005*. School of Public Policy Research Paper, Vol. 6(24) (Calgary: the School of Public Policy, 2013).

Osberg, Lars. *What's So Bad About More Inequality? Annual Symposium, Levelling the Spirit: Addressing the Social Impacts of Economic Inequality*. Canberra, Australia, November 12, 2013 (version March 5, 2014). http://myweb.dal.ca/osberg/conference.htm (accessed November 21, 2014)

Veall, Michael. "Top Income Shares in Canada: Recent Trends and Policy Implications," *Canadian Journal of Economics* 45(4) (2012): 1247-1272.

CHAPTER 7

Arrow, Kenneth J. *Social Choice and Individual Values*. New York: John Wiley and Sons, 1951.

Auerbach, Alan J. *Federal Budget Rules: The US Experience*. Working Paper No. 14288. Cambridge, MA: National Bureau of Economic Research, 2008.

Baylis, Kathy, and Hartley Furtan. "Free-Riding on Federalism: Trade Protection and the Canadian Dairy Industry." *Canadian Public Policy* 29(2) (2003): 145-161.

Blair, Douglas H., and Robert A. Pollak. "Rational Collective Choice." *Scientific American* 249(2) (August 1983): 88-95.

Boothe, Paul. *The Growth of Government Spending in Alberta*. Canadian Tax Paper No. 100. Toronto: Canadian Tax Foundation, 1995.

Brennan, Richard. "Hard Times for Big Three Automakers." *The Toronto Star*, Feb 3, 2007, p. F3.

Buchanan, James M. "Social Choice, Democracy, and Free Markets," in *Fiscal Theory and Political Economy—Selected Essays*, ed. James M. Buchanan, pp. 75-89. Chapel Hill: University of North Carolina Press, 1960.

Carrick, R. "Balanced Budget Legislation Draws Criticism from Martin." *The [Windsor] Star*, 2 September 1995, H8.

CBC.ca. "CBC asks: Many Canadians distrustful of federal politics," March 25, 2015. http://www.cbc.ca/news/politics/cbc-asks-many-canadians-distrustful-of-federal-politics-poll-indicates-1.3005779

Delacourt, Susan. "Losing Interest." *The Globe and Mail*, Saturday, April 1, 1995, p. D1.

Erickson, Lynda, and Brenda O'Neill. "The Gender Gap and the Changing Woman Voter in Canada." *International Political Science Review* 23(4) (October 2002): 373-392.

Fattah, Hassan M. "First Time Out, Kuwaiti Women Become a Political Force." *New York Times*, June 26, 2006, p. A3.

Flanagan, Thomas. *Game Theory and Canadian Politics*. Toronto: University of Toronto Press, 1998.

Gidengil, Elisabeth, Joanna Everitt, André Blais, Patrick Fournier, and Neil Nevitte. "Back to the Future? Making Sense of the Canadian Election outside Quebec." *Canadian Journal of Political Science* 39(1) (March 2006): 1-25.

Gonzalez, Francisco, and Jean-François Wen. "A Theory of Top Income Taxation and Social Insurance." *The Economic Journal* 125(587) (September 2015).

Keller, Bill. "Same Old Bureaucracy Serves New South Africa" *New York Times*, June 4, 1994, p. A1.

Keynes, John Maynard. *The General Theory of Employment, Interest, and Money*. New York: Harcourt Brace and World, 1965 (1936).

Kneebone, Ronald D. "Deficits and Debt in Canada: Some Lessons from Recent History." *Canadian Public Policy* 20(2) (1994): 152-164.

Landon, Stuart, Melville L. McMillan, Vijay Muralidharan, Mark Parsons. "Does Health Care Spending Crowd out Other Provincial Government Expenditures?" *Canadian Public Policy* 32(2) (2006): 121-141.

Lee, Chulhee. "Rising Family Income Inequality in the United States, 1868-2000: Impacts of Changing Labor Supply, Wages, and Family Structure." *International Economic Journal* 22(2) (2008): 253-272.

Levin, Jonathan, and Barry Nalebuff. "An Introduction to Vote-Counting Schemes." *Journal of Economic Perspectives* 9 (Winter 1995): 3-26.

Lindahl, E. "Just Taxation—A Positive Solution," in *Classics in the Theory of Public Finance*, ed. R.A. Musgrave and A.T. Peacock. New York: St. Martin's Press, 1958.

Lott, John R. "Public Schooling, Indoctrination, and Totalitarianism." *Journal of Political Economy* Part II (December 1999): S127-S157.

Martin, Paul. "The Canadian Experience in Reducing Budget Deficits and Debt." *Federal Reserve Bank of Kansas City Economic Review*, First Quarter (1996): 11-25.

Massie, Robert K. *Peter the Great—His Life and World*. New York: Random House, 1980.

Meltzer, Allan H., and Scott F. Richard. "A Rational Theory of the Size of Government." *Journal of Political Economy* 89(5) (October 1981): 914–27.

Milligan, Kevin S., and Michael Smart. "Regional Grants as Pork Barrel Politics." *CESifo Working Paper Series No. 1453*. Available at SSRN: http://ssrn.com/abstract=710903.

Moene, Karl Ove, and Michael Wallerstein. "Inequality, Social Insurance, and Redistribution." *American Political Science Review* 95(4) (2001): 859–874.

Niskanen, William A., Jr. *Bureaucracy and Representative Government*. Chicago: Aldine, 1971.

Olive, David. *Canadian Political Babble*. Toronto: John Wiley and Sons, 1993.

Organisation for Economic Co-operation and Development. *OECD Economic Outlook* Volume 2015, Iss. 1. Paris: June 2015.

Peacock, A.T., and J. Wiseman. *The Growth of Public Expenditure in the United Kingdom*, 2nd ed. London: Allen and Unwin, 1967.

Peterson, Rick. "Message to the Conservatives: Go Mainstream or Go Home." *Policy Options*, September (2004).

Philipps, Lisa C. "The Rise of Balanced Budget Laws in Canada: Legislating Fiscal (Ir)responsibility." *Osgoode Hall Law Journal* 34(4) (1997): 681–740.

Savoie, Donald J. *The Politics of Public Spending in Canada*. Toronto: University of Toronto Press, 1990.

Savoie, Donald J. *Whatever Happened to the Music Teacher: How Government Decides and Why*. McGill-Queen's University Press, 2013.

Savoie, Donald J. "Fixing the Bureaucracy." *Policy Options* (July, 2013).

Schorske, Carl E. *Fin-de-Siècle Vienna—Politics and Culture*. New York: Vintage Books, 1981.

Smith, Julie P. *Taxing Popularity: The Story of Taxation in Australia*. Canberra: Federalism Research Centre, Australian National University, 1993.

Stephenson, Amanda. "Alberta's dairy farmers say supply management not a threat to Canada-EU beef deal." *Calgary Herald*, May 27, 2013. http://www.calgaryherald.com/business/Alberta+dairy+farmers+supply+managment+threat+Canada+beef+deal/8446526/story.html

Tanzi, Vito, and Ludger Schuknecht. "Reforming Government: An Overview of Recent Experience." *European Journal of Political Economy* 13 (September 1997).

Treff, Karin, and David Perry. *Finances of the Nation, 2006*. Toronto: Canadian Tax Foundation, 2007.

Treff, Karin, and Deborah Ort. *Finances of the Nation, 2010*. Toronto: Canadian Tax Foundation, 2011.

Young, Robert A. "Budget Size and Bureaucratic Careers," in *The Budget-Maximizing Bureaucrat: Appraisals and Evidence*, ed. André Blais and Stéphane Dion, pp. 33–58. Pittsburgh: University of Pittsburgh Press, 1991.

Young, Walter D. *The Anatomy of a Party: The National CCF, 1932–61*. Toronto: University of Toronto Press, 1969.

IN THE NEWS

Krugman, Paul. "The Conscience of a Liberal." *The New York Times*, July 5, 2015. http://krugman.blogs.nytimes.com/2015/07/05/austerity-arithmetic/

Menton, Jessica. "Greek Referendum 2015: What does a 'Yes' or 'No' Vote Mean for Greece's Debt Crisis?" *International Business Times*, July 4, 2015. http://www.ibtimes.com/greek-referendum-2015-what-does-yes-or-no-vote-mean-greeces-debt-crisis-1995189

Stamouli, Nektaria, and Markus Walker. "How Alexis Tsipras's Greek Referendum Call Came After Creditors Covered His Proposals in Red Ink." *The Wall Street Journal*, June 28, 2015. http://www.wsj.com/articles/first-red-ink-then-tsiprass-call-for-greek-referendum-1435524517

Papadimas, Lefteris, and Renee Malzezou. "Greeks defy Europe with overwhelming referendum 'No'." Reuters, July 5, 2015. http://www.reuters.com/article/2015/07/05/us-eurozone-greece-idUSKBN0P40EO20150705

Tsipras, Alexis. "An End to the Blackmail." Translated by Stathis Kouvelakis in *Jacobin Magazine*, online, June 27, 2015. https://www.jacobinmag.com/2015/06/tsipras-speech-referendum-bailout-troika/

CHAPTER 8

Albouy, David. *Evaluating the Efficiency and Equity of Federal Fiscal Equalization*. Journal of Public Economics 96(9–10) (2012): 824–839.

Baker, Michael, A. Abigail Payne, and Michael Smart. "An Empirical Study of Matching Grants: The 'cap on CAP.'" *Journal of Public Economics* 72(2) (May 1999): 269–88.

Banzhaf, H., and R. Walsh. "Do People Vote with Their Feet: An Empirical Test of Tiebout's Mechanism." *American Economic Review* 98(3) (2008): 843–863.

Bayer, P., F. Ferreira, and R. McMillan. "A Unified Framework for Measuring Preferences for Schools and Neighborhoods." *Journal of Political Economy* 115(4) (2007): 588–638.

Bird, Richard, and Andrey Tarasov. "Closing the Gap: Fiscal Imbalances and Intergovernmental Transfers in Developed Federations." *Environment and Planning C: Government and Policy*, 22(1) (2004): 77–102.

Blöchliger, H., and C. Vammalle. *Reforming Fiscal Federalism and Local Government: Beyond the Zero-Sum Game*. OECD Fiscal Federalism Studies, Paris: OECD Publishing, 2012. DOI: http://dx.doi.org/10.1787/9789264119970-en

Boadway, Robin. "Should the Canadian Federation Be Rebalanced?" Working Paper 2004a(1), Queen's University.

Boadway, Robin. "The Theory and Practice of Equalization." *CESifo Economic Studies*, 50(1) (2004b): 211–254.

Boadway, Robin, and Frank Flatters. *Equalization in a Federal State: An Economic Analysis*. Ottawa: Supply and Services Canada for the Economic Council of Canada, 1982.

Boothe, Paul, and Jeffrey Petchey. "Assigning Responsibility for Regional Stablization: Evidence from Canada and Australia," in *Reforming Fiscal Federalism for Global Competition*, ed. P. Boothe, pp. 141–62. Edmonton: University of Alberta Press, 1996.

Breton, Albert, and Anthony Scott. *The Economic Constitution of Federal States*. Toronto: University of Toronto Press, 1978.

Buchanan, James M. "An Economic Theory of Clubs." *Economica* 32 (February 1965): 1–14.

Canada. *Report of the Royal Commission on Dominion–Provincial Relations*. Ottawa, 1940.

Chernick, Howard. "An Economic Model of the Distribution of Project Grants." in *Fiscal Federalism and Grants-in-Aid*, eds. P. Mieszkowski and W. Oakland, pp. 81–103. Washington, D.C.: Urban Institute Press, 1979.

Courchene, Thomas. "Interprovincial Migration and Economic Adjustment." *Canadian Journal of Economics* 3(1970): 550–76.

Council of the Federation. *Reconciling the Irreconcilable: Addressing Canada's Fiscal Imbalance*. Report of the Advisory Panel on Fiscal Imbalance (2006).

Dahlby, Bev. "The Marginal Cost of Public Funds and the Flypaper Effect." *International Tax and Public Finance*, 18(2011): 304–321.

Day, Kathleen, and Stanley Winer. "Internal Migration and Public Policy: A Research Proposal." Mimeo. February 1997.

Day, Kathleen, and Stanley Winer. "Internal Migration and Public Policy: An Introduction to the Issues and a Review of Empirical Research in Canada," in *Issues in the Taxation of Individuals*, ed. Allan Maslove, pp. 3–61. Toronto: University of Toronto Press, 1994.

Expert Panel on Equalization and Territorial Formula Financing. *Achieving a National Purpose: Putting Equalization Back on Track*. Ottawa: Expert Panel on Equalization and Territorial Formula Financing, 2006.

Feehan, Jim. *Canada's Equalization Formula: Peering Inside the Black Box . . . and Beyond*. School of Public Policy Research Paper, Vol 7(24), September. Calgary: The School of Public Policy, 2014.

Feldstein, Martin, and Marian Vailliant Wrobel. "Can State Taxes Redistribute Income?" *Journal of Public Economics* 68 (June 1998): 369–396

Filimon, R., T. Romer, and H. Rosenthal. "Asymmetric Information and Agenda Control: The Bases of Monopoly Power and Public Spending." *Journal of Public Economics* 17 (1982): 51–70.

Fischel, William. "Property Taxation and the Tiebout Model: Evidence for the Benefit View from Zoning and Voting." *Journal of Economic Literature* 30(1) (March, 1992): 171–177.

Government of Canada. *A History of the Health and Social Transfers*. Retrieved May 3, 2011 from Finance Canada website: http://www.fin.gc.ca/fedprov/his-eng.asp.

Government of Canada. *Federal Support to Provinces and Territories*. Retrieved May 3, 2011 from Finance Canada website: http://www.fin.gc.ca/fedprov/mtp-eng.asp.

Government of Canada. *The Budget Plan 2007*. Ottawa: Department of Finance Canada, 2007. http://www.budget.gc.ca/2007/plan/bptoc-eng.html

Government of Canada. *The Budget Plan 2009*. Ottawa: Department of Finance Canada, 2009. http://www.budget.gc.ca/2009/plan/bptoc-eng.html

Gramlich, Edward M., and Daniel L. Rubinfeld. "Microestimates of Public Spending Demand Functions and Test of the Tiebout and Median-Voter Hypotheses." *Journal of Political Economy* 90 (June 1982): 536–60.

Hamilton, Bruce. "Zoning and Property Taxation in a System of Local Governments." *Urban Studies* 12 (June 1975): 205–11.

Inman, Robert P. *The Flypaper Effect*. NBER Working Paper No. 14579 (December 2008).

Inman, Robert P. "Fiscal Allocations in a Federalist Economy: Understanding the 'New' Federalism," in *American Domestic Priorities—An Economic Appraisal*, ed. John M. Quigley and Daniel L. Rubinfeld, pp. 3–33. Berkeley: University of California Press, 1985.

Knight, B. "Endogenous Federal Grants and Crowd-Out of State Government Spending: Theory and Evidence from the Federal Highway Aid Program." *American Economic Review* 92 (March 2002): 71–92.

Lin, Z. "Interprovincial Labour Mobility: The Role of Unemployment Insurance and Social Assistance." Human Resources Development Canada, 1995.

Mark, Stephen T., Therese J. McGuire, and Leslie E. Papke. "The Influence of Taxes on Employment and Populations Growth: Evidence from the Washington, D.C. Metropolitan Area." *National Tax Journal* (March 2000): 105–124.

Mieszkowski, Peter, and George R. Zodrow. "Taxation and the Tiebout Model." *Journal of Economic Literature* (September 1989): 1098–146.

Moffitt, Robert. "Incentive Effects of the U.S. Welfare System: A Review." *Journal of Economic Literature* 30(1) (March 1992): 1–61.

Oates, Wallace E. *Fiscal Federalism*. New York: Harcourt Brace, 1972.

Oates, Wallace E. "An Essay on Fiscal Federalism." *Journal of Economic Literature* 37 (September 1999): 1120–1149.

Oates, Wallace E. "On the Evolution of Fiscal Federalism" *National Tax Journal* 61(2) (2008): 313–334.

Palmon, Oded, and Barton A. Smith. "New Evidence on Property Tax Capitalization." *Journal of Political Economy* 106 (October 1998): 1099–1111.

Panizza, Ugo. "On the Determinants of Fiscal Centralization: Theory and Evidence." *Journal of Public Economics* 74 (October 1999): 97–140.

Rathelot, R., and P. Sillard. "The Importance of Local Corporate Taxes in Business Location Decisions: Evidence from French Micro Data." *The Economic Journal* 118 (March 2008): 499–514.

Rhode, P., and K. Strumpf. "Assessing the Importance of Tiebout Sorting: Local Heterogeneity from 1850 to 1990." *American Economic Review* 93(5) (2003): 1648–1677.

Rubinfeld, Daniel. "The Economics of the Local Public Sector," in *Handbook of Public Economics*, 2, ed. Alan J. Auerbach

and Martin Feldstein, Ch. 11. Amsterdam: North-Holland, 1987.

Sandler, Todd, and John T. Tschirhart. "The Economic Theory of Clubs: An Evaluative Survey." *Journal of Economic Literature* 18(4) (December 1980): 1481–521.

Smart, M. "Taxation and Deadweight Loss in a System of Intergovernmental Transfers." *Canadian Journal of Economics* 31(1) (1998): 189–206.

Smart, M. "Raising Taxes through Equalization." *Canadian Journal of Economics* 40(4) (2007): 1188–1212.

Smart, M. "The Evolution of Federal Transfers Since the O'Brien Report," in *The 2009 Federal Budget: Challenge, Response and Retrospect*, eds. C. Beach, B. Dahlby, and P. Hobson, pp. 199–221. Montreal-Kingston: McGill-Queen's University Press (2010).

Snoddon, T., and P. Hobson. "Cost-Sharing and Federal-Provincial Fiscal Relations." in *The 2009 Federal Budget: Challenge, Response and Retrospect*, eds. C. Beach, B. Dahlby, and P. Hobson, pp. 181–198. Montreal-Kingston: McGill-Queen's University Press (2010).

Stegarescu, Dan. "The Effects of Economic and Political Integration on Fiscal Decentralization: Evidence from OECD Countries." *Canadian Journal of Economics* 42(2) (2009): 694–718.

Strumpf, K, and F. Oberholzer-Gee. "Endogenous Policy Decentralization: Testing the Central Tenet of Economic Federalism." *Journal of Political Economy* 110 (2002): 1–36.

Tiebout, Charles. "A Pure Theory of Local Expenditures." *Journal of Political Economy* 64 (1956): 416–24.

Treff, Karin, and Deborah Ort. *Finances of the Nation, 2010*. Toronto: Canadian Tax Foundation, 2011.

Turcotte, Martin, and Mireille Vézina. "Migration from Central to Surrounding Municipalities in Toronto, Montréal and Vancouver." *Canadian Social Trends* (Cat. No. 11-008-X). Ottawa: Statistics Canada, 2010.

Watson, William. "A Estimate of the Welfare Gain from Fiscal Equalization." *Canadian Journal of Economics* 19 (1986): 298–308.

Wilson, L.S. "Equalization, Efficiency and Migration: Watson Revisited" *Canadian Public Policy* 29(4) (2003): 385–396.

Winer, Stanley, and Denis Gauthier. *Internal Migration and Fiscal Structure: An Econometric Study of the Determinants of Interprovincial Migration in Canada*. Ottawa: Supply and Services Canada for the Economic Council of Canada, 1982.

IN THE NEWS

Robson, William. "More Money for Provinces? Just Say No, Mr. Harper," *The Globe and Mail*. Tuesday, Oct. 7, 2014.

Smart, M., and R. Bird. "Earmarking Grants and Accountability in Government." Rotman School of Management Working Paper No. 1498775 (October 2009).

CHAPTER 9

Alberta. *A Framework for Reform: Report of the Premier's Advisory Council on Health*. Government of Alberta, 2001.

Boothe, Paul, and Barbara Johnston. *Stealing the Emperor's Clothes: Deficit Offloading and National Standards in Health Care*. Toronto: C.D. Howe Institute, 1993.

Canada. *Commission on the Future of Health Care in Canada: Final Report*. Ottawa: Minister of Public Works and Government Services, 2002.

Canadian Institute for Health Information. *Prescribed Drug Spending in Canada 2012 Report*. Ottawa: Canadian Institute for Health Information, 2014.

Canadian Institute for Health Information. *National Health Expenditure Trends, 1975 to 2014*. http://www.cihi.ca/cihi-ext-portal/internet/en/documentfull/spending+and+health+workforce/spending/nhex_product_2014 (accessed May 21, 2015)

Canadian Institute for Health Information. *Wait Times in Canada—A Comparison by Province*. 2011. https://secure.cihi.ca/estore/productSeries.htm?locale=en&pc=PCC395 (accessed May 21, 2015)

Canadian Institute for Health Information. *Wait Times for Priority Procedures in Canada, 2015*. https://secure.cihi.ca/estore/productSeries.htm?locale=en&pc=PCC395 (accessed May 21, 2015)

Cohen, Alma, and Peter Siegelman. "Testing for Adverse Selection in Insurance Markets." *Journal of Risk and Insurance* 77(1) (2010): 39–84.

Courchene, Thomas. "A Reforming Medicare Budget." *National Post*, January 3, 2002, p. A14.

Curtis, Lori J., and William MacMinn. "Health Care Utilization in Canada: Twenty-five Years of Evidence." *Canadian Public Policy* 34(1) (March 2008): 65–87.

Cutler, David M., and Sarah J. Reber. "Paying for Health Insurance: The Trade off Between Competition and Adverse Selection." *Quarterly Journal of Economics*, 113(2) (1998): 433–66.

Dahlby, Bev. "Adverse Selection and Pareto Improvement through Compulsory Insurance." *Public Choice* 37(3) (1981): 547–558.

Davis, K., K. Stremikis, D. Squires, and C. Schoen. *Mirror, Mirror on the Wall, 2014 Update: How the U.S. Health Care System Compares Internationally*. The Commonwealth Fund, June 2014. http://www.commonwealthfund.org/publications/fund-reports/2014/jun/mirror-mirror (Accessed May 21, 2015).

DeNavas-Walt, Carmen, Bernadette D. Proctor, and Jessica C. Smith. *Income, Poverty, and Health Insurance Coverage in the United States: 2011*. U.S. Department of Commerce, Economics and Statistics Administration, U.S. Census Bureau (September 2012).

Flood, Colleen M., and Tom Archibald. "The Illegality of Private Health Care in Canada." *Canadian Medical Association Journal* 164(6) (March 2001): 825–830.

Health and Welfare Canada. *Report on Health of Canadians*. Ottawa: Minister of Public Works and Government Services, 1996.

Krugman, Paul. "First, Do More Harm." *New York Times*, December 16, 2006.

Landon, S., M. L. McMillan, V. Muralidharan, and M. Parsons. "Does Health-care Spending Crowd out Other Provincial Government Expenditures." *Canadian Public Policy* 32(2) (2006): 121–141.

Luo, Zhong-Cheng, R. Wilkins, M. Heaman, P. Martens, J. Smylie, L. Hart, F. Simonet, S. Wassimi, Y. Wu, and W.D. Fraser. "Birth Outcomes and Infant Mortality by the Degree of Rural Isolation Among First Nations and Non-First Nations in Manitoba, Canada." *Journal of Rural Health* 26 (2010): 175–181.

National Forum on Health. "Striking a Balance Working Group Synthesis Report," in *Canadian Health Action: Building on the Legacy, Volume II of the Report of the National Forum on Health*. Ottawa: Minister of Public Works and Government Services, 1997.

Newhouse, Joseph P., and the Insurance Experiment Group. *Free for ALL? Lessons from the RAND Health Insurance Experiment*. Cambridge, MA: Harvard University Press, 1993.

O'Neill, June E., and Dave M. O'Neill. "Health Status, Health Care and Inequality: Canada vs. the U.S." *Forum for Health Economics & Policy, Berkeley Electronic Press* 10(1) (2008).

Pauly, Mark V. "Overinsurance and Public Provision of Insurance: the Roles of Moral Hazard and Adverse Selection." *The Quarterly Journal of Economics* 88(1) (February 1974): 44–62.

Pauly, Mark. "Taxation, Health Insurance and Market Failure in the Medical Economy." *Journal of Economic Literature* 24(2) (June 1986): 629–75.

Public Health Agency of Canada and Canadian Institute for Helath Information. *Obseity in Canada*. Ottawa: Her Majesty the Queen in Right of Canada, 2011.

Phelps, Charles E. *Health Economics*, 4th edition. Boston: Addison Wesley, 2010.

Québec. *Guaranteeing Access: Meeting the Challenges of Equity, Efficiency and Quality* [consultation document]. Québec: Direction des communications du ministére de la Santé et des Services Sociaux, 2006.

Rothschild, Michael, and Joseph Stiglitz. "Equilibrium in Competitive Insurance Markets: An Essay on the Economics of Imperfect Information." *The Quarterly Journal of Economics* 90(4) (November 1976): 629–648.

Saskatchewan. *Caring for Medicare: Sustaining a Quality System*. Saskatchewan: Government of Saskatchewan, 2001.

Senate. *The Health of Canadians—The Federal Role: Final Report*. Ottawa: Minister of Public Works and Government Services, 2002.

Smith, Jessica C., and Carla Medalia. *Health Insurance Coverage in the United States: 2014*. U.S. Department of Commerce, Economics and Statistics Administration, U.S. Census Bureau (September 2015).

Van Doorslaer, Eddy. "Equity in Health and Health Care in Canada in International Perspective," in *Financing Health Care: New Ideas for a Changing Society*, eds. Mingshan Lu, and Egon Jonsson. Weinheim: Wiley-VCH: Chapter 10, 2008.

Woolhandler, Steffie, M.D., M.P.H., Terry Campbell, M.H.A., and David U. Himmelstein, M.D. *New England Journal of Medicine* (349) (August 21, 2003): 768–775. DOI: 10.1056/NEJMsa022033

IN THE NEWS

Gagnon, Marc-André. "The Case for National Pharmacare," *National Post*, June 10, 2013. http://news.nationalpost.com/full-comment/marc-andre-gagnon-the-case-for-national-pharmacare (accessed May 21, 2015)

Goodman, Lee-Anne. "Call Growing Louder for National Prescription Drug Plan," *The Globe and Mail*, October 5, 2015. http://www.theglobeandmail.com/news/politics/call-growing-louder-for-national-prescription-drug-plan/article20937357/ (accessed May 20, 2015)

Morgan, S., J. Daw, and M. Law. *Rethinking Pharmacare in Canada*. C.D. Howe Institute Commentary No. 384. Toronto: C.D. Howe Institute, 2013.

Morgan, S., M. Law, J. Daw, L. Abraham, and D. Martin. "Estimated Cost of Universal Public Coverage of Prescription Drugs in Canada," *Canadian Medical Association Journal* 187(7) (April 2015): 491–497.

Stueck, Wendy. "Two New Reports Call for National Prescription Drug Plan," *The Globe and Mail*, December 3, 2014. http://www.theglobeandmail.com/news/british-columbia/two-new-reports-call-for-national-prescription-drug-plan/article21942209/ (accessed May 21, 2015)

CHAPTER 10

Baker, Michael, Miles Corak, and Andrew Heisz. "Unemployment in the Stock and Flow." Discussion Paper No. 97, Business and Labour Market Analysis. Ottawa: Statistics Canada, 1996.

Busby, Colin, and David Gray. *Mending Canada's Employment Insurance Quilt: The Case for Restoring Equity*. C.D. Howe Institute Backgrounder, No. 144, November 2011.

Chan, Ping Ching Winnie, René Morissette, and Marc Frenette. *Workers Laid-off During the Last Three Recessions: Who Were They, and How Did They Fare?* Statistics Canada Analytical Studies Research Paper Series, No. 2011337. Ottawa: Ministry of Industry, 2011. http://www.statcan.gc.ca/pub/11f0019m/11f0019m2011337-eng.pdf.

Christofidies, L. N., and C. J. McKenna. *Employment Patterns and Unemployment Insurance*. Unemployment Insurance Evaluation Series, Human Resources Development Canada. Ottawa: Ministry of Supply and Services, 1995.

Corak, Miles. "Unemployment Insurance, Work Disincentives, and the Canadian Labor Market: An Overview," in *Unemployment Insurance: How to Make It Work*, ed. John Richards and William G. Watson, pp. 86–159. Toronto: C. D. Howe Research Institute, 1994.

Dahlby, Bev. "Payroll Taxes," in *Business Taxation in Ontario*, ed. Allan Maslove, pp. 80–170. Published for the Ontario Fair Tax Commission by the University of Toronto Press, Toronto, 1993.

Day, Kathleen M., and Stanley L. Winer. "What Do We Know about the Relationship between Regionalized Aspects of the Unemployment Insurance System and Internal Migration in Canada? CESifo Working Paper No. 3479 (May 2011).

Finnie, Ross, and Ian Irvine. "The Redistributional Impact of Canada's Employment Insurance Program, 1992–2002." *Canadian Public Policy* 37(2) (2011): 201–218.

Forget, Claude. *Report of the Commission of Inquiry on Unemployment Insurance*. Ottawa: Supply and Services Canada, 1986.

Gray, David. *Has EI Reform Unravelled? Canada's EI Regime in the 2000s*. C. D. Howe Institute Backgrounder. Toronto: C.D. Howe Institute, 2006.

Green, David, and Craig Riddell. "Qualifying for Unemployment Insurance: An Empirical Analysis for Canada." Unemployment Insurance Evaluation Series, Human Resources Development Canada. Ottawa: Ministry of Supply and Services, 1995.

Green, David, and Craig Riddell. "The Economic Effects of Unemployment Insurance in Canada: An Empirical Analysis of Unemployment Insurance Disentitlement." *Journal of Labor Economics* 11(1, part 2) (January 1993): pp. S96–147.

Guest, Dennis. *The Emergence of Social Security in Canada*. Vancouver: University of British Columbia Press, 1980.

Human Resources Development Canada. *Chief Actuary's Report on Employment Insurance Premium Rates for 2001*. Ottawa: Human Resources Development Canada.

Human Resources and Skills Development Canada. *Employment Insurance Monitoring and Assessment Report 2013-14*. Ottawa: Human Resources and Skills Development Canada, 2014.

Krueger, Alan B., and Andreas Mueller. "Job Search and Unemployment Insurance: New Evidence from Time Use Data." *Journal of Public Economics* 94 (2010): 298–307.

Kuhn, Peter, and Chris Riddell. "The Long-Term Effects of Unemployment Insurance: Evidence from New Brunswick and Maine, 1940–1991. *Industrial and Labor Relations Review* 63(2) (2010): 183–204.

Marsh, Leonard Charles. *Report on Social Security for Canada*. Toronto: University of Toronto Press, 1975. This report was originally published in 1943 by the Government of Canada.

May, Doug, and Alton Hollett. *The Rock in a Hard Place*. The Social Policy Challenge 9. Toronto: C.D. Howe Institute, 1995.

Mortensen, D. T. "Unemployment Insurance and Job Search Decisions." *Industrial and Labor Relations Review* 30(4) (1977): 505–517.

Mowat Centre. *What the New EI Rules Mean*. Toronto: Mowat Centre for Policy Innovation, 2012.

Mowat Centre Employment Insurance Task Force. *Making It Work: Final Recommendations of the Mowat Centre Employment Insurance Task Force*. Toronto: Mowat Centre for Policy Innovation, 2011.

Phipps, Shelley. "Working for Working Parents: The Evolution of Maternity and Parental Benefits in Canada." *IRPP Choices* 12(2) (May 2006).

Riddell, W. Craig, and Xueda Song. "The Impact of Education on Unemployment Incidence and Re-employment Success: Evidence from the U.S. Labour Market." *Labour Economics* 18 (2011): 453–463.

Shannon. Michael, and Michael P. Kidd. "Institutional Specifics and Unemployment Insurance Eligibility in Canada: How Sensitive are Employment Duration Effects." *Empirical Economics* 25 (2000): 327–350.

Statistics Canada. *Canadian Economic Observer*. Historical Statistical Supplement 1994–1995. Ottawa, 1995.

Tal, Benjamin. *Dimensions of Youth Employment in Canada*. CIBC World Markets Inc., Economics, 2013. (online resource).

Tatsiramos, K., and J. C. van Ours. "Labour Market Effects of Unemployment Insurance Design," *Journal of Economic Surveys* 28(2) (2014): 284–311.

TD Economics. *One Indicator to Rule Them All*. Special Report, October 23, 2014. Available at: http://www.td.com/economics/analysis/canada/national-economy/national.jsp.

IN THE NEWS

Bédard, Michel and Pierre Fortin. "*Onze propositions pour un meilleur régime d'assurance-emploi*", IRPP Research Paper, July 2015

MacEwen, Angella. (2015) "How to make Employment Insurance more accessible." *The Globe and Mail*, February 17, 2015. http://www.theglobeandmail.com/report-on-business/rob-commentary/how-to-make-employment-insurance-more-accessible/article23015874/

McKenna, Barrie. (2011) "Employment Insurance system unjust and inefficient, report finds." *The Globe and Mail*, November 15, 2011. http://www.theglobeandmail.com/news/national/time-to-lead/employment-insurance-system-unjust-and-inefficient-report-finds/article554698/

Woolley, Frances. "Canada's shame: EI is stealing from the young," *The Globe and Mail*, June 7, 2012. http://www.

theglobeandmail.com/report-on-business/economy/economy-lab/canadas-shame-ei-is-stealing-from-the-young/article4238254/

CHAPTER 11

Attanasio, Orazio P., and Agar Brugiavini. Social Security and Households' Saving. *Quarterly Journal of Economics* 118(3) (August 2003): 1075–1120.

Attanasio, Orazio P., and Susann Rohweddder. Pension Wealth and Household Saving: Evidence from Pension Reforms in the United Kingdom. *American Economic Review* 93(5) (December 2003): 1499–1521.

Baker, Michael, Jonathan Gruber, and Kevin Milligan. "The Retirement Incentive Effects of Canada's Income Security Programs." *Canadian Journal of Economics* 36(2) (May 2003): 261–290.

Battle, Ken. "A New Old Age Pension," in *Reform of Retirement Income Policy: International and Canadian Perspectives*, ed. Keith G. Banting and Robin Boadway, pp. 135–90. School of Policy Studies, Queen's University, Kingston, Ontario, 1996.

Chiappori, Pierre-André and Bernard Salanié. "Testing for Asymmetric Information in Insurance Markets." *Journal of Political Economy* 108(1) (February 2000): 56–78.

Diamond, Peter A. "A Framework for Social Security Analysis." *Journal of Public Economics* 8(3) (December 1977): 275–98.

Federal, Provincial, and Territorial Governments of Canada. *An Information Paper for Consultations on the Canada Pension Plan*. Ottawa: February 1996.

Fougère, Maxime, Simon Harvey, Yu Lan, André Léonard, and Bruno Rainville. "Incentives for Early Retirement in Canada's Defined-Benefit Public and Private Pension Plans: An Analysis with a Dynamic Life-Cycle CGE Model," in *Retirement Policy Issues in Canada*, ed. Abbott, Michael G., Beach, Charles M., Boadway, Robin W., and James G. MacKinnon. Kingston: John Deutsch Institute, 2009.

Godbout, Luc, Yves Trudel, and Suzie St-Cerny. "Differential Returns by Year of Retirement under the Canada Pension Plan." *Canadian Public Policy* 40(4) (December 2014): 364–376.

Government of Canada. *The Seniors Benefit: Securing the Future*. Ottawa: 1996.

Government of Canada. *CPP and OAS Annual Statistics Tables* (Ottawa: 2014).

http://www.servicecanada.gc.ca/eng/services/pensions/statistics/.

Human Resources Development Canada. *Securing the Canada Pension Plan: Agreement on Proposed Changes to the CPP*. Ottawa: 1997.

Human Resources Development Canada. *Annual Statistics on the Canada Pension Plan and Old Age Security*. Ottawa: December 1994.

Human Resources and Skills Development Canada. *Canada Pension Plan, Old Age Security: Statistical Bulletin*. Ottawa: Service Canada, January 2011.

Human Resources and Skills Development Canada. *Canada Pension Plan, Old Age Security: Statistical Bulletin*, June 2015 (Ottawa: Service Canada).

Modigliani, Franco. "Life Cycle, Individual Thrift, and The Wealth of Nations." *American Economic Review* 76(3) (June 1986): 297–313.

Office of the Superintendent of Financial Institutions Canada (OSFIC). *9th Actuarial Report on the Old Age Security Program*. Ottawa: Minister of Public Works and Government Services, 2011.

Office of the Superintendent of Financial Institutions Canada (OSFIC). *26th Actuarial Report of the Canada Pension Plan*. Ottawa: 2013.

Office of the Superintendent of Financial Institutions Canada (OSFIC). *25th Actuarial Report of the Canada Pension Plan*. Ottawa: 2010.

Office of the Superintendent of Financial Institutions (OSFIC). *Canada Pension Plan: Fifteenth Actuarial Report*. Ottawa: 1995.

Office of the Superintendent of Financial Institutions (OSFIC). *Canada Pension Plan: Sixteenth Actuarial Report*. Ottawa: 1997.

Oreopoulos, Philip. "Bad Tasting Medicine: Removing Intergenerational Inequity from the CPP." *Choices* 2(5) (November 1996). Institute for Research on Public Policy, Montreal, Quebec.

La Régie des rentes du Québec. *Régime de rentes du Québec Statistiques de l'année 2014*. Quebec: 2015.

Schlesinger, Joel. "Marge, 69, fears she will outlive her $400,000 RRSP." *The Globe and Mail*, February 13, 2014. http://www.theglobeandmail.com/globe-investor/personal-finance/retirement-rrsps/marge-69-fears-she-will-outlive-her-400000-rrsp/article16826652/

Service Canada. *Quarterly Report of the Canada Pension Plan and Old Age Security*, July–September 2015, Cat. ISPB-258-04-13E (July 2015).

Statistics Canada. Deaths 2007. Catalogue 84F0211X. Ottawa: Ministry of Industry, 2010.

Statistics Canada. *Income in Canada* 2009. Catalogue 75-202-XWE. Ottawa: 2011.

Statistics Canada. *Generations in Canada: Age and Sex*, 2011 Census. Catalogue 98-311-X2011003. Ottawa: 2012.

Townsend, Monica. *Our Aging Society: Preserving Retirement Incomes into the 21st Century*. Ottawa: Canadian Centre for Policy Alternatives, 1995.

Vaillancourt, François, Charles Lammam, Ian Herzog, and Pouya Ebrahimi. Compulsory Government Pensions vs. Private Savings: The Effect of Previous Expansion to the Canada Pension Plan. Fraser Institute (July 2015).

IN THE NEWS

Artuso, Antonella. "Feds, Province scrap over Ontario pension plan." *The Toronto Sun*, July 30, 2015. http://www.torontosun.com/2015/07/30/sousa-slams-feds-for-lack-of-pension-plan-help

Ferguson, Rob. "Ottawa slammed for refusing to help run Ontario pension plan." *thestar.com*, July 30, 2015. http://www.thestar.com/news/canada/2015/07/30/charles-sousa-slams-ottawa-for-refusing-to-help-run-ontario-pension-plan.html

Geddes, John. "Harper on CPP: It's about individual responsibility." *Maclean's*, December 19, 2013. http://www.macleans.ca/politics/harper-clarifies-his-cpp-stance-its-about-individual-responsibility/

McFarland, Janet. "Ontario's proposed pension plan excludes half of workers." *The Globe and Mail*, May 1, 2014. http://www.theglobeandmail.com/report-on-business/ontarios-proposed-pension-plan-excludes-half-of-workers/article18373313/

CHAPTER 12

Allen, Douglas. "Welfare and the Family: The Canadian Experience." *Journal of Labour Economics* 11(1) (1993): S201–23.

Barrett, Gary F., and Michael I. Cragg. "Dynamics of Canadian Welfare Participation." Discussion Paper No. 95-08. Department of Economics, University of British Columbia, 1995.

Battle, Ken, Michael Mendelson, and Sherri Torjman. "The Modernization Mantra: Toward a New Architecture for Canada's Adult Benefits." *Canadian Public Policy* 31(4) (2005): 431–437.

Boessenkool, Kenneth J. *Back to Work: Learning from the Alberta Welfare Experiment*. C.D. Howe Institute Commentary 90. Toronto: C.D. Howe Institute, 1997.

Charette, M., and R. Meng. "The Determinants of Welfare Participation of Female Heads of Households in Canada." *Canadian Journal of Economics* 27(2) (1994): 290–306.

Clavet, Nicholas-James, Jean-Yves Duclos, and Guy Lacroix. "Fighting Poverty: Assessing the Effect of Guaranteed Minimum Income Proposals in Quebec." *Canadian Public Policy*, 39(4) (2013): 491–516.

Duclos, Jean-Yves. "A Better Income Security System for All Canadians," in *A Canadian Priorities Agenda: Policy Choices to Improve Economic and Social Well-Being*, eds. Jeremy Leonard, Christopher Ragan, and France St-Hilaire, pp. 233–266. Montreal: Institute for Research on Public Policy, 2007.

Feng, Yan, Sangita Dubay, and Bradley Brooks. "Persistence of Low Income Among the Non-elderly Unattached Individuals." Catalogue No. 75F0002MIE, no. 005, Ottawa: Ministry of Industry, 2007.

Finnie, Ross, Ian Irvine, and Roger Sceviour. *Social Assistance Use in Canada: National and Provincial Trends in Incidence, Entry and Exit*. Analytical Studies Branch Research Paper Series. Ottawa: Ministry of Industry, 2005.

Fortin, B., G. Lacroix, and S. Drolet. "Welfare Benefits and the Duration of Welfare Spells: Evidence from a Natural Experiment in Canada." *Journal of Public Economics* 88 (2004): 1495–1520.

Fortin, B., G. Lacroix, and H. Roberge. "The Dynamics of Welfare Spells in Quebec." Department of Economics, Laval University, 1995.

Fortin, Bernard, Michel Truchon, and Louis Beausejour. "On Reforming the Welfare System: Workfare Meets the Negative Income Tax." *Journal of Public Economics* 51(2) (June 1993): 119–51.

Gueron, Judith M. "Welfare Reform in the United States: Strategies to Increase Work and Reduce Poverty," in *Income Security in Canada: Changing Needs, Changing Means*, ed. Elisabeth B. Reynolds, pp. 171–87. Montreal: Institute for Research on Public Policy, 1993.

Kneebone, Ronald D., and Katherine White. "Fiscal Retrenchment and Social Assistance in Canada." *Canadian Public Policy*, 35(1) (2009): 21–40.

Kneebone, Ronald, and Katherine White. *The Rise and Fall of Social Assistance Use in Canada, 1969–2012*. School of Public Policy Research Paper, Vol 7(5), February. Calgary: The School of Public Policy, 2014.

Krashinsky, Michael. "Putting the Poor to Work: Why 'Workfare' Is an Idea Whose Time Has Come," in *Helping the Poor: A Qualified Case for "Workfare,"* eds. J. Richards and W.G. Watson, pp. 91–120. Toronto: C.D. Howe Institute, 1995.

Laurin, Alexandre, and Finn Poschmann. *What Has Happened to Quebecers' Marginal Effective Tax Rates?* C. D. Howe Institute e-brief, May 18, 2011.

Lemieux, T., and K. Milligan. "Incentive Effects of Social Assistance: A Regression Discontinuity Approach." *Journal of Econometrics* 142(2) (2008): 807–828.

Lightman, Ernie S. "You Can Lead a Horse to Water; but . . .: The Case against Workfare in Canada," in *Helping the Poor: A Qualified Case for "Workfare,"* eds. J. Richards and W.G. Watson, pp. 151–83. Toronto C.D. Howe Institute, 1995.

Milligan, K., and M. Stabile. "The Integration of Child Tax Credits and Welfare: Evidence from the Canadian National Child Benefit Program." *Journal of Public Economics* 91 (2007): 305–326.

Milligan, K., and M. Stabile. "Child Benefits, Maternal Employment, and Children's Health: Evidence from Canadian Child Benefit Expansions." *American Economic Review: Papers and Proceedings* 99(2) (2009): 128–132.

National Council of Welfare. *Welfare Incomes 2009*. Ottawa: Minister of Public Works and Government Services Canada, 2010.

National Council of Welfare. *Welfare in Canada*. Ottawa: Minister of Supply and Services Canada, 1987.

Ontario Social Assistance Review Advisory Council. *Report of the Social Assistance Review Advisory Council*. May 2010. http://www.mcss.gov.on.ca/en/mcss/publications/social/sarac/toc_sarac.aspx

Poschmann, Finn. *Still High: Marginal Effective Tax Rates on Low-Income Families*. C.D. Howe Institute Backgrounder, No. 113 (2008).

Royal Commission on the Economic Union and Development Prospects for Canada Report. 1985. Volumes I, II, and III. Ottawa: Minister of Supply and Services Canada.

Scarth, W. and L. Tang. "An Evaluation of the Working income Tax Credit." *Canadian Public Policy* 34(1) (2008): 25–36.

Sheikh, M. *Report of the Commission for the Review of Social Assistance in Ontario: Taking Stock Two Years Later*. School of Public Policy Research Paper, Vol 8(8),

March. Calgary: The School of Public Policy, 2015.

Tweedle, Anne, Ken Battle, and Sherri Torjman. *Welfare in Canada 2013*. Caledon Institute of Social Policy, November 2014.

IN THE NEWS

Coyne, Andrew. "Fewer people sit below the poverty line now than ever before. Why are we not talking about it?" *National Post*, July 22, 2013. http://news.nationalpost.com/full-comment/andrew-coyne-fewer-people-sit-below-the-poverty-line-now-than-ever-before-why-are-we-not-talking-about-it

Editorial. "Defining Necessities." *The Globe and Mail*, December 4, 2009. http://www.theglobeandmail.com/news/national/defining-necessities/article4196703/

Matern, Richard, Michael Mendelson, and Michael Oliphant. *Testing the Validity of the Ontario Deprivation Index*. Caledon Institute on Social Policy and the Daily Food Bank. December 2009. http://www.caledoninst.org/

Monsebraaten, Laurie. "Where are you on the Deprivation Index?" *The Toronto Star*, December 2, 2009. http://www.thestar.com/life/health_wellness/2009/12/02/where_are_you_on_the_deprivation_index.html.

CHAPTER 13

Acemoglu, Daron, Simon Johnson, James A. Robinson, and Pierre Yared. "From Education to Democracy?" Working Paper 11204. Cambridge: MA: National Bureau of Economic Research, 2005.

Angrist, Joshua, and Victor Lavy. "Using Maimonides' Rule to Estimate the Effect of Class Size on Scholastic Achievement." *Quarterly Journal of Economics* 114 (1999): 533–575.

Auld, Douglas, and Harry Kitchen. *Financing Education and Training in Canada*. Canadian Tax Paper No. 110. Toronto: Canadian Tax Foundation, 2006.

Bird, Richard M. *Charging for Public Services*. Toronto: Canadian Tax Foundation, 1976.

Bird, Richard M., and Enid Slack. *Urban Public Finance in Canada*. Toronto: Butterworths, 1983.

Boudarbat, Brahim, Thomas Lemieux, and W. Craig Riddell. "The Evolution of the Returns to Human Capital in Canada, 1980–2005." *Canadian Public Policy* 36(1) (2010): 63–89.

Burbidge, J., Lonnie Magee, and A. Leslie Robb. "The Education Premium in Canada and the United States." *Canadian Public Policy* 28(2) (2003): 203–217.

Canadian Council on Learning. Tallying the Costs of Post-Secondary Education: The Challenge of Managing Student Debt and Loan Repayment in Canada. Ottawa: Canadian Council on Learning, 2010.

Constantatos, C., and E. G. West. "Measuring Returns from Education: Some Neglected Factors." *Canadian Public Policy* 17(2) (June 1991): 127–138.

Dee, Thomas. "Are There Civic Returns to Education." *Journal of Public Economics* 88 (2004): 1697–1720.

Deming, David J., Justine S. Hastings, Thomas J. Kane, and Douglas O. Staiger. "School Choice, School Quality and Postsecondary Attainment." Working Paper No. 17438. Cambridge: MA: National Bureau of Economic Research, 2011.

Dickson, Vaughan, William J. Milne, and David Murrell. "Who Should Pay for University Education? Some Net Benefit Results by Funding Source for New Brunswick." *Canadian Public Policy* 22(4) (December 1996): 315–329.

Dynarski, Susan, Joshua M. Hyman, and Diane Whitmore Schanzenbach. "Experimental Evidence on the Effect of Childhood Investments on Postsecondary Attainment and Degree Completion." Working Paper No. 17533. Cambridge: MA: National Bureau of Economic Research, 2011.

Easton, Stephen T. *Education in Canada: An Analysis of Elementary, Secondary and Vocational Schooling*. Vancouver: The Fraser Institute, 1988.

Emery, Herb. "Total and Private Returns to University Education in Canada: 1960–2030 and in Comparison to Other Post-Secondary Training," in *Higher Education in Canada*, eds. Charles M. Beach, Robin W. Boadway, and R. Marvin McInnis (pp. 77–112). John Deutsch Institute, 2005.

Ferrer, Ana, and W. Craig Riddell. "Education, Credentials, and Immigrant Earnings." *Canadian Journal of Economics* 41(1) (2008): 186–216.

Figlio, David N. *Testing Crime and Punishment*. NBER Working Paper No. 11194. Cambridge, MA: National Bureau of Economic Research, 2005.

Figlio, David, and Cassandra M. D. Hart. "Competitive Effects of Means-Tested School Vouchers." *American Economic Journal: Applied Economics* 6(1) (2014): 133–56.

Fischel, William A. "School Finance Litigation and Property Tax Revolts: How Undermining Local Control Turns Voters Away from Public Education." *Lincoln Institute of Land Policy Working Paper*. Cambridge, MA., 1998.

Frenette, Marc. "Why are Lower-Income Students less Likely to Attend University? Evidence from Academic Abilities, Parental Influences, and Financial Constraints," in *Who Goes? Who Stays? What Matters? Accessing and Persisting in post-Secondary Education in Canada*, eds. Ross Finnie, Richard Mueller, Arthur Sweetman, and Alex Usher (pp. 279–298). Kingston: School of Policy Studies, Queen's University, 2008.

Friedman, W., M. Kremer, E. Miguel, and R. Thornton. *Education as Liberation*. NBER Working Paper No. 16939 (April 2011).

Garcea, Joseph, and Dustin Munroe. "Reforms to Funding Education in Four Canadian Provinces." *Canadian Journal of Educational Administration and Policy*, Issue 159: 2014.

Glaeser, Edward L., Giacomo A. M. Ponzetto, and Andrei Shleifer. "Why Does Democracy Need Education?" NBER Working Paper No. 12128. Cambridge, MA: National Bureau of Economic Research, 2006.

Government of Canada. *Improving Social Security in Canada*. Ottawa: October 1994.

Hanson, Jorgen. *Returns to University Level Education: Variations within Disciplines, Occupations and Employment Sectors*. Ottawa: Human Resources and Social Policy Development, 2006.

Hanushek, Eric A. "Publicly Provided Education," in *Handbook of Public Economics*, eds. Alan J. Auerbach and Martin Feldstein (pp. 2045–2141). Amsterdam: Elsevier, 2002.

Hanushek, Eric A., Charles Ka Yui Leung, and Kuzey Yilmaz. "Redistribution through Education and Other Transfer Mechanisms." *Journal of Monetary Economics* 50(8) (November 2003): 1719–1750.

Hanushek, Eric A., and Margaret Raymond. "Does School Accountability Lead to Improved Student Performance?" *Journal of Policy Analysis and Management* 24(2) (2005): 297–327.

Heywood, John S., and Ziangdong Wei. "Education and Signalling: Evidence from a Highly Competitive Labor Market." *Education Economics* 12(1) (2004): 1–16.

Hoxby, Caroline M. "Is There an Equity-Efficiency Trade-off in School Finance? Tiebout and a Theory of the Local Public Goods Producer." NBER Working Paper No. 5265. Cambridge, MA: National Bureau of Economic Research, 1995.

Hoxby, Caroline. "The Effects of Class Size on Student Achievement: Evidence from Population Variation." *Quarterly Journal of Economics* 115(4) (2000): 1239–1285.

Hoxby, Caroline. "School Choice and School Competition: Evidence from the United States." *Swedish Economic Policy Review* 10(2) (2003): 9–65.

Human Resources and Skills Development Canada. *Formative Evaluation of the Additional Canada Education Savings Grant and the Canada Learning Bond (Final Report)*. Ottawa: Human Resources and Skills Development Canada, November 2009.

Jacob, Brian. "Accountability, Incentives and Behaviour: The Impact of High-Stakes Testing in the Chicago Public Schools." *Journal of Public Economics* 89 (2005): 761–796.

Jacob, Brian, and Steven D. Levitt. "Rotten Apples: An Investigation of the Prevalence and Predictors of Teacher Cheating." *Quarterly Journal of Economics* 118(3) (2003): 834–877.

Jepson, Christopher, and Steven Rivkin. *What Is the Trade-off Between Smaller Classes and Teacher Quality?"* NBER Working Paper No. 9205. Cambridge, MA: National Bureau of Economic Research, 2002.

Johnson, David. *Signposts of Success: Interpreting Ontario's Elementary School Test Scores*. C. D. Howe Institute Policy Study 40. Toronto: C. D. Howe Institute, 2005.

Johnson, David. "How is Variation in Tuition across Canadian Provinces Related to University Participation in the Youth in Transition Survey?" in *Who Goes? Who Stays? What Matters? Accessing and Persisting in post-Secondary Education in Canada*, eds. Ross Finnie, Richard Mueller, Arthur Sweetman, and Alex Usher (pp. 299–326). Kingston: School of Policy Studies, Queen's University, 2008.

Ladd, Helen F. "School Vouchers: A Critical View." *Journal of Economic Perspectives* 16(4) (2002): 3–24.

Löfgren, Karl-Gustaf, Torsten Persson, and Jorgen W. Weibull. "Markets with Asymmetric Information: The Contributions of George Akerlof, Michael Spence, and Joseph Stiglitz," *The Scandinavian Journal of Economics* 104(2) (2002): 195–211.

McMullen, Kathryn. "Changes in Participation in Adult Education and Training, 2002 and 2008." *Education Matters: Insights on Education, Learning and Training in Canada*, vol. 6, no. 6. Statistics Canada Cat. No. 81-004-X: December 2010. http://www.statcan.gc.ca/pub/81-004-x/2009006/article/11126-eng.htm (accessed July 12, 2011)

McMullen, Kathryn. "Recent Trends in Adult Education and Training in Canada." *Education Matters: Insights on Education, Learning and Training in Canada*, Statistics Canada Cat. No. 81-004-X: December 2004. http://www.statcan.gc.ca/pub/81-004-x/200412/7737-eng.htm (accessed July 12, 2011)

Milligan, Kevin, Enrico Moretti, and Philip Oreopoulos. "Does Education Improve Citizenship? Evidence from the United States and the United Kingdom." *Journal of Public Economics* 88 (2004): 1667–1695.

Moussaly-Sergieh, Karim, and François Vaillancourt. *Extra Earning Power: The Financial Returns to University Education in Canada*. C. D. Howe Institute e-brief. Toronto: C. D. Howe Institute, 2009.

Neill, Christine. "Tuition Fees and the Demand for University Places." *Economics of Education Review* 28 (2009): 561–570.

Oreopoulos, P. "Do Dropouts Drop Out Too Soon? Wealth, Health and Happiness from Compulsory Schooling." *Journal of Public Economics* 91(11–12) (2007): 2213–2229.

Poterba, James M. "Government Intervention in the Markets for Education and Health Care: How and Why." NBER Working Paper No. 4916. Cambridge, MA: National Bureau of Economic Research, 1994.

Spence, Michael. "Job Market Signalling." *Quarterly Journal of Economics* 87(3) (1973): 355–374.

Statistics Canada. *Summary Elementary and Secondary School Indicators for Canada, the Provinces and Territories, 2006/2007 to 2010/2011*. No 81-595-M, No. 099. Ottawa: Ministry of Industry, 2013.

Treff, Karin, and Deborah Ort. *Finances of the Nation, 2012*. Toronto: Canadian Tax Foundation, 2013.

IN THE NEWS

Johnson, David. *Value for Money? Teacher Compensation and Student Outcomes in Canada's Six Largest Provinces*. C. D. Howe Institute Commentary No 434. Toronto: C.D. Howe Institute, September 2015.

Richarz, Allan. "Ontario teachers are overpaid." *National Post*, August 25, 2015. http://news.nationalpost.com/full-comment/allan-richarz-ontarios-teachers-are-overpaid

Ross, Selena. "Ontario teachers' union endorse tentative agreement with schools." *The Globe and Mail*, August 22, 2015. http://www.theglobeandmail.com/news/national/ontario-teachers-union-endorse-tentative-agreement-with-schools/article26064887/

CHAPTER 14

Banerjee, Sidhartha. "Quebec Carbon Tax Put in Place Amid Outcry." *The Globe and Mail*, October 1, 2007.

Beck, Marisa, Nicholas Rivers, Randall Wigle, and Hidemichi Yonezawa. "Carbon tax and revenue recycling: Impacts on households in British Columbia." *Resource and Energy Economics* 41 (August 2015): 40–69.

Burtraw, Dallas, Richard Sweeney, and Margaret Walls. "The Incidence of U.S. Climate Policy: Alternative Uses of Revenues from a Cap-and-Trade Auction." Resources for the Future Discussion Paper no. 09-17-REV, June 2009.

Congressional Budget Office (CBO). "The Distribution of Household Income and Federal Taxes, 2008 and 2009." July 2012. https://www.cbo.gov/sites/default/files/112th-congress-2011-2012/reports/43373-AverageTaxRates_screen.pdf

Congressional Budget Office (CBO). *The Economic Effects of Comprehensive Tax Reform*. Washington, DC: US Government Printing Office, 1997.

Davies, James B. "Tax Incidence: Annual and Lifetime Perspectives in the United States and Canada," in *Canada–U.S. Tax Comparisons*, eds. John B. Shoven and John Whalley (pp. 151–88). Chicago: University of Chicago Press, 1992.

Davies, J., F. St-Hilaire, and J. Whalley. "Some Calculations of Lifetime Tax Incidence." *American Economic Review* 74(4) (September 1984).

Dyck, Dagmar. "Fiscal Redistribution in Canada, 1994–2000." *Canadian Tax Journal* 53(4) (2005): 974–1006.

Eaton, B. Curtis, Diane F. Eaton, and Douglas W. Allen. *Microeconomics: Theory with Applications*, 8th ed. Toronto: Pearson, 2012.

Friedman, Milton. *A Theory of the Consumption Function*. Princeton, NJ: Princeton University Press, 1957.

Fuchs, Victor, Alan B. Krueger, and James M. Poterba. "Economists' Views about Parameters, Values, and Policies: Survey Results in Labor and Public Economics." *Journal of Economic Literature* 36(3) (September 1998): 1387–1425.

Fullerton, Don, and Diane Lim Rogers. "Neglected Effects on the Uses Side: Even a Uniform Tax Would Change Relative Goods Prices." *American Economic Review* 87 (May 1997): 120–125.

Fullerton, Don, and Garth Heutel. "The General Equilibrium Incidence of Environmental Taxes." *Journal of Public Economics* 91 (2007): 571–591.

Fullerton, Don, and Garth Heutel. "Analytical General Equilibrium Effects of Energy Policy on Output and Factor Prices." *The B.E. Journal of Economic Analysis & Policy* 10(2), Berkeley Electronic Press, (2011).

Galbraith, John W., and Murray Kaiserman. "Taxation, Smuggling, and Demand for Cigarettes in Canada: Evidence from Time Series Data." *Journal of Health Economics* 16(3) (June 1997): 287–301.

Gillespie, W. Irwin. "On the Redistribution of Income in Canada." *Canadian Tax Journal* 24(4) (July–August 1976): 419–50.

Gillis, Malcolm, and Charles E. McLure. "Excess Profits Taxation: Post-Mortem on the Mexican Experience." *National Tax Journal* 32(4) (December 1979): 501–11.

Harberger, Arnold C. "The Incidence of the Corporation Income Tax," in *Taxation and Welfare*, ed. Arnold C. Harberger (pp. 135–62). Boston: Little, Brown, 1974.

Hassett, Kevin A., Aparna Mathur, and Gilbert E. Metcalf. "The Incidence of a U.S. Carbon Tax: A Lifetime and Regional Analysis." *The Energy Journal* 30(2) (2009): 155–178.

Kesselman, R. Jonathan, and Ron Cheung. "Tax Incidence, Progressivity, and Inequality in Canada." *Canadian Tax Journal* 52(3) (2004): 709–789.

Kleven, Henrik Jacobsen, Camille Landais, and Emmanuel Saez. "Taxation and International Migration of Superstars: Evidence from the European Football Market." *American Economic Review*, 103(5) (August 2013): 1892-1924.

Lee, Marc. "Eroding Tax Fairness: Tax Incidence in Canada, 1990–2005." Toronto: Canadian Centre for Policy Alternatives (November 2007).

McKenzie, Kenneth, and Jack Mintz. "Tax Effects on the Cost of Capital," in *Canada–U.S. Tax Comparisons*, eds. John B. Shoven and John Whalley. Chicago: University of Chicago Press, 1992.

Schaafsma, Joseph. "Forward Shifting of the Personal Income Tax by Self-Employed Canadian Dentists." *Canadian Journal of Economics* 25(3) (August 1992): 636–51.

Vermaeten, Arndt, W. Irwin Gillespie, and Frank Vermaeten. "Who Paid the Taxes in Canada, 1951–1988?" *Canadian Public Policy* 21(3) (September 1995): 317–43.

Vermaeten, Frank, W. Irwin Gillespie, and Arndt Vermaeten. "Tax Incidence in Canada." *Canadian Tax Journal* 42(2) (1994): 348–416.

IN THE NEWS

Henry, Samuel. "French football clubs threaten strike over 75 per cent super tax." *The Telegraph*, October 17, 2013. http://www.telegraph.co.uk/news/worldnews/europe/france/10386961/French-football-clubs-threaten-strike-over-75-per-cent-super-tax.html

Love, Brian. "Soccer-French court strikes down Monaco tax status deal." *Reuters*, July 9, 2015. http://sports.yahoo.com/news/soccer-french-court-strikes-down-monaco-tax-status-105426715–finance.html

National Post Wire Services. "France's 75% millionaire tax approved by country's high court." *Financial Post*, December 30, 2013. http://business.financialpost.com/news/france-millionaire-tax-approved

NBER Digest. *Taxes and the International Migration of Superstars.* *NBER Digest*, August 25, 2015. http://www.nber.org/digest/apr11/w16545.html

Smith, Adam. "English Soccer Tackles High Taxes and a Weak Pound." *Time*, July 27, 2009. http://content.time.com/time/world/article/0,8599,1912935,00.html

Viscusi, Gregory. "France to Apply 75% Tax to Soccer Players' Compensation." *Bloomberg*, April 2, 2013. http://www.bloomberg.com/news/articles/2013-04-02/france-to-apply-75-tax-to-soccer-players-compensation

CHAPTER 15

Adichie, Chimamanda Ngozi. "A Country's Frustration, Fueled Overnight." *New York Times*, January 17, 2012.

Bishop, Robert L. "The Effects of Specific and Ad Valorem Taxes." *Quarterly Journal of Economics*, May 1968: 198–218.

Boskin, Michael J. "Efficiency Aspects of the Differential Tax Treatment of Market and Household Economic Activities." *Journal of Public Economics* 4 (1975): 1–25.

Chandler, William. "The Value of Household Work in Canada, 1992." *Canadian Economic Observer*, April 1994.

Dahlby, Bev. "The Marginal Cost of Funds from Public Sector Borrowing." *Topics in Economic Analysis & Policy* 6(1) (2006): Article 1.

Fortin, B., and G. Lacroix. "Labour Supply, Tax Evasion, and the Marginal Cost of Public Funds: An Empirical Investigation."

Journal of Public Economics 55 (November 1994): 407–31.

Harberger, Arnold C. "Efficiency Effects of Taxes on Income from Capital," in *Taxation and Welfare*, ed. Arnold C. Harberger (pp. 163–70). Boston: Little, Brown, 1974.

Hines, James R., Jr. "Three Sides of Harberger Triangles." *Journal of Economic Perspectives*, Spring 1999: 167–88.

Jorgenson, Dale W., and Kun-Young Yun. *Investment, Volume 3, Lifting the Burden: Tax Reform, the Cost of Capital, and US Economic Growth.* Cambridge, MA: MIT Press, 2001.

Kaplow, Louis. *The Theory of Taxation and Public Economics.* Princeton, NJ: Princeton University Press, 2008.

Mankiw, Gregory N., and Matthew Weinzierl. "The Optimal Taxation of Height: a Case Study of Utilitarian Income Redistribution." *American Economic Journal: Economic Policy* 2(1) (February 2010): 155–176.

Oum, Tae Hoon, W.G. Waters, and Jong-Say Yong. "Concepts of Price Elasticities of Transport Demand and Recent Empirical Estimates: An Interpretive Survey." *Journal of Transport Economics and Policy* 26 (May 1992): 139–54.

Parry, Ian W.H., and Wallace Oates. "Policy Analysis in the Presence of Distorting Taxes." *Journal of Policy Analysis and Management* 19(4) (Autumn 2000): 603–613.

Sandmo, Agnar. "Optimal Taxation—An Introduction to the Literature." *Journal of Public Economics* 6 (1976): 37–54.

U.S. Bureau of the Census, 2009.

Whalley, John, and Deborah Fretz. *The Economics of the Goods and Services Tax.* Toronto: Canadian Tax Foundation, 1990.

IN THE NEWS

Bennett, Jamie. "Mill rates down, poll tax up." *The Western Star*, December 18, 2012. http://www.thewesternstar.com/News/Local/2012-12-18/article-3142251/Mill-rates-down,-poll-tax-up/1

Hayward, Shawn. "Poll tax remains." *The Packet*, December 31, 2013. http://www.thepacket.ca/News/Local/2013-12-31/article-3560899/Poll-tax-remains/1

CBC News. "Poll tax burden too much, advocate says," April 29, 2013. http://www.cbc.ca/news/canada/newfoundland-labrador/poll-tax-burden-too-much-advocate-says-1.1360169

CHAPTER 16

Becker, Gary S. "Crime and Punishment: An Economic Approach." *Journal of*

Political Economy 76 (March–April 1968): 169–217.

Becker, Gary S., and Casey B. Mulligan. "Deadweight Costs and the Size of Government." *Journal of Law and Economics* 46(2) (October 2003): 293–340.

Bird, Richard, and Michael Smart. "Tax Policy and Tax Research in Canada," in *The State of Economics in Canada: Festschrift in Honour of David Slater*, eds. Patrick Grady and Andrew Sharpe. Kingston: John Deutsch Institute, 2001.

Blumenthal, Marsha, Charles Christian, and Joel Slemrod. "Taxpayer Response to an Increased Probability of Audit: Evidence from a Controlled Experiment in Minnesota." *Journal of Public Economics* 79(3) (2001): 455–483.

Boadway, Robin, Nicolas Marceau, and Maurice Marchand. "Investment in Education and the Time Inconsistency of Redistributive Tax Policy." *Economica* 63(250) (May 1996): 171–189.

Canadian Tax Foundation. *The National Finances*, 1994. Toronto: Canadian Tax Foundation, 1994.

Chandoevwit, Worawan, and Bev Dahlby. "The Marginal Cost of Public Funds for Excise Taxes in Thailand." *eJournal of Tax Research* 5(1) (July 2007): 135–167.

Clotfelter, Charles T. "Tax Evasion and Tax Rates: An Analysis of Individual Returns." *Review of Economics and Statistics* 65(3) (August 1983): 363–73.

Corlett, W. J., and D. C. Hague. "Complementarity and the Excess Burden of Taxation." *Review of Economic Studies* 21 (1953): 21–30.

Cowell, Frank A. *Cheating the Government.* Cambridge, MA: MIT Press, 1990.

Dahlby, Bev, and Ergete Ferede. "Estimating the Tax Base Elasticities and the Marginal Cost of Public Funds for Canadian Provinces." Mimeo, June 2015.

Diamond, Peter A. "A Many-Person Ramsay Tax Rule." *Journal of Public Economics* 4 (1975): 335–42.

Edgeworth, F. Y. "The Pure Theory of Taxation," reprinted in *Readings in the Economics of Taxation*, eds. Richard A. Musgrave and Carl S. Shoup (pp. 258–96). Homewood, IL: Richard D. Irwin, 1959.

Feldstein, Martin S. "On the Theory of Tax Reform." *Journal of Public Economics* 6 (1976): 77–104.

Frank, Robert. "'Emergency' Tax on the Rich Roils Britain." *CNBC*, August 29, 2012. www.cnbc.com/id/48825978.

Giles, David E. A., and Lindsay M. Tedds. *Taxes and the Canadian Underground Economy.* Toronto: Canadian Tax Foundation, 2001.

Goolsbee, Austan, and Amil Petrin. "The Consumer Gains from Direct Broadcast Satellites and the Competition with Cable Television." *Econometrica* 72(2) (2004): 351–381.

Groves, Harold. *Financing Government.* New York: Henry Holt, 1946.

Gruber, Jonathan, and Emmanuel Saez. "The Elasticity of Taxable Income: Evidence and Implications." *Journal of Public Economics* 84(1) (April 2002): 1–33.

Holcombe, Randall. "The Ramsey Rule Reconsidered." *Public Finance Review* 30(6) (November 2002): 562–578.

House of Commons, Standing Committee on Finance. *Replacing the GST: Options for Canada.* June 1994.

Judge, Timothy A., and Daniel M. Cable. "The Effect of Height on Workplace Success and Income: Preliminary Test of a Theoretical Model." *Journal of Applied Psychology* 89(3) (2004): 428–441.

Lemieux, Thomas, Bernard Fortin, and Pierre Frechette. "The Effect of Taxes on Labor Supply in the Underground Economy." *American Economic Review* 84(1) (March 1994): 231–54.

Mankiw, N. Gregory, Matthew C. Weinzierl, and Danny Yagan. "Optimal Taxation in Theory and Practice." *Journal of Economic Perspectives* 23(4) (Fall 2009): 147–174.

Mirus, Rolf, Roger S. Smith, and Vladimir Karoleff. "Canada's Underground Economy Revisited: Update and Critique." *Canadian Public Policy* 20(3) (1994): 235–52.

Musgrave, Richard A. *The Theory of Public Finance.* New York: McGraw-Hill, 1959.

Pigeon, Marc-André. "The Underground Economy: Measurement and Consequences." Library of Parliament Research Publication PRB-04-40E: Ottawa, 2004.

Rabushka, Alvin. "Could a Degressive Tax Be Better Than a Flat Tax?" *The Daily Report.* The Hoover Institution, 2003.

Ramsey, Frank. "A Contribution to the Theory of Taxation." *Economic Journal* 37: 47–61.

Schuetze, Herb J. "Profiles of Tax Non-Compliance Among the Self-Employed in Canada." *Canadian Public Policy* 28(2) (June 2002): 219–237.

Smith, Philip. "Assessing the Size of the Underground Economy: The Statistics Canada Perspective." *Canadian Economic Observer* 3 (May 1994): 16–33.

Sørensen, Peter. "The Theory of Optimal Taxation: What is the Policy Relevance?" *International Tax and Public Finance* 14(4) (August 2007): 383–406.

Speer, Sean, Milagros Palacios, Marco Lugo, and François Vaillancourt. *The Cost to Canadians of Complying with Personal Income Taxes.* Vancouver: Fraser Institute, April 2014.

Spiro, Peter S. "Estimating the Underground Economy: A Critical Evaluation of the Monetary Approach." *Canadian Tax Journal* 42(4) (1994): 1059–81.

Stern, Nicholas H. "On the Specification of Models of Optimal Income Taxation." *Journal of Public Economics* 6(1 and 2) (July–August 1976): 123–62.

Vaillancourt, Francois. *The Administrative and Compliance Costs of the Personal Income Tax and Payroll Tax System in Canada, 1986.* Toronto: Canadian Tax Foundation, 1989.

Vaillancourt, François, Édison Roy-César, and Maria Silvia Barros. *The Compliance and Administrative Costs of Taxation in Canada.* Vancouver: Fraser Institute, 2013.

Vaillancourt, François, Jason Clemens, and Milagros Palacios. *Compliance and Administrative Costs of Taxation in Canada.* Vancouver: Fraser Institute, 2007.

Winer, Stanley, and Walter Hettich. "The Political Economy of Taxation: Positive and Normative Analysis When Collective Choice Matters," in *The Encyclopedia of Public Choice,* eds. C. Rowley and F. Scheinder. Kluwer Academic, 2004.

IN THE NEWS

CTV News Montreal. "Quebec report recommends $5.9B in tax cuts, higher consumption taxes." March 19, 2015. http://montreal.ctvnews.ca/quebec-report-recommends-5-9b-in-tax-cuts-higher-consumption-taxes-1.2288153

Gordon, Stephen. "Quebec budget starts the structural reform the province needs." *Maclean's,* March 26, 2015. http://www.macleans.ca/economy/economicanalysis/the-quebec-budget-starts-the-structural-reform-the-province-needs/

Hadekel, Peter. "Quebec must follow through on tax reform." *The Gazette,* June 17, 2015. http://montrealgazette.com/business/local-business/quebec-needs-to-show-resolve-on-tax-reform

CHAPTER 17

Allen, J. R., D. A. Dodge, and S. N. Poddar. "Indexing the Personal Income Tax: A Federal Perspective." *Canadian Tax Journal* 22(4) (July–August 1974).

Ault, Hugh J., and David Bradford. "Taxing International Income: An Analysis of the U.S. System and Its Economic Premises," in *Taxation in the Global Economy,* eds. Assaf Razin and Joel Slemrod (pp. 11–54). Chicago: University of Chicago Press, 1990.

Bird, Richard M. "The Tax Kaleidoscope: Perspectives on Tax Reform in Canada." *Canadian Tax Journal* 18(5) (September–October 1970).

Bittker, Boris. "Federal Income Taxation and the Family." *Stanford Law Review* 27 (July 1975): 1392–463.

Brown, W. Mark, and Afshan Dar-Brodeur. "Income from Owner-occupied Housing, 1969 to 2011: New Evidence from the Survey of Household Spending and the Survey of Financial Security." *Statistics Canada, Economic Insights* (11-626-X) No. 54 (December 10, 2015).

Burbidge, John, Deborah Fretz, and Michael R. Veall. "Canadian and American Saving Rates and the Role of RRSPs." *Canadian Public Policy* 24(2) (June 1998): 259–263.

Canada Revenue Agency. *Income Statistics–Interim Statistics (2012 tax year)* (Ottawa, 2014). Available at http:www.cra-arc.gc.ca.

Chandler, William. "The Value of Household Work in Canada." *Canadian Economic Observer* (April 1994).

Cloutier, A. Pierre, and Bernard Fortin. "Converting Exemptions and Deductions into Credits: An Economic Assessment," in *The Economic Impacts of Tax Reform,* eds. Jack Mintz and John Whalley. Toronto: Canadian Tax Foundation, 1989.

Davies, James B., and Junsen Zhang. "Measuring Marginal Income Tax Rates for Individuals in Canada: Averages and Distributions over Time." *Canadian Journal of Economics* 29(4) (November 1996): 959–75.

Department of Finance Canada. *Tax Expenditures and Evaluations 2012.* Ottawa, 2015. Available at http://www.fin.gc.ca.

Duclos, Jean-Yves, Bernard Fortin, and Andrée-Anne Fournier. "An Analysis of Effective Marginal Tax Rates in Quebec." *Canadian Public Policy* 35(3) (September 2009): 343–371.

Emes, Joel, and Jason Clemens. *Flat Tax: Principles and Issues,* 2001 Fraser Institute Critical Issues Bulletin. Vancouver, B.C.: The Fraser Institute, 2001.

Ernst and Young. Tax information on their website at http://www.ey.com/ca.

Feldstein, Martin S. "On the Theory of Tax Reform." *Journal of Public Economics* 6 (1976): 77–104.

George, Henry. *Progress and Poverty.* New York: Doubleday, 1914, Book VII.

Hossain, Belayet, and Laura Lamb. "Price Elasticities of Charitable Giving across Donation Sectors in Canada: Is the Tax Incentive Effective?" *International Scholarly Research Network ISRN Economics* Volume 2012, Article ID 421789. doi:10.5402/2012/421789, 6 pages (December 2012a).

Hossain, Belayet, and Laura Lamb. "Does the Effectiveness of Tax Incentives on the Decision to Give Charitable Donations Vary across Donation Sectors in Canada?" *Applied Economics Letters* 19(15) (March 2012b): 1487–1491.

Howard, R., G. C. Ruggeri, and D. Van Wart. "Federal Tax Changes and Marginal Tax Rates, 1986 and 1993." *Canadian Tax Journal* 43(4) (1995): 906–22.

Hull, Brian, and Lawrence Leonard. "Indexing the Personal Income Tax: An Ontario Perspective." *Canadian Tax Journal* 22(4) (July–August 1974).

Ivkovich, Zoran, James M. Poterba, and Scott Weisbenner. "Tax-Motivated Trading by Individual Investors." *American Economic Review* 95(5) (December 2005): 1605–1630.

Jarvis, Gregory, and Roger S. Smith. "Real Income and Average Tax Rates: An Extension for the 1970–75 Period." *Canadian Tax Journal* 25(2) (March–April 1977).

Kesselman, Jonathan R. "The Child Tax Benefit: Simple, Fair, Responsive?" *Canadian Public Policy* 19(2) (June 1993).

Kitchen, Harry, and Richard Dalton. "Determinants of Charitable Donations by Families in Canada: A Regional Analysis," *Applied Economics* 22 (1990): 285–299.

Kitchen, Harry. "Determinants of Charitable Donations in Canada: A Comparison over Time," *Applied Economics* 24 (1992): 709–713.

Milligan, Kevin. "Do Tax-Sheltered Savings Crowd Out Other Savings? Implications, Evidence, and Explanations." Mimeo prepared for the Department of Finance (August, 1998).

McLure, Charles. "Thinking Straight about the Taxation of Electronic Commerce: Tax Principles, Compliance Problems, and Nexus," in *Tax Policy and the Economy, Volume 16*, ed. James M. Poterba. Cambridge, MA: MIT Press, 2002.

Mintz, Jack. "Taxing Families: Does the System Need an Overhaul?" *IMFC Review*, Spring/Summer 2008: 15–17.

OECD. *Revenue Statistics, 1965–2013.* Paris: OECD, 2014.

Perry, D. B. "The Cost of Indexing the Federal Income Tax System." *Canadian Tax Journal* 33(2) (March–April 1985).

Royal Commission on Taxation. *Report*, vol. III. Ottawa: Queen's Printer, 1966.

Simons, Henry C. *Personal Income Taxation.* Chicago: University of Chicago Press, 1938.

Statistics Canada. *Public Finance Historical Data 1965/66–1991/92*, Cat. no. 68-512 occasional. Ottawa: Minister of Industry, 1992.

Statistics Canada. *Canadian Economic Observer: Historical Statistical Supplement 2009–10*, Cat. no. 11-210-XWE. Ottawa: Minister of Industry, 2010.

Stewart, James B. "At 102%, His Tax Rate Takes the Cake." *New York Times*, February 3, 2012.

Urquhart, M. C., and K. A. H. Buckley. *Historical Statistics of Canada*, 2nd ed. Ottawa: Minister of Supply and Services, 1983.

Vukelich, George. "The Effect of Inflation on Real Tax Rates." *Canadian Tax Journal* 20(4) (July–August 1972).

IN THE NEWS

Geddes, John. "Who really benefits from income-splitting." *Maclean's*, April 24, 2015. http://www.macleans.ca/politics/ottawa/about-that-big-tax-break-for-the-richest-15-of-canadians/

Lahey, Kathleen. "Income splitting won't help parents who really need a tax break." *The Globe and Mail*, October 30, 2014. http://www.theglobeandmail.com/globe-debate/income-splitting-wont-help-parents-who-really-need-a-tax-break/article21382476/

CHAPTER 18

Beach, Charles M., Robin W. Boadway, and Neil Bruce. *Taxation and Savings in Canada.* Ottawa: Economic Council of Canada, 1988.

Benjamin, Daniel J. "Does 401K Eligibility Increase Saving? Evidence from Propensity Score Subclassification." *Journal of Public Economics* 87(5–6) (May 2003): 1259–1290.

Bong-Chan Kho, René M. Stulz, and Francis E. Warnock. "Financial Globalization, Governance, and the Evolution of the Home Bias." *Journal of Accounting Research* 47(2) (2009): 597–635.

Break, George F. "Income Taxes and Incentives to Work." *American Economic Review* 47 (1957): 529–49.

Brewer, Mike, and James Browne. "Can More Revenue be Raised by Increasing Income Tax Rates for the Very Rich?" Institute for Fiscal Studies, IFS Briefing Note BN84, 2009.

Carroll, Chris, and Lawrence H. Summers. "Why Have Private Saving Rates in the United States and Canada Diverged?" *Journal of Monetary Economics* 20 (September 1987): 249–279.

Dahlby, Bev and Ergete Ferede. "Estimating the Tax Base Elasticities and the Marginal Cost of Public Funds for Canadian Provinces." School of Public Policy, University of Calgary, Working Paper, August 2015.

Davies, James B., and Stanley Winer. "Closing the 49th Parallel: An Unexplored Episode in Canadian Economic and Political History." *Canadian Public Policy*, forthcoming, 2011.

Department of Finance Canada. *Tax Expenditures and Evaluations 2014.* Ottawa: Queen's Printer, 2015.

Engen, Eric M., William G. Gale, and John Karl Scholz. "The Illusory Effects of Saving Incentives on Saving." *Journal of Economic Perspectives* 10(4) (Fall 1996): 113–138.

Engelhardt, Gary V. "Tax Subsidies and Household Saving: Evidence from Canada." *Quarterly Journal of Economics* 111(4) (November 1996): 1237–1267.

Feldstein, Martin. "The Effects of Taxes on Economic Behavior." *The National Tax Journal* 61(1) (March 2008): 131–139.

Government of Canada. *Public Accounts of Canada 2014.* Ottawa: Public Works and Government Services Canada, 2015.

Hamermesh, D., and S. Woodbury. "Taxes, Fringe Benefits, and Faculty." *Working Paper 3455.* Cambridge, MA: National Bureau of Economic Research, 1990.

Heim, Bradley T. "The Effect of Recent Tax Changes on Taxable Income: Evidence from a New Panel of Tax Returns." *Journal of Policy Analysis and Management* 28(1) (Winter 2009): 147–163.

Helliwell, John, and Ross McKitrick. "Comparing Capital Mobility between Provincial and National Borders." *Canadian Journal of Economics* 32(5) (November 1999): 1164–73.

Hemming, Richard. "Income Tax Progressivity and Labour Supply." *Journal of Public Economics* 14(1) (August 1980): 95–100.

Hubbard, R. Glenn, and Jonathan S. Skinner. "Assessing the Effectiveness of Saving Incentives." *Journal of Economic Perspectives* 10(4) (Fall 1996): 73–90.

Hum, Derek, and Wayne Simpson. *Income Maintenance, Work Effort, and the Canadian Mincome Experiment.* Ottawa: Economic Council of Canada, 1991.

Hum, Derek, and Wayne Simpson. "Labour Supply Estimation and Public

Policy." *Journal of Economic Surveys* 8(1) (March 1994): 57–81.

Ibbotson, Roger G. and Laurence B. Siegel. "Real Estate Returns: A Comparison with Other Investments," *AREUEA Journal 12* (Fall 1984): 219–243.

Joint Committee on Taxation. *Macroeconomic Analysis of Various Proposals to Provide $50 Billion in Tax Relief* (March 1, 2005): JCX-4-05.

Jump, Gregory V. "Tax Incentives to Promote Personal Saving: Recent Canadian Experience," in *Saving and Government Policy*. Conference Series No. 25 (pp. 6–64). Boston: Federal Reserve Bank of Boston, 1982.

Kim, Bong-Han, and Keun-Yeob Oh. "Capital Mobility in Saving and Investment: A Time-Varying Coefficients Approach." *Journal of International Money and Finance* 27(5) (September 2008): 806–815.

Kho, Bong-Chan, René M. Stulz, and Francis E. Warnock. "Financial Globalization, Governance, and the Evolution of the Home Bias." *Journal of Accounting Research* 47(2) (May 2009): 597–635.

Laffer, Arthur B. "Statement Prepared for the Joint Economic Committee, May 20," reprinted in *The Economics of the Tax Revolt: A Reader*, ed. Arthur B. Laffer and Jan P. Seymour (pp. 75–79). New York: Harcourt Brace Jovanovich, 1979.

McLure, Charles E., Jr. "Taxes, Saving, and Welfare: Theory and Evidence." *National Tax Journal* 33(3) (September 1980).

Meghir, Costas, and David Phillips. "Labour Supply and Taxes." Prepared for the Report of a Commission on Reforming the Tax System for the 21st Century, Chaired by Sir James Mirrlees, Institute for Fiscal Studies, 2008.

Meyer, Bruce D., and Dan T. Rosenbaum. "Welfare, the Earned Income Tax Credit, and the Labor Supply of Single Mothers." *Quarterly Journal of Economics* 116(3) (August 2011): 1063–1114.

Milligan, Kevin. "Tax-Preferred Savings Accounts and Marginal Tax Rates: Evidence on RRSP Participation." *Canadian Journal of Economics* 35(3) (August 2002): 436–456.

Milligan, Kevin, and Michael Smart. "Taxation and Top Incomes in Canada." *Canadian Journal of Economics*, forthcoming. Working paper available at http://faculty. arts.ubc.ca/kmilligan/research/papers/ cje-5.0.pdf (January 2014).

Morissette, René, and Marie Drolet. "Pension Coverage and Retirement Savings of Young and Prime-Aged Workers in Canada, 1986–1997." *Canadian Journal of Economics* 34(1) (February 2001): 100–119.

Morissette, Charles. "The Underground Economy in Canada, 1992 to 2011." Statistics Canada Income and Expenditure Accounts Technical Series, Catalogue no. 13-604-M-No. 73 (2014).

Poterba, James M. "Taxation and Housing Markets," in *Canada–U.S. Tax Comparisons*, eds. John B. Shoven and John Whalley (pp. 275–94). Chicago: University of Chicago Press, 1992.

Poterba, James M., and Andrew A. Samwick. "Taxation and Household Portfolio Composition: U.S. Evidence from the 1980s and 1990s." *Journal of Public Economics* 87(1) (January 2003): 5–38.

Poterba, James M., Steven F. Venti, and David A. Wise. "How Retirement Saving Programs Increase Saving." *Journal of Economic Perspectives* 10(4) (Fall 1996): 113–138.

Prescott, Edward C. "Why Do Americans Work So Much More Than Europeans?" *Federal Reserve Bank of Minneapolis Quarterly Review* 28(1) (July 2004): 2–13.

Roberts, Paul C. "The Keynesian Attack on Mr. Reagan's Plan." *The Wall Street Journal*, March 19, 1981, p. 26.

Rogerson, Richard, and Johanna Wallenius. "Micro and Macro Elasticities in a Life Cycle Model with Taxes." *Journal of Economic Theory* 144 (November 2009): 2277–92.

Sabelhaus, John. "Public Policy and Saving in the United States and Canada." *Canadian Journal of Economics* 30(2) (May 1997): 253–75.

Sand, Benjamin M. "Estimating Labour Supply Responses Using Provincial Tax Reforms." Mimeo, Vancouver: University of British Columbia, 2005.

Schneider, Friedrich, and Dominik H. Enste. "Shadow Economies: Size, Causes, and Consequences." *Journal of Economic Literature* 38(1) (March 2000): 77–114.

Smith, Lawrence B., Kenneth T. Rosen, and George Fallis. "Recent Developments in Economic Models of Housing Markets." *Journal of Economic Literature* 26 (March 1988).

Spiro, Peter S. "Estimating the Underground Economy: A Critical Evaluation of the Monetary Approach." *Canadian Tax Journal* 42(4) (1994): 1059–81.

Statistics Canada. *Changing Patterns in Canadian Homeownership and Shelter Costs, 2006 Census.* Ottawa: Ministry of Industry, 2008.

Statistics Canada. *The Assets and Debts of Canadians.* Ottawa, Ministry of Industry, 2001.

Tobin, James. "Liquidity Preference as Attitude toward Risk." *Review of Economic Studies* 25 (February 1958): 65–86.

Wall Street Journal. "Non-Stop Taxes." April 19, 2001, p. A18.

Watanabe, Katsunori, Takayuki Watanabe, and Tsutomu Watanabe. "Tax Policy and Consumer Spending: Evidence from Japanese Fiscal Experiments." *Journal of International Economics* 53(2) (April 2001): 261–281.

Webb, James R, and Jack H. Rubens. "Tax Rates and Implicit Rates of Return on Owner-Occupied Single-Family Housing," *Journal of Real Estate Research* 2 (Winter 1987): 11–28.

IN THE NEWS

Den Tandt, Michael. "Justin Trudeau's tax plan difficult to attack, even for Conservatives." Full Comment, *National Post*, May 6, 2015. http://news. nationalpost.com/full-comment/michael- den-tandt-justin-trudeaus-tax-plan- difficult-to-attack-even-for-conservatives

Curry, Bill. "Trudeau's new high-income bracket may encourage tax avoidance, economists warn." *The Globe and Mail*, May 5, 2015. http://www. theglobeandmail.com/news/politics/ liberals-new-high-income-bracket- may-encourage-tax-avoidance- economists-warn/article24263994/

Clark, Scott and Peter DeVries. "Exploding the myth of the wealthy tax refugee." *iPolitics*, May 25, 2015. http:// ipolitics.ca/2015/05/25/exploding-the- myth-of-the-wealthy-tax-refugee /

CHAPTER 19

Aaron, Henry J. "Introduction and Summary," in *The Value-Added Tax: Lessons from Europe*, ed. Henry J. Aaron (pp. 1–18). Washington, DC: Brookings Institution, 1981.

Altig, David, Alan J. Auerbach, Laurence J. Kotlikoff, Kent A. Smetters, and Jan Wallise. "Simulating Fundamental Tax Reform in the United States." *American Economic Review* 91(3) (June 2001): 574–595.

Andrews, William D. "The Achilles' Heel of the Comprehensive Income Tax," in *New Directions in Federal Tax Policy for the 1980s*, eds. Charles E. Walker and Mark A. Bloomfield (pp. 278–84). Cambridge, MA: Ballinger, 1983.

Atkinson, A.B., and J.E. Stiglitz. *Lectures on Public Economics.* New York: McGraw-Hill, 1980.

Beach, Charles M., Robin W. Boadway, and Neil Bruce. *Taxation and Savings in Canada.* Ottawa: Economic Council of Canada, 1988.

Becker, Gary S., and Casey B. Mulligan. "Deadweight Costs and the Size of Government." *Journal of Law and*

Economics 46(2) (October 2003): 293–340.

Bird, Richard M. "Policy Forum: Visibility and Accountability–Is Tax-Inclusive Pricing a Good Thing?" *Canadian Tax Journal* 58(1) (2010): 63–76.

Bird, Richard M. *Where Do We Go From Here? Alternatives to the GST.* Toronto: KPMG Centre for Government, April 1994.

Bird, Richard M., and Eric M. Zolt. "The Limited Role of the Personal Income Tax in Developing Countries." *Journal of Asian Economics* 16(6) (December 2005): 928–46.

Bird, Richard M., and Michael Smart. "The Impact on Investment of Replacing a Retail Sales Tax by a Value-Added Tax: Evidence from Canadian Experience." *National Tax Journal* 62(4) (December 2009): 591–609.

Browning, Martin, and Thomas F. Crossley. "The Life-Cycle Model of Consumption and Saving." *Journal of Economic Perspectives* 15(1) (Winter 2001): 3–22.

Chait, Jonathan. "Trading Little Loopholes for a Giant One." *New York Times,* August 7, 1996, p. A17.

Dahlby, Bev, and Ergete Ferede. "Estimating the Tax Base Elasticities and the Marginal Cost of Public Funds for Canadian Provinces." Mimeo (May 25, 2015).

Davies, J., F. St-Hilaire, and J. Whalley. "Some Calculations of Lifetime Tax Incidence." *American Economic Review* 74(4) (September 1984).

Department of Finance. *Goods and Services Tax: An Overview.* Ottawa: August 1989.

Department of Finance, The Honourable Michael H. Wilson. *The White Paper: Tax Reform 1987.* Ottawa: June 18, 1987.

Dynan, Karen E., Jonathan Skinner, and Stephen P. Zeldes. "Do the Rich Save More?" *Journal of Political Economy* 112(2) (April 2004): 397–444.

Economic Council of Canada. *Road Map for Tax Reform: The Taxation of Savings and Investment.* Ottawa: 1987.

Feldstein, Martin. "The Effect of Taxes on Efficiency and Growth." Working Paper No. 12201. Cambridge MA: National Bureau of Economic Research (March 2006).

Friedman, Milton. *A Theory of the Consumption Function.* Princeton, NJ: Princeton University Press, 1957.

Government of Canada. *Public Accounts 2014.* Ottawa: Public Works and Government Services Canada (October 2014).

Hall, Robert E. and Alvin Rabushka. *The Flat Tax,* revised 2nd ed. Stanford, CA: Hoover Institution Press, 2007.

Hamilton, Bob, and John Whalley. "Efficiency and Distributional Effects of the Tax Reform Package," in *The Economic Impacts of Tax Reform,* eds. Jack Mintz and John Whalley. Toronto: Canadian Tax Foundation, 1989.

Hobbes, Thomas. *Leviathan.* New York: Meridian Books, 1963 (1651).

House of Commons, Standing Committee on Finance. *Replacing the GST: Options for Canada.* Ottawa: June 1994.

Kaplow, Louis. "On the Undesirability of Commodity Taxation Even When Income Taxation is Not Optimal." *Journal of Public Economics* 90(6–7) (August 2006): 1235–1250.

Keen, Michael. "VAT Attacks!" *International Tax and Public Finance* 14(4) (August 2007): 365–381.

Kesselman, Jonathan R. "Assessing a Direct Consumption Tax to Replace the GST." *Canadian Tax Journal* 42(3) (1994): 709–803.

Lazear, Edward P., and James M. Poterba. "Reforming Taxes to Promote Economic Growth." *The Economists' Voices* 3(1): Article 3 (January 2006).

McLure, Charles Jr. "What Can the United States Learn from the Canadian Sales Tax Debate?" Chapter 10 in *Canada-U.S. Tax Comparisons* eds. John B. Shoven and John Whalley Chicago: University of Chicago Press, 1992.

Metcalf, Gilbert E. "Life Cycle Versus Annual Perspectives on the Incidence of a Value Added Tax," in *Tax Policy and the Economy,* Volume 8, ed. J. Poterba. Cambridge: MIT Press, 1994.

OECD. *International VAT/GST Guidelines.* Paris: *Centre for Tax Policy and Administration* (February 2006).

Sandford, C., M. Godwin, and P. Hardwick. *Administrative and Compliance Costs of Taxation.* Perrymead: Fiscal Publications, 1989.

Sørensen, Peter Birch. "The Theory of Optimal Taxation: What Is the Policy Relevance?" *International Tax and Public Finance* 14(4) (August 2007): 383–406.

Spiro, Peter, "Estimating the Underground Economy: A Critical Evaluation of the Monetary Approach." *Canadian Tax Journal* 42(4) (1994).

Spiro, Peter. "Evidence of a Post-GST Increase in the Underground Economy." *Canadian Tax Journal* 41(2) (1993).

Stockfisch, J. A. "Value-Added Taxes and the Size of Government: Some Evidence." *National Tax Journal* 38(4) (December 1985): 547–52.

Tait, Alan A. *Value Added Tax: International Practice and Problems.* Washington, DC: International Monetary Fund, 1988.

Venti, Stephen F., and David A. Wise. "Choice, Chance, and Wealth Dispersion at Retirement," in *Aging Issues in the United States and Japan,* eds. Seiritsu Ogura, Toshiaki Tachibanaki, and David A. Wise. Cambridge, MA: National Bureau of Economic Research, 2001.

Vermaeten, A., W.I. Gillespie, and F. Vermaeten. "Who Paid the Taxes in Canada, 1951–1988." *Canadian Public Policy* 21(3) (September 1995).

IN THE NEWS

Artuso, Antonella. "Up to 10¢/L gas tax hike to fund Ontario transit, panel recommends." *Toronto Sun,* December 12, 2013. http://www.torontosun.com/2013/12/12/up-to-10-gas-tax-hike-for-transit-ontario-advisory-panel-recommends.

Kalinowsky, Tess. "Raise gas tax and add road tolls, expert tells Ontario." *thestar.com,* July 15, 2015. http://www.thestar.com/news/investigations/2015/07/15/raise-gas-tax-and-add-road-tolls-expert-tells-ontario.html

Wood, Joel. "Is It Time to Raise the Gas Tax? Optimal Gasoline Taxes for Ontario and Toronto." *Canadian Public Policy* 41(3) (September 2015): 179–190.

CHAPTER 20

Altus Group. "2015 Property Tax Rate Analysis," prepared for Real Property Association of Canada. September 2015.

Broadbent Institute. "Haves and Have-Nots: Deep and Persistent Wealth Inequality in Canada." September 2014. https://d3n8a8pro7vhmx.cloudfront.net/broadbent/pages/32/attachments/original/1430002827/Haves_and_Have-Nots.pdf?1430002827

Brueckner, J. K., and H. A. Kim. "Urban Sprawl and the Property Tax." *International Tax and Public Finance* 10(1) (January 2003): 5–23.

Brzozowski, Matthew, Martin Gervais, Paul Klein, and Michio Suzuki. "Consumption, Income, and Wealth Inequality in Canada." *Review of Economic Dynamics* 13(1) (January 2010): 52–75.

Dachis, Ben, Gilles Duranton, and Matthew A. Turner. "The effects of land transfer taxes on real estate markets: Evidence from a natural experiment in Toronto." *Journal of Economic Geography* 12(2) (March 2012): 327–54.

Davies, James B. "The Distributive Effects of Wealth Taxes." *Canadian Public Policy* 17 (September 1991): 17.

Davies, James B. "The Relative Impact of Inheritance and Other Factors on

Economic Inequality." *The Quarterly Journal of Economics* 97 (August 1982).

Davies, James B., France St-Hilaire, and John Whalley. "Some Calculations of Lifetime Tax Incidence." *American Economic Review* 74(4) (September 1984): 633–49.

Hamilton, Bruce. "Property Taxes and the Tiebout Hypothesis: Some Empirical Evidence," in *Fiscal Zoning and Land Use Controls: The Economic Issues*, eds. Edwin S. Mills and Wallace E. Oates (pp. 13–30). Lexington, MA: Lexington Books, 1975.

Harris, C. Lowell. "Property Taxation after the California Vote." *Tax Review* 39(8) (August 1978): 35–38.

Heal, Geoffrey. "Bundling Public and Private Goods: Are Development and Conservation Necessarily in Conflict?" Working Paper. New York: Columbia Business School, July 2001.

Jorgenson, Dale W., and Kun-Young Yun. "The Excess Burden of Taxation in the U.S.," in *Empirical Approaches to Fiscal Policy Modelling*, eds. Alberto Heimler and Daniele Muelders. London: Chapman and Hall, 1993.

Mieszkowski, Peter M. "The Property Tax: An Excise Tax or a Profits Tax?" *Journal of Public Economics* 1 (1972): 73–96.

Mieszkowski, Peter M., and George R. Zodrow. "Taxation and the Tiebout Model." *Journal of Economic Literature*, September 1989: 1098–146.

Morissette, René, and Xuelin Zhang. "Revisiting Wealth Inequality." *Perspectives on Labour and Income* 7(12) (2006). Ottawa: Statistics Canada.

Newcomer, Mabel, and Ruth Gillette Hutchinson. "Taxation of Land Values in Canada." *Journal of Political Economy* 40(3) (June 1932): 366–378.

Nguyen-Hoang, Phuong, and John Yinger. "The Capitalization of School Quality into House Values: A Review." *Journal of Housing Economics* 20(1) (March 2011): 30–48.

Oates Wallace. "The Effects of Property Taxes and Local Spending on Property Values: An Empirical Study of Tax Capitalization and the Tiebout Hypothesis." *Journal of Political Economy* 77 (1969): 957–71.

Oates, Wallace E., and Robert. M. Schwab. "The Impact of Urban Land Taxation: The Pittsburgh Experience." *National Tax Journal* 50(1) (March 1997): 1–21.

Oates, Wallace E., and Robert M. Schwab. "The Window Tax: A Case Study in Excess Burden." *Journal of Economic Perspectives* 29(1) (Winter 2015): 163–180.

Organisation for Economic Co-operation and Development. *Revenue Statistics, 1965–2013*. Paris: OECD, 2014.

Slack, Enid. *Assessment Limits for Ontario. Could We Live with the Consequences?* Toronto: Association of Municipalities of Ontario, 2010.

Smith, Roger S. *Personal Wealth Taxation: Canadian Tax Policy in a Historical and an International Setting*. Toronto: Canadian Tax Foundation, 1993.

Smith, Roger S. "Why the Canadian Property Tax(payer) Is Not Revolting." *Canadian Tax Journal* 38(2) (March–April 1990).

Smith, Roger S. "Personal Wealth Taxation and the European Union," a paper prepared for the Conference on Tax Policy in the European Union. The Hague: Ministry of Finance, November 2001. Mimeo.

Van Rompaey, Catherine, Michael Palardy, and John Trstenjak. "Measuring the Canadian Wealth Distribution—Issues and Challenges Vis-à -Vis the LWS." Statistics Canada Working Paper Prepared for the Luxembourg Wealth Study Technical Conference, December 14–15, 2006.

Vermaeten, A., W. I. Gillespie, and F. Vermaeten. "Who Paid the Taxes in Canada, 1951–1988?" *Canadian Public Policy* 21(3) (September 1995).

Wolff, Edward N. "Recent Trends in the Size Distribution of Household Wealth." *Journal of Economic Perspectives* 12(3) (Summer 1998): 131–150.

Wolff, Edward N. "Recent Trends in Household Wealth in the United States: Rising Debt and the Middle-Class Squeeze—an Update to 2007." Levy Economics Institute of Bard College Working Paper No. 589, March 2010.

IN THE NEWS

Ipsos Public Affairs. 2015 Citizen Satisfaction Survey: Final Report. Prepared for the City of Calgary, November 11, 2015.

Kaufman, Bill. "Nenshi: Calgary Citizen Satisfaction Survey shows 'extraordinarily high' number of people satisfied." *Calgary Sun*, November 23, 2015. http://www.calgarysun.com/2015/11/23/nenshi-calgary-citizen-satisfaction-survey-shows-extraordinarily-high-number-of-people-satisfied

660 News. "Results are in from 2015 Citizen Satisfaction Survey & Research on Calgary's Economy." November 23, 2015. http://www.660news.com/2015/11/23/results-are-in-from-2015-citizen-satisfaction-survey-research-on-calgarys-economy/.

Slack, Enid. "The Property Tax – in Theory and Practice." IMFG Papers on Municipal Finance and Governance, No. 2, 2011, Munk School of Global Affairs, University of Toronto.

CHAPTER 21

Arnold, Brian J., and Neil H. Harris. "NAFTA and the Taxation of Corporate Investment: A View from Within NAFTA." *Tax Law Review* 49(4) (Summer 1994): 560–76 (in particular).

Boadway, Robin W. *Public Sector Economics*. Cambridge: Winthrop, 1979.

Bossons, John. *The Impact of Inflation on Income and Financing of Large Non-Financial Corporations*. Ontario Commission on Inflation Accounting, Supplementary Paper No. 5. Toronto: 1977.

Chen, Duanjie, and Jack Mintz. "The 2014 Global Tax Competitiveness Report: A Proposed Business Tax Reform Agenda." *University of Calgary, SPP Research Papers* vol. 8(4) (February 2015).

Chen, Duanjie, and Jack Mintz. *Business Tax Reform: More Progress Needed*. C. D. Howe Institute e-brief, June 20, 2006.

Chen, Duanjie, and Jack Mintz. Federal/Provincial Combined Marginal Effective Tax Rates on Capital 1997–2006, 2010. *Supplementary Information for Business Tax Reform: More Progress Needed*. (C.D. Howe e-brief, June 20, 2006).

Chetty, Raj, and Emmanuel Saez. "Dividend Taxes and Corporate Behavior: Evidence from the 2003 Dividend Tax Cut." *Quarterly Journal of Economics* 120(3) (August 2005): 791–833.

Chirinko, Robert S. "Business Fixed Investment Spending: A Critical Survey of Modeling Strategies, Empirical Results, and Policy Implications." *Journal of Economic Literature* 31(4) (December 1993): 1875–911.

Chirinko, Robert S. "Corporate Taxation, Capital Formation, and the Substitution Elasticity between Labor and Capital." *National Tax Journal* 55(2) (June 2002): 339–355.

Chirinko, Robert S., Steven M. Fazzari, and Andrew P. Meyer. "How Responsive is Business Capital Formation to Its User Cost? An Exploration with Micro Data." *Journal of Public Economics* 74 (October 1999): 53–80.

Cnossen, Sijbren. "What Kind of Corporation Tax?" *Bulletin for International Fiscal Documentation* 47(1) (January 1993).

Cnossen, Sijbren. "Taxing Capital Income in the Nordic Countries: A Model for the European Union?" In *Taxing Capital*

Income in the European Union: Issues and Options for Reform, ed. Sibren Cnossen (pp.180–213). Oxford: Oxford University Press, 2000.

Dahlby, Bev, and Ergete Ferede. "What Does it Cost Society to Raise a Dollar of Tax Revenue?" C. D. Howe Institute Commentary No. 324 (March 2011).

Daly, Michael J., Pierre Mercier, and Thomas Schweitzer. "Chapter 3: Canada," in *Tax Reform and the Cost of Capital*, ed. D. Jorgenson and R. Landau. Washington, DC: Brookings Institution, 1993.

Department of Finance, Canada. *Report of the Technical Committee on Business Taxation*. Ottawa: December 1997.

Department of Finance, Canada. *Tax Expenditures and Evaluations, 2014*. Ottawa: Public Works and Government Services Canada, 2015.

Fama, Eugene F., and Merton H. Miller. *The Theory of Finance*. New York: Holt, Rinehart and Winston, 1972.

Fuchs, Victor R., Alan B. Kruger, and James M. Poterba. "Economists' Views About Parameters, Values, and Policies: Survey Results in Labor and Public Economics." *Journal of Economic Literature* 36(3) (September 1998): 1387–1425.

Goolsbee, Austan. "The Impact and Inefficiency of the Corporate Income Tax: Evidence from State Organizational Form Data." *Journal of Public Economics* 88(11) (September 2004): 2283–99.

Goolsbee, Austan. "Investment Subsidies and Wages in Capital Goods Industries: To the Workers Go the Spoils?" *National Tax Journal* 56(1) (March 2003): 153–165.

Gordon, Roger H., and Young Lee. "Do Taxes Affect Corporate Debt Policy? Evidence from US Corporate Tax Return Data." *Journal of Public Economics* 82(2) (November 2001): 195–224.

Graham, John. "Taxes and Corporate Finance: A Review." *Review of Financial Studies* 16(4) (Winter 2003): 1074–1128.

Jenkins, Glenn P. *Inflation: Its Financial Impact on Business in Canada*. Ottawa: Economic Council of Canada, 1977.

Jorgenson, Dale W. "Capital Theory and Investment Behavior." *American Economic Review* 53(2) (May 1963): 247–59.

Jorgenson, Dale W., and Kun-Young Yun. *Investment, Vol. 3, Lifting the Burden: Tax Reform, the Cost of Capital, and US Economic Growth*. Cambridge: MIT Press, 2001.

McKenzie, Kenneth J. "Income Taxes, Integration, and Income Trusts." *Canadian Tax Journal* 54(3) (2006): 633–656.

McKenzie, Kenneth J., and Natalia Sershun. "Taxation and R&D: An Investigation of the Push and Pull Effects." *Canadian Public Policy* 36(3) (September 2010): 307–324.

Poterba, James M. "Dividends, Capital Gains, and the Corporate Veil: Evidence from Britain, Canada, and the United States," in *National Saving and Economic Performance*, eds. Douglas B. Bernheim and John B. Shoven (pp. 49–71). Chicago: University of Chicago Press, 1991.

Schaller, Huntley. "Estimating the Long-Run User Cost Elasticity." *Journal of Monetary Economics* 53(4) (May 2006): 725–736.

Statistics Canada. *Quarterly Financial Statistics for Enterprises, Second Quarter, 2015*, Cat. No. 61-008-X. Ottawa: September 2015.

Stein, Jeremy. "Agency, Information and Corporate Investment," in *Handbook of Economics of Finance, Vol. 1A*. eds. G. M. Constantinides, M. Harris, and R. M. Stulz. Amsterdam: North Holland, 2003.

Stiglitz, Joseph E. "Taxation, Corporate Financial Policy, and the Cost of Capital." *Journal of Public Economics* 2 (1973): 1–34.

Treff, Karin, and David B. Perry. *Finances of the Nation, 2006*. Toronto: Canadian Tax Foundation, 2007.

Treff, Karin, and Deborah Ort. *Finances of the Nation, 2010*. Toronto: Canadian Tax Foundation, 2011.

U.S. Department of the Treasury. *Integration of the Individual and Corporate Tax Systems*. Washington, DC: U.S. Government Printing Office, 1992.

IN THE NEWS

Bowles, Rachel. "Harold Crooks on The Price We Pay." The Skinny, September 8, 2015. http://www.theskinny.co.uk/festivals/uk-festivals/film/harold-crooks-on-the-price-we-pay

Smart, Michael, and Qing Hong. "In Praise of Tax Havens: International Tax Planning and Foreign Direct Investment." *European Economic Review* 54(1) (January 2010): 82–95.

Tencer, Daniel. "Canadian Corporations had $200 Billion in World's Top Tax Havens Last Year: Report." *The Huffington Post*, Canada, June 16, 2015. http://www.huffingtonpost.ca/2015/05/16/corporate-tax-havens-canada_n_7293410.html

Thompson Reuters. "U.S. companies stashed $2.1 trillion offshore to avoid taxes: Report." CBCNews Business, October 6, 2015. http://www.cbc.ca/news/business/fortune-500-offshore-taxes-1.3258516

Index